P9-CCW-723

INTRODUCTION TO COMPUTER SYSTEM PERFORMANCE EVALUATION

McGraw-Hill Computer Science Series

Ahuja: *Design and Analysis of Computer Communication Networks*
Donovan: *Systems Programming*
Filman and Friedman: *Coordinated Computing: Tools and Techniques for Distributed Software*
Hamacher, Vranesic, and Zaky: *Computer Organization*
Hayes: *Computer Architecture and Organization*
Hutchison and Just: *Programming Using the C Language*
Hwang and Briggs: *Computer Architecture and Parallel Processing*
Kant: *Introduction to Computer System Performance Evaluation*
Keller: *A First Course in Computer Programming Using Pascal*
Kohavi: *Switching and Finite Automata Theory*
Korth and Silberschatz: *Database System Concepts*
Levi and Agrawala: *Real-Time System Design*
Liu: *Elements of Discrete Mathematics*
Liu: *Introduction to Combinatorial Mathematics*
Madnick and Donovan: *Operating Systems*
Manna: *Mathematical Theory of Computation*
Milenkovic: *Operating Systems: Concepts and Design*
Newman and Sproull: *Principles of Interactive Computer Graphics*
Payne: *Introduction to Simulation: Programming Techniques and Methods of Analysis*
Rice: *Matrix Computations and Mathematical Software*
Rich and Knight: *Artificial Intelligence*
Salton and McGill: *Introduction to Modern Information Retrieval*
Shooman: *Software Engineering: Design, Reliability, and Management*
Siewiorek, Bell, and Newell: *Computer Structures: Principles and Examples*
Tremblay and Bunt: *An Introduction to Computer Science: An Algorithmic Approach*
Tremblay, DeDourek, and Bunt: *An Introduction to Computer Science: An Algorithmic Approach, Pascal Edition*
Tremblay and Sorenson: *The Theory and Practice of Compiler Writing*
Tucker: *Computer Science: A Second Course Using Modula-2*
Tucker: *Programming Languages*
Tucker, Bradley, Cupper, and Garnick: *Fundamentals of Computing I: Logic, Problem Solving, Programs, and Computers*
Wiederhold: *Database Design*

INTRODUCTION TO COMPUTER SYSTEM PERFORMANCE EVALUATION

K. Kant

Department of Computer Science
The Pennsylvania State University

With Contributions by M. M. Srinivasan

Industrial and Operations Engineering Department
The University of Michigan, Ann Arbor

McGraw-Hill, Inc.

New York St. Louis San Francisco Auckland Bogotá
Caracas Lisbon London Madrid Mexico Milan Montreal
New Delhi Paris San Juan Singapore Sydney Tokyo Toronto

This book was set in Computer Modern Roman by the author.
The editor was Eric M. Munson;
the production supervisor was Friederich W. Schulte.
The cover was designed by Rafael Hernandez.
Project supervision was done by Publication Services.
R. R. Donnelley & Sons Company was printer and binder.

INTRODUCTION TO COMPUTER SYSTEM PERFORMANCE EVALUATION

Copyright © 1992 by McGraw-Hill, Inc. All rights reserved.
Printed in the United States of America. Except as permitted under the United States Copyright Act of 1976, no part of this publication may be reproduced or distributed in any form or by any means, or stored in a data base or retrieval system, without the prior written permission of the publisher.

2 3 4 5 6 7 8 9 0 DOC DOC 9 0 9 8 7 6 5 4 3 2

ISBN 0-07-033586-9

Library of Congress Cataloging-in-Publication Data

Kant, K. (Krishna)
Introduction to computer system performance evaluation / K. Kant; with contributions by M.M. Srinivasan.
p. cm. — (McGraw-Hill computer science series)
Includes bibliographical references and index.
ISBN 0-07-033586-9
1. Electronic digital computers—Evaluation. I. Srinivasan, M. M. II. Title. III. Series.
QA76.9.E94K36 1992
004′.029′7—dc20 91-21266

CREDITS

The text includes the following material from other copyrighted sources, taken by permission of the respective publishers, when necessary. The citation here is in the same form as in the bibliographic notes. The full reference to the source may be found in the references section.

1. Classification of computer systems in Section 1.1. Adapted from Siewiorek and Swarz (1982).
2. Figure 13-10 illustrating use of success diagrams. From Siewiorek and Swarz (1982).
3. Comparison of alternate designs in Section 3.5.1 and its justification in Section 3.5.2. Adapted from Law and Kelton (1982).
4. Table E.1 and all four tables in Section E.2. From Law and Kelton (1982).
5. The sample behavior sequence in Figure 4-3 and the results in Table 4.1. From Buzen and Denning (1980).
6. The lemmas and proofs in Section 6.1.2 and the discussion in Section 6.1.3. Rephrased from Kelly (1979).
7. Exercises 6.2, 6.3, and 6.4 are taken from Kelley (1979).
8. Discussion on decomposability in Section 8.4 based on Courtois (1977).
9. Discussion on MVA-based modeling of channel contention in Section 8.2.5 adapted from Lazowska, Zahorjan, Graham and Sevcik (1984).
10. Discussion on conservation laws in Section 9.2.2 based on Gelenbe and Mitrani (1980).
11. Discussion on RECAL in Section 10.2.1 based on Conway and Georganas (1986).
12. Discussion on the MVAC algorithm in Section 10.2.2 based on Conway, Silva, Lavenberg (1986).
13. Discussion on Tree-convolution algorithm in Section 10.3.1 based on Lam and Lien (1983).
14. Tolerance errors for generalized linearizer algorithm in Table 7.3 taken from Krzeinski and Greyling (1985).
15. Figure 12-10 illustrating confusion in GSPN's. From Marson, Balbo, Chiola and Conte (1987).
16. Figure 12-11 showing a GSPN model of a multiprocessor system. From Marson, Balbo and Conte (1986).

TO MY BROTHER,
Keshav Kant,
for Everything

CONTENTS

PREFACE

1. MOTIVATION

The book provides an up-to-date treatment of the fundamental techniques and algorithms of computer system performance evaluation. My motivation in writing the book was two-fold. First, it should be usable as a text for a one or two semester graduate course in the theory and practice of performance evaluation with strong emphasis on analytic modeling. Second, it should be useful as a reference to both researchers and practitioners in the performance evaluation field. Because of this latter purpose, the book contains discussion on many more topics and in more depth than may be appropriate in a book that is only intended to be a text book. I shall later comment on what may be omitted in a "typical" course in performance evaluation.

The material originally grew out of many years of teaching experience of the author. Despite the existence of many books on the topic, the selection of appropriate reading material for the students has always been a difficult and challenging task. Several factors contribute to this.

The field of performance evaluation has progressed rapidly in the past ten years and it is only now begun to approach maturity. Consequently, many of the important developments in the field are available only in technical journals. This has consistently made the coherent treatment of the material difficult. Analytic performance modeling is somewhat peculiar with regard to its mathematical content. The mathematics is rarely advanced, but the proliferation of mathematical symbols and nonstandard notation often makes it look unapproachable.

I believe that a comprehensive course on performance evaluation should discuss measurement, simulation, and analytic modeling in sufficient depth (including topics like model calibration, data analysis, etc.). This often requires the use of more books, thereby further aggravating the problems of incoherence and nonuniform notation. I have also found that the students generally lack adequate background in probability theory and stochastic processes, which further adds to the problems.

2. CONTENT OVERVIEW

The selection of the material for this book has been guided primarily by the goals and problems stated above. For the background material, Appendix B provides a quick review of the probability theory, and includes discussion on most concepts that are needed in performance modeling. The chapters in the book have been divided up into two parts. Part 1 includes chapters 1–8 and is particularly suited for a typical one-semester course in performance evaluation. Part 2 includes the remaining chapters, and generally discusses more advanced topics.

Topics other than analytic modeling appear in the first four chapters. Chapter 1 provides an overview of the techniques of performance evaluation, workload characterization, and benchmarking. Chapter 2 contains a detailed discussion on hardware, software, and hybrid instrumentation of computer systems. Chapter 3 is concerned with the design of measurement and simulation experiments and the analysis of experimental data. Chapter 4 introduces various features of queuing network models and shows how to calibrate and validate such models. It also has a rather comprehensive discussion on the fundamental relationships between various operational quantities. The material in chapters 3 and 4 should be adequate to work effectively with queuing network based simulation models of computer systems.

Chapters 5 and 9 are concerned with the essentials of stochastic analysis. While much of the material in these chapters is classical, I have tried to include at least a brief discussion on many topics that are often missed in elementary discussions of queuing theory. These include characterization of output processes, conservation laws, semi-Markov processes, difficulties in using transform methods, modeling of arrival processes, and matrix analytic methods of solution.

Chapter 6 discusses a variety of concepts related to product-form, such as local balance, reversibility, quasi-reversibility, station balance, etc. It also shows how product-form solution comes about in open and closed networks with single and multiple chains or classes. Chapter 7 presents both Convolution and Mean Value Analysis algorithms for solving closed product-form networks. It also shows how these algorithms can be applied to mixed networks.

Chapter 8 discusses aggregation, decomposition, and heuristic mean value analysis, that form the basis for hierarchical modeling and various types of approximations. The use of these techniques is illustrated by considering the modeling of several features of real computer systems.

Chapter 10 discusses product-form networks with several advanced features (e.g., variable population, state-dependent routing, etc.). It also discusses a number of algorithms that exploit various characteristics of the network for an efficient solution. Chapter 11 discusses performance bounds, which are useful when many alternatives need to be evaluated quickly.

Chapter 12 discusses both untimed and timed Petri net models and shows how they could be used in analyzing situations involving synchronization between concurrent activities. Chapter 13 discusses some selected applications of the techniques discussed in earlier chapters. In particular, it talks about the modeling of token-ring local area networks, performance optimization in a distributed system, performance modeling of situations where jobs have internal concurrency, and transient analysis of performance and reliability, particularly in the context of gracefully degrading systems.

Appendices C and D show how to use the techniques discussed in the rest of the book to analytically model various aspects of real computer systems. These appendices are primarily intended for class use, but may also be of independent interest.

I am pleased to acknowledge here that the entire Chapter 11, the first two sections in Chapter 13, and the corresponding bibliographic notes were written by Dr. M. M. Srinivasan. I would also like to thank him for letting me take the liberty of making substantial editorial changes to these portions to keep a single-authorship style.

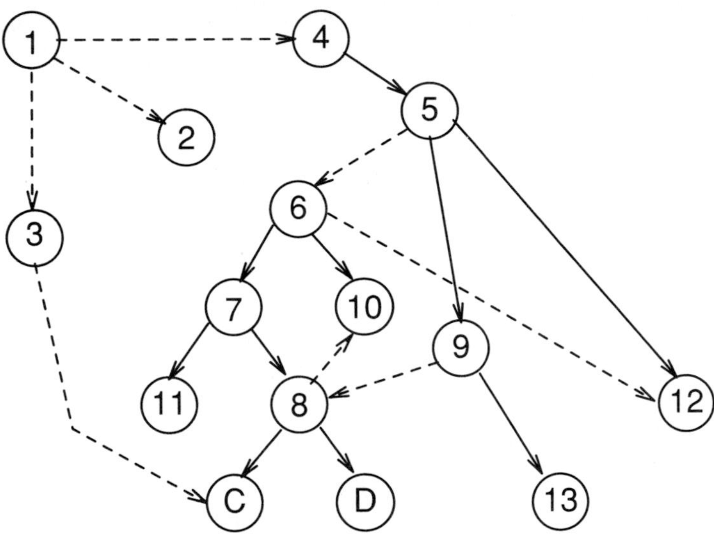

The diagram above shows the dependence relationships between the various chapters. This diagram should be useful both for self-study and class use. The solid arcs indicate a strong dependence and the dotted ones only a minor one. Arcs for transitive dependencies are not shown explicitly. In examining this diagram, please keep in mind that not everything in the prerequisite chapter is needed in the dependent chapter. Often, a conceptual understanding along with a few equations is all that is needed to make progress.

3. COURSE USE

Ideally, the material presented in this text should be covered over a 2-semester period, where the first semester concentrates on measurement, simulation, and simple analytic modeling, whereas the second one deals with more advanced analysis techniques. However, to be widely applicable, I shall describe the text use only for a single-semester course. It is also possible to use portions of the book in an advanced seminar setting, and I shall make some comments regarding such a use.

3.1 INTRODUCTORY COURSE

The material in the text is organized according to the order it may be lectured in a class. Chapter 1 provides an overview of the field and discusses important topics of workload characterization and benchmarking. The exercises at the end of this chapter are specifically intended to encourage the students to immediately start exploring monitoring tools (1.1 and 1.2), simulation tools (1.3), workload modeling (1.4), and system selection (1.5). While these exercises are necessarily stated in generic terms, it should be easy to give site-specific assignments based on them. Chapter 2 discusses hardware and software measurement techniques and highlights difficulties in accurate measurements. It is very valuable for students to write some monitoring routines based on this discussion. While the measurement of system activity may require access to privileged information (e.g., kernel data structures) and familiarity with the operating system, instrumentation of user-written programs can be done easily. Chapter 3 discusses issues related to simulation and data analysis. This is the point for the students to learn how to use an available simulation package, organize simulation runs, analyze data, etc. The use of a powerful simulation package (such as SES™ or Q+™) would be very helpful in minimizing the time needed for writing and debugging simulation program). The simulation skills are needed later for the validation of analytic models. Sections 3.5 and 3.6 can be disposed off with only a brief overview. I would recommend requiring the students to use the variance reduction techniques discussed in Section 3.7 in their simulation experiments.

Chapter 4 discusses the basics of queuing network based modeling that are crucial for both simulation and analytic modeling. However, to save time, Section 4.4 can be disposed off with only an overview. The students may be given a simple central-server model of the computer facility that they are using and asked to calibrate it based on the discussion in Section 4.5. (See, for example, exercises 4.9 and 4.10). Such an exercise is invaluable in making the students appreciate the difficulties involved in calibrating even simple models. The model could actually be given to them a bit earlier (with calibration parameters chosen arbitrarily) so that they can write a simulation program for it. This is also the right time to start learning how to use an analytic modeling package. Having done so, the students would be able to both simulate and analytically solve the model that they have calibrated, and compare the results. This whole exercise can progress in parallel with the discussion on next three chapters.

Chapter 5 covers the essentials of basic queuing theory. Except for abridging the details, it should be covered completely. It would also be desirable to briefly mention a few results from Chapter 9 including the PASTA property, residual life, conservation laws, embedded Markov chains, and the Pollaczek-Khinchine formula for a M/G/1 queue.

Chapter 6 discusses the basics of product-form queuing networks. While much of the material in this chapter is important, Section 6.1 should probably be disposed off with only a brief discussion on local balance. (The multiplicity of concepts here could be confusing to the novice.) Chapter 7 discuss the basic computational algorithms for product-form networks, and should be covered in detail. The section on mixed networks may appear a bit threatening, but if the derivations are ignored, the final results are really very simple and easily usable. Chapter 8, in my view, is crucial and should be covered in detail. However, certain sections (e.g., 8.2.3, 8.2.4, 8.4.3, and 8.4.4) may be discussed only briefly.

Appendix C discusses a modeling project that has been used as a semester project for the performance evaluation class taught by the author. The project has been laid out as a sequence of subgoals, so that the students can make steady progress on it in parallel with the coverage of relevant topics in the lectures. The writeup starts with a detailed description of the computer system to be modeled, and then goes through the process of abstraction, model building and calibration. Unfortunately, this "realism" often causes a lot of confusion, and a detailed class discussion is essential.

Appendix D presents a case study in performance tuning using analytic techniques, and can be covered after Chapter 8. The writeup tries to convey several insights into why the system is behaving the way it is, how to look for a good tuning strategy, how to interpret the program output, etc. I believe that a close study of this material, along with the modeling extensions indicated, would provide valuable insights into the practice of performance modeling.

As I found out from my own experience, even the above-mentioned coverage often turns out to be too much for a semester, and further cuts may have to be made. I would recommend prerequisite courses on probability theory, operating systems, and computer architecture to avoid wasting time on trivialities.

3.2 ADVANCED COURSE

For the outline presented here, I shall assume that the course shall start out in the lecture format and eventually move to a group discussion and/or student seminar format (although one could very well maintain a lecture-only format). The starting point of the course would be a review of the basics learnt in the introductory course. The most important topics to review are basic queuing theory (chapter 5), product-form networks (chapter 6), and aggregation (chapter 8). Chapter 9 can be covered in depth at this point, possibly by picking up additional material from the sources cited. Other important topics are reversibility (chapter 6) and product-form networks with advanced features (chapter 10). The specialized algorithms in Chapter 10 serve well for student seminars and implementation projects. The decomposition approximation in Section 8 can also be explored in some more depth, if necessary. Performance bounds discussed in Chapter 11 is another good topic to be covered in a few student seminars. I would also recommend a detailed discussion of both untimed and timed Petri-nets (chapter 12). It would be helpful to have a Petri-net based modeling package (e.g., SPAN or ULTRASAN™) available which the students can use for verifying correctness and temporal aspects of applications involving synchronization (e.g., communication protocols, concurrency control, and flexible manufacturing systems). Towards the end of the course, one may pick up a few interesting applications and show how the analysis techniques can be applied to them. Chapter 13 discusses four such applications, but surely there are many others.

As a final note, the material in chapters 12 and 13 could be of independent value in an advanced course dealing with various issues concerning parallel and distributed systems. For example, a course on the specification and verification of concurrent systems could also go into the performance issues and use Chapter 12.

4. SELECTION RATIONALE

Because of the vastness of the performance evaluation field, many topics have been omitted from the book. Also, as the suggestions above indicate, the book includes a lot of material that probably will never be used in a typical one-semester course. In the following, I briefly describe the selection rationale. Because I wanted the book to be a useful reference, the rationale is not limited to pedagogy alone.

As stated earlier, I believe that the material in chapters 1–3 is essential to give a balanced view of performance modeling. However, I decided not to delve too deep into simulation, primarily because excellent treatment of the subject exists in many other books. I have also avoided talking about how to write simulation programs. The wide availability of high-level simulation packages obviates such a discussion; besides, I wanted to project the view that experiment design and data analysis are far more important topics to learn than the trivialities of programming.

The material on analytic modeling covers the subject fairly well, however, some comments are in order. I believe that matrix analytic methods need more exposure than they have received in the past. I have, therefore, not hesitated to devote a considerable number of pages to this topic in Chapter 9. With regard to classical queuing theory, my attempt has been more to present the basic ideas than the details. Thus, while M/G/1 queue is analyzed in detail, G/M/1 is not, since the methods of attack are identical. The reason for including product-form networks with advanced features in Chapter 10 is to stimulate their greater use in practice. Other algorithms in Chapter 10 are interesting in different ways, however, because of the lack of space, they are considerably abbreviated. One important omission has been a detailed discussion on the computation of flow-time distributions. Because of the difficulty of the topic, the results here are limited in scope and difficult to present. I therefore decided to omit them altogether.

I believe Chapter 8 includes most of the important concepts in the engineering of performance modeling, although the choice of specific approximate algorithms is somewhat arbitrary. For example, I did not include approximate algorithms for dealing with blocking or adaptive routing. Chapter 11 covers several bounding techniques, but not all of them. We really did not think that including all bounding techniques would be appropriate.

Chapter 12 concentrates only on the aspects of Petri-Nets that are most essential for performance modeling. I have omitted or abbreviated topics such as invariant analysis, properties of Petri-net languages, etc., since they are not of direct interest. The analysis of high-level Petri-nets is also omitted, primarily because of the infancy of the subject. I believe that most of the important results on timed Petri-nets are included in this chapter.

The selection of topics for Chapter 13 has been difficult because there are so many interesting applications to consider. The list of topics was shuffled many times, until we came up with the current selections. Some of the other topics that were considered are: analysis of database concurrency control protocols, performance issues in computer communication networks (routing, flow control, etc.), performance modeling of multiprocessor systems, control of queuing systems, and flexible manufacturing systems. The decision to drop them does not reflect their lack of importance, but only the impracticality of including them.

5. MISCELLANEOUS NOTES

Here are a few points regarding the contents that I wish to get across all readers. For brevity, the equations have been numbered using the syntax (⟨section no⟩.⟨equation no⟩) in each chapter. Equations in the same chapter are referenced using this syntax; equations from a different chapter are referenced using the syntax (⟨chapter no⟩.⟨section no⟩.⟨equation no⟩). With a few exceptions, the notation is consistent throughout the text and is summarized in Appendix A. Instead of wasting space on a separate chapter summary, we have tried to make the opening paragraph in each chapter a summary of the topics covered in that chapter. Finally, the bibliographic notes at the end of each chapter are not limited to the discussion in the text — they also provide pointers to selected literature on other related topics.

Perhaps, a disclaimer is in order regarding the last item in this list. In a vast field like performance modeling, with thousands of interesting articles and may be a hundred books, this "selection" of additional material is necessarily arbitrary, primarily based upon what we happened to see. Whenever possible, we have tried to include survey articles or other articles that contain a rich bibliography, as this helps to keep the reference list short. There is also a clear bias toward books and easily accessible articles. Also, old references have generally been eliminated, although the bibliographic notes do attempt to properly credit the work of the originator of the idea.

Finally, I would very much appreciate knowing about any and all the bugs that you find in this text, so that I could at least prepare an errata, and in due course, eliminate them from the text. I can be contacted via email at kant@cs.psu.edu.

ACKNOWLEDGMENTS

I am grateful to the Computer Science Department of the Pennsylvania State University and Bell Communications Research for providing the facilities necessary for the development and typesetting of this book. Several people have contributed to the book. First, I would like to thank M. M. Srinivasan for his contributed material to the book. Some of the proofs in Chapter 6 were originally written and debugged by Mohammad Ghodsi. Korrinn P. Fu contributed in numerous ways in producing the first troff draft of the book. Daqin Liu generated most of the pictures, "fixed" them over and over again, and also helped considerably in the difficult task of converting the original troff document to latex. Comments from many people were helpful in improving the presentation of the material and compiling the reference list. In particular, I would like to thank M. M. Srinivasan, Chip McGuire, Dominico Ferrari, Edward Lazowska, and John Zahorjan. A few of the references were taken from the lists provided by Harry Rubin and Eugene Miya.

McGraw-Hill and the author would like to thank the following reviewers for their many helpful comments and suggestions: David Finkel, Worchester Polytechnic Institute; Herman Hughes, Michigan State University; Richard Muntz, University of California at Los Angeles; and Zary Segall, Carnegie Mellon University.

K. Kant

INTRODUCTION TO COMPUTER SYSTEM PERFORMANCE EVALUATION

Part I

Basic Concepts

CHAPTER

1

Performance Measures and Evaluation Techniques

In this chapter we discuss the need for and methods of evaluating the performance of computer systems. To start with, we shall take a very general view of performance and introduce a variety of measures for its many aspects. We then look at some evaluation methods for the more traditional performance measures. We also discuss problems of workload characterization and benchmarking of both conventional and highly parallel computer systems.

1.1 Evaluation Metrics

A computer system, like any other engineering machine, can be measured and evaluated in terms of how well it meets the needs and expectations of its users. It is desirable to evaluate the performance of a computer system because we want to make sure that it is suitable for its intended applications, and that it satisfies the given efficiency and reliability requirements. We also want to operate the computer system near its optimal level of processing power under the given resource constraints. The interesting performance measures and the desired operational requirements of a computer system depend on the domain of application. For example, the requirements for a system to be used in a short-term unmanned space mission are very different from those for a manned space station. Thus, it is essential for us to define the performance measures that are important in various application domains.

Broadly speaking, all performance measures deal with three basic issues: (1) how quickly a given task can be accomplished, (2) how well the system can deal with failures and other unusual situations, and (3) how effectively the system uses the available resources. Since a computer system will typically run several types of tasks, the measures in the first category should be evaluated separately for each workload type. Possible classifications for workload are real-time control, transaction processing, interactive computing and batch. Similarly, the faults afflicting a system differ in the damage done to it; thus, all measures in the second category should be evaluated for each fault type. For illustration, we shall use only two categories of failures: catastrophic and benign. (A failure is defined as the observable effect of a fault.) Catastrophic failures are those that cause a substantial loss of information. For example, in most well-designed systems, a CPU crash would be benign, but a disk head crash may be catastrophic. Now we can categorize the performance measures as follows.

Responsiveness: These measures are intended to evaluate how quickly a given task can be accomplished by the system. Possible measures are waiting time, processing time, conditional waiting time (waiting time for tasks requiring a specified amount of processing time), queue length, etc. In some cases, mean values of these measures are adequate; in others, higher moments, percentiles, or the entire distribution may be needed. It may be necessary to evaluate these measures for each important category of the workload.

Usage Level: These measures are intended to evaluate how well the various components of the system are being used. Possible measures are throughput and utilization of various resources. The objectives behind these measures conflict with those behind the responsiveness measures, since a well-utilized system would generally respond more slowly than a less-utilized system.

Missionability: These measures indicate if the system would remain continuously operational for the duration of a mission. Possible measures are the distribution of the work accomplished during the *mission time*, interval availability (probability that the system will keep performing satisfactorily throughout the mission time), and life-time (time when the probability of unacceptable behavior increases beyond some threshold). These measures are useful when repair/tuning is impractical or when the unacceptable behavior may be catastrophic.

Dependability: These measures indicate how reliable the system is over the long run. Possible measures are number of failures/day, MTTF (mean time to failure), MTTR (mean time to repair), long-term availability, and cost of a failure.[1] These measures are useful when repairs *are* possible and failures are tolerable.

[1]A measure called MTBF (mean time between failures) is also commonly used. It is defined as MTTF+MTTR.

Productivity: These measures indicate how effectively a user can get his or her work accomplished. Possible measures are user friendliness, maintainability, and understandability. Because these measures are difficult to quantify, we shall not consider them.

The measures introduced above consider responsiveness aspect separate from the reliability aspect. In certain systems, such a clear separation is not possible, and one must consider measures that have to do with both aspects simultaneously. For example, in a multiprocessor system, the total failure of an individual processor may only degrade the overall processing rate. For such systems we need to characterize performance at various levels of operability. The relevant measures here are *performability measures*, and will be studied in Chapter 13.

The relative importance of various measures depends on the application involved. In the following, we provide a broad classification of computer systems according to the application domains, indicating which measures are most relevant:

1. **General purpose computing:** These systems are designed for general purpose problem solving. Relevant measures are responsiveness, usage level, and productivity. Dependability requirements are modest, especially for benign failures.
2. **High availability:** Such systems are designed for transaction processing environments (bank, airline, or telephone databases, switching systems, etc.). The most important measures are responsiveness and dependability. Both of these requirements are more severe than for general purpose computing systems; moreover, any data corruption or destruction is unacceptable. Productivity is also an important factor.
3. **Real-time control:** Such systems must respond to both periodic and randomly occurring events within some (possibly hard) timing constraints. They require high levels of responsiveness and dependability for most workloads and failure types and are therefore significantly over-designed. Note that the utilization and throughput play little role in such systems.
4. **Mission Oriented:** These systems require extremely high levels of reliability over a short period, called the mission time. Little or no repair/tuning is possible during the mission. Such systems include fly-by-wire airplanes, battlefield systems, and spacecrafts. Responsiveness is also important, but usually not difficult to achieve. Such systems may try to achieve high reliability during the short term at the expense of poor reliability beyond the mission period.
5. **Long-life:** Systems like the ones used for unmanned spaceships need long life without provision for manual diagnostics and repairs. Thus, in addition to being highly dependable, they should have considerable intelligence built in to do diagnostics and repair either automatically or by remote control from a ground station. Responsiveness is important but not difficult to achieve.

In general purpose and transaction-processing systems, the users of the system may have performance concerns that are different from the system level concerns. To illustrate this, consider two computer systems, A and B. For a given failure type, system A has a large MTTF and small MTTR, but the failure might result in the loss or corruption of many user files. System B has a smaller MTTF, longer MTTR, but loses few files. In this case, the user might consider system B better, even though the MTTF, MTTR, and cost criteria might favor system A. As another example, a system that is easy to use may be considered better than another system that provides greater functionality, which in turn makes it harder to use. Many other examples abound. It is important to consider the measures that are most relevant to the performance concerns of the users, otherwise, a well designed system may fail to gain acceptance among the user community. Unfortunately, the user level concerns are often subjective and difficult to quantify. Therefore, we shall also consider the "standard" system-level measures.

This text is primarily concerned with the responsiveness and usage-level aspects of performance evaluation. In such an evaluation, we assume that the system under study does not change its physical characteristics; i.e., failures, repairs, degradation, etc. are not considered. Thus, we shall study only the phenomenon of queuing, resource possession, and synchronization. However, many of the techniques and tools used here (simulation, Markov modeling, etc.) can also be employed in evaluating the effect of physical changes. We shall return to the latter topic briefly in Section 13.4.

1.2 Techniques of Performance Evaluation

There are three basic techniques for performance evaluation: (1) measurement, (2) simulation, and (3) analytic modeling. The latter two techniques can also be combined to get what is usually known as *hybrid modeling*. In the following, we discuss these briefly and point out their comparative advantages and disadvantages.

1.2.1 Measurement

Measurement is the most fundamental technique and is needed even in analysis and simulation to calibrate the models. Some measurements are best done in hardware, some in software, and some in a hybrid manner. Chapter 2 examines the details of measurement techniques, highlighting the precautions necessary to obtain accurate data. Since there are several uncontrolled (or uncontrollable) factors in a measurement experiment, the data collected from measurements must be analyzed by statistical techniques to draw meaningful conclusions. One must also carefully select what output parameters need to be measured, how they should be measured, and what values should be selected for input combinations that *are* under the control of the experimenter. Chapter 3 examines the issues of data analysis and experiment design.

As an illustration of the importance of designing a measurement experiment carefully, suppose that we wish to study the behavior of some output parameter Y as a function, say f, of some input parameters $x_1, \ldots, x_n$. If each x_i can take k distinct values, the experiment must be run k^n times to capture all the effects. However, a careful selection of the "input vectors" would usually be able to capture all the major effects at a much lower cost.

1.2.2 Simulation Modeling

Simulation involves constructing a model for the behavior of the system and driving it with an appropriate abstraction of the workload. The major advantage of simulation is its generality and flexibility; almost any behavior can be easily simulated. However, there are many important issues that must be considered in simulation:

1. It must be decided what not to simulate and at what level of detail. Simply duplicating the detailed behavior of the system is usually unnecessary and prohibitively expensive.
2. Simulation, like measurement, generates much raw data, which must be analyzed using statistical techniques.
3. Similar to measurements, a careful experiment design is essential to keep the simulation cost down.

In general, the simulation can be done at several levels of detail, depending on the objectives of the study. For example, to estimate the average response time experienced by terminal users from a computer system, there is no need to simulate individual instructions or even individual operating system commands. It is probably adequate to consider the distribution of the processing and I/O times required by the commands issued by the terminal users. On the other hand, if the objective is to study the effectiveness of cache or pipelining, an instruction level simulation becomes necessary. Typically, in a given simulation study, different components of the system are simulated at different levels of detail. For example, in the above instruction level simulation example, the I/O subsystem specifics are not very important and thus may be represented in even less detail than in a response time model. One could also have several different models of the same system at various levels of detail, such that the results of a more detailed model are used to calibrate the next higher-level model.

Both measurement and simulation involve careful experiment design, data gathering, and data analysis. These steps could be tedious; moreover, the final results obtained from the data analysis only characterize the system behavior for the range of input parameters covered. Although extrapolation can be used to obtain results for nearby parameter values, it is not possible to ask "what if" questions for arbitrary parameter values.

1.2.3 Analytic Modeling

Analytic modeling involves constructing a mathematical model of the system behavior (at the desired level of detail) and solving it. The main difficulty here is that the domain of tractable models is rather limited. Thus, analytic modeling will fail if the objective is to study the behavior in great detail. However, for an overall behavior characterization, analytic modeling is an excellent tool. The major advantages of analytic modeling over the other two techniques are (a) it generates good insight into the workings of the system that is valuable even if the model is too difficult to solve; (b) simple analytic models can usually be solved easily, yet provide surprisingly accurate results, and (c) results from analysis have better predictive value than those obtained from measurement or simulation.

The simplicity required by tractable analytic models is not necessarily a handicap and may even be desirable for several reasons. First, simpler models tend to be more robust than the more complex ones; i.e., small errors in parameter values affect the results less significantly. Second, simpler models are easier to understand, calibrate, and modify and thus avoid many pitfalls that more complex models may not. Third, in many situations the input parameters are not known reliably or the desired results are not well defined. For example, the *average* number of users on the system may be between 10 and 20; the exact number depends on factors that are not yet known. (Notice that we speaking of the average number of users; so the uncertainty is *not* caused by the randomness in user behavior.) Similarly, it may be desirable to have *average* response time less than 3 seconds, the exact value being unimportant. In such cases, a very accurate modeling is pointless: all we need is to be able to separate the "bad" choices from "good" ones. Simple-minded analytic models are desirable here, since simulation is expensive and does not give any formulae that can be used to discriminate between the "good" and "bad" choices.

As with simulation, it is often desirable to do analytic modeling at several levels of detail, with the more detailed model generating inputs for the higher-level model. We shall discuss analytic modeling of queuing systems in much detail in later chapters of the book.

1.2.4 Hybrid Modeling

A complex model may consist of several submodels, each representing certain aspect of the system. Only some of these submodels may be analytically tractable; the others must be simulated. For example, in a computer system using dynamic partitioned memory allocation, the fraction of memory wasted due to fragmentation may be difficult to estimate analytically, even though the other aspects of system behavior can be modeled analytically. In such cases, we can take the hybrid approach, which will proceed as follows:

1. Solve the analytic model assuming no fragmentation of memory and determine the distribution of memory holding time.

2. Simulate only memory allocation, holding, and deallocation, and determine the average fraction of memory that could not be used because of fragmentation.
3. Recalibrate the analytic model of step 1 with reduced memory and solve it. (It may be necessary to repeat these steps a few times to get convergence.)

In the above example, one could also do a purely simulation modeling; however, such an approach may be less desirable for the following reasons: (a) since the cost of simulation is proportional to the number of events handled, simulating the full model may be much more expensive than simulating only the memory allocation/deallocation; and (b) so long as the job arrival rate and memory holding time do not change significantly, the hybrid approach would allow us to study the model analytically as a function of various other input parameters.

We shall not discuss hybrid modeling explicitly in the balance of the book. However, whenever one is faced with the problem of modeling a complex system, it is worth reviewing the available analytic techniques to see what aspects of system behavior can be studied adequately by using those techniques. Only the remaining aspects then need be studied by simulation.

1.3 Applications of Performance Evaluation

Performance modeling and evaluation may be needed for a variety of purposes; however, the following needs stand out:

1. **System design:** In designing a new system, one typically starts out with certain performance/reliability objectives and a basic system architecture, and then decides how to choose various parameters to achieve the objectives. This involves constructing a model of the system behavior at the appropriate level of detail, and evaluating it to choose the parameters. At higher levels of design, simple analytic reasoning may be adequate to eliminate bad choices, but simulation becomes an indispensable tool for making detailed design decisions and avoiding costly mistakes.
2. **System selection:** Here the problem is to select the "best" system from among a group of systems that are under consideration for reasons of cost, availability, compatibility, etc. Although direct measurement is the ideal technique to use here, there might be practical difficulties in doing so (e.g., not being able to use them under realistic workloads, or not having the system available locally). Therefore, it may be necessary to make projections based on available data and some simple modeling.
3. **System upgrade:** This involves replacing either the entire system or parts thereof with a newer but compatible unit. The compatibility and cost considerations may dictate the vendor, so the only remaining problem is to choose quantity, speed, and the like. Often, analytic modeling is adequate

here; however, in large systems involving complex interactions between subsystems, simulation modeling may be essential. Note that a direct experimentation would require installing the new unit first, and thus is not practical.

4. **System tuning:** The purpose of tuneup is to optimize the performance by appropriately changing the various resource management policies. Some examples are process scheduling mechanism, context switching, buffer allocation schemes, cluster size for paging, and contiguity in file space allocation. It is necessary to decide which parameters to consider changing and how to change them to get maximum potential benefit. Direct experimentation is the simplest technique to use here, but may not be feasible in a production environment. Since the tuning often involves changes to aspects that cannot be easily represented in analytic models, simulation is indispensable in this application.

5. **System analysis:** Suppose that we find a system to be unacceptably sluggish. The reason could be either inadequate hardware resources (CPU, memory, disk, etc.) or poor system management. In the former case, we need system upgrade, and in the latter, a system tuneup. Nevertheless, the first task is to determine which of the two cases applies. This involves monitoring the system and examining the behavior of various resource management policies under different loading conditions. Experimentation coupled with simple analytic reasoning is usually adequate to identify the trouble spots; however, in some cases, complex interactions may make a simulation study essential.

We now examine the application of simulation/analysis to some of these problems in a little more detail. Consider first the system design. In the initial stages of design, we have to decide on a number of system features and capabilities, and their potential benefits and costs. Few things are frozen or even known at this stage, and a large number of possibilities must be evaluated. Clearly, it is neither desirable nor possible to construct a prototype or a detailed simulation model at this stage. What we need is the ability to quickly answer "what if" type of questions. Simple, "back of the envelope" calculations, combined with experience with similar systems, and rules of thumb are the appropriate techniques to use at this stage. Asymptotic analysis is often useful at this stage, since it provides limits on what is achievable and what is not. For example, we can obtain a lower bound on the response time by assuming that there are no queuing delays, and an upper bound by assuming that the most heavily loaded devices are saturated. Somewhat sharper results can often be obtained quickly by making various simplifying assumptions, e.g., all devices are equally loaded. As the design matures, so does the need for more sophisticated modeling and more accurate solutions. For example, a simple queuing model may evolve into a set of interrelated models, each one of which deals with multiple work-load types. At the same time, we may have to drop one or more of the simplifying assumptions in the analysis. However, one should not lose sight of two facts (a) the answers need be only as accurate as the uncertainties in the model structure or its calibration parameters, and (b) so long as these uncertainties are large, a simple asymptotic analysis that yields lower and upper bounds may be more valuable than estimates of "average" behavior. During later stages of development, certain aspects may need a more thorough investigation than what a simple analysis is able to provide. At this time we can opt for hybrid modeling, whereby the intractable aspects are simulated and the results are used to calibrate simplified analytic models. This is preferable to immediately switching to simulation for two reasons: (a) we retain the advantages of analytic modeling as far as possible, and (b) it is much easier to develop simulation programs for selected aspects than for the entire system. A hybrid simulation tool that provides a convenient staged migration from analytic to simulation model would be very helpful here. Prototype building and measurements on it would constitute the final stage, and may not even be undertaken.

Performance tuning by adjusting the controllable system parameters is probably best done by direct experimentation; however, the experimenter needs to have a clear idea of what parameter settings are good and worth trying. If this is not the case or there are many settings to consider, some analysis is needed to narrow down the choices. Two approaches are possible for this: (a) run a set of preliminary experiments where the parameters of interest take very small and very large values; (b) construct a simple model and solve it analytically. The main problem with (a) is that a large number of experiments may be required. Analytic modeling is a viable option here because high accuracy is not needed, and the model need only track the change in the output due to changes in the input parameter rather than predicting the actual output values.

1.4 Workload Characterization

Irrespective of which of the three basic performance evaluation techniques we use, we need to provide certain inputs to the real system or its model. There are two categories of relevant inputs. The first category includes parameters that can be controlled by the system designer/administrator, e.g., the scheduling disciplines, interconnections between devices, and resource allocation policies. The second category includes inputs generated by the environment in which the system is used, e.g., the interarrival times and service demands of incoming jobs, and are usually not under the control of the system designer/administrator. These inputs can be used for driving the real system (as in measurement) or its simulation model, and for determining distributions for analytic/simulation modeling. We refer to these inputs as the *workload*. Workload characterization is one of the central issues in performance evaluation because it is not always clear what aspects of the workload are important, in how much detail the workload should be recorded, and how the workload should be represented and used. We illustrate some of these difficulties by an example.

Suppose that we are considering the expansion of an existing computing facility. For this, we need to do some measurements under the real work-load (with the controllable parameters fixed at desired levels), and use them to make expansion decisions. There are several difficulties in doing this. First, we need to decide when and for how long the measurements should be taken. The desired period is not necessarily the one at peak load, since a measurement during such periods may give a highly skewed picture of the system. The duration is important since we want all parts of the system to be exercised during the measurement period and the mix of running jobs to be "representative" of the workload. It is also important to realize here that we want to characterize the workload for the expanded system, not for the existing system. Thus, we need to project if the expansion would have any effect on the nature of the workload itself. Finally, to determine how much of each resource to acquire, we may need to do some modeling using the collected data for calibration and validation. As we shall see in Section 2.5.2, this is not necessarily straightforward even if the measurements are quite detailed.

The workload characterization problem becomes more difficult when direct measurement is not possible. This happens when designing or evaluating a system for an anticipated need. In this case, we must generate the representative workload artificially. In many situations, one does not have a clear idea of what the representative workload should be and precisely which aspects are important and adequate. Yet another difficulty is that workloads evolve over time, and may not only increase in intensity, but also change their composition. Projections based on past trends are often useful, but may lead to false conclusions at times.

It is important to note that *workload characterization only builds a model of the real workload*, since not every aspect of the real workload may be captured or is relevant. The level of abstraction in this model depends on how the workload will be used. Analytic modeling usually requires a rather abstract workload model (e.g., characterization in terms of statistical properties) whereas simulation can use a very detailed model (e.g., a trace of actual events). For reasons of cost-effectiveness and robustness, it is desirable to keep the model (and hence the characterization of the workload driving it) as abstract as possible. For example, when evaluating the effectiveness of an instruction pipeline or a cache, we need information on instruction sequences in addition to the relative frequency of various instructions. However, we should not immediately jump to the conclusion that the actual instruction traces are necessary for effective workload characterization. It may be adequate to capture only the "first order" sequencing effects represented by the probabilities (or relative frequencies) of the form p_{ij} which gives the probability that the jth instruction will immediately follow the ith instruction. Such an information is not only less expensive to collect but is also less sensitive to minor changes in the workload. Of course, the real difficulty may be in convincing oneself that this model is adequate.

A workload model may be executable or nonexecutable. For example, recording the arrival instants and service durations of jobs creates an executable model (which can drive a real system directly), whereas only determining the distributions creates a nonexecutable model. An executable model need not be a record of inputs, it can also be a program that generates the inputs. Workload characterization then amounts to determining the parameters that control the behavior of the program. The parameters themselves can be considered as a nonexecutable representation of the workload. Executable workloads are useful in direct measurements and trace-driven simulations, whereas nonexecutable workloads are useful for analytic modeling and distribution-driven simulations.

In the next section, we discuss the problem of benchmarking computer systems. Since workload characterization is an important aspect of benchmarking, we shall see the use of both executable and nonexecutable workload models at several levels of detail.

1.5 Benchmarking Computer Systems

When selecting a machine for a given application environment, it is useful to have some comparative benchmarks available that can be used to either narrow down the choices or make a final selection. In a selection scenario, it is usually not possible to actually access the machine and do a detailed evaluation; instead, one must depend on the published data on the machine. The benchmarks are primarily intended to provide an overall assessment of various machines on the market. Benchmarks are usually run by vendors or third parties for "typical" configurations and workloads, and not by the user interested in the selection process. Although this is a necessary limitation for practical reasons, it also leaves a lot of room for misinterpretation and misuse of the measures both by the vendors and the users. It is therefore important to examine the advantages and disadvantages of commonly used measures. We shall do this first for traditional computer systems, and then turn to highly parallel ones.

1.5.1 Traditional Computer Systems

Two popular measures of the processing rate for conventional computer systems are MIPS (million instructions per second) and MFLOPS (million floating point instructions per second). Taken literally, these measures must necessarily be worthless, since the instruction formats, complexity, and execution times vary widely even for a single-machine type. In fact, even if we do an elaborate weighted averaging over all the instruction types of a machine, the result is still useless because (a) there is no reasonable way to obtain weighting factors, and (b) the instructions on machines with very different architecture are not comparable. For example, the instructions on a RISC (reduced instruction set computer) are much simpler and highly optimized compared to those on a CISC (complicated instruction set computer). Thus, RISC instructions will typically execute much faster than the CISC instructions. This difference does not directly translate into faster program execution because the same program will take fewer CISC instructions to code.

It is clear that any reasonable approach must necessarily examine the running times of real programs written in a high-level language. Thus, the first problem is to characterize the application domain by a set of "typical" programs. There are two ways to do this: (a) choose a small subset of real application programs, known as *application benchmarks*, that are programs representative of the application domain of interest, or (b) design some artificial programs, known as *synthetic benchmarks*, that mimic a real program execution environment by using statistical data about real high-level language programs. Some examples of the relevant statistical data are:

- Fraction of statements of each type (assignment, conditionals, for-loops, etc.).
- Fraction of variables of each type (integer, real, character, etc.) and locality (local or global).
- Fraction of expressions with certain number and type of operators and operands.

Since these characteristics vary widely over different application domains and programming constructs, it is more useful to have a separate benchmark (application or synthetic) for each application domain and programming language class. The main advantage of a synthetic benchmark over an application benchmark is that overall application domain characteristics can be closely matched by a single program. However, since a synthetic benchmark is not designed to do anything meaningful, it may show the following strange characteristics:

1. Since the expressions controlling conditional statements are chosen randomly, a significant amount of unreachable (or "dead") code may be created, much of which can be eliminated by a "smart" compiler. This makes the code-size highly dependent on the quality of the compiler.
2. The random selection of statements may result in unusual locality properties, thereby defeating well-designed paging algorithms.
3. The benchmark may be small enough to fit entirely in the cache and thereby result in an unusually good performance.

Because of these problems, both real and synthetic benchmarks have been developed over the years. In the following we briefly survey a few of them.

The *Whetstone* is a synthetic benchmark based upon the characteristics of Fortran programs doing extensive floating-point computation. A single Whetstone "instruction" is defined as a mix of basic high-level operations, and the results are reported as mega-Whetstones per second. This benchmark, although still very popular, represents outdated and arbitrary instruction mixes and is thus not very useful for machines with a high degree of internal parallelism (pipelining, vectored computation, etc.), particularly in conjunction with optimizing and parallelizing compilers.

Dhrystone is a synthetic benchmark written in C, and is designed to represent applications involving primarily integer arithmetic and string manipulation in a block-structured language. This benchmark is only 100 statements long, and thus would fit in the instruction cache of most systems. Also, since it calls only two simple procedures, strcpy() and strcmp(), a compiler that replaces these procedure calls by inline code can cause a very significant speed-up. The results are quoted as Dhrystones/sec, which refers to the rate at which the individual statements of the benchmark are executed.

A popular application benchmark is *Linpack*, which solves a dense 100×100 linear system of equations using the Linpack library package. There are two problems with this benchmark: (a) Over 80% of the time is spent in doing $A(I) = B(I) + C \times D(I)$ type of calculation, thereby making the results highly dependent on how well such a computation is handled, and (b) the problem is too small.

More recently, a number of other benchmarks have become very popular. These include (1) *Spice*, a large analog circuit simulation package, mostly written in Fortran, which uses both integer and floating point arithmetic, (2) *gcc*, based on the GNU C compiler, (3) *li*, a lisp interpreter written in C, and (4) *nasa7*, a synthetic benchmark consisting of a set of seven kernels doing double-precision arithmetic in Fortran.

Given a benchmark program, we can compare various machines in terms of their running times. Since different benchmarks have different sizes, it is more convenient to normalize their running times with respect to those on a reference machine. For historical reasons, the VAX11/780 is still a popular reference machine; moreover, it is regarded to be a typical 1 MIPS machine. Thus, if an integer benchmark takes 80 seconds of CPU time on a VAX11/780, and 4 seconds on machine A, we can claim that A is an 80/4=20 MIPS machine. Notice that this notion of MIPS (and similarly of MFLOPS) is quite meaningful (but has nothing to do with a similar machine language-level measure).

When comparing machines using a benchmark program, some care is needed to eliminate the effect of extraneous factors. For example, a highly optimizing compiler can often speed up the code by a factor of 2 compared with an ordinary compiler. Therefore, it is necessary that the benchmarks for all machines be compiled using compilers with similar features and settings. Also, the details of the machine configuration should be spelled out clearly, so that, for example, one could not claim much shorter times by just increasing the cache-size.

Since there are many different capabilities of the machine to be tested out (integer arithmetic, floating point arithmetic, cache management, paging, I/O, etc.), we can either have a suite of benchmarks for them, or come up with a single *synthetic program* that can exercise all these capabilities. A synthetic program can be thought of as a control program that takes some parameters to define the nature of the desired workload and then generates such a workload. Thus, a synthetic program can be used to generate both CPU-intensive and I/O-intensive workloads. For example, in a Unix-like environment, the synthetic program could be a shell-script that generates some controlled mixture of commands to do editing, compilation, file/directory manipulation, CPU-intensive computing, process creation/destruction, etc.

Apart from simplifying the job of studying system performance for a wide range of parameters, synthetic programs also allow realistic simulation of the computing environment. Notice that the classical benchmark programs only measure the CPU performance, and even that when the benchmarks are run in isolation. In contrast, a synthetic program such as a shell-script can easily mimic the behavior of a terminal user in an interactive environment, by running several copies of the script concurrently (or by spawning several processes that do various things). Thus, we can not only study the CPU performance in a realistic setting, but also measure quantities like system throughput which indirectly reflect all aspects of the system. Synthetic programs are also useful in investigating alternatives, since they generate reproducible workload. Thus, for performance tuning studies, one can set up a synthetic program to generate workload similar to the actual workload, and then use it to explore various system configurations and operating system policies. The reproducibility helps in revealing minor differences between the alternatives.

Synthetic programs have a few disadvantages as well: (1) such programs are complex and are usually operating system-dependent; (2) it may be difficult to choose parameters such that they approximate the real workload well; and (3) they generate much raw data that needs to be reduced and interpreted.

Yet another method is to use a *script* as the input workload. A script is a record of all the actions of the users of a real computing environment. Since a script represents everything in the real workload, it is very useful in comparing two different versions of the same system (e.g., the system with and without some hardware and/or software upgrade). However, scripts may be undesirable in other situations, because of the following problems:

1. Since a script contains real commands, it may be installation-dependent, and may not work elsewhere even on the same machine model and under the same operating system. One could say that a script includes too many dependencies.
2. A script is available only when the intended user community is already using some computing facility. Since scripts cannot be changed, they cannot reflect any future or altered needs of this user community.
3. If the goal of the evaluation is to identify a machine that would take some load off the existing facility, a script may be useless because of a possible change in the nature of the workload owing to the new equipment.
4. A script is an accurate model of workload, but not a compact one. It may be unwieldy, hard to interpret, and for many applications unnecessary.

Recognizing the need for high quality standardized benchmarks and benchmark data on contemporary computer systems, a number of vendors have collectively established an organization called System Performance Evaluation Cooperative (SPEC). It publishes a quarterly newsletter containing benchmark data on contemporary systems as it becomes available. For CPU performance, SPEC has defined a suite of ten benchmarks, four of which (gcc, espresso, li, and eqntott) do primarily integer arithmetic, and the other six (spice, doduc, nasa7, matrix, fpppp, and tomcatv) primarily floating point. The reference machine used is VAX11/780. The geometric mean of the integer benchmark results is known as *SPECint*, and those of others as *SPECfp*. The geometric mean of SPECint and

System	CPU/FPU	Mem	O/S	MARK	INT	FP
CDC CD4680	R6000A/6010	32 Mb	EP/IX 1.2.3	46.5	45.8	46.9
DEC DS5500	R3000/3010	32 Mb	Ultrix 4.1	21.5	21.9	21.1
HP 9000/400s	MC68040/int	16 Mb	HP UX 8.0	11.8	12.9	11.0
IBM RS6000/550	4164/int	64 Mb	AIX 3.1	54.3	34.5	73.5
Intel i860/40	i860/int	16 Mb	Unix860/4.0	26.7	19.9	32.5
MIPS RC6280	R6000/6010	32 Mb	Risc/OS4.52	46.5	45.0	47.6
SGI 4D/320S	R3000/3010	64 Mb	IRIX 3.3	19.5	22.6	17.6
Sun Sparcstn-2	CY7C601/TI	16 Mb	SunOS 4.1.1	21.2	20.7	21.5

TABLE 1.1: Benchmark data for some selected workstations.

SPECfp is known as *SPECmark*, and has become a popular measure. Table 1.1 lists these three measures for a few systems (denoted as MARK, INT, and FP). The CPU/FPU column in this table gives the chips used for CPU and floating point unit respectively, where "int" means that the floating point arithmetic is integrated into the main CPU. Thus, SPARCstation-2 is about 21.2 times faster than a VAX11/780 on integer operations. The data shown here is for illustrative purposes only, and *not* intended for a direct comparison, since the selected systems do not necessarily fall in the same price/performance category. Also, some important information such as cache size, compiler version, background load, etc., is not indicated.

SPEC has developed two other measures. *SPECthruput* is a measure of CPU performance under moderate CPU contention. To obtain this measure for a multi-processor with n processors, two copies of the SPEC benchmark are run concurrently on each CPU, and the elapsed time is noted. For reference, two copies are run concurrently on a VAX11/780. The ratio of the times then gives a rating similar to SPECmark, except that the effect of CPU contention is also reflected. For the overall system performance, SPEC has developed a benchmark, called System Development Multitasking (SDM). It is a shell-script that exercises various components of the system in a multitasking Unix environment. The measure is reported in terms of the number of scripts executed per hour as a function of the degree of multiprogramming. It takes into account not only the processing speed, but also the I/O speed and O/S overhead.

In the above, we indicated that an average measure such as SPECint is obtained by taking the geometric mean of individual benchmark results. Arithmetic mean may seem more natural for averaging, but is undesirable for several reasons. One problem is that arithmetic mean does not preserve running time ratios, such as those in Table 1.1. To see this, let σ_{t1} and σ_{t2} denote the running times of two benchmarks on a test machine, and σ_{r1} and σ_{r2} those on the reference machine. Let AM denote arithmetic mean. It is easy to see that

$$AM\left(\frac{\sigma_{t1}}{\sigma_{r1}}, \frac{\sigma_{t2}}{\sigma_{r2}}\right) \neq \frac{AM(\sigma_{t1}, \sigma_{t2})}{AM(\sigma_{r1}, \sigma_{r2})} \tag{5.1}$$

The significance of this result is that if we compute the arithmetic mean using the numbers given in Table 1.1, we will not get the same results as those obtained by taking the ratios of averaged times on the desired machine and VAX11/780. Harmonic mean also has the same problem, but geometric mean does not. Because of this, published benchmarks always report geometric means. There is another advantage of geometric means, which is seen more easily by considering an extreme case. Suppose that the normalized speeds of two benchmarks are 10 and 90 respectively. Then the arithmetic mean (= 50) is considerably higher than the geometric mean (= 30). Here the arithmetic mean essentially depends on the "good" numbers, and tends to ignore the poor ones. On the other hand, if we were looking at running times instead of speeds, arithmetic mean will do the opposite! Geometric mean, on the other hand, will not be affected by this change.

1.5.2 Highly Parallel Architectures

Most of the traditional performance measures and the techniques for obtaining them are geared toward uniprocessor or transparent multiprocessor systems. When dealing with modern machines with a large number of processors connected via an interconnection network, possibly with multiple levels of pipelining and vector processing capabilities in each processor, the characterization and measurement of performance becomes difficult. In the following, we briefly examine some of these problems.

Let us start with speed characterization in terms of MIPS or MFLOPS. In spite of the problems with these measures, they are easily understood and useful for conventional machines. For example, if two RISC machines A and B have the specified ratings of 40 and 20 MFLOPS respectively, there is little risk in predicting that A would be significantly faster than B for compute-intensive floating-point applications. Unfortunately, in the absence of further information, this assessment may well be totally wrong if A and B were parallel machines! The problem is that in the case of a parallel machine, the raw processing power is *not* the only dominant factor in determining the observed speed; *a lot depends on how much inherent parallelism the application has, and to what extent this parallelism can be exploited by the machine*. Naturally, if the machine provides far greater parallelism than can be reasonably exploited, a large gap may exist between the peak MIPS/MFLOPS claim of the machine and what is observed on real applications. As an example, consider a vector machine that takes, on the average, 250 nanoseconds per floating point operation and has vector registers of size 500. Such a machine can claim a maximum speed of 2 Giga-FLOPS; however, achieving this speed requires that most vectors have 500 or more elements. With a more realistic average vector size of 50, the machine can only provide a throughput of 200 MFLOPS, which is only 10% of the peak rate. In this situation, a machine that takes 125 nanoseconds per operation and has vector registers of size 50 appears 5 times slower, but is actually twice as fast!

The above comments apply equally well with respect to inherent parallelism of the applications. Some applications have large inherent parallelism and thus can benefit from a large number of processors, but others cannot. For example, consider two machines: machine A that has 64 processors each rated at 8 MIPS, whereas machine B has 16 processors each rated at 16 MIPS. It appears that machine A is twice as powerful as machine B; however, an application that has no more than 16 parallel activities would run twice as fast on machine B. On the other hand, an application that can be divided up into 64 parallel activities may run *more than twice as fast* on machine A because of the lack of process switching overhead.

To further illustrate the importance of inherent parallelism, consider a simple result known as *Amdahl's Law*. Suppose that the fraction f of a program is parallelizable, and the other $1 - f$ is purely sequential. Also assume that the parallelizable part has linear speedup, i.e., with n processors, it will take $1/n$th the time needed on one processor. Then the effective speed with n processors, denoted $S(n)$, is given by

$$S(n) = \frac{S(1)}{1 - f + f/n} \tag{5.2}$$

Note that as $n \to \infty$, $S(n)$ approaches $S(1)/(1 - f)$. Thus, if $f = 0.5$, we can get only a two-fold increase in speed even with an infinite number of processors. Of course, the assumption of sustained linear speed up is itself unrealistic. Also, we have ignored all the data propagation and management overhead.

In view of these difficulties, MIPS/MFLOPS ratings may be totally useless for a parallel machine. Let us now assess the usefulness of synthetic benchmarks. It is immediately seen that unlike sequential machine benchmarks like Whetstone and Dhrystone, we cannot construct synthetic benchmarks for parallel machines by only using statistical measures like the fraction of statements and variables of each type. We also need to characterize the inherent parallelism in the programs. Naturally, this requires a careful definition for what is meant by *inherent parallelism*. To be accurate, we must distinguish between *data parallelism* and *code parallelism*. Data parallelism refers to the manipulation of multiple data items in parallel by the same operation and is the type of parallelism exploited by SIMD (single-instruction, multiple-data) machines. Such parallelism arises in working with structured data such as vectors, matrices, lists, and sets. Data parallelism can be characterized by the average number and fraction of data items that can be manipulated in parallel. (The first measure depends on the size of the problem, but the latter only on the nature of the problem.) Code parallelism refers to how finely the code can be divided up into logical pieces that can run in parallel. (Each such piece may internally have data parallelism that the machine can also exploit.) A possible measure here is the "average parallelism", denoted σ, that we can define as follows:

$$\sigma = \sum_{n=1}^{\infty} n f(n) \tag{5.3}$$

where $f(n)$ is the fraction of code that can be split into at most n parallel activities. This measure may be difficult to compute without estimating $f(n)$ explicitly. Unfortunately, $f(n)$ is not a well-defined quantity since it says nothing of the interactions between the n parallel activities, or about the data dependencies between these and other activities. To accurately reflect the latter, we can use a task-graph or data-flow model of the application, but it is difficult to characterize the information contained there by a few simple measures.

The effective exploitation of inherent parallelism is another important issue in comparing parallel machines. This is a very complex issue to address. Let us start from the algorithm side. In the case of a conventional machine, the algorithm used does not matter since we can run the same (or almost same) high-level language program on all the machines that we wish to compare. Unfortunately, this is not so in the case of a parallel machine. The problem is that a well-designed parallel algorithm depends on several architectural characteristics of the machine on which it is supposed to run. Some of these characteristics are number of processors (few or many), interconnection pattern (bus, crossbar, mesh, etc.), interaction mechanism (shared memory or message passing), and vector register size. For example, it is unfair to take an algorithm that assumes the availability of a large shared memory and expect it to run well on a machine that doesn't have any shared memory. An obvious approach to getting around this problem is to pick the optimal algorithm for each machine under consideration. Unfortunately, picking the best algorithm for a given machine is itself a formidable problem. Furthermore, even for a given machine type (e.g., a hypercube), the optimal algorithm would usually depend on how many processors were installed!

Even if we can identify a good algorithm for a given architecture, several other aspects may come into play. For example, the capabilities of the language in which the algorithm is expressed could have a major impact on how well or poorly the algorithm can be implemented. For example, an unoptimized implementation of Ada-like entry call mechanism on shared memory machine may be much less efficient than a routine implementation of monitor-based interaction. Thus, a parallel algorithm has an even greater language and compiler dependency than a sequential algorithm. Many other characteristics of the machine and/or the operating system may affect how well a given algorithm can be implemented. These are timing characteristics (e.g., how the communication time compares against the computation time), process management (e.g., whether light-weight processes are available and whether multiprogramming is supported), scheduling mechanism, and so on. Finally, in using a benchmark, one should ensure that the demands placed on the system resources are sufficiently high to be representative of "real-life"; otherwise, it is possible to get misleading results simply because those resources happened to be plentiful during the benchmark tests. Although these problems apply to both sequential and parallel machines, the latter are more likely to have plentiful resources, and may require more care. Here are several examples of problematic situations:

1. If the benchmark is sufficiently small in size, it may reside completely in the cache; therefore, machines with large caches may appear to be much superior to those with smaller caches. For example, Dhrystone benchmark suffers from this problem.

2. A large memory may eliminate paging for medium-size programs and thus result in small execution times, even if the paging scheme is poorly designed.
3. If I/O performance is of interest, but the benchmark does not provide adequate I/O load, good performance may be obtained simply because there is enough buffer space to drastically reduce the real I/O frequency.
4. If the benchmark contains a lot of dead code or code that can be optimized, it is possible to get a small execution time at the expense of a much longer compilation time. Similar comments apply with respect to parallelism.

To summarize, although synthetic benchmarks are useful for parallel machines, it is difficult to design good benchmarks without due consideration to various features of the machine in question including size, architecture, operating system, and compiler. With such dependencies in the benchmark, observing the performance of the same benchmark on different systems may be of questionable value. (This also gives vendors plenty of opportunity to discredit direct comparisons and instead publicize their own measurements!) What is needed is the design of different "versions" of a benchmark starting from a common high-level specification. This is not only a difficult task, but also leaves room for disagreement since different versions may have very different sizes. One further consequence of these difficulties is that the benchmarking on parallel machines may not have the same kind of predictive value as on a conventional machine. For example, consider programs A and B that are functionally similar but B involves twice as much computation as A on a sequential machine. In this situation, it may be nearly impossible to estimate a priori how the running time of B will compare against that of A on a parallel machine, or how the running time of A will change if the number of processors is doubled. Synthetic programs also suffer from similar problems, and moreover would be extremely difficult to design because of the need to select proper algorithms based on architectural and operating system characteristics.

One trend in parallel numeric computation is to let the user write programs without regard to parallelism, and shift the burden of exploiting parallelism to the compiler. In such cases, synthetic benchmarks developed for sequential machines can be used directly, but this still does not solve the problem. Basically, this approach passes the buck to the compiler, so a well-crafted compiler could show a relatively slow machine in a much more favorable light. The problem of inherent parallelism still remains. That is, if the benchmark code is mostly nonparallelizable, a highly parallel machine may not do much better than a modest single-processor machine. For example, Whetstone, Dhrystone, and Spice benchmarks contain little vectorizable code and thus would only provide worst case performance for a vector machine. On the other hand, Linpack, Livermore Fortran Kernel, and Stanford floating point benchmarks all contain quite a bit of vectorizable code, and thus would show a vector machine in a favorable light.

There are two commonly used measures for describing both inherent and exploitable parallelism of a given algorithm. These are *speedup* and *efficiency*. Speedup, denoted $S(p)$, is defined as the running time of the best possible sequential algorithm divided by the running time of the given parallel algorithm using p processors. Efficiency is defined as $S(p)/p$. These measures can be used for inherent parallelism under an idealized model of a machine with p identical processors: no overhead, zero or constant communication costs, etc. This makes these measures useful for comparing two different algorithms for the same problem at an abstract level. Speedup and efficiency can also be used to characterize exploitable parallelism by measuring them on a real machine. Of course, the measured values depend on various characteristics of the machine and the results may not extend easily if the problem or machine characteristics are changed slightly. For example, doubling the size of the problem may not retain the same value for speedup or efficiency.

1.6 Exercises

1. In the computing environment you use, find out what monitoring facilities are available for estimating usage of various system resources (CPU, memory, disk, channels, and communication network). Study documentation on each one of these, and run them to get a feel for the information they gather.
2. Many compilers come with a *profiler* utility, which can provide you with a break-up of the time spent in various procedures of the program, and the number of times each procedure is called. Find out how to use the profiler and run it on a reasonably complex program that you may have written. Examine the output and state what valuable information you have obtained from the profiler that would help you in improving the performance of your program.
3. Find out what discrete event simulation packages are available at your site. Select one package and explore how you would simulate a simple single-server queuing system using it.
4. Characterize the workload on your computer system. In particular, determine if there are several classes of users with very different resource requirements, and characterize the resource requirements of these classes. What difficulties (other than inadequate data) might you encounter in doing such a study?
5. Suppose that you are considering setting up a small local area network consisting of a file server and a few (at least 4) diskless workstations. Suppose that your budgeting limit is $100,000, disk requirements between 1.5 and 2 GB, and at least 12 Mb memory per workstation. You also want to have a tape drive for back-ups (cartridge or reel), a printer, and adequate memory on the server to handle all clients. One major application that you wish to support is simulation of complex queuing systems. Collect information on products that appear viable, and carefully study technical data on them. How would you decide which system is best, performance-wise? What factors, other than performance, should be considered in making a selection?

6. Consider a multiprocessor system with n processors. If k out of n processors are working, we say that the system is in state k. In each state, the system exhibits a given throughput. Discuss what interesting performance and reliability measures you can obtain from such a model.
7. Consider the problem of designing an instruction pipeline for a computer. The specific question of interest is how many stages should this pipeline have? Which of the four techniques discussed in Section 1.2 is most suited for answering this question?

Bibliographic Notes

A survey of the performance evaluation field may be found in Heidelberger and Lavenberg (1984), which also contains a rich bibliography on the subject. A recent survey of the field that also includes an assessment of the progress in the past 25 years appears in Reiser (1991). There are many text books on performance modeling, a few recent books that are not referenced elsewhere in this text are Wolff (1989), Jain (1990) and King (1990). Siewiorek and Swarz (1982) and Johnson (1989) provide comprehensive surveys of reliability characterization and evaluation in computing systems. Our classification in Section 1.1 is partly based on the former. These books also include case studies on many highly reliable computer systems for a range of applications.

A survey of hybrid modeling appears in Shanthikumar and Sargent (1983). Detailed treatment of workload characterization may be found in Ferrari (1978, 1984), and Ferrari, Serazzi, and Zeigner (1983). Some more recent work appears in Calzarossa and Ferrari (1986). The Whetstone benchmark is reported in Curnow and Wichman (1976). The Dhrystone benchmark appears in Weicker (1984). A recent discussion on several benchmarks and comparison tables for many computer systems can be found in Price (1989). Dongarra, Martin, and Worlton (1987) discuss the pitfalls in benchmarking. Detailed discussion on the problem of selecting computer systems may be found in Ferrari (1978). A recent survey article on parallel architectures appears in Duncan (1990). Lubeck, Moore, and Mendez (1985) provides benchmark comparisons of three supercomputers. Lipovski and Malek (1987) contains a collection of articles on recent architectures. The concept of "average parallelism" was motivated by Eager, Zahorjan and Lazowska (1989). This paper also gives bounds on speedup and efficiency based on average parallelism. Several books are devoted to a detailed discussion of parallel architectures and algorithms, such as Hwang and Briggs (1984) and Hennessy and Patterson (1990). For detailed benchmark data on contemporary systems, the reader should consult the quarterly newsletter published by SPEC.

CHAPTER

2

Measurement Techniques

In this chapter we discuss the three fundamental techniques for measuring performance parameters of a computer system: hardware, software, and hybrid. We also examine certain auxiliary topics such as the use of measurements in real-time control of performance, measurability limitations, and monitoring of parallel and distributed systems.

2.1 Classification of Measurement Techniques

A real measurement experiment could be rather involved, but if we can identify the measurement primitives needed to support it, the entire problem becomes easy to solve. Before discussing these primitives, let us introduce the concepts of event and state. The *state* of the system is defined by the values contained in various storage elements, be they memory locations, registers, or flip-flops. In any measurement situation, only a few of these state holders (or *state variables*) are relevant. Depending on the measurement objectives, some of these may be used to define the *relevant states* and others to provide further information about what is happening in those states. We call the former *primary variables* and others *auxiliary*. For example, the relevant states may be only the busy/idle condition of the paging disk, but we may be interested in knowing the number of free memory blocks whenever a page I/O is initiated. We refer to a change in a relevant state variable as an *event*. The events could also be classified as primary or auxiliary depending on what type of state variables are involved. Now we can enumerate the primitive measurements as follows:

1. The number of times a given state is visited during a given time interval. (Sometimes, we may want relative frequencies, instead of absolute numbers, but that is a trivial change.) Some examples are the number of times a data structure is referenced, relative frequency of executing a given instruction, number of times the I/O is done from cylinder 0 of some disk, etc. In the last example, the relevant state is defined by the situation where I/O is in progress on cylinder 0 and the primary event is the initiation of such an I/O operation. We call these measurements type $\mathcal{A}$.
2. The values of auxiliary state variables whenever a relevant state is entered. For example, we may wish to record the number of processes in the ready list whenever an I/O operation is initiated. We call these type $\mathcal{B}$ measurements.
3. The fraction (or amount) of time for which the system is in a given state. As an example, we may want to know what fraction of the time the disk head stays on cylinder 0. We call these type $\mathcal{C}$ measurements.

It is clear that if we can choose the relevant states any way we want, these three measurement types cover all the information that we may be interested in obtaining. Thus, there are two issues in measurement: (a) how do we recognize conditions for measurement and (b) how do we actually measure the quantity of interest. The "condition for measurement" can be recognized in two ways:

1. As being in a relevant state. A natural way to do this is to sample the system and check if the primary state variables have the desired values. For example, to check if the control is inside a given procedure, we sample the program counter and see if it contains an address that belongs to that procedure. This leads to *sampled monitoring*.
2. As an event that brings the system to a relevant state. Thus, to check if the control is inside a given procedure, we explicitly look for the events of entry to and exit from the procedure. This leads to *trace monitoring*.

It is easy to see that we can do measurements of all three types using trace monitoring. Type $\mathcal{A}$ measurements cannot be done using sampling, since the sampling would fail to count all instances when the system was in the desired state. Even relative frequencies cannot be estimated properly by sampling, because if two consecutive samples show the system to be in the same state, we cannot tell if the system has been in that state or is visiting it the next time. However, if the duration of desired states is shorter than the inter-sample gap, relative frequencies can be estimated reliably. Similar comments apply to type $\mathcal{B}$ measurements. However, type $\mathcal{C}$ measurements are possible by sampling since the computed relative frequency really gives an estimate of the fraction of time spent in the desired state. Multiplying this by the measurement duration, we can also get an estimate of total time spent in the desired state. Of course, sampling only gives us an estimate, not the exact answer.

It may appear from the above discussion that trace monitoring is always preferable to sampling, but this is not true. We shall comment on this aspect later, but first we introduce another dimension for classifying the measurement techniques. This dimension has to do with the type of instrumentation used in monitoring. The instrumentation can be broadly divided into the following three classes:

Hardware monitoring: This technique employs additional monitoring hardware that is interfaced with the system under measurement in a nonintrusive way. The main advantage of this technique is that the measurement does not interfere with the normal functioning of the monitored system and fast events can be captured. However, it is expensive and has difficulty in doing software-level measurements. Typical applications of this technique are in measurements of types $\mathcal{A}$ and $\mathcal{C}$ for fast occurring events, e.g., in measuring device utilizations, cache hit rate, and pipeline flush rate.

Software monitoring: This technique uses some measurement code either embedded in the existing software or as a separate set of routines. The main advantage of this technique is its generality and flexibility. The disadvantages are that it may seriously interfere with the normal functioning of the system and cannot be used to capture fast occurring events. This technique is most appropriate for obtaining user program and operating system related information, such as the time spent executing a particular routine, page-fault frequency, and average number of processes in each possible state.

Hybrid monitoring: This technique draws upon the advantages of both hardware and software monitoring. All relevant signals are collected under software control and sent to another machine for measurement and processing. The advantages are that it is flexible and that its domain of application overlaps those of both hardware and software monitoring. The disadvantages are that the synchronization requirements between the measuring and measured system may cause some interference, and it is expensive and cumbersome to obtain detailed program or O/S-level measurements.

We shall discuss these three techniques in the next three sections. Subject to the limitations mentioned above, each technique can use both sampling and trace monitoring, and we shall discuss both types in each case. In illustrating the techniques, we shall mostly draw on examples that are appropriate for the type of measurement under discussion. It is therefore important to note at the outset the criteria for deciding which technique is most suitable for a given problem. The most important issues in the selection are as follows:

1. *Accessibility.* As already indicated, the hardware may be unaware of the software-level information and thus unable to obtain it. An example is the information regarding the allocation of various system resources to a process. Similarly, the functions that are handled entirely in hardware such as cache management, address translation, and physical layer of networking may be inaccessible to software.

2. *Event frequency.* If the events occur too rapidly, the software may be unable to track them. Thus, we have to either select hardware monitoring or a sampled measurement in software. (The slow sampling rate by software may or may not be a handicap in obtaining accurate information.)
3. *Monitor artifact.* The interference caused by measurement may perturb the workload significantly. For example, if we monitor the I/O traffic on a disk and record the information on that disk itself, the measurements are no longer accurate. If there is no easy way to compensate for monitor artifact, we may have to try a different monitoring technique.
4. *Overhead.* In some situations, the interference may either not affect the measurement accuracy or may be easy to compensate for. Nevertheless, the interference may be unacceptable because of a significant reduction in useful work. (This aspect is relevant only when measuring under a "live" workload.)
5. *Flexibility.* This issue has to do with how easy it is to modify or upgrade the instrumentation and/or the information being collected. Generally, software instrumentation is easier to change than hybrid instrumentation, which in turn is easier to change than hardware instrumentation.

Often one encounters peculiar problems different from the inherent limitations of the chosen technique. One such problem is that certain signals or state variables may be off-limits for reasons of security, privacy, protection, lack of documentation, unavailability of source code, and inability to access (e.g., signals/registers buried inside a chip). We shall discuss more details on this in Section 2.5.2. Another problem is poor *event resolution*, i.e., the events of interest can be monitored, but the information needed to classify them is inadequate. For example, we may be able to count the total number of I/O operations initiated on a given disk, but we cannot tell how many of those came from batch jobs and how many from interactive jobs. Yet another problem is poor *clock resolution*, which results in inaccurate timing of fast occurring events. Unfortunately, in contemporary systems, most of these problems are a rule, rather than an exception, and may dictate the monitoring technique. For example, a poor timer resolution at the software level may force us to settle for hardware monitoring, even though the latter may not be suitable according to other criteria. Even worse, no technique may yield satisfactory information, and one may have to depend on assumptions, approximations, and indirect measurement. For example, if the breakdown of I/O initiations by job categories is not available, one may have to estimate relative frequency of the I/O initiated by interactive jobs using some other information.

2.2 Hardware Monitoring

In hardware monitoring, the conditions for measurement are indicated by a logic signal S, synthesized using more primitive logic signals available from the machine backplane. Here S is a single-bit signal, but it may be synthesized using both single-bit and multi-bit signals. Thus, in addition to normal boolean functions, the synthesizer should also provide functions such as comparison of multi-bit signals, AND of all bits, OR of all bits, etc., that take multi-bit signals and yield single-bit outputs. By convention, we assume that a 0 to 1 transition in S takes us to a relevant state, and a 1 to 0 transition takes us out of such a state. For example, suppose that the condition of interest is the simultaneous operation of two devices, say D_1 and D_2. Also suppose that the busy condition for device D_i is indicated by a boolean flag F_i in the backplane. Then $S = F_1 \wedge F_2$. In general, $S = 1$ only indicates that we are in *some relevant state*. If there is more than one such state and the measurement calls for distinguishing among them, a multi-bit signal, say S', synthesized using auxiliary state variables, will also be required. For example, if we wish to determine the relative frequency of executing each instruction, a 0 to 1 transition in S may indicate that a new instruction has been fetched into the instruction register, and S' is the set of bits that represent the opcode.

With the above setup, type $\mathcal{A}$ measurements involve incrementing a counter whenever S makes a 0 to 1 transition. The counter is chosen from an array indexed by S'. (The signal S' may be valid only when $S = 1$ as in the instruction frequency example above.) For type $\mathcal{B}$ measurements, we use the leading edge of S to transfer auxiliary state information from the backplane to hardware registers (or to a memory module that is a part of the monitor). In discussing type $\mathcal{C}$ measurement, let us assume that S is already synthesized appropriately; i.e., there is no S' to worry about. The measurement can be done using either the trace or the sampling technique. In the trace technique, we can accumulate the duration for which $S = 1$ by keeping track of the times when S makes 0 to 1 and 1 to 0 transitions. This is nearly impossible to do considering the rapid rate at which hardware signals change. Because of this, *type $\mathcal{C}$ measurements in hardware are almost invariably done by sampling*. The idea is to use S to gate clock pulses, which are then counted by a hardware counter.

It is important to note that a hardware monitor is only supposed to act as a "silent observer" of the system activity. That is, the monitor should have its own counters, timers, logic synthesizers, memory modules, etc., rather than sharing the hardware provided by the system under measurement. The measured system may still be responsible for starting measurements and storing or displaying final results, but the effect of these is usually insignificant. Thus, *hardware monitors generally do not contribute to monitor artifact*. By their very nature, hardware monitors can easily capture fast occurring events, but are poor in obtaining detailed software-level information.

In the following, we consider some details of sampled monitoring of type $\mathcal{C}$. The general setup is shown in Fig. 2-1. At the beginning of the measurement interval, the counter is set to 0. The function synthesizer generates the event signal S using the raw inputs available from the machine backplane. The boolean function that defines the event in terms of the raw input signals is itself selected by putting the appropriate code in the event definition register. The output signal S is then ANDed with the clock signal and used to increment the counter. The interrupt generator circuit detects the end of the measurement period and sets the interrupt flag. Notice that the clock signal is effective only while the interrupt flag is clear. Thus, setting the interrupt flag freezes the counter. The value contained in the counter at this point gives the duration for which the condition of interest prevailed during the measurement interval. It can be read by the interrupt handler (implemented either via additional hardware or in the software of the system under measurement).

If the purpose of the experiment is to measure the fraction of time, it is desirable to choose the measurement interval as 2^N clock pulses (where N is the number of bits in the counter), as this avoids explicit division for computing the fraction. In this case, the interrupt generator circuit is nothing more than an N-bit straight binary counter with a logical NOR of its outputs. We shall see this explicitly in Example 2.1.

Although the measurements can be done completely autonomously, it is preferable to let the measured system interact with the monitor at the start and end of a measurement session. This requires two facilities. First, there should be a machine instruction or a system call that starts the measurement (i.e., clears the counter, interrupt generator, and the interrupt flag, and loads the event definition register with the appropriate selection code). Second, the CPU should be able to recognize the interrupt posted by the measurement circuit and read the value contained in the counter. The implementation of these facilities is easy if the CPU can interact with the hardware monitor as it would interact with a device. That is, the hardware monitor would have an entry in the interrupt vector of the machine, and its event definition register and counter would appear like command and data registers to the CPU. The interaction then takes place via the normal bus interface. This arrangement also has the advantage that the signals available on the data bus directly (e.g., instruction opcodes, operand addresses, and operand values). can be picked up without any special purpose interfacing. For other signals, the following two approaches are possible:

1. Deliberately put the signals on the data bus so that the monitor can pick them off. For example, any information contained in a memory location (general purpose register) can be accessed by a load (store) type of instruction. When the CPU instructs the monitor to start up, it can also indicate what information will be coming on the data bus and in what order. The monitor can store this information into its own registers for later use.
2. Directly tap the pins on various chips. The desired information may exist on a pin only at certain times, so the monitor needs to save it for later use.

The main problem with the first approach is that the software running on the measured system must issue appropriate instructions to put the relevant information on the bus. Doing so amounts to hybrid monitoring (monitoring by hardware under software control), instead of hardware monitoring (a silent observation of what is going on). This problem does not exist with the second approach. However, we now have two other difficulties. First, any signal that is buried inside a VLSI chip and not available on the pins cannot be measured.

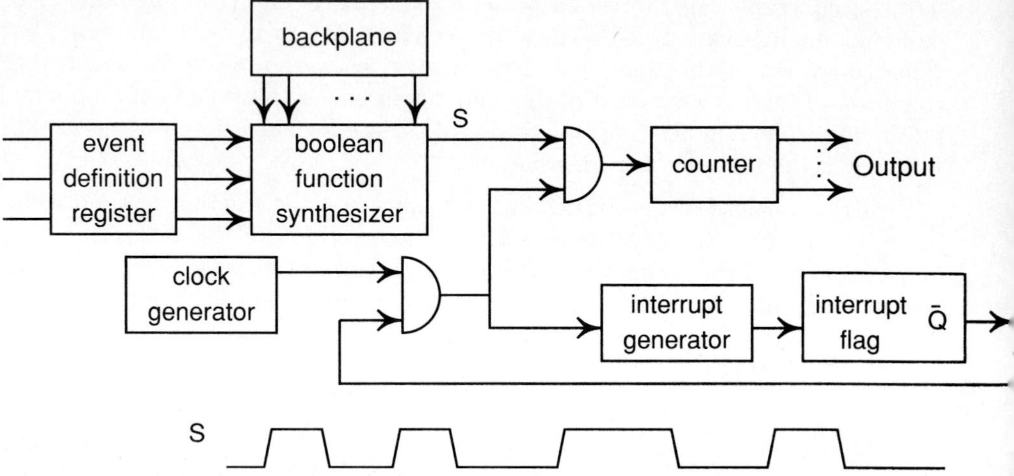

FIGURE 2-1: Instrumentation for sampled hardware monitoring.

Second, a haphazard tapping of signals at various points in a circuit board is something that should never be allowed! Thus, only those signals that have been explicitly brought out to a special connector by the board manufacturer are really accessible. Also, in the absence of any standardization of what these additional signals are, it is difficult to design a general purpose monitor (even for a given bus type). It is clear that providing a comprehensive hardware monitor as an afterthought is a nearly impossible task. We now illustrate the measurement procedure by a concrete example.

Example 2.1 Consider a system with one CPU and n channels. Show the setup for measuring the fraction of time the CPU and k channels (for a given $k \in 1\,..\,n$) are busy simultaneously.

Solution The required input signals are the CPU-busy bit (denoted CpB) and the channel-busy bits (denoted ChB_i for channel i). We assume that these are available from the backplane. Let $f_{k/n}$ denote the boolean function that generates the output 1 if exactly k out of its n boolean inputs are at logic 1. Then the function synthesizer component of Fig. 2-1 must compute the boolean function S as follows:

$$S = CpB \wedge f_{k/n}(ChB_1, \ldots, ChB_n) \tag{2.1}$$

The details of the setup are shown in Fig. 2-2. For each clock pulse, if S is high and the measurement interval is not over, the duration counter will be incremented by 1. The N-bit binary counter along with the NOR gate acts as an interrupt generator. Obviously, the NOR gate output will make a 0-to-1 transition when the counter overflows (i.e., after 2^N clock pulses have been generated). This, in turn, will set the latch and freeze the duration counter. The measurement can be controlled at the program level by providing a system call

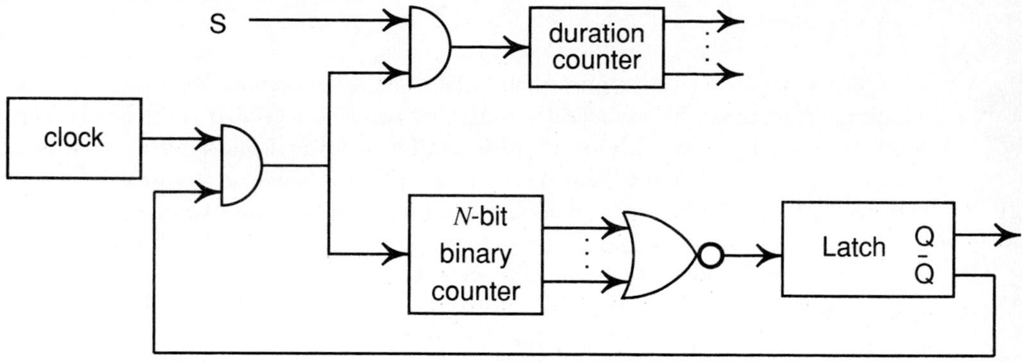

FIGURE 2-2: Setup for CPU-Channel overlap measurement.

such as IO_OVERLAP(k, X) (where X indicates the memory location in which the measurement result is returned). The system call could spawn a surrogate process to do the following:

1. Determine the function code to load into the event definition register using the parameter k.
2. Initialize the event definition register, clear both counters, and reset the interrupt latch (should be done last). The monitoring would then start automatically.
3. Block until the monitor posts an interrupt. Then read the value from the duration counter, convert it to a real number, put it in location X, and exit.

□

Sampled measurement may yield erroneous results unless one is careful in the experimental setup. For example, consider the setup for measuring CPU utilization (e.g., Fig. 2-2 with $k = 0$). We can make the following observations regarding this setup:

1. The number of samples used in the experiment is fixed ($= 2^N$). Since sampling gives only statistical information, it is necessary to make N sufficiently large. Given that we are dealing with a random signal, the considerations in choosing N are the same as those in choosing the number of observations in a simulation experiment.
2. Let f denote the sampling frequency (same as the clock rate). Then the measurement interval T is given by $2^N/f$. For good accuracy, it is essential that the signal S makes many transitions during the period T. (This would be necessary even in trace monitoring.)
3. Any synchronization between the sampling and sampled signal should be avoided. To see the problem, note that if the two signals were perfectly

synchronized, the measured utilization will be 100% (in phase) or 0% (out of phase).

For a fixed N, the requirement (2) gives an *upper bound* on f, i.e., the sampling rate must be sufficiently small to observe signal S sufficiently long. Within reasonable time limits, there is really no lower bound on f! This is an important result, since it allows us to do sampling in software (which is slow), if software monitoring is more convenient than hardware monitoring. For example, if the O/S schedules a special *idle process* when there is no regular process on the ready list, the CPU busy bit will always be on, and hardware monitoring is not possible without access to the id of the running process. In this situation, it is much more convenient to periodically sample the id of the running process at the software level and thereby estimate the CPU utilization.

In most cases, the sampled signal is random (at least relative to the sampling signal) and the synchronization problem mentioned in (3) above does not arise. If however, the sampled signal is periodic (or nearly periodic), some care is needed to avoid erroneous results. Notice that the well-known *Nyquist criterion* applies in this case and requires that f is larger than twice the frequency of the sampled signal. An alternate method is to "randomize" the sampling signal itself. To this end, we can start with a high-frequency clock and feed it to a counter with a pseudo random period. The output could then be used for sampling. Although this scheme is a bit more complex, it would yield greater accuracy if the number of samples 2^N is fixed.

As stated earlier, hardware monitoring may be inconvenient for measuring software-level characteristics. We illustrate this by an example.

Example 2.2 Devise a sampled measurement technique for estimating the time spent by a program within a given loop.

Solution The setup is sketched in Fig. 2-3. The "sync" signal indicates that: (a) the address bus has a valid address, and (b) the address is for an instruction, rather than for data. A 0 to 1 transition in the sync signal is used to transfer instruction address from the bus to a register. This address is then checked against a lower and upper bound to find out if it corresponds to the sequence of instructions belonging to the loop in question. The output of the comparator is the desired signal S, which can be used to gate clock pulses and count them exactly as in Fig. 2-2. (The details of counting are not shown.) The final count, multiplied by the clock period gives an estimate of the time spent in the loop. There are a few points worth mentioning about this setup:

1. Since the address bus always carries real addresses, this scheme will not work in a virtual memory system, or any other system where the physical addresses are not guaranteed to be contiguous. In memory management schemes where the programs are dynamically relocated but contiguous, the bound registers in Fig. 2-3 must be reloaded every time the program is moved.

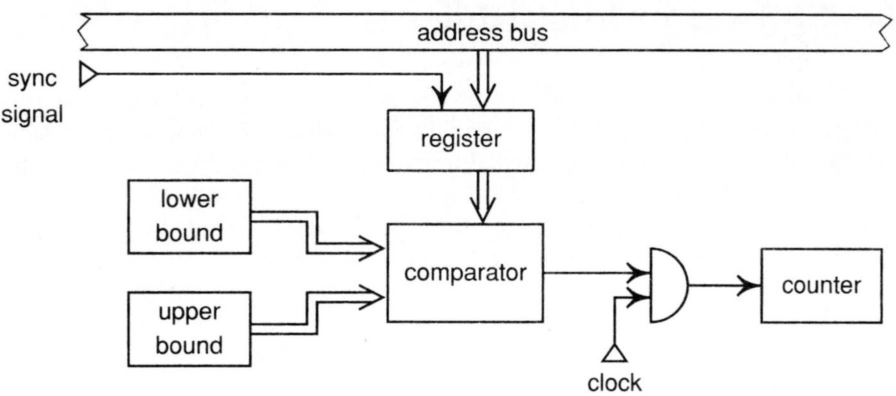

FIGURE 2-3: Measuring time spent in a loop.

2. Since the program counter (PC) holds only the instruction addresses, and these addresses are virtual (and hence contiguous), it is natural to ask why we have to get addresses from the address bus. The reason is that the PC lies inside the microprocessor chip and cannot be accessed directly (without using the bus). Virtual addresses also have the disadvantage that several programs could have the same set of virtual addresses.

3. Because of sampled measurement, the time duration obtained from the experiment is only an approximation. Its accuracy depends on how the sampling is carried out.

□

Obtaining process-specific measurements is also cumbersome using hardware monitoring. For example, suppose that we want to measure the CPU utilization attributable to process n. For this, the function synthesizer will AND the CPU-busy signal with the output of a comparator that checks if the id of the currently running process is n. Unfortunately, the monitor cannot obtain the process id just by tapping into some signals on the backplane. Instead, the system must maintain the id of the currently running process in some register that is accessible to the monitor. Obtaining the CPU utilization attributable to several (or all) processes requires a bit more work, since the same duration counter must be shared by all of them. This is done as follows: whenever a process, say n, releases the CPU, the contents of the counter are stored away in the nth element of an array, say L, so that the counter can be correctly restored when process n is rescheduled. Note that L must be a part of the monitoring hardware, and loading and saving should be done in response to process switches on the monitored system. Obviously, the clock must be blocked from reaching the counter while the reloading is being done. All these requirements make the monitoring rather cumbersome. We shall see in Section 2.4 that this problem is very nicely solved by hybrid monitoring.

2.3 Software Monitoring

Software monitoring is most suited for program-level measurements and requires some support from the operating system and the hardware. The most important facility is a *programmable timer*, needed for controlling time durations. It can be loaded with the desired time interval. Once started, it counts down and generates an interrupt when the remaining time reaches zero. The interrupt handling routine could then take appropriate actions, such as reading state variables or processing collected data and closing down the experiment. Another important facility is a *virtual clock*, which is needed for measuring process-specific time durations. The virtual clock for a process P_i can be thought of as a real-time clock that runs only while process P_i is under execution. A single physical clock is adequate to provide a virtual clock for every process running on the CPU. Basically, the idea is to reserve a slot in the process control block (PCB) of each process for storing timer contents. When a given process P_i is switched out, the timer contents are stored in its PCB slot. Later when P_i is switched back in, the timer contents are restored. It is also useful to have a *programmable virtual timer*, i.e., a programmable timer that runs down only when the corresponding process is executing. It should also be possible to associate an arbitrary routine with a programmable timer (real or virtual), so that desired actions can be taken whenever the timer expires. This capability is similar to that available for installing new device-drivers, and is supported by many contemporary operating systems. The measurements often involve reading and modifying privileged information, such as the one contained in various kernel data structures. This is usually provided via *system calls*, some of which may be usable only in privileged mode. User-level multiprocessing, i.e., mechanisms for creating/destroying processes, and for interprocess communication and synchronization, are often very handy in software monitoring.

Both trace and sampling are useful in the context of software monitoring. We discuss these briefly in the next two subsections. The discussion that follows applies to all three measurement types ($\mathcal{A}$, $\mathcal{B}$, or $\mathcal{C}$) with differences arising only in terms of precisely what is recorded.

2.3.1 Trace Monitoring

Trace monitoring involves adding some extra code to a program to record certain information whenever events of interest occur. For example, to measure the I/O rate for each device, we only need to maintain a counter for each device that is incremented on each I/O initiation. Similarly, the average time taken per I/O operation on a given device can be measured by also keeping track of the sum of all I/O durations on that device.

The main advantage of trace monitoring is flexibility, since it only involves inclusion of appropriate statements in the system/application software. However, this flexibility could also be a major drawback for several reasons: (a) one must clearly understand the functioning of the programs to instrument them,[1] (b) the added code could contain bugs and make the programs misbehave, and (c) the added code could interfere with the program in unexpected ways. We shall see an example of these problems shortly. In many cases, instrumentation may not even be possible either because the source code is not available for proprietary reasons or is inadequately documented and difficult to understand.

One example of a trace monitoring facility is the *gprof utility* available under Berkeley Unix™ . To use gprof, a user compiles the program with "-pg" option, which inserts monitoring code for each procedure call. When such a program is run, the average time taken by each procedure is computed and put into a separate file. The time taken by a called procedure is included in the calling procedure. The tool can handle self-recursive and mutually recursive procedures. It is also possible to obtain time taken by major program blocks by using the "-a" option.

Trace monitoring can be made more convenient by providing an interactive environment in which instrumentation code can be dynamically added, deleted, and modified. The support required here is similar to the one provided by interactive program debuggers. Some commercial packages are available that allow these facilities. Often the monitoring needs cannot be fully anticipated at the time of program development. To ease later changes to monitoring code, it is usually a good idea not to insert optional monitoring code directly, but only to provide *hooks* at appropriate places. A hook can be in the form of a conditional procedure call or trap (the condition indicating whether or not the monitoring is enabled). Normally, the called routine would do nothing, but as the monitoring needs develop, appropriate code can be added to these routines.

Example 2.3 A newly developed compiler for Pascal was found to be much slower than expected. After some preliminary investigation, it was suspected that the compiler was spending too much time manipulating the symbol table. Show how the fraction of time used for symbol table manipulations, denoted *frac*, can be measured accurately.

Solution We start by noting that the fraction of time spent in manipulating symbol tables depends on the program to be compiled; therefore, we must use a number of randomly selected programs, and then analyze the data using statistical techniques. Consider one such experiment. Let "Tot_time" denote the total time needed for compilation and "ST_time" the time spent manipulating the symbol table. Then $frac = \text{ST\_time}/\text{Tot\_time}$. In most systems, "Tot_time" (the total CPU time used by a process) is available directly, but we shall compute it explicitly. To keep track of the CPU time used by the process that executes the compiler, we need a virtual clock. At the beginning of compilation, we initialize and start the virtual clock, and at the end read it. This could be done either by modifying the compiler code, or at the command level (by preparing a command file containing clock operations around the compilation command). Even in the

[1]The word "instrument" in the context of software monitoring means the insertion of appropriate code.

```
entry procedure P_i(<formal parameters>);
......
var start, finish: integer;
begin
  if measure_flag then start := Read_virtual_clock();
     .
     .
     .
  if measure_flag then
  begin
    finish := Read_virtual_clock();
    ST_time := ST_time + (finish-start);
  end
end ;
```

FIGURE 2-4: Instrumentation of a compiler routine.

latter case, we have to introduce some code in the compiler, and we shall use a global boolean variable called "measure_flag" to control the execution of these statements. Presumably, this flag can be turned on/off by specifying a measure option in the compilation command.

We assume that the symbol table is organized as an abstract datatype with entry procedures $P_1, \ldots, P_n$. To localize code modification, we shall instrument only P_i's, rather than calls to them from other parts of the compiler. The instrumented code for P_i is shown in Fig. 2-4.

Now we note two important points regarding this instrumentation. First, we need to address the issue of monitor artifact. The additional code affects the values of both "ST_time" and "Tot_time", however, the effect on "ST_time" is less pronounced and we shall ignore it. Whether the effect on "Tot_time" is significant depends on the length of the procedure and the relative frequency of its call. If most procedures have only a few lines, the enabling of "measure_flag" would increase "Tot_time" dramatically. This, in turn, means that the measured *frac* could be severely underestimated. One way to correct for this is to measure "Tot_time" while keeping the code in Fig. 2-4 uninstrumented; this will give us the true value that we are looking for. (The overhead of just measuring "Tot_time" can be considered negligible.) Another way is to estimate the time needed by the instrumentation code and subtract this from "Tot_time".

A second point regarding our instrumentation concerns the hidden overhead of procedure calls. In a language like Pascal, the time needed to build the stack-frame for a procedure call could be significant, but we have excluded that by reading the starting value of the virtual clock inside the procedures. Similarly, if the procedure is a function returning a complicated data structure, the time needed by the clean-up operations before return may be significant. We have ignored that also by reading the ending value inside the procedures. Thus, if the procedures are short, we could severely underestimate "ST_time", and hence *frac*. One way to correct for this is by instrumenting each call to a procedure, as shown below:

```
start := Read_virtual_clock();
call P_i(<actual parameters>);
finish := Read_virtual_clock();
ST_time := ST_time + (finish−start);
```

However, this solution requires modifications to the entire program rather than just the module of interest. For a large program like a compiler, this solution is totally unacceptable unless we have a reliable tool that can automatically instrument all calls. The alternate solution is to estimate the frame construction and destruction time explicitly for each procedure by doing a separate instrumentation of the code. For example, to estimate frame construction time, we need to read the virtual clock just before the procedure call and then inside the procedure just before its first executable statement. Except for situations where a variable number of parameters could be passed to a procedure, instrumenting a single call should suffice for this estimation. We also need to record the total number of calls to each procedure in this case. □

The discussion above illustrates the need for a careful consideration of all possible sources of monitor artifact and mechanisms for either avoiding them or accounting for them. *If the measurement is complicated or if the functioning of the system is not well understood, it is easy to miss out on some of the sources of monitor artifact, which could make the results unreliable.* This is one of the dangers of software monitoring. Another is that simple compensations of artifact, such as the one used here, may not be adequate. The main problem is an alteration in the overall workload because of the measurement overhead. For example, if the measurement substantially increases the execution time, the overall workload becomes more compute-bound than in its "natural state". This may in turn affect how the O/S schedules processes, how page faults are handled, etc. Thus, if we put extra code in kernel routines dealing with process scheduling in order to construct a histogram of ready-list size, the perturbations caused by it may be very difficult to account for accurately. In such cases, it is necessary to carefully examine if the effect is likely to be significant, and if so, come up with an alternate method of measurement.

2.3.2 Sampled Monitoring

For sampled monitoring in software, we generate interrupts periodically by using a programmable timer (or a programmable virtual timer, if process-specific measurements are desired), and read the appropriate state information in the interrupt handling routine. For example, to determine how much time a program spends within a given procedure, we check the program counter on every timer interrupt, and increment a counter if the instruction address lies within the procedure. The final count multiplied by the interrupt interval gives an estimate of the total time spent in the procedure. As mentioned in Section 2.2, sampling frequency and the number of samples should be chosen carefully to get acceptable accuracy.

Advantages of this method are that no program instrumentation is needed, and thus we do not face the dangers of program modification. Also, if we do not have access to the source code, or the source code is not well understood, sampling may be the only way to do software monitoring. Localized corrections for monitor artifact are also easier to make because (a) we are only "freezing" the program execution periodically, instead of altering its execution time characteristics, and (b) the time spent on each invocation of the interrupt handler can be easily estimated. However, the activities that do go on while the system state is being sampled (e.g. I/O), would result in a perturbed overall workload.

Sampling has several other disadvantages as well. First, sampling yields only statistical results, as was noted earlier. Second, sampling involves extra overhead of interrupt handling (and possible context switches). Finally, certain measurements may be awkward or impossible to do accurately if we are restricted to only sampling the system state periodically. We shall illustrate this by a simple example.

Example 2.4 Discuss the suitability of sampled software monitoring for estimating the distribution of seek distances for a moving head disk.

Solution We assume that the file-system maintains the current head position in a variable called CYL, i.e., every time a seek operation is initiated, the file-system puts the desired cylinder number in CYL. Thus, the difference between two consecutive values of CYL gives the seek distance. For sampled monitoring, we simply read the value of CYL periodically. If the sampling rate is too low, several adjacent displacements will be collapsed together. If the rate is too high, many samples will indicate zero movement. Irrespective of whether duplicate samples are retained, the frequency of zero seeks cannot be estimated accurately. This difficulty is not surprising, since what we want here is a type $\mathcal{A}$ measurement, which cannot be done accurately using sampling. Of course, the problem can be solved if the number of I/O operations could also be counted, but this too is a type $\mathcal{A}$ measurement. In contrast, the trace monitoring would keep track of the cylinder requested by each I/O initiation, and thus can estimate the distribution accurately. □

We now make a few general comments regarding software monitoring. In the context of tuning, software monitoring can be used both for *system tuning* and *program tuning*. System tuning refers to the alteration of some operating system parameters so that all users experience better response from the system, whereas program tuning refers to the tuning of programs that are of interest to only individual users. The distinction is important, since in the former case, the accessibility is usually limited and only certain predefined parameters can be changed, whereas in the latter case, arbitrary source modifications may be possi-

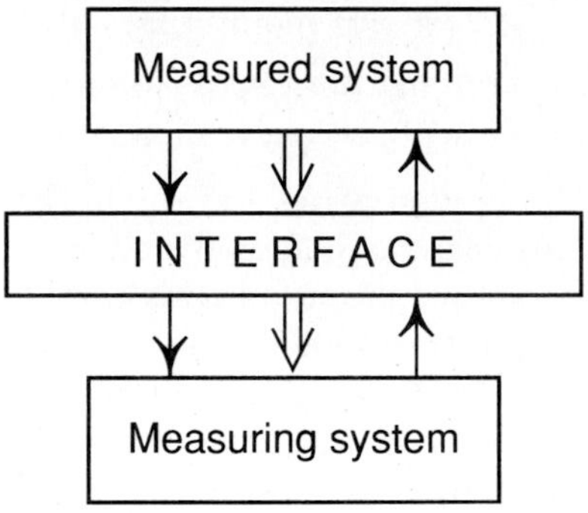

FIGURE 2-5: Setup for hybrid measurement.

ble. This difference dictates how the measurements are made and what should be measured. For example, in the former case, sampled monitoring may be the only feasible technique, and the measurement of the time spent in each procedure is probably useless. On the other hand, with a personal or locally developed piece of software, trace monitoring may be the most convenient method, and timing measurements such as those given by the *gprof* utility (see Section 2.3.1) are highly valuable. This is because many programs follow the so called "90-10 rule", i.e., 90% of the time is spent in 10% of the code! Thus, if we can identify the procedures or blocks where the program spends most of its time, we can concentrate on making this portion more efficient, and thereby get a big payoff for a relatively small effort. Some of the actions to consider in making the code faster are the use of a better data structure and/or algorithm, replacing value and value-result parameters by reference parameters, replacing procedure calls by inline code, using higher levels of optimization during compilation, etc.

2.4 Hybrid Monitoring

Hybrid monitoring involves transferring relevant information under software control from the system under measurement to a set of interface registers where it can be picked up by a measuring system. The overall setup is shown in Fig. 2-5. The main idea is to allow complex measurements without intolerable perturbation in the workload of the measured system. To show the need for hybrid monitoring, let us consider the measurement of the relative frequency of instruction usage. We start by considering the hardware and software monitoring techniques to solve the problem, mainly to show their inadequacy.

To solve the problem using hardware monitoring, we can pick the instruction opcode from the data bus whenever an instruction is fetched. We can use a counter array, say COUNT, with each element initially set to 0. For each instruction executed, we increment the element of COUNT corresponding to the opcode. Relative frequency of usage can be obtained by dividing the final counts by the number of instructions executed. Note that none of the resources of the measured system (e.g., memory, registers, ALU) should be used for this monitoring.

It is clear that this method is not desirable. Not only does it require a lot of hardware to do a little bit of measuring, it is also awkward and inflexible.

Next consider a purely software solution. The counter array now sits in the main memory of the measured system and is initialized as before. We assume that it is possible to cause a trap after every instruction execution (this can be done on MC68000 class of machines by enabling the trap mode of execution). The trap handler would then increment the appropriate array element using the opcode as the index (assuming that the opcode is accessible at the software level). It is important to turn off the instruction trapping while the control is in the trap handling routine! Clearly, the overhead of this setup is enormous, i.e., a trap routine must be executed for every instruction. One also has to be careful that the instructions executed for measurement purposes do not affect the measurement.

We can conclude from these observations that neither the hardware nor software technique is tightly fitted for this problem. A good solution is to do the job partly in hardware and partly in software by using two general purpose computers: one under measurement, and one to measure. The first system outputs the opcode to an interface register. The second system picks up the opcode from this register and uses it to increment the COUNT array, which is now stored in the main memory of the measuring system. One clear advantage of this setup over the hardware technique is that we have a full-fledged computer system to do the measurement; therefore, a change in the measurement objectives will not require any new hardware. A second advantage is that the control software running on the measured system can be designed to place any relevant information on the system bus, from where it can be picked up by the interface. As mentioned in the context of hardware monitoring, this approach can be used to expose information in main memory, machine registers, and even devices (in case of memory-mapped I/O). It is also possible to provide DMA (direct memory access) capability in the interface, so that the measuring system can transfer large chunks of information to/from the main memory of the measured system without any active cooperation by the latter. The advantage over the software technique is that the measurement now has very little effect on the functioning of the measured system; and fast, hardware level signals can be captured.

Let us consider some further details of hybrid measurement. Before the measuring can begin, there is usually a setup phase, initiated by a user logged into the measuring system. The setup phase provides the following information:

1. The control program(s), if any, to be run on the measured system. This information is usually passed to the measured system via some networking interface (as opposed to the monitoring interface).
2. What information the monitoring interface should capture and when. The interface will typically have a number of general purpose registers and flags, and the setup phase will decide what information goes into what register/flag, when it is written and read, etc.

Measured System	Measuring system
loop	**loop**
Process next instruction;	Wait until $F_1 = 1$;
busy-wait until $F_2 = 1$;	Reset F_1;
Reset F_2;	Read opcode from R;
$R \leftarrow$ instruction opcode;	Increment COUNT[<opcode>];
Set F_1;	Set F_2;
forever;	**forever**;

FIGURE 2-6: Two-way synchronization in hybrid measurement.

3. How the measuring system should retrieve the information from the interface and what to do with it (display, store, reduce, etc.).
4. How the measured and measuring system would synchronize. The synchronization would use some flags in the interface and a protocol must be set up for setting and clearing these flags.

Let us examine these steps for our instruction frequency measurement assuming that the measuring system is sufficiently fast. Here the control program to be run on the measured system is the benchmark program for which instruction frequency measurement is desired. The interface assignments include a register, say R, to hold the instruction opcode, and a flag, say F_1, to indicate that a new opcode has been placed in R. (R and F_1 can be set by the interface itself; the control program running on the measured system need not explicitly emit any codes to set them.) If the measuring system does not have any other urgent activities to attend to, it could do busy-waiting on F_1 to receive opcodes; otherwise, F_1 might be used to post an interrupt to the measuring system. In either case, for each opcode received, all that the measuring system has to do is to increment the appropriate element of COUNT array and reset flag F_1.

If the measuring system is not sufficiently fast to process one opcode before the next one is received, we need a two-way synchronization. If we look at the two systems as processes and the interface register R as a buffer, then we have the classical single-slot producer-consumer problem. The solution then requires yet another interface flag (or semaphore) F_2, and is shown in Fig. 2-6. Initially, $F_1 = 0$ and $F_2 = 1$. If the measured system finds $F_2 = 0$, it means that the measuring system is still not done with the previous opcode and therefore, the execution of the next instruction of the benchmark should be deferred. Similarly, $F_1 = 0$ means that the new opcode has not yet been placed in R. Although this handshake mechanism eliminates loss of information, it causes monitor artifact. In our present example, this interference does not cause any inaccuracies, but in general it could. Also, the control program to be run on the measured system is now as shown in Fig. 2-6, and not simply the benchmark program itself. Because of these difficulties, a two-way synchronization should be avoided whenever possible.

The hybrid technique can be used for a variety of measurements by appropriately assigning the interface flags and registers to hold relevant information. For example, to measure the fraction of time that both the CPU and the channel are busy, we can assign one flag for the CPU busy condition and another one for the channel busy condition. (It is assumed that the interface can tap the CPU-busy and channel-busy signals.) We then take the logical AND of the two signals: this could be done either by having a function synthesizer (as in hardware monitoring) or in software by the measuring system. In applications like overlap measurements, the software solution is impractical because the signals typically change too fast. In any case, the measuring system would be responsible for using the flag outputs appropriately. If the flag output changes infrequently, the measuring system could use software means to determine the amount of time the flag stays in a given state; otherwise, we need to equip the interface with hardware similar to that in hardware monitoring.

Hybrid monitoring has problems of its own. In addition to bringing out miscellaneous signals to the interface (as in hardware monitoring), it should be possible to do an on-demand assignment of signals to various interface flags and registers. This makes hybrid monitoring interfaces expensive and awkward for complex measurements. Furthermore, the only way to obtain software-level information and achieve a two-way synchronization is by running a control program on the measured system that would interact with the interface as it would with a device. This causes several difficulties:

1. The program to be run on the measured system must be instrumented so that it executes instructions that would carry out the relevant information transfer. (The code in Fig. 2-6 can be regarded as such an instrumented benchmark program.) This could be complicated and causes monitor artifact.
2. Only a limited amount of software level information can be provided to the interface, partly because of storage limitation in the interface and partly because we want to keep monitor interference small.
3. Since the information obtained by the interface via bus (as opposed to direct tapping) is a copy of what exists in main memory or registers, some care is needed to ensure that this copy is up to date. Problems could arise if some synchronization is done based on this duplicate information (e.g., having a copy of a semaphore variable).

Thus, even though hybrid monitoring using a fast measuring system can greatly alleviate the interference problem, it still does not have the flexibility of software monitoring. Also, if the signals change too fast, special purpose hardware may be the only way to capture all the events. This may undermine the reasons for using a standard computer system for carrying out the measurements.

Hybrid monitoring can use both trace and sampling techniques. Until now, we have really described the trace technique, where the measured system outputs the relevant information to the interface registers and then sets a flag to inform the measuring system to pick up the information. Thus, in a sense, the measuring system operates under the control of the measured system, similar to the trace monitoring code in software that is executed only when a significant event occurs. Trace monitoring gives exact results, but proper synchronization is essential between the two systems. (If the monitoring system is very fast, only one-way synchronization is necessary.)

In sampling, the two systems operate autonomously. The measured system puts the information into the interface registers whenever necessary, whereas the measuring system examines them periodically. To avoid synchronization problems, the interface can provide two sets of registers, say, S_1 and S_2. The measured system puts information into S_1 whenever it desires, and the interface transfers information from S_1 to S_2. The set S_2 is also accessed by the measuring system. The advantage of this scheme is that if S_2 is being sampled by the measuring system when the measured system wants to put new information, the measured system is not delayed. Instead, the interface simply defers transferring the information from S_1 to S_2 until the measuring system has finished access. This scheme still requires mutual exclusion over S_2, but that is easy to provide without affecting the measured system.

As an example of hybrid monitoring, consider the seek distribution measurement of Example 2.4. This would require having an interface register that maintains a copy of the contents of CYL. In the trace monitoring, we also need a flag that is set by the monitoring interface and cleared by the measuring system. The details remain essentially the same as before. In particular, sampled monitoring would give incorrect results.

2.5 Other Issues in Measurement

In this section we briefly touch upon the following issues in measurement: real-time performance control, measurability limitations, and special considerations in measuring parallel and distributed systems.

2.5.1 Real-Time Control of Performance

The measurements obtained from a system can be used in various ways, including comparison between alternate configurations, model calibration, and real-time control of system performance. Of these, the last application needs special treatment from a measurement-technique point of view, since the data collection, reduction, and usage should all occur on the fly.

The general setup for real-time performance control is shown in Fig. 2-7. We measure the performance parameter of interest (e.g., response time, throughput, or memory usage) for each transaction in the system and then compute an appropriate *performance index* (PI). The performance index may be defined either as the average value of the measured quantity (average response time,

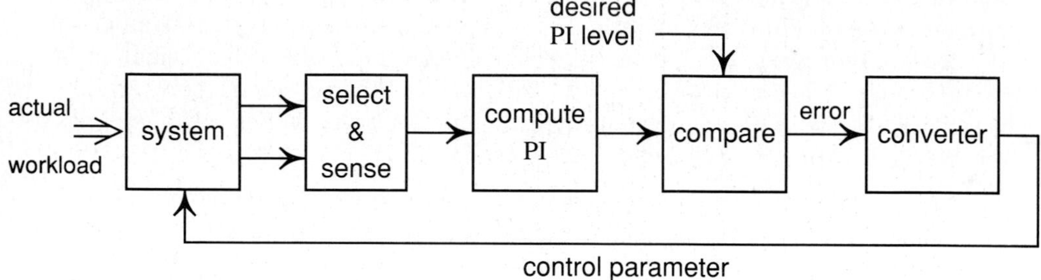

FIGURE 2-7: Real-time control of system performance.

average throughput, etc.), or a percentile measure (e.g., a value such that 90% of the response times are smaller than this value). The computed PI is compared against the desired value to generate the error signal. The *converter* translates this error signal into a change in the desired *control parameter* (CP). The CP may be chosen as either the input workload or the attributes of some resource management policies. It is possible that different CP's are used depending on the system state and the magnitude of error. In any case, the intended effect of the control is to reduce the error.

The most interesting issues in this setup are (1) how we estimate PI, (2) how we convert the "error" signal to a change in CP, and (3) how we actually apply the control. We shall discuss these issues with the following running example: we are given an interactive computer system where the average system response time experienced by terminal users, denoted R, must be maintained below T seconds.

The PI can be estimated using any of the techniques discussed earlier; however, the real-time nature of measurement imposes some restrictions: (a) the measurement must be done continuously under live workload and thus should not cause significant overhead, (b) long measurement intervals cannot be used, and (c) it should be possible to use the measurement results in the control loop directly. To measure R in our example, we can use either a hybrid or a software technique. Suppose that we measure the response time experienced by n successive user commands. Let R_i denote the response time of the ith command. Then the PI can be estimated as

$$PI = \frac{1}{n}\sum_{i=1}^{n} R_i \tag{5.1}$$

Because of the need for continuous monitoring, we have to first clarify which n commands to use for computing PI. The obvious answer may be the last n commands, but this could change PI on every command. Since a change in PI would cause a change in CP, the net result would be a very jittery control. To avoid this problem, we instead consider commands in blocks of size n. Here, a new average will be computed only when we move from one block to the next.

To further smooth out the PI value, we also retain a bit of past history. That is, let

$$\overline{R}(k) = \frac{1}{n}\sum_{i=1}^{n} R_i(k) \tag{5.2}$$

where $R_i(k)$ is the ith response time during the kth block. Define $PI(k)$, the performance index for the kth block, as

$$PI(k) = \alpha PI(k-1) + (1-\alpha)\overline{R}(k) \tag{5.3}$$

Here, the constant α (in the range $0 < \alpha < 1$) is the *damping factor*. A higher value of α will give greater importance to the past behavior. Note that for any $\alpha < 1$, the effect of past behavior will be damped exponentially, since

$$PI(k) = \sum_{j=1}^{k} \alpha^{k-j}(1-\alpha)\overline{R}(j) \tag{5.4}$$

Because of this, the operation in (5.3) is also known as *exponential averaging*. The "sample size" n should also be chosen carefully. If n is too small, the control will be jittery, since the performance index is not being computed reliably. On the other hand, if n is large, the control will be sluggish and may "lag"; that is, the control may be applied after the conditions leading to the control action have vanished.

The error signal in our example is $\max[PI(k) - T, 0]$. Now to specify the converter box, we have to choose the control parameter (CP). In this regard, we need to look for practical ways of reducing the response time. The following are some of the possibilities, in the order of increasing severity:

1. Alter memory management parameters. For example, in a demand paging environment, reducing the degree of multiprogramming or altering working-set sizes could help considerably.
2. Suspend background processing (e.g., mail processing, accounting, and logging), and any other activities that do not have any timing constraints.
3. Suspend (or terminate) batch processes started by users, and do not allow any more batch submissions.

These actions determine the appropriate control parameters. Now to actually apply the control, we need to know the relationship between the error signal and the CP. Usually, such a relationship is difficult to quantify, and a workable approach is to use *successive approximation*, i.e., to "guess" an amount by which the CP should be altered, and then observe the effect of actually doing so. For example, to bring the response time below T, we may suspend batch processes one by one, until the desired objective is achieved. Another strategy would be something like a "binary search", where we may start by suspending many batch processes and then possibly restart some, if necessary. These simple

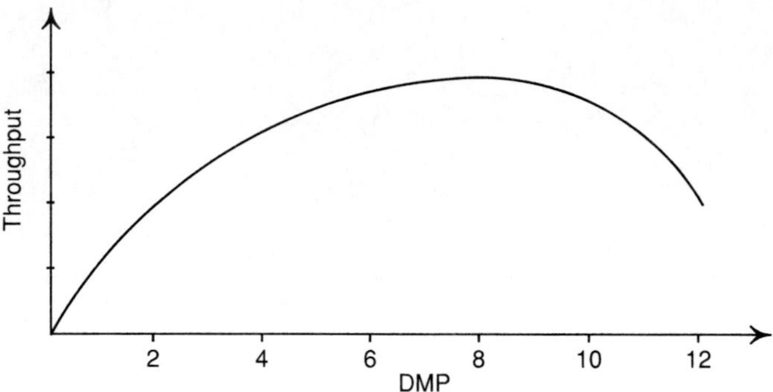

FIGURE 2-8: A plot of throughput versus degree of multiprogramming.

strategies may be adequate in noncritical applications such as the current one; but in others, naive methods may cause jittery response, excessive lag, or even instability.

If none of the actions taken to reduce the error signal is entirely effective, on-line control may not be possible. The system then needs to be analyzed carefully to determine what off-line modifications in software and hardware are needed to achieve the desired performance.

Example 2.5 Consider a computer system with demand-paged memory management. Show how a real-time control mechanism can be used to keep system throughput near the optimum value.

Solution A well-known way of solving this problem is by an adaptive control of the degree of multiprogramming (DMP). That is, the DMP can be used as the CP in this problem. The general behavior of throughput as a function of DMP is shown in Fig. 2-8. On the low end, the throughput is small because there are not enough jobs in the system, and on the high end, the throughput is small because of *thrashing* (i.e., most jobs waiting to read a page from the paging device). The optimum throughput occurs when the DMP is high enough to keep the paging device busy, but not too high to overload it. Let F denote the average time between successive page-faults that do require a disk read, and S the average time needed to swap-in a page. Then if we can maintain $F \approx S$, the desired condition can be achieved. (For those familiar with queuing theory, note that $F \leq S$ does not represent an unstable situation, because the number of jobs generating page-faults is finite.)

Since F depends not only on the DMP but also on the locality, size, and other characteristics of programs, it should be estimated on the fly. For any reasonable disk-scheduling algorithm, S will decrease with the number of pending I/O requests, and thus may also show dependence on various system parameters. However, it is reasonable to determine an "average" value of S by a separate experimentation, and we shall assume this to be the case. We could then regard

F as the performance index (PI) and S as its target value. The time between successive page-faults is best measured by trace monitoring in the page-fault handling routine. If this routine determines that the requested page must be read from the disk, it notes the current wall clock time and computes the time since the last such page-fault. The damped averaging discussed in the context of response-time control can be used here as well. If the DMP is too high, the desired control action is to swap out certain processes. If the DMP is too low, we can swap in previously swapped out processes, if any, or bring in new processes. Note that if there are not enough jobs in the system, the optimum DMP cannot be achieved. □

2.5.2 Measurability Limitations

Although much of the measurement is straightforward in theory, a variety of practical problems may make accurate measurements of desired quantities very difficult or impossible. An awareness of these limitations on *measurability* is important not only in planning and executing specific experiments, but also in designing new, more measurable systems.

The first limitation on measurability comes because not all the desired hardware signals are available on the system backplane. Certain signals, essential for the desired measurement, may reside inside a chip, which would make them inaccessible. With high levels of integration in digital circuits, and because the pins are the most precious resource on a VLSI chip, only a few signals are available externally. A possible solution is to multiplex many signals on a few pins to allow both diagnosis and measurements, but manufacturers rarely design chips with these goals. Often, one can expose many of these signals by executing instructions that would either put them on the bus or result in some other observable effect.

A second measurability limitation comes from circuit considerations such as fan-out limits, time skew because of additional loading, problems in accessing those signals on the circuit board that have not been brought out to connector pins, and so on. Some of these problems, as mundane as they might seem, could severely limit hardware and hybrid monitoring unless the designer gives careful thought to the need for measurement.

Even if the hardware allows all reasonable measurements to be obtained, that is not enough because the hardware is as such unaware of the software-level information. Thus, software-level measurements would require some support from the operating system either in the form of retaining the necessary information in the kernel data structures or making it available for hardware monitoring. Thus, the measurability may be severely compromised because of the software. A related issue is one of privacy and security. It is typically undesirable to allow a user to access information about processes, files, directories, etc., belonging to other users. One solution is to have full measurability at the machine level, but let only "trusted users" use it. This is not always feasible and may complicate the security problems considerably. Other software-level problems include lack of documentation or the unavailability of source code. One very common problem is the poor resolution of the clocks and timers provided by the O/S. The problem is often a result of how the O/S handles interrupts, process management, and related things. For example, if sleeping processes are examined only once each second, it does little good to let a process specify delay time to less than a second!

One important application of measurements is in the calibration of simulation and analytic models of performance. Even if the operating system can measure and report on many events, the information provided is not necessarily useful in calibrating performance models. The difficulty arises when a useful model of the system must abstract out many details of the physical system, thereby causing a severe mismatch between what can be directly measured and what the model needs for calibration. It is important to note here that *just having very detailed measurements on the system activities does not guarantee that a simple and abstract model of the system can be calibrated*. For example, many systems using demand-paged memory management can provide detailed statistics on aspects like page-fault rate, page read/write rate, average cluster size for swap-in, and scan rate (for detecting page references). However, a simple model of the system may not even represent paging explicitly and thus require average degree of multiprogramming (ADMP) only. With paging and complex swapping of working sets, it is not at all clear what ADMP is and how it should be measured. As another example, the system may provide detailed information on various types of workloads, except that the assumed groupings are different from what the modeler is interested in.

It should be clear from the above discussion that *model calibration is a difficult task and usually the biggest source of errors*. It would be ideal to have an elaborate and flexible measurement facility incorporated into the operating system (and supported by hardware, to the extent necessary), but most systems ignore this aspect completely. Moreover, it is not at all clear what criteria should be used to design such a facility, or how its complexity and overhead are to be managed.

Surprisingly, *our inability to calibrate models accurately can be used as an argument in favor of choosing simple analytic models over elaborate simulation models*. First, as the complexity of the model increases, so do the number of calibration parameters and hence, the reliability and robustness of the model decreases. It is not unusual to find that a simple model yields better results than a more elaborate one. Second, since simulation is typically much more expensive than analysis, it would be pointless to do simulation if the model itself is not reliably calibrated.

2.5.3 Monitoring Parallel and Distributed Systems

Although the techniques discussed until now apply to parallel and distributed systems as well, a few additional points are worth noting regarding such systems. In hardware monitoring, we implicitly assumed that the monitor is able to track all relevant events. In hybrid monitoring also, we clearly preferred a fast measuring system so that a two-way synchronization between the measured and measuring system is avoided. *A high-end parallel machine would probably already use the fastest available logic, and thus the convenient assumption of a faster monitoring logic may be unrealistic.* The parallelism (whether in form of pipelining or multiple computational units) only serves to make matters worse. A type $\mathcal{A}$ measurement may still be feasible by using the signal itself as a clock driving a counter provided that we use fast logic and minimize gate depth. Sampled monitoring is fine for type $\mathcal{B}$ measurements if the auxiliary variables of interest change slowly and thus need not be examined on every event. A related problem is that of dealing with the measured data. If the data comes sufficiently fast, it may not be possible to reduce it on-line or store it on a secondary storage device. Instead, it may be necessary to provide a large buffer in the monitor itself.

The obvious way to tackle parallelism is by doing monitoring in parallel on various components of the machine. If all components reside on a single chip (e.g., stages of a pipeline), this may be infeasible owing to accessibility limitations. Even when the approach is feasible (e.g., in monitoring processors of a multiprocessor system), it makes the monitor expensive and dependent on the degree of parallelism in the machine (e.g., the number of processors in a multiprocessor). It may be difficult to overdesign individual monitoring units, which means that each unit would have little time to do anything beyond recording data. Thus, large amounts of unprocessed data may have to be held in buffers. The off-line analysis of these data streams may or may not need any correlation between them. For example, suppose that we wish to study an instruction pipeline having n stages. Normally, the ith stage will be working on the $(n-i)$th instruction following the instruction that is in the last stage of execution. However, this is not the only possible scenario. If the ith stage finishes its work, but the $(i+1)$st stage is still busy, the former will get *blocked* until the $(i+1)$st stage becomes free. (This scenario assumes that there are no buffers between stages.) Also, if the execution of a (possibly conditional) branch instruction is in progress, and at the ith stage it is determined that the branch will indeed be taken, all instructions in stages 1 through $i-1$ must be aborted. Suppose that the performance parameters of interest are the pipeline throughput λ and the average instruction execution time $E[R]$. It is easy to estimate λ by counting the number of completions in the last stage. Let R_i denote the time spent in the ith stage by an instruction that is not aborted. Then $R = \sum_{i=1}^{n} R_i$, which means that $E[R] = \sum_{i=1}^{n} E[R_i]$. Unfortunately, we cannot estimate $E[R_i]$'s, because in the ith stage we know nothing of the instructions that are aborted in a later stage. This has two consequences: (a) each "reading" obtained in the ith stage must be tagged so that we could later identify whether it corresponds to an aborted instruction, and (b) on-line data reduction *at* stage i is not possible, even if there is enough extra time to maintain a running sum of individual R_i's. The tagging could add a substantial overhead for data collection. It is also worth noting that even in situations where there is no abortion, an untagged parallel measurement of R_i's in each stage is inadequate. This is because the R_i's of various stages are almost always mutually dependent, and we cannot obtain moments of R from those of R_i's. For example,

$$\sigma_R^2 \neq \sum_{i=1}^{n} \sigma_{R_i}^2$$

and a simple-minded measurement of variance will therefore fail. In our current example, the dependence arises because of the blocking phenomenon. As we shall see in Section 5.5.7, flow times are mutually dependent in almost all interesting cases. Dealing with monitor artifact is also more difficult in a parallel system because of complex interactions between different components and the rather high speed of events.

An important characteristic of loosely coupled parallel systems and distributed systems is the communication between various components via messages. In such systems, tracking the messages flowing between various components is essential for capturing the cause-effect relationships between various activities. In measuring this aspect, careful consideration must be given to the level of detail desired, which in turn determines how the monitoring must be done. For example, consider a distributed system with an ISO-OSI type of layered communication model. At the application layer, we cannot track messages that are handled by lower layers (e.g., acknowledgments, flow-control messages, and routing table updates.). Also, for the messages that we can track, not all the information may be available. For example, at this level we have no idea how the message will be routed to its destination. Similarly, at the network level, problems such as lost and corrupted packets are not visible. The lower layers (especially physical and data link) may be implemented directly in hardware, and hardware/hybrid monitoring may be essential to get at such information. Going too low in the hierarchy may also be undesirable, since at that level we can only monitor the information contained in the packet/message but not necessarily the context of the message. Even if the context is discernible, we have to examine every packet passing by to identify which ones are of interest. This, in turn, means that monitoring may need substantial computing resources even if the packets of interest flow at a very low rate! The problems here are similar to the ones in the context of hardware versus software measurement, except that now we have many more layers of information.

The hierarchical nature of system organization naturally leads to hierarchical monitoring. One such hierarchy comes from the hardware organization. At the lowest level is an individual machine, and several machines may be connected into a cluster. The clusters in turn may be connected into larger clusters, and so on. Thus, each machine can be monitored separately to obtain local information. The clustering medium (such as a bus) can be monitored to obtain interaction between machines of a cluster, etc. The second hierarchy comes from software structure as discussed above. The information from different levels may have to be gathered using a variety of monitoring routines, possibly operating in different protection domains. Thus, an important issue is the correlation of all the information gathered. Although manual correlation based on tags may be adequate for simple systems, it would be very helpful to the analyst if the monitoring tool (now consisting of a coherent set of modules working together) itself can correlate the information and present a complete view to the user. There is also the reverse problem: Given a set of measurement objectives, the tool itself should be able to decide at what levels the monitoring is needed and in how much detail. A few experimental performance tools have addressed these issues with varying degrees of success, as discussed in the bibliographic notes.

Whether dealing with a conventional or a parallel system, one may expect the monitoring tool to do more than just record data and do some simple data reduction. The tool itself, or some other program that works in conjunction with the tool, could try to compute various performance measures, locate trouble spots, formulate remedial actions, and perhaps even apply them! Although certain systems have attempted to do this, the last three activities are likely to be exceedingly difficult even in simple systems. A rule-based approach appears natural here, but its practicality is far from obvious.

2.6 Exercises

1. Consider the problem of "optimizing" the instruction set of a microprogrammable machine. The vendor provides a default set of 50 instructions, denoted X_i, $i = 1..50$. To evaluate what modifications, if any, are needed to the instruction set, a measurement experiment is to be done while running "typical" application programs. The purpose of the experiment is to estimate (a) relative frequency (or probability) of occurrence of each instruction, and (b) probability that after executing instruction X_i, the instruction X_j, $i, j \in 1..50$, will be executed.

   (a) What type of measurement scheme would you recommend: hardware, software, or hybrid? State pros and cons of each scheme.

   (b) Suppose that you decided to do hybrid measurement. Clearly state all steps of the setup phase and specify the program to be run on the measuring system.

   (c) How would you use the measurement results to decide (i) which instructions should be eliminated, and (ii) what new instructions should be formed by combining a sequence of existing instructions?

2. Consider the problem of measuring memory utilization (defined as the fraction of memory being occupied) in a computer system that uses dynamic partitioned memory management. The measurement is to be done on a continuous basis, with average utilization computed over every 5 minute interval and stored in a specific memory location. Show the details of the trace and sampled monitoring in software.

3. Consider a multiprocessor system with 5 processors, 4 memory modules (MM), and 2 shared busses. The state of various resources (processor, bus, and memory) is given by 3 register arrays denoted P, B, and M respectively with the following interpretations:

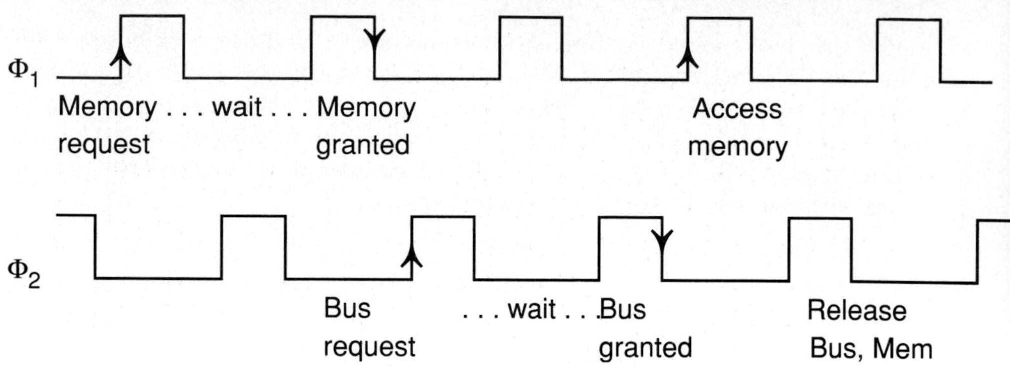

FIGURE 2-9: Timing diagram for a multiprocessor system.

$P(i) = k$	Processor i accessing or waiting for memory k
$B(j) = i$	Bus j allocated to processor i
$M(k) = i$	Memory module k allocated to processor i

Also, $P(i) = 0$ means that processor i is doing local computation, and $B(j) = 0$ and $M(k) = 0$ mean that those resources are free. The system operates with a common two-phase clock having a cycle time of 100 ns. The two clock phases and the actions of a processor in accessing an MM are depicted in Fig. 2-9.

The MM (bus) is requested on the leading edge of ϕ_1(ϕ_2) and granted on the trailing edge of ϕ_1 (ϕ_2). The arbiter itself does not take any extra time for decision making, but there may be additional delays if the requested resource is busy. Each MM access takes a complete clock cycle, and a processor may make any number of accesses before releasing the MM. The bus is also released along with the MM. The state of the registers may change only at the trailing edge of a phase. For each processor, we want to measure the fraction of requests directed to each MM, and the average number of cycles spent waiting for an MM, waiting for a bus, and accessing an MM.

(a) Show a suitable instrumentation for this measurement. State any precautions that are necessary to ensure correctness of the results.

(b) Discuss what conclusions can be drawn from these measurements. For example, what does a severe imbalance between the access frequency of various MM's mean? How would you tell if the system needs more busses, more MM's, or fewer MM's but with higher capacity?

4. Design a general function synthesizer for the CPU-channel overlap problem discussed in Section 2.2. The inputs are k, CpB and $ChB_1, \ldots, ChB_n$ where k could take any value between 0 and n. Assume that $n = 3$. The design should be minimal.

5. Devise a suitable scheme (hardware, hybrid, or software) for monitoring the page swap-in rate of a computer system. Pay special attention to any significant monitor artifacts and synchronization requirements.
6. Consider the control strategy of Example 2.5. Devise a scheme for predetermining S as required in the example. Next, suppose that we estimate both F and S in the control loop. Discuss how such a scheme might work and what instrumentation is needed.

Bibliographic Notes

Svobodova (1976) contains a comprehensive discussion on the three measurement techniques discussed here. It also shows the details of interface register assignments for various types of hybrid measurements. Some of our discussion on measurement techniques is based on this. Ferrari (1978) and Ferrari, Serazzi, and Zeigner (1983) provide further classification of various measurement techniques. Bucher and DePrycker (1982) discusses systematic development of monitoring systems for high-level language programs. Miller, Macrander, and Sechrest (1985) discusses monitoring tools for distributed programs running under Berkeley Unix. Burkhart and Milen (1989) discusses measurement tools for multiprocessor systems. Kerola and Schwetman (1987) reports a program for analyzing data collected from such systems. Joyce, Lomow, Slind, and Unger (1987) describes a general purpose monitoring system for distributed systems. Segall and Rudolph (1985) describes an integrated instrumentation environment that organizes information from various levels in a multiprocessor using relational database ideas. Yang and Miller (1989) discusses a hierarchical approach to measuring performance of parallel and distributed systems and locating potential performance problems based on the data gathered. A recent book edited by Simmons, Koskela, and Bucher (1990) contains several articles on the monitoring of both shared-memory and distributed-memory parallel processing systems.

CHAPTER

3

Experiment Design and Data Analysis

When dealing with measurement or simulation, a careful experiment design and data analysis are essential for reducing costs and drawing meaningful conclusions. The two issues are coupled, since it is usually not possible to select all parameters of an experiment without doing a preliminary run and analyzing the data obtained. In this chapter we discuss various aspects of experiment design and data analysis. In most cases, the techniques apply equally well to both measurement and simulation, and there is no need to specify what we are dealing with. However, some of the topics (e.g., variance reduction techniques) are particularly important for simulations.

The widespread availability of high-level simulation packages obviates a detailed discussion on the mechanics of writing simulation programs. Such packages typically take the model description along with the calibration data and run-length control as an input and produce the results. Therefore, we only provide a brief overview of simulation techniques in Section 3.1, and then move on to the topics of experiment design and data analysis. Other aspects of simulation, namely model calibration and validation, are shared by analytic modeling as well, and are deferred until Chapter 4.

3.1 Simulation Techniques

The kind of simulation of interest to us is *discrete event simulation*, where the state of the system is updated every time an event occurs. The most common phenomenon that we shall be dealing with is the queuing of customers at a station either to receive service or to acquire some resource (buffers, channels, etc.). In such cases, the relevant events are the arrival of a customer at a station, service completion at a station, resource acquisition, resource release, etc. In dealing with parallel/distributed processing systems, other features such as fork/join of customers and timeouts are also important. In all of these cases, there are three basic operations that a simulation program needs to perform: event generation, event handling, and statistics collection. In the following, we discuss these topics briefly.

Event generation can be either *trace driven* or *distribution driven*. In the first case, the time of occurrence of the event (and the magnitude of auxiliary variables associated with the event, if any) are obtained from measurements on a real system and then used directly in the simulation. In the latter case, they are generated to follow a given (continuous or discrete) distribution. Trace-driven simulations may be necessary if detailed characteristics of the input (e.g., locality, sequencing, and correlation properties) must be preserved. In most other cases, distribution-driven simulations are preferred because distributions provide a compact, reproducible, and easily modifiable model of the workload. The issue is essentially one of workload characterization, as discussed in Section 1.4.

Distribution-driven simulations require the generation of random numbers that follow a given distribution. This is done in two steps. First, we generate "unif(0,1)" random numbers, i.e., random numbers that are uniformly distributed in the range 0 through 1. Next, we transform these into random numbers having the desired distribution. Most languages (simulation or otherwise) provide unif(0,1) generators, so the implementation details may be unnecessary. However, should manual generation be required, it is important that only the proven generators be used because a generator may have the required number-theoretic and statistical properties, and yet fail in subtle ways. One reasonably good generator is as follows: The nth random number can be obtained as $Z_n/(2^{31}-1)$ where Z_n is generated using the recurrence relation

$$Z_n = (16807\, Z_{n-1}) \bmod (2^{31}-1) \tag{1.1}$$

The initial number Z_0, called the *seed*, can be chosen to be any nonzero integer. With the usual 32 bit integer representations, this generator would require the simulation of double precision integer arithmetic.

For the transformation step, let Y be a unif(0,1) random variable, and $X = G^{-1}(Y)$. Then,

$$F_X(x) \triangleq Pr[G^{-1}(Y) < x] = Pr[Y \le G(x)] = G(x) \tag{1.2}$$

That is, the distribution of X is $G(x)$. Thus, to generate an instance x_0 of X, we first generate an instance y_0 of Y and then let $x_0 = G^{-1}(y_0)$. In some cases,

G^{-1} cannot be expressed in a closed form, and alternate generation methods are needed. For example, if the distribution of X is Erlang or hyperexponential, we only have to exploit the relationship of these distributions to the exponential distribution. (See Appendix B.)

Next, we consider the topic of event handling and statistics collection. The usual method for doing this is to always advance the simulation clock to the time of occurrence of the next event and then update the system state correspondingly. An alternate method is to advance simulation time in unit increments and then handle all events scheduled to occur during that time interval. This approach may be necessary when the system parameters are a function of time, as is the case for a nonhomogeneous Markov chain (see Section 5.2) or when periodic activities are involved. In most other cases, this approach is unnecessary and expensive. In any case, the occurrence of an event would typically enable some other events, and the occurrence of these events must be scheduled. For example, the departure of a customer from a station would allow the next waiting customer (if any) to be put into service, and hence a new completion must be scheduled to occur at a later time. Usually, all scheduled events are maintained on a linked data structure that allows efficient processing of insert, delete, and min operations. The programming details are straightforward and omitted here.

When using a high-level simulation package for complex simulations, the experimenter must carefully examine the order in which the package handles events that occur at the same simulation clock time. The potential for incorrect handling typically arises when the model contains many activities that take zero simulation time (e.g., allocation or release of passive resources, computation of some parameters, routing of customers, etc.) perhaps mixed with some synchronization between customers (e.g., splits and joins). Failure to address these issues may lead to subtle errors that may be difficult to detect.

Lately, there has been a considerable interest in parallel simulation. Typically, the simulation model is a network of queuing stations that operate in parallel. Therefore, in a multiple-processor environment, it seems natural to assign the functionality of each station to a separate processor and thereby expect a considerable speed-up in the simulation. Unfortunately, this intuition is flawed because the correct time ordering of the events must be maintained. In the *pessimistic parallel simulation*, correct event ordering is always enforced, which usually results in very poor speed-ups. In the *optimistic parallel simulation*, events are executed immediately if they are currently not known to violate any ordering constraint. If a violation is later detected, the simulation rolls back and does things in the correct order. It is possible to get significant speed-ups using the optimistic approach, but a considerable amount of application-specific information must be exploited to avoid frequent rollbacks. Only a few commercial packages currently support parallel simulation.

3.2 Fundamentals of Data Analysis

The most fundamental aspect of the systems of interest to us is that they are driven by a nondeterministic workload. This randomness in the inputs makes the outputs also random. Thus, no single observation from the system would give us a reliable indication of the performance of the system. One way to cope with this randomness is to use several observations in estimating how the system will behave "on the average". This immediately raises several questions:

1. How do we use several observations to estimate the average performance, i.e., what is a good estimator based on several observations?
2. Is an estimate based on several observations necessarily more reliable than the one based on a single observation?
3. How do we characterize the error in our estimate as a function of the number of observations? Or, put another way, given the tolerable error, how do we determine the number of observations?
4. How do we perform experiments so that the error characterization is itself reliable?
5. If the number of needed observations is found to be too large, what can we do to reduce it?

Answers to these questions lie at the very core of data analysis and experiment design. In this section, we discuss only the first four issues. The last issue is taken up in Section 3.7.

Let X denote a performance measure of interest (e.g., the response time). We can regard X as a random variable with some *unknown* distribution. Let s and σ^2 denote its mean and variance respectively.[1] Suppose that we obtain the observations $X_1, X_2, \ldots, X_n$. We can associate a random variable with each observation as well, i.e., regard X_i as the value of *a random variable that represents the ith observation of the system*. It is a common practice to denote this random variable also by the symbol X_i, since there is rarely any confusion. We shall also adopt this practice. Notice that by its very definition, each of the X_i's should have the same distribution as X, and hence $E(X_i) = s$ and $\text{Var}(X_i) = \sigma^2$.

Now, suppose that we compute an expected value estimate of X, denoted $\hat{X}$, using $X_1, \ldots, X_n$. We could regard $\hat{X}$ also as a random variable. We say that $\hat{X}$ is an *unbiased estimator* if $E(\hat{X}) = s$. It is desirable to use an estimator that remains unbiased *even when the observations are not mutually independent*. One such estimator is the *sample mean*, usually denoted as $\overline{X}$, because

$$E[\overline{X}] = \frac{1}{n} E\left[\sum_{i=1}^{n} X_i\right] = \frac{1}{n}\sum_{i=1}^{n} E[X_i] = s \tag{2.1}$$

[1] Much of the statistics literature uses μ to denote the mean, whereas much of the queuing theory uses μ as a rate parameter. Retaining this dual interpretation tends to hopelessly confuse "service times" and "service rates"; therefore, we shall use the symbol s for mean.

irrespective of whether the X_i's are mutually independent. In fact, the sample mean is the only nontrivial estimator with this property. Another desirable property of an estimator is that it should be more reliable than a single observation; i.e., it should have a smaller variance. Let σ_Y^2 be the general notation for the variance of a random variable Y. Also, let $\text{Cov}(X, Y)$ denote the covariance of X and Y, and ρ_{XY} their correlation coefficient. (See appendix B for a definition of these parameters.) Since $E(\overline{X}) = s$, we have

$$\begin{aligned}
\sigma_{\overline{X}}{}^2 &= E[(\overline{X} - s)^2] = \frac{1}{n^2}\sum_{i=1}^{n}\sum_{j=1}^{n} E[(X_i - s)(X_j - s)] \\
&= \frac{1}{n^2}\sum_{i=1}^{n} E[X_i - s]^2 + \frac{1}{n^2}\sum_{i=1}^{n}\sum_{j=1, j\neq i}^{n} E[(X_i - s)(X_j - s)] \\
&= \frac{\sigma^2}{n} + \frac{2}{n^2}\sum_{i=1}^{n}\sum_{j=i+1}^{n} \text{Cov}(X_i, X_j) \qquad (2.2)
\end{aligned}$$

Now if $X_1, \ldots, X_n$ are independent, $\text{Cov}(X_i, X_j) = 0$, and $\sigma_{\overline{X}}^2 = \sigma^2/n$. Hence, *the use of n mutually independent observations reduces the variance by a factor of n.* Also, since $|\rho_{XY}| \leq 1$, taking the sample mean can never hurt. In fact, if σ is finite and $|\rho_{XY}| < 1$, we have

$$\lim_{n\to\infty} \sigma_{\overline{X}}^2 = 0 \qquad (2.3)$$

That is, the sample mean will converge to the expected value as $n \to \infty$. This is one form of the *law of large numbers*. Note that if the observations are positively correlated (i.e., $\rho_{XY} > 0$), taking the mean becomes less effective. On the other hand, if they are negatively correlated, the variance will be less than σ^2/n. This last observation is the basis for the *variance reduction techniques* discussed in Section 3.7.

It is clear from the above discussion that the sample mean $\overline{X}$ is a desirable estimator of $E[X]$ (or s). However, we also need to see how good the estimator is by determining an interval around $\overline{X}$ that contains s with a given probability. This requires an estimate of the variance σ^2, which is also unknown. We estimate σ^2 by the *sample variance*, denoted δ_X^2, and defined as

$$\delta_X^2 = \frac{1}{(n-1)}\sum_{i=1}^{n}(X_i - \overline{X})^2 \qquad (2.4)$$

Let us examine the expected value of δ_X^2. For this, let

$$\phi = \sum_{i=1}^{n} E[X_i - s + s - \overline{X}]^2 = \sum_{i=1}^{n} E\left[(X_i - s) - \frac{1}{n}\sum_{j=1}^{n}(X_j - s)\right]^2 \qquad (2.5)$$

Expanding the square, taking the expectation operator inside, and noting that $E[(X_i - s)^2] = \sigma^2$ for any i, we have

$$\begin{aligned}\phi &= \sum_{i=1}^{n}\left[\sigma^2 - \frac{\sigma^2}{n} - \frac{2}{n}\sum_{j\neq i}\mathrm{Cov}(X_i,X_j) + \frac{1}{n^2}\sum_{j=1}^{n}\sum_{k\neq j}\mathrm{Cov}(X_j,X_k)\right] \\ &= (n-1)\sigma^2 - \frac{2}{n}\sum_{i=1}^{n}\sum_{j=i+1}^{n}\mathrm{Cov}(X_i,X_j) \qquad (2.6)\end{aligned}$$

It is easy to see that $E[\delta_X^2] = \phi/(n-1)$. Thus, we see that if X_i's are mutually independent, δ_X is an unbiased estimator of σ, but not otherwise in general. Henceforth, *we shall assume that all X_i's are independent*. Since $\mathrm{Var}(\overline{X}) = \sigma^2/n$ in this case, we can also define an unbiased estimator of $\mathrm{Var}(\overline{X})$, denoted $\delta_{\overline{X}}^2$, as simply δ_X^2/n.

The measures $\overline{X}$ and $\delta_{\overline{X}}^2$ give us some idea about the real value of s. For a more concrete characterization, we would like to obtain an interval of width e around $\overline{X}$, such that the real value s lies somewhere in the range $\overline{X} \pm e$. Since $\overline{X}$ is a random variable, we can specify such a finite range only with some probability $P_0 < 1$. The parameter P_0 is called the *confidence level*, and must be chosen a priori. Typical values are 0.90, 0.95 or 0.99 depending on how reliable we want the results to be. Thus, our problem is to determine e such that

$$Pr(|\overline{X} - s| \leq e) = P_0 \qquad (2.7)$$

The parameter $2e$ is called the *confidence interval*, and is expected to increase as P_0 increases. To determine its value, we need to know the distribution of $\overline{X}$. To this end, we use the *central limit theorem*, and conclude that if n is large, the distribution of $\overline{X}$ can be approximated as $\mathcal{N}(s, \sigma/\sqrt{n})$, i.e., normal with mean s and variance σ^2/n. (See Appendix B.) Let

$$Y = (\overline{X} - s)\sqrt{n}/\sigma \qquad (2.8)$$

Then the distribution of Y must be $\mathcal{N}(0,1)$. Fig. 3-1 shows the density function of Y where e' is chosen such that $Pr(|Y| \leq e') = P_0 \triangleq 1 - \alpha$. Since the normal density is symmetric about the mean, $\alpha/2$ mass must be contained in each tail. That is, $F_Y(-e') = \alpha/2$, or $e' = -F_Y^{-1}(\alpha/2)$. Thus, given α, e' can be obtained from the tables of standard normal distribution. Henceforth we shall denote e' as $Z_{\alpha/2}$, which means that $Pr(|Y| \leq Z_{\alpha/2}) = 1 - \alpha$.

Using the definition of Y from equation (2.8), we thus get an expression for the confidence interval of s, but it contains an unknown parameter σ. We can substitute δ_X for σ, but that will not work because the distribution of the random variable $(\overline{X} - s)\sqrt{n}/\delta_X$ is unknown and may differ substantially from the normal distribution. To get around this difficulty, we assume that the distribution of each X_i itself is normal, i.e., $\mathcal{N}(s, \sigma)$. Then, $Y = (\overline{X} - s)\sqrt{n}/\delta_X$ has the standard *t-distribution* with $(n-1)$ degrees of freedom. We denote the latter as $\Phi_{t,n-1}(.)$. The density function of this distribution is also symmetric about the mean (and

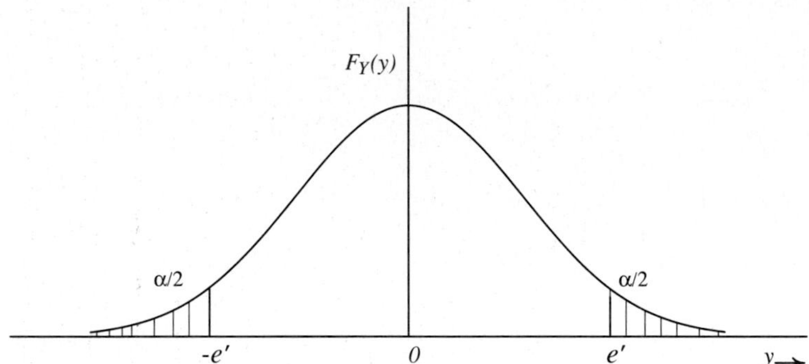

FIGURE 3-1: Plot of the standard normal density function.

indeed looks much like the normal density except for a slower decay). Therefore, by proceeding exactly as in the above, we get

$$Pr(|Y| \leq t_{n-1,\alpha/2}) = 1 - \alpha \quad \text{where } t_{n-1,\alpha/2} = -\Phi_{t,n-1}^{-1}(\alpha/2) \tag{2.9}$$

$t_{n-1,\alpha/2}$ may be found from Table E.1. Now by using equation (2.8), we get

$$Pr\left[\left|\frac{(\overline{X} - s)\sqrt{n}}{\delta_X}\right| \leq t_{n-1,\alpha/2}\right] = 1 - \alpha \tag{2.10}$$

We can put this equation in the following alternate form

$$Pr[\overline{X} - \beta \leq s \leq \overline{X} + \beta] = 1 - \alpha \quad \text{where } \beta = \frac{\delta_X t_{n-1,\alpha/2}}{\sqrt{n}} \tag{2.11}$$

This formula can be used in two ways: (a) to determine confidence interval for a given number of observations, or (b) to determine the number of observations needed to achieve a given confidence interval. For the latter, suppose that the desired error (i.e., fractional half-width of the confidence interval) is q. Then

$$\frac{\delta_X \; t_{n-1,\alpha/2}}{\sqrt{n}} \leq q\overline{X} \quad \Rightarrow \quad n \geq \frac{\delta_X^2 t_{n-1,\alpha/2}^2}{q^2 \overline{X}^2} \tag{2.12}$$

Since δ_X, $\overline{X}$, and $t_{n-1,\alpha/2}$ depend on n, we should first "guess" some value for n and determine δ_X, $\overline{X}$, and $t_{n-1,\alpha/2}$. Then we can check if equation (2.12) is satisfied. If it is not, more observations should be made.

In the above we assumed a two-sided confidence interval. In some applications, we only want to find out whether the performance measure of interest exceeds (or remains below) some given threshold. The only difference in the analysis here is that we consider the tail of t-distribution only on one side. For example, to assert that the actual value s exceeds some threshold $\overline{X} - e$, let $Y = (\overline{X} - s)\sqrt{n}/\delta_X$. Then

$$\begin{aligned} Pr(s \geq \overline{X} - e) &= P_0 \quad \Rightarrow \quad Pr(Y \leq e') = P_0 \\ \Rightarrow \quad 1 - F_Y(-e') &= 1 - \alpha \quad \Rightarrow \quad e' = t_{n-1,\alpha} \end{aligned}$$

which gives the following one-sided equivalent of equation (2.9)

$$Pr(Y \leq t_{n-1,\alpha}) = 1 - \alpha \tag{2.13}$$

Note that the left-hand side of this equation contains α (instead of $\alpha/2$) because the entire mass is now on the lower end. Substituting for Y, we get

$$Pr(s \geq \overline{X} - \beta) = 1 - \alpha \qquad \text{where } \beta = \delta_X t_{n-1,\alpha}/\sqrt{n} \tag{2.14}$$

We could follow the same procedure to assert that s is less than some threshold; however, because of the symmetry of the t distribution, the result will be identical. That is, (2.14) will continue to hold with the inequality reversed. We shall illustrate one-sided confidence intervals by means of an example.

Example 3.1 Five independent experiments were conducted for determining the average flow rate of the coolant discharged by the cooling system. One hundred observations were taken in each experiment, the means of which are reported below:

3.07 3.24 3.14 3.11 3.07

Based on this data, could we say that the mean flow rate exceeds 3.00 at a confidence level of 99.5%? What happens if we degrade the confidence level down to 97.5%?

Solution The sample mean and sample standard deviation can be calculated from the data as: $\overline{X} = 3.126$, $\delta_X = 0.0702$. From Table E.1, we get $t_{4,0.005} = 4.604$, and the lower bound becomes $3.126 - 0.0702 \times 4.604/\sqrt{5} = 2.9815$. Therefore, $Pr(s \geq 2.9815) = 0.995$, and with 99.5% confidence, we can claim that the mean flow rate exceeds 2.9815. In other words, at this confidence level, we cannot be sure that the flow rate exceeds 3.00. However, at 97.5% confidence level, the lower bound can be calculated to be 3.039, which allows us to accept the claim. This may sound anomalous, but note that the lowering of the confidence level would allow us to raise the lower bound. □

Often we are interested in constructing confidence intervals for the variance as well. If X_i's are mutually independent, equation (2.4) gives an unbiased estimator of the variance, but the distribution of δ_X^2 is unknown. So we again assume that X_i's have normal distribution. Then δ_X^2 has *chi-square distribution*. To get the standard chi-square distribution, we consider the random variable

$$\chi_{n-1}^2 = \frac{(n-1)\delta_X^2}{\sigma^2} = \sum_{i=1}^{n} \left[\frac{X_i - \overline{X}}{\sigma}\right]^2 \tag{2.15}$$

where the subscript $(n-1)$ indicates the degrees of freedom. The χ_n^2 measure has the following properties: $E(\chi_n^2) = n$, $\text{Var}(\chi_n^2) = 2n$, and χ_n^2/n has gamma distribution. (See Exercise 3.7). Since chi-square density is not symmetric about the mean, if we insist on a symmetric confidence interval, the two tails will contain unequal probabilities. Similarly, if we insist on equal probabilities, the confidence interval will be asymmetric about the mean. Computationally, it is more convenient to allocate the residual probability α equally to the two tails. This gives the following expression for the confidence interval of σ^2

$$Pr\left[\chi_{n-1,\alpha/2} \leq \frac{(n-1)\delta_X^2}{\sigma^2} \leq \chi_{n-1,1-\alpha/2}\right] = 1-\alpha \tag{2.16}$$

where $\chi_{n,\alpha}$ is the value of the inverse chi-square distribution function with n degrees of freedom evaluated at argument value α. Tables of these values can be found in most books on statistics. We also note that, if needed, one could construct a one-sided confidence interval for the variance by allocating the entire mass to one end.

Let us now take a second look at what we have achieved. We have been able to get expressions for the confidence interval; however, several assumptions were needed in the process. *It is important that these assumptions hold in practice, else the computed intervals will be incorrect and worthless.* First, we want X_i's to be independent. Second, we want all of them to have a normal distribution. We shall discuss the consequences of these requirements in the next section.

3.3 Organizing Simulation Runs

Most experiments are concerned with steady-state behavior; therefore, any data obtained from the transient period must be discarded. Informally speaking, we can say that the system has reached steady state when the distribution of the desired output parameter has become time invariant.[2] It is, of course, possible that a system does not show steady-state behavior; however, such situations are usually not difficult to detect and avoid. Theoretically, the steady state is reached only as $t \to \infty$, and the rate of approach depends on system parameters in a complex way. Thus, it may be difficult to distinguish slow approach to steady state from the situation where the system is already close to steady state. Added to this is the problem of constructing empirical distributions that could be used for verifying approach to the steady state. There are two ways of constructing empirical distributions: (a) by observing the evolution of a single instance of the system over a period of time, and (b) by observing several instances of the system at the same point in their evolution. As we shall see in 5.3.4, certain systems may yield different results with the two methods! In either case, the verification may well require more data than what is necessary for the studying the performance of the system.

Because of these difficulties, the length of the transient period is usually chosen based upon rules of thumb and educated guesses. For example, we may discard all data until the slowest device in the model has processed at least a few-hundred requests. Although such a rule is probably safe, it is not necessarily a good idea to be safe! The problem is that the reduction in variance achieved

[2]Strictly speaking, this is not sufficient for steady state, as discussed in Section 5.1, but the violations are rare.

by discarding less data may more than compensate for the error caused by the transient effects.

In the last section we identified two requirements on X_i's to allow reliable data analysis. These are (a) each X_i should be normally distributed, and (b) all X_i's should be independent. To satisfy the first requirement, we invoke the central limit theorem (CLT). That is, if we obtain X_i as the arithmetic mean of a sufficiently large batch of individual observations, say $X_{i1}, \ldots, X_{im}$, we can expect its distribution to be close to normal. It is important to note here that the ordinary form of CLT would require $X_{i1}, \ldots, X_{im}$ to be independent, but *a series of individual observations from an experiment could never be independent.* Thus, we are really using the meta form of the CLT. Practically, this means that the batch size m may have to be chosen rather large, usually in a few-hundreds. Although in theory we can "guess" a value of m and then verify whether the corresponding batch means (X_i's) are normally distributed, this method of choosing m would be extremely expensive. That is, *checking if our data analysis is valid may be much more expensive than the analysis itself*! Fortunately, in this case it does not hurt to err on the side of safety.

We now discuss several ways of organizing simulations so as to obtain the n data points $X_1, \ldots, X_n$ needed for the analysis.

1. Independent Replication Method:

Here we obtain each data point X_i as a sample mean from a separate run (of length m). If these runs are started with different random number seeds, we can easily satisfy the requirement that all X_i's be independent. The main problem with this method is that we must discard transient data for every run. With some packages, proper reseeding of all random number sources may also be difficult.

2. Single-Run Method:

Here we make one long run of size $m \times n$, and divide it into n subruns, each of size m. The motivation for this method is that transient data needs to be discarded only once. The main difficulty is that the subruns, and hence the X_i's in the analysis, are no longer independent. However, the correlation between X_i and X_{i+1} for any i is expected to decrease as m increases. To choose an appropriate value of m, we first pick it as discussed above, and then check if the corresponding *autocorrelation coefficient* is sufficiently small (< 0.02). The autocorrelation coefficient of lag k is given by $\mathcal{R}(k)/\mathcal{R}(0)$ where the *autocovariance* $\mathcal{R}(k)$ can be defined as

$$\mathcal{R}(k) = \frac{1}{n-k} \sum_{i=k+1}^{n} [X_{i-k} - \overline{X}][X_i - \overline{X}] \tag{3.1}$$

Often, it is adequate to consider only $k = 1$, which gives autocorrelation between successive batches.

Given a long simulation run, there are many ways to create batches. In the above we kept the batches nonoverlapping. Even in this case, there is some freedom: is it better to use a few long batches, or many small ones? Experiments have suggested a good range for n is 10 through 30; i.e., it is better to have a few long batches. Typical batch size is in the range of a few-hundreds, as already indicated above. There is another method, called the *overlapping batch* (OB) method which, with due care, performs better than the nonoverlapping batch method. A simple rule is to let each new observation start a new batch of m observations. In this way, if we start with a total of n individual observations, we get $n - m + 1$ batches, each of size m. The variance of sample mean is now estimated using the following formula

$$\delta^2_{\overline{X}} = \frac{m}{n-m} \sum_{j=1}^{n-m+1} \frac{[X_j - \overline{X}]^2}{n-m+1} \tag{3.2}$$

where, as usual, X_j is the sample mean of the jth batch. The confidence interval formula remains essentially the same; i.e., with $Y = (\overline{X} - s)/\delta_{\overline{X}}$, we have

$$Pr(|Y| \leq t_{\ell,\alpha/2}) = 1 - \alpha \qquad \text{where } \ell = 1.5(\lfloor n/m \rfloor - 1) \tag{3.3}$$

Comparing this expression against the one for the nonoverlapping batch (NB) method, we see a gain by a factor of 1.5 in terms of the degrees of freedom. Furthermore, for large n, $\delta^2_{\overline{X}}$ is also smaller. In fact, as $n \to \infty$, $\delta^2_{\overline{X}}$ for OB method is about 2/3 of that for the NB method. Yet, the bias in $\delta^2_{\overline{X}}$ (as an estimate of true variance of $\overline{X}$) remains about the same. Thus, the OB method is generally more desirable than the NB method.

3. Regenerative Method:

A detailed discussion of this method requires several concepts from Chapter 5; therefore, we discuss it here only briefly and informally. We start by defining a renewal (or regenerative) state. A system state is called regenerative if the behavior of the system, following entry to this state, is independent of all past history. Under steady state, each state (including the regenerative ones) must occur infinitely often. Let the period between successive entry to the same regenerative state be called a *cycle*. The cycles are probabilistic replicas of one another (i.e., in each cycle, the observations are identically distributed) and are mutually independent. Furthermore, the system exhibits steady-state behavior in each cycle. That is, if the system is started in a regenerative state, then there is no transient period to be discarded. For the purposes of simulation, we can start the system in a regenerative state and treat each subsequent cycle as an independent run.

Appealing as it may sound, this method has two serious problems. First, the experimenter has no control over the cycle length. Some cycles may be too short to be useful, whereas others so long that they have to be terminated prematurely. The unequal cycle lengths also complicate data analysis, since a long cycle would yield a more reliable estimate than a short one. The second problem is that we may not be able to find a regenerative state that occurs sufficiently often. This is an especially serious problem for networks, where we need a global state in which every station is simultaneously in a regenerative state. Because of these difficulties, regenerative simulation is usually not practical.

In closing this section, we again emphasize that the batch-sizes and the number of batches must be chosen carefully, or else the analysis will predict a confidence interval whose *coverage* (i.e., the probability that the expected value lies in the interval) is far lower than the assumed confidence level.

3.4 Selection of Inputs

In many instances, the purpose of a simulation exercise is to study the effect of changes in the values of various input parameters on the system performance. Suppose that we have k controllable input parameters, each with n different values. Then the number of possible combinations is n^k, and a *factorial experiment design* would consider all these combinations. Obtaining reliable confidence intervals may already require long runs for each combination, so having to deal with too many combinations may be infeasible. Thus, one has to be careful in choosing the input parameters (also known as *factors*) to be varied and the combination of values used for them. Less important factors may either be held constant or assigned only a few values. Similarly, if two factors interact weakly, they need not be varied simultaneously.

During initial stages of study, it is not known what factors are important and should be studied carefully. The usual approach then is to assign only high and low values to every factor. The values chosen would typically be the minimum and maximum values encountered. With proper scaling, we can represent them as simply 0 and 1. Suppose that there are k factors, denoted $f_1, \ldots, f_k$. Then a factorial design will consider all 2^k combinations. Let c_i denote the value (0 or 1) for the ith factor, and $\mathbf{c} = c_1, \ldots, c_k$ an *input vector*. Let $X_\mathbf{c}$ denote the value of the output parameter X corresponding to the input vector $\mathbf{c}$. Then the *main effect* (or first order effect) of factor i is given by

$$e_i = \frac{1}{2^{k-1}} \left[\sum_{\forall \mathbf{c}: c_i = 1} X_\mathbf{c} - \sum_{\forall \mathbf{c}: c_i = 0} X_\mathbf{c} \right] \tag{4.1}$$

This can be interpreted as the average change in the output parameter when the ith factor is changed from low to high value. (Note that for a given value of the ith factor, there are 2^{k-1} possible values for others.) The main effect can be used to make some decisions concerning further experimentation. Let $\overline{X}$ denote the average value of X, i.e.,

$$\overline{X} = \frac{1}{2^k} \sum_{\forall \mathbf{c}} X_\mathbf{c} \tag{4.2}$$

Then if $e_i \ll \overline{X}$, and the effect of ith factor on the output is expected to be roughly monotonic, we can simply fix this factor at some suitable intermediate value for further experiments. (The monotonicity condition is important; otherwise the results may be incorrect. For example, if we measure throughput at a degree of multiprogramming of 1 and 20 in a paging system, we may find the main effect to be very small.) If monotonicity does not hold, more intermediate values should be chosen to capture all major peaks and valleys in X.

The main effect does not quantify interaction between factors. That is, it does not tell us whether two factors, both of which are considered important on the basis of their main effect, should be varied simultaneously or individually. For this, we need to consider higher-order effects. Let $m_{ij}(x)$ denote the main effect of ith factor when factor j is fixed at value x. That is,

$$m_{ij}(x) = \frac{1}{2^{k-2}}\left[\sum_{\forall \mathbf{C}:c_i=1,\ c_j=x} X_{\mathbf{C}} - \sum_{\forall \mathbf{C}:c_i=0,\ c_j=x} X_{\mathbf{C}}\right] \tag{4.3}$$

Then, the *simple interaction effect* between factors i and j is defined as

$$e_{ij} = \frac{m_{ij}(1) - m_{ij}(0)}{2} \tag{4.4}$$

That is, e_{ij} *is one-half the change in the main effect of factor i, when factor j is changed from high to low.* It is also interesting to note that

$$e_i = \frac{m_{ij}(1) + m_{ij}(0)}{2} \tag{4.5}$$

It is easy verify from (4.4) that $e_{ji} = e_{ij}$, i.e., the ordering does not matter. We could also define higher-order interactions similarly. For example, the third order effect would be one-half the change in the second order effect when the third parameter is changed from 0 to 1. In many situations, third and higher-order effects are of magnitude comparable to errors, and can be ignored.

The concepts introduced above can be extended to situations where each factor assumes more than two values; however, the computations become increasingly involved. For example, suppose that we have two factors A and B, each with 3 values. Let us denote these as $a_0 .. a_2$ and $b_0 .. b_2$ respectively. Let X_{ij} denote the output parameter value when the inputs are a_i and b_j. Then if B is held constant, say at b_0, we need two parameters to describe the change in the output because of A. For example, we can speak of the overall change (or linear change) defined as $X_{20} - X_{00}$ and the quadratic change defined as $X_{20} - 2X_{10} + X_{00}$. Thus, the main effect of A should be described by a pair of changes, each element in the pair being the average of changes over each of the three levels of B. The quadratic term is zero if and only if the output parameter is a linear function of the input values.

As commented above, factorial designs may be too expensive in general. Factorial designs are essential if all effects are important, but in the usual case where only the main and a few interaction effects are needed, we could do much better. The corresponding experiment designs are known as *fractional factorial designs* and involve $m < 2^k$ combinations. An important concept here is one of *confounding*. Suppose that we eliminate some of the 2^k input parameter combinations, and compute various interaction effects using the results for the rest. It is then possible that the expressions for two distinct effects, say $E1$ and $E2$, become identical. Thus, we cannot separate $E1$ from $E2$, and we say that the two effects have been confounded. As an example, consider an experiment with $k = 4$. Suppose that we choose combinations with an even number of zeros (i.e., an even number of factors are given the low value). This yields only 8 combinations instead of the total of 16. Using (4.4), it is easy to verify that e_{ij} will now be confounded with e_{kl}, where k and l are the remaining two factors. Surely, we want the main and simple interaction effects not to get mixed up with one another, but we may not care if others are confounded (with one another or with main and simple interaction effects). This is the criterion for choosing the combinations. Methods exist to choose combinations that keep the desired effects clear (possibly at the cost of confounding others) but we shall not get into those here. Das and Giri (1986) provides much further detail on this topic.

3.5 Comparison of Alternate Designs

In this section we briefly look at the techniques for selecting one or more systems from a given set according to some performance criteria. For example, in computer systems, the performance criteria might be the throughput, interactive response time, or some combination of several parameters. In this discussion we will assume that a *smaller* performance parameter value is a better one. Completely analogous results apply when a larger value is more desirable.

One simple way to select the best system from a set is by doing a pair-wise comparison. For example, if we have to select among four systems, we could first compare systems 1 and 2, and pick the best one, say x. We then compare systems 3 and 4 and pick the best one, say y, and finally we compare x and y. This process can be represented naturally via a binary tree. Let P_c be the probability of correct selection in a comparison, and let k be the number of systems to be compared. The final choice will be correct if a correct selection is made at each nonleaf node along the path from the best system to the root. That is, the final choice will be correct only with a probability of $P_c^{\lceil \log_2 k \rceil}$. In the following we look at a different method where the probability of correct selection does not deteriorates with k.

We shall consider three selection problems: (a) selection of the best system in the set, (b) selection of a subset of size m containing the best system, and (c) selection of m best systems. Problem (a) is relevant when performance is the only criterion for selection (i.e., the performance-based selection is to be done from among a set of systems that already satisfy other desired criteria). In many cases, problem (c) is most relevant, but too expensive to solve. As a compromise, one may settle for the selection criteria stated in problem (b), which is expected to be the least expensive of the three. Section 3.5.1 discusses the selection procedure.

Its justification is the subject of Section 3.5.2.

3.5.1 Selection Procedures

Let P_0 denote the desired probability of correct selection, and s_i the expected value of the performance measure for the ith system. Let d denote the *indifference amount* indicating the minimum difference between two systems that is considered to be *practically significant*. We assume that $\forall i \forall l (|s_i - s_l| \geq d)$. Of course, we do not know if this condition holds. If it does not, the results will be accurate only up to the value of d.

The selection procedure for all three problems involves two steps. For each system $j \in 1..k$, we start with n measurements, denoted $x_{j1}, \ldots, x_{jn}$. Let M_j and S_j^2 denote the sample mean and sample variance computed from this data for the jth system. Typical values of n are between 15 and 25. Since the chosen n may be inadequate for some of the systems, the second step calls for more measurements. It is important to note that each x_{ji} is assumed to have a normal distribution; therefore, *it should be obtained as a sample mean of suitably many individual observations*. The steps to deal with problem (a) can now be summarized as follows:

1. Find out if we need more observations. That is, for $1 \leq i \leq k$, let

$$N_i = \max\left(n+1, h_1^2 S_i^2 / d^2\right) \tag{5.1}$$

   where h_1 is listed in Table E.2. As expected, h_1 increases with both k and P_0.

2. Make $N_i - n$ more replications of the ith alternative, and find the sample mean of these additional observations. Let us call this sample mean M_i'.

3. Define the weighting factors W_i as follows:

$$W_i = \frac{n}{N_i}\left(1 + \left[1 - \frac{N_i}{n}\left[1 - (N_i - n)\frac{d^2}{h_1^2 S_i^2}\right]\right]^{1/2}\right) \tag{5.2}$$

4. Perform linear interpolation between the sample means M_i and M_i' using the weight W_i, i.e., $\tilde{M}_i = W_i M_i + (1 - W_i) M_i'$. The best system is the one with the smallest $\tilde{M}_i$ value.

For problems (b) and (c), the selection procedure remains unchanged except that in equation (5.1), the parameter h_1 gets replaced by h_2 and h_3 respectively. Note that $h_3 > h_1 > h_2$, as expected.

3.5.2 Validity of Selection Procedures

The purpose of this section is to briefly justify the procedures of Section 3.5.1 and show how the values for h_1, h_2, and h_3 in Appendix E can be computed.

All three procedures are based on the fact that for $i = 1, 2, \ldots, k$, the random variable

$$T_i = \frac{\tilde{M}_i - s_i}{d/h} \tag{5.3}$$

has the standard t-distribution with $n-1$ degrees of freedom, where h is h_1, h_2, or h_3. The T_i's are also mutually independent. The expression for the weight W_i in (5.2) is chosen specifically to make T_i have this t-distribution.

For *notational convenience*, we assume that the systems are indexed such that $s_i < s_j$ if and only if $i < j$. Then system 1 is the best one. Let d be the indifference amount and P_0 the desired lower bound on the probability of correct selection. Let $P\{CS\}$ denote the probability of correct selection that we actually achieve. Obviously, we want $P\{CS\} \geq P_0$. A correct selection is made if and only if $\tilde{M}_1$ is the smallest of the $\tilde{M}_i$'s. Thus, if we let f and F denote the density and distribution function of the standard t-variate with $n-1$ degrees of freedom, we can write

$$\begin{aligned}
P\{CS\} &= Pr[\tilde{M}_1 \leq \tilde{M}_2, \ldots, \tilde{M}_1 \leq \tilde{M}_k] \\
&= Pr\left[\frac{\tilde{M}_1 - s_1}{d/h_1} \leq \frac{\tilde{M}_l - s_l}{d/h_1} + \frac{s_l - s_1}{d/h_1} \quad \text{for } l = 2, \ldots, k\right] \\
&= Pr\left[T_l \geq T_1 - \frac{s_l - s_1}{d/h_1} \quad \text{for } l = 2, \ldots, k\right] \\
&= \int_{-\infty}^{\infty} \prod_{l=2}^{k} F\left[\frac{s_l - s_1}{d/h_1} - t\right] f(t)\, dt
\end{aligned} \tag{5.4}$$

The last step in this equation follows by conditioning on $T_1 = t$ and by the independence of the T_i's. This equation also exploits the symmetry of t density, i.e., $1 - F(x) = F(-x)$.

Since $s_l - s_1 \geq d$ for all l, and a distribution function is always nonnegative and monotone-increasing, we get a lower bound on $P\{CS\}$ by substituting d for $s_l - s_1$ in (5.4). Now with a change of variable from t to $-t$ and using $f(t) = f(-t)$, we finally get

$$P\{CS\} \geq \int_{-\infty}^{\infty} [F(t + h_1)]^{k-1} f(t)\, dt \tag{5.5}$$

The equality holds in equation (5.5) when $s_1 + d = s_2 = \cdots = s_k$. This arrangement of s_i's is called the *least favorable configuration* since it yields the smallest probability of correct selection. Thus, for this choice of s_i's, we can substitute P_0 on the left-hand side of (5.5) and change the inequality to equality. Then, given a value for P_0 and k, h_1 can be obtained by numerically solving (5.5).

Demonstrating the validity of the subset selection procedures is more complicated but follows a similar line of reasoning. The details are explored in Exercise 3.10. For problem (b),

$$P\{CS\} \geq m \binom{k'}{m} \int_{-\infty}^{\infty} F(t + h_2)[F(t)]^{m-1}[F(-t)]^{k'-m} f(t)\, dt \tag{5.6}$$

where $k' = k - 1$. The least favorable configuration for this problem is the same as for problem (a). Now by replacing $P\{CS\}$ with P_0, we get an equality in (5.6), and h_2 can be solved for numerically. Finally, for problem (c),

$$P\{CS\} \geq m \int_{-\infty}^{\infty} [F(t + h_3)]^{k-m} [F(-t)]^{m-1} f(t)\, dt \tag{5.7}$$

from which we can solve for h_3. For this problem, however, the least favorable configuration occurs when $s_1 + d = \cdots = s_m + d = s_{m+1} = \cdots = s_k$.

3.6 Regression Analysis

The controllable input parameters in a performance study can be classified as qualitative or quantitative. We designate a parameter x as *quantitative*, if a total order exists among the set of values taken by x; otherwise, we call it *qualitative*. For example, in the context of paged memory management, a qualitative parameter is the page replacement algorithm, and a quantitative parameter is the page size. The significance of the total order is that it allows us to do interpolation and extrapolation of the functions defined over the set. For example, given the system throughput under FIFO and LRU page-replacement schemes, we cannot say anything concerning the throughput under other page replacement schemes. However, given the throughput under page sizes of 2K and 4K, we can predict the throughput for page size 3K fairly accurately. Designs with different values of a qualitative variable could be evaluated using the method described in Section 3.5. For a quantitative variable, however, we want to find a functional relationship that can be used for interpolation and extrapolation. We address this problem in this section. For simplicity, we shall only consider the single input parameter case. Extensions to the multiple-parameter case are briefly outlined in Section 3.6.3.

3.6.1 General Treatment

Let X and Y denote the input and output parameters of interest. Let X_i, $i \in 1..n$ denote an increasing set of values of the input parameter, and Y_i, $i \in 1..n$ the corresponding *observed values* of the output parameter. Then we want to determine a function $Y = f(X)$ that is consistent with these observations. Because of the effect of uncontrolled variables and measurement errors, we will not observe the true value $f(X_i)$ at point X_i. Instead, what we get is

$$Y_i = f(X_i) + \mathcal{E}_i \tag{6.1}$$

where $\mathcal{E}_i$ is a random variable representing the unknown error. Note that we have assumed the error to be *additive*, which may not always be realistic. In general, the error can affect the output parameter in arbitrary ways, but it becomes very difficult to deal with complex models of the error. It is convenient to assume that $\mathcal{E}_i$ does not have a bias, i.e., $E[\mathcal{E}_i] = 0$. If the error does have a bias, we should work to either eliminate the bias by proper experiment design, or estimate the bias and include its effect in the value of the output parameter. Since all observations come from the same system, we can assume that $\mathcal{E}_i$'s are identically distributed, with a common variance denoted as σ^2.

In general, the form of f is not known; therefore, the best we can do is to assume a form with some unknown parameters. These parameters are then estimated from the data in such a way that gives the best fit for the assumed function. In other words, the parameters are chosen to minimize the variation of the observed values about the values estimated by the application of f. This observation leads to the familiar *least squares method* for estimating the functional parameters. If the resulting minimum variation is still too large, one may conclude that the assumed functional form is unacceptable. In the analysis itself, we think of the assumed f function as the *actual function*.

Let $\alpha_1, \ldots, \alpha_k$ denote the k unknown parameters of the assumed function f. For clarity, we will write f as $f(X;\ \alpha_1, \ldots, \alpha_k)$. Presumably, α_j's have some *actual values*, that we do not know. All we can do is to estimate their values from the data. We shall denote the estimated values by using the circumflex (ˆ) symbol. Thus, $\hat{f}(X) = f(X; \hat{\alpha}_1, \ldots, \hat{\alpha}_k)$. As for Y's, there are three types of values to consider:

1. Actual values: denoted $\mathcal{Y}$, e.g., $\mathcal{Y}_i = f(X_i; \alpha_1, \ldots, \alpha_k)$.
2. Observed values Y_i's, related to $\mathcal{Y}_i$ as $Y_i = \mathcal{Y}_i + \mathcal{E}_i$.
3. Estimated values: denoted $\hat{Y}$, e.g., $\hat{Y}_i = \hat{f}(X_i) = f(X_i; \hat{\alpha}_1, \ldots, \hat{\alpha}_k)$.

Again, we do not know $\mathcal{Y}_i$'s, but stating some of the properties will involve their use. The total variation of the observed values about the estimated values is given by Q_E,

$$Q_E = \sum_{i=1}^{n} [Y_i - \hat{f}(X_i)]^2 \tag{6.2}$$

The estimation now involves finding values of α_i's such that Q_E is minimized. The resulting estimate is called the *regression* of Y over X. We now state an important result without proof, that gives conditions under which the least squares method yields a "good" estimator.

Lemma 3.1 (Gauss-Markov theorem). The least squares method yields an unbiased estimator of α_i's, and minimizes variance in estimated values if the following conditions are satisfied:

1. $f(X)$ is linear in α_i's. That is, $f(X) = \alpha_1 g_1(X) + \cdots + \alpha_k g_k(X)$, where g_i's are arbitrary but fully known functions.
2. There is no uncertainty (or error) in the values X_i's.
3. Error in the observed values of Y (i.e., $\mathcal{E}_i$) has zero mean.
4. All measurements are uncorrelated.

□

We will assume that these conditions are true for the analysis that follows. Unbiased estimator means that $E[\hat{\alpha}_j] = \alpha_j$, and $E(\hat{Y}) = \mathcal{Y}$. It can also be shown that

$$\mathrm{Var}(\hat{Y}) = \sum_{i=1}^{k} g_i^2(X)\mathrm{Var}(\hat{\alpha}_i) \tag{6.3}$$

Thus, minimum variance estimation of $\hat{\alpha}_i$'s implies minimum variance for $\hat{Y}$. From the definition of Q_E, we have

$$Q_E = \sum_{i=1}^{n}[Y_i - \hat{\alpha}_1 g_1(X_i) - \cdots - \hat{\alpha}_k g_k(X_i)]^2 \tag{6.4}$$

Consider Q_E as a function of some α_j. Then with the obvious choice of the constants a_i and b_{ij}, we can write

$$Q_E(\alpha_j) = \sum_{i=1}^{n}(a_i + b_{ij}\alpha_j)^2 \ \triangleq\ A + B\alpha_j + C\alpha_j^2$$

where $A > 0$ and $C > 0$. Thus, Q_E is convex in α_j's, and we can find the global minima by setting partial derivatives with respect to α_j's equal to zero. This gives

$$\sum_{i=1}^{n} g_j(X_i)[Y_i - \hat{\alpha}_1 g_1(X_i) - \cdots - \hat{\alpha}_k g_k(X_i)] = 0 \qquad \text{for} \quad j = 1\,..\,k$$

which can be put in the following matrix form

$$\Pi\boldsymbol{\alpha} = \boldsymbol{\theta} \tag{6.5}$$

where $\boldsymbol{\alpha} = [\alpha_1, \ldots, \alpha_k]$ and $\boldsymbol{\theta} = [\theta_1, \ldots, \theta_k]$ are column vectors, and $\Pi = [\pi_{jm}]$ is a $k \times k$ matrix. The elements of Π and $\boldsymbol{\theta}$ are defined as follows:

$$\pi_{jm} = \sum_{i=1}^{n} g_j(X_i)g_m(X_i) \qquad \text{and} \qquad \theta_j = \sum_{i=1}^{n} g_j(X_i)Y_i \tag{6.6}$$

Example 3.2 Suppose that the hypothesized "actual" function is quadratic and is given by

$$\mathcal{Y} = f(x) = a_1 + a_2 x + a_3 x^2 \tag{6.7}$$

Find expressions for estimated values of a_i's.

Solution Throughout this problem we assume that the summations are over i ranging from 1 to n. Let $z_j = \sum x_i^j$ for $j = 1\,..\,4$. Then from equation (6.5), the equations satisfied by a_i's are as follows:

$$\begin{bmatrix} n & z_1 & z_2 \\ z_1 & z_2 & z_3 \\ z_2 & z_3 & z_4 \end{bmatrix} \begin{bmatrix} \hat{a_1} \\ \hat{a_2} \\ \hat{a_3} \end{bmatrix} = \begin{bmatrix} \sum Y_i \\ \sum x_i Y_i \\ \sum x_i^2 Y_i \end{bmatrix} \tag{6.8}$$

from which we can get expressions for a_i's. It is also easy to show from here that $E[\hat{a_1}] = a_1$, i.e., the estimates are unbiased, but let's relegate the details to Exercise 3.12. □

3.6.2 Linear Regression

Linear regression arises in practice quite often, and we shall discuss it in some detail in this section. Since X_i's cannot be random variables according to the Gauss-Markov theorem, we will use lower-case x from now on. Let $\mathcal{Y} = f(x; \alpha, \beta) = \alpha + \beta x$, $\bar{x} = \sum_i x_i/n$, and $\overline{Y} = \sum_i Y_i/n$. It is easy to verify that equation (6.5) gives the following estimates of β and α.

$$\hat{\beta} = \sum_{i=1}^{n} (x_i - \bar{x})Y_i \Big/ \sum_{i=1}^{n} (x_i - \bar{x})^2 \tag{6.9}$$

$$\hat{\alpha} = \overline{Y} - \hat{\beta}\bar{x} \tag{6.10}$$

Since $\hat{Y} = \hat{\alpha} + \hat{\beta}x$, from equation (6.10) we also get

$$\hat{Y} = \overline{Y} + \hat{\beta}(x - \bar{x}) \tag{6.11}$$

Let $\overline{\mathcal{Y}}$ denote the sample average of $\mathcal{Y}_i$'s. Since $\mathcal{Y}_i = \alpha + \beta x_i$, we have $\overline{\mathcal{Y}} = \alpha + \beta\bar{x}$. Thus, we get an equation similar to equation (6.11) for the actual values.

$$\mathcal{Y}_i = \overline{\mathcal{Y}} + \beta(x_i - \bar{x}) \tag{6.12}$$

Under the assumptions of the Gauss-Markov theorem, all Y_i's are uncorrelated, with mean $\mathcal{Y}_i$ and variance σ^2. We now show that the estimates of α and β are unbiased. That is, $E[\hat{\beta}] = \beta$ and $E[\hat{\alpha}] = \alpha$. Let $z_i = x_i - \bar{x}$ and $\gamma = \sum_{i=1}^{n} z_i^2$. Since $Y_i = \mathcal{Y}_i + \mathcal{E}_i$, $E[Y_i] = \mathcal{Y}_i$. Using equation (6.9), we have

$$E(\hat{\beta}) = \frac{1}{\gamma}\sum_{i=1}^{n} z_i E[Y_i] = \frac{1}{\gamma}\sum_{i=1}^{n} z_i \mathcal{Y}_i = \frac{1}{\gamma}\left[\sum_{i=1}^{n} \overline{\mathcal{Y}} z_i + \sum_{i=1}^{n} \beta z_i^2\right] = \beta$$

where we have used equation (6.12) and the fact that $\sum_{i=1}^{n} z_i = 0$. Now from equation (6.10),

$$E(\hat{\alpha}) = E[\overline{Y} - \hat{\beta}\bar{x}] = \overline{\mathcal{Y}} - \beta\bar{x} = \alpha$$

This also means that $\hat{Y}$ is an unbiased estimate of $\mathcal{Y}$. By similar manipulations, we can show that $\hat{\beta}$ and $\overline{Y}$ are uncorrelated, i.e., $E(\hat{\beta}\overline{Y}) = \beta\overline{\mathcal{Y}}$. From equation (6.9), we can also compute the variance of $\hat{\beta}$, which turns out to be simply σ^2/γ. Since Y_i's are all uncorrelated, we have $\text{Var}(\overline{Y}) = \sigma^2/n$. Also, since $\text{Cov}(\hat{\beta}\overline{Y}) = 0$, from (6.10), we have

$$\text{Var}(\hat{\alpha}) = \text{Var}(\overline{Y}) + \bar{x}^2\text{Var}(\hat{\beta}) = \frac{\sigma^2}{n} + \frac{\bar{x}^2\sigma^2}{\gamma} = \frac{\sigma^2 \sum x_i^2}{n\sum(x_i - \bar{x})^2} \tag{6.13}$$

Therefore, from equation (6.11), the variance of $\hat{Y}$ can be computed as

$$\mathrm{Var}(\hat{Y}) = \sigma^2 \left[\frac{1}{n} + \frac{(x-\bar{x})^2}{\sum_i (x_i - \bar{x})^2}\right] \tag{6.14}$$

We can now construct confidence intervals for the true values α, β, and $\mathcal{Y}$ with the assumption that $\mathcal{E}_i$'s (and hence Y_i's) are approximately normally distributed. However, σ is unknown and must be replaced by the sample variance as in Section 3.2. Since $\hat{Y}_i$ is an unbiased estimate of $\mathcal{Y}_i$, we can estimate sample variance as

$$\delta^2 = \frac{1}{(n-2)} \sum_{i=1}^{n} (Y_i - \hat{Y}_i)^2 = \frac{Q_E}{(n-2)} \tag{6.15}$$

where we have used $(n-2)$ in the denominator to make δ an unbiased estimate of σ. An intuitive explanation of why this choice makes the estimate unbiased is that two degrees of freedom are lost in obtaining $\hat{\alpha}$ and $\hat{\beta}$ from the data. Let $\mathcal{V}^2(\hat{Y})$ denote the variance of $\hat{Y}$ when σ is replaced by δ in (6.14). Then $(\hat{Y} - \mathcal{Y})/\mathcal{V}(\hat{Y})$ will have the standard t-distribution. Let $\gamma = 1 - P_0$ where P_0 is the confidence level. Then as in Section 3.2, we get the following expression for the confidence interval of $\mathcal{Y}$.

$$Pr\left[\hat{Y} - \mathcal{V}(\hat{Y})t_{n-2,\gamma/2} \le \mathcal{Y} \le \hat{Y} - \mathcal{V}(\hat{Y})t_{n-2,\gamma/2}\right] = 1 - \gamma \tag{6.16}$$

Similar expressions can be written for the confidence intervals of α and β. As is emphasized in Section 3.2, these formulae require that each data point Y_i be obtained as a sample mean of a sufficiently large batch. Fig. 3-2 shows a plot of the lower and upper bounds of the confidence interval for $\mathcal{Y}$ as a function of x. It can be seen that the confidence band has minimum width at $x = \bar{x}$ and expands on both sides. The plot clearly shows that *the extrapolation of the regression curve into a region far removed from the observation interval may yield highly unreliable results.*

3.6.3 Other Issues in Regression Analysis

One important issue in regression analysis is to ensure that the assumed functional form explains the data adequately. One way to do this to look at the confidence intervals of α_i's and check if they are sufficiently narrow. However, there is an easier way to approach to the problem. Let us define:

$Q_T = \sum_i (Y_i - \overline{Y})^2$: Total variation about the mean.

$Q_R = \sum_i (\hat{Y}_i - \overline{Y})^2$: Variation explained by regression.

$Q_E = \sum_i (Y_i - \hat{Y}_i)^2$: Variation not explained by regression (i.e., error).

We minimized Q_E earlier to estimate α_i's. By using equations (6.9) and (6.11) in the above definitions, it is easy to show that $Q_T = Q_R + Q_E$. (Also see Exercise 3.11.) Thus, if Q_E/Q_T is small (say, < 0.10), we can claim that we have

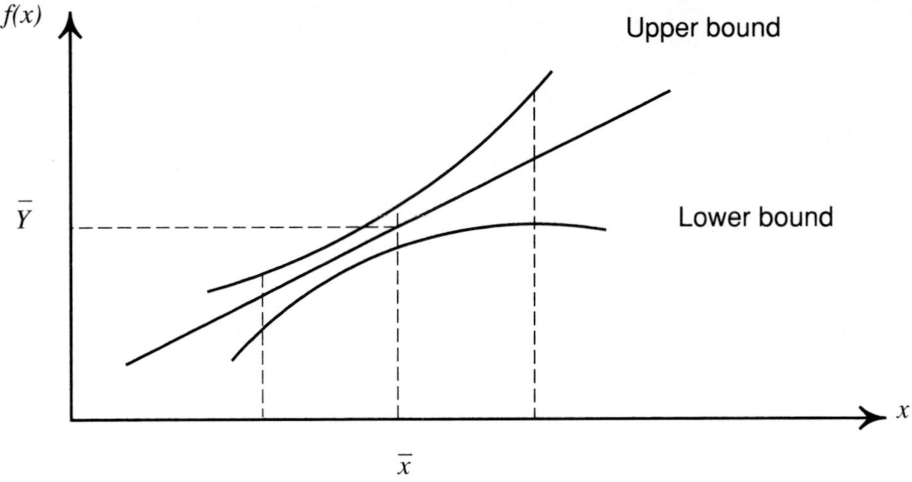

FIGURE 3-2: Lower and upper bounds of confidence interval for $\mathcal{Y}$.

a good regression model; otherwise, we may have one or more of the following situations: (a) measurement errors are large, (b) the number of data points is too small, and/or (c) the assumed functional form is incorrect. Situation (a) calls for a better controlled experiment, whereas situation (b) calls for more data points. If we have already taken care of these aspects, we should look for other plausible functions that could be used in the regression model.

In some situations we may find that the poor fit results because the output parameter is significantly affected by another factor that cannot be realistically fixed at a constant level. This points toward the need for *multiple-regression* that considers all important factors. In the following, we very briefly examine multiple-regression. Suppose that there are m independent (or orthogonal) factors, and let

$$\mathcal{Y} = f(X^1, X^2, \ldots, X^m; \alpha_1, \alpha_2, \ldots, \alpha_k) \tag{6.17}$$

such that $\mathcal{Y}$ is linear in $\alpha_1, \alpha_2, \ldots, \alpha_k$. Suppose that X^j takes n_j values, denoted $X^j_1, \ldots, X^j_{n_j}$. Then the observed values are $Y_{i_1,\ldots,i_m}$ versus $(X^1_{i_1}, \ldots, X^m_{i_m})$ where $i_j \in 1 \mathinner{..} n_j$. We assume that the conditions of the Gauss-Markov theorem hold here as well. Then the least square method obtains $\alpha_1, \ldots, \alpha_k$ by minimizing

$$Q_E = \sum_{i_1=1}^{n_1} \sum_{i_2=1}^{n_2} \cdots \sum_{i_m=1}^{n_m} (Y_{i_1,\ldots,i_m} - \hat{f}(X^1_{i_1}, \ldots, X^m_{i_m}))^2 \tag{6.18}$$

The function in equation (6.18) is convex; therefore, the global minima can be found by equating partial derivatives of Q_E with respect to α_i's to zero. The details are similar to those for the case of single-variable regression and are left as an exercise. The major problem with multiple-regression is that it is difficult to come up with a suitable but compact function in several variables. Using a

X	Y	X	Y	X	Y
2	0.09	4	0.25	6	0.45
8	0.60	10	0.85	12	1.45
14	1.80	16	2.15	18	2.55
20	3.00	22	3.40		

TABLE 3.1: System response-time as a function of number of terminals.

canonical form (i.e., a sum of the products of powers of X^j's) would require too many α_i's, and hence too many data points for a reliable estimate. The difficulty here is similar to the one we faced in experiment design. Just as the experiment design can be simplified if only certain effects are important, so can the regression analysis. For example, if only the main effects are important, we need to vary only one parameter at a time, which means that f can be expressed as a sum of single-factor functions. Similarly, if only the main and simple interaction effects are important, we can write f as a sum of terms, each of which contains no more than two variables. This would considerably reduce the number of α_i's, and hence the data points needed to estimate them reliably.

Let us now discuss another important issue in regression analysis. Recall that the Gauss-Markov theorem requires that the assumed function be linear in its parameters. Often one must deal with functions that do not have this property. The least squares method is not guaranteed to give unbiased estimates in such cases. Moreover, if Q_E is not a convex function of α_i's, determining α_i's that minimize Q_E may become exceedingly difficult. Sometimes it is possible to linearize the function by some transformation. The standard analysis then applies to the transformed domain. For example, consider the function $\mathcal{Y} = f(x) = \alpha_1 e^{\alpha_2 x}$, which is nonlinear in α_2. Here $\ln(\mathcal{Y})$ becomes linear in parameters (we can call $\ln(\alpha_1)$ something else without causing any problems). However, we need to be careful in applying such transformations. Note that in the analysis above, the error was assumed to be additive, i.e., $Y = f(x) + \mathcal{E}$. Additive error is usually (but not always) realistic. But to do the log transformation, we must assume the error to be multiplicative, which may be unacceptable. Note that $Y_i = \alpha_1 e^{\alpha_2 x_i} + \mathcal{E}_i$ cannot be linearized. Thus, the type of error we can allow depends directly on the transformations involved.

Example 3.3 Consider the behavior of 90 percentile response time (Y) as a function of number of active users (X) for an interactive system. The data is given in Table 3.1. From this data, it appears that Y may be related to X as $Y = aX^b$ for some a and b. Determine $\hat{a}$ and $\hat{b}$. What is the maximum number of terminals that the system can safely support and yet provide a response time of 3.0 seconds, or less, 95% of the time?

Solution We can linearize the equation as $\log Y = \log a + b \log X$ (logarithms are to the base 10 here). Using equations (6.9) and (6.10), we get $\log \hat{a} = -1.54148$ and $\hat{b} = 1.54259$. Let $Z = \log Y$ and $V = \log X$. From Table 3.1 we get $\overline{V} = 0.99204$ and $\overline{Z} = -0.011165$. From equation (6.15), $\delta = 0.025938$. From Table

E.1, $t_{9,\,0.025} = 2.262$. Therefore, the bounds on $\hat{Z}$ (as a function of V) are given by

$$(-1.5415 + 1.5426V) \pm 0.05867\sqrt{\frac{1}{11} + \frac{(V - 0.9920)^2}{2.5063}}$$

The narrow confidence intervals should show that the linear approximation is very good. In particular, the ratio Q_R/Q_T turns out to be 0.992044. To get the number of terminals that can be supported, we find the value of X such that the upper bound of Y does not exceed 3.0 seconds. This value turns out to be 19. For $X = 19$, the predicted value of Y is 2.70 seconds, and the upper bound is 2.83 seconds. □

3.7 Variance Reduction Techniques

For a given confidence level, the width of the confidence interval is proportional to the sample standard deviation; therefore, the cost of an experiment can be reduced if the sample variance could be reduced. In this section we shall examine three techniques to do this. Although we discuss these techniques separately, it is possible to combine them, as explored in exercises 3.15 and 3.16.

3.7.1 Common Random Numbers

Consider the problem of comparing two systems, Sys-1 and Sys-2. Let $X_1, \ldots, X_n$ denote n independent, normally distributed, data points from Sys-1, and let $Y_1, \ldots, Y_n$ denote those from Sys-2. Let $Z_i = X_i - Y_i$ and $E[Z_i] = s$. We assume that the Z_i's are also mutually independent. This means that although X_i and Y_i may be mutually dependent, X_i and Y_j with $j \neq i$ must be mutually independent. Then we can get the confidence interval for s in the usual way (e.g., from equation (2.11) with X replaced by Z). This confidence interval would quantify the difference in the expected performance of the two systems. If the confidence interval includes 0, the difference between the two systems is not *statistically significant*, and we cannot identify the better system. This may happen because the sample variance δ_Z is too high. Since δ_Z is an estimate of σ_Z, let us look at the components of σ_Z. Let σ_X and σ_Y denote the variances of X_i's and Y_i's respectively. Then for any pair of data points (X_i, Y_i), we have

$$\sigma_Z^2 = E[(Z_i - E(Z_i))^2] = \sigma_X^2 + \sigma_Y^2 - 2\text{Cov}(X_i, Y_i) \tag{7.1}$$

It is clear that to reduce σ_Z, X_i and Y_i must be positively correlated. This corresponds to the intuitive notion of using *identical experimental conditions* to obtain the observations X_i and Y_i. In measurement experiments, this can be achieved by ensuring that the two systems are subjected to identical workloads and have their tuning parameters set identically. In simulation experiments, the experimental conditions *are* the various random numbers; therefore, positive correlation can be achieved by using the same random numbers for the same purpose in each of the systems under comparison. Hence, the technique is known as the *common random number* (CRN) technique.

A careful use of this technique can result in a significant reduction in the sample variance. As an extreme, but realistic, example, consider two computer systems A and B, where A has a single CPU, but B has two CPU's, each half as fast as A's CPU. Suppose that both interarrival and service times are exponentially distributed. Starting with an empty system, both systems were simulated for the first 100 jobs at traffic intensity of 0.9, and the sample variance of the response time was computed. When both systems used different random numbers, this variance was found to be 25.491, but dropped to 0.0103 when identical random numbers were used for both arrivals and services! In this example, the variance drops so much because the two systems to be compared are very similar. In general, one system may need more random numbers than the other one, possibly because it has some features not possessed by the other. Thus, to achieve significant variance reduction, it is necessary to use the *same random number in both systems for the activities that are common or similar*. It is important to note that the problem being addressed here is not just one of programming; if an activity in one system is broken down into two lower-level activities in the other system, it is not clear how to use the CRN technique. Yet another problem is that the two systems might respond differently to the large or small values of a random number, and thus the desired positive correlation may not be induced. In fact, it is not hard to construct examples where the effects will be opposite, and hence the induced correlation will be negative. With due care, however, the CRN technique rarely backfires (and it is very easy to use).

3.7.2 Antithetic Variable Method

Unlike CRN, this technique is intended for experimenting with a *single* system. For example, if we want to estimate the average response time provided by a computer system, antithetic variable technique will be useful. The technique requires that the output parameter show monotonic behavior (increasing or decreasing) with respect to the input parameter being manipulated. For example, the *average* response time will typically increase monotonically with *average* service time and decrease monotonically with average interarrival time.

Suppose that we make *two separate simulation runs* with equal numbers of service completions. Let us consider the service for the ith customer in both of these runs. Let X_{i1} and X_{i2} be the values of the unif(0,1) random number used in generating the two service times and let R_{i1} and R_{i2} be the corresponding values of response times. Suppose that instead of generating X_{i2} independently of X_{i1}, we simply set $X_{i2} = 1 - X_{i1}$. Then if X_{i1} is large, X_{i2} will be small, and vice versa. Because of the monotonicity, this dependence between X_{i1} and X_{i2} is reflected in the outputs as well. That is, R_{i2} would be small if R_{i1} is large, and vice versa. In other words, we have artificially induced a *negative correlation* between the observations R_{i1} and R_{i2}. Let $U_i = (R_{i1}+R_{i2})/2$. The idea is then to use U_i, instead of R_{i1} and R_{i2}, for further analysis. Since R_{i1} and R_{i2} represent observations from the same system, they must be identically distributed. Let σ^2 denote their common variance. It is easy to see that

$$\mathrm{Var}(U_i) = \frac{\sigma^2 + \mathrm{Cov}(R_{i1}, R_{i2})}{2} \tag{7.2}$$

Since $\mathrm{Cov}(R_{i1}, R_{i2}) < 0$, each U_i contributes less than $\sigma^2/2$ to the variance. In contrast, if we had simply used two independent observations, the contributed variance would be $\sigma^2/2$. Thus, *for the same total simulation time*, we gain by using the antithetic variable method.

As in the CRN technique, proper synchronization is important here as well, but can be achieved easily. One only has to make sure that a separate random number stream is used for each different random variable. Then for any given random variable, if the first run uses the value u, the second one can use $1-u$. However, if all random numbers come from the same underlying generator, simply substituting $1-u$ for u in the code for the second run will not work.

Although this technique appears attractive, a substantial reduction in variance is not always guaranteed. There are several reasons for this. First, in a complex system, the required monotonicity may not hold. Second, a given input parameter may not influence the output parameter sufficiently strongly. Third, the method may not induce much negative correlation even if the first two problems do not exist. To demonstrate this, let us go back to our response time example. Even though the average response time is strongly influenced by average service time, this is *not* what is being exploited by equation (7.2). There we have two individual customers, one of whom has a small service time and the other a large service time. Surely this will affect the service time component of their response time directly. But the waiting time component of their response time depends entirely on the service times of the customers that are served ahead of or with them. Thus, the phenomenon that is primarily responsible for variance reduction is that if one system is experiencing a burst of large service times, the other will be experiencing a similar burst of small service times. We cannot count on such bursts being of any substantial length; otherwise, our random number generator is not truly random! Moreover, such bursts will become less and less likely as the system becomes more complex. In spite of all these problems, the method is almost trivial to use; it makes sense to exploit it even if the results are not very significant.

3.7.3 Control Variate Method

This method is also intended for experimenting with a single system. Let X represent the desired output from the simulation. Let $s = E[X]$ be the parameter that we wish to estimate. Let Y represent another random variable *with known mean* ν that is known to be correlated (positively or negatively) with X. Then $X_c = X - a(Y - \nu)$ is also an unbiased estimate of s for any constant a. Therefore, the idea is to use X_c instead of X in the data analysis. Obviously,

$$\mathrm{Var}(X_c) = \mathrm{Var}(X) + a^2\mathrm{Var}(Y) - 2a\mathrm{Cov}(X, Y) \tag{7.3}$$

For X_c to be the preferred variate, we must have $\mathrm{Var}(X_c) < \mathrm{Var}(X)$. This requires that $2\mathrm{Cov}(X, Y)/a > \mathrm{Var}(Y)$.[3] Since $\mathrm{Var}(Y)$ must be positive, this means that if X and Y are positively correlated, a must be positive, and negative otherwise. Typically, one restricts a to be $+1$ or -1; however, other values may be more desirable. For example, from (7.3) we can find the optimal value of a, denoted a^*, that minimizes $\mathrm{Var}(X_c)$. It is easy to verify that $a^* = \mathrm{Cov}(X, Y)/\mathrm{Var}(Y)$. Substituting this in equation (7.3), we get:

$$\mathrm{Var}(X_c) = \mathrm{Var}(X) - \frac{[\mathrm{Cov}(X, Y)]^2}{\mathrm{Var}(Y)} = (1 - \rho_{XY}^2)\mathrm{Var}(X) \qquad (7.4)$$

where ρ_{XY} is the correlation coefficient between X and Y. The significance of this equation is that *with optimal value of a, variance reduction will be achieved so long as some correlation exists between X and Y.* This is not necessarily true with other values of a. However, determining the optimal value would require reliably estimating $\mathrm{Cov}(X, Y)$ and $\mathrm{Var}(Y)$ from the data, and might prove expensive.

The random variable Y is known as the *control variate*. There are two common ways of choosing it. The *internal method* picks a random variable from the experiment itself. For example, if the output parameter is the response time of a station, we can pick the service time of the station as the control variate. The service time is surely positively correlated with the response time and has a known mean. However, the variance reduction may be limited by two factors. First, the correlation between the response time and the service time of a given customer may not be sufficiently strong. (The reasons for this are essentially the same as in the antithetic variable method.) Second, if the response time is much larger than the service time, a^* may be much larger than 1, which makes $a = 1$ a poor choice.

The *external method* picks the control variate from a similar, but much simpler model. For example, if we are simulating a queuing network model $\mathcal{Z}$ that does not have a product-form solution (see Section 6.1), we can consider another model $\mathcal{Z}^*$, which is derived from $\mathcal{Z}$ by changing service-time distributions, resource constraints, etc., so that $\mathcal{Z}^*$ satisfies conditions for product-form solution. Thus, $\mathcal{Z}^*$ can be solved analytically and the average response time determined exactly. We then simulate $\mathcal{Z}$ and $\mathcal{Z}^*$ in parallel and use the outputs as X and Y, respectively. If the two models are sufficiently similar, a strong positive correlation should exist between X and Y. This method is quite worthwhile if the necessary software exists to analytically solve simplified models.

---

[3] Cautionary note: Since a may be positive or negative, we cannot put a on either side. For example, it would be wrong to claim that $2\mathrm{Cov}(X, Y) > a\mathrm{Var}(Y)$.

3.8 Exercises

1. Consider Example 7.1, which analytically solves a single-chain model of an interactive computer system. Assume that the service-time distribution at the CPU is exponential stage-type and the scheduling discipline is round-robin. Suppose that the coefficient of variation (CV) is 1 and the time slice (TS) is 5 ms. Other parameters are the same as in that example.

   (a) Write a simulation program for this problem. Initially, place all N customers at the terminal station. Run the model for 400 command completions and clear the statistics. Now run the model for an *additional* 2000 commands, while outputting statistics every 400 command completions. The statistics of interest are the average response times at the CPU and disk. The experiment will give you five sets of CPU and disk response times.

   (b) Assume that the sample means obtained above are independent and normally distributed, and construct 95% confidence intervals for CPU and disk response times. Check whether the intervals contain the exact values obtained from the analytic solution. (The analytic solution assumes PS discipline, but since the time slice is very small, the results should also apply to the round-robin discipline.)

   (c) Next, simulate the system for the four combinations resulting from TS of 1 ms and 10 ms, and CV of 0.25 and 4. Compare simulation results against the same analytical results and comment on the differences.

2. For each of the five experiments in Exercise 3.1, find the sample mean of system response time (R) experienced by the terminal users. Estimate the number of data points needed to get 95% confidence interval for R with fractional half-width of 0.05.

3. Complete all steps in the derivation of equation (2.16).

4. In Exercise 3.1, compute the main and interaction effects of CV and TS using the CPU response time from the last four experiments. Which of the two factors is more important? Would you consider the interaction between them significant?

5. Two simulation experiments were made to compare FIFO and LRU page replacement algorithms. For each experiment, 16 independent simulation runs of length 1000 each were made and the average page-fault rate was determined. The results are listed in Table 3.2.

   (a) At 95% confidence level, is the difference between the two algorithms statistically significant? Would you consider it practically significant?

   (b) How many data points do we need to estimate expected page-fault rate for each algorithm with an accuracy of 5% at 95% confidence level?

i	X_i(FIFO)	X_i(LRU)	i	X_i(FIFO)	X_i(LRU)
1	293.51	273.97	9	193.84	196.36
2	271.13	225.24	10	219.29	203.20
3	187.85	199.42	11	220.84	167.00
4	221.31	191.97	12	184.90	194.33
5	204.38	219.60	13	268.05	235.25
6	240.31	230.80	14	255.17	273.82
7	173.60	192.78	15	206.39	178.30
8	256.45	239.29	16	247.28	225.92

TABLE 3.2: Page-fault rates for FIFO and LRU replacement schemes.

6. Let X_i, $i \in 1..n$ be mutually independent random variables with distribution $\mathcal{N}(s_i, \sigma_i)$. Show that the arithmetic average of X_i's also has the normal distribution.

7. In this problem we shall study the properties of χ_n^2 variate. Using equation (2.15), show that $E(\chi_n^2) = n$. Next, using the fact that each X_i in equation (2.15) is $\mathcal{N}(s, \sigma)$, show that χ_n^2/n has gamma distribution with parameter $s = 1$ and $\alpha = n/2$. From this, show that $\text{Var}(\chi_n^2) = 2n$.

8. Consider a fractional factorial experiment design with $k = 5$. Devise a scheme that avoids all confoundings between main and simple interaction effects while using a minimum number of combinations.

9. Suppose that the two levels in an experiment design are represented by -1 and $+1$. Consider a two-factor experiment involving factors X and Y. Show that determining the main and simple interaction effects in this case is equivalent to determining the coefficients b, c, and d for the following curve fitted through the outputs corresponding to the four input combinations.

$$f(X, Y) = a + bX + cY + dXY \tag{8.1}$$

10. Proceeding as we did for deriving equation (5.5), verify equation (5.7). Do the same for equation (5.6).

11. The *sample correlation coefficient* between two sequences $\{X_i\}$ and $\{Y_i\}$ can be defined as

$$\gamma_{XY} = \sum_i (X_i - \overline{X})(Y_i - \overline{Y}) \Big/ \sqrt{\sum_i (X_i - \overline{X})^2 \sum_i (Y_i - \overline{Y})^2} \tag{8.2}$$

Show that for linear regression, $\gamma_{XY}^2 = Q_R/Q_T$, and thus can also be regarded as a measure of the goodness of linear regression.

12. Using equation (6.8) show that in Example 3.2

$$\hat{a_1} = \frac{(z_1 z_4 - z_3^2)\sum Y_i + (z_2 z_3 - z_1 z_4)\sum x_i Y_i + (z_1 z_3 - z_2^2)\sum x_i^2 Y_i}{n(z_2 z_4 - z_3^2) - z_1(z_1 z_4 - z_2 z_3) + z_2(z_1 z_3 - z_2^2)} \tag{8.3}$$

Next obtain expressions for $\sum \mathcal{Y}_i$, $\sum x_i \mathcal{Y}_i$, and $\sum x_i^2 \mathcal{Y}_i$ by taking expected values in (6.8). Substitute these in the expression for $E[\hat{a_1}]$ to show that $E[\hat{a_1}] = a_1$, i.e., $\hat{a_1}$ is an unbiased estimate of a_1. Do the same for $\hat{a_2}$ and $\hat{a_3}$. Also, show that $Q_T = Q_E + Q_R$ holds here as well.

13. Fit the equation $Y = \alpha\beta^X$ through the following data: (the ordinate values can be assumed to be $1, 2, 3, \dots$).

    3.93, 5.31, 7.24, 9.64, 12.87, 17.07, 23.19, 31.44

14. Show that Q_E for multiple-regression given in (6.18) is a convex function of α_i's. Find a matrix equation similar to (6.5) for the estimates of α_i's. Specialize these equations for multiple linear regression.

15. Suppose that we use both CRN and antithetic variable methods to reduce the variance in a comparison study. Let U_i and V_i denote the ith data point for the first and second system respectively. CRN is used to induce positive correlation between U_i and V_i. Antithetic variable is used for individual systems. Thus, U_i is the average of U_{i1} and U_{i2}. Similarly, V_i is the average of V_{i1} and V_{i2}. Find an expression for the variance of $(U_i - V_i)$ and discuss under what conditions variance reduction can be achieved. What synchronization problems arise in this method?

16. Show how you can combine the CRN technique with the control variate method to reduce the variance. Are there any special problems in doing so?

Bibliographic Notes

Much of the material in this chapter is classical and may be found in standard books on statistics and systems modeling, for example, Box, Hunter, and Hunter (1978), Kobayashi (1978), and Law and Kelton (1982). These books also discuss the topic of writing simulation programs. I particularly like Law and Kelton (1982) because of its numerous insights into various aspects of performing simulations and analyzing data.

Shantikumar and Sargent (1983) discusses hybrid simulation. Wagner and Lazowska (1989) and Fujimoto (1990) provide surveys of various issues in both optimistic and pessimistic parallel simulation. The topic of experiment design is covered in detail in Das and Giri (1986). Our discussion in Section 3.5.1 comes from Dudewicz and Dalal (1975). Both Kobayashi (1978) and Law and Kelton (1982) discuss analysis of variance, a topic that we have glossed over. Our discussion on variance reduction techniques is partly based on Law and Kelton (1982). More detailed discussion on these and other techniques can be found in Kleijnen (1974). The IEEE tutorial volume on discrete event simulation edited by Dudewicz and Karian (1985) contains many interesting articles on various topics. A recent survey on steady-state simulation may be found in Pawlikowski (1990).

CHAPTER

4

Fundamentals of Queuing Models

In this chapter we discuss the fundamentals of queuing-network oriented modeling of systems. We introduce open and closed networks, and define various input and output parameters for them. We next show several relationships between these parameters under various operational assumptions. We also consider modeling of several more advanced features of queuing network models, including classes and chains, and extend the operational analysis to models with multiple chains and classes. Finally, we discuss the calibration and validation of queuing network models of computer systems.

4.1 Structure and Performance Parameters

A queuing network model (QNM) of a computer system is a collection of service stations connected via directed paths along which the customers of the system move. The *stations* represent various system resources, and the *customers* represent jobs, processes, or other active entities. The customers move from one station to another, queuing up at each for some service. The service requirement of a customer at a station is a random variable that is described by a probability distribution. In general, a QNM may also have some special types of stations, such as those involved in resource allocation and deallocation; however, we shall

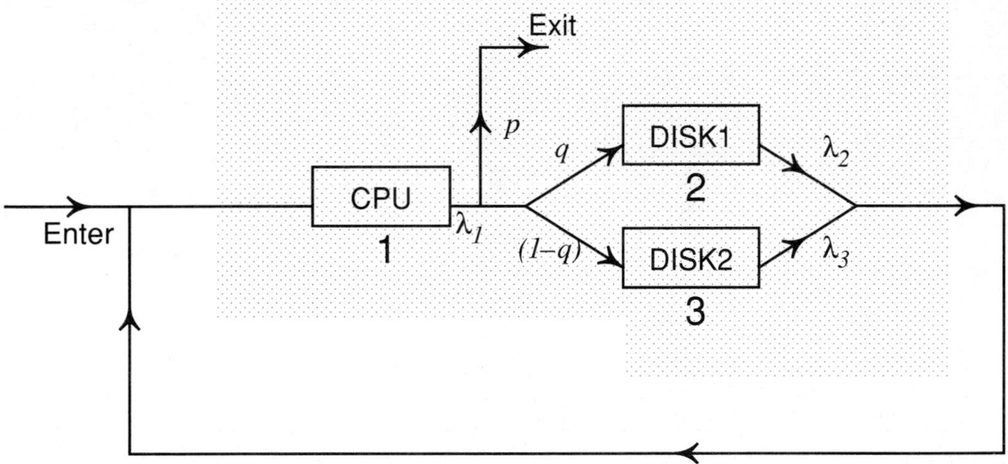

FIGURE 4-1: An open model of a computer system.

not consider them in this chapter.

4.1.1 Open and Closed Models

A QNM in which there is no restriction on the number of customers is called an *open* or *infinite population* model. In such models, the customers initially arrive from an external source and eventually leave the system. Fig. 4-1 shows an example of an open model. Here an entering job first queues up at the CPU to do some computation. After finishing this computation, the job may either be done and leave the system, or need some disk I/O. The first situation occurs with probability p, and the latter with $1 - p$. These probabilities are known as *routing probabilities*. A job going towards disks chooses disk1 with probability q and disk2 with probability $1 - q$. After the requested I/O operation is complete, the job comes back to the CPU for more computation.

In models where the number of customers is fixed (i.e., no arrivals from, or departures to, the external world), the model is called a *closed* or *limited population* model with the number of circulating customers known as the *population*. In a closed model, the arrival rate to any station must drop to zero if all circulating customers are already queued up at that station. Fig. 4-2 shows an example of a closed model. This model is similar to the one in Fig. 4-1, except that the customers are the terminal users (or more accurately, the terminal processes.) In this model, the exit of a customer from the terminal station represents the issuing of a command, and its return to the terminal represents the completion. If a terminal user must wait for the response to the issued command before proceeding, the population of the model is the same as the number of active terminals.

In a closed model, the "completion" of a job or customer is represented

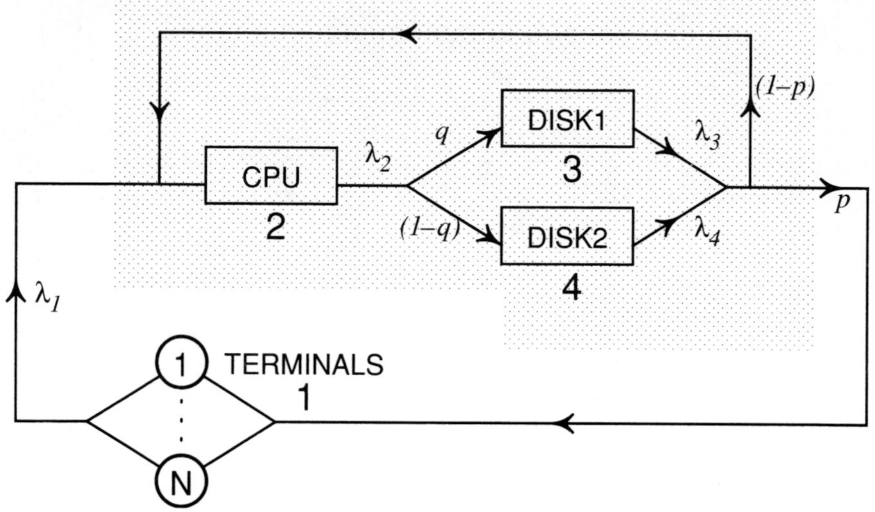

FIGURE 4-2: A closed model of a computer system.

only indirectly. For example, in Fig. 4-2, when a customer returns to the terminal station, we can say that that particular customer finishes and goes out of the system, but another statistically identical customer takes its place. In this way, a closed model can represent the behavior of a real system, where the customers do indeed enter and exit the system. This also means that the job completion rate in a closed model will be the throughput along an appropriately chosen branch of the network. Closed models are generally more realistic than open models, since they can capture physical limitations better. For example, in a computer system, the restriction on the number of resident processes can be modeled accurately by choosing population equal to the desired degree of multiprogramming. Unfortunately, closed models are also harder to solve, and a considerable portion of this text is devoted to solution algorithms for closed models.

A computer system may process several distinct types of workload. This aspect can be modeled by using the concepts of *chains* and *classes*, and is discussed in sections 4.3 and 4.4. For now, we assume that all customers in the model are statistically identical. We shall refer to such a model as a *simple model*.

We call a QNM *well-formed* if it is connected and has a well-defined long-term behavior. We defer the details concerning this property to Section 4.4.1 and only state the results for simple QNM's. A closed QNM is well-formed if every station is reachable from all others with a nonzero probability. The same definition applies to an open, connected QNM if we add a hypothetical station H that generates all external arrivals and absorbs all departing customers. We shall henceforth assume that all QNM's that we consider are well-formed.

4.1.2 Performance Parameters

A *simple* QNM requires the following inputs: (a) number of stations, henceforth denoted as M, (b) service-time distribution and scheduling discipline at each station, (c) routing probabilities of customers among stations, and (d) population (for closed models) or interarrival-time distribution (for open models). The output parameters of interest are the various performance measures at each station, such as response time, queue length, throughput, and utilization. In much of this text, we are concerned with only the steady-state behavior of the system. Also, we shall often be dealing with only the average parameters, instead of the probability distributions. In the following list, we define certain basic input and output parameters for the stations of a simple queuing network and establish notations for them. The subscript i refers to the station to which the parameters apply. The network in question may be open or closed. In the latter case, it is customary to include the population level N as an argument of the output parameters.

1. *Average service time* s_i: Average time spent in serving a customer at station i. We shall often speak of the (average) *service rate*, denoted μ_i. This is defined as simply $1/s_i$.
2. *External arrival rate* Λ_i: Average rate at which customers arrive to station i, *from the external world*. This applies to open networks only.
3. *Routing probability* q_{ij}: Fraction of departures from station i headed to station j next.
4. *Throughput* λ_i *or* $\lambda_i(N)$: Average number of service completions per unit time at station i.
5. *Average response time* R_i *or* $R_i(N)$: Average time a customer spends at station i, either waiting to be served or receiving service.
6. *Average waiting time* W_i *or* $W_i(N)$: Average time a customer spends at station i waiting to be served.
7. *Average queue length* Q_i *or* $Q_i(N)$: Average number of customers at station i, *including those being serviced.*
8. *Average waiting line length* L_i *or* $L_i(N)$: Average number of customers at station i, *excluding those being serviced.*
9. *Utilization* U_i *or* $U_i(N)$: Fraction of time that station i is busy. (As such, this definition applies only when s_i is independent of n; a more general definition is introduced in Section 4.3.2).
10. *Queue-length distribution* $P_i(n)$ *or* $P_i(n|N)$: Probability of finding n customers at station i. (Notice the | separating n and N.)

The list includes only the most frequently encountered measures; we shall introduce others when necessary. We shall use these notations consistently, except that the station subscript i and population indicator N may be dropped when no confusion arises. Also, in the next section, we shall use the symbol X_i to denote overall arrival rate to station i. In most other places, X_i will be the same as the throughput λ_i, and no separate notation is needed for it.

The average service time often depends on the number of customers present at the station, denoted n. In such a case, we shall use the notation $s_i(n)$ and refer to $s_i(1)$ as s_i°. Similarly, we shall use the notations $\mu_i(n) \triangleq 1/s_i(n)$ and $\mu_i^\circ \triangleq 1/s_i^\circ$. There is one more aspect regarding service times (or rates) that should be noted. The "work" brought by a customer is typically measured in some units other than time. For example, the processing requirements of a job may be measured in terms of the number of instructions to be executed, the I/O requirements in terms of the number of bytes of data to be transferred, etc. Let w_i denote the average *work requirement* of a customer. The server has certain *work capacity* measured as the number of units of work done per second. For example, the work capacity of a CPU can be specified as the number of instructions executed per second, the work capacity of an I/O device as the number of bytes transferred per second, etc. Let us denote the work capacity as r_i. Note that r_i may depend on the number of customers present, but w_i does not. We could now define the mean service time $s_i(n)$ as $w_i/r_i(n)$. In calibrating a model, a separate specification of w_i and $r_i(n)$ is desirable because it allows us to alter the two parameters independently. (In the computer system context, w_i can be viewed as a software parameter, whereas $r_i(n)$ is a hardware parameter.) However, in the analysis per se, it is adequate to consider $s_i(n)$ only. Therefore, we shall not speak of the w_i and $r_i(n)$ parameters from now on, and "service rate" to us shall always mean $r_i(n)/w_i$, rather than $r_i(n)$.

4.2 Operational Analysis of Queuing Models

In this section, we derive several relationships between various performance parameters. We shall use the *operational approach* for deriving these, rather than the *stochastic approach*. In the operational approach, we deal with behavior sequences and their properties, rather than with random processes. Therefore, we will have no occasion to specify or use the interarrival time and service-time distributions. We shall return to the stochastic approach in Chapter 5. We first introduce relevant behavioral properties and operational measures, and then discuss relationships between the measures. It turns out that many of the operational results are identical to those obtained by stochastic analysis, but have the advantage of being more intuitive and applicable to nonstochastic systems as well.

4.2.1 Behavioral Properties

Suppose that we observe a queuing system for a time period T and record all interesting events (arrivals and service completions at each station) during this period. There are three properties of particular interest concerning such a behavior sequence: homogeneity, flow balance, and one-step behavior. The concept of homogeneity applies to arrivals, services, and routing. *Homogeneous arrivals* means that the *average* arrival rate to a station is independent of the number of customers present there. Similarly, *homogeneous service* means that the *average* service rate is independent of the number of customers at the station. Note that the service rate must be zero when the station is empty, and in a closed network, the arrival rate must drop to zero when all N customers are present at the station. The definition of homogeneity does permit this essential form of dependence. *Routing homogeneity* means that the routing probabilities do not depend on the number of customers present at the source, destination, or any other station. We shall implicitly assume routing homogeneity throughout this section.

Flow balance refers to the property that the total number of arrivals to a station during the period T equals the total number of departures from the station. Flow balance is an appropriate assumption in most situations, and is essential for studying the long-term behavior of the system. *One-step behavior* means that (a) arrivals do not coincide with departures, and (b) at any instant, only one arrival or one departure can occur. As we shall see, many of our results need this assumption. Intuitively, the one-step property is important because without it, the state of the system as seen by an arriving or departing customer is not well defined. For example, if two customers arrive at once when there are already n customers in the system, how many customers does each one of them see on arrival: n or $n+1$?

An important point to keep in mind concerning these and other operational properties is that they are defined directly in terms of the given behavior sequence. *Thus, by "average" we really mean sample average, and by "probability", we mean relative frequency*. For example, to find the arrival rate while the station has n customers queued, we simply count how many arrivals occurred over the period when the station actually contained n customers. Whether we have "enough" samples in this exercise is totally irrelevant! We shall shortly cast these definitions in precise mathematical terms, which will allow us to verify if the alleged properties hold for the behavior sequence at hand.

As an example, consider the behavior sequence shown in Fig. 4-3 for a station in a closed system with a population of three. Here the upward transitions indicate arrivals, and the downward transitions indicate departures. Thus, the vertical axis gives the number of customers present in the system. The labels on the horizontal segments show the time units for which the system stays in the corresponding state. (The fact that all time durations are integers is not significant.) This behavior sequence is one-step because only one event (a single arrival or departure) occurs at any time. It is also flow balanced because all incoming customers during time T depart during T (i.e., the final "state" of the system is the same as the initial state). We can make this behavior sequence persistent by simply repeating the given behavior indefinitely. Thus, we would have a system operating under steady state, but the system is neither stochastic nor does it satisfy any of the usual assumptions such as exponentially distributed service time. The results are still the same as would hold in a stochastic system with exponential distributions. This shows that the operational assumptions are

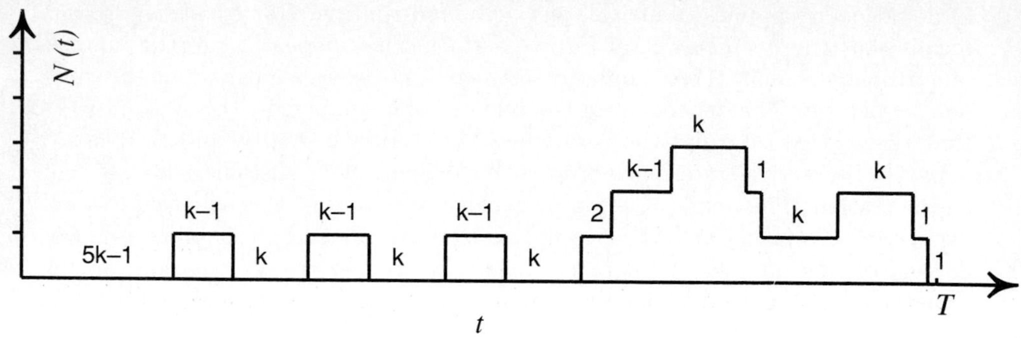

FIGURE 4-3: A sample behavior sequence.

weaker than the corresponding stochastic assumptions.

4.2.2 Operational Definitions of Performance Measures

In this section, we derive a number of relationships between various performance measures. As such, these relationships only apply to the observation period T; however, if the underlying system is persistent and the observation period T covers a complete "regeneration cycle", then the behavior in all subsequent cycles will be statistically identical, and hence the results will hold in general.

Suppose that the system of interest is station i belonging to a closed network with population N. Let us define the following parameters over the observation period T:

- $A_i(n)$ Number of arriving customers who find n customers at station i.
- $D_i(n)$ Number of departing customers who leave behind $n-1$ customers at station i (i.e., the number of departures while the station is in state n).
- $T_i(n)$ Duration of time for which there are n customers at station i.

Note that $A_i(N) = 0$ and $D_i(0) = 0$, but $T_i(n)$ may be nonzero for all values of $n \in 0 \mathinner{..} N$. Let B_i denote the total busy period. Obviously,

$$B_i = T - T_i(0) = \sum_{n=1}^{N} T_i(n) \tag{2.1}$$

Let A_i and D_i denote, respectively, the total number of arrivals and departures during time T. Then

$$A_i = \sum_{n=0}^{N-1} A_i(n) \quad \text{and} \quad D_i = \sum_{n=1}^{N} D_i(n) \tag{2.2}$$

Let $X_i(N)$ denote the overall arrival rate to station i. Then,

$$X_i(N) = A_i/T \tag{2.3}$$

Let $Y_i(n|N)$ denote the arrival rate to station i when n customers are present there. This is often known as *restricted arrival rate* and is given by

$$Y_i(n|N) = \frac{A_i(n)}{T_i(n)}, \qquad 0 \le n \le N-1 \tag{2.4}$$

Note that $Y_i(N|N) = 0$. The departure rate or throughput of station i, denoted $\lambda_i(N)$, is given by

$$\lambda_i(N) = D_i/T \tag{2.5}$$

The average service time of station i when n customers are present there, denoted $s_i(n)$, is given by

$$s_i(n) = \frac{T_i(n)}{D_i(n)}, \qquad 1 \le n \le N \tag{2.6}$$

In analogy with $Y_i(n|N)$, we can think of the service rate $\mu_i(n)$ as the *restricted departure rate*. If the services are homogeneous, we denote $s_i(n)$ and $\mu_i(n)$ as simply s_i and μ_i respectively. If the arrivals are homogeneous, $Y_i(n|N)$ is independent of n for $n < N$, and denoted as $Y_i(N)$. Flow balance means that $A_i = D_i$, which implies that $X_i(N) = \lambda_i(N)$.

In a queuing system, there are three interesting distributions of the number of customers present at a station:

- Distribution seen by an arriving customer, denoted $PA_i(.|.)$. By definition, the probability that an arriver finds n customers in the system is given by

$$PA_i(n|N) = A_i(n)/A_i \quad \text{for} \quad 0 \le n < N \tag{2.7}$$

- Distribution seen by a departing customer, denoted $PD_i(.|.)$. The probability that a departer leaves behind n customers in the system is given by

$$PD_i(n|N) = D_i(n+1)/D_i \quad \text{for} \quad 0 \le n < N \tag{2.8}$$

- Distribution seen by a random observer, denoted $P_i(.|.)$. This is the fraction of time the system contains n customers, and is given by

$$P_i(n|N) = T_i(n)/T \quad \text{for} \quad 0 \le n \le N \tag{2.9}$$

We shall see detailed relationships involving these distributions in sections 4.2.4 and 4.2.5. As a simple example, the utilization $U_i(N)$, as defined earlier, can be expressed as

$$U_i(N) = \frac{B_i}{T} = \frac{T - T_i(0)}{T} = 1 - P_i(0|N) \tag{2.10}$$

4.2.3 Forced Flows and Visit Ratios

This section concerns the analysis of queuing networks operating under flow balance. This is the most frequently encountered situation in practice, and we shall show how the throughputs of all stations can be related in such a case. These results hold in stochastic systems as well, if we examine their steady-state behavior. The results follow from a simple conservation property, often known as the *forced-flow law*, which states that at any branch or join point in a network, there is no net accumulation or loss of customers.

Let λ_i denote the throughput of station i in a flow-balanced network with M stations. Then for any station i, the total *arrival rate* should also be λ_i. This arrival rate can be expressed in terms of the throughputs of other stations by accounting for all the flows into station i. This gives

$$\lambda_i = \Lambda_i + \sum_{j=1}^{M} \lambda_j q_{ji}, \qquad 1 \le i \le M \tag{2.11}$$

where Λ_i is the external arrival rate to station i, and q_{ji} is the probability that a customer exiting station j goes to station i directly. We can put these equations in the following matrix form

$$\mathbf{A}.\boldsymbol{\lambda} = \boldsymbol{\Lambda} \tag{2.12}$$

where $\mathbf{A}$ is a $M \times M$ matrix of q_{ij}'s, and $\boldsymbol{\lambda}$ and $\boldsymbol{\Lambda}$ are $M \times 1$ vectors of λ_i's and Λ_i's respectively. If the network is open, the system (2.12) is nonhomogeneous, and will have a unique solution so long as the network is well-formed. This means that given the external arrival rates, we can determine the throughputs of all stations exactly. If the network is closed, the system (2.12) becomes homogeneous and does not have a unique solution. However, if the network is well-formed, the rank of $\mathbf{A}$ is $M-1$, which means that we have exactly $M-1$ linearly-independent equations, which can be solved to determine the ratios of throughputs.

Because throughput ratios can be determined easily in both open and closed networks, it is convenient to introduce the notion of *relative throughputs* or *visit ratios*. The reference station for computing these ratios can be chosen arbitrarily, since the results will be independent of this choice. We shall denote the visit ratio for station i as v_i. By definition, for any two stations i and j,

$$v_i/v_j = \lambda_i/\lambda_j \tag{2.13}$$

If station k is chosen as the reference station, we can also interpret v_i as the number of visits to station i for each visit to station k. As we shall see in later chapters, visit ratios often provide adequate information to calibrate and solve a model, and the routing probabilities are not needed.

Example 4.1 Compute the relative throughputs for each station in figures 4-1 and 4-2 respectively.

Solution Let Λ denote the external arrival rate, and λ_i the throughput of station i. Then for Fig. 4-1, we can write the following equations

$$\begin{aligned}\lambda_1 &= \Lambda + \lambda_2 + \lambda_3 \\ \lambda_2 &= (1-p)\lambda_1 \times q \\ \lambda_3 &= (1-p)\lambda_1 \times (1-q)\end{aligned}$$

Suppose that we define visit ratios relative to the external source, i.e., $v_i = \lambda_i/\Lambda$. Then the equations above yield the following solution:

$$v_1 = 1/p \qquad v_2 = q(1-p)/p \qquad \text{and} \quad v_3 = (1-q)(1-p)/p$$

Note that here we can determine exact throughputs. For example, if $p = 0.1$, $q = 0.8$, and $\Lambda = 10/\text{sec}$, then $\lambda_1 = 100/\text{sec}$, $\lambda_2 = 72/\text{sec}$, and $\lambda_3 = 18/\text{sec}$.

For the model of Fig. 4-2, we have

$$\lambda_2 = \lambda_1 + (1-p)(\lambda_3 + \lambda_4), \qquad \lambda_3 = q\lambda_2, \qquad \lambda_4 = (1-q)\lambda_2$$

It is easy to see that these equations are linearly independent, but we cannot write any more independent equations. Thus, exact throughputs cannot be determined, but visit ratios can. For example, if we let $v_2 = 1$, $p = 0.2$, and $q = 0.6$, then $v_1 = 0.2$, $v_3 = 0.6$, and $v_4 = 0.4$. □

4.2.4 Some Fundamental Results

In this section we prove three important operational relationships, which hold under very general conditions. We start with a simple property known as the *throughput law*. By the definition of throughput, we have

$$\lambda_i(N) = \frac{D_i}{T} = \frac{1}{T}\sum_{n=1}^{N} D_i(n) = \sum_{n=1}^{N} \frac{D_i(n)}{T_i(n)}\frac{T_i(n)}{T} = \sum_{n=1}^{N} \frac{P_i(n|N)}{s_i(n)}$$

Put in standard form, the throughput law then states

$$\lambda_i(N) = \sum_{n=1}^{N} \mu_i(n) P_i(n|N) \tag{2.14}$$

Note that (2.14) would hold for any behavior sequence since its derivation does not need any assumptions (homogeneity, one-step behavior or flow balance). In particular, *throughput law would continue to hold even in the context of stochastic analysis, where we are dealing with the statistical properties of the system, instead of the observable properties of finite behavior sequences*. If the services are homogeneous, i.e., $\mu_i(n) = \mu_i$ for all $n > 0$, (2.14) reduces to

$$\lambda_i(N) = \mu_i[1 - P_i(0|N)] \tag{2.15}$$

Using equation (2.10), we get

$$U_i(N) = \lambda_i(N) s_i \tag{2.16}$$

This simple property is known as the *utilization law*. It also holds in the stochastic sense, provided that the service rate is independent of the "load" at station i. A more direct way of obtaining the utilization law is as follows:

$$U_i(N) = \frac{B_i}{T} = \frac{B_i}{D_i} \times \frac{D_i}{T} = s_i \lambda_i(N)$$

Throughput and service rate describe the behavior of a station on its "output end". Quite analogously, arrival rate and restricted arrival rates describe the behavior on the "input end" of the station. Thus, like the throughput law, we have the following *arrival law*.

$$X_i(N) = \sum_{n=0}^{N-1} Y_i(n|N) P_i(n|N) \tag{2.17}$$

The proof follows trivially from the definition (without any assumptions).

$$X_i(N) = \frac{A_i}{T} = \sum_{n=0}^{N-1} \frac{A_i(n)}{T_i(n)} \frac{T_i(n)}{T} = \sum_{n=0}^{N-1} Y_i(n|N) P_i(n|N)$$

Under flow balance, the arrival rate is the same as throughput, which means that equations (2.14) and (2.17) give two ways of expressing the throughput. If the arrivals are homogeneous, i.e., $Y_i(n|N) = Y_i(N)$ for all $n < N$, equation (2.17) yields the following simple relationship

$$X_i(N) = Y_i(N)(1 - P_i(N|N)) \tag{2.18}$$

Notice the complementary nature of equations (2.15) and (2.18). A simple way to remember them is to note that services cannot occur if the station is empty, and arrivals cannot occur if the station is full.

Next we discuss *Little's law*, which relates average response time to the average queue length. Consider a closed region Ω enclosing some portion of a queuing network. Let λ_Ω be the output rate (or throughput) of this region, Q_Ω the average number of customers in the region, and R_Ω the average time spent by a customer inside the region. Then Little's law states that

$$\lambda_\Omega \times R_\Omega = Q_\Omega \tag{2.19}$$

The following is a sketch of the proof of this important law. Suppose that we start observing the subsystem enclosed by region Ω at a time when it is empty and a customer has just arrived. Without loss of generality, we can let this time instant be $t = 0$. Fig. 4-4 shows the number of arrivals and departures that have occurred by time t. We denote these as $\mathcal{A}(t)$ and $\mathcal{D}(t)$ respectively. $\mathcal{A}(t)$ makes a jump of unit magnitude whenever a customer arrives and $\mathcal{D}(t)$ makes a similar jump when a customer departs. Therefore, at any time t, the difference $\mathcal{A}(t) - \mathcal{D}(t)$ gives the number of customers in the subsystem. Suppose that at $t = \tau$, the subsystem is about to go into the next busy period. Then

$\mathcal{A}(\tau^-) = \mathcal{D}(\tau^-)$, and thus the flow balance holds over the period $(0, \tau)$. Let n denote the number of customers serviced during time τ and let $R_\Omega(i)$ be the response time of the ith departing customer. Also let *area* denote the area of the shaded region in Fig. 4-4 (between time instants 0 and τ). Suppose, for simplicity, that the customers are served by the subsystem in a first-in first-out pipeline fashion. Then, the average response time R_Ω is given by

$$R_\Omega \triangleq \frac{1}{n}\sum_{i=1}^{n} R_\Omega(i) = \frac{area}{n} \tag{2.20}$$

This follows because $R_\Omega(i)$ is the time between the ith upward transition of $\mathcal{A}(t)$ and that of $\mathcal{D}(t)$ and also equals the area of the "horizontal rectangle" of unit height formed by these two transitions. Since the *area* can be interpreted as the integral of the number of customers present in the subsystem, the average number of customers is simply $area/\tau$. (In this view, we think of *area* as composed of a sequence of "vertical rectangles" separated by transitions in $\mathcal{A}(t)$ and $\mathcal{D}(t)$.) Since $\lambda_\Omega = n/\tau$ by equation (2.5), we have

$$Q_\Omega = \frac{area}{\tau} = \frac{area}{n} \times \frac{n}{\tau} = R_\Omega \lambda_\Omega \tag{2.21}$$

Notice that we did not need to assume homogeneity or one-step behavior to derive this identity. The assumptions that we did make, namely, the first-in first-out pipelined service and special choice of starting and ending points, can also be relaxed. The first assumption was used only to simplify the interpretation of Fig. 4-4, and is not important for the proof. The proof is based only on two basic identities, namely $R_\Omega = area/n$ and $Q_\Omega = area/\tau$, where *area* is simply the total "backlog" during the time interval τ. This backlog will remain invariant under any kind of service mechanism. Thus, *Little's law holds under any type of scheduling discipline*. With respect to the other assumption, note that what we have considered is a complete *regeneration cycle* for the subsystem. If the starting and ending point of the observation interval are chosen arbitrarily, the validity of Little's Law hinges on whether $area/n$ can be reasonably interpreted as the average response time. For example in Fig. 4-4, there is no problem with choosing the endpoint of the interval between τ' and τ, but other choices may require us to pretend that the partially served and waiting customers have also finished by the endpoint. Similarly, a move of the start point may mean that only the residual response times are included for some customers. Of course, the perturbation caused by these "end effects" will become negligible as $T \to \infty$ provided that there is no indefinite accumulation or depletion of customers. It follows that *Little's Law applies in the stochastic sense to any system operating under steady state*.

Since Little's law applies to any closed region, we can obtain a number of interesting results by choosing this region in special ways. For example, there are three ways to apply Little's law to a single station i:

1. To the entire station, which gives $Q_i = \lambda_i R_i$.

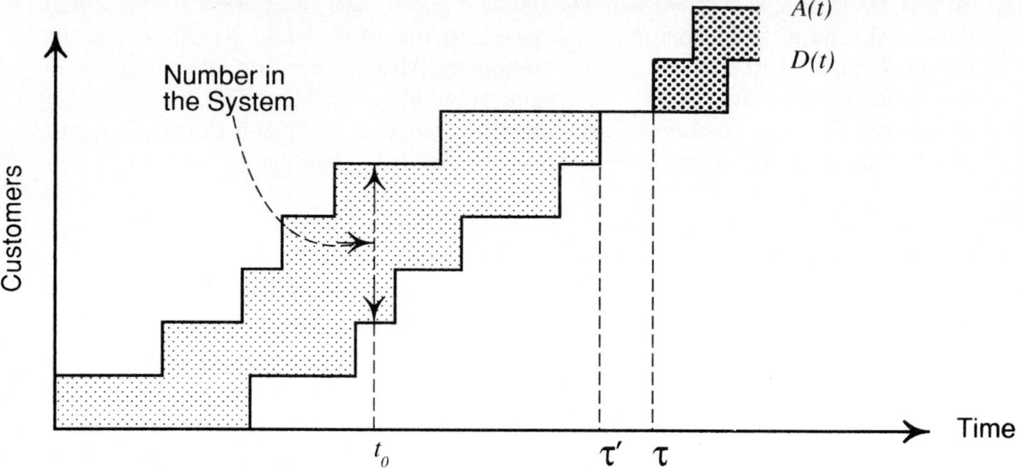

FIGURE 4-4: Arrival and departure functions.

2. To only the waiting line at the station, which gives $L_i = \lambda_i W_i$.
3. To only the "service box" of the station. This is most useful if the services are homogeneous. In this case, the average number of customers in the "service box" is same as the probability that the server is busy, which in turn is the utilization. Thus, we get the utilization law $U_i = \lambda_i s_i$.

Often, Little's law is used on subnetworks to compute the *flow time* of jobs through that subnetwork. In this application, we first add up the queue lengths at all the stations in the subnetwork, and then multiply this by the throughput. Sometimes, it is useful to apply Little's law to an entire closed network. Suppose that we have already computed the response time of each station in a closed network containing M stations and N customers. Now consider the *cycle-time* $CT_k(N)$ at some station k, i.e., the average time a customer takes to return to station k since its last visit. During this cycle time, the customer will make, on the average, v_i/v_k visits to station i, each time spending $R_i(N)$ time units there. Therefore, $CT_k(N) = \sum_{i=1}^{M} v_i R_i(N)/v_k$ and by applying Little's law to the entire network, we get

$$\lambda_k(N) = \frac{N v_k}{\sum_{i=1}^{M} v_i R_i(N)} \tag{2.22}$$

We shall use this relation in Section 7.2 in the mean value analysis algorithm.

4.2.5 Properties of Queue Length Distributions

In this section we show several important properties of the three queue length distributions under various operational assumptions. We start by considering the consequences of one step-behavior. If the arrivals (departures) occur singly, then in any system state n, at most one arrival (departure) can remain unmatched by a departure (arrival). This happens because the system cannot return to state n unless an opposite event occurs. It follows that

$$\forall n \; |A_i(n) - D_i(n+1)| \leq 1 \tag{2.23}$$

where $D_i(n+1)$ can exceed $A_i(n)$ only if we start with a nonempty system. Under flow balance, we cannot have an arriver who has not departed, or vice versa, and hence equation (2.23) reduces to $A_i(n) = D_i(n+1)$. This also implies $A_i = D_i$, as expected. Thus, we get the important result that *under flow balance and one-step behavior, the arriver's distribution is the same as that of the departer's*, i.e.,

$$PA_i(n|N) = PD_i(n|N) \tag{2.24}$$

We can also get recursive equations for random observer's and arriver's distributions under these two assumptions. By definition,

$$P_i(n|N) = \frac{T_i(n)}{T} = \frac{T_i(n)}{D_i(n)}\frac{D_i(n)}{T} = \frac{T_i(n)}{D_i(n)}\frac{A_i(n-1)}{T_i(n-1)}\frac{T_i(n-1)}{T}$$

where we have used the identity $D_i(n) = A_i(n-1)$. Recognizing various terms, we get

$$P_i(n|N) = s_i(n)Y_i(n-1|N)P_i(n-1|N) \tag{2.25}$$

Similarly, for the arriver's distribution we get

$$PA_i(n|N) = \frac{A_i(n)}{A_i} = \frac{A_i(n)}{T_i(n)}\frac{T_i(n)}{D_i(n)}\frac{D_i(n)}{A_i} = Y_i(n|N)s_i(n)\frac{A_i(n-1)}{A_i}$$

which yields

$$PA_i(n|N) = s_i(n)Y_i(n|N)PA_i(n-1|N) \tag{2.26}$$

We can show another interesting result popularly known as the *arrival theorem*. It states that

$$PA_i(n|N) = P_i(n|N-1) \tag{2.27}$$

That is, *under flow balance and one-step behavior, an arriving customer sees the random observer's distribution with itself removed from the network*. The proof of this result is a little involved and will not be presented. Note that in an open network, equation (2.27) states that the arriver's distribution must be the same as that of the random observer's. Coupled with equation (2.24), we have the following result:

> For a station in an open network that exhibits flow balance and one-step behavior, we have $PA_i(n) = P_i(n) = PD_i(n)$ for all n.

The departer's distribution can be related to the random observer's distribution (without any assumptions) as follows:

$$PD_i(n|N) = \frac{D_i(n+1)}{T_i(n+1)}\frac{T_i(n+1)}{T}\frac{T}{D_i} = \frac{\mu_i(n+1)}{\lambda_i(N)}P_i(n+1|N) \tag{2.28}$$

Under flow balance and one-step behavior, using (2.24) we get

$$PA_i(n|N) = \mu_i(n+1)P_i(n+1|N)/\lambda_i(N) \tag{2.29}$$

Furthermore, using the arrival theorem, we get the so called *marginal local balance theorem*, which can be restated as

$$\mu_i(n)P_i(n|N) = \lambda_i(N)P_i(n-1|N-1) \tag{2.30}$$

We shall prove this equation using stochastic means in Section 7.2.

In practice, the arrivals are often homogeneous, and we can show some interesting results under this assumption. By definition

$$PA_i(n|N) = \frac{A_i(n)}{A_i} = \frac{A_i(n)}{T_i(n)}\frac{T_i(n)}{T}\frac{T}{A_i} = \frac{Y_i(N)}{X_i(N)}P_i(n|N)$$

Therefore, by equation (2.18) we get the following relationship (without assuming one-step behavior or flow balance).

$$PA_i(n|N) = \frac{P_i(n|N)}{1-P_i(N|N)} \tag{2.31}$$

That is, *in a closed network under homogeneous arrivals, the arriver's distribution is a simple renormalization of the random observer's distribution.* For an open network, this equation means that the arriver's and random observer's distributions are identical. If the system shows one-step behavior and flow balance as well, we can use (2.29) to get

$$P_i(n|N) = \frac{\lambda_i(N)}{\mu_i(n)}\frac{P_i(n-1|N)}{1-P_i(N|N)} \triangleq \alpha(n)P_i(n-1|N) \tag{2.32}$$

This recurrence relation, along with the requirement that all probabilities sum to 1, gives us the following expression for $P_i(n|N)$

$$P_i(n|N) = \prod_{i=1}^{n}\alpha(i)\left[1+\sum_{k=1}^{N}\prod_{j=1}^{k}\alpha(j)\right]^{-1} \tag{2.33}$$

Although $\alpha(n)$ involves $P_i(N|N)$, we can obtain $P_i(N|N)$ by letting $n = N$ in equation (2.33). Thus, if we know the throughput $\lambda_i(N)$ at station i (e.g., by measurement or some other means), we can compute random observer's distribution (and hence the other two distributions, queue-length moments, average response time, and utilization). Since the throughputs of all stations are proportional to their visit ratios, all parameters of other stations can also be computed. If the

n	$A_i(n)$	$D_i(n)$	$T_i(n)$	$P_i(n)$	$PA_i(n)$	$PD_i(n)$	$X_i(n)$	$s_i(n)$
0	4	-	$8k$	8/15	4/7	4/7	$1/(2k)$	-
1	2	4	$4k$	4/15	2/7	2/7	$1/(2k)$	k
2	1	2	$2k$	2/15	1/7	1/7	$1/(2k)$	k
3	-	1	k	1/15	-	-	-	k

TABLE 4.1: Performance parameters for the behavior sequence in Fig. 4-3.

network in question is open, we get an even simpler result, since $\alpha(n) = \lambda_i/\mu_i(n)$ and λ_i is known. That is, in an open network, equation (2.33) provides a simple and explicit expression for the queue length distribution.

Finally, under homogeneous services, flow balance, and one-step behavior, (but arrivals not necessarily homogeneous), equation (2.29) reduces to $P_i(n|N) = U_i(N)PA_i(n-1|N)$, which means that

$$Q_i(N) \triangleq \sum_{n=1}^{N} nP_i(n|N) = U_i(N)\sum_{n=1}^{N} nPA_i(n-1|N)$$

which along with Little's law gives the following interesting relationship

$$R_i(N) = s_i(1 + QA_i(N)) \tag{2.34}$$

where $QA_i(N)$ is the average queue length seen by an arriving customer. Note that by the arrival theorem, $QA_i(N) = Q_i(N-1)$. This substitution gives us the well-known *mean value theorem*, which we shall prove using stochastic means in Section 7.2.

Example 4.2 Characterize the behavior sequence shown in Fig. 4-3 and compute the three distributions for it.

Solution We already noted that this behavior sequence is one-step and flow balanced. The performance parameters corresponding to Fig. 4-3 can be computed using the relationships given above and are shown in Table 4.1. Note that $A_i = D_i = 7$ as expected from the flow balance property, which also means that the arrival rate $X_i(N)$ and throughput $\lambda_i(N)$ should be the same $(= 7/15k)$. Both arrivals and services are homogeneous since $Y_i(n|N)$ and $s_i(n)$ are independent of n. Note that the utilization law applies because $U_i = 1 - P_i(0) = 7/15$ and $s_i\lambda_i = k \times 7/(15k) = 7/15$. Also $PA_i(n)$ is simply a renormalization of $P_i(n)$, and $PD_i(n) = PA_i(n)$ as expected. □

4.2.6 Comparison of Operational and Stochastic Analysis

As we saw in the preceding subsections, operational analysis deals with behavior sequences rather than random processes. Therefore, it relies on behavioral assumptions rather than those about the statistical properties of the random processes. The results apply to finite behavior sequences, and in some cases can be extended to infinite behavior sequences as well. In contrast, the results obtained from stochastic arguments must necessarily assume infinite behavior sequences and nondeterministic behavior. In spite of this difference, under comparable assumptions, many of the results obtained from the two approaches are identical. In this sense, the operational analysis can be considered as an extension to the classical stochastic analysis. It also has the advantage of providing simple and intuitive proofs to several results that would be difficult to prove stochastically.

The *comparable assumptions* in the two approaches are as follows. One-step behavior corresponds to exponentially distributed interarrival and service times, because with exponential distribution the probability of two or more events occurring in a short interval is negligible. (This will be shown in Section 5.1.3). Flow balance corresponds to the assumption of steady state, and homogeneity corresponds to state independence.

Although this correspondence between operational and stochastic assumptions is useful, there is no suggestion that these assumptions are identical. For example, flow balance means that the total number of arrivals during the observation period equals the total number of departures, whereas steady-state operation means that the statistical properties of the random process representing system state are invariant under time shifts. *An operational assumption is a concrete property of a given behavioral realization, whereas the corresponding stochastic assumption is a statistical statement about all possible behavior sequences.* Equating the two properties naively will often lead to incorrect conclusions. For example, suppose that we equate state independence to homogeneity. Consider a D/D/1 system; i.e., a load-independent station with deterministic interarrival and service times, denoted as a and b, respectively. Assume that $a > b$ to ensure stability. Let n denote the number of customers present at the station. We may regard n as the "state" of the system, and since a is independent of n, claim that the arrivals are homogeneous. From (2.31), it then follows that the arriver's distribution should be the same as the random observer's. However, this is not true because an arriver in this system will never find anyone present, whereas a random observer will see a customer with probability b/a. The problem is that the assumption of homogeneous arrivals is wrong here. To see this, note that this system has the property that whenever a customer is present, no more can arrive until it leaves. Thus, in any concrete behavior realization of the system, we will find that $Y_i(0|\infty) > 0$, whereas $Y_i(n|\infty) = 0$ for $n > 0$, i.e., the arrivals are nonhomogeneous.

In previous sections, we generalized a few operational identities (e.g., Little's law) to apply in the stochastic sense. Such a generalization requires a lot of care, and is often not easy because we must account for all possible behavior sequences. For example, the arriver's distribution is the same as the random observer's only if the interarrival-time distribution is exponential, even though that may seem to be true whenever the arrival rate is state-independent. (See Section 9.2.1).

It is, however, true that all our operational results obtained under one-step behavior assumption carry over to the stochastic domain (with exponential distribution assumption). Viewed another way, although operational analysis is useful in explaining stochastic results under exponential distributions, it cannot replace stochastic techniques for tackling more complex queuing problems.

4.3 General Features of Queuing Models

In this section we briefly consider some extensions to simple QNM's that are useful in modeling complex characteristics of real systems. We shall also indicate the level of difficulty in solving models containing these features.

4.3.1 Classes and Chains

In a simple queuing model, it is convenient to assume that all customers are statistically identical; that is, their service time requirements at a given station are drawn from the same probability distribution and they are all routed similarly. A real computer system, however, may serve many categories of jobs such that the level of service provided and/or the routing depends on the category. For example, the characteristics of batch jobs may be different from those of the interactive jobs. This aspect can be represented in a queuing network model by introducing the concept of a *chain*. Thus, we may have a batch chain, an interactive chain, and so forth. *A chain forms a permanent categorization of jobs; a job belonging to one chain cannot switch to another chain.*

In addition to the permanent categorization of jobs, it is also desirable to allow the customers to go through different phases of processing in the system. This necessarily requires the ability to switch from one phase to another, and thus needs a concept other than chains. We refer to these phases as *classes* and allow several classes within a chain. For example, the execution of both batch and interactive jobs would involve two distinct phases: program loading from disk into the main memory, and the actual execution. We can represent this by having two classes in each chain, such that all customers of a chain start out in class 1 to do program loading, and then switch to class 2 for execution. (In a closed model, class 2 jobs would switch back to class 1 after finishing execution.)

Most of the results for simple QNM's extend to QNM's with multiple chains or classes, as we shall see in Section 4.4 and in later chapters of the book. However, the difficulties in model calibration, solution, and validation typically increase rapidly with the number of chains/classes; thus the introduction of many job categories may not always be worthwhile.

4.3.2 Load-Dependent Stations

In Section 4.2, we introduced the concept of homogeneous service and proved several results under homogeneous and nonhomogeneous service. In this section we shall study the corresponding stochastic concepts of load-independent and load-dependent service rates. There are many practical situations where the average service rate of a station depends on its loading level. For example, suppose that station i contains k identical servers, each capable of serving at the average rate of μ_i°. Let n denote the number of customers at the station. Then for $n \leq k$, the effective service rate of the station will be $n\mu_i^\circ$, because only n out of k servers could be busy. For $n > k$, the effective service rate will be fixed at $k\mu_i^\circ$, since all the servers will be busy. Therefore,

$$\mu_i(n) = \begin{cases} n\mu_i^\circ & \text{for } n < c \\ c\mu_i^\circ & \text{for } n \geq c \end{cases} \tag{3.1}$$

As another example, if a CPU uses round-robin discipline, no switching overhead is incurred when there is only one process on the ready list, and otherwise each time-slice expiry results in a context switch.

We shall henceforth refer to $\mu_i(1)$ as the *basic service rate* and denote it as μ_i°. Similarly, we denote the basic service time as s_i°. Let

$$\mu_i(n) = \mu_i^\circ C_i(n) \tag{3.2}$$

where $C_i(n)$ is called the *capacity function*, and by definition, $C_i(1) = 1$. By the throughput law, we have

$$\lambda_i(N) = \sum_{n=1}^{N} \mu_i(n) P_i(n|N) = \mu_i^\circ \sum_{n=1}^{N} C_i(n) P_i(n|N)$$

Now we define the utilization of station i as

$$U_i(N) = \frac{\text{Throughput}}{\text{Basic service rate}} = \sum_{n=1}^{N} C_i(n) P_i(n|N) \tag{3.3}$$

Note that $U_i(N)$ *can* be greater than 1. One interpretation of this definition is that the *utilization is the expected value of the capacity function*. If the station is a multiple-server station, the utilization can be interpreted as the expected number of busy servers. If the station is load-independent, i.e., $\forall n\ C_i(n) = 1$, equation (3.3) gives the familiar result $U_i(N) = 1 - P_i(0|N)$. Thus, for a load-independent station, our present definition of utilization agrees with our earlier definition. The new definition is needed because it is meaningless to talk of "fraction of time the station is busy" when the station has multiple servers. Note that with the new definition,

$$U_i(N) = \lambda_i(N) s_i^\circ \tag{3.4}$$

which agrees with the utilization law, *except that it now holds irrespective of whether station i is load-independent*.

We are now in a position to derive a simple but useful result. Let station i be *either load-independent or a multiserver*. In both cases, each customer requires the same amount of service time, independent of the load. Therefore,

$$R_i = W_i + s_i^\circ \tag{3.5}$$

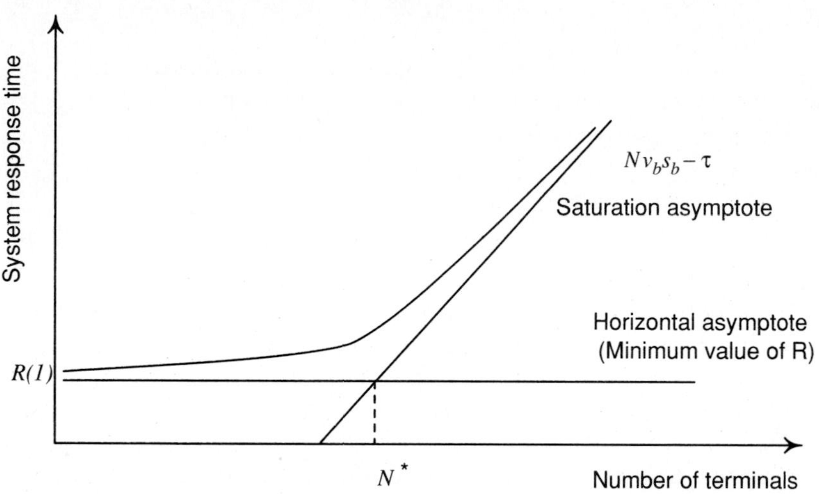

FIGURE 4-5: System response time as a function of number of terminals.

Multiplying both sides of this equation by λ_i, and then applying Little's law, we get

$$Q_i = L_i + U_i \tag{3.6}$$

We shall need this relation in Section 9.2.

An important special case of load-dependent stations is a *delay station*. Such a station does not have a waiting line, i.e., $L = 0$. It can be characterized as a load-dependent station with the capacity function of $C(n) = n$. In other words, if there are n customers at the station, n servers are also available, so that no customer has to wait. Terminals in a computer system are appropriately modeled as delay stations, with *think time* as the basic service time. Note that for a delay station i in a simple network, $R_i(N) = s_i^\circ$, where s_i° is the basic service time. By applying Little's law to this, we get $U_i(N) = Q_i(N)$. This relation is not surprising, since with no queuing, the expected number of busy servers must be the same as the expected number of customers at the station.

At this point we consider a simple application to illustrate the usefulness of various concepts. Consider the model of an interactive system such as the one in Fig. 4-2. We would like to find the optimum number of terminals for such a system. Let us designate the terminal as station 1 and the rest as stations $2..M$. The terminal station is of delay type, and we assume the rest to be load-independent. The subsystem consisting of stations $2..M$ is often referred to as the *central subsystem*. Let us suppose that all visit ratios are defined relative to the terminal station. Let $R(N)$ denote the response time experienced by the terminal users at population N. Then $R(N)$ will show the general behavior depicted in Fig. 4-5. This curve has two asymptotes:

1. When $N = 1$, there is no queuing anywhere in the central subsystem; therefore, $R_i(N) = s_i$, and hence $R(1) = \sum_{i=2}^{M} v_i s_i$. This gives the asymptote

for the low end.

2. When N is sufficiently large, some station in the central subsystem will become a bottleneck; i.e., will have utilization approaching 1. Since $\lambda_i(N) = v_i\lambda_1(N)$, by the utilization law,

$$U_i(N) = \lambda_1(N)v_i s_i, \qquad 1 \le i \le M \tag{3.7}$$

Therefore, *the station to first reach saturation will be the one with the largest value of* $v_i s_i$. Let us denote this station by the subscript b (where b stands for "bottleneck"). Since $U_b(N) \approx 1$, from equation (3.7), $\lambda_1(N) \approx 1/(v_b s_b)$ under saturation. By applying Little's law over the entire network, we get $N = \lambda_1(N)[R(N) + \tau]$ where $\tau = R_1(N)$ is the mean think time. Thus, $R(N) = N v_b s_b - \tau$ gives the asymptote for the high end.

Let N^* denote the abscissa of the intersection between the two asymptotes. If $N \ll N^*$, the system is underutilized, and if $N \gg N^*$, each new job interferes completely with the existing ones (thereby leading to a linear increase in response time). Thus, N^* can be regarded as the optimum number of terminals, often referred to as the *saturation point* in the literature. Obviously,

$$N^* = \left[\sum_{i=2}^{M} v_i s_i + \tau\right] \Big/ v_b s_b \tag{3.8}$$

The above formula may give a fractional number. We can round it to the nearest integer to get the desired value.

This example also shows how to do *asymptotic analysis* of a closed queuing network. Basically, the idea is to identify the most heavily loaded station (i.e., the one with the largest value of $v_i s_i$), and assume that it is saturated. Since the throughputs of all stations are related, we immediately get the maximum possible throughputs of all the stations. It is also possible to get response times, since we can consider the bottleneck station as a source/sink and treat the rest of the network as open. As we shall see in later chapters, open networks are generally easier to analyze than closed networks.

4.3.3 Other Features and Limitations

Here we briefly mention some other important features of real systems and comment on whether they can be incorporated into QNM's. We start with *nonconservative* systems. Although we did not make it explicit, we have consistently assumed that there is no artificial loss or creation of work, i.e., the system is conservative. This means, for example, that the server does not stay idle while there are customers to serve, a customer does not "withdraw" from the system after partial service, etc. In some systems, such assumptions must be relaxed. Consider, for example, the problem of parallel search on a multiprocessor system. The search is started in parallel along different paths on each of the processors, and as soon as any of them finds the target, the search is aborted on all others.

Such systems are generally very difficult to analyze. There are other systems that are *pseudo-conservative*, i.e., nonconservative in a restricted sense. For example, in a token-ring local-area network, the token (which *is* the server) may not be present at a node even when some packets are queued there. If the time needed to switch from one node to the next is zero, the server is nonconservative only with respect to individual nodes; there is still no loss of work in the system as a whole. With nonzero switching time, only a certain portion of service capacity is dedicated to transmitting packets. Section 13.1 examines some of these systems.

In our characterization of QNM's, we assumed that the routing probabilities are fixed numbers, independent of the number of customers at various stations. (In operational terms, this is the same as assuming homogeneous routing.) In real systems, it is often desirable to keep some information about the congestion levels at various service facilities, so that a service request could be routed to a lightly loaded facility. This *adaptive routing* can be modeled easily in QNM context, but the efficient solution is possible in only very limited cases.

A fundamental characteristic of QNM's is that a customer can occupy only one service station or resource at a time, but in reality, there are many instances of *simultaneous resource possession*. For example, in a computer system, a job will typically acquire main memory, tape drives, etc., *before* it begins execution and may hold them throughout its lifetime. Similarly, before a process can start I/O on a disk, it might have to explicitly request and get hold of an I/O channel. Such features are totally out of the purview of QNM's, though indirect modeling is possible. This problem is addressed briefly in Section 8.2.

Customers in a real system may show other types of complex behavior. For example, a process in a computer system may spawn several child processes, all of which work concurrently on various parts of the problem. These processes may later merge together (or terminate) at some point. This aspect can be modeled, but efficient solution is feasible only in some simple cases. More generally, processes may synchronize in arbitrary ways. Timed Petri-net models can represent such synchronization naturally and are, therefore, preferred. The eventual solution to these models, however, uses the same techniques as needed by QNM's. Thus, the difference between QNM's and timed Petr-net models is only in the representational power rather than in the solution power. We shall explore Petri-net based modeling in Chapter 12.

4.4 Analysis of Multiple-Class Networks

In this section we show how we can identify the chains and classes in a network with several categories of activities. Next we show how to determine visit ratios in such networks. Finally, we show that most of the operational definitions and results of Section 4.2 extend easily to such networks as well.

4.4.1 Characterization of Classes and Chains

In this section we consider the following questions concerning a network with multiple categories of customers:

1. How do we check if the network is *consistent*, i.e., connected and structurally sound?

2. How do we identify the chains, and the classes contained within those chains?

3. How do we check if the network is *well-formed*, i.e., has a well-defined long-term behavior?

In examining these issues, we shall use the network of Fig. 4-6 as a running example. This network is *alleged* to contain six categories (or classes) of jobs, whose routing is shown with lines of different styles. Customers switch from one class to another in several parts of this network; this is shown by an abrupt change in line style. For example, a class 1 customer coming out of the terminal (shown in solid line) has three choices: (a) stay in class 1 and go to disk1, (b) switch over to class 2 (shown in dashed-dotted lines) and go to the CPU, or (c) switch over to class 3 (shown in dashed lines) and go to disk2. The *switching probabilities* corresponding to these three events are 0.3, 0.5, and 0.2 respectively. When a class 2 customer at the CPU finishes its service and exits, it changes back to class 1 with probability 0.75 and stays in class 2 with probability 0.25. In the former case, it goes to disk2, gets serviced, and then unconditionally changes back to class 2. In the latter case, it goes to disk1, and switches over to class 1 unconditionally after exiting disk1. A class 3 customer at disk2 changes to class 1 (with probability 0.6) or to class 2 (with probability 0.4) after exiting. The network does receive external arrivals, which come in as members of class 5. It also has departures to the external world as customers of class 6. Class 6 customers can switch over to classes 4 and 5, and so on.

Given a complex model such as the one in Fig. 4-6, it is not obvious whether the category assignments made by the modeler result in a meaningful network. For example, the modeler may have designated activities in two different parts of the model as belonging to the same category (possibly because those activities have similar characteristics in the real system), but the model structure indicates this to be impossible. Let us see how this may happen. Let us first eliminate external arrivals and departures by introducing a hypothetical station H in the model such that all departures to the external world go to H and all external arrivals come from H. If Ω is the original model, we shall denote this modified model as Ω'. Now consider two distinct path segments, say x and y in Ω', designated as belonging to the same category c. Then it is essential that a customer on path x, after a finite number of class switchings, be able to take path y, and vice-versa. If this were not the case, the two paths could not possibly belong to the same category. On the other hand, if this property holds for every pair of paths from every category, the model can be claimed to be *consistent*.

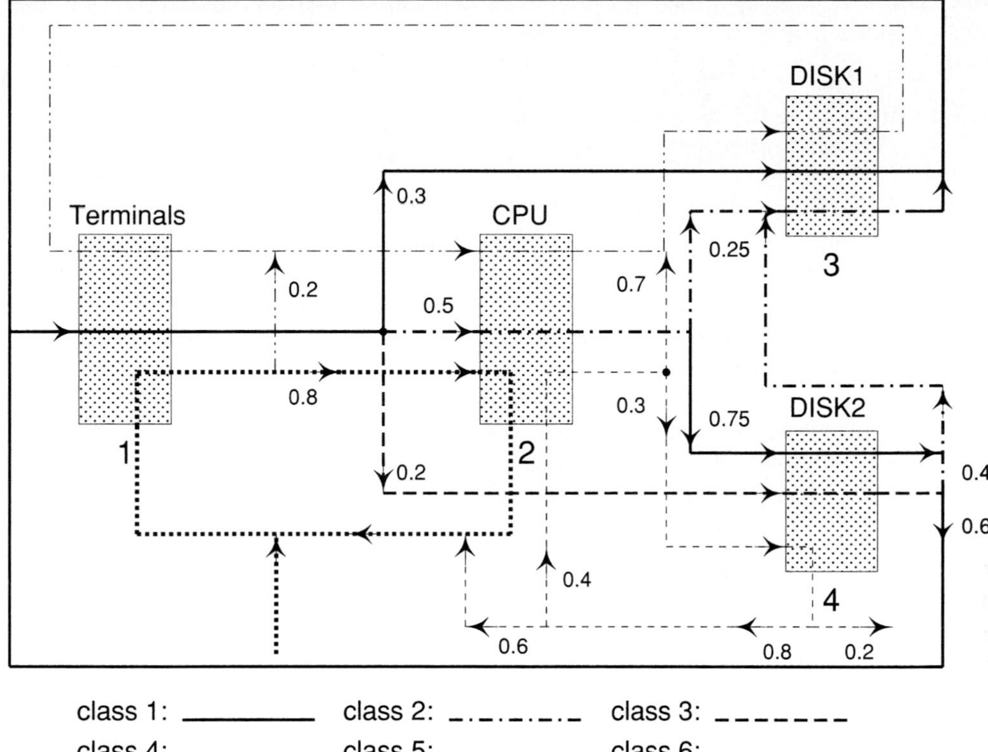

FIGURE 4-6: A computer system model with six categories of jobs.

The model in Fig. 4-6 is easily seen to be consistent according to the requirements above. However, had we tried to lump classes 2 and 5 into a single class, it is easy to verify that the model would become inconsistent. We shall henceforth assume that all models are consistent.

A consistent network need not be well-formed, i.e., its long-term behavior may be ill-defined. For example, if the network of Fig. 4-6 is allowed to operate for a long time, customers will be pumped into class 4 indefinitely but cannot leave. Also, class 6 will eventually be devoid of any customers and should be removed. To identify these situations, we use a graph model, known as the *reachability graph* (RG). The nodes of a RG are the classes, and an arc from node c to node d means that a class c customer can switch to class d directly (with a nonzero probability). Let $S_1, \ldots, S_k$ be the strongly connected components (SCC) of RG. All classes in a SCC must show similar long-term behavior, because any class in a SCC can transform to any other within the same SCC. Each SCC can be classified into one of the following four categories:

Closed if in the long run it will have a finite number of customers permanently locked in it.

Open if it will have both arrivals from and departures to the external world (either directly or via the classes of other SCC's).

Transient if in the long run it will have no customers in it.

Unstable if in the long run it receives customers from the external world or classes of other SCC's, but does not shed any.[1]

Now we can characterize well-formedness. *A consistent network is well-formed if and only if it does not have any unstable or transient SCC's.* In a well-formed network, closed SCC's can be identified as closed chains, and open SCC's can be further grouped into open chains. The classification algorithm itself is straightforward, and is sketched briefly in the following. We start with the reachability graph, say G, of the given model, and proceed as follows:

1. Construct a reduced reachability graph, say G_r, by replacing the SCC's of G by individual nodes. In G_r, an arc from node i to node j indicates that some class in the SCC S_i can switch to some class in the SCC S_j with nonzero probability.
2. If class i customers arrive from the external world, regard this as as switch from a "dummy class" to class i. Similarly, regard class i departures to the external world as a switch from class i to yet another dummy class. Add nodes and arcs to G_r corresponding to these dummy classes. Let the new graph be denoted as G'_r.
3. Label all nodes of G'_r as O, C, T or U (for open, closed, transient and unstable) recursively as follows:
   (a) Label all "dummy nodes" as O, and all isolated nodes as C.
   (b) If a node has no incoming arc but at least one outgoing arc, label it as T.
   (c) If a node has at least one incoming arc and at least one outgoing arc, label it as follows: if all its source nodes are labeled as T, label it as T, else label it as O.
   (d) If a node has no outgoing arc but at least one incoming arc, label it as follows: if all its source nodes carry the label T, label it as C, else label it as U.
4. Remove from G'_r, all dummy nodes and nodes labeled as T or U. (The corresponding arcs are also removed.) Call the resulting graph G''_r.
5. All nodes marked as C in G''_r must be isolated and represent closed chains (with SCC population as the chain population). Of the remaining nodes, each connected component represents an open chain.

The intuition behind this algorithm is as follows: A node which only has transient sources and generates output, must be transient itself. All SCC's represented by isolated nodes or those nodes that receive input only from transient

[1]The concept of stability here is weaker than the one normally used in characterizing open networks (which also requires knowledge of parameters other than routing).

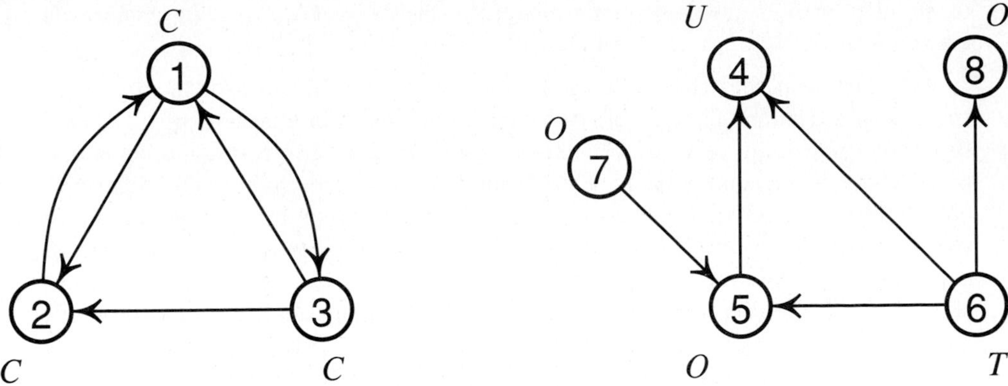

FIGURE 4-7: Reachability graph for the model in Fig. 4-6.

nodes will eventually have a finite population and must be closed. Finally, a SCC that receives inputs from a permanent source but has no output must be unstable.

Example 4.3 Check if the model in Fig. 4-6 is well-formed. Also classify all open and closed classes into chains.

Solution Fig. 4-7 shows the RG for the model in Fig. 4-6, and has two connected components (CC) as shown. The CC on the left-hand side makes an isolated SCC, and thus classes 1-3 are closed. In the other CC, there is no nontrivial SCC. Step 2 of the algorithm adds nodes 7 and 8 to this CC, and step 3 labels it as shown. Thus, we identify class 4 as unstable, class 5 as open, and class 6 as transient. Consequently, the model is not well-formed. If we ignore classes 4 and 6, the model has only two chains, one closed, containing classes 1-3, and the other open, containing class 5. □

4.4.2 Characteristics of Multiple-Class Networks

As shown in the last section, all classes in a well-formed network can be grouped into open and closed chains. If all the chains in the model are closed, we call the model closed, if all are open, we call the model open, and if some chains are closed and some open, we call the model *mixed*. We now say a few words about open and closed chains. For generality, we consider a mixed model with K chains, such that chains $1 \,..\, C$ are closed, and the rest are open. We also assume that the network can achieve steady-state operation. This requires that the open chains occupy less than 100% of the capacity of each server.

The main motivation for grouping the classes into different chains is that the customers belonging to one chain cannot move to another chain. This means that each closed chain has its own population, which represents the set of customers that always behave in a particular way. We shall denote the population of chain i as N_i, and the *population vector* as $\mathbf{N} = (N_1, \ldots, N_K)$ where by convention, $N_i = \infty$ for an open chain.

It turns out that the distinction between classes and chains is inconsequential for open chains. That is, we can regard each class in chains $C+1..K$ as a separate open chain, or view all such classes as belonging to a single open chain, or pick any other combination. This is not true of closed chains. The difference comes from the fact that a class belonging to an open chain can have any number of customers at any of the stations it passes through, whereas the number of customers in a class belonging to a closed chain cannot exceed the chain population. Thus, the classes belonging to an open chain can be dealt with like different chains. Conversely, two different open chains can be treated like two classes of an open chain. Because of this, *it is adequate to consider only one open chain in an open or mixed model*. For the class of networks that we deal with in much of this book, handling multiple classes is almost trivial, but this is not the case with chains. Therefore, we shall mostly discuss multiple-chain networks with one class per chain.

The input/output parameters of a multiple-chain network must be specified on a per-chain basis; therefore, we now require a second subscript in our notations. Thus, $\lambda_{ir}(\mathbf{N})$ denotes the throughput of chain r at station i when the network population is given by the vector $\mathbf{N}$. Other notations are contained in Appendix A. As in single-chain networks, under flow balance, the forced-flow law yields the following equation for the throughputs

$$\lambda_{ir} = \Lambda_{ir} + \sum_{j=1}^{M} \lambda_{jr} q_{jir} \tag{4.1}$$

where q_{jir} is the routing probability of chain r customers from station j to station i, and Λ_{ir} is the external arrival rate of chain r customers to station i. Equation (4.1) gives an independent system of equations for each chain r. We shall assume that the network is well-formed. Then the comments in Section 4.2.3 apply to each chain. That is, if chain r is open, equation (4.1) gives the throughputs exactly, and if it is closed, it gives them to within a constant. In any case, all visit ratios v_{ir}'s are easily determined.

If the chains contain several classes, we also need to include a subscript for class in our notations. Thus, the visit ratio for class c of chain r at station i will be denoted as v_{irc}. Let q_{jdicr} denote the routing probability for a chain r job going to station i as a member of class c after being serviced at station j as a member of class d. Then the visit ratios satisfy the following equation

$$v_{irc} = \Lambda_{irc} + \sum_{j=1}^{M} \sum_{d=1}^{nc(r)} v_{jrd} q_{jdicr} \tag{4.2}$$

where $nc(r)$ is the number of classes in chain r. The situation is still similar to the one discussed above. That is, for each chain r, equation (4.2) gives an independent system of equations; the only difference is that now we have $M \times nc(r)$ equations for chain r instead of M equations. Thus, if chain r is open, equation (4.2) gives exact throughput of every class at every station, and if it is closed, it gives only the visit ratios for them.

Example 4.4 Compute all visit ratios for the model in Example 4.3 (after the removal of classes 4 and 6).

Solution We shall denote the chain containing classes 1-3 as chain 1, and the one containing class 5 as chain 2. The class subscript is redundant for chain 2, and we shall omit it. Suppose (arbitrarily) that $v_{111} = v_{12} = 1$. Obviously, for chain 2, $v_{22} = 0.8 \times v_{12} = 0.8$. Chain 1 contains classes 1-3, which satisfy the following equations:

$$
\begin{aligned}
v_{212} &= 0.50 \times v_{111} = 0.50 \\
v_{311} &= 0.30 \times v_{111} = 0.30 \\
v_{411} &= 0.75 \times v_{212} = 0.375 \\
v_{413} &= 0.20 \times v_{111} = 0.20 \\
v_{312} &= 0.25 \times v_{212} + v_{411} + 0.40 \times v_{413} = 0.125 + 0.375 + 0.08 = 0.580
\end{aligned}
$$

In writing these equations for, say, class c at station i, we always consider the rate at which class c customers *arrive* at station i. A class c customer may switch to another class immediately after exiting station i, but that does not affect the visit ratio of station i. All visit ratios not explicitly computed above are zero. □

4.4.3 Operational Analysis of Multiple-Chain Networks

In this section we show that most of the operational definitions and laws discussed in Section 4.2 in the context of single-chain networks can be carried over to multiple chain/class networks. For simplicity in stating the results, we only consider multiple-chain networks with one class per chain. Similar results can be obtained for the more general case as well. We assume that the network has M stations and K chains. The state of a station in such a network can be described by a vector, called the *occupancy vector*. We denote it as $\mathbf{n}_i = (n_{i1}, \ldots, n_{iK})$, whose components n_{ir} give the number of chain r customers at station i. When there is no confusion, we shall shorten this notation to $\mathbf{n}$ with chain r component denoted as n_r. Obviously, $\mathbf{n}$ can range from $\mathbf{0}$ to $\mathbf{N}$. We also need the notation e_r which is a vector with K elements, of which the rth element is 1 and all others are zero. We call this *a unit vector in rth dimension*. Suppose that we observe station i for T time units. Then we can introduce the following three measures for each chain $r \in [1 \mathinner{..} K]$.

$A_{ir}(\mathbf{n})$: Number of arriving chain r customers who find $\mathbf{n}$ customers at station i.

$D_{ir}(\mathbf{n})$: Number of chain r departures while the station is in state $\mathbf{n}$ (i.e., the number of departing customers that leave behind $\mathbf{n} - e_r$ customers).

$T_{ir}(\mathbf{n})$: Duration of time for which there are $\mathbf{n}$ customers at station i.

Let

$$A_{ir} = \sum_{n_1=0}^{N_1} \cdots \sum_{n_{r-1}=0}^{N_{r-1}} \sum_{n_r=0}^{N_r-1} \sum_{n_{r+1}=0}^{N_{r+1}} \cdots \sum_{n_K=0}^{N_K} A_{ir}(\mathbf{n}) \tag{4.3}$$

We shall abbreviate summations like these by specifying the range of $\mathbf{0}$ to $\mathbf{N}-e_r$ for the vector $\mathbf{n}$. Thus, we define

$$A_{ir} = \sum_{\mathbf{n}=\mathbf{0}}^{\mathbf{N}-e_r} A_{ir}(\mathbf{n}), \qquad D_{ir} = \sum_{\mathbf{n}=e_r}^{\mathbf{N}} D_{ir}(\mathbf{n}) \tag{4.4}$$

Let $X_{ir}(\mathbf{N})$ denote the total arrival rate of chain r customers to station i. Then,

$$X_{ir}(\mathbf{N}) = A_{ir}/T \tag{4.5}$$

Let $Y_{ir}(\mathbf{n}\|\mathbf{N})$ denote the restricted arrival rate of chain r to station i when $\mathbf{n}$ customers are present there. Then

$$Y_{ir}(\mathbf{n}|\mathbf{N}) = \frac{A_{ir}(\mathbf{n})}{T_i(\mathbf{n})}, \qquad \mathbf{0} \leq \mathbf{n} \leq \mathbf{N}-e_r \tag{4.6}$$

The throughput of chain r at station i, denoted $\lambda_{ir}(\mathbf{N})$ is given by

$$\lambda_{ir}(\mathbf{N}) = D_{ir}/T \tag{4.7}$$

Let the average service time of chain r customers at station i when $\mathbf{n}$ customers are present there, be denoted as $s^*_{ir}(\mathbf{n})$. (The reason for using s^* instead of s will be clear shortly.) Obviously,

$$s^*_{ir}(\mathbf{n}) = \frac{T_i(\mathbf{n})}{D_{ir}(\mathbf{n})}, \qquad e_r \leq \mathbf{n} \leq \mathbf{N} \tag{4.8}$$

As in the single-chain case, it is often convenient to use service rate, which is simply the inverse of service time, i.e., $\mu^*_{ir}(\mathbf{n}) = 1/s^*_{ir}(\mathbf{n})$. Unlike the single-chain case, however, homogeneous service *does not* imply that s^*_{ir} (or μ^*_{ir}) is independent of $\mathbf{n}$, because $\mu^*_{ir}(\mathbf{n})$ is the *effective rate* at which the server can process chain r customers. Since this server is also being used by other chains, it cannot devote 100% of its capacity to chain r. Thus, we can view $\mu^*_{ir}(\mathbf{n})$ as the product of the following two terms:

1. The fraction of service capacity devoted to chain r. This depends on the scheduling discipline. We assume a *processor sharing* (PS) discipline where the server is equally shared among all customers present at the station. This discipline can be regarded as the limiting case of the round-robin discipline when the time slice becomes infinitesimally small.

2. The *inherent service rate* for chain r (i.e., the service rate for chain r if the server serves only this chain). We shall denote the inherent service rate as μ_{ir} (and inherent service time as s_{ir}). In general, the inherent service rate could itself depend on the occupancy vector $\mathbf{n}$.

That is,

$$\mu^*_{ir}(\mathbf{n}) = \frac{n_r}{|\mathbf{n}|}\mu_{ir}(\mathbf{n}) \qquad \text{where } |\mathbf{n}| = \sum_{k=1}^{K} n_k \tag{4.9}$$

We have chosen PS discipline here because it is one of the "symmetric disciplines" that are easy to handle by stochastic means. We shall see more on this in Section 6.1.

Homogeneity only means that $\mu_{ir}(\mathbf{n})$ is independent of $\mathbf{n}$; i.e., $\mu_{ir}(\mathbf{n}) = n_r\mu^\circ_{ir}/|\mathbf{n}|$.

The three basic distributions for the multiple-chain case can be defined as follows:

Distribution seen by chain r arrivers

$$PA_{ir}(\mathbf{n}|\mathbf{N}) = A_{ir}(\mathbf{n})/A_{ir}, \quad \mathbf{0} \leq \mathbf{n} \leq \mathbf{N} - e_r \tag{4.10}$$

Distribution seen by chain r departers

$$PD_{ir}(\mathbf{n}|\mathbf{N}) = D_{ir}(\mathbf{n} + e_r)/D_{ir}, \quad \mathbf{0} \leq \mathbf{n} \leq \mathbf{N} - e_r \tag{4.11}$$

Distribution seen by a random observer

$$P_i(\mathbf{n}|\mathbf{N}) = T_i(\mathbf{n})/T \quad \mathbf{0} \leq \mathbf{n} \leq \mathbf{N} \tag{4.12}$$

Notice that the definition of arriver's and departer's distributions is chain-specific. We could also define the distributions seen by a random arriver/departer, but those are not very useful.

We now prove the multiple-chain counterparts of the results shown in sections 4.2.4 and 4.2.5. The *throughput law* holds, since

$$\begin{aligned}\lambda_{ir}(\mathbf{N}) &= \frac{D_{ir}}{T} = \frac{1}{T}\sum_{\mathbf{n}=e_r}^{\mathbf{N}} D_{ir}(\mathbf{n}) = \sum_{\mathbf{n}=e_r}^{\mathbf{N}} \frac{D_{ir}(\mathbf{n})}{T_i(\mathbf{n})}\frac{T_i(\mathbf{n})}{T} \\ &= \sum_{\mathbf{n}=e_r}^{\mathbf{N}} \mu^*_{ir}(\mathbf{n})P_i(\mathbf{n}|\mathbf{N}) \end{aligned} \tag{4.13}$$

If the services are homogeneous, the station will be occupied by chain r customers with probability $n_r/|\mathbf{n}|$ in state $\mathbf{n}$. Therefore,

$$\lambda_{ir}(\mathbf{N}) = \mu^\circ_{ir}\sum_{\mathbf{n}=e_r}^{\mathbf{N}} \frac{n_r}{|\mathbf{n}|}P_i(\mathbf{n}|\mathbf{N}) = \mu^\circ_{ir}U_{ir}(\mathbf{N}) \tag{4.14}$$

which is simply the *utilization law* $U_{ir}(\mathbf{N}) = \lambda_{ir}(\mathbf{N})s^{\circ}_{ir}$. Similarly, we can prove the *arrival law*

$$X_{ir}(\mathbf{N}) = \frac{A_{ir}}{T} = \sum_{\mathbf{n}=\mathbf{0}}^{\mathbf{N}-e_r} \frac{A_{ir}(\mathbf{n})}{T_i(\mathbf{n})}\frac{T_i(\mathbf{n})}{T} = \sum_{\mathbf{n}=\mathbf{0}}^{\mathbf{N}-e_r} Y_{ir}(\mathbf{n}|\mathbf{N})P_i(\mathbf{n}|\mathbf{N}) \tag{4.15}$$

If the arrivals are homogeneous, $Y_{ir}(\mathbf{n}|\mathbf{N})$ becomes independent of $\mathbf{n}$, and we get

$$X_{ir}(\mathbf{N}) = Y_{ir}(\mathbf{N})(1 - P_{ir}(N_r|\mathbf{N})) \tag{4.16}$$

where $P_{ir}(n|\mathbf{N})$ denotes the probability of finding n chain r customers at station i. Under flow balance, $X_{ir}(\mathbf{N}) = \lambda_{ir}(\mathbf{N})$, and the throughput can be obtained using either (4.13) or (4.15). Also, under homogeneous arrivals, we have

$$PA_{ir}(\mathbf{n}|\mathbf{N}) = \frac{A_{ir}(\mathbf{n})}{A_{ir}} = \frac{Y_{ir}(\mathbf{N})}{X_{ir}(\mathbf{N})}P_i(\mathbf{n}|\mathbf{N}) = \frac{P_i(\mathbf{n}|\mathbf{N})}{1 - P_{ir}(N_r|\mathbf{N})} \tag{4.17}$$

The comments concerning equation (2.31) apply here as well.

Next we discuss *Little's law*. Applied to chain r over a closed region Ω, it states

$$Q_{\Omega r} = \lambda_{\Omega r} R_{\Omega r} \tag{4.18}$$

The proof and other comments surrounding (4.18) stay basically the same as in Section 4.2.4. Fig. 4-4 also applies if we consider only chain r. In particular, (4.18) still applies to any kind of scheduling discipline. The application of (4.18) to the "service box" of a homogeneous server gives the utilization law in (4.14). As in the single-chain case, *in the case of a multiserver and a load-independent station*, we have

$$R_{ir} = W_{ir} + s_{ir} \tag{4.19}$$

And, by applying Little's law to this identity, we get

$$Q_{ir} = L_{ir} + U_{ir} \tag{4.20}$$

If chain r is closed, by applying (4.18) to the entire network, we get

$$\lambda_{kr}(\mathbf{N}) = \frac{N_r v_{kr}}{\sum_{i=1}^{M} v_{ir} R_{ir}(\mathbf{N})} \tag{4.21}$$

We now derive a few results assuming one-step behavior and flow balance. As in Section 4.2.5, each upward transition must be matched by a downward transition in this case, i.e., $A_{ir}(\mathbf{n}) = D_{ir}(\mathbf{n} + e_r)$ for all $\mathbf{n}$. Therefore,

$$PA_{ir}(\mathbf{n}|\mathbf{N}) = PD_{ir}(\mathbf{n}|\mathbf{N}) \tag{4.22}$$

The multiple-chain equivalents of equations (2.25) and (2.26) (i.e., the recursions for arriver's and random observer's distributions) can be derived exactly as in Section 4.2.5. They are

$$P_i(\mathbf{n}|\mathbf{N}) = s^*_{ir}(\mathbf{n})Y_{ir}(\mathbf{n}-e_r|\mathbf{N})P_i(\mathbf{n}-e_r|\mathbf{N}) \tag{4.23}$$

$$PA_{ir}(\mathbf{n}|\mathbf{N}) = s^*_{ir}(\mathbf{n})Y_{ir}(\mathbf{n}|\mathbf{N})PA_{ir}(\mathbf{n}-e_r|\mathbf{N}) \tag{4.24}$$

The *arrival theorem* also extends, and has the following form

$$PA_{ir}(\mathbf{n}|\mathbf{N}) = P_i(\mathbf{n}|\mathbf{N}-e_r) \tag{4.25}$$

That is, the distribution seen by a chain r arriver is the random observer's distribution with the arriver removed. If chain r is open, this further implies that

$$\forall \mathbf{n}\ [PA_{ir}(\mathbf{n}) = P_i(\mathbf{n}) = PD_{ir}(\mathbf{n})] \tag{4.26}$$

The multiple-chain version of equation (2.28) is

$$PD_{ir}(\mathbf{n}|\mathbf{N}) = \mu^*_{ir}(\mathbf{n}+e_r)P_i(\mathbf{n}+e_r|\mathbf{N})/\lambda_{ir}(\mathbf{N}) \tag{4.27}$$

This also requires no assumptions and can be proved as easily as (2.28). Under flow balance and one-step behavior, we can use (4.22) to get

$$PA_{ir}(\mathbf{n}-e_r|\mathbf{N})\lambda_{ir}(\mathbf{N}) = \mu^*_{ir}(\mathbf{n})P_i(\mathbf{n}|\mathbf{N}) \tag{4.28}$$

which along with (4.25) gives the multiple-chain version of the *marginal local balance theorem*. If the services are homogeneous, we can use the definition of μ^*_{ir} and sum over all $\mathbf{n}$ in (4.28) to get

$$\sum_{\forall \mathbf{n}, n_r>0} n_r P_i(\mathbf{n}|\mathbf{N}) = U_{ir}(\mathbf{N}) \sum_{\forall \mathbf{n}, n_r>0} |\mathbf{n}| PA_{ir}(\mathbf{n}-e_r|\mathbf{N})$$

The left-hand side of this equation is simply the chain specific queue-length $Q_{ir}(\mathbf{N})$, and the summation on the right-hand side can be written as

$$\sum_{k=1}^{|\mathbf{N}|} \sum_{|\mathbf{n}|=k, n_r>0} |\mathbf{n}| PA_{ir}(\mathbf{n}-e_r|\mathbf{N}) = \sum_{k=1}^{|\mathbf{N}|} k PA_{ir}(k-1|\mathbf{N}) = 1 + QA_i^{(r)} \tag{4.29}$$

where $QA_i^{(r)}(\mathbf{N})$ is the average *total* queue length seen by an arriving chain r customer. Putting everything together and applying Little's law, we get the multiple-chain equivalent of equation (2.34).

$$R_{ir}(\mathbf{N}) = s^\circ_{ir}(1 + QA_i^{(r)}(\mathbf{N})) \tag{4.30}$$

By the arrival theorem, $QA_i^{(r)}(\mathbf{N}) = Q_i(\mathbf{N}-e_r)$, which gives the *mean value theorem* for multiple-chain networks.

Finally, we extend the results of Section 4.3.2 to multiple-chain networks. Note that when speaking of nonhomogeneous service, we allowed μ_{ir} to depend on the occupancy vector $\mathbf{n}$. Although this is very general, such an elaborate dependence is extremely expensive to work with and is usually avoided. In many situations, it is adequate to let the inherent service rate depend only on the *total* number of customers at the station, without any regard to the chains to which they belong. We could then define the *capacity function* much as for the single-chain case, i.e.,

$$\mu_{ir}(\mathbf{n}) = \mu^\circ_{ir} C_i(|\mathbf{n}|) \tag{4.31}$$

In this case, most of the single-chain results extend rather easily. In particular, *we can define utilization of chain r as the expected capacity devoted to chain r*, which in turn yields the utilization law $U_{ir}(\mathbf{N}) = \lambda_{ir} s^{\circ}_{ir}$, irrespective of whether station i is load-independent. For a delay station the capacity function is simply $C_i(\mathbf{n}) = |\mathbf{n}|$, and the relations derived in Section 4.3.2 for a delay station continue to hold, i.e.,

$$R_{ir}(\mathbf{N}) = s^{\circ}_{ir}, \qquad \text{and} \qquad U_{ir}(\mathbf{N}) = Q_{ir}(\mathbf{N}) \tag{4.32}$$

where the second equation follows from the first by Little's law.

4.5 Calibration of Queuing Models

In this section we consider the problem of calibrating and validating queuing network models of computer systems. The techniques discussed here apply to both analytic and simulation modeling, though analytic models generally involve fewer and coarser parameters. For example, if we calibrate a model for simulation purposes, it is generally desirable to obtain the service-time distribution; however, the corresponding analytic model may just use the first (or first two) moments of the service-time distribution. Thus, analytic models are generally easier to calibrate, but this not always the case, as discussed in Section 2.5.2.

The input parameters of a QNM can be classified as (a) static or workload-independent, and (b) dynamic or workload-dependent. Static parameters include job categories, device speeds, device capacities, interconnections, resource limitations, allocation policies, and scheduling policies. Although, by definition, these need not be measured, there are often situations where we need a much simpler characterization than what exists in reality. This characterization would often need some measurements either to choose from among several possible approximations or to validate them. We shall see examples of this throughout this section.

The dynamic parameters include resource requirements, service times, routing probabilities, arrival rates, etc., and must be either estimated or obtained by direct measurement. The output parameters typically include response times, queue lengths, etc. Ideally, the input parameters of the model should be used for calibration, and output parameters for validation. In practice, however, some of the output parameters may be easy to measure, and it makes sense to use those in the calibration. For example, device utilizations and completion counts (which basically represent throughputs) are typically easy to obtain and routinely used in model calibration. In such cases, these parameters cannot be used for a reliable model validation.

For simplicity we shall only consider single-chain networks with multiple classes and multiple-chain networks with one class per chain. We shall mostly speak of the latter case in our discussion, but the same techniques apply to the former case as well. The following are the main input parameters for multiple-chain models of computer systems:

1. Number of job chains or classes
2. Queuing discipline at each station,
3. Population for each closed chain
4. Mean service time at each station.
5. Higher moments or distribution of service times
6. Passive resource requirements
7. Routing probabilities or visit ratios
8. Overhead and load-dependent behavior for each station.

We discuss these in some detail in the following. The reader should keep in mind that the techniques and approximations discussed below are only suggestive; they are not to be regarded as the only way to proceed.

Before proceeding, we make a few general remarks regarding modeling. The three important steps in modeling are construction, calibration, and validation of the model. Although in theory these three steps should proceed sequentially, this is not so in practice. Apart from the objectives of the modeling study, *the most important factor affecting the model is the data needed to calibrate and validate the model*. Often, the structure of the model is dictated by what data can or cannot be obtained reliably. Therefore, our discussion on calibration will often delve into issues that are really concerned with model construction. Yet another point to remember is that since model construction involves abstraction, *the calibration parameters are defined relative to the model, and how we measure them depends on the correspondence between the model and the real system*. For example, to calibrate the CPU station in a central-server type of model, we need the total CPU time that a job receives from the time it is put on the ready list until it either terminates or issues an I/O request. That is, in counting the number of completions (e.g., for equation (5.2) discussed later), such things as the expiration of time slice or the interruption by the arrival of a higher-priority process should be ignored. Thus, it is important to examine what the reported counts do and do not include, so that adjustments can be made.

4.5.1 Number of Chains or Classes

There are two aspects to be considered here. The first problem is one of modeling; i.e., how many chains or classes should we use and what should their characteristics be. The second problem is one of obtaining other category specific parameters. Because of the measurement difficulties, the two aspects cannot be considered independently. The categories are originally defined based upon the objectives of the modeling study. In the next phase we examine whether the data can be gathered according to this classification. If not, we have to either resort to some approximations based upon the available data, or eliminate some classes by merging them with others.

In high-level models used for predicting end-to-end response times, the categories of interest are often those defined by the system itself. In such cases the statistics reported by the measurement utility can be used directly in the calibration. However, if class switches occur, the available information may be inadequate. For example, suppose that a job starts out in the interactive category, but because of its heavy resource usage, it is treated like a batch job from some point onwards. In such cases the monitoring utility may not correctly apportion the service demands of such jobs between the two categories, and some adjustments to the data may be necessary. Another possibility is that certain measurements may not be reported on a per category basis. If this happens in only a few cases, we can still resort to data adjustments; otherwise, it may be preferable to merge certain categories together so that the available data can be used directly for calibration.

In some situations the modeler does not know what classes should be used in the model. This often happens when we do not clearly understand the mix of job types exercising the system. The usual approach is then to collect raw data over a relatively long period and then attempt to classify the jobs based on relevant factors such as CPU time, I/O time, memory requirement, etc. A *clustering analysis* would then be used to find the relevant classes.

In principle, it is possible to have a sufficiently flexible software monitor that can accept class definitions in general terms, and assign each activity of interest to the appropriate class. However, such a monitor will be very complex and might cause significant interference with the normal system operation. We are not aware of the existence of any such monitor. An alternative is to do a detailed logging of every event and then do an off-line analysis to extract the relevant information and its context. This could also be very expensive. Thus, although the calibration of multiple-chain models is conceptually no harder than that for single-chain models, obtaining adequate data may be nearly impossible (except when modeler's classes are same as those used by the system). Educated guesses based on observed characteristics of the system are often used in calibration, but such schemes are highly ad hoc and of questionable accuracy. In fact, *a detailed model with unreliable calibration is often worse than a well-calibrated but simplistic model*. Thus, having many chains/classes is not necessarily a good idea.

4.5.2 Queuing Discipline

A simulation model can directly use the real queuing discipline at various devices; however, an analytic model is unable to do so either because the real discipline is too complex, or because it is based upon some dynamic parameters of the system. In such cases we try to find a simple approximation for the real discipline. For example, the round-robin discipline is generally quite difficult to analyze, but if the time-slice is small compared with the mean service time, we can approximate it by the processor sharing (PS) discipline. Similarly, the multi-level round-robin discipline, a popular choice for CPU scheduling, can be approximated by the *biased processor sharing* discipline, which in turn can be analyzed approximately. In these cases if the real-system varies the time-slice dynamically in a complex way, we need to measure the average time-slice value at each priority level to find out if the approximation of PS or biased PS is good.

In some situations we can model the effect of complex scheduling disciplines indirectly. That is, we retain a simple scheduling discipline such as FCFS or PS, but alter the service time, capacity function, or other parameters to account for the effect of the real discipline. For example, consider the typical scheduling algorithms for a moving head disk (e.g., SSTF or SCAN). The main characteristic of all such algorithms is that the average seek time decreases with load. Thus, instead of trying to model them directly, we can account for them indirectly by making the disk a load-dependent station with an appropriate increasing capacity function. (Appendix C provides some hints on how to do so.) If the justification for a proposed simplification is not clear, it may be worthwhile to run a small simulation or measurement experiment using the proposed changes and examine the difference in results, instead of immediately regressing to a more complicated modeling.

4.5.3 Chain Population

In the computer system context, the chain population is the number of processes that actively circulate through the chain (also known as the *degree of multiprogramming*). Thus, the calibration involves taking a snapshot of the system and counting the number of active processes. Two difficulties arise in this regard: (a) each snapshot may show a different number of active processes, and (b) it is not always clear what is meant by an active process. Problem (a) arises because in reality, the number of active processes is almost always a random variable with some distribution. Let us denote this as $\mathcal{N}_r$ for chain r. If $\mathcal{N}_r$ is not highly variable, we can simply use its average value $\overline{\mathcal{N}}_r$ in the model. In other cases, we can obtain the empirical distribution of $\mathcal{N}_r$ and solve the model for each of its feasible values (say, $1..N$). Then if X is some performance measure (e.g., average queue length or average response time), we can obtain its overall value by a simple weighted summation:

$$X = \sum_{n=1}^{N} X(n) Pr(\mathcal{N}_r = n) \tag{5.1}$$

Taking a snapshot to estimate $\overline{\mathcal{N}}_r$ or its distribution is basically sampled monitoring in software. Most systems have built-in commands to provide such information (e.g., "ps" command in Unix^{TM}). A different way is to use trace monitoring in software. This technique requires access to the system routines and is best suited for the monitor utility specifically developed for the system. The idea is to record necessary information (e.g., update the time-integral of the degree of multiprogramming) whenever any process changes its state.

Although a snapshot will generally indicate whether a process is running, ready, waiting, etc., the information provided is still inadequate for our purposes. For example, a terminal process may be idle because the terminal user may be either thinking or gone. The only way to distinguish between the two situations is by comparing the idle period against some predetermined threshold. It is not entirely clear how to choose this threshold. Also, the counting of various system processes depends upon whether their activities are represented explicitly in the model. For example, if a printer is present in the model, the printer demon process is a legitimate customer and should be included. Otherwise, it can be ignored. In the latter case, any resources of the model used by the print demon would only contribute to the "overhead", which is accounted for indirectly because the mean service time as obtained by equation (5.2) given later, will include the effect of the demon processes on the utilization but not on the number of completions. (See Section 4.5.8 for more on this.) If a *user process* visits a device not explicitly included in the model, we can consider the process to have disappeared while it is at that device. Basically, this would result in the inclusion of the average number of processes that are inside the modeled portion of the system. For example, swapped-out processes need be counted only if the swap device is included in the model.

Although the above rule for counting system processes is straightforward, problems may arise with respect to the calibration of other parameters. For example, the demon processes considered as "overhead" should not be counted towards the device throughput. But chances are that the monitor doesn't care about the identity of the process and includes all of them in the completion counts. If we have some way of estimating the fraction of completions that correspond to the demon processes, we are still fine; otherwise, we cannot ignore any processes. Now we have two possibilities: (a) include a station in the model to represent the blocked duration of these processes and always count them, or (b) do not include any extra station, but count the demon processes only while they are not blocked. Generally, method (a) would be more accurate since method (b) can be thought of as an approximation that includes the average number of active demon processes instead of all of them. In either case, the model includes some processes that behave differently from the explicitly represented processes. Thus, we may have to add some more chains to our model. In the absence of any detailed information, we may have to assume that these processes behave like others at the regular stations that they visit.

4.5.4 Mean Service Times

In this section we only consider load-independent and delay stations. We start with load-independent stations. The measurement can be done either by trace technique or via sampling. The trace technique would essentially involve accumulating the integral of the service time over the measurement period and then dividing it by the number of customers served. Often the monitoring utilities do not report the average service time directly, but only provide some related information that can be used for computing it. The resulting technique is closer to sampled monitoring. Unfortunately, different estimation techniques may be necessary for different devices. In the following we show how the service times can be obtained for CPU, disks, and terminals.

Mean service time (MST) for the CPU is usually computed using the CPU utilization and the number of completions at the CPU, since these parameters are readily available. For chain r in the model, we can obtain the $MST(r)$ as follows:

$$MST(r) = \frac{\text{Duration of test period} \times \text{utilization for chain } r}{\text{Number of chain } r \text{ completions during the test period}} \tag{5.2}$$

Equation (5.2) is merely the utilization law, since the right-hand side can be interpreted as U_r/λ_r. The only difficulty here is that if the reported completion count includes those processes that we consider overhead, some adjustments are necessary. These are discussed in Section 4.5.8.

In estimating the disk service times, we must account for all three phases of service, namely seek, latency, and transfer. A monitor would typically report such things as number of seeks per unit time (ns) and average seek duration (st). For moving head disks, the rotational delay (rd) can be assumed to be one-half of the disk revolution time, but for fixed head disks using sector queuing, more information is needed. Average time per transfer (tt) and number of transfers per unit time (nt), or some related parameters, are almost always reported by the monitor. Thus, the mean service time s can be estimated as

$$s = rd + tt + st \times ns/nt \tag{5.3}$$

Notice that this estimation does not account for delays caused by channel or control unit contention; those aspects must be modeled separately. Channels and control units can be treated like passive resources that are acquired by processes before the data transfer can begin. (Of course, the connectivity restrictions that dictate which control units and channels can be used by a disk-drive must also be observed.) Accurate analytic modeling of these aspects is difficult and is briefly discussed in Section 8.2.5. It may be possible to simplify this modeling if the monitor provides some contention-related data (e.g., the probability of missing a connection on a drive with rotational position sensing capability).

As in the case of CPU, the above method works for both single-chain and multiple-chain cases but difficulties may arise if the monitor does not provide all the information on a chain-by-chain basis. Certain assumptions can often be used in such cases. For example, if the information used by different chains is not confined to specific areas of the disk, one may assume that all chains have similar seek characteristics.

There is another problem that we have to consider in the case of disks. As stated before, for any reasonable disk scheduling algorithm, the average seek time per request will decrease as the load increases. Therefore, a disk should be modeled as a load-dependent station, but the monitors rarely provide any direct information on this load-dependent behavior. There are two ways to estimate load-dependence. One is to measure average seek time and congestion at the disk at different times when the load is expected to vary widely, e.g., late at night (possibly very light load), in the morning (moderate load), and afternoon (heavy load), and fit a simple curve through the measured data. The second method is to construct a mathematical model by using information regarding the distribution of requested cylinder numbers. Appendix C illustrates one such approach.

Next, we consider the calibration of service time for a delay station. In most applications of a delay station, the monitor can directly measure the delay (or flow time) across such a station. However, there is one special case that presents some problems. This concerns the "think time" for terminals in an interactive system. This parameter is rarely reported by monitors; besides, it is not even well defined. (Do we really want to consider the "think time" of a user who signs on and then goes away for an hour?) This parameter is best determined indirectly. Let Z_r denote the average think time, R_r the system response time, and N_r the population for chain r. We have already seen how to measure N_r; R_r is either reported directly by the monitor or can be obtained from the response times of various devices in the system. By Little's law, $Z_r = N_r/\lambda_r - R_r$, where λ_r is the completion rate and is usually available. Thus, Z_r can be computed.

4.5.5 Service-Time Distribution

Service-time distributions are needed primarily in simulation modeling. Here we first construct a histogram (either on-line or off-line), and then fit a suitable analytic distribution through it, if necessary. Analytic models usually do not need distributions directly, but may need the first few (usually two) moments. We have already seen how to get the first moment. Getting higher moments or distribution requires trace monitoring of individual service times and updating the running sum or frequency counts.

Suppose that we have obtained a histogram of service times, and want to fit a suitable analytic distribution through it. The distributional form is chosen a priori depending on the physical characteristics of the system being modeled and such considerations as the ease of dealing with that distribution in the analysis. The next step is to check how good the fit is and determine the parameters of the distribution from the data. In the following we briefly illustrate how this may be done for a distribution that takes two parameters: mean m and variance σ^2

Let X denote the random variable of interest, $H(x)$ its empirical distribution function (or *cumulative histogram*), and $G(x, m, \sigma)$ its assumed distribution function. Let $Y = (X - m)/\sigma$. It is easy to verify that the distribution function of Y, denoted G^*, is $G^*(y) = G(y, 0, 1)$, which is known completely (e.g., standard normal). As shown in Exercise 4.11, if the assumed distribution is a good approximation, then the plot of ${G^*}^{-1}[H(x)]$ versus x must be approximately linear. We could then determine m and σ easily by regression analysis, since the least square line fitted through the plot will have the slope of $1/\sigma$ and intercept of $-m/\sigma$.

4.5.6 Passive Resource Demands

This measurement is somewhat similar to service time measurement, but what is measured depends on whether or not piecemeal allocation is involved. We shall illustrate the difficulties using memory allocation as an example, but the discussion applies to other types of passive resources, including buffers, channels, etc. First suppose that there is no piecemeal allocation; i.e,, each program must be loaded completely into memory before beginning execution. We could then take system snapshots to determine the distribution of the memory occupied by a process. If only the average memory requirement per process is desired, we need only record the number of memory resident processes and the total used memory in each snapshot.

With piecemeal allocation (as in the case of demand paging), the required parameters depend on the details of the model. In a detailed simulation model, we may explicitly need the page reference pattern so that the page-fault handling can be simulated directly. For an analytic model, we need only the number of memory-resident processes, denoted L, and the mean time between page-faults, denoted $\phi(L)$, as a function of L. This function is known as the *life-time function*. The distribution of L can be obtained easily from system snapshots as mentioned above, but $\phi(L)$ must be measured by a system utility.

If swapping of complete programs is also used (for example, to maintain the degree of multiprogramming at an optimum level), we also need to measure swap frequency, possibly as a function of the number of resident processes. This information can be gathered from snapshots since swapped-out processes are usually so marked.

4.5.7 Routing Probabilities and Visit Ratios

Let q_{ijr} denote the routing probability of chain r jobs from station i to station j. We can estimate q_{ijr} as C_{ir}/A_{ijr}, where C_{ir} is the number of chain r completions at station i, and A_{ijr} is the number of chain r arrivals to station j from station i.

We saw in sections 4.2.3 and 4.4.2 how to compute visit ratios from routing probabilities. In a network with M stations we could have up to $M(M-1)$ routing probabilities (per chain), but only M visit ratios. Visit ratios are also easier to measure, since we only need to know the number of completions at each device for each chain during the measurement interval. Thus, if visit ratios are adequate for solving the model, routing probabilities need not be measured. This is often true with analytic modeling; however, accurate simulation needs routing probabilities. For the product-form analytic models, it is even possible to go a step further and eliminate the need for visit ratios as well. This is done by working with *service demands* instead of service times. For station i and chain r, the service demand, denoted d_{ir}, is defined as

$$d_{ir} = v_{ir} s_{ir} \tag{5.4}$$

Since the throughputs are proportional to visit ratios, we can use the analogy of equation (5.4) with the utilization law and refer to d_{ir} as *relative utilization*. As we shall see in later chapters, the analytic solution involves only d_{ir}'s; therefore, if we are willing to settle for only system throughput (instead of throughputs of individual stations) and residence times (instead of response times) at each station, it is enough to measure only d_{ir}'s. The *residence time*, denoted R^*_{ir} for station i and chain r, is defined as the response time multiplied by the visit ratio, i.e.,

$$R^*_{ir} = v_{ir} R_{ir} \tag{5.5}$$

4.5.8 Overhead and Load Dependence

In most modeling situations, we can identify two types of activities: those that are explicitly represented in the model, and those that are not. Let us identify these as class 1 and class 2 activities respectively. Let U_i, λ_i and S_i respectively denote the utilization, throughput and mean service time of some station m for class i activities. By the utilization law $U_i = \lambda_i S_i$. First suppose that both U_i and λ_i can be obtained for each class separately (either directly or indirectly). Then a good way to model the situation is to have two classes (or chains, if appropriate) passing through station m with service times of S_1 and S_2 respectively. This would also require the introduction of a station that is visited by class 2 customers while they are idle. Thus, the idle time also needs to be measured. (See Section 4.5.3.)

Next suppose that the monitor only reports overall utilization (U), but individual throughputs are available (or the fraction of completions belonging to class 2 is known). An appropriate approach is then to use only class 1 in the model whose service time is determined as U/λ_1. This technique artificially increases resource requirements of class 1 to account for the resources consumed by the overhead activities. (In this case class 2 customers should not be counted toward population or any other parameter.) Now suppose that the monitor only reports overall throughput $\lambda = \lambda_1 + \lambda_2$, but the utilizations are known individually. In this case, we assume that $S_1 = S_2$. By the utilization law, it then follows that $S_1 = U/\lambda$ where $U = U_1 + U_2$. Then we could either use a 2-class model as explained above, or a single-class model with service time of $S' = U/\lambda_1 = S \times U/U_1$.

Finally, if the monitor only gives the overall utilization and overall throughput, we can assume that the computed service time applies to both classes and thus use a 2-class model as explained above. (If mean service time is the only aspect that distinguishes between these two classes, we effectively get a single-class model with customers of both classes counted toward the population.) Notice that a single-class model wherein we completely ignore class 2 and increase the service time of class 1 is not possible here!

These techniques apply to any station in the network. In the special case of a CPU, the two classes might be user processes (that contribute to user-mode utilization) and system processes (that contribute primarily to supervisor-mode utilization). However, further difficulties may arise in more refined models. For example, if we wish to explicitly model some (but not all) of the supervisor-mode activities, but the monitor only provides overall supervisor-mode utilization, we may need some heuristics to apportion this utilization correctly among explicit and implicit components. Similar problems may arise with respect to attributing the overall utilization to various chains.

Next we consider the calibration of stations showing load-dependent behavior. Since chain-independent capacity functions are adequate for most purposes, we shall consider only those here. Although, in principle, the calibration of more general capacity functions is no harder, the measurability limitations usually make such an exercise infeasible. In calibrating load-dependent stations, it helps to know the reason for such behavior. Three common reasons for a station, say i, to be load-dependent, are the following.

1. It represents several identical devices of the physical system that operate like a multiserver station. For example, in a closely coupled multiprocessor system, all CPU's can be represented by a single multiserver station.
2. The load dependence merely represents the *overhead* that varies with load. For example, the process management overhead per insertion/deletion may be $O(log\, n)$ or $O(n)$. Similarly, a communication link may work more efficiently as the load increases, because it can piggyback more acknowledgments in regular packets.
3. Load-dependence is an inherent property of the station. For example, the average seek time of a disk decreases with the number of requests queued up.

In case (1), if the measurements could be made separately for each physical device, the calibration methods for load-independent stations still apply. (There may be a few minor problems, however, as discussed in Exercise 4.12). In case (2), the load-dependence is usually weak, and it is reasonable to consider the station as load-independent, operating under some "average overhead". Since the method of Section 4.5.4 gives an overall average for the service time, the average overhead need not be estimated separately. This technique can also be used for case (3) if the load-dependence is weak. In some cases we can estimate load-dependence analytically by considering an idealized model (e.g., the one discussed in the context of seek times in Section 4.5.4). In general, however, we need to accumulate the functions $D_i(n)$ and $T_i(n)$, as defined in Section 4.2.2, for each value of n. If this is not feasible, we can measure the average service time at several loading levels and then estimate the capacity function by fitting a simple function through this data. (See Exercise 4.13).

4.5.9 Output Parameters and Model Validation

Since throughputs and utilizations are typically used in model calibration, the most interesting average output parameters to use in validation are response times and queue lengths. More generally, we may be interested in measuring queue length distribution, since both simulation and analytic modeling generally provide it. If we have full control over the measurements, we can use a trace technique. That is, we keep track of the location of each customer (with respect to the stations in the model) and use this information to construct a histogram of the queue length at each station. If however, we are limited to using only the standard measurement utilities, the distribution may have to be obtained by sampling. For example, if the processes represent customers, we can periodically examine the number of processes in each state. If the state of a process (hibernating, running, ready, blocked for disk I/O, etc.) is adequate to identify the device in the model where that process must be residing, each sample gives us a snapshot of the queue lengths at various devices in the system. *It is important that the reported values be instantaneous values, rather than averages over some interval.* However, if this interval can be set to a small value, reasonable estimates can still be obtained.

If the computed values of validation parameters differ significantly from the measured ones, the models must be examined for possible deficiencies. There are several possible reasons why the validation may fail: (a) the measurements needed for calibration were performed incorrectly or are unreliable; (b) the calibration was done improperly; (c) certain activities that have a significant impact on the performance have not been accounted for either directly or indirectly; or (d) the model is inaccurate. These aspects should be looked at carefully and remedial actions taken. After the model has passed this preliminary validation, it is advisable to do more thorough validation before trusting its results. For this, the measurements should be done under changed workload conditions and the results compared against the computed results. For example, if the model represents an interactive system, it would be desirable to validate the model for two extreme situations, one with a large number of active terminals, and the other with very few. In a real workload environment this may be done by making measurements at different times during the day so long as we can be reasonably confident that the nature of the workload itself does not change appreciably. If not, we may need synthetic programs to generate artificial workload that can drive the system while it is nearly idle. If the model passes the preliminary test, but fails the more thorough test, several new aspects need to be looked at:

1. The new workload has a different qualitative constitution than the one for which the model was originally constructed. In this case, the model is valid, but is not applicable to the new workload.
2. Certain aspects of the workload are not being modeled in sufficient detail. For example, all system activities might have been lumped as "overhead". The remedy in this case is to use a more refined model.
3. The model is not robust; i.e., a small change in certain input parameters causes a large change in the results, and thus the inaccuracies in the original model (in modeling or calibration) are exaggerated if the workload is changed. In this case, the remedy might well be a simplification in the model! Remember that simpler models are more likely to be robust than

the more complex ones.

A model of a complex system might require several iterations before reasonable results are obtained. In some cases we may be unable to accurately calibrate certain aspects of the model that would make it faithful. Modeling is unlikely to be very useful in such a situation, unless data gathering can be improved.

4.6 Exercises

1. Assuming one-step behavior, flow balance, homogeneous arrivals, and homogeneous service at a single-server station i, which is a part of a network with population N, show that the mean queue length can be expressed as

$$Q_i(N) = U_i(N)\frac{1 - U_i(N) - P_i(N|N)}{1 - (N+1)P_i(N|N)} \tag{6.1}$$

   Use equations (2.31) and (2.34). Also show the same thing by using equation (2.32) directly. What simplifications can you make to this equation as $N \to \infty$, assuming that station i is not a bottleneck?

2. Show that the proof of Little's formula holds for last-come first-served and processor sharing disciplines by verifying that *area* still represents the total backlog.

3. Consider a station where the arrivals occur in packets of size 1 or 2, but the services occur singly. The packet size is randomly chosen, and the probability of it being of size 1 is q. Both arrivals and services are homogeneous and the system is flow-balanced. The interarrival and service times are constant and given by a and b respectively. Show by a counterexample that the arriver's distribution is different from the departer's distribution, which, in turn, is different from a random observer's distribution.

4. Consider the computer system model shown in Fig. 4-8. Let $P(n)$ denote the probability that a customer coming out of the terminal will make n visits to the CPU-disk subsystem before returning back to the terminal. Find an expression for $P(n)$, $n = 1 .. \infty$.

5. Consider the model in Fig. 4-8 again. Assume $q_1 = 0.6$, $q_2 = 0.8$, and population $N = 10$. A few other parameters are given below. Compute the remaining output parameters, i.e., throughputs, utilizations, and average queue lengths.

Terminal	Delay station, Average think time = 1.00 sec.
CPU	Load-dependent: capacity $C(n) = 1/(0.9 + 0.1n)$, Average basic service time = 50 ms, Average response time = 233 ms.
Disk	Load-independent, Average service time = 100 ms, Average response time = 400 ms.

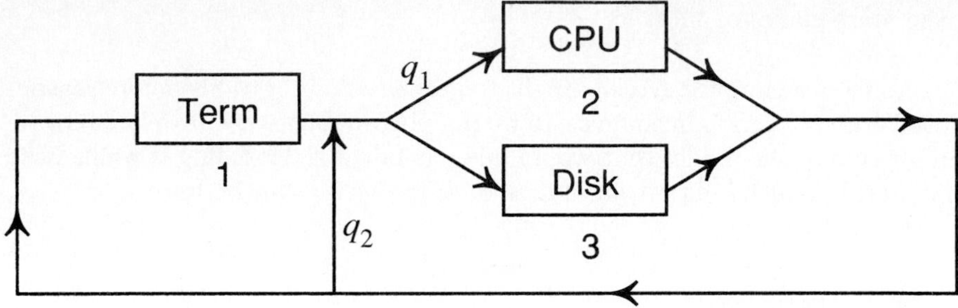

FIGURE 4-8: A closed model of an interactive computing system.

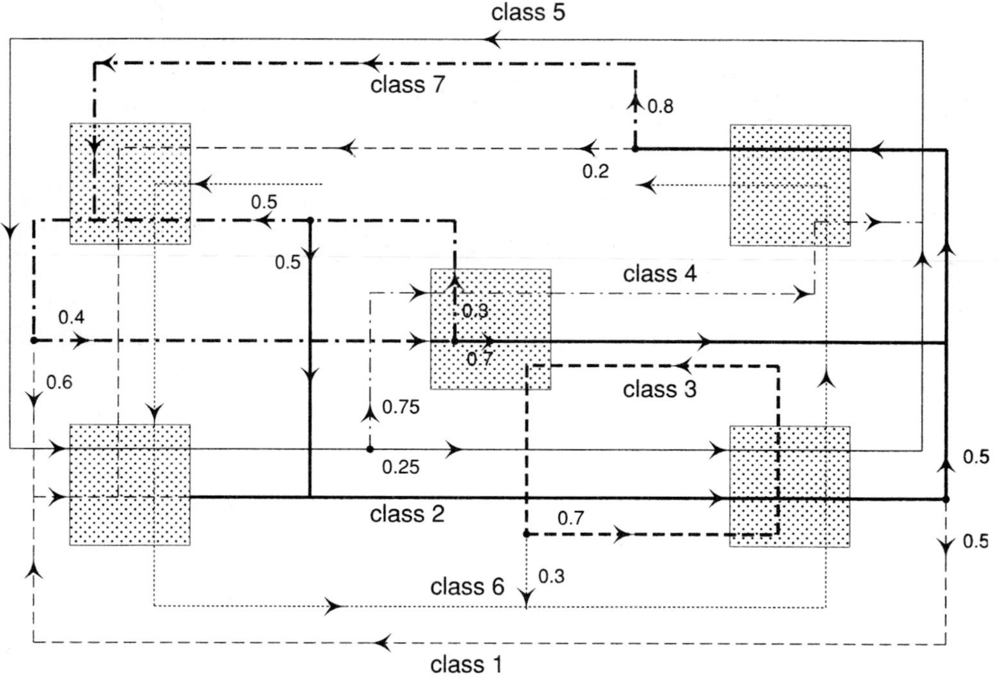

FIGURE 4-9: A multiple-class model.

6. Consider the model in Fig. 4-8 again with CPU as a load-independent station. What is the optimum number of terminals that this system can support?

7. Consider the multiple-class model in Fig. 4-9. Show that the model is consistent. Show its reachability graph, and identify the chains and the classes contained in them. Can the network be made well-formed (after removing transient classes)? Classify the network as open, closed or mixed. By choosing a suitable reference station for each chain, determine the visit ratios for all classes of the chain.

8. If each chain in a multiple-chain network consists of several classes, we can represent the occupancy vector as a matrix $\vec{\mathbf{n}} = (\mathbf{n}_1, \ldots, \mathbf{n}_K)$ where $\mathbf{n}_i = n_{i1}, \ldots, n_{i\,nc(i)}$, and $nc(i)$ is the number of classes in chain i, and n_{ij} is the number of customers belonging to class j of chain i present at the station. Show that with these definitions, all the operational identities in Section 4.4.2 extend to this more general case.

9. Find out what performance monitoring facilities are available on the computer system that you work on. Discuss to what extent a central server model such as the one in Fig. 4-2 can be calibrated and validated using the available data. Clearly indicate the possible errors in measuring parameters that are not available directly.
(Note: For those working with Berkeley Unix™ , the following commands are useful for calibration: vmstat(1), pstat(8), iostat(1), ps(1), and pstat(1)).

10. A central server model applies to a workstation environment as well, since we can treat the file server as the central server and the clients as peripheral devices. In most cases, the communication medium (e.g., ethernet) is not a performance limiting resource and can be ignored. Show how such a model can be calibrated using the available measurement facilities. [Note: Under Berkeley Unix, there are a few commands available to capture network traffic, such as netstat(8c) and nfsstat(8c)].

11. With reference to the curve fitting problem discussed in Section 4.5.5, show that $H(x) \triangleq Pr(X \leq x) \approx G^*(\frac{x-m}{\sigma})$. From this, show that if the assumed distribution function is correct, the plot of ${G^*}^{-1}[H(x)]$ versus x must be linear.

12. Consider a machine with k identical CPU's, each one of which picks up processes from a common ready list. Suppose that we measure the average service time for each CPU using the method of Section 4.5.4. Let the measured values be $S_1, \ldots, S_k$. The model for the machine represents all CPU's by a single multiserver station with the service rate of $\mu(n)$. Devise a suitable approximation for $\mu(n)$ assuming that S_i's do not differ very much. How does the overhead get accounted for in this calibration?

13. Suppose that we wish to determine the service rate function $\mu_i(n)$ for station i in a closed model with population N. Suppose that the station is load-independent except for the overhead, which increases slowly with load. So we assume that the station capacity decreases linearly with n with rate δ. The system reports utilization, denoted $U_i^*(N)$, as the fraction of time the station is busy. Starting with the throughput theorem, show that

$$\mu_i(n) = \frac{U_i^*(N)(1+\delta-\delta n)}{\overline{S}[U_i^*(N)(1+\delta) - \delta Q_i(N)]} \tag{6.2}$$

where $\overline{S}$, $U_i^*(N)$ and $Q_i(N)$ are the measured values of service time, utilization and queue length respectively. That is, $\overline{S} = U_i^*(N)/\lambda(N)$, $U_i^*(N) = 1 - P(0|N)$, and $Q(N) = \sum_{n=1}^{N} nP(n|N)$. Devise a procedure for estimating δ.

Bibliographic Notes

The operational approach to queuing system analysis was developed by Buzen and Denning and is surveyed in Denning and Buzen (1978) and in Buzen and Denning (1980). The marginal local balance theorem is proved in Reiser and Lavenberg (1980). Our terminology of classes and chains is taken from Sauer and Chandy (1981). Lazowska, et al. (1984) refers to chains as simply classes. The arrival theorem for multiple-chain networks is proved in Lavenberg and Reiser (1980) and Sevcik and Mitrani (1981). Calibration of queuing network models of computer systems is discussed in Lazowska, et al. (1984) and a survey appears in Rose (1978). Lazowska, et al. (1984) also discusses some heuristics for calibrating multiple-chain models when the monitor does not break everything down on a chain-by-chain basis.

CHAPTER

5

Elementary Stochastic Analysis

In this chapter we discuss basics of stochastic analysis: characterization of random processes, analysis of discrete and continuous time Markov chains, long-term behavior of random processes, birth and death processes, and the method of stages. In this chapter, we shall mostly be dealing with the analysis of an isolated service station. In the classical queuing theory, an isolated service station is often characterized by *Kendall's notation* which is X/Y/c, where X represents interarrival-time distribution, Y represents service-time distribution, and c is the number of servers. For example, a G/G/1 system refers to the situation where both interarrival and service-time distributions are general and there is but one load-independent server at the station. Exponential distributions are often denoted by the letter M in this notation (M stands for "memoryless"); thus the notation M/M refers to a system where both interarrival and service-time distributions are exponential.

5.1 Random Processes

A *random process* can be thought of as a random variable that is a function of time. That is, if $X(t)$ is a random process, then at any given time instant $t = \tau$, $X(\tau)$ is an ordinary random variable with distribution denoted as $F_{X(\tau)}(x)$. A random process is used to describe the "state" of a stochastic system as a function of time. For example, the number of customers in a queuing system as a function of time is a random process. Sometimes, the state description itself involves a time parameter, an example being the number of arrivals to a queuing system during the time interval $(t, t+\tau)$. In such cases, the parameter t describes the time when we look at the state of the system, and τ is an *auxiliary time parameter*. Although this distinction seems obvious here, it may be confusing if not stated explicitly. For example, if we let $N(t)$ denote the number of arrivals during the time interval $(0, t)$, t is still an auxiliary time parameter.

5.1.1 Classification of Random Processes

Random processes can be classified according to the following four criteria:

1. *State space*, i.e., the domain of values taken by $X(t)$, which could be *discrete* or *continuous*. For example, the number of buffers in use for I/O has a discrete state space, whereas the noise in a communication channel has a continuous state space. If the state space is discrete (or countable), we shall use the word *chain*. If it is continuous, or when the distinction is not important, we shall use the word *process*.

2. *Time parameter*, which could be discrete or continuous. In the first case, the phenomenon is usually referred to as a *stochastic sequence* or time series. Often a useful stochastic sequence may be found embedded in the continuous time random process that describes the state of the system at all time instants.

3. *Variability*, which refers to the time-related behavior of the random process. We shall shortly examine the concept of a stationary process, which, roughly speaking, means that the random process does not change its properties with time.

4. *Correlation aspects*: Let $t_1 < t_2 < \cdots < t_n$. Then the random variable $X(t_n)$ may be independent of $X(t_1), \ldots, X(t_{n-1})$, dependent on only $X(t_{n-1})$, etc. We shall consider some important cases shortly.

With respect to state space, we shall mostly deal with random chains, though much of the material extends easily to random processes. The nature of the time parameter requires some care in interpretation. Although there are applications in which the time is truly discrete (e.g., slotted communication protocols, where a transmit or a receive is attempted only at the beginning of a "time-slot"); in most others, events can occur at any point in real time. Discrete time random processes are still useful because we can often identify a useful embedded random process at certain discrete points of the original continuous time process. Such discrete points of interest are *usually not equally spaced with respect to real time*. To keep this distinction clear, we shall henceforth speak of *discrete parameter* and *continuous parameter* processes. The phrase *discrete time process* will be reserved for the special case where the time is truly discretized. For a discrete parameter process, "time" is measured as the number of points since the beginning at which a change of state (or "transition") could have occurred. (There is no requirement that a change in state occur at each such point.) If time is truly discrete, this measure is related to the elapsed real time in an obvious way; but in other cases, it has no direct relation to the real time. For a continuous parameter process, "time" always means real time, and every transition changes the state of the process.

With respect to variability, we shall mostly deal with *stationary processes*, so let us examine this concept. Consider a random process $X(t)$ at an ordered set of time instants $t_1 < t_2 < \cdots$. If $X(t)$ changes its properties with time, this could imply the following:

(a) For some i, the random variables $X(t_i)$ and $X(t_{i+1})$ have different distributions.

(b) For given i and $j > i$, the dependence between the random variables $X(t_i)$ and $X(t_j)$ varies with the time origin t_i.[1]

It is important to note that these two types of time-dependencies are distinct properties. For example, all $X(t_i)$'s may be identically distributed, and yet the dependencies between them may vary with the time origin. That is, the time independence of $F_{X(t)}$ is not sufficient for stationarity. Formally, we can define stationarity by the requirement that all joint distributions (including individual ones) of the random variables $X(t_i)$'s are invariant with respect to shifts in the time origin. This characterization is highly restrictive and is often known as *strict sense stationarity*. In practice, one often uses a much weaker definition, known as *wide sense stationarity*. This definition disallows the time-dependence of types (a) and (b) discussed above only in a weak sense. That is, instead of requiring that the individual distribution $F_{X(\tau)}$ be independent of time parameter τ, we only require that $E[X(\tau)]$ be independent of τ. Similarly, instead of requiring the joint distributions to be independent of time origin, we only require that the covariance of any pair $X(t_i)$, $X(t_j)$ have this property (i.e., depend only on the time difference $t_j - t_i$). These two properties essentially capture the "first order effects". They are easy to verify in practice and adequate for most purposes.

With respect to the correlation aspects, we are most interested in two types of processes: (a) *Markov processes*, where the future behavior depends only on the present but not the past, and (b) *Independent processes*, where the $X(t_i)$'s are independent. In the following, we characterize the properties of these two types of random processes.

5.1.2 Markov Processes

Let $t_1 < t_2 < \ldots$ denote ordered time instants, and $P(X(t_n) = j)$ the probability of finding the system in state j at time t_n. The time parameter could be continuous or discrete; it does not matter. Although our notation for state suggests a

[1]The variation in dependence as a function of $t_j - t_i$ is a distinct property and is characterized by the correlation aspect mentioned above.

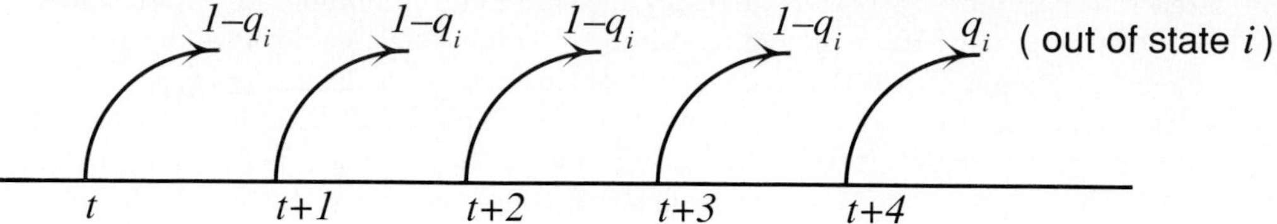

FIGURE 5-1: Distribution is geometric for the discrete parameter case.

discrete state space, this aspect is also irrelevant. Then, the Markovian property states that

$$Pr[X(t_n) = j|X(t_{n-1}) = i_{n-1},\ X(t_{n-2}) = i_{n-2},\ X(t_{n-3}) = i_{n-3}, \dots\ ] \\ = Pr[X(t_n) = j|X(t_{n-1}) = i_{n-1}] \quad (1.1)$$

That is, all information concerning the states through which the system has gone through in the past is irrelevant. It is important to emphasize that in equation (1.1), the time instants $t_{n-1}, t_{n-2}, \dots$ can be chosen completely arbitrarily. This has several implications. First, if we choose t_{n-1} sufficiently further back than t_n, the probability of the system being in state j at time t_n may not even depend on the state at time t_{n-1}. The property in equation (1.1) does not rule out this possibility. Second, if t_n is a time instant just after a transition to state j, and t_{n-1} a time instant just prior to the transition, equation (1.1) says that the state after the transition depends only on the state just prior to the transition. This alone is normally regarded as the Markovian property, but equation (1.1) has a third implication as well. That is, if we choose t_n such that the process has already been in state j for some time, we can still choose t_{n-1}, t_{n-2}, etc. arbitrarily close to t_n. This means that the probability of finding the system in state j at time t_n depends on state j, but not on how long the system has already been in state j. We can say that *the process is memoryless not only with respect to the states visited in the past, but also with respect to the time already spent in the current state.*

The last point mentioned implies that the *state residence time* of a Markov process (i.e., the time for which the Markov process stays in a given state) cannot have an arbitrary distribution. In fact, for a homogeneous Markov process, the distribution is geometric for the discrete parameter case and exponential otherwise. The discrete parameter case is shown in Fig. 5-1. Suppose that the system is in state i and the probability of it going to some other state at the next time instant is q_i. (Recall that "time" is not the real time for discrete parameter case.) It is easy to see from Fig. 5-1 that

$$Pr(\text{Residence time } = n) = (1-q_i)^{n-1}q_i \quad (1.2)$$

which is the standard geometric distribution. For the continuous parameter case, let T denote the time spent by the process in a given state. Then, because of the memoryless property, for any value of τ, $P(T > t+\tau|T > \tau)$ must be a function of only t. Let us denote this function as $h(t)$. Using $\tau = 0$, we can express $h(t)$

as simply $P(T > t)$. By the definition of conditional probability,

$$P(T > t + \tau | T > \tau) = \frac{P(T > t + \tau \;\&\; T > \tau)}{P(T > \tau)} = \frac{P(T > t + \tau)}{P(T > \tau)} \triangleq h(t)$$

Therefore,

$$P(T > t + \tau) = P(T > t)P(T > \tau) \tag{1.3}$$

The only function that has this property is the exponential function, i.e., $P(T > t) = e^{-ct}$ for some c (See Exercise 5.1). Thus, the residence time in a continuous parameter Markov process must be exponentially distributed.

The above restriction on the residence time limits the usefulness of Markov processes. Often one encounters systems where the residence time is arbitrary, but the next state depends only on the current state. Such systems are known as *semi-Markov*. More precisely, equation (1.1) characterizes a semi-Markov process if we choose $t_1, t_2, \ldots$ denote times *just after successive transitions*. Another way to describe such systems is to say that the random process has a discrete-parameter *embedded Markov process* at transition points. That is, the behavior is Markovian at transition points, but arbitrary otherwise. In Section 9.2, we shall see how to analyze a queuing system by identifying an embedded Markov chain/process at appropriate time instants.

5.1.3 Independent Processes

In this section, we briefly study an important class of independent processes that have numerous applications in the modeling of queuing systems. Consider a sequence of events and let X_i denote the time between the occurrence of ith and $(i+1)$st event. If the X_i's are independent, identically distributed random variables, we call the resulting random process X_i, $i = 1, 2, \ldots$ a *renewal process*. Note that a renewal process is a special case of the class of independent processes, and by definition must be stationary. It is a discrete parameter process, where "time" is really the event number.

One common example of a renewal process is the arrival process to a queuing system. Often, the times between successive arrivals are independent and identically distributed. We assume this to be the case for all the queuing systems studied in this chapter. To make this aspect clear, one often uses the notation GI/M/c and GI/G/c (instead of G/M/c and G/G/c) where I stands for independent. Renewal processes occur in many other contexts as well, such as successive failures of system components and successive references to the same page in a paging system.

Let $F_X(t)$ and $f_X(t)$ denote, respectively, the distribution and density functions of the interevent times X_i's, and let $S_n = X_1 + \cdots + X_n$. Then S_n gives the time until the occurrence of nth event. Because X_i's are iid (independent and identically distributed), the distribution of S_n is n-fold convolution of $F_X(t)$ with itself, henceforth denoted as $F_{(n)}(t)$. The process S_n is also known as the *random walk process*. (In a general random walk process, X_i's can take both negative and positive values.) This designation results from the fact that if we interpret each event as a step, and X_i as the step size, then S_n gives the position after n steps. Let $N(t)$ denote the number of renewals in time $(0, t]$. This process is called the *renewal counting process*; it is a stationary, discrete state random process.[2] It is easy to see that $F_{(n)}(t)$ is the complementary distribution function of $N(t)$, because

$$P[N(t) \geq n] = P(S_n \leq t) = F_{(n)}(t) \tag{1.4}$$

We now consider a very special renewal process, namely the one where X_i's are exponentially distributed, i.e., $f_X(x) = \lambda e^{-\lambda t}$ for some λ. Thus, $F_{(n)}(t)$ becomes the n-stage Erlang distribution, and from equation (1.4) it is easy to verify that $N(t)$ has the Poisson distribution with rate λ, i.e.,

$$P(N(t) = n) = \frac{(\lambda t)^n}{n!} e^{-\lambda t} \tag{1.5}$$

The Poisson process plays a central role in queuing theory because it possesses a number of interesting properties:

1. *Relation to exponential distribution*: Interevent time is exponentially distributed with rate λ, as we have already seen.
2. *Uniformity*: Probability of more than one arrival in a small time interval Δt is negligible, i.e., of order $(\Delta t)^2$. From (1.5), this probability can be seen to be $1 - (1 + \lambda\Delta t)e^{-\lambda\Delta t}$, which is $O((\Delta t)^2)$.
3. *Memorylessness*: Past behavior is totally irrelevant; i.e., the probability of occurrence of an event is independent of how many events have occurred in the past and the time since the last event.
4. *Mixture*: Sum of k independent Poisson streams with rates $\lambda_1, \ldots, \lambda_k$ is also Poisson with rate $\lambda = \lambda_1 + \cdots + \lambda_k$.
5. *Probabilistic split*: A k-way probabilistic split of a Poisson stream with probabilities $q_1, \ldots, q_k$ creates k independent Poisson substreams with rates $q_1\lambda, \ldots, q_k\lambda$.
6. *Limiting theorem*: Let $A_1(t), \ldots, A_k(t)$ be k *independent* renewal counting processes, each having an arbitrary interevent-time distribution with finite mean (m_i) and finite variance (σ_i^2). Then the "average" random process

$$X(t) = [A_1(t) + \cdots + A_k(t)]/k \tag{1.6}$$

has Poisson distribution with rate $k\big/\sum_{i=1}^{k} \frac{1}{m_i}$ as $k \to \infty$ and certain regularity conditions hold.

Property (3) follows from the fact that the Poisson process is a renewal process with exponentially distributed interevent time. Properties (4) and (5) are easy

[2] As explained earlier, t is an auxiliary time parameter here.

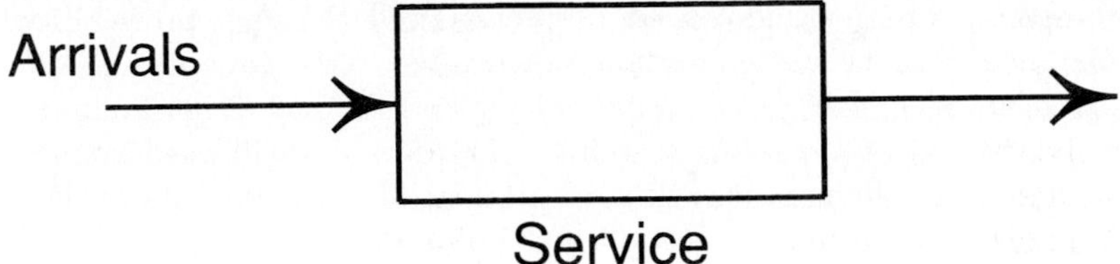

FIGURE 5-2: An isolated queuing system.

to prove and are explored in Exercise 5.2. The proof of property (6) can be approached much like that for the central limit theorem, but is omitted here. Note that because of property (6), one can often assume that the overall traffic is approximately Poisson, even though the individual constituents are not.

5.2 Analysis of Markov Chains

Consider the behavior of an isolated queuing station, such as the one shown in Fig. 5-2. The relevant random process is $X(t)$, the number of customers in the system at time t. Obviously, the state space of $X(t)$ is Z^+, the set of all nonnegative integers. The time parameter could be continuous or discrete, and we shall consider both. *We assume that the arrival and service processes are stationary, mutually independent and Markovian in nature.* The last property means that the probability of an arrival or service completion within a given time interval is independent of all past history, including the time of last arrival or service. We are interested in finding the *state probabilities* $\pi_j(t) = P(X(t) = j)$, i.e., the probability that there are $j \in 0 \,..\, \infty$ customers in the system at time t. These probabilities would depend on the *initial distribution* $P(X(0) = i)$, which is assumed to be given. Let

$$P_{ij}(u,t) \triangleq P[X(t) = j | X(u) = i] \tag{2.1}$$

denote the probability that the system is in state j at time t, given that it was in state i at time u. We call this as the *transition probability*. This quantity is same as the one used in equation (1.1) to characterize the Markovian property. We could then write

$$\pi_j(t) = \sum_{i=0}^{\infty} \pi_i(u) P_{ij}(u,t) \tag{2.2}$$

This equation results from the fact that to be in state j at time t, the system must have been in some state i at time u from which it transited to state j by time t (in one or more transitions). It is convenient to write (2.2) in a matrix form. For this, we define $\Pi(t) = [\pi_0(t),\ \pi_1(t),\ \ldots\ ]$ as a *row vector*, and $H(u,t)$ as the square matrix of $P_{ij}(u,t)$'s. Then (2.2) can be rewritten as

$$\Pi(t) = \Pi(u) H(u,t) \tag{2.3}$$

This is a fundamental equation and can be adapted to give the state probability vector $\Pi(t)$ for both discrete and continuous parameter cases. Notice that the number of feasible states in the system, and hence Π and H, may either be finite or infinite. In the context of a queuing system, a closed model will have a finite number of states, and an open model will have an infinite number of states. For now, this distinction is irrelevant.

5.2.1 Discrete Parameter Case

Assume that the time starts at 0 and is represented by the set of nonnegative integers. Define $Q(n)$ as $H(n, n+1)$ and let $u = n$ and $t = n+1$ in equation (2.3). This results in the following recurrence equation for the discrete parameter chain

$$\Pi(n+1) = \Pi(n)Q(n) \tag{2.4}$$

which in turn gives $\Pi(n)$ in terms of $\Pi(0)$. Let us now see the meaning of $Q(n)$. A representative element of $Q(n)$ is $P_{ij}(n, n+1)$, henceforth denoted as $q_{ij}(n)$. It is the probability of going from state i to state j at the next time instant after n (i.e., at time $n+1$). We call $q_{ij}(n)$ a *one-step transition probability*. Notice that in each row of $Q(n)$, all elements must sum to 1 since this sum represents the total probability of transition in a given state. Of course, all $q_{ij}(n)$'s should also lie in the range [0,1]. Matrices that have these two properties are usually known as *stochastic* or *d-stochastic* where "d" stands for discrete parameter domain. (The latter is not a standard terminology, but we use it to avoid confusion.)

A discrete parameter Markov chain is called *homogeneous* if all $q_{ij}(n)$'s are independent of the time parameter n. Obviously, *in a homogeneous chain, the transition process is stationary*. Henceforth, we shall only consider homogeneous chains, since this is practically the most important case. With Q defined as $[q_{ij}]$, equation (2.4) simplifies to

$$\Pi(n+1) = \Pi(n)Q \tag{2.5}$$

Since $\Pi(0)$ is known, equation (2.5) can be used to compute the first few values of $\Pi(n)$; however, to obtain a general expression for the transient solution, it is convenient to use z-transforms. Let the z-transform of $\Pi(n)$ be denoted as $\Phi(z)$. Like $\Pi(n)$, $\Phi(z)$ is a row vector $[\phi_0(z), \phi_1(z), \ldots]$ where $\phi_i(z)$ is the z-transform of the probability of being in state i. That is,

$$\phi_i(z) = \sum_{k=0}^{\infty} \pi_i(k) z^k \tag{2.6}$$

Multiplying both sides of equation (2.5) by z^{n+1}, summing over all n, we get $\Phi(z) - \Pi(0) = \Phi(z)Qz$, which simplifies to give

$$\Phi(z) = \Pi(0)[I - Qz]^{-1} \tag{2.7}$$

where I is the identity matrix. This form is most useful when Q is finite and we shall assume this to be the case. $\Pi(n)$ could then be retrieved by inverting $\Phi(z)$.

The equation $\det(I - Qz) = 0$ (where "det" denotes the determinant) is known as the *characteristic equation* of the Markov chain, and its roots are known as the *characteristic roots*. Recall that given a matrix Q, the equation $xQ = \lambda x$ has a nontrivial solution x if and only if $(Q - \lambda I)$ is singular (or $\det(Q - \lambda I) = 0$). It follows that *the characteristic roots of Q are simply the inverse of its eigenvalues*. This explains the importance of characteristic roots in analyzing the behavior of $\Pi(n)$. Consider the partial-fraction expansion of $\phi_i(z)$ for any state i. The terms in this expansion will have denominators of the form $(z - r)^k$ (where r is a characteristic root and k is a positive integer). Therefore, from Appendix E, the inversion of $\phi_i(z)$ to get $\pi_i(n)$ will yield a sum of terms, each of which contains terms like r^{-n}. Now if the system is stable, such terms cannot blow up as $n \to \infty$.[3] Therefore, *every nonunity root r of the characteristic equation must have a magnitude larger than 1*. Also, since at least one of the $\pi_i(n)$'s must be nonzero as $n \to \infty$, *at least one of the roots of the characteristic equation should always be unity*. These properties also follow from the fact that Q is a stochastic matrix. It can be shown that all eigenvalues of such matrices are positive and the largest eigenvalue is 1. That is, *the spectral radius of a stochastic matrix is 1*.

Often we are interested only in the limiting (or steady-state) behavior of the system. We define the *limiting distribution*, henceforth denoted as Π, as simply $\lim_{n\to\infty} \Pi(n)$. For now, we assume that this limit does exist. From the properties just mentioned, it follows that to get limiting distribution, we only need to consider those terms in the partial-fraction expansion of $\phi_i(z)$ that have $(z - 1)$ in the denominator. However, if we know that the limiting distribution is independent of the initial conditions, we can obtain it much more easily. Let $\mathbf{e}$ denote a *column vector* of all 1's. It is clear from equation (2.5) that the limiting distribution Π must satisfy the following system of linear equations

$$\Pi = \Pi Q \quad \text{and} \quad \Pi \cdot \mathbf{e} = 1 \tag{2.8}$$

where the second part in (2.8) comes from the fact that all probabilities must sum to 1.

A Markov chain can be represented by a directed graph, known as the *state transition diagram*. In this graph, the nodes represent the states, and the arcs represent the transitions. The arcs are labeled by transition probabilities. We shall use this graph model in Section 5.3 to study some properties of Markov chains. For now, we only consider an example.

Example 5.1 Consider a discrete parameter Markov chain with the following single-step transition probability matrix

$$Q = \begin{bmatrix} 2/3 & 1/3 & 0 \\ 1/2 & 0 & 1/2 \\ 0 & 0 & 1 \end{bmatrix}$$

Draw the state transition diagram for this chain. Assuming that the system is in state 1 initially, compute the state probability vector $\Pi(n)$ for $n = 1, 2, \ldots, \infty$.

[3] Keep in mind that n here represents time and not state.

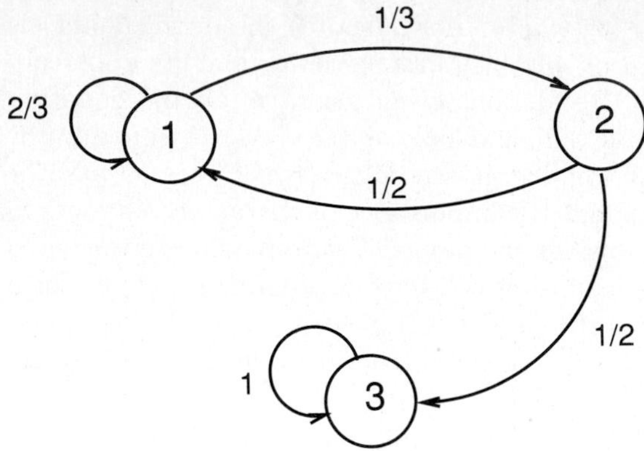

FIGURE 5-3: State transition diagram for Example 5.1.

Also compute the characteristic roots of Q and characterize the limiting behavior of the chain.

Solution The state transition diagram is shown in Fig. 5-3. The first few values of $\Pi(n)$ can be obtained by simple matrix multiplications. For the general case, equation (2.7) gives

$$I - Qz = \begin{bmatrix} 1-2z/3 & -z/3 & 0 \\ -z/2 & 1 & -z/2 \\ 0 & 0 & 1-z \end{bmatrix}$$

The characteristic equation is $(1-z)(1-2z/3-z^2/6) = 0$, and gives the following three roots

$$z_0 = 1, \qquad z_1 = -2+\sqrt{10}, \qquad z_2 = -2-\sqrt{10}$$

As expected, one root is unity, and the others have magnitude larger than 1. From Fig. 5-3 we can see that as $n \to \infty$, the system will settle in state 3 with probability 1. Therefore, we know that the unity root should appear only in $\phi_3(z)$. The other two roots will appear in all ϕ_i's and will lead to a damped oscillatory effect, which would eventually die down to zero. To illustrate this, let us compute $\pi_1(n)$. Since $\Pi(0) = [1 \;\; 0 \;\; 0]$, the first row of $[I - Qz]^{-1}$ is itself $[\phi_1(z) \; \phi_2(z) \; \phi(z)]$. It is easy to verify that $\phi_1(z) = -6/(z^2+4z-6)$. Therefore, $\pi_1(n)$ is the same as $f^*(n)$ in Example B.2, i.e.,

$$\pi_1(n) = 0.9487[z_1^{-n-1} - z_2^{-n-1}]$$

$\pi_2(n)$ and $\pi_3(n)$ can be computed similarly. □

5.2.2 Continuous Parameter Case

We again start with equation (2.3). Let $u = t - \Delta t$. Then

$$\Pi(t) - \Pi(t-\Delta t) = \Pi(t-\Delta t)[H(t-\Delta t, t) - I]$$

Dividing by Δt, and taking the limit as $\Delta t \to 0$, we get the following basic equation for the continuous parameter case

$$\frac{\partial \Pi(t)}{\partial t} = \Pi(t)Q(t) \quad \text{where} \quad Q(t) = \lim_{\Delta t \to 0} \frac{H(t-\Delta t, t) - I}{\Delta t} \tag{2.9}$$

Equation (2.9) is known as the (forward) *Chapman-Kolmogorov equation.* Let $q_{ij}(t)$ denote the (i,j)th element of $Q(t)$. Also, let δ_{ij} denote the *Kronecker delta function*; i.e., $\delta_{ij} = 1$ for $i = j$ and zero otherwise. Then by the definition of $Q(t)$, we have

$$q_{ij}(t) = \lim_{\Delta t \to 0} \frac{P_{ij}(t-\Delta t, t) - \delta_{ij}}{\Delta t} \tag{2.10}$$

Let Δt be a small interval. Then equation (2.10) implies that

$$\begin{aligned} 1 - P_{ii}(t-\Delta t, t) &\approx -q_{ii}(t)\Delta t \\ P_{ij}(t-\Delta t, t) &\approx q_{ij}(t)\Delta t \quad \text{for } i \neq j \end{aligned} \tag{2.11}$$

where the approximation becomes exact as $\Delta t \to 0$. Thus, $q_{ij}(t)$ for $i \neq j$ can be interpreted as the rate at which the system goes from state i to j at time t. Similarly, $-q_{ii}(t)$ can be interpreted as the rate at which the system departs from state i at time t. Because of this interpretation, $Q(t)$ is called the *transition rate matrix*. Since the total transition probability from any state i (back to state i or to other states) must be 1, we have

$$\sum_{j \neq i} P_{ij}(t-\Delta t, t) + P_{ii}(t-\Delta t, t) = 1 \tag{2.12}$$

Applying (2.11) and taking the limit as $\Delta t \to 0$, we get

$$\sum_{j=0}^{\infty} q_{ij}(t) = 0 \tag{2.13}$$

That is, *all elements in a row of $Q(t)$ must sum to 0. Also, while the off-diagonal elements of $Q(t)$ must be nonnegative, those along the diagonal must be negative.* Although not a standard terminology, we shall call such matrices *c-stochastic*, where "c" refers to the continuous parameter domain.

The first order differential equation in (2.9) is easy to solve and gives

$$\Pi(t) = \Pi(0) \exp\left[\int_0^t Q(u)\, du\right] \tag{2.14}$$

As in the discrete parameter case, we are primarily interested in homogeneous chains. A continuous parameter chain is called homogeneous if the *transition rates* are independent of time. In this case, equation (2.9) reduces to the following

$$\frac{\partial \Pi(t)}{\partial t} = \Pi(t)Q \tag{2.15}$$

Also, equation (2.14) reduces to $\Pi(t) = \Pi(0)\exp(Qt)$. However, this form is not suitable computationally, and it may be more convenient to work with Laplace transforms. Let $\Psi(s)$ denote the Laplace transform of $\Pi(t)$. Using the differentiation property of Laplace transforms, equation (2.15) yields

$$\Psi(s) = \Pi(0)[sI - Q]^{-1} \tag{2.16}$$

Notice the similarity between this and equation (2.7). Here also we can speak of characteristic roots, *which in this case are simply the eigenvalues of* Q. Before pursuing this aspect, let us examine the limiting distribution, which again is defined as $\lim_{t\to\infty} \Pi(t)$. If this distribution exists and is independent of the initial conditions, the derivative in equation (2.15) must be zero, and we get the following system of linear equations

$$\Pi Q = 0 \quad \text{and} \quad \Pi \cdot \mathbf{e} = 1 \tag{2.17}$$

Again notice the similarity between the systems (2.17) and (2.8). Such similarities are not incidental; we can indeed go from a discrete parameter system to a continuous one and vice versa, depending on what is more convenient to work with. Suppose that we start with a continuous parameter chain $\mathcal{Z}$. Since the corresponding Q matrix must be c-stochastic, its diagonal elements must be negative and largest in magnitude in each row. Let δ denote some positive number, strictly larger in magnitude than all diagonal elements of Q. Let

$$Q' = \delta^{-1}Q + I \tag{2.18}$$

Obviously, Q' is a d-stochastic matrix and therefore can be considered as a transition probability matrix of some discrete parameter Markov chain $\mathcal{Z}'$. Let Π' denote the limiting distribution of $\mathcal{Z}'$, i.e.,

$$\Pi' Q' = \Pi' \quad \text{and} \quad \Pi' \cdot \mathbf{e} = 1$$

By using equation (2.18) in the above equation, it is trivial to verify that $\Pi' = \Pi$. That is, $\mathcal{Z}$ and $\mathcal{Z}'$ have identical steady-state distribution. Therefore, *all steady-state results on discrete parameter chains can be translated to corresponding results for continuous parameter chains, and vice-versa.* In particular, (2.18) implies that *all nonzero eigenvalues of Q must be negative, and if the limiting distribution exists, at least one eigenvalue must be zero*. We shall see in Section 13.4.4 that the transient distributions of $\mathcal{Z}$ and $\mathcal{Z}'$ can also be related.

We shall have many other occasions to use equation (2.18). One point to note about it is that δ must be finite for the transformation to work. In some cases, this is not possible. An example is the delay station, where the transition rate in state i is $i\mu$ and thus $\lim_{i\to\infty} q_{ii} = -\infty$. If we want to work with a discrete parameter chain in such cases, we instead have to use the embedded chain at transition points. Extraction of such a chain is discussed in Section 9.2.4.

Our discussion until now has been rather abstract. Let us now interpret the results in the context of the queuing system shown in Fig. 5-2. In this queuing system, the interarrival and service times must be exponentially distributed, but the arrivals and departures may occur in batches of arbitrary size. We shall see in Section 5.6 that by defining the system state differently, we can actually cover a much larger class of queuing systems in the same framework, but let us ignore that aspect for now. In the discrete parameter case, q_{ij}'s can be specified in terms of the probabilities of one or more arrivals and services, and in the continuous parameter case, they can be specified in terms of the arrival and service rates. For example, in the discrete parameter case, q_{35} would represent the probability of the simultaneous arrival of two customers while there are three customers already queued up at the station. In the next example, we show how the analysis above can be applied to a simple Markovian system where both arrivals and services occur singly and have state-independent rates.

Example 5.2 Obtain steady-state queue-length distribution for an open M/M/1 system, i.e., a system with Poisson arrivals and a single exponential server.

Solution Let λ and μ denote the rate parameters for the exponential distributions characterizing the interarrival and service times. Let t denote some arbitrarily chosen point in time and T_a the time interval from t until next arrival. Also let Δt be a small time interval. Because of the memoryless property of the exponential distribution, we can speak of $Pr(T_a \leq \Delta t)$ without knowing how long it has been since the last arrival. Thus, for any system state k, we have

$$P_{k,k+1}(t, t+\Delta t) = Pr(T_a \leq \Delta t) = 1 - e^{-\lambda \Delta t} = \lambda \Delta t + o(\Delta t) \qquad (2.19)$$

where $o(x)$ refers to terms that go to zero faster than x. By the definition of q_{ij}'s for a continuous time Markov chain, it then follows that $q_{k,k+1} = \lambda$ for any k. Similarly, we can show that $q_{k,k-1} = \mu$ for any $k > 0$. Thus, λ and μ are not only the arrival and service rates, but also the forward and backward transition rates. Since multiple arrivals and services are not permitted, no transitions are possible between states that differ by more than 1. By equation (2.13), this means that $q_{kk} = -(\lambda + \mu)$ for all $k > 0$. Thus, we are able to characterize the transition rate matrix Q completely. It will be shown later that the limiting distribution exists if $\lambda < \mu$. Assuming this to be the case, the steady-state equation $\Pi Q = 0$ takes the following form

$$[\pi_0 \ \pi_1 \ \pi_2 \ \cdots \ ] \begin{bmatrix} -\lambda & \lambda & 0 & 0 & \cdots \\ \mu & -(\lambda+\mu) & \lambda & 0 & \cdots \\ 0 & \mu & -(\lambda+\mu) & \lambda & \cdots \\ 0 & 0 & \mu & -(\lambda+\mu) & \cdots \\ \cdot & \cdot & \cdot & \cdot & \cdots \end{bmatrix} = [0] \qquad (2.20)$$

This infinite system has a very simple solution. The first equation in (2.20) gives $-\lambda\pi_0 + \mu\pi_1 = 0$, or $\pi_1 = \rho\pi_0$ where $\rho = \lambda/\mu$. The second equation gives

$$\lambda\pi_0 - (\lambda + \mu)\pi_1 + \mu\pi_2 = 0$$

Combining the two equations, we get $\pi_2 = \rho^2\pi_0$. Continuing in this manner, it is easy to see that the general solution is $\pi_n = \rho^n\pi_0$. Now by using the requirement that all probabilities sum to 1, we get $\pi_0 = (1-\rho)$, and we have the full solution. We shall return to this system in Section 5.5. □

As in the discrete parameter case, we can represent a continuous parameter Markov chain by a directed graph. The only difference is that we label the arcs with transition rates. This graph is often known as the *transition rate diagram*.

5.3 Long-Term Behavior of Markov Chains

In this section, we present a number of results that are useful in checking whether a random process is "well behaved" with respect to its long-term behavior. These results are of crucial importance not only in analytic modeling of stochastic systems, but also in their simulation. Although much of our discussion is geared toward Markov chains, the concepts are also important for general random processes. We shall mostly deal with discrete parameter chains in this section, because one can examine the properties of a continuous parameter chain by examining the discrete parameter chain embedded at its transition points.

5.3.1 Limiting and Stationary Distributions

Consider a discrete parameter Markov chain $\mathcal{Z}$. The limiting distribution Π for $\mathcal{Z}$ is defined as $\lim_{n\to\infty} \Pi(n)$. We noted in the last Section that if this limit exists and is unique, we can get the limiting distribution by solving equation (2.8). In general, however, (2.8) may have a solution even in other cases, and we shall denote it as Π^*. Because of the fixed-point nature of (2.8), Π^* must be such that if the system is started with this as the initial distribution, it will retain this distribution forever. Therefore, the solution to (2.8) is known as the *stationary distribution*. Now, $\mathcal{Z}$ is started with a different (and arbitrary) initial distribution, three possibilities exist.

1. It always settles with Π^*; in which case we have a unique limiting distribution, which is the same as the stationary distribution.
2. It never settles down. In this case, no limiting distribution exists.
3. It always settles, but the long-term distribution depends on the initial state. In this case, the limiting distribution exists, but is nonunique.

These three scenarios apply to continuous parameter chains as well. In the next subsection, we shall introduce the notion of *ergodicity* and show that an ergodic system always exhibits scenario (1). We can consider such systems as "well-behaved", and indeed most practical systems whose long-term behavior is of interest, are of this type. We shall also see how to tell when scenarios (2) and (3) apply. In Section 5.3.3, we shall see how to obtain limiting distributions when scenario (3) applies.

5.3.2 State Classification and Ergodicity

In this section, we introduce a number of concepts that are useful in identifying the conditions under which a Markov chain will have a unique limiting distribution. If the chain under consideration is a continuous parameter chain, we shall really be dealing with an embedded chain; therefore, we can speak of transition probability in either case. Let $f_{ii}^{(n)}$ denote the probability that thc system, after making a transition while in state i, goes back to state i for the *first time* in exactly n transitions. Note that if state i has a self-loop, the system can go back to state i in a single transition, and hence $f_{ii}^{(1)} > 0$ in this case. Otherwise, $f_{ii}^{(1)}$ will be zero. $f_{ii}^{(0)}$ is always zero. Let f_{ii} denote the probability that the system ever returns to state i. Obviously,

$$f_{ii} = \sum_{n=1}^{\infty} f_{ii}^{(n)} \tag{3.1}$$

Let us examine the behavior of state i when the system is observed over a long period of time. If $f_{ii} = 1$, every time the system leaves state i, it must return to this state with probability 1. That is, during an infinitely long period of time, the system must return to state i infinitely often. For this reason, we call such a state *recurrent*. If, however, $f_{ii} < 1$, each time the system leaves state i, there is a finite probability that it does not come back to state i. Thus, over an infinitely long observation period, the system can visit state i only finitely often. For this reason, we call such a state *transient*. The motivation for the classification is, of course, that the transient states are of no interest for the long-term behavior of the system. Recurrent states can be further classified depending on whether the eventual return can occur in a finite amount of time. Suppose that the system has just entered state i, and let θ_{ii} denote the *expected time* until it reenters state i. Let us note a few points about this definition to ensure its correct interpretation:

1. The notion of "time" depends on the parameter type. For a discrete parameter chain, the time is measured as the number of transitions or "hops", whereas for a continuous parameter chain, time is simply the real time.

2. The very next transition could well be back to state i itself. This situation is *not* excluded in defining θ_{ii}. (In this case, the system comes back to state i in a single transition.)

3. If the chain under consideration is fully Markovian (as opposed to semi-Markov), we need not insist that the "system has just entered state i", and instead just say that the system *is* in state i.

We shall measure θ_{ii} in terms of number of transitions for the discussion that follows. This means that if the given chain is continuous parameter, we must use a suitable embedded chain. Since $f_{ii} = 1$ for a recurrent state i, we can regard $f_{ii}^{(n)}$ as the mass function of the number of transitions needed to return to state i. Therefore, by the definition of expected value, we have

$$\theta_{ii} = \sum_{n=1}^{\infty} n f_{ii}^{(n)} \tag{3.2}$$

Notice that $f_{ii}^{(n)}$'s must eventually decay faster than $O(n^{-2})$ for the series in (3.2) to converge. If this does not happen, then $\theta_{ii} = \infty$ and we refer to state i as *null recurrent*. Otherwise, we refer to state i as *positive recurrent*. If $f_{ii}^{(n)} > 0$ only when n equals some integer multiple of a number $k > 1$, we refer to state i as *periodic* with period $= k$. Otherwise (i.e., if $f_{ii}^{(n)} > 0$ and $f_{ii}^{(n+1)} > 0$ for some n), state i is called *aperiodic*. A Markov chain is called *irreducible* if every state is reachable from every other state in one or more transitions (i.e., the state transition graph is strongly connected). We now state, without proof, a few important results for irreducible Markov chains.

Lemma 5.1 All states of an irreducible Markov chain are of the same type (i.e., transient, null recurrent, periodic, or positive recurrent and aperiodic). Furthermore, in the periodic case, all states have the same period.

□

A consequence of this theorem is that we can name an irreducible chain according to state types. Thus, the phrase "recurrent chain" means an irreducible chain with recurrent states. A Markov chain is called *ergodic* if it is irreducible, positive recurrent, and aperiodic. Actually, *aperiodicity is relevant only for discrete time chains*. We shall see why this is the case after discussing Example 5.4. The concept of ergodicity can also be defined in a different but equivalent way, as we shall see in Section 5.3.4. Here we state an important result on ergodic Markov chains.

Lemma 5.2 An ergodic Markov chain has a unique limiting distribution, independent of the initial state. It is given by system (2.8) for the discrete case, and system (2.17) for the continuous case.

□

We mention one more result concerning irreducible Markov chains that is theoretically important, but possibly not of much practical use.

Lemma 5.3 An irreducible discrete parameter Markov chain is transient if and only if the system of equations $Z_i = \sum_{j=1}^{\infty} q_{ij} Z_j$ has a nonzero bounded solution.

□

It is clear that for an ergodic Markov chain the limiting and stationary distributions are the same and given by (2.8) or (2.17). If a discrete time chain only violates the aperiodicity requirement, the limiting distribution does not

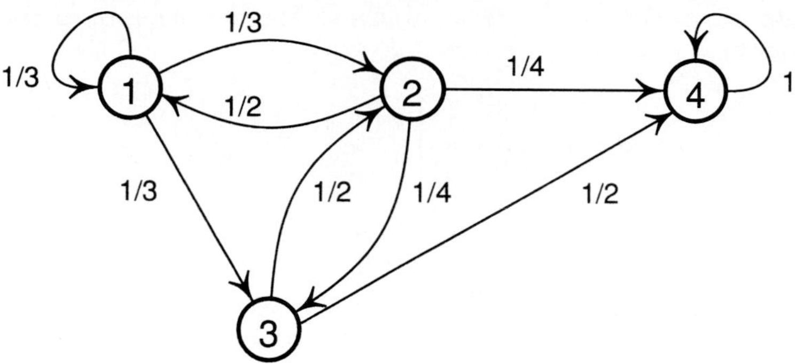

FIGURE 5-4: State transition diagram for Example 5.3.

exist, but a unique stationary distribution does. *An irreducible finite Markov chain must be positive recurrent* because every infinitely long sequence of hops must use certain states infinitely often, and because of irreducibility, if one state is visited infinitely often, so should all of them. If an infinite state, irreducible Markov chain is transient or null recurrent, the limiting probability of any finite state is 0 and no stationary distribution exists. We now illustrate these ideas through a series of examples.

Example 5.3 Classify all states of the discrete parameter Markov chain whose state diagram is shown in Fig. 5-4.

Solution From the diagram, it is clear that $f_{11}^{(1)} = 1/3$, $f_{11}^{(2)} = (1/3)(1/2) = 1/6$, and $f_{11}^{(3)} = (1/3)(1/2)(1/2) = 1/12$. Continuing in this manner, we get

$$f_{11}^{(n)} = \frac{1}{3} \cdot \left(\frac{1}{2} \cdot \frac{1}{4}\right)^{\frac{n-3}{2}} \cdot \frac{1}{2} \cdot \frac{1}{2} \qquad \text{for } n > 3 \text{ and odd}$$

$$f_{11}^{(n)} = \frac{1}{3} \cdot \left(\frac{1}{4} \cdot \frac{1}{2}\right)^{\frac{n-2}{2}} \cdot \frac{1}{2} \qquad \text{for } n > 2 \text{ and even}$$

Therefore,

$$f_{11} = \sum_{n=1}^{\infty} f_{11}^{(n)} = \frac{1}{3} + \frac{1}{6} \sum_{m=0}^{\infty} \left(\frac{1}{8}\right)^m + \frac{1}{12} \sum_{m=0}^{\infty} \left(\frac{1}{8}\right)^m = \frac{13}{21}$$

Thus, state (1) is transient. State (4) is obviously recurrent since $f_{44} = f_{44}^{(1)} = 1$. Without computing f_{22} and f_{33}, we can claim that states (2) and (3) are transient since the subgraph consisting of nodes 1, 2, and 3, is strongly connected. The entire chain is, however, reducible and consists of two strongly connected components. □

Example 5.4 Consider a discrete time Markov chain with Q matrix shown below. Classify its states and the long-term behavior. Next consider $(Q - I)$ as the transition rate matrix for a continuous parameter Markov chain. Show the long-term behavior here as well.

$$Q = \begin{bmatrix} 0 & 0 & 1 \\ 1 & 0 & 0 \\ 0 & 1 & 0 \end{bmatrix}$$

Solution It is easy to see that the chain is irreducible, and because of the finite number of states, it is positive recurrent. Since the chain cycles through its three states sequentially, it is periodic with period 3. This can also be seen by noting that for all i, $f_{ii} = f_{ii}^{(3)} = 1$. Suppose that the chain is in state 1 initially, i.e., $\Pi(0) = [1 \;\; 0 \;\; 0]$. It is then easy to verify using the relation $\Pi(n) = \Pi(0)Q^n$ that

$$\Pi(n) = \begin{cases} [1\,0\,0] & \text{for } n = 0, 3, 6, \ldots \\ [0\,1\,0] & \text{for } n = 1, 4, 7, \ldots \\ [0\,0\,1] & \text{for } n = 2, 5, 8, \ldots \end{cases} \tag{3.3}$$

Therefore, $\lim_{n\to\infty} \Pi(n)$ does not exist and there is no limiting or steady-state distribution. However, if we let $\Pi(0) = [1/3 \;\; 1/3 \;\; 1/3]$, we get $\Pi(n) = \Pi(0)$ for all n; i.e., the system never leaves the initial state. This is the stationary distribution that one would get by solving equation (2.8). This shows that for a nonergodic chain, the limiting distribution may depend on the initial distribution. Now if we treat the chain as continuous time, the periodicity is no longer relevant and the *limiting distribution* can be easily obtained as $[1/3 \;\; 1/3 \;\; 1/3]$. □

It is clear from this example that a periodic chain may fail to have a limiting distribution because it may get locked into a synchronized oscillatory behavior. In fact, this is the only reason for not having a limiting distribution (assuming, of course, that the chain is irreducible and positive recurrent). We can also see that such a behavior is possible only in discrete time. For a continuous parameter chain, the real time between transitions is not fixed, and thus any synchronization that exists initially must fade away in the long run. In other words, although a continuous parameter chain may keep cycling through a sequence of states in an orderly manner, it will not be in a given state at certain predefined points in time. This is the reason why we said that periodicity is irrelevant for ergodicity of continuous parameter Markov chains. The same argument applies to an embedded Markov chain, as long as the transition points come from a continuous time domain.

Example 5.5 Characterize the Markov chain for the simple M/M/1 queuing system of Example 5.2. What would happen in the limited population case?

Solution The transition rate diagram here is the same as in Fig. 5-6, except that the arrival and service rates are state-independent. Clearly, the Markov chain for this system, denoted $\mathcal{Z}$, is irreducible. Therefore, by Lemma 5.1, all states must be of the same type. Now to compute $f_{ii}^{(n)}$'s, we can use equation (2.18) to get a discrete parameter chain, denoted $\mathcal{Z}^*$, that has the same long-term behavior.

The state classification of $\mathcal{Z}^*$ then also applies to $\mathcal{Z}$. Since $\mathcal{Z}^*$ is irreducible, f_{ii}'s must be same for all states. If $\lambda > \mu$, we find that $f_{ii} < 1$, and hence $\mathcal{Z}$ is transient. (Another way to confirm this is to use Lemma 5.3). For $\lambda \leq \mu$, $f_{ii} = 1$ and $\mathcal{Z}$ is recurrent. If $\lambda < \mu$, $\mathcal{Z}$ is positive recurrent. Therefore, for $\lambda < \mu$, $\mathcal{Z}$ is ergodic, and the steady-state distribution derived in Example 5.2 is unique. If $\lambda = \mu$, the chain is null recurrent. In this case, the average queue length is infinite, even though any given state can be visited infinitely often with probability 1. Finally, in the finite population case, the chain will always be positive recurrent *irrespective of the value of* λ.

We note here that we could have also analyzed this system by considering the discrete parameter chain embedded at the transition points of $\mathcal{Z}$. Even though this discrete parameter chain is periodic with period 2, the periodicity is irrelevant because we are dealing with an embedded chain with transition points coming from a continuous time domain. □

5.3.3 Analysis of Reducible Chains

In most practical applications where we wish to study long-term behavior, the Markov chain of interest is irreducible, and can be analyzed as discussed in the last section. However, reducible chains do occasionally arise, and it is important to understand how to analyze them correctly. The limiting behavior of a reducible chain necessarily depends on the initial distribution, because not every state is reachable from every initial state. This is not a problem, since in practical applications involving reducible chains, the initial distribution is a part of the problem specification.

Let $\mathcal{Z}$ denote a reducible chain. We can decompose $\mathcal{Z}$ into maximal strongly connected components (SCC's) and work with them. From Lemma 5.1, all states in a SCC must be of the same type. In the long run, the system could only be in one of the *recurrent* SCC's, so these SCC's are of particular interest. First, we claim that a recurrent SCC cannot have any transition to any state outside that SCC. To see this, suppose that there is a transition from a state α of a recurrent SCC to some outside state β. Since we have assumed the SCC's to be maximal, we cannot have a path from β to α, but this means that α must be transient. This property further means that there could be no paths between various recurrent SCC's. It then follows that the limiting distribution of $\mathcal{Z}$ can be obtained from those of the recurrent SCC's. If a state i in a recurrent SCC has $\theta_{ii} < \infty$ and is aperiodic (needed only for the discrete time case), then this SCC is ergodic and must have a unique limiting distribution, independent of the initial state. Thus, if all recurrent SCC's have a unique limiting distribution, then so does $\mathcal{Z}$ (where the latter is relative to the given initial distribution).

Now to determine the effect of transient states, we construct an aggregated Markov chain $\mathcal{Z}^*$ by replacing each recurrent SCC in the original Markov chain by a single state. The transition rates (or probabilities) for $\mathcal{Z}^*$ can be determined easily. Because of the property shown above, the only new rates (or probabilities) are those from a transient state, say i, to a recurrent SCC, say j. We can compute

q^*_{ij} as

$$q^*_{ij} = \sum_{\forall k \in SCC(j)} q_{ik} \tag{3.4}$$

We can now solve $\mathcal{Z}^*$ and determine the limiting state probabilities for it. Obviously, only the states corresponding to recurrent SCC's will have a nonzero probability in $\mathcal{Z}^*$. Let us denote these probabilities as $P_1, \ldots, P_K$ where P_i corresponds to the ith recurrent SCC. Since $\mathcal{Z}^*$ is reducible, we cannot obtain these probabilities using equations (2.8) or (2.17). Instead, we must compute them using transform methods, as discussed in Section 5.2. For example, for a continuous parameter chain, only a term like α/s in the partial-fraction expansion of the Laplace transform is relevant, and gives α as the limiting probability. Similarly, in the discrete parameter case, the coefficient of the $1/(1-z)$ term in the z-transform is relevant. Let $\Pi_i = [\pi_{i1}, \pi_{i2}, \ \ldots\ ]$ denote the stationary distribution for the ith SCC. Then the limiting probability for state k of SCC i is simply $P_i \pi_{ik}$.

Let us illustrate the ideas with a few examples. The chain in Fig. 5-3 is reducible and has two SCC's, one consisting of states {1,2} and the other {3}. Since any starting state will eventually lead to state 3, we have a degenerate situation where a unique limiting distribution exists even though the chain is reducible. It is easy to see that [0 0 1] is also the unique solution to the system (2.8). A similar situation exists in Fig. 5-4. In the following, we consider a more complicated example.

Example 5.6 Characterize the limiting distribution for the discrete parameter chain shown in Fig. 5-5(a) assuming that the system is initially in state 1.

Solution The complete chain $\mathcal{Z}$ has two recurrent SCC's, shown enclosed in dotted boxes in Fig. 5-5(a). SCC1 is unconditionally ergodic whereas SCC2 is ergodic if the time is not discrete. The corresponding limiting distributions are [1/2 1/2] and [1/3 1/3 1/3] respectively. The aggregation is trivial here, and the aggregated chain $\mathcal{Z}^*$ is shown in Fig. 5-5(b). Since $\Pi(0) = [1 \;\; 0 \;\; 0]$, we only need to compute the first row of the matrix $[I - Qz]^{-1}$ for $\mathcal{Z}^*$. It is given by

$$\left[\frac{1}{1-0.2z} \quad \frac{0.3z}{(1-z)(1-0.2z)} \quad \frac{0.5z}{(1-z)(1-0.2z)} \right]$$

We can now do a partial-fraction expansion of each row element and consider only the terms with denominator $(1-z)$. The resulting distribution is [0 0.375 0.625]. Of course, in this simple example, we can obtain this result by inspection. From Fig. 5-5(a), it is obvious that the system will get locked into SCC1 $0.3/0.8 = 37.5\%$ of the time. It is easy to see that the equation $\Pi = \Pi Q$ does not have a solution here, thus no stationary distribution exists. □

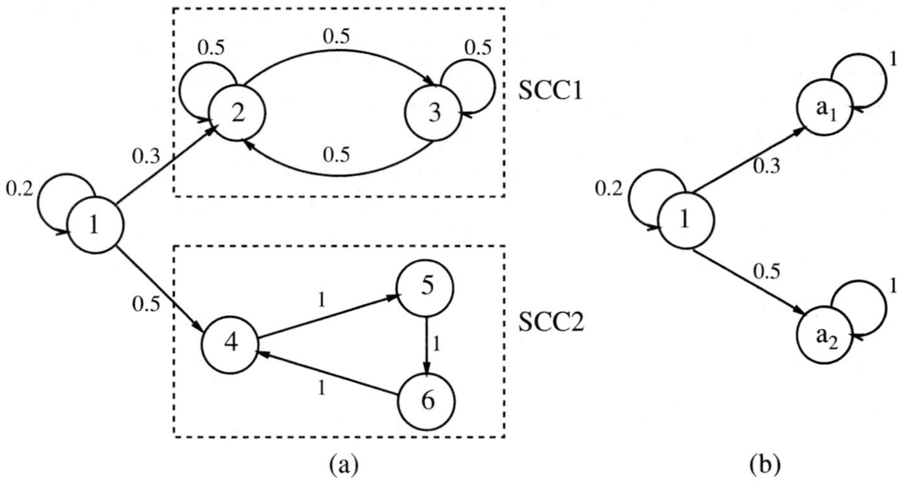

FIGURE 5-5: (a) Complete chain $\mathcal{Z}$ and (b) Aggregated chain $\mathcal{Z}^*$.

5.3.4 Ergodicity of General Random Processes

Let us now leave Markov chains and consider random processes in general. Since the notions of state and transitions between states apply to any random process, so do the concepts of irreducibility, recurrence, periodicity, ergodicity, stationary distribution, and limiting distribution. However, it may be difficult or impossible to provide mathematical equations that allow us to verify various properties or compute distributions. For example, we can always define stationary distribution Π^* as the one such that if the system is started in Π^*, it will stay in it forever. But, in general, we do not have any explicit equations to compute the stationary distribution. Similarly, we can define the limiting distribution as the one that the system will possess as time $t \to \infty$, but we have no equations to characterize it. Operationally (e.g., in the context of simulation), we can define these distributions as follows. Consider the following two ways of estimating the distribution of a stationary random process:

1. Observe one instance of the process evolve over time and thereby estimate the *time-averaged distribution*. The stationary distribution corresponds to such a time average from one sample path.
2. Start up a number of instances of the process with the same initial conditions, and observe all of them at the same time instant in their evolution. This gives an estimate of the *sample-averaged distribution*. The limiting distribution corresponds to such an average over several sample paths.

We say that *the random process is ergodic if the sample-averaged distribution is the same as the time-averaged distribution*. Note that in Example 5.4, each state is visited exactly once in each cycle and hence the time average over one sample path (i.e., the average over an arbitrarily large number of cycles) gives the distribution [1/3 1/3 1/3]. However, if we look at several samples at the same time instant, we will always find them to be perfectly "synchronized" because of the periodicity. Thus, for any value of t, the sample average will be the same as a single sample. We already know that no limit exists for this as $t \to \infty$. Thus, the system is not ergodic (for discrete time case). With continuous time, no such "synchronization" will be maintained, and the average of a sufficiently large number of samples at any given time instant will yield the distribution [1/3 1/3 1/3]. Thus, the system will be ergodic for the continuous time case.

It is clear from the discussion above that ergodicity is crucial in the study of a random process. In particular, if we are dealing with a reducible random process, we should first decompose it into its irreducible components. Similarly, positive recurrence is essential for the convergence of expressions involving infinite sums of probabilities. Therefore, a first step in the analysis of a queuing system is often finding conditions under which the stochastic process of interest is positive recurrent. The characterization of ergodicity in terms of the equivalence of sample and time averages is an important concept for intuitive understanding, but is not of much practical value in checking whether a given system is ergodic. The characterization in terms of irreducibility, aperiodicity, and positive recurrence applies in general, but may also be difficult to verify, particularly in non-Markovian systems. Irreducibility (or lack thereof) is generally obvious in a well-formulated problem, but no general and easily verifiable criterion for it can be given. Similar comments apply to aperiodicity. Given an irreducible system, positive recurrence nearly always amounts to ensuring that the queuing system is stable, i.e., none of the queues can grow indefinitely. This, in turn, means that π_0 (the probability of the system being empty) is strictly greater than zero. In a work-conserving system, the conditions for $\pi_0 > 0$ are usually trivial to find and will be discussed in Section 6.2.1. For other systems, finding the stability condition may almost amount to solving the system. If the system is Markovian (or can be modeled as such by identifying an embedded Markov chain), and the transition rate (or probability) matrix has a special structure, specific conditions are possible for positive recurrence. We shall see an example of this in Section 9.5.

It is important to note that the concepts of ergodicity, positive recurrence, etc. remain crucial even if we only wish to study the system by simulation. For example, before we attempt a steady-state simulation of the system, we must ensure that it is positive recurrent, otherwise, the result will only be a program abort with an out-of-memory condition. An even more troublesome situation can arise if the system is reducible (and hence nonergodic). In simulation, we compute all performance parameters as time averages over a single sample path; therefore, what we get is the stationary distribution. On the other hand, the statistical parameters such as the expected value are always defined as sample averages and are thus based on the limiting distribution. Another way to look at this mismatch is that what we want is how the system will behave at a single point as $t \to \infty$, but what we get from simulation is the average over the simulation period. Thus, *the simulation results may be misleading for a nonergodic system.* To see this, consider simulating the system of Example 5.6 using the single-run

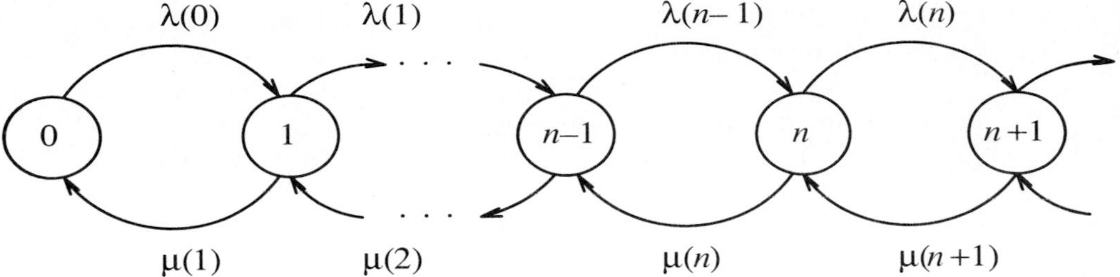

FIGURE 5-6: Transition rate diagram for a birth-death model.

method. (See Section 3.3). After a while, the system may well fall into SCC1 and would stay there from then on. Thus, irrespective of how long the simulation is run, it would claim that in the long run, the system spends one-half of its time in state 2 and the other half in state 3. Clearly, this is not how the system behaves "on the average", because if we performed a large number of experiments, the system would fall into SCC1 in only 37.5% of the instances! The only correct way to simulate this system is to perform a large number of simulation runs, and obtain sample averages. Also note that a casual use of the independent replication method may give unreliable results, because we may have decided to do just 5 replications (but made each run very long) of which say, 3, brought the system into SCC1.

5.4 Birth and Death Processes

In this section we study a special type of continuous-time Markov chain where the transitions can occur only between adjacent states. That is, if $Q = [q_{ij}]$ denotes the transition rate matrix of the Markov chain, then for any state $k > 0$, we have

$$\begin{aligned} q_{k,k+1} &= \lambda(k) && \text{– Arrival (birth) rate in state } k \\ q_{k,k-1} &= \mu(k) && \text{– Departure (death) rate in state } k \\ q_{i,j} &= 0 && \text{– for } |i-j|>1 \end{aligned} \tag{4.1}$$

The rate at which the system moves out of state k is $-q_{kk} = [\lambda(k) + \mu(k)]$. The transition rate diagram for this system is shown in Fig. 5-6. Although we can analyze this system also using equations (2.15) and (2.17), it is instructive to approach the problem more directly.

In this system, an upward transition can only be caused by an arrival, the rate of which depends only on the current system state (and not on the amount of time for which the system has been in this state). Therefore, interarrival times must be exponentially distributed. By a similar argument, we find that the service-time distribution must also be exponential. Therefore, the probability of more than one arrival or service completion in a small time Δt is negligible (see Section 5.1.3). Furthermore, since the arrival and service processes are independent, the probability of an arrival and departure coinciding is also negligible. This system is therefore the classical M/M system. Now,

$$\text{Prob(one arrival in time } \Delta t | \text{ system in state } k) = \lambda(k)\Delta t,$$
$$\text{Prob(one service in time } \Delta t | \text{ system in state } k) = \mu(k)\Delta t,$$
$$\text{Prob(no arrivals/services in } \Delta t | \text{ system in state } k) = 1 - \lambda(k)\Delta t - \mu(k)\Delta t.$$

Let $P(n,t)$ denote the probability of finding n customers in the system at time t.[4] Then for $n \geq 1$, there are three ways for the system to be in state n at time $t + \Delta t$: (a) system is in state $n-1$ at time t, and an arrival occurs during time Δt, (b) system is in state $n+1$ at time t, and a service completion occurs during Δt, or (c) system is in state n at time t and no arrival or service completion occurs during Δt. Therefore, $P(n, t + \Delta t)$ can be expressed as follows:

$$\begin{aligned} P(n, t+\Delta t) &= P(n-1,t)\lambda(n-1)\Delta t + P(n+1,t)\mu(n+1)\Delta t \\ &+ P(n,t)[1 - \lambda(n)\Delta t - \mu(n)\Delta t] \end{aligned} \tag{4.2}$$

Rearranging terms and taking the limit as $\Delta t \rightarrow \infty$, we get

$$\begin{aligned} \frac{dP(n,t)}{dt} &= \lambda(n-1)P(n-1,t) + \mu(n+1)P(n+1,t) - [\lambda(n) + \mu(n)]P(n,t) \\ \frac{dP(0,t)}{dt} &= \mu(1)P(1,t) - \lambda(0)P(0,t) \end{aligned} \tag{4.3}$$

The above differential-difference equations describe the transient behavior of a M/M system. It is possible to write such equations without even going through the earlier steps. In the right-hand side of equation (4.3), the first two terms give the net rate at which the system enters state n, and the last one gives the net rate at which it moves out of state n. The difference is the rate of change in $P(n,t)$, which by definition is its time derivative. We shall use this approach in Section 5.5.6 for characterizing the output process of a M/M system.

Unfortunately, a solution to these equations, even when λ and μ are state-independent, is extremely complicated. Although we can avoid analytic complexity by solving these differential equations numerically, such an approach fails to provide an insight into the system behavior. Because of this, much of the performance analysis literature deals with steady-state solutions only, even though the transient behavior is often of great interest. In Section 9.5.2 we shall see how to partially overcome this limitation without leaving the domain of steady-state solutions.

To examine the steady-state solution, let us see under what conditions the present system will be ergodic. The only relevant properties in this regard are irreducibility and positive recurrence. Irreducibility requires that if $\lambda(n) > 0$

[4]Notice the change in notation from π to P. The latter is more common, and we shall use it from this point onward. The earlier use of π was intended to avoid confusion with transition probabilities.

only when $n_1 \leq n \leq n_2$, the same should hold for $\mu(n)$. A sufficient, but not necessary, condition for positive recurrence is as follows:

$$\exists k \, \forall n > k \, [\lambda(n)/\mu(n+1) < 1] \tag{4.4}$$

Intuitively, this condition states that if the system contains more than k customers, the traffic intensity $\rho(n+1) = \lambda(n)/\mu(n+1)$ falls below 1. This means that eventually the work can be handled faster than it arrives, and therefore an infinite accumulation of customers is avoided. Obviously, this condition is satisfied vacuously if we are dealing with closed (i.e., finite population) systems. This condition is not strictly necessary, because if for a finite number of states n with $n > k$, $\rho(n) \geq 1$, we could still have a stable system. However, in practice, such irregularities are unlikely to arise, and (4.4) can also be considered as necessary.

Henceforth, we assume that the ergodicity conditions are satisfied. Then under steady state, the derivatives in (4.3) must vanish, and we get a set of difference equations. These equations can be interpreted as *flow conservation equations*, since under steady state, the effective rate with which the system enters state n should be equal to the effective rate with which it exits state n. We can write such balance equations directly from the transition rate diagram of Fig. 5-6. It is convenient to assume that $\lambda(-1) = \mu(0) = 0$ and write one generic equation for all n. This is

$$\lambda(n-1)P(n-1) + \mu(n+1)P(n+1) = [\lambda(n) + \mu(n)]P(n) \tag{4.5}$$

The conservation law just mentioned can be stated in a more general form as follows: *For any closed boundary, the effective flow inward must equal the effective flow outward.* In obtaining (4.5), the boundary was chosen to contain only state n, but any other closed boundary will also do. In fact, by choosing the boundary properly, one can often come up with simpler balance equations. For example, if the boundary contains states 0 through $n-1$, we get

$$\lambda(n-1)P(n-1) = \mu(n)P(n) \tag{4.6}$$

which, compared with (4.5), is trivial to solve. The solution is

$$P(n) = \frac{\lambda(0)\lambda(1)\cdots\lambda(n-1)}{\mu(1)\mu(2)\cdots\mu(n)} P(0) \tag{4.7}$$

where $P(0)$ can be obtained using the requirement that all probabilities sum to 1. Once all the probabilities are known, various performance parameters (e.g., queue-length moments and average response time) can be computed easily. Obtaining response-time distribution is much more difficult, and is discussed later.

The equations obtained above are known as *global balance equations* (GBE). It will be seen in Section 6.1 that certain systems, including the present one, also satisfy *local balance equations* (LBE). Roughly speaking, a local balance equation considers transitions because of only one type of activity at a time. We shall see an example of this in Section 5.6.3, where the LBE's are obtained by considering only one stage of service at a time. Although the LBE's written this way will always satisfy the GBE's, we should ensure that they are all mutually consistent. If they are not, that means the system under consideration is not a local balance system (or the local balance equations were not identified correctly).

Before closing this section, we examine two special cases of equation (4.3). One special case arises when there is no service. This is called the *pure birth process*. If λ is state-independent, the resulting equations can be solved for $P(n,t)$, which turns out to be the Poisson process, as shown in Section B.2.1. Similarly, if there are no arrivals, and we start with a nonempty system, we get a *pure death process*.

5.5 Steady-State Analysis of M/M Systems

In this section, we derive detailed results for several important M/M systems. All results are based on the solution given in equation (4.7). This equation holds for any scheduling discipline that is work-conserving and independent of the service time requirement of the customers. Henceforth, we refer to such scheduling disciplines as SI. We now enhance our usual notation for queuing systems by adding three more parameters: scheduling discipline, storage capacity, and population. Storage capacity means the maximum number of customers allowed to be queued up (including those in service) at the station. Thus, the notation M/G/c/FCFS/K/N means Poisson arrivals, general service-time distribution, c identical servers, FCFS scheduling discipline, storage capacity of K, and population of N. We note that all results in this section can also be obtained by the operational analysis, as mentioned in Section 4.2.6. In the following, X denotes the random variable that gives the number of customers at the station under steady state.

5.5.1 Simple M/M/1/SI/∞/∞ Queue

This is the classical M/M/1 queue that we have already analyzed in Example 5.2. Here both $\lambda(n)$ and $\mu(n)$ are independent of the state n and are denoted as λ and μ. Let $\rho = \lambda/\mu$. For ergodicity, equation (4.4) implies that $\rho < 1$ and we assume this to be the case. Then equation (4.7) gives $P(n) = \rho^n P(0)$. Since all probabilities must sum to 1, we have $\sum_{n=0}^{\infty} \rho^n P(0) = 1$, which means that $P(0) = (1-\rho)$. Therefore,

$$P(n) = (1-\rho)\rho^n \tag{5.1}$$

That is, *in a simple M/M/1 system, the queue length distribution is geometric with parameter* ρ. Various performance parameters can now be obtained by using their definitions and the fundamental results derived in Section 4.2. For example, by the utilization law, the utilization works out to be ρ. This is also the average number of customers in service. Since we are dealing with a load-independent station, we can also use (4.2.10) to get the same result, as shown below. The queue length is obtained by its definition, response time by Little's law, etc.[5]

$$\text{Utilization } (U) = 1 - P(0) = \rho \tag{5.2}$$

$$\text{Avg. queue length } (Q) = E[X] = \sum_{n=1}^{\infty} nP(n) = \frac{\rho}{(1-\rho)} \tag{5.3}$$

$$\text{Avg. response time } (R) = \frac{E[X]}{\lambda} = \frac{1}{\mu(1-\rho)} \tag{5.4}$$

$$\text{Avg. number waiting } (L) = \sum_{n=1}^{\infty}(n-1)P(n) = Q - \rho = \frac{\rho^2}{(1-\rho)} \tag{5.5}$$

$$\text{Avg. waiting time } (W) = R - \frac{1}{\mu} = \frac{\rho}{\mu(1-\rho)} \tag{5.6}$$

$$\text{Queue-length variance } (\sigma_X^2) = E[(X - E(X))^2] = \frac{\rho}{(1-\rho)^2} \tag{5.7}$$

The waiting time W can also be obtained as Q/μ, since an arriving customer will find Q customers on the average, each one which requires $1/\mu$ units of service.

Fig. 5-7 shows the mean queue length (Q) and queue length variance (σ_X^2) as a function of ρ. Note that both of these parameters increase slowly at first, but beyond $\rho = 0.8$ the increase is very sharp. As expected, with $\rho \to 1$, both Q and σ_X^2 become unbounded. The coefficient of variation of the queue length is $1/\sqrt{\rho}$, which decreases with ρ and eventually approaches 1. It is clear that to get good performance, the system should not be loaded beyond about 70%. Put another way, if we want to provide good service to the customers (i.e., low response time), we cannot keep the server busy most of the time!

5.5.2 M/M/c/SI/∞/∞ Queue

This is the multiple-server extension to the system examined in the last subsection. An example of such a system is a homogeneous multiprocessor, where each processor picks processes to run from a common ready list. To analyze this system, we only have to choose $\lambda(k)$ and $\mu(k)$ properly, and then use equation (4.7). Here $\forall n, \lambda(n) = \lambda$, and

$$\mu(n) = \begin{cases} n\mu_\circ & \text{for } n < c \\ c\mu_\circ & \text{for } n \geq c \end{cases} \tag{5.8}$$

where $\mu_\circ$ is the basic service rate of the station. (For a discussion on equation (5.8) see Section 4.3.2 which introduces load-dependent stations.) Let $\rho = \lambda/c\mu_\circ$. Substituting for λ and $\mu(n)$ in equation (4.7) and simplifying, we get

$$P(n) = \begin{cases} \dfrac{\lambda^n P(0)}{\mu_\circ^n n!} = \dfrac{(c\rho)^n}{n!}P(0) & \text{for } n \leq c \\ \dfrac{\lambda^n P(0)}{\mu_\circ^n c! c^{n-c}} = \dfrac{(c\rho)^n}{c! c^{n-c}}P(0) & \text{for } n \geq c \end{cases} \tag{5.9}$$

[5]The reader is urged to review all the relationships developed in Section 4.2 and see how they apply here.

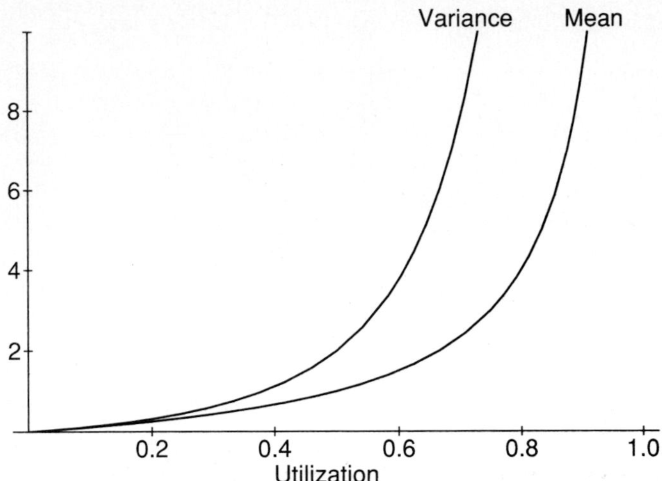

FIGURE 5-7: Mean and variance of queue length as a function of ρ.

By the utilization law, $U = \lambda/\mu_\circ = c\rho$; therefore, ρ can be interpreted as the utilization of each server. Notice that $0 \leq \rho < 1$. By summing (5.9) over all n, we obtain the following expression for $P(0)$.

$$P(0)^{-1} = \sum_{n=0}^{c-1} \frac{(c\rho)^n}{n!} + \frac{(c\rho)^c}{c!(1-\rho)} \tag{5.10}$$

It is also possible to get a compact expression for the queue length, and it is given by

$$Q = \sum_{n=1}^{\infty} nP(n) = \frac{(c\rho)^c \rho P(0)}{c!(1-\rho)^2} + c\rho \tag{5.11}$$

Other parameters could then be obtained by using their definitions and the fundamental laws. For example, the response time R is Q/λ. The average number of customers in service is the same as the average number of busy servers. This, by the definition in equation (4.3.3), is the same as the station utilization $c\rho$. This also means that

$$Q = L + c\rho \tag{5.12}$$

Dividing both sides by λ, we also get $R = W + 1/\mu$, as expected. The probability that all servers are busy, denoted $\mathcal{C}(\rho, c)$, can be verified to be

$$\mathcal{C}(\rho, c) = \frac{(c\rho)^c/c!}{(1-\rho)\sum_{n=0}^{c-1} \frac{(c\rho)^n}{n!} + \frac{(c\rho)^c}{c!}} \tag{5.13}$$

This formula is often known as *Erlang's C formula*.

It is interesting to compare the results for this case with the one where we have a single-server with rate $c\mu_\circ$. The question is whether a single CPU with a processing rate of $c\mu_\circ$ is better or worse than a multiprocessor system with c CPU's, each having the processing rate of $\mu_\circ$. Single-server has the advantage that the full processing power of the station can always be dedicated to serving customers. With multiple servers, if the number of customers present at the station is less than c, some servers will go idle. Thus, the average queue length, and hence the average response time, will be smaller for the single-server case. However, for a given scheduling discipline under heavy traffic, the coefficient of variation for the response time will be expected to be smaller for the multiple-server case because of better spreading of the service capacity among customers. Multiple servers, of course, have the reliability advantage too (assuming that the failure of one does not affect others).

5.5.3 Simple M/G/∞/SI/∞/∞ Queue

This is the *delay station* case discussed in Section 4.3.2. Again, the arrival rate is state-independent, and $\forall n > 0, \mu(n) = n\mu_\circ$. Substituting in equation (4.7), we get

$$P(n) = \frac{\lambda^n}{\mu_\circ^n n!}P(0) = \frac{\rho^n P(0)}{n!}$$

where $\rho = \lambda/\mu_\circ$. $P(0)$ can be computed by the requirement that all probabilities sum to 1. Since $\sum_{n=0}^{\infty} \rho^n/n! = e^\rho$, we have

$$P(n) = \frac{\rho^n}{n!}e^{-\rho} \tag{5.14}$$

Thus, the distribution is Poisson with mean ρ. Therefore, $Q = \rho$, and by the definition of utilization, $U = \rho$. Thus, we get the familiar result that the utilization is the same as the queue length for a delay station. Since there is no queuing at a delay station, we expect $R = 1/\mu_\circ$, and the application of Little's law gives us exactly this.

This system is about the only one where the transient solution is easy to obtain. This can be done by solving the first order differential equation in (4.3). The distribution turns out to be Poisson with mean $\rho(1 - e^{-\mu_\circ t})$.

The most important point to note about a delay server is that *the distribution of service time, other than the mean, is irrelevant*. That is why the heading for this subsection says M/G rather than M/M. Intuitively, this happens because there is no queuing and each arriving customer can act independently. It is possible to prove this result formally by analyzing a Semi-Markov process, embedded at departure points, that keeps track of the remaining service time of each customer.

5.5.4 Simple M/M/c/SI/K/∞ Queue

This is the finite storage case, where the system can hold at most K customers (including those in service). An arriving customer is rejected and discarded if the system is already full. Thus, $\lambda(n)$ can be defined as follows:

$$\lambda(n) = \begin{cases} \lambda_\circ & \text{for } n < K \\ 0 & \text{for } n = K \end{cases} \tag{5.15}$$

We also have c identical servers available at the station, each with the processing rate of $\mu_\circ$. Because of finite storage capacity, if $K < c$, the service rate will be limited by the storage capacity, and otherwise by the number of servers. That is,

$$\mu(n) = \min(n, c, K)\mu_\circ \tag{5.16}$$

$P(n)$ can now be obtained by substituting these definitions in equation (4.7) and simplifying. The details can be worked out easily, and are omitted. Note that this system has only $\min(c, K) + 1$ feasible states (unlike others considered until now, which all had an infinite number of states).

Finite storage situation occurs often in practice. For example, in a computer network, each node has only a certain amount of buffer space to hold incoming packets. If the packets arrive while all buffers are full, they may be dropped. This is known as *rejection blocking*, and this is what we analyzed in the above. However, other types of blocking are also possible. For example, in a manufacturing environment, if the input hopper of a machine if full, the previous machine may have to just stop until the finished part can be moved out. This is known as *production blocking*. We shall revisit blocking in Chapter 10.

If the storage capacity is no more than the number of servers, we have an interesting special case, known as the *loss system*. Because there is no queuing in a loss system, we can expect that the *results depend only on the mean service time*. Thus, the loss system that we analyze here can be denoted as M/G/K/-SI/K/∞. The loss system is commonly used in modeling telephone switching stations where the servers are the number of voice channels provided by the switch. Any caller to whom a voice channel cannot be assigned gets a busy tone and must hang up (i.e., be rejected). For a M/G/K/SI/K/∞ system, $\lambda(n)$ is given by equation (5.15), and $\mu(n) = n\mu_\circ$ for $n \le K$. Let $\rho = \lambda_\circ/\mu_\circ$ and $\psi(n) = \rho^n/n!$. Then from equation (4.7), $P(n) = \psi(n)P(0)$. Therefore,

$$P(0)^{-1} = \sum_{n=0}^{K} \psi(n) \quad \Rightarrow \quad P(n) = \psi(n) \Big/ \sum_{k=0}^{K} \psi(k) \tag{5.17}$$

Thus, the queue length distribution here is truncated Poisson. Notice that the M/G/∞ system considered earlier is the limiting case of this as $K \to \infty$. The probability that an arriving customer is rejected, denoted P^*, is given by

$$P^* = P(K) = \psi(K) \Big/ \sum_{n=0}^{K} \psi(n) \tag{5.18}$$

This is known as *Erlang's loss formula* or *Erlang's B formula*, and is useful in analyzing telephone switching systems. In this application, P^* is commonly referred to as the *blocking probability*.

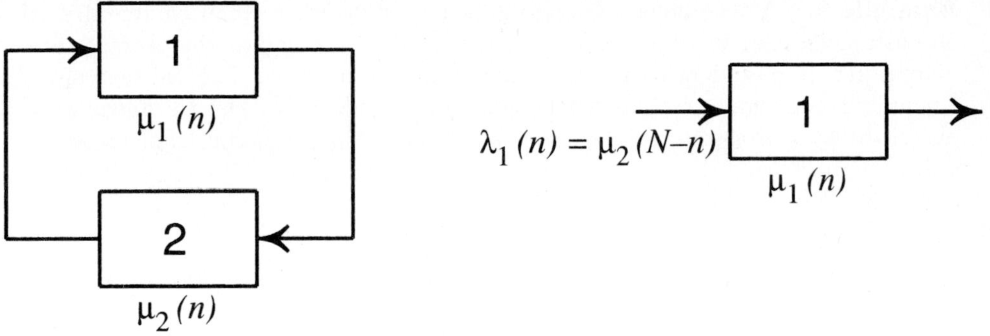

FIGURE 5-8: Equivalence between a closed network and an isolated station.

5.5.5 Finite Population Systems

Let N denote the total number of customers in the "universe" containing the service station of interest and n the number of customers present at the station. The key feature of finite population system is that the arrival rate λ depends on n; however, the exact nature of this effect depends on the underlying physical situation. Two useful models of the arrival process are as follows:

(a) Each customer has its own independent arrival rate ($\lambda_\circ$); therefore, the overall arrival rate is proportional to the number of customers left in the universe. That is, $\lambda(n) = (N - n)\lambda_\circ$

(b) The customers are released sequentially, one at a time, to the service station. In this case, the arrival rate remains constant as long as not all N customers have been released to the station.

As an example, consider a M/M/1/SI/K/N station with type (a) arrival model. Then $\mu(n) = \mu_\circ$ and

$$\lambda(n) = \begin{cases} (N-n)\lambda_\circ & \text{for } n < \min(N, K) \\ 0 & \text{for } n \geq \min(N, K) \end{cases} \tag{5.19}$$

The state probabilities and performance parameters could then be obtained from equation (4.7). Note that this system suffers from blocking if $K < N$.

An isolated station with finite population can be viewed as a closed network of two stations as shown in Fig. 5-8. Here the second station represents the arrival process from the universe. In particular, the arrival model (a) corresponds to the case where the second station is a delay station with average think time of $1/\lambda_\circ$ and model (b) to the case where the second station is a load-independent station with service rate of $\lambda_\circ$. The main significance of this equivalence is that *a two-station closed network model can be analyzed like an isolated station*, that is, by using equation (4.7).

Example 5.7 A telephone exchange is to be set up for a small community of 50 customers, each of whom independently attempts to call at the average rate of one per hour and talks for 12 minutes on the average. The call attempts (including reattempts by customers who get a busy tone) can be adequately described by a Poisson process. The telephone exchange has a capacity of K voice channels. Find the minimum value of K such that the probability of service denial is 2% or less.

Solution The system can be modeled as a M/G/K/SI/K/N system with $N = 50$. The arrival rate is given by equation (5.19) and $\mu(n) = n\mu_\circ$, where $\lambda_\circ = 1/60$ per minute and $\mu_\circ = 1/12$ per minute. Let $\rho = \lambda_\circ/\mu_\circ = 0.2$. From equation (4.7) for $n = 0, \ldots, K$, we have

$$P(n) = \rho^n \binom{50}{n} P(0)$$

Thus, the probability of a rejected call, $P(K)$, is given by

$$P(K) = \rho^K \binom{50}{K} \left[\sum_{n=0}^{K} \rho^n \binom{50}{n}\right]^{-1}$$

Setting $P(K) \le 0.02$ and solving the equation, we get $K = 14$. It may be noted that $P(K)$ decreases rapidly with K. Thus, $P(10) = 0.14473$, and $P(15) = 0.00815$. □

5.5.6 Output Process in M/M/c Queues

In this section we show that the output (or departure) process of a M/M/c/-SI/∞/∞ system is identical to its arrival process, i.e., it is Poisson with rate λ. Although we expect the mean output rate to be λ, the Poisson nature of the output process is somewhat surprising. Let D denote the random variable for the interdeparture time and let us choose the time origin just after some departure. Let $G_n(t)$ denote the joint probability that at time t there are n customers in the system and the next departure has not yet occurred. That is,

$$G_n(t) = Pr[X(t) = n \;\&\; D > t] \tag{5.20}$$

where the distribution of $X(t)$ is given by equation (5.9). Let $F_D(t)$ and $f_D(t)$ denote, respectively, the distribution and density functions of D. From equation (5.20),

$$Pr(D > t) = \sum_{n=0}^{\infty} G_n(t) \quad \Rightarrow \quad F_D(t) = 1 - \sum_{n=0}^{\infty} G_n(t) \tag{5.21}$$

To determine $G_n(t)$, we write a set of flow equations much like those in Section 5.4. To do this, we regard equation (5.20) as giving the probability of a "state". For $n > 0$, the flow equation is

$$\frac{dG_n(t)}{dt} = -[\lambda + \mu \min(n, c)]G_n(t) + \lambda G_{n-1}(t) \tag{5.22}$$

In this equation, the first term on the right-hand side is the total rate at which the system moves out of state n and the second term gives the total rate at which the system comes to such a state. The difference is the rate of change, which is the same as the derivative of $G_n(t)$. Similarly, for $n = 0$ we have

$$\frac{dG_0(t)}{dt} = -\lambda G_0(t) \tag{5.23}$$

To get a boundary condition for this differential-difference equation, note that by definition $G_n(0) = Pr[X(0) = n]$. That is, $G_n(0)$ is the probability that there are n customers in the system right after a departure. In other words, $G_n(0)$ is the departer's distribution. By using the stochastic versions of the arguments in Section 4.2.5 we can show that this distribution must be the same as the random observer's distribution given in Section 5.5.2. It is easy to show that (5.22) and (5.23) have a particularly simple solution, given by

$$G_n(t) = Pr[X(t) = n]e^{-\lambda t} \tag{5.24}$$

Now if we sum both sides of (5.24) over all n, the right-hand side becomes $e^{-\lambda t}$ because all probabilities must sum to 1. Therefore by equation (5.21), we get

$$F_D(t) = 1 - e^{-\lambda t} \tag{5.25}$$

That is, the interdeparture time is exponentially distributed. This, in turn, means that the departure process is Poisson.

The characterization of the departure process is important if we feed the output of one station to another, i.e., when we consider networks of M/M/c stations. Here the results are somewhat nonintuitive. If the network does not have any feedback, i.e., if customers cannot return to previously visited stations, the output processes of all stations are still Poisson, with mean rate dictated by the flow-balance requirement. However, if there are feedbacks, *the output stream from a station, that directly or indirectly receives any fed-back customer, directed to another station, is non-Poisson.* This output is not even a renewal process, since the successive interdeparture times are not identically distributed. *Yet, all output streams from any station to the external world are still Poisson and mutually independent*! Also, as we shall see in Section 6.2, the system behaves as if it consisted of a set of independent M/M/c stations. With closed networks, the situation is even more curious: None of the flows in the network are Poisson (because the customers do return to previously visited stations), yet, the system acts like a collection of independent M/M/c stations (except for a normalization constant).

For illustration, we prove only a simple result. Consider a M/M/1 system in steady state where the output is fed back with probability q, as shown in Fig. 5-9. We will show that the composite arrival process to the station is not Poisson, but instead a mixture of two exponentials. Yet, the departures to the external world remain Poisson. Obviously, in Fig. 5-9, the composite arrival rate $\lambda^* = \lambda/(1-q)$. Let $\rho = \lambda^*/\mu$ denote the utilization of the station. For ease of reference, let an arrival refer to external arrival, and an "input" to either

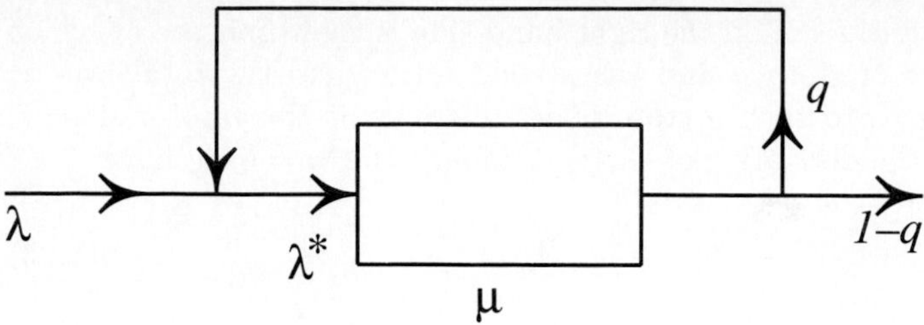

FIGURE 5-9: A M/M/1 station with feedback.

external arrival or feedback. Suppose that an input occurs at time τ, and denote the entering customer as $\mathcal{A}$. Let X denote the time from τ until the first feedback, if any, of the customers who have arrived by time τ (including $\mathcal{A}$ itself). The reason for excluding the arrivals after time τ is that we are only interested in the time period from τ until the first external arrival or feedback. Let X_n denote the conditional value of X, conditioned on the fact that there were n customers *just before* time τ. Let $P(n)$ denote the probability that $\mathcal{A}$ finds n customers in the system. Now if $\mathcal{A}$ is an external arriver, it will see the arriver's distribution, but if it is a fed back customer, it will see the departer's distribution. Since these two distributions are the same as that of a random observer, we have $P(n) = (1-\rho)\rho^n$ irrespective of where $\mathcal{A}$ came from. It follows that,

$$f_X(x) = \sum_{n=0}^{\infty}(1-\rho)\rho^n f_{X_n}(x) \tag{5.26}$$

Let us now see how to get $f_{X_n}(x)$. Since a customer that finishes service feeds back only with probability q, the number of service completions before a feedback, denoted $\mathcal{N}$, has a geometric distribution given by $Pr(\mathcal{N} = i) = (1-q)^{i-1}q$. Since the service time of each customer is exponentially distributed, the time needed for i services has i-stage Erlang distribution. Therefore, the density function of the time until first feedback can be obtained as

$$f_{X_n}(x) = \sum_{i=1}^{n+1}(1-q)^{i-1}q\frac{\mu^i x^{i-1}e^{-\mu x}}{(i-1)!} \tag{5.27}$$

where the upper limit is $(n+1)$ because we do not want to include any external arrivals after time τ. Since none of the existing $n+1$ customers may be fed back, we expect $f_{X_n}(x)$ to be a *defective density*, i.e., $\int_0^\infty f_{X_n}(x)dx < 1$.

By substituting (5.27) in (5.26) and simplifying, we find that X has a defective exponential distribution given by

$$f_X(x) = q\mu e^{-(\mu-\lambda)x} \qquad F_X(x) = \frac{q\mu}{\mu-\lambda}[1-e^{-(\mu-\lambda)x}] \tag{5.28}$$

Let Y denote the time from τ until the next input. Then

$$Pr(Y > y) = Pr(\text{No arrival in } y) \times Pr(X > y) = e^{-\lambda y}[1-F_X(y)] \tag{5.29}$$

Let $\alpha = q\mu/(\mu - \lambda)$. Then the last equation can be written in the following compact form

$$Pr(Y > y) = (1 - \alpha)e^{-\lambda y} + \alpha e^{-\mu y} \tag{5.30}$$

It is clear that $Pr(Y > y)$ is a linear combination of two exponentials, one due to arrivals, and the other due to service completions. That is, the overall arrival process (and hence the overall departure process) is non-Poisson. Now to prove that the departures to the external world are still Poisson, we can start with equation (5.20) with D now interpreted as the time until the next departure to the external world. This would result in the multiplier $(1 - q)$ for μ in equation (5.22). The final result still remains the same, i.e., the departures to the external world are Poisson with rate λ. The details are left as an exercise.

5.5.7 Response-Time Distributions

In this section, we briefly discuss the problem of determining response-time distribution for a M/M type of queuing system. The general approach is to pick a *tagged customer* and account for all the delays that it encounters from entry until exit. We shall illustrate this for a M/M/1/FCFS/∞/∞ system. Let $\mathcal{R}$ denote the response time of the tagged customer and X the number of customers that it finds on arrival. Then we can express the distribution function of $\mathcal{R}$ as follows:

$$F_{\mathcal{R}}(t) = Pr(\mathcal{R} \leq t) = \sum_{n=0}^{\infty} Pr(\mathcal{R} \leq t | X = n) Pr(X = n) \tag{5.31}$$

where the first term, henceforth denoted as $\mathcal{R}(n)$, is the response time of the tagged customer given that it finds n customers ahead of itself. Let $\mathcal{S}_i$ denote the service time of the ith customer (the tagged customer being the $(n+1)$-st customer). Then for $n > 0$, $\mathcal{R}(n) = \mathcal{R}_1 + \mathcal{S}_2 + \cdots + \mathcal{S}_n + \mathcal{S}_{n+1}$ where $\mathcal{R}_1$ is the remaining service time (or *residual life*) of the customer currently receiving service. Each $\mathcal{S}_i$ has exponential distribution with mean $1/\mu$. Because of the memoryless property of the exponential distribution, the distribution of $\mathcal{R}_1$ is the same as that of $\mathcal{S}_1$. Thus, $\mathcal{R}(n)$ is a sum of $n+1$ independent, identically distributed (iid) exponential random variables. (This also means that the case $n = 0$ does not need any special handling.) Therefore, the distribution of $\mathcal{R}(n)$ is $(n+1)$-stage Erlang. The term $Pr(X = n)$ is the arriver's distribution, which is the same as in (5.1). Let f denote the density function of $\mathcal{R}$. Then,

$$\begin{aligned} f_{\mathcal{R}}(t) &= \sum_{n=0}^{\infty} f_{\mathcal{R}(n)}(t) Pr(X = n) = \sum_{n=0}^{\infty} \left[\frac{\mu(\mu t)^n}{n!} e^{-\mu t} \right] (1 - \rho)\rho^n \\ &= \mu(1 - \rho)e^{-\mu t} \sum_{n-0}^{\infty} \frac{(\rho \mu t)^n}{n!} = \mu(1 - \rho)e^{-\mu(1-\rho)t} \end{aligned} \tag{5.32}$$

Thus, the response-time distribution is also exponential! The mean of this distribution is $1/\mu(1-\rho)$, as we might expect from equation (5.4). A similar analysis is possible for a M/M/c/FCFS/∞/∞ system also. The distribution is now a sum of two exponentials. The details are somewhat difficult and are omitted. The final expression is

$$f_{\mathcal{R}}(t) = \frac{\mu(\rho - 1 + \eta/c)e^{-\mu t} - (1-\eta)(\rho - 1)\mu e^{-(c\mu - \lambda)t}}{\rho - 1 + 1/c} \tag{5.33}$$

where $\rho = \lambda/(c\mu)$ and $\eta = 1 - (c\rho)^c P(0)/[c!(1-\rho)]$. One can use the same approach for other scheduling disciplines as well. In most cases, it is difficult to obtain explicit expressions, and it helps to switch to the Laplace transform domain. One could then obtain response time moments by differentiation in the usual way.

Response-time distribution is practically a very important output parameter, but quite difficult to compute in general. The first problem is that it depends on the details of the scheduling discipline, even though the mean response time is the same for all SI disciplines. An even greater problem arises when dealing with queuing networks. As discussed in the last section, internal flows in a network of M/M/c stations are not Poisson in the presence of feedbacks, *even though the queue length distribution can be obtained by considering each station in isolation.* This non-Poisson nature further complicates the computation of response-time distribution. In fact, there are no exact results available in the literature for general networks with feedback. In *feed-forward networks*, however, we can treat each station in isolation and compute the response-time distribution for it.

In a queuing network, we often want to compute the *flow-time distribution* (or first few moments of it). Flow time is defined as the total time needed to pass through a designated set of stations. For example, in a computer system model, we may wish to compute the distribution of the system response time, which is the same as the flow time through the central subsystem. Computing flow-time distribution is an even more difficult problem because of the possible dependencies between the response times of various stations. To see this, suppose that we are only dealing with nonpreemptive scheduling disciplines. Consider two stations i and j and two customers A and B. Suppose that A is served before B at station i. If A and B can take different paths from station i to station j, it is possible that at station j, customer A will be served *after* customer B. This overtaking makes the response-time distributions at stations i and j dependent, and the analysis becomes intractable. Thus, the only flow time results available in the literature are for *overtake-free networks* under FCFS discipline. Let us see the restrictions for such networks. First, such networks can allow at most one path from any station to any other. In other words, the network must look like a directed tree, often known as an *arborescent network*. Second, the internal stations of the network should have only single-servers; otherwise, overtaking is still possible. This is because customer A may finish before customer B at station i, and after customer B at station j, if station j were to be a multiserver.

To see the nonintuitive nature of the results, consider a network with three FCFS stations connected in series. Obviously, this network is arborescent. Suppose that the middle station (station 2) is a multiserver, thereby violating the above mentioned restriction. Let $\mathcal{R}_i$ denote the response time of station i. It can be shown here that $\mathcal{R}_1$ and $\mathcal{R}_2$ are independent, $\mathcal{R}_2$ and $\mathcal{R}_3$ are independent, but $\mathcal{R}_1$ and $\mathcal{R}_3$ are not! An even more curious situation arises when the middle station is also a single-server. In this case, all $\mathcal{R}_i$'s are independent, but if we considered waiting times (instead of response times), we lose the independence!

5.6 Batch Systems and Method of Stages

In this section we show that the analysis tools that we have developed until now also apply to systems more general than M/M systems. One generalization is batch arrivals and/or services, i.e., systems where several customers may arrive or get served as a group. This only involves allowing transitions to nonadjacent states, and is analyzed in Section 5.6.1. The second generalization is to allow those interarrival and service-time distributions that can be represented by a network of exponential stages. In each stage of such a distribution, the behavior is Markovian; therefore, we can construct a Markovian state transition diagram, obtain global balance equations, and solve them. This technique is usually known as the *method of stages* and is discussed in later subsections. The analysis here uses transform methods. We shall show in Section 9.5 that all these problems can also be solved using matrix analytic methods.

The method of stages is of practical importance because we can approximate any given distribution function $\psi(x)$ by a suitable distribution function based on the exponential distribution. Let us denote this approximate representation as $\psi^*(x)$. In practice, it is usually enough if $\psi^*(x)$ can match the mean and variance of $\psi(x)$, because the higher moments either do not affect the results very much or the distribution itself is not very reliably known. (Recall the difficulties in model calibration, as discussed in Section 4.5). Since a branching Erlang representation with k stages can provide any coefficient of variation larger than or equal to $1/\sqrt{k}$, $\psi^*(x)$ is commonly chosen to have branching Erlang (or one of its special cases, such as Erlang or hyperexponential) distribution.

5.6.1 Analysis of Batch Systems

In this section we briefly discuss how systems with batch arrivals or batch services can be analyzed. We note at the outset that the purpose of this section is only to illustrate standard solution techniques in the context of batch systems, rather than studying the batch systems per se. The book by Chaudhry and Templeton (1983) is an excellent reference on the analysis of batch systems.

Batch arrivals/services occur commonly in practice because it is often more economical to collect a number of items (orders, jobs, machine parts, etc.) before servicing them or sending them over to another service facility. In other situations, the arrivals may not actually occur in batches, but the arrival process may be bursty. In such cases, it is unrealistic to assume the arrivals to be Poisson, but it may be adequate to use the *batch-Poisson* model considered in this section (with the calibration parameters chosen according to the aggregate properties of the real arrival stream.) For the discussion that follows, it is convenient to define the notion of a "logical unit". For arrivals, a logical unit is a batch if the arrivals occur in batches; otherwise it is a single customer. The same applies to services. We shall assume throughout this section that the *arrival and service processes are Poisson in terms of logical units*. We shall also assume that the service station contains but one load-independent server and the scheduling discipline is FCFS.

We start with systems where the batch size is fixed. We can show that such systems are similar to the stage type of systems. (The assumption of single-server is essential here.) In particular, suppose that the arrivals occur in batches of size k, but the services occur singly with rate μ. We denote this system as $\mathrm{M}^{(\mathrm{k})}/\mathrm{M}/1$. We can view this situation differently as follows: Think of each batch as consisting of but one customer, except that this customer has to go through k sequential stages of service, each with rate μ. Under FCFS discipline, this customer will have the same service-time distribution as the k customers of a batch in the original system. Therefore, this batch arrival system is equivalent to a $\mathrm{M}/\mathrm{E_k}/1$/FCFS system, i.e., one where the arrivals are Poisson and the service-time distribution is k-stage Erlang. We shall analyze $\mathrm{M}/\mathrm{E_k}/1$/FCFS system in Section 5.6.2. Notice that this equivalence is only in terms of batches. It is also possible to relate the customer-level performance parameters of the two systems, as we shall see in Section 5.6.2.

Now suppose that the arrivals are Poisson with rate λ, but the server waits until k customers have arrived, and then serves them all as a single unit. We denote this system as $\mathrm{M}/\mathrm{M}^{(\mathrm{k})}/1$. This system is similar to the one where the service times are exponentially distributed but the interarrival times have a k-stage Erlang distribution. To see this, consider a Poisson arrival process with rate $k\lambda$ such that only every kth customer is admitted into the system. Then the net arrival rate to the station is λ, but we must have k arrivals before a service will take place. This is exactly the behavior of the batch service system. Thus, the batch service system is equivalent to the $\mathrm{E_k}/\mathrm{M}/1$/FCFS system discussed in Section 9.1. In the following we consider batch arrivals where the batch size is a random variable but the services occur singly. Such systems are often denoted as $\mathrm{M}^{(\mathrm{X})}/\mathrm{M}/1$ in the literature.

Suppose that the batch arrival rate is λ, and the batch size is a random variable denoted C. Let $\mathrm{Prob}(C = k) = c_k$. Services occur singly with rate μ. The state of the system is described by n, the number of customers present at the station. The transition rate diagram is shown in Fig. 5-10. Since services occur singly, backward transitions occur only to adjacent states and have the rate μ. The forward transitions from state n can occur to any state $n+k$, $k > 0$, and happen with rate $c_k\lambda$. It is easy to see from the transition diagram that for $n > 0$, the global balance equations are given by

$$\lambda \sum_{k=1}^{n} P(n-k)c_k + \mu P(n+1) = (\lambda + \mu)P(n) \tag{6.1}$$

and for $n = 0$ the equation is $\lambda P(0) = \mu P(1)$. Let $\Phi_C(z) = \sum_{n=0}^{\infty} z^n c_n$ denote the z-transform of the sequence $c_1, c_2, \ldots$. Also let $\overline{C} = \Phi'_C(1)$ denote the expected batch size and $\rho = \lambda/\mu$. Multiplying both sides of equation (6.1) by z^n and summing over all n, we get

$$\rho \sum_{n=1}^{\infty} z^n \sum_{k=1}^{n} P(n-k)c_k + \sum_{n=1}^{\infty} z^n P(n+1) = (1+\rho) \sum_{n=1}^{\infty} z^n P(n)$$

Let $\Phi(z)$ denote the z-transform of state probabilities. Changing the order of summation and replacing $n-k$ by n in the first term, and simplifying, we get

$$\rho \sum_{k=1}^{\infty} z^k \sum_{n=0}^{\infty} z^n P(n)c_k + \frac{1}{z}[\Phi(z) - zP(1) - P(0)] = (1+\rho)[\Phi(z) - P(0)]$$

Now recognizing the z-transforms and applying $\rho P(0) = P(1)$, we get

$$\rho\Phi_C(z)\Phi(z) + \frac{1}{z}[\Phi(z) - P(0)] = (1+\rho)[\Phi(z) - P(0)]$$

which simplifies to

$$\Phi(z) = \frac{(1-z)P(0)}{1 - z - \rho z(1 - \Phi_C(z))} \tag{6.2}$$

The unknown probability $P(0)$ can be obtained in several ways. One method is to use the fact that $\Phi(1) = 1$, which results from the requirement that all probabilities sum to 1. Another method is to use the utilization law, which must hold here because of homogeneous service. By definition, $1 - P(0) = U = \lambda_{\text{total}}/\mu$ where λ_{total} is the effective arrival rate to the station. Obviously, $\lambda_{\text{total}} = \overline{C}\lambda$, and hence

$$P(0) = (1 - \overline{C}\rho) \tag{6.3}$$

Let us examine the ergodicity condition at this point. Basically, we only have to ensure positive recurrence here, which requires that $P(0) > 0$. That is, the ergodicity condition is simply $\rho < 1/\overline{C}$.

We can now use the moment generation property of z-transforms to obtain queue-length moments from (6.2). This is possible directly when modeling a situation where the arrivals actually occur in batches. If the batch arrival model is used only to approximately account for the bursty nature of arrivals, we need to assume a form for the distribution of C with some unknown parameters, and then estimate these parameters using various performance measures. One simple and popular model in this regard assumes geometric distribution for batch sizes, i.e.,

$$c_k = (1-\alpha)\alpha^{k-1} \quad \text{for} \;\; k = 1..\infty, \; 0 < \alpha < 1 \tag{6.4}$$

For this model, it is easy to verify that

$$\Phi_C(z) = z(1-\alpha)/(1-\alpha z) \quad \text{and} \quad \overline{C} = \Phi'_C(1) = 1/(1-\alpha) \tag{6.5}$$

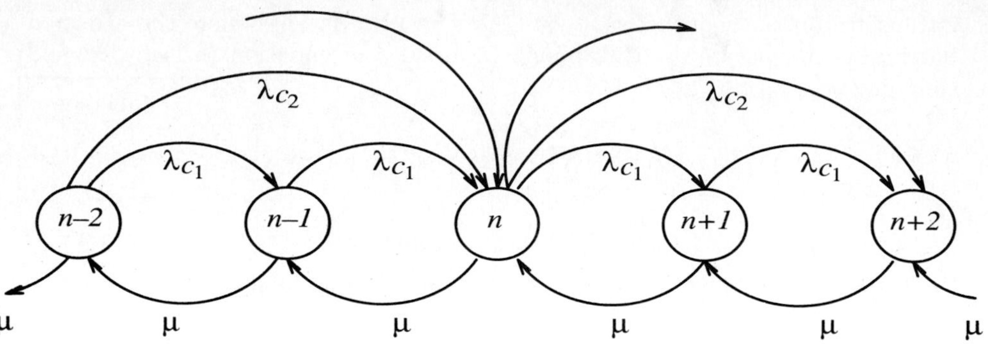

FIGURE 5-10: Transition-rate diagram for the batch arrival case.

The expression for $\Phi(z)$ then simplifies to

$$\Phi(z) = \frac{(1-\alpha-\rho)(1-\alpha z)}{(1-\alpha)(1-z(\alpha+\rho))} \tag{6.6}$$

which yields the following expression for the average queue length

$$Q = \frac{\overline{C}\rho}{(1-\overline{C}\rho)}\overline{C} \tag{6.7}$$

The main advantage of the geometric model is its simplicity. It has only one calibration parameter, α, that can be chosen appropriately to model the "batchiness" of the arrivals by matching the measured value of Q against the one computed by (6.7). We also note the similarities and differences between (6.7) and the queue length for a M/M/1 station given in equation (5.3). Note that under similar loading, $Q_{\text{batch}} = Q_{\text{expo}}\overline{C}$. That is, the queue length is now significantly larger. This is a result of the lack of orderliness in the arrival process.

Example 5.8 Consider a computer installation where a user may submit at most 2 jobs at a time. Let a batch of size 2 occur with probability q. Assuming that the batch arrival rate is λ and job service rate is μ, write the global balance equations and obtain an explicit expression for $P(n)$.

Solution Let n denote the number of customers in the system. A transition to state n can occur only from the states $(n-2)$, $(n-1)$, and $(n+1)$ with rates λq, λr, and μ, respectively, where $r = 1-q$. Therefore, we have the following global balance equations.

$$\mu P(1) = \lambda P(0) \qquad \text{(because } r+q=1\text{)}$$
$$\mu P(2) + \lambda r P(0) = (\mu+\lambda)P(1)$$
$$\mu P(n+1) + \lambda r P(n-1) + \lambda q P(n-2) = (\mu+\lambda)P(n) \qquad \text{for } n \geq 2$$

Let $\rho = \lambda/\mu$. The z-transform can now be obtained easily and works out to be

$$\Phi(z) = \frac{P(0)}{(1-\rho z - q\rho z^2)} \tag{6.8}$$

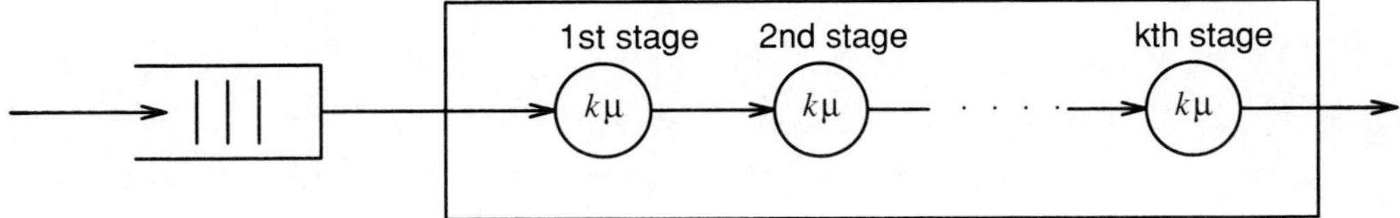

FIGURE 5-11: A k-stage representation of service-time distribution.

We could also obtain this directly from equation (6.2) by using $\Phi_C(z) = (1 - q) + qz$. To invert (6.8), we decompose the denominator into partial fractions. The quadratic equation $z^2 + z/q - 1/\rho q = 0$ gives $z = -a \pm \sqrt{b}$ where $a = 1/(2q)$ and $b = 1/(4q^2) + 1/(\rho q)$. Therefore,

$$\Phi(z) = \frac{P(0)}{2\sqrt{b}\rho q}\left[\frac{1}{(z+a+\sqrt{b})} - \frac{1}{(z+a-\sqrt{b})}\right]$$

Using the inversion formula $1/(z+\alpha) \rightarrow (-1)^n/\alpha^{n+1}$, we get

$$P(n) = \frac{P(0)(-1)^n}{2\rho q\sqrt{b}}\left[(a+\sqrt{b})^{-n-1} - (a-\sqrt{b})^{-n-1}\right]$$

$P(0)$ is trivial to get, as we have already seen in the general case. We have $P(0) = 1 - (1+q)\rho$, which means that the stability (or ergodicity) condition is $\rho < 1/(1+q)$. □

5.6.2 Staged Service with FCFS Scheduling

In this section we show how to analyze a system involving stage-type distributions by considering the example of a M/E$_k$/1/FCFS/∞/∞ queue, i.e., the one where the service time has a k-stage Erlang distribution. (We shall see in Section 9.2.2 that the same results also apply to a few scheduling disciplines other than FCFS). The k-stage Erlang system is shown in Fig. 5-11 where at most one customer is allowed to enter the "service box". Let the average service rate of the station be μ, which means that the service rate of each stage is $k\mu$. Then the system state can be represented by the pair (n, j) where n gives the total number of customers at the station and $j = 1..k$ is the stage in which the currently served customer is receiving service. Note that with $n = 0$, the stage of service is meaningless, therefore, it suffices to have only one such state. With this state description, the behavior of the system is Markovian, since the service time within a stage is exponentially distributed. The transition diagram is shown in Fig. 5-12. For $n > 1$, the global balance equations are as follows:

$$\begin{aligned}(\lambda + k\mu)P(n,1) &= \lambda P(n-1,1) + k\mu P(n+1,k) \quad \text{for } j = 1 \\ (\lambda + k\mu)P(n,j) &= \lambda P(n-1,j) + k\mu P(n,j-1) \quad \text{for } j > 1\end{aligned} \tag{6.9}$$

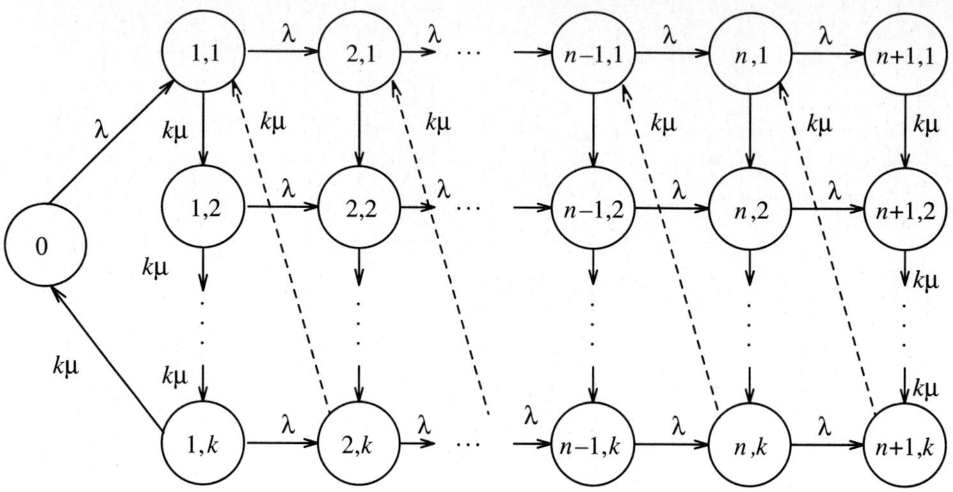

FIGURE 5-12: State transition diagram for Erlang service.

For $n = 0$ we have $\lambda P(0) = k\mu P(1,k)$, and for $n = 1$,

$$\begin{aligned}(\lambda + k\mu)P(1,1) &= \lambda P(0) + k\mu P(2,k) \\ (\lambda + k\mu)P(1,j) &= k\mu P(1,j-1) \quad \text{for } j > 1\end{aligned} \tag{6.10}$$

Let $\rho = \lambda/(k\mu)$. $P(0)$ can be found easily by the utilization law, i.e.,

$$U = 1 - P(0) = \lambda/\mu = k\rho \quad \Rightarrow \quad P(0) = 1 - k\rho \tag{6.11}$$

There are several ways to solve the system of equations (6.9). Note that we are only interested in the probability of finding n customers in the system, denoted $P(n)$. Obviously,

$$P(n) = \sum_{j=1}^{k} P(n,j) \tag{6.12}$$

One solution method is to use two-dimensional z-transform of $P(n,j)$, i.e.,

$$\Phi^*(y,z) = \sum_{j=1}^{k}\sum_{n=1}^{\infty} y^j z^n P(n,j) \tag{6.13}$$

This definition is somewhat different from the standard definition of z-transforms, because the upper bound of j is finite and the probability $P(0)$ has been left out. The first difference is out of necessity, the second, out of convenience. It really does not matter how one defines the z-transform as long as one can make a good use of it. Let $\Phi(z)$ denote the standard z-transform of $P(n)$. It is easy to see that

$$\Phi(z) \triangleq \sum_{n=0}^{\infty} z^n P(n) = P(0) + \Phi^*(1,z) \tag{6.14}$$

Thus, if we first find $\Phi^*(1, z)$, we can determine $\Phi(z)$. We omit the algebra and report only the expression for $\Phi(z)$.

$$\Phi(z) = \frac{(1 - k\rho)(1 - z)}{1 - z[1 + \rho(1 - z)]^k} \tag{6.15}$$

Differentiating $\Phi(z)$ and evaluating at $z = 1$, we get the average queue length

$$Q = \frac{k\rho[2 - \rho(k - 1)]}{2(1 - k\rho)} \tag{6.16}$$

Response time could then be obtained as Q/λ. Note that the *queue length is smaller than for a comparable M/M queue and decreases monotonically with k*. This is expected because as k increases, the randomness in the system decreases. In particular, as $k \to \infty$ with the utilization $U = \lambda/\mu = k\rho$ held constant, we get the following result for the deterministic service case:

$$Q_{\mathrm{M/D/1}} = \frac{U(1 - U/2)}{1 - U} \tag{6.17}$$

There are two other ways of solving (6.9), and it is instructive to look at them briefly. The first technique is quite general and applies in a number of other situations as well. Suppose that we define a set of *partial generating functions*, defined as follows:

$$\Phi_j(z) = \sum_{n=1}^{\infty} z^n P(n, j) \qquad \text{for} \quad 1 \le j \le k \tag{6.18}$$

Then equation (6.9) will give us a system of k linear equations in $\Phi_j(z)$'s. Since these equations involve z, they must be solved *symbolically*. Then we can get $\Phi(z)$ as

$$\Phi(z) = P(0) + \sum_{j=1}^{k} \Phi_j(z) \tag{6.19}$$

This technique will work whenever the second parameter (e.g., k in the $\mathrm{M/E_k/1}$ case) is finite. Here $\Phi_j(z)$ can be regarded as the z-transform of phase-dependent state probabilities and can be used to compute phase-dependent performance parameters (although these are not interesting in our $\mathrm{M/E_k/1}$ system).

The symbolic solution required by this method is expensive, but can be avoided if we are only interested in the first few moments of the queue length. The idea is to write expressions for the required moments (which will involve derivatives of $\Phi(z)$ at $z = 1$). However, there is one important point to note. Suppose that we start with the linear system $A(z)\mathbf{\Phi}(z) = b(z)$, where $A(z)$ is a $k \times k$ matrix, $\mathbf{\Phi}(z)$ is a $k \times 1$ vector of $\Phi_j(z)$'s, and $b(z)$ is also a $k \times 1$ vector. First let us consider the system $A(1)\mathbf{\Phi}(1) = b(1)$. Here $A(1)$ must be singular, because we do have the additional equation $\mathbf{e}^T \cdot \mathbf{\Phi}(1) = 1$, i.e., all probabilities sum to 1. However, using this additional equation, we can solve for $\mathbf{\Phi}(1)$. Now, differentiating $A(z)\mathbf{\Phi}(z) = b(z)$, we get

$$A(z)\mathbf{\Phi}'(z) \triangleq c(z) = b'(z) - A'(z)\mathbf{\Phi}(z) \tag{6.20}$$

Now a direct solution of the system $A(1)\mathbf{\Phi}'(1) = c(1)$ will fail because of the singularity of $A(1)$, so the approach is to first eliminate the $z - 1$ factor from both $\det[A(z)]$ and $c(z)$, and then let $z = 1$.

The final method exploits the fact that *every nonzero state in the model consists of exactly k phases*. This means that we could map the pair (n, j) to a single number m and then use ordinary z-transforms. We let $m = kn - (j - 1)$ for $n \geq 1$, and $m = 0$ for $n = 0$. With this mapping, m can be interpreted as the number of outstanding phases of service in the system. Each new customer brings k such phases, and each service completion in a stage reduces the number of phases by 1. The generating function under this view, denoted $G(z)$, is easy to compute and is given by:

$$G(z) \triangleq \sum_{m=0}^{\infty} z^m P(m) = \frac{(1 - k\rho)(1 - z)}{1 - z(1 + \rho) + \rho z^{k+1}} \tag{6.21}$$

Then $G'(1)$ gives the expected number of outstanding phases in the system, each of which will delay an incoming customer by $1/(k\mu)$ units. Therefore, the average waiting time W experienced by an incoming customer is $G'(1)/(k\mu)$. Since $R = W + 1/\mu$, by Little's law, the average queue length *seen by an arriver* is

$$Q = \rho G'(1) + k\rho \tag{6.22}$$

We shall show in Section 9.2.1 that the arriver's distribution is the same as the random observer's distribution for any M/G/1 queue. Therefore, equation (6.22) also gives the average queue length seen by a random observer.

It is easy see that the quantity m above would be the same as the number of customers present in a comparable batch-arrival system, i.e., a $\mathrm{M}^{(\mathrm{k})}/\mathrm{M}/1$ system with batch arrival rate of λ and the service rate of $k\mu$. (See introductory remarks in Section 5.6.1). Therefore, $G(z)$ above should be the same as the generating function for this batch system, say, $G_b(z)$. With state-independent arrivals and services the queue length distribution should depend only on the traffic intensity; therefore, $G(z)$ should also be the same as $G_b(z)$ for a system with batch arrival rate of λ/k and service rate of μ. This can be verified by substituting $\Phi_C(z) = z^k$ in equation (6.2). Thus, $G'(1)$ is the queue length for the batch arrival case and from (6.22) we have

$$Q_{\mathrm{M/E_k/1}} = \rho Q_{\mathrm{batch}} + k\rho \tag{6.23}$$

The important point to remember is that *the average queue length is not the same for* $\mathrm{M}^{(\mathrm{k})}/\mathrm{M}/1$ *and* $\mathrm{M/E_k/1}$ *systems*; the equivalence holds only at the batch level.

5.6.3 Staged Service with PS Scheduling

In this section we consider staged service under processor sharing (PS) discipline. The purpose of doing this is twofold: first, to illustrate that we now need a different definition of "state", and second, to show that this system has a very different, though rather simple, solution. We could again choose an arbitrary number of stages, but for simplicity, we shall consider a two-stage system. The two stages will be connected in series as before, but will have different service rates, denoted as μ_1 and μ_2 respectively. The arrival rate is still denoted as λ.

For a preemptive discipline like PS, the earlier view that the customers enter the box of Fig. 5-11 one by one must be changed. We now immediately admit an incoming customer into the box and let it proceed to stage 1. Because of the PS scheduling, this customer will immediately start sharing stage 1 with other customers in their stage 1 of processing. Let S denote the service time requirement of this customer at stage 1 (an exponentially distributed random variable with mean $1/\mu_1$). Thus, the customer will stay in stage 1 until it has received S units of service. It will then proceed to stage 2, where it is again served according to the PS discipline until it has received its stage 2 service requirement. We can now define the system state by the pair (n_1, n_2) where n_i is the number of customers in stage i. Since there is only one server, both stages cannot be active simultaneously. Therefore, because of equal sharing enforced by the PS discipline, stage i customers receive only $n_i/(n_1+n_2)$ fraction of the server. In other words, the effective service rate in stage i is $\mu_i n_i/(n_1+n_2)$. The global balance equation for a general state (n_1, n_2) is given by

$$\left[\lambda + \frac{n_1\mu_1}{n_1+n_2} + \frac{n_2\mu_2}{n_1+n_2}\right] P(n_1,n_2) = \frac{(n_2+1)\mu_2}{n_1+n_2+1} P(n_1,n_2+1)$$
$$+\lambda P(n_1-1,n_2) + \frac{(n_1+1)\mu_1}{n_1+n_2} P(n_1+1,n_2-1) \qquad (6.24)$$

Again, we could approach the solution in several ways. One is the recursive substitution, which will actually work in this case, but is hardly the right thing to do. The second method is to get two-dimensional z-transform. Notice that unlike equation (6.13), we now have a true 2-D transform since both n_1 and n_2 range from 0 to ∞. Define $\rho_i = \lambda/\mu_i$ for $i = 1, 2$. We omit the calculational details, and only report the final result, which is

$$\Phi(z_1,z_2) = \sum_{n_1=0}^{\infty}\sum_{n_2=0}^{\infty} z_1^{n_1} z_2^{n_2} P(n_1,n_2) = \frac{P(0,0)}{1-\rho_1 z_1 - \rho_2 z_2} \qquad (6.25)$$

where $P(0,0)$ can be obtained as $1-(\rho_1+\rho_2)$ either by using the requirement that $\Phi(1,1) = 1$ or the fact that $\rho_1+\rho_2$ is the station utilization. However, we should warn the reader of our extreme luck! Two (and higher) dimensional z-transforms are rarely so easy to get with only a few unknown parameters. In general, the z-transform may involve functions like $\Phi(z_1, 0)$ and/or $\Phi(0, z_2)$ on the right-hand side, which are not available directly. Finding expressions for these functions may require several advanced concepts from the complex variable theory.

The double transform in (6.25) can be inverted in two steps using the formulae in Appendix E. In the first step, we treat z_1 as a constant and thus invert the function $1/(a - \rho_2 z_2)$, where $a = 1 - \rho_1 z_1$. The result is $\rho_2^{n_2}/a^{n_2+1}$. In the second step, we invert with respect to z_1 and get the following result

$$P(n_1, n_2) = \left[\frac{(n_1 + n_2)!}{n1!n_2!}\right] \rho_1^{n_1} \rho_2^{n_2} P(0, 0) \tag{6.26}$$

The above method is included here only for illustration. Actually, we can solve the problem much more easily because this system satisfies local balance. Since we have not seen a precise characterization of local balance until now, here we only state an informal rule for writing the local balance equations for stage i while the system is in state (n_1, n_2): *Equate the total flow into stage i caused by an arrival to the total flow out of stage i due to a service completion.*

The flow into stage 1 due to an arrival is $\lambda P(n_1 - 1, n_2)$, and the flow out of stage 1 due to service completion is $P(n_1, n_2)\mu_1 n_1/(n_1 + n_2)$. We equate these two flows to get

$$P(n_1, n_2) = \frac{\lambda}{\mu_1} \frac{n_1 + n_2}{n_1} P(n_1 - 1, n_2) \tag{6.27}$$

Similarly, the total flow into stage 2 due to an arrival is

$$P(n_1 + 1, n_2 - 1)(n_1 + 1)\mu_1/(n_1 + n_2)$$

and the total flow out of stage 2 due to a service completion is

$$P(n_1, n_2)\mu_2 n_2/(n_1 + n_2)$$

We equate these two flows also, to get

$$P(n_1, n_2) = \left[\frac{n_1 + 1}{n_1 + n_2}\right] \left[\frac{n_1 + n_2}{n_2}\right] \frac{\mu_1}{\mu_2} P(n_1 + 1, n_2 - 1) \tag{6.28}$$

Substituting (6.27) and (6.28) into (6.24), we get the third equation

$$\lambda P(n_1, n_2) = \frac{(n_2 + 1)\mu_2}{n_1 + n_2 + 1} P(n_1, n_2 + 1)$$

which can be rewritten as

$$P(n_1, n_2) = \frac{\lambda}{\mu_2} \left[\frac{n_1 + n_2}{n_2}\right] P(n_1, n_2 - 1) \tag{6.29}$$

It is clear from equation (6.27) that

$$P(n_1, n_2) = \rho_1^{n_1} \frac{(n_1 + n_2)(n_1 + n_2 - 1) \cdots (n_2 + 1)}{n_1!} P(0, n_2)$$

Now from equation (6.29), $P(0, n_2) = \rho_2 P(0, n_2 - 1)$. By using this equation recursively, we get $P(0, n_2) = \rho_2^{n_2} P(0, 0)$. Thus, we get an expression for $P(n_1, n_2)$

that is the same as the one in equation (6.26). However, if we had not obtained (6.26) earlier by a different method, we still couldn't be sure whether the solution at this point is correct because we have not used (6.28), which could be an independent equation. Also, we used only a special case of equation (6.29). If the solution is to be valid, it must satisfy all these equations in general. It is easy to verify that our solution indeed has this property, and so (6.26) must be the only and correct solution. Now we note thc following things about our solution:

1. The solution is the same as for a two-chain M/M/1 system with μ_i as the service rate for chain i, and λ as the arrival rate for each chain. Actually, what we have obtained is the product-form solution for the two chain case, as we shall see in Section 6.2.3.

2. Let $P(n)$ denote the probability of finding n customers in the system. Then

$$P(n) = \sum_{n_1=0}^{n} P(n_1, n-n_1) = \sum_{n_1=0}^{n} \binom{n}{n_1} \rho_1^{n_1} \rho_2^{n-n_1} P(0,0) = \rho^n P(0,0)$$

where $\rho = \rho_1 + \rho_2$ is the overall utilization of the station. Thus, the overall distribution is the same as for a M/M/1 queue. In fact, it can be shown that the *PS discipline gives the same result with any service-time distribution that has a rational Laplace transform.*

5.7 Exercises

1. Prove that the only solution to equation (1.3) is the exponential function. [Hint: Subtract both sides of (1.3) from $Pr(T > t)$ and divide by τ. Then take the limit as $\tau \to 0$, and solve the resulting first order differential equation].

2. Prove properties (4) and (5) in Section 5.1.3. Let $N_i(t)$ denote the counting process for the ith stream and $N(t)$ for the combined stream. Let $\Phi_i(z)$ and $\Phi(z)$ denote, respectively, the z-transforms of the mass functions of $N_i(t)$ and $N(t)$. Using equation (B.3.2) and the convolution property, show that $\Phi(z) = e^{-\lambda(1-z)}$. To prove property (5), first show that

$$Pr[N_i(t) = n_i] = \sum_{n=n_i}^{\infty} Pr[N_i(t) = n_i | N(t) = n] Pr[N(t) = n] \qquad (7.1)$$

where the first term on the right-hand side is the binomial distribution $B(n, n_i, q_i)$ from equation (B.2.2).

3. Let $Y_1, Y_2, \ldots$ denote a set of iid random variables and let N be another independent random variable. Let $X = Y_1 + Y_2 + \cdots + Y_N$. Show that $E[X] = E[N]E[Y]$ where $E[Y]$ denotes the common mean of Y_i's.

4. Consider a discrete parameter Markov chain with the following transition probability matrix

$$Q = \begin{bmatrix} 1/2 & 1/4 & 0 & 1/4 \\ 1/3 & 0 & 1/3 & 1/3 \\ 1/2 & 0 & 1/4 & 1/4 \\ 0 & 0 & 1/2 & 1/2 \end{bmatrix}$$

Draw the state transition diagram for this chain and classify all four states (as transient, null recurrent, nonnull recurrent, or periodic). Is this chain ergodic? Suppose that the system is in state 1 initially. Compute the state probability vector $\Pi(t)$ for $t = 1$, $t = 2$, and $t = \infty$.

5. Show that if a discrete parameter Markov chain has a unique limiting distribution, then $\lim_{n\to\infty} Q^n = Q^*$, where Q^* is a matrix with all identical rows. Also show that $\Pi(\infty)$ forms the rows of Q^*. [Hint: $\Pi(\infty)$ must be independent of $\Pi(0)$].

6. Draw the state transition diagram and classify all the states of a discrete time Markov chain with the following transition probability matrix

$$Q = \begin{bmatrix} 0 & 1 & 0 & 0 \\ 0 & 1/2 & 1/2 & 0 \\ 0 & 0 & 0 & 1 \\ 1/2 & 0 & 0 & 1/2 \end{bmatrix}$$

Suppose that the process is in state 1 initially. Show by explicit calculations of limiting and stationary distributions that they are identical.

7. Consider a M/M/c/SI/24/∞ queuing system that represents the behavior of service windows in a bank. There are a total of six windows, but not all of them are always manned. All customers form a single queue. The mean interarrival time is one minute, and the mean service time per customer is four minutes. Let n denote the number of customers in the system. If $0 \le n \le 4$, only one window provides service. Whenever $n > 4$, another window is opened up, and whenever $n \le 4$, the extra window is closed down. Thus, for $5 \le n \le 8$, two windows are operational. The same happens for higher values of n; that is, for $9 \le n \le 12$, three windows will be open, and so on. Solve this system and determine the average queue length and the average number of open windows.

8. Consider the problem of selecting the number of dial-up ports to be provided on a computer system. The arrival process is Poisson with a rate of 20 users/hour. The mean connection time is 30 minutes. If all the ports are busy, an attempted dial-up is rejected. How many dial-up ports are needed to ensure a rejection probability of 5% or less?

9. Consider the closed queuing network model of a dedicated system shown in Fig. 5-13 with population 3. The service-time distribution at the CPU is exponential with mean 1, and at the disk it is two-stage Erlang with mean 1. Let the pair (n_2, j) define the state of this system where n_2 gives the number of customers in the disk queue and j gives the stage (=1 or 2) of service.

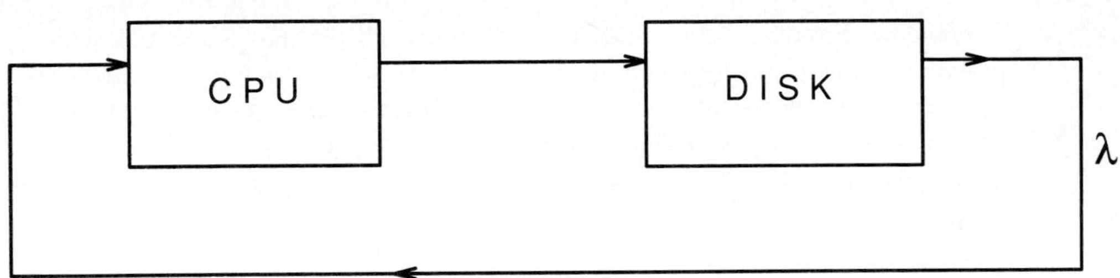

FIGURE 5-13: A model of a dedicated system.

(a) How many states does this system have? Draw the state transition diagram and write down the global balance equations.

(b) Solve the balance equations and obtain explicit expressions for state probabilities. Then compute the average queue length and the utilization of the disk.

(c) Find the throughput λ_{disk}. By applying Little's law to the entire network, find the response time of the CPU. Compute all other performance parameters for CPU and disk using the fundamental laws.

10. Complete the proof of the claim that in Fig. 5-9, the departures to the external world form a Poisson process.

11. Consider a $M/E_2/1/FCFS/3/3$ queuing system with mean arrival rate of 2/sec and the mean service rate of 4/sec. After serving one customer, the server takes a vacation with exponentially distributed time if and only if there are no waiting customers. The mean vacation time is 0.5 seconds.

    (a) Choose a suitable definition of system "state" and draw the complete state transition diagram.

    (b) Write down global balance equations considering boundary in a way that yields the simplest set of equations.

    (c) Solve the equations and obtain expressions for the probability of finding n customers in the system.

    (d) Using the throughput law, compute the system throughput. Also compute the average queue length and average response time of the station. What would be an appropriate definition of utilization in this problem?

12. Consider a $M/H_2/1/FCFS/\infty/\infty$ queue in steady state. Here H_2 means that the service-time distribution is two-stage hyperexponential. Let λ be the arrival rate, and μ_i the service rate of stage i ($i = 1, 2$). Suppose that the customer goes to stage 1 with probability of 0.5. Give an appropriate definition of the system state and draw the state transition diagram. Write down the global balance equations for the general state and solve them using z-transforms.

13. Reconsider Exercise 5.12 under PS scheduling discipline. Show that the global balance equations can now be split into local balance equations by considering flows into and out of each stage. Solve the local balance equations to get an explicit solution for the state probabilities.

14. This problem concerns some extensions to the batch arrival problem in Example 5.8. Suppose that the system can hold at most four jobs. Thus, when a new batch arrives, the system checks if there is room for it. If not, the entire batch is thrown away. Construct the state diagram and write down global balance equations for each state. Obtain expressions for the state probabilities.

Bibliographic Notes

Much of the material included in this chapter is classical in nature and can be found in most books on queuing theory. Excellent treatment of the subject is available in Kleinrock (1975), Trivedi (1982), Gross and Harris (1985), and to a limited extent in Kobayashi (1978). A concise compilation of most results may be found in Kleinrock (1976). Ross (1970, 1983) provide an in-depth mathematical treatment of renewal theory, classification of states of Markov chains, and many other topics not covered in this chapter. Disney and Kiessler (1987) contains a detailed discussion on the characterization of various traffic processes, including output processes of queuing systems. Our discussion in sections 5.5.6 and 5.5.7 is partly based on Gelenbe and Mitrani (1980), which provides an in-depth treatment of a number of topics in queuing theory. Chaudhry and Templeton (1983) is an excellent source for detailed treatment of batch systems. The introductory chapter in this text provides a concise compilation of results in basic queuing theory.

CHAPTER

6

Product-Form Queuing Network Models

In this chapter we start the study of product-form (PF) queuing networks. We first discuss several related properties that lead to the PF solution. These are local balance, reversibility, quasi-reversibility, station balance, and the $M \Rightarrow M$ property. We then derive the PF solution for single and multiple-chain networks. We consider both open and closed PF networks. Open PF networks are generally easy to solve, and the solution algorithms are given in this chapter. For closed PF networks, we only provide an overview and a classification of the solution algorithms. We also discuss multiple-class models, and show that if the capacities are chain-independent, multiple classes are trivial to deal with.

6.1 Characterization of Product-Form Solution

Consider a queuing network with M stations, such that $\mathcal{S}_i$ describes the state-space of the ith station. Then a network state is given by $\mathbf{s} = \{s_i \in \mathcal{S}_i, 1 \leq i \leq M\}$. Now if the transitions between the network states can be described by a Markov process, the standard techniques discussed in Chapter 5 still apply, but several difficulties arise. If the network is open, we would require multi-dimensional z-transforms, which are rarely easy to work with. If the network is closed, the number of states will usually be too large to allow a direct solution of global balance equations. A related problem is that a numerical solution, even if feasible, gives little insight into the workings of the systems and makes it difficult to ask "what if" types of questions. Therefore, it is important to study a special class of queuing network models where we can obtain an explicit symbolic solution. This solution turns out to be in the form of a product of the terms corresponding to each station, and we call such queuing networks *product-form networks*. Although the class of queuing networks having product-form solutions is by itself rather limited, it is often possible to account for non-product-form features approximately and still retain the simplicity of product-form solutions. This allows acceptable modeling of several features of real systems. Such extended applications make the study of product-form networks especially important.

6.1.1 Local Balance and Product-Form Solution

The key to product-form solution is local balance, a property that we mentioned briefly in Section 5.6.3. Here we provide a more precise characterization of this important property and show how it leads to product-form solution.

Consider a queuing network with M stations and K chains. Let n_{ir} denote the number of chain r customers at station i and let $\mathbf{n}_i = (n_{i1}, \ldots, n_{iK})$ denote the occupancy vector at station i. Then for product-form networks, it is adequate to represent the system state by the vector $(\mathbf{n}_1, \ldots, \mathbf{n}_M)$. Let e_{ir} denote a *unit vector* in the $M \times K$ two-dimensional state space of the system. That is, if we let e_r denote a vector of size K that has a 1 in rth place and zeros elsewhere, $e_{ir} = (\mathbf{0}, \ldots, \mathbf{0}, e_r, \mathbf{0}, \ldots, \mathbf{0})$, where e_r appears in the ith position and $\mathbf{0}$ is a vector of K zeros. Let S and S' denote a pair of *adjacent states*, i.e., in an open system, $S = S' + e_{ir}$ and in a closed system $S = S' + e_{ir} - e_{jr}$ for some station $j \neq i$. The difference in the definitions results because in a closed system the new customer must have come from another station j. Let $\mu_{ir}(S)$ denote the departure rate of chain r customers from station i in state S. Similarly, let $a_{ir}(S')$ denote the total rate with which chain r arrivals to station i bring the system to state S. Under local balance, $P(S)$, the probability of finding the system in state S can be expressed as follows.

$$\mu_{ir}(S) \times P(S) = a_{ir}(S') \times P(S') \tag{1.1}$$

That is, the effective rate at which the system leaves state S due to the service completion of a chain r customer at station i, equals the effective rate at which the system enters state S due to an arrival of chain r customer to station i. In contrast, global balance is characterized by the property that the total flow into a state equals the total flow out of that state. It is important to note that local balance *does not* necessarily say that the effective flow rate from S to S' equals the effective rate in the opposite direction. To see this, note that following a service completion in state S, the finished customer may go to any one of the other $M - 1$ stations (or to the outside world in an open system). Each such possibility will lead the system to a different state. However, μ_{ir} in equation (1.1) is merely the total departure rate due to the service completion of a chain r customer at station i. Similarly, a_{ir} is the total rate with which the system moves into state S due to the arrival of a chain r customer to station i; we do not care which station this chain r customer is coming from. In a closed network, even though S' is defined as $S - e_{ir} + e_{jr}$, the station index j only acts as a reference point and can be chosen arbitrarily. For example, nothing will change if we choose station j such that a chain r customer exiting from station j has zero probability of being routed to station i directly! These aspects will be clearer later when we actually derive local balance equations for open and closed product-form networks.

In the above we considered the simple multiple-chain case for illustration. We can similarly define local balance for a number of other situations. In the single-chain case, the local balance equations reduce to

$$\mu_i(S) \times P(S) = a_i(S') \times P(S') \tag{1.2}$$

where S and S' now only give the number of customers at each station. In general, each chain passing through station i could consist of several classes. For this case, the state description should specify the number of customers of each class of each chain at the station. Let S and S' be two adjacent states such that an arrival of class c customer of chain r takes the station from state S' to state S. In this case, we can generalize equation (1.1) as follows:

$$\mu_{irc}(S) \times P(S) = a_{irc}(S') \times P(S') \tag{1.3}$$

where $\mu_{irc}(S)$ denotes the departure rate of class c, chain r customers from station i in state S, and $a_{irc}(S')$ is the rate at which the system enters the state S due to the arrival of a class c, chain r customer to station i.

With certain scheduling disciplines, local balance can be shown to hold even when the service-time distribution is represented by a network of exponential stages. In such cases, the state description would include the stage of service of each customer (or the number of customers in each stage). Then the local balance equation becomes

$$\mu_{ircl}(S) \times P(S) = a_{ircl}(S') \times P(S') \tag{1.4}$$

where μ_{ircl} denotes the flow out of stage l due to the departure of a class c, chain r customer while the system is in state S, and a_{ircl} denotes the flow into stage l that brings the system to state S due to a class c, chain r arrival. We used a special case of such equations in Section 5.6.3.

If local balance holds, the solution assumes a simple product-form. For example, consider a single-chain, single-class closed network with exponentially distributed service times. Let $\mu_i(n)$ denote the service rate of station i at load n. Recall from Section 4.3.2, that $\mu_i(n)$ can be expressed as $\mu_i^\circ C_i(n)$ where $C_i(n)$ is the capacity function for station i. Let v_i be the visit ratio of station i, and $u_i = v_i/\mu_i^\circ$ the relative utilization. Finally, let

$$V_i(n) = \prod_{j=1}^{n} C_i(j) \tag{1.5}$$

We shall show in Section 6.3 that local balance yields the following solution

$$P(n_1, \ldots, n_M) = \frac{1}{G} \prod_{i=1}^{M} \frac{u_i^{n_i}}{V_i(n_i)}$$

where n_i denotes the number of customers at station i, and G is the *normalization constant* to ensure that all probabilities sum to 1. From equation (5.4.7), the ith product term in the above equation can be seen to be proportional to the probability of finding n_i customers at station i when station i is considered in isolation. Thus, the network-state probability can be obtained (up to a multiplicative constant) by multiplying together the state probabilities for each station in isolation. In later sections we shall see the same result for more general networks. Thus, *local balance yields a solution with the product-form property.* For scheduling disciplines that do not distinguish customers on the basis of their chain/class affiliation (e.g., nonpriority disciplines), it is possible to show the opposite; i.e., product-form implies local balance. Also, no priority disciplines leading to the product-form solution are known, and probably none exist. Because of this, *we shall use local balance and product-form interchangeably.*

Local balance is related to a number of other concepts explored in the literature. One such concept is the $M \Rightarrow M$ property. An open queuing system is said to have the $M \Rightarrow M$ property, if feeding it with independent Poisson arrival streams results in independent Poisson departure streams. It can be shown that if each station in a queuing network has the $M \Rightarrow M$ property, the network has a product-form solution. Furthermore, if the network is open or mixed, it itself has the $M \Rightarrow M$ property. It can be shown that if a station satisfies local balance, it must have $M \Rightarrow M$ property. The opposite also holds for nonpriority disciplines. Thus, local balance and $M \Rightarrow M$ can be considered as equivalent properties.

Reversibility and quasi reversibility are other related concepts, which we shall study in some detail shortly. We shall show that both of these concepts lead to product-form solution. The main virtue of these concepts is that they lead to simple proofs of properties that may otherwise require considerable effort.

As one might expect, every SI scheduling discipline under exponentially distributed service times yields local balance. However, there are certain SI disciplines, usually known as *symmetric disciplines*, that yield local balance irrespective of the nature of the service-time distribution. Such disciplines can be described as follows: Suppose that we mark each queue position at the station and keep track of the *category* (i.e., the class within a chain) of the customer waiting there (if any). Then symmetry means that the rate with which a customer at any given queue position receives service is proportional to the probability that a customer of the corresponding category will arrive at that position.[1]

Let us see a more precise characterization of symmetric disciplines for single-chain, single-class systems. Suppose that we number queue positions (starting from the head of the queue) as $1, 2, \ldots, n$ while there are n customers at a service station. Let $\phi(l, n)$ denote the fraction of service capacity dedicated to

[1] The term *station balance* has also been used in the literature to described this situation.

a customer in position l while n customers are present. Let $\psi(l,n)$ denote the probability that if a customer arrives while there are n customers already at the station, it will be placed in position $l \in \{1 .. n+1\}$ (by shifting others, if necessary). A scheduling discipline is called symmetric if it is possible to characterize it in such a way that the following equation is satisfied.

$$\phi(l, n+1) = \psi(l, n) \tag{1.6}$$

Note that the use of n instead of $n+1$ on the LHS is necessary because the placement of the new customer will result in a total of $n+1$ customers.

As an example, the PS discipline can be characterized as follows: Since the server is shared equally among all customers, we have $\phi(l, n+1) = 1/(n+1)$ for all l. If we view PS as the idealization of the round-robin discipline, we would put an incoming customer at the "tail end of the queue", which would mean that $\psi(n+1, n) = 1$. However, as the time slice shrinks down to zero, it really does not matter where we put an incoming customer. Thus, *we can choose* $\psi(l,n) = 1/(n+1)$, which means that an incoming customer is equally likely to be placed in any one of the $n+1$ positions. It follows that we can describe the PS discipline in a way that equation (1.6) is satisfied. With FCFS discipline, $\phi(1, n+1) = 1$, since only the customer at the head of the queue gets served. Also, we must choose $\psi(n+1, n) = 1$, which means that equation (1.6) cannot be satisfied. (Exercise 6.5 explores a similar description of other scheduling disciplines.)

It is possible to show a number of interesting results concerning symmetric disciplines (albeit under the assumption of a particular algebraic form of the solution):

1. Symmetric discipline (or station balance) implies local balance.
2. The steady-state probabilities depend only on the mean of the service-time distribution, and not on its higher moments. This property is often known as the *insensitivity property* of product-form networks.
3. product-form solution under nonexponential service-time distribution implies station balance. That is, the symmetric disciplines are the only ones that give product-form solution under nonexponential service!
4. A symmetric discipline must start serving a customer as soon as it enters the system. Thus, none of the nonpreemptive scheduling disciplines will yield a product-form solution under non-exponential service-time distribution.

Because of the above results, the class of networks with station balance is the same as the one with local balance under nonexponential service-time distributions. The same is true with exponential service times if the mean service time depends on the class/chain. However, if all classes and chains have identical exponential distribution, any SI discipline will yield local balance, even if it does not satisfy station balance. That is, *station balance is sufficient but not necessary for local balance.*

It can be shown that under some mild restrictions, all symmetric disciplines can be characterized by a single concrete discipline, known as *last batch processor sharing* (LBPS). In this discipline, every incoming job is assigned a "batch number", and the batches are scheduled according to LCFSPR (last come first served, with preemptive resume) discipline. That is, if batch i is currently in service, and a batch $j \neq i$ job arrives, the service for batch i is preempted and batch j goes into service. The resumption occurs according to the LCFS discipline. All jobs within a batch are scheduled according to processor sharing (PS) discipline. LBPS reduces to PS if there is only one batch, and reduces to LCFS if each job is a batch by itself.

6.1.2 Reversible Markov Processes

To understand the concept of reversibility intuitively, suppose that we make a film of the behavior of an isolated service station and then run the film backward. The departing customers in the real system will be seen as arrivers in the backward run, and vice versa. Let $X(t)$ denote the random process describing the number of customers at the station, and $X_b(t)$ the corresponding process in the backward run of the film. Then if $X_b(t)$ and $X(t)$ are statistically identical, we say that $X(t)$ is reversible. More formally, we can define the concept as follows:

> A random process $X(t)$ is reversible, if for any finite sequence of time instants $t_1, \ldots, t_k$ and a parameter τ, the joint distribution of $X(t_1), \ldots, X(t_k)$ is the same as that of $X(\tau - t_1), \ldots, X(\tau - t_k)$.

An example of a reversible system is the classical M/M/c queue. One way to see this is to recall that the departure process of a M/M/c system is Poisson with the same rate, and hence the reversed system will be indistinguishable from the original system. An example of a nonreversible system is a M/M/1 queue with batch arrivals. Clearly, the departures do not occur in batches in such a system, and hence the system could not be reversible.

A reversible random process must be stationary, since by definition, $X(\tau + t_1), \ldots, X(\tau + t_k)$ has the same distribution as $X(-t_1), \ldots, X(-t_k)$, which again, by definition, has the same distribution as $X(t_1), \ldots, X(t_k)$. That is, all joint distributions are independent of time shifts, as required for stationarity. This property means that we cannot hope to characterize transient behavior of Markovian systems using reversibility.

Reversible Markov processes can be characterized by an important property known as *detailed balance*.

Lemma 6.1 Let $X(t)$ be a stationary, discrete parameter Markov chain with $Q = [q(i,j)]$ as its one-step transition probability matrix. If $X(t)$ is reversible, then its state probabilities $P(i)$'s satisfy the following detailed balance equation

$$P(i)q(i,j) = P(j)q(j,i) \tag{1.7}$$

Conversely, if we can find probabilities $P(i)$'s with $\sum_{\forall i} P(i) = 1$ satisfying (1.7), then $X(t)$ is reversible and $P(i)$'s form its stationary distribution.

Proof For brevity, let us denote the event $X(t) = i$ as simply (t, i). Suppose that $X(t)$ is reversible, and consider the joint probability of events (t, i) and $(t+1, j)$ at $t = n$. Since $X(t)$ is stationary and Markovian, for any n, we have

$$\begin{aligned} Pr[(n,i),(n+1,j)] &= Pr[(n,i)]Pr[(n+1,j)|(n,i)] \\ &= P(i)q(i,j) \end{aligned} \tag{1.8}$$

Now by using $\tau = 2n + 1$ in the definition of reversibility, we conclude that $Pr[(n,i),(n+1,j)] = Pr[(n,j),(n+1,i)]$. Like equation (1.8), the latter probability can be expressed as $P(j)q(j,i)$, and we have the proof.

For the converse, suppose that (1.7) holds. By summing over all j, we get the global balance equations $P(i) = \sum_{\forall j} P(j)q(j,i)$. Therefore, by equation (5.2.8), $P(i)$'s form the stationary distribution of $X(t)$. Let $i_0, \ldots, i_k$ be some set of states. By using equation (1.7) recursively for this set of states, we can conclude that

$$P(i_0)q(i_0,i_1)\cdots q(i_{k-1},i_k) = P(i_k)q(i_k,i_{k-1})\cdots q(i_1,i_0) \tag{1.9}$$

However, for any time instant $t = n$, by the definition of conditional probability, we have [see equations (B.1.2) and (B.1.3)]

$$\begin{aligned} &Pr[(n,i_0),\ldots,(n+k,i_k)] \\ &\quad = P(i_0)Pr[(n+1,i_1),\ldots,(n+k,i_k)|(n,i_0)] \\ &\quad = P(i_0)Pr[(n+1,i_1)|(n,i_0)]Pr[(n+2,i_2),\ldots|(n,i_0),(n+1,i_1)] \\ &\quad = P(i_0)q(i_0,i_1)Pr[(n+2,i_2),\ldots,(n+k,i_k)|(n+1,i_1)] \end{aligned}$$

where we have used the Markovian property of $X(t)$ in the last two steps. Therefore, by induction we get the left-hand side of (1.9), i.e.,

$$Pr[(n,i_0),\ldots,(n+k,i_k)] = P(i_0)q(i_0,i_1)\cdots q(i_{k-1},i_k)$$

Similarly, the right-hand side of (1.9) can be shown to be $Pr[(n',i_k),\ldots,(n'+k,i_0)]$ for any n'. That is,

$$Pr[(n,i_0),\ldots,(n+k,i_k)] = Pr[(n',i_k),\ldots,(n'+k,i_0)]$$

Substituting $n' = \tau - (n+k)$ in the right-hand side, we get

$$Pr[(n,i_0),\ldots,(n+k,i_k)] = Pr[(\tau-n,i_0),\ldots,(\tau-n-k,i_k)]$$

This equation is almost the definition of reversibility except that the time instants $n, n+1, \ldots$ are consecutive (instead of being arbitrary). This, however, is not a problem since we can remove the term for any time instant $n+j, 0 \le j \le k-1$ by summing over all values of i_j. Thus, we have the result. □

Using (5.2.18), which relates discrete and continuous parameter Markov chains, it is easy to see that *Lemma 6.1 applies to continuous parameter chains as well if we interpret $q(i,j)$'s as the transition rates*. We also have the following interesting result.

Corollary 6.1 A Markov process is reversible if and only if its Q matrix can be written as the product $D \times A$ where D is a diagonal matrix of $1/P(i)$'s and A is a symmetric matrix.

Proof From equation (1.7), $q(i,j) = a_{ij}/P(i)$ where a_{ij} is a constant such that $a_{ij} = a_{ji}$. The result then follows. □

We can also obtain another interesting result, known as the *Kolmogorov criterion*.

Lemma 6.2 (Kolmogorov criterion). A stationary Markov chain is reversible if and only if for every finite sequence of states $i_0, \ldots, i_k$ the transition probabilities (or rates in the continuous parameter case) satisfy the following equation

$$q(i_0,i_1)q(i_1,i_2)\cdots q(i_{k-1},i_k)q(i_k,i_0) = q(i_k,i_{k-1})q(i_{k-1},i_{k-2})\cdots q(i_1,i_0)q(i_0,i_k) \qquad (1.10)$$

Proof Suppose that the chain is reversible. Multiplying both sides of equation (1.9) by $q(i_k, i_0)$, and applying (1.7) once more, we get (1.10).

For the converse, let us multiply both sides of (1.10) by $P(i_0) \triangleq Pr[(n, i_0)]$. Because of the Markovian property, the left-hand side can be expressed as (see the second part of the proof of Lemma 6.1)

$$Pr[(n,i_0),\ldots,(n+k,i_k),(n+k+1,i_0)]$$

whereas the right-hand side becomes

$$Pr[(n',i_0),(n'+1,i_k),\ldots,(n'+k,i_1),(n'+k+1,i_0)]$$

Therefore by choosing $n' = \tau - (n+k+1)$, we find that the equality of the last two equations implies reversibility. □

Lemma 6.1 can also be exploited to obtain results when the transition rates of a reversible Markov chain are altered. First, it is obvious that if both $q(i,j)$ and $q(j,i)$ are multiplied by the same constant, nothing is changed. However, a more interesting result is as follows:

Lemma 6.3 Let A be a subset of the set of all states S, and suppose that we multiply all $q(i,j)$'s where $i \in A$, $j \in \{S - A\}$ by a constant c. Then the state probabilities for the resulting system, denoted $P'(i)$'s, are given as follows:

$$P'(i) = \begin{cases} \delta P(i) & \text{if } i \in A \\ \delta c P(i) & \text{if } i \in S - A \end{cases} \qquad (1.11)$$

where δ is the normalizing constant to ensure that all probabilities sum to 1.

Proof Because of equation (1.7), the probability of any state i can be expressed as a product of $P(0)$ and the ratios of forward and backward transition probabilities (or rates) along any simple path from state 0 to state i. It is then easy to see that multiplying the forward probabilities (or rates) along the boundary separating A from $S - A$ would result in equation (1.11). □

If in Lemma 6.3 we choose $c = 0$, we effectively truncate the state space from S to A. This *truncated chain* is still reversible and its state probabilities become $\delta P(i)$, i.e., a simple renormalization of the original state probabilities. However, we must choose the set A in this case such that the truncated chain remains irreducible.

Let us now reexamine the detailed balance condition in equation (1.7). It states that *for a Markov chain to be reversible, for any pair of states i and j, either there should be transitions in both directions or neither*. If $X(t)$ represents the state of a queuing system, detailed balance also implies local balance. However, local balance does not require transitions in both directions between a pair of states, and thus *local balance does not imply detailed balance*. Also, though the local balance is described in terms of single arrivals and departures (as we did in Section 6.1.1), no such requirement applies to detailed balance. That is, it is possible to have detailed balance even when the transitions can occur between nonadjacent states. We note here that in the literature, detailed balance is sometimes used as a synonym for local balance, but we do not take this approach.

We now examine the reversed process $X(\tau - t)$ corresponding to an arbitrary stationary Markov process $X(t)$. This is often useful in proving reversibility and characterizing the departure process from a queue. The next lemma applies to both continuous and discrete parameter chains; therefore, we state it in general terms.

Lemma 6.4 Let $X(t)$ denote an ergodic Markov chain with transition matrix Q. Then $X(\tau - t)$ has the same stationary distribution as $X(t)$. Also let $Q^* = [q^*(i,j)]$ denote the transition matrix of $X(\tau - t)$. Then,

$$q^*(i,j) = P(j)q(j,i)/P(i) \tag{1.12}$$

Proof Since $X(t)$ is ergodic, it has a unique stationary distribution. By the definition of stationarity, this distribution should apply to $X(\tau - t)$ as well. In the continuous parameter case, for a small time interval Δt, we have

$$\begin{aligned} q^*(i,j)\Delta t &= Pr[(\tau - t - \Delta t, j)|(\tau - t, i)] = Pr[(t,j)|(t + \Delta t, i)] \\ &= Pr[(t,j)]Pr[(t + \Delta t, i)|(t,j)]/Pr[(t + \Delta t, i)] \end{aligned}$$

where in the second step, we simply moved the process "forward" by an amount $2t + \Delta t - \tau$. Now, dividing by Δt and taking the limit as $\Delta t \to 0$, we get equation (1.12). A similar proof can be given for the discrete parameter case as well. □

It is important to note the similarity between equations (1.12) and (1.7). These equations show that if $X(t)$ is reversible, then $q^*(i,j)$ (the rate from i to j in the reversed process) should be same as $q(i,j)$ (the rate from i to j in the original process). In other words, for a reversible process, $Q = Q^*$, which is simply another way of saying that time reversal does not affect the process. However, if the process is not reversible, $q(i,j)$ may well be zero whereas $q^*(i,j)$ is not.

We now show how the concept of reversibility can be used to prove some interesting results. From Lemma 6.1 and equation (5.4.6) it should be obvious that the queue length process of a M/M/c system is reversible. This immediately gives the following result:

Lemma 6.5 The departure process of a M/M/c system is Poisson and the number in the queue at any time t is independent of the departure process prior to t.

Proof Let $X(t)$ denote the queue length process. In forward time, the departures cause downward jumps in $X(t)$; in reverse time, they cause corresponding upward jumps. Because of reversibility, these upward jumps should correspond exactly to the arrival process, which is Poisson. Therefore the departure process should also be Poisson. Since in forward time, the arrivals after time t are independent of the queue length at time t, and hence in reverse time, the departures before time t must be independent of queue length at time t, and the second part of the lemma follows. □

This lemma immediately leads to several well-known results for a feed-forward network of M/M stations. Suppose, for the moment, that external arrivals occur to only one station, say station number 1. Let us number other stations based on the partial order created by the feed-forward routing. Let $X_i(t)$ denote the queue length process of station i. Then by Lemma 6.5, for any time instant t_0, $X_1(t_0)$ is independent of the departures prior to time t_0, but $X_i(t_0)$ for $i > 1$ could only depend on the departures before t_0. Thus, $X_1(t)$ must be independent of $X_i(t)$, $i \geq 2$. By induction, it follows that all $X_i(t)$'s must be independent. This argument can be made with respect to each arrival stream, and thus holds even if multiple stations receive external arrivals. It follows that all flows in a feed-forward network are Poisson (see Section 5.5.6), which in turn implies product-form solution. Also, if the scheduling is overtake-free, all response times must be independent (see Section 5.5.7). In a more general network, we can use essentially the same arguments to show that all departures to the external world are Poisson (as stated in Section 5.5.6). These results also extend to multiple-chain networks.

6.1.3 Quasi-Reversible Queuing Systems

Let $X(t)$ denote the queue length process at a queuing system. Then

> $X(t)$ is quasi-reversible if for any time instant t_0, $X(t_0)$ is independent of (a) arrival times of customers after t_0, and (b) departure times of customers prior to t_0.

This definition holds for the multiple-chain/class case as well. Property (a) implies that the arrival times of customers after t_0 are independent of the system state at t_0. This requires that at any time t following an arrival, the probability of an arrival in an interval $(t, t+\tau)$ should be independent of t. (See the comments regarding the PASTA property in Section 9.2.1). Therefore, *all arrival streams to a quasi-reversible system should be independent and Poisson.* Similarly, property (b) implies that *all departure streams should be independent and Poisson.* Thus, a quasi-reversible system exhibits the $M \Rightarrow M$ property discussed earlier. The opposite is also true because of the basic properties of the Poisson process.

It is important to make a careful distinction between reversible and quasi-reversible systems. Reversibility requires that for any pair of states i and j, either there is no transition in either direction, or a transition can occur in both directions. Quasi reversibility does not mandate transitions in both directions. In this sense, quasi reversibility is more general than reversibility. However, quasi reversibility also imposes an additional restriction, which makes it incomparable with reversibility. In a quasi-reversible queue, the arrivals after time t must be independent of the state of the queue at time t; that is, the arrival rate cannot be state-dependent. It should be clear from Lemma 6.1 that reversibility does not require this assumption.

Quasi reversibility helps to explain the local balance equations that were suggested in Section 6.1.1. Consider an *isolated* quasi-reversible queue that receives customers of several classes (or chains, the distinction being irrelevant). Let us denote the queue length process as $X(t)$. Let S and S' denote two states such that the arrival of a class c customer takes the system from state S to S'. (There is no suggestion that S' is unique.) Let us now consider the reversed process $X(\tau - t)$ and denote its parameters by using asterisks, e.g., P^* for state probability, Q^* for transition rate matrix, etc. By equation (1.12) we then have

$$P(S)q^*(S, S') = P(S')q(S', S) \tag{1.13}$$

Let λ_c denote the total rate with which the system moves out of state S due to the arrival of a class c customer. Note that λ_c does not depend on S because the arrivals must be state-independent under quasi reversibility. Let $\Omega_c(S)$ denote the set of all those states wherein there is one more class c customer in the system than in state S. Then,

$$\lambda_c = \sum_{S' \in \Omega_c(S)} q(S, S') \tag{1.14}$$

Since we are considering steady-state behavior, $X(t)$ must be stationary, which in turn means that the arrival rate for class c must be the same for both $X(t)$ and $X(\tau - t)$. Therefore,

$$\sum_{S' \in \Omega_c(S)} q(S, S') = \sum_{S' \in \Omega_c(S)} q^*(S, S') \tag{1.15}$$

By summing (1.13) over $\Omega_c(S)$ and using (1.15), we finally get

$$P(S) \sum_{S' \in \Omega_c(S)} q(S, S') = \sum_{S' \in \Omega_c(S)} P(S')q(S', S) \tag{1.16}$$

These equations are known as *partial balance equations*, because they lie somewhere between detailed balance and global balance equations. These equations say that *the effective rate at which the system moves out of state S due to the arrival of a class c customer at the station equals the effective rate at which the system moves into state S due to the departure of a class c customer from the station*. These equations can be used to obtain local balance equations, as we shall see in later sections. When dealing with symmetric disciplines and stage type service-time distributions, it is easy to show that the partial balance equations hold with respect to each stage (in addition to the station). This explains the local balance equations of the type (1.4).

It is interesting to note that quasi reversibility leads to the same kind of results as reversibility. In particular, if we consider an open network of quasi-reversible queues, we find that the queue length processes at all queues are mutually independent (which implies product-form solution), departures to the external world are Poisson, and the whole system is itself quasi-reversible. These properties, in turn, imply that *we can write partial balance equations for each station in an open network of quasi-reversible stations*. Note that the set Ω_c can contain more than one member only in a network (because of the routing of customers among different stations). Similar results hold for closed networks, although the proof given above will not go through.

It is important to note that neither reversibility nor quasi reversibility in the context of a queuing system requires exponentially distributed service times. The distribution can be arbitrary so long as the scheduling discipline is symmetric. This is the same property that we mentioned in the context of station balance. We mentioned earlier that quasi-reversible systems are identical to those having the $M \Rightarrow M$ property. Since $M \Rightarrow M$ systems are identical to those satisfying local balance, we have a somewhat anomalous situation because quasi reversibility does not allow state-dependent arrivals, but local balance does (e.g., the birth-death process). However, we can allow for state-dependent arrivals in quasi-reversible systems in a somewhat indirect way. Suppose that we are given a network of quasi-reversible queues, denoted Ω. Let us add an extra quasi-reversible station to Ω that takes state-independent arrivals from the external world and feeds the stations of Ω with its output. In this case, the arrivals to the stations of Ω can depend on the total number of customers of each class in Ω, and yet we can show that all the results (including product-form solution) hold. This has two consequences. First, since local balance in open networks permits only this type of state dependence of the arrival rate (as discussed later in this chapter), the anomaly is resolved. Second, the trick of adding an extra station allows us to make the network closed and thereby extend the open network results to closed networks as well. (See Section 5.5.5).

6.2 Open Queuing Network Models

In this section we study open product-form queuing networks. In Section 6.2.1, we consider the stability conditions, which actually apply to non product-form networks as well. In later subsections we derive the solution for single and multiple-chain open product-form networks. We also show that multiple chains are trivial to handle if the arrival rate is state-independent.

6.2.1 Stability Conditions

When analyzing an open or mixed network of queues, the first problem is to ensure that the steady-state solution indeed exists; i.e., none of the stations goes into saturation. So long as the scheduling discipline is work conserving, the stability condition depends only on the average arrival and service rates of each station and is independent of the distributional form. Thus, *the discussion in this section applies to any type of queuing network, including non-Markovian ones.* The requirements we place are that the network is well-formed, the scheduling discipline at each station is work conserving, and the arrival and service rates at any station do not depend on the state of other stations. The method is to essentially apply equation (5.4.4) to each station of the network. To this end, the first step is to assume flow balance and use the equations in Section 4.2.3 or 4.4.2 to determine the throughputs. For single-chain networks, we could then directly apply equation (5.4.4) to each station. Note that even though (5.4.4) was derived for Poisson arrivals and exponential service, it applies in general. This equation says that the arrival rate should eventually fall below the service rate. If this is the case, the station cannot have infinite queue length irrespective of the nature of arrivals and service.

Let us now consider multiple-chain/class networks. If we are dealing with a mixed network, we can simply ignore closed chains. This works because the closed chains can increase the queue length at any station by at most a finite number. Also, since the distinction between chains and classes is irrelevant for stability, we can consider a station i with a total of J classes passing through it. Let $\mathbf{n} = (n_1, \ldots, n_J)$ denote the occupancy vector at station i. Then the multiple-class analog of equation (5.4.4) is given by

$$\exists \mathbf{k}\, \forall \mathbf{n} > \mathbf{k} \left[\sum_{c=1}^{J} \frac{\lambda_{ic}(\mathbf{n} - e_c)}{\mu_{ic}(\mathbf{n})} < 1 \right] \tag{2.1}$$

where $\mu_{ic}(\mathbf{n})$ is the inherent service rate. Since $\lambda_{ic}(\mathbf{n} - e_c)/\mu_{ic}(\mathbf{n})$ gives the traffic intensity of class c at load $\mathbf{n}$, this equation states that eventually the total traffic intensity must fall below 1. In the usual situation where the arrival rates are state-independent and the station capacities are class-independent, $\mu_{ic}(\mathbf{n}) = \mu_{ic}^{\circ} C_i(n)$, and equation (2.1) reduces to $\forall k\, \exists n\, [U_i/C_i(n) < 1]$, where U_i is the overall station utilization. In effect, we can characterize stability by considering an aggregated single-class network with station capacities as $C_i(n)$, and other parameters defined as follows:

$$\lambda_i = \sum_{c=1}^{J} \lambda_{ic}, \qquad U_i = \sum_{c=1}^{J} \frac{\lambda_{ic}}{\mu_{ic}^{\circ}}, \qquad \text{and} \qquad \mu_i^{\circ} = \frac{\lambda_i}{U_i} \tag{2.2}$$

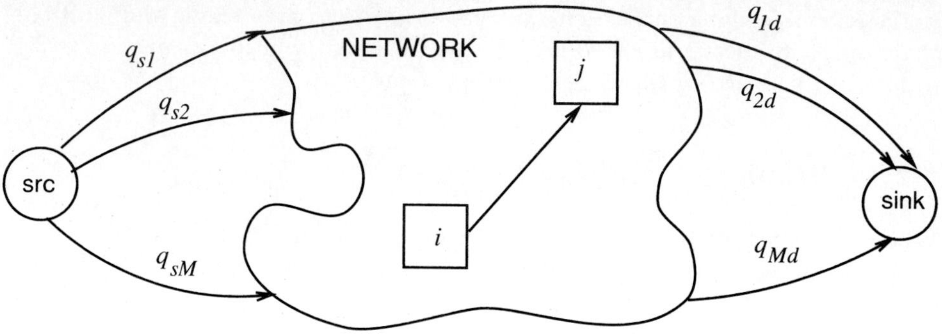

FIGURE 6-1: Representation of an open, single-chain network.

It is important to note that this aggregation is only for characterizing stability. In general, the aggregated network will not give the same overall queue length, response time, etc., as the original network.

Although our discussion on networks until now has assumed homogeneous routing, a limited form of nonhomogeneous routing is practically useful and can be analyzed easily. The special case of interest is the one where the routing probability from any station i to any other station j, denoted q_{ij}, depends only on the state of the destination station. In such cases the arrival rate to station i becomes state-dependent. Although the above equation allows this, but we can no longer compute exact throughputs using the equations from Section 4.2 or 4.4. This is not a problem, since the stability concerns only the situation when the number of customers is large. Thus, to compute λ_{ic}'s for equation (2.1), we can use the value $\lim_{n_j\to\infty} q_{ij}(n_j)$ for each state-dependent routing probability $q_{ij}(n_j)$.

6.2.2 Single-Chain Product-Form Networks

Suppose that the network has M stations. We add two fictitious stations to the network: *source* and *sink*. The source station generates all external arrivals and the sink absorbs all customers leaving the system. This is shown in Fig. 6-1. We use q_{si} to denote the probability that an external arrival is directed to station i. Similarly, we use q_{id} to denote the probability that a customer that finished its service at station i leaves the system. Finally, we use q_{ij} to denote the routing probability from station i to station j. We will show that local balance holds in this system under the following conditions:

1. Generation of customers at the source is a Poisson process with the mean rate of $\Lambda(n)$ where n is the number of customers currently in the network. The rate of *external arrivals* to station i, denoted $\Lambda_i(n)$, is thus $\Lambda(n)q_{si}$. Since we want our Markov chain to be irreducible, we assume that if $\Lambda(k) = 0$ for some k, then for all $n > k$, $\Lambda(n) = 0$.

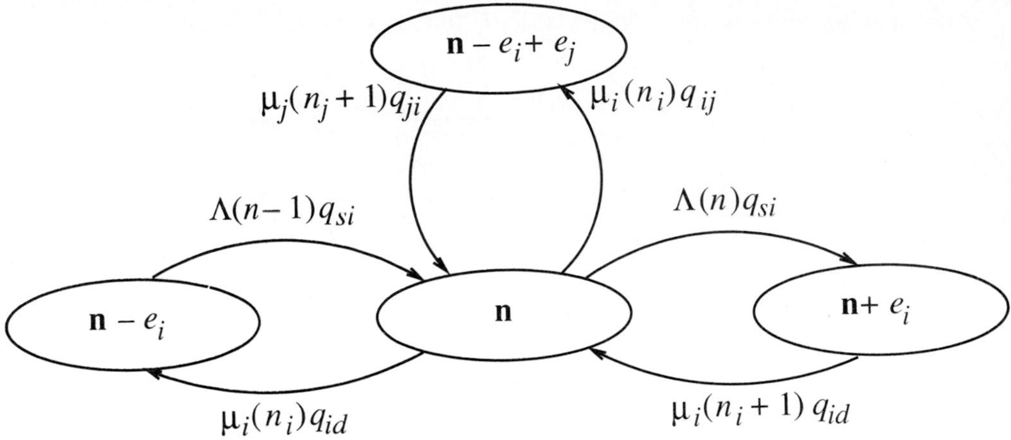

FIGURE 6-2: State transition diagram for an open network.

2. Service-time distribution at every station is exponential and the scheduling discipline is SI. The basic service rate of station i is μ_i° and the capacity is $C_i(n)$ at load n.

Let v_i denote the visit ratio of station i relative to the source node, and $\lambda_i(n)$ its arrival rate when there are n customers *in the entire network*. Since a customer makes v_i visits to station i for each visit to the source, we have $\lambda_i(n) = v_i\Lambda(n)$. Since the visit ratio for the source is 1, the visit ratio for the destination should also be 1. Therefore, by flow balance we have the following relationships

$$\sum_{i=1}^{M} q_{si} = 1 \qquad \text{and} \qquad \sum_{i=1}^{M} v_i q_{id} = 1 \tag{2.3}$$

$$q_{id} = 1 - \sum_{j=1}^{M} q_{ij} \qquad \text{and} \qquad v_i = q_{si} + \sum_{j=1}^{M} v_j q_{ji} \tag{2.4}$$

The state of the network is defined by the vector $\mathbf{n} \triangleq (n_1, \ldots, n_M)$ where n_i is the number of customers at station i. Let n denote the total number of customers *in the entire network*, i.e., $n = |\mathbf{n}|$. A part of the state diagram of this system is shown in Fig. 6-2. Here e_i represents the unit vector in the ith dimension (over the M-dimensional state space of the system). That is, $e_i = (0, \ldots, 0, 1, 0, \ldots, 0)$ where the 1 is in ith position. We first write down the global balance equation for state $\mathbf{n}$. For $n > 0$, the rate at which the system leaves state $\mathbf{n}$ due to an arrival or completion at station i is $\Lambda(n)q_{si} + \mu_i(n_i)q_{id} + \sum_{j=1}^{M} \mu_i(n_i)q_{ij}$ or $\Lambda(n)q_{si} + \mu_i(n)$. Therefore, by equating the total in-flow and out-flow for state $\mathbf{n}$, Fig. 6-2 yields the following equation:

$$P(\mathbf{n})\sum_{i=1}^{M}[\Lambda(n)q_{si}+\mu_i(n_i)] = \sum_{i=1}^{M}\sum_{j=1}^{M}\mu_j(n_j+1)P(\mathbf{n}-e_i+e_j)q_{ji}$$
$$+\sum_{i=1}^{M}\Lambda(n-1)P(\mathbf{n}-e_i)q_{si}+\sum_{i=1}^{M}\mu_i(n_i+1)P(\mathbf{n}+e_i)q_{id} \quad (2.5)$$

and for $n = 0$,

$$\Lambda(0)P(\mathbf{0}) = \sum_{i=1}^{M}\mu_i(1)P(e_i)q_{id} \quad (2.6)$$

It is clear from Fig. 6-2 that this system is not reversible. (For example, we may have $q_{si} = 0$ and $q_{id} > 0$ for some station i, which means that the detailed balance cannot hold.) However, since all stations are individually quasi-reversible, the entire network should also be quasi-reversible. Therefore, we can write partial balance equations with respect to each station in the network. [See the discussion following equation (1.16)]. To write these equations relative to station i, let us choose $S = \mathbf{n} - e_i$. The arrival of a customer to station i takes the system to state $\mathbf{n}$, thus $\Omega_{ic}(S)$ contains only $\mathbf{n}$ as the member. The effective rate of going from state $\mathbf{n}-e_i$ to $\mathbf{n}$ is $\lambda_i(n-1)$, the total arrival rate to station i. The effective rate of going from $\mathbf{n}$ to $\mathbf{n} - e_i$ is the service rate $\mu_i(n_i)$. Therefore, the partial balance equation becomes

$$\mu_i(n_i)P(\mathbf{n}) = \lambda_i(n-1)P(\mathbf{n}-e_i) \qquad i = 1\,..\,M \quad (2.7)$$

We note that we could have identified (2.7) as a local balance equation as well. Now to verify that the assumption of partial (or local) balance is indeed correct, we substitute for q_{si} from equation (2.4) into (2.5). Then by using (2.7), we can show that (2.5) reduces to the second identity in equation (2.3). The details are left as an exercise. It is easy to see that (2.6) is also satisfied. Now we use (2.7) to obtain the solution as follows:

$$P(\mathbf{n}) = \frac{\lambda_i(n-1)}{\mu_i(n_i)}P(\mathbf{n}-e_i) = \frac{u_i}{C_i(n_i)}\Lambda(n-1)P(\mathbf{n}-e_i) \quad (2.8)$$

where we have used the identity $\lambda_i(n) = v_i\Lambda(n)$. Applying this equation recursively, we get

$$P(\mathbf{n}) = \frac{u_i^{n_i}}{V_i(n_i)}\prod_{k=1}^{n_i}\Lambda(n-k)P(\mathbf{n}-n_ie_i) \quad (2.9)$$

where V_i is the product of capacities defined in (1.5). Starting with (2.9) and doing a similar *reduction* over all other stations, we get the desired product-form solution

$$P(\mathbf{n}) = \prod_{k=0}^{n-1}\Lambda(k)\prod_{i=1}^{M}\frac{u_i^{n_i}}{V_i(n_i)}P(\mathbf{0}) \quad (2.10)$$

The state dependence of the arrival rate in equation (2.10) makes the network behave like a closed network. To see this, suppose that $\Lambda(k)$ drops to zero for $k \geq N$ for some finite N. (This is to be expected in any practical situation.) Then, following the discussion in Section 5.5.5, we can add one more station, numbered $M+1$, to the network. The network now becomes closed and has population N. The new station has state-dependent service rate of $\mu_{M+1}(n) = \Lambda(N-n)$. Because of this equivalence, an open network with state-dependent arrivals can be analyzed using the methods of Section 6.3. Therefore, we henceforth assume that $\Lambda(n) = \Lambda$ for all n. In this case the state-dependent arrival rate must be the same as the throughput, i.e., $\lambda_i(n) = \lambda_i = v_i\Lambda$. It follows that

$$P(\mathbf{n}) = \prod_{i=1}^{M} \frac{U_i^{n_i}}{V_i(n_i)} P(\mathbf{0}) \tag{2.11}$$

where $U_i = \lambda_i/\mu_i^\circ$ is the actual utilization. Let $P_i^{(iso)}(n)$ denote the probability of finding n customers at station i when that station is considered in isolation. From equation (5.4.7), $P_i^{(iso)}(n) = P_i^{(iso)}(0)U_i^n/V_i(n)$. Therefore,

$$P(\mathbf{n}) = P(\mathbf{0}) \prod_{i=1}^{M} \frac{P_i^{(iso)}(n_i)}{P_i^{(iso)}(0)} \tag{2.12}$$

Summing both sides of this equation over the entire state space, we get

$$\sum_{\forall \mathbf{n}} P(\mathbf{n}) = \frac{P(\mathbf{0})}{\prod_{i=1}^{M} P_i^{(iso)}(0)} \sum_{n_1=0}^{\infty} P_i^{(iso)}(n_1) \cdots \sum_{n_M=0}^{\infty} P_i^{(iso)}(n_M)$$

Since all probabilities must sum to 1, we get $P(\mathbf{0}) = \prod_{i=1}^{M} P_i^{(iso)}(0)$. Therefore,

$$P(\mathbf{n}) = \prod_{i=1}^{M} P_i^{(iso)}(n_i) \tag{2.13}$$

That is, the network state probability can be obtained by considering each station in isolation. Let $P_i(n)$ denote the *marginal queue length distribution* of station i; i.e., the probability of finding $n \in 0\,..\,\infty$ customers at station i when this station is considered as a part of the network. By summing over all states of stations other than i in the last equation, it easily follows that $P_i(n) = P_i^{(iso)}(n)$ for all n, i.e., the presence of other stations does not affect the marginal distribution. In other words, *in an open product-form network with state-independent arrivals, each station behaves as if it were in isolation.* It is important to remember, however, that *all such claims regarding product-form networks only apply to the marginal distribution, and thus to queue-length moments and the average response time.* The response-time distribution depends on all sorts of details of the network, and we shall not consider it in our analysis. With this understanding, it is safe to claim that a single-class open PF network can be analyzed trivially as follows:

1. Compute steady-state throughput of each station using (4.2.12), and check for stability.

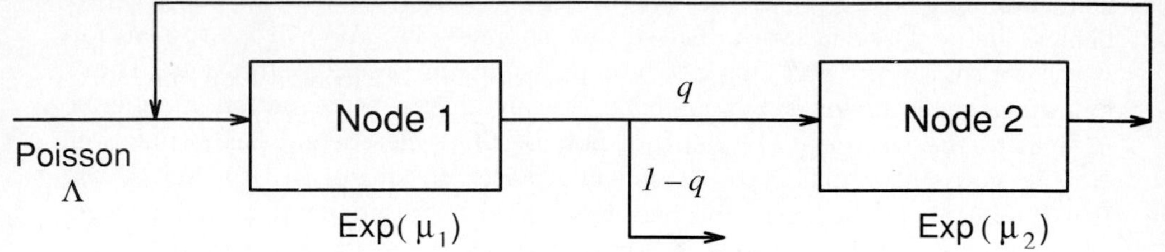

FIGURE 6-3: A simple model of a distributed system.

2. Consider each station separately and use the formulas in Section 5.5 to get their performance parameters.

Other network-wide parameters could then be obtained easily. We illustrate this by an example.

Example 6.1 A simple model of a distributed computer system consisting of two nodes is shown in Fig. 6-3. Jobs are always submitted and completed at node 1, but during execution, a job may move to node 2 (with probability q) to access a resource not available at node 1. Assuming that the product-form solution holds, do the following:

1. Find the steady-state distribution of $P(n_1, n_2)$ where n_i is the number of customers at node i, $i = 1, 2$.
2. Let $\Lambda = 20/\text{min}$, $\mu_1 = 250/\text{min}$, $\mu_2 = 190/\text{min}$, and $q = 0.9$. Does this problem have a steady-state solution? Find queue length and response time at each node and for the entire system.
3. Does this network have any bottlenecks?

Solution Let λ_1 and λ_2 denote the throughputs of nodes 1 and 2 respectively. Then,

$$\lambda_1 = \Lambda + \lambda_2, \qquad \lambda_2 = q\lambda_1$$

Solving these equations, we get $\lambda_1 = \Lambda/(1-q)$ and $\lambda_2 = \Lambda q/(1-q)$. Since both stations are load-independent, from equation (5.5.1), $P_i(n_i) = \rho_i^{n_i}(1-\rho_i)$ where $\rho_i = \lambda_i/\mu_i$. Thus, $P(n_1, n_2)$ can be obtained as $P_1(n_1)P_2(n_2)$, and from equation (5.5.3), $Q_i = \rho_i/(1-\rho_i)$. Let $E[X]$ denote the average number of customers in the system. Then $E[X] = Q_1 + Q_2$. To find the system response time, denoted R, we can use Little's formula, i.e., $R = E[X]/\Lambda$.

For the values given, $\lambda_1 = 200/\text{min}$ and $\lambda_2 = 180/\text{min}$. Therefore, $\rho_1 = U_1 = 0.8$ and $\rho_2 = U_2 = 0.9474$. Since both U_1 and U_2 are less than 1, the steady-state solution exists. Now

$$Q_1 = \frac{0.8}{0.2} = 4, \qquad Q_2 = \frac{0.9474}{0.0526} = 18$$

Therefore, $E[X] = 22$, and $R = 22/20 = 1.1$ minutes.

Obviously, the major contribution to the response time comes from node 2. Thus, any effort in performance improvement should concentrate on this node. For example, suppose that we increase its processing rate slightly, from the current 190/min to 200/min. Then $\rho_2 = 0.9$, $Q_2 = 0.9/0.1 = 9$, and $R = 13/20 = 0.65$ min. That is, the response time reduces by about 40%. □

6.2.3 Multiple-Chain Product-Form Networks

Suppose that we have K chains in the network, and let n_{ir} represent the number of chain r customers at station i. Then the state of the system is defined by the matrix $\vec{\mathbf{n}} = (\mathbf{n}_1, \mathbf{n}_2, \ldots, \mathbf{n}_M)$, where $\mathbf{n}_i = (n_{i1}, \ldots, n_{iK})$ is the occupancy vector at station i. In our analysis, we shall use the unit vectors e_r and e_{ir} defined exactly as in Section 6.1.1. That is, $e_r = (0, \ldots, 0, 1, 0, \ldots, 0)$ is of length K, with a 1 in the rth position. Notice carefully that *this definition of e_r is different from the one for single-chain networks*, where e_r is a unit vector in the M-dimensional state space of station occupancies. Also, $e_{ir} = (\mathbf{0}, \ldots, \mathbf{0}, e_r, \mathbf{0}, \ldots, \mathbf{0})$ gives a unit vector in the $M \times K$ dimensional state space of the entire network. (In this definition, the vector e_r appears in position i).

Because of the insensitivity property of product-form networks, we can assume that the scheduling discipline at each station is processor sharing. Then, assuming a chain-independent capacity function, equation (4.4.9) yields

$$\mu^*_{ir}(\mathbf{n}_i) = \frac{n_{ir}}{n_i}\mu^\circ_{ir}C_i(n_i) \tag{2.14}$$

As with single-chain networks, we shall initially assume that the arrival rate is state-dependent. The allowed form of dependence here is a simple extension of the one in single-chain networks. Let N_r denote the number of chain r customers in the network. That is,

$$N_r = \sum_{i=1}^{M} n_{ir} \tag{2.15}$$

Then the external arrival rate of chain r can depend on N_r, and will be denoted as $\Lambda_r(N_r)$.

As in single-chain networks, we add the fictitious source and destination nodes to our network. Let v_{ir} denote the visit ratio for chain r at station i, where the visit ratio of the source node is assumed to be 1 for each chain. Let $\Lambda_{ir}(N_r)$ and $\lambda_{ir}(N_r)$ denote the external and total arrival rate of chain r to station i. Then $\Lambda_{ir}(N_r) = q_{sir}\Lambda_r(N_r)$ and $\lambda_{ir}(N_r) = v_{ir}\Lambda_r(N_r)$. Here q_{sir} is the probability that a newly generated chain r customer arrives at station i. The visit ratios satisfy the following equation

$$v_{ir} = q_{sir} + \sum_{j=1}^{M} v_{jr}q_{jir} \tag{2.16}$$

where q_{jir} is the routing probability for chain r customers from station j to station i. Most of the details here closely parallel those for single-chain networks and are omitted. To write down the partial balance equations with respect to station i and chain r, let $S = \vec{\mathbf{n}} - e_{ir} = (\mathbf{n}_1, \ldots, \mathbf{n}_i - e_r, \ldots, \mathbf{n}_M)$, and consider the arrival of a chain r customer to station i. The rate of this arrival is $\lambda_{ir}(N_r - 1)$, and it takes the system to state $\vec{\mathbf{n}}$. The total departure rate in state $\vec{\mathbf{n}}$ is $\mu_{ir}^*(\mathbf{n}_i)$. Therefore, we get the following partial balance (and also local balance) equation for $i = 1..M$ and $r = 1..K$.

$$\mu_{ir}^*(\mathbf{n}_i)P(\vec{\mathbf{n}}) = \lambda_{ir}(N_r - 1)P(\vec{\mathbf{n}} - e_{ir}) \tag{2.17}$$

Let $u_{ir} = v_{ir}/\mu_{ir}^\circ$ denote the relative utilization of chain r at station i. Using equation (2.14), we can rewrite this equation as follows:

$$P(\vec{\mathbf{n}}) = \frac{n_i}{C_i(n_i)} \times \frac{u_{ir}}{n_{ir}} \times \Lambda_r(N_r - 1)P(\vec{\mathbf{n}} - e_{ir}) \tag{2.18}$$

By applying this equation recursively n_{ir} times, we can reduce the ith element of $\vec{\mathbf{n}}$ on the right-hand side to $\mathbf{n}_i - n_{ir}e_r$. We then do a similar *reduction* with respect to other chains, one by one. This gives a product over all chains and reduces the ith element of $\vec{\mathbf{n}}$ to $\mathbf{0}$. That is,

$$P(\vec{\mathbf{n}}) = \frac{n_i!}{V_i(n_i)} \prod_{r=1}^{K} \frac{u_{ir}^{n_{ir}}}{n_{ir}!} \prod_{k_r=1}^{n_{ir}} \Lambda_r(N_r - k_r) \times P(\mathbf{n}_1, \ldots, \mathbf{n}_{i-1}, \mathbf{0}, \mathbf{n}_{i+1}, \ldots, \mathbf{n}_M)$$

Next, we apply the same set of steps with respect to the remaining stations. This yields the following product-form solution.

$$P(\vec{\mathbf{n}}) = P(\vec{\mathbf{0}}) \prod_{i=1}^{M} \left[\frac{n_i!}{V_i(n_i)} \prod_{r=1}^{K} \frac{u_{ir}^{n_{ir}}}{n_{ir}!} \right] \times \prod_{r=1}^{K} \prod_{k=0}^{N_r-1} \Lambda_r(k) \tag{2.19}$$

As with single-chain networks, the dependence of the external arrival rate on the network population essentially results in a closed network of $M+1$ stations where the new station models the arrival process. Therefore, for now, we assume that $\Lambda_r(n) = \Lambda_r$ for each r and n. Then $\prod_{k=0}^{N_r-1} \Lambda_r(k) = \Lambda_r^{N_r} = \prod_{i=1}^{M} \Lambda_r^{n_{ir}}$. Also $\lambda_{ir} = v_{ir}\Lambda_r$. Let $U_{ir} = \lambda_{ir}/\mu_{ir}^\circ = u_{ir}\Lambda_r$ be the actual utilization of chain r at station i. Then equation (2.19) yields the following solution

$$P(\vec{\mathbf{n}}) = P(\vec{\mathbf{0}}) \prod_{i=1}^{M} X_i(\mathbf{n}_i) \tag{2.20}$$

where

$$X_i(\mathbf{n}_i) = \frac{n_i!}{V_i(n_i)} \prod_{r=1}^{K} \frac{U_{ir}^{n_{ir}}}{n_{ir}!} \tag{2.21}$$

Now suppose that we consider station i in isolation. Then the solution would be the same as in (2.20) with $M = 1$. That is,

$$P_i^{(iso)}(\mathbf{n}_i) = P_i^{(iso)}(\mathbf{0})X_i(\mathbf{n}_i) \tag{2.22}$$

Therefore, as in Section 6.2.2, we can show the following

$$P(\vec{\mathbf{n}}) = \prod_{i=1}^{M} P_i^{(iso)}(\mathbf{n}_i) \tag{2.23}$$

which, in turn, means that *the marginal distribution for a station in the network is the same as the distribution in isolation*. We can also show that *if the customers are not distinguished based on their chain membership, the resulting expression for state probability is identical to equation (2.11)*. Let $P(n_1, \ldots, n_M)$ denote the probability that each station i contains a total of n_i customers. Then from equation (2.20),

$$P(n_1, \ldots, n_M) = P(\vec{\mathbf{0}}) \prod_{i=1}^{M} \frac{1}{V_i(n_i)} \left[\sum_{|\mathbf{n}_i|=n_i} n_i! \prod_{r=1}^{K} \frac{U_{ir}^{n_{ir}}}{n_{ir}!} \right] \tag{2.24}$$

Invoking the *multinomial theorem* of combinatorics, the bracketed term is simply $U_i^{n_i}$, where $U_i = \sum_{i=1}^{M} U_{ir}$ is the overall utilization of station i. Also, $P(\vec{\mathbf{0}})$ can also be written as $P(\mathbf{0}) = P(n_1 = 0, \ldots, n_M = 0)$. Therefore, equation (2.24) reduces to (2.11). The significance of this result is that given a multiple-chain network $\mathcal{Z}$, we can obtain chain-independent results by simply constructing a single-chain network, denoted $\mathcal{Z}^*$. The input parameters for station i in $\mathcal{Z}^*$ are as follows:

$$\lambda_i = \sum_{r=1}^{K} \lambda_{ir}, \qquad U_i = \sum_{r=1}^{K} \frac{\lambda_{ir}}{\mu_{ir}^{\circ}}, \qquad \mu_i^{\circ} = \frac{\lambda_i}{U_i} \tag{2.25}$$

and the capacity functions of $\mathcal{Z}$ apply to $\mathcal{Z}^*$ as well. This aggregation is the same as the one in Section 6.2.1, except that now it can also be used for computing exact aggregated performance measures. Now to get a relationship between chain-independent and chain-dependent parameters, let us consider equations (2.20) and (2.11) for $M = 1$. It is clear that

$$P_i(\mathbf{n}_i) = P_i(n_i) n_i! \prod_{r=1}^{K} \frac{\rho_{ir}^{n_{ir}}}{n_{ir}!} \qquad \text{where } \rho_{ir} = \frac{U_{ir}}{U_i} \tag{2.26}$$

That is, *the chain-dependent distribution can be obtained from the chain-independent distribution by a simple combinatorial partitioning argument*! Using this, we can also derive relationships between Q_i and Q_{ir}. For notational convenience, we shall do this for $r = 1$, but the same applies to any chain. By definition,

$$Q_{i1} = \sum_{k=1}^{\infty} \sum_{n_{i2}=0}^{\infty} \cdots \sum_{n_{iK}=0}^{\infty} k P_i(k, n_{i2}, \ldots, n_{iK}) \tag{2.27}$$

Note the lower bound of 1 for k. Substituting equation (2.26), we have

$$Q_{i1} = \sum_{k=1}^{\infty} \sum_{n_{i2}=0}^{\infty} \cdots \sum_{n_{iK}=0}^{\infty} P_i(n_i) \frac{n_i! \, \rho_{i1}^{k}}{(k-1)!} \prod_{r=2}^{K} \frac{\rho_{ir}^{n_{ir}}}{n_{ir}!} \tag{2.28}$$

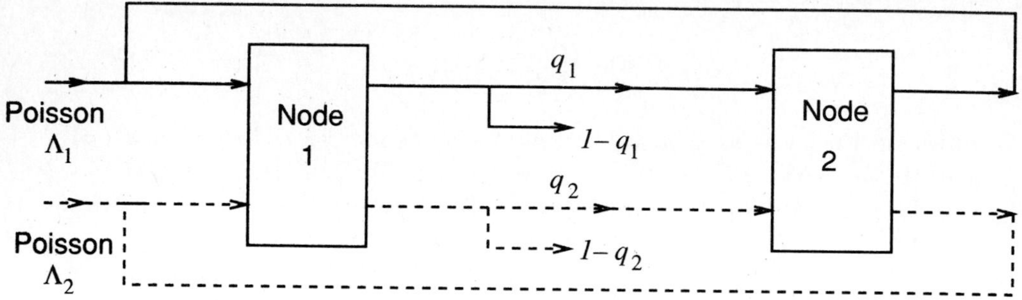

FIGURE 6-4: A two-chain model of a distributed system.

Pulling out ρ_{i1}, and then substituting $k+1$ for k, we get

$$Q_{i1} = \rho_{i1} \sum_{k=0}^{\infty} \sum_{n_{i2}=0}^{\infty} \cdots \sum_{n_{iK}=0}^{\infty} P_i(n_i+1) \frac{(n_i+1)!\ \rho_{i1}^k}{k!} \prod_{r=2}^{K} \frac{\rho_{ir}^{n_{ir}}}{n_{ir}!}$$

Putting together all terms corresponding to each possible value of n_i, we can write this as follows:

$$Q_{i1} = \rho_{i1} \sum_{n_i=0}^{\infty} (n_i+1) P_i(n_i+1) \sum_{\sum_{\forall r} n_{ir}=n_i} n_i! \prod_{r=1}^{K} \frac{\rho_{ir}^{n_{ir}}}{n_{ir}!}$$

Now, applying the multinomial theorem, and realizing that $\sum_{r=1}^{K} \rho_{ir} = 1$, we get

$$Q_{i1} = \rho_{i1} \sum_{n_i=0}^{\infty} (n_i+1) P_i(n_i+1) = \rho_{i1} \sum_{n_i=1}^{\infty} n_i P_i(n_i) = \rho_{i1} Q_i \tag{2.29}$$

Thus, for any station i, once we have the average queue length for the aggregated model, we can get chain-dependent queue lengths by the following simple relationship

$$Q_{ir} = \frac{U_{ir}}{U_i} Q_i \tag{2.30}$$

Since λ_{ir}'s are already known, we can compute chain-dependent response times R_{ir} as Q_{ir}/λ_{ir}. It is important to remember, however, that *none of this would apply if the capacities were chain-dependent*.

Example 6.2 Suppose that in Example 6.1 we have two types of jobs: interactive (chain 1) and batch (chain 2). Fig. 6-4 shows the modified model. The parameters for the two chains are as follows:

External arrival rates: Λ_1=100/min, Λ_2=10/min.

Routing probabilities: $q_1 = 0.75$, $q_2 = 0.9$.

Service rates for station 1: $\mu_{11} = 1200/\text{min}$, $\mu_{12} = 200/\text{min}$.

Service rates for station 2: $\mu_{21} = 1000/\text{min}$, $\mu_{22} = 150/\text{min}$.

Compute the average performance parameters for each chain at each station.

Solution Using the same approach as in Example 6.1, we get

$\lambda_{11} = 400/\text{min}$, $\lambda_{12} = 100/\text{min}$, $\lambda_{21} = 300/\text{min}$, and $\lambda_{22} = 90/\text{min}$.

Therefore, by the utilization law,

$U_{11} = 0.25$, $U_{12} = 0.5$, $U_{21} = 0.3$, and $U_{22} = 0.6$.

Now we can construct $\mathcal{Z}^*$. For this,

$\lambda_1 = 500/\text{min}$, $\lambda_2 = 390/\text{min}$, $U_1 = 0.75$, and $U_2 = 0.9$.

Since both U_1 and U_2 are less than 1, the network does have a steady-state solution. From equation (5.5.3),

$Q_1 = 0.75/0.25 = 3$, and $Q_2 = 0.9/0.1 = 9$.

Therefore, $Q_{11} = 1$, $Q_{12} = 2$, $Q_{21} = 3$, and $Q_{22} = 6$. Using Little's law,

$R_{11} = 0.15$ sec, $R_{12} = 1.2$ sec, $R_{21} = 0.6$ sec, and $R_{22} = 4$ sec.

The system response time for chain 1 is $(1+3) \times 60/100 = 2.4$ sec, and for chain 2, it is $(2+6) \times 60/10 = 48$ sec. □

6.3 Closed Product-Form Networks

Consider a closed network with M stations and K closed chains with population vector denoted as $(N_1, \ldots, N_K)$. We shall refer to the entire network as Ω, formally defined as the set of all stations $1 \mathinner{..} M$. As with open multiple-chain networks, the state of the network Ω is again given by the matrix $\vec{\mathbf{n}} = (\mathbf{n}_1, \ldots, \mathbf{n}_M)$ where $\mathbf{n}_i = (n_{i1}, \ldots, n_{iK})$. However, n_{ir}'s must now satisfy the following condition

$$\forall r \in [1 \mathinner{..} K] \quad \sum_{i=1}^{M} n_{ir} = N_r \tag{3.1}$$

Let S_r denote the set of all feasible states for chain r, and $\mathbf{S}$ the set of all feasible network states. Obviously, $|S_r|$ is the number of ways of distributing the N_r customers of chain r over M stations. Therefore, as shown in Exercise 6.7,

$$|\mathbf{S}| = \prod_{r=1}^{K} |S_r| \quad \text{where } |S_r| = \binom{N_r + M - 1}{M - 1} \tag{3.2}$$

Notice that the number of states increases exponentially with the number of chains. Also, for any given chain r, the number of states increases as $O(N_r^{M-1})$

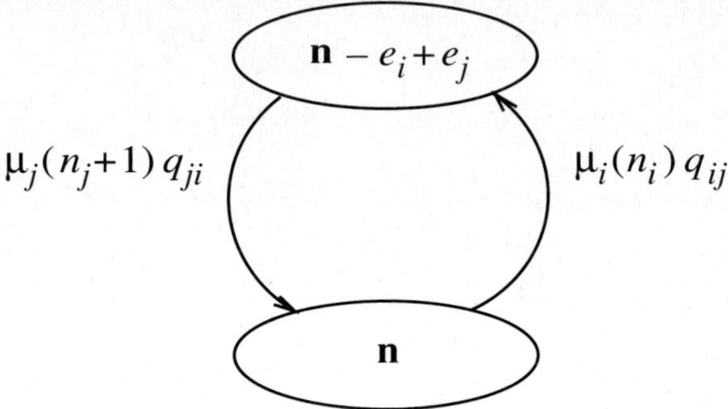

FIGURE 6-5: State transition diagram for a closed network.

for large N_r. The product-form solution for closed networks is similar to that for open chain networks, except for a constant of proportionality, known as the *normalization constant*, which depends on the number of states. Consequently, the complexity of solving closed networks is partially governed by the number of feasible states. This is unlike open networks that are trivial to solve, even though the state space is infinite.

6.3.1 Single-Chain Networks

As in open networks, we start with the state transition diagram and write down the global balance equations; then show that the local balance holds. Again, we shall assume exponential distribution for the service times and PS discipline in our derivations. A part of the state transition diagram is shown in Fig. 6-5. The notation here is identical to that for the open chain case. That is, q_{ij} is the probability that a customer enters station j after leaving station i and e_i is the unit vector in the jth dimension in the M-dimensional state space. The visit ratio v_i's satisfy the following equation

$$v_i = \sum_{j=1}^{M} v_j q_{ji} \tag{3.3}$$

The global balance equations are

$$\sum_{i=1}^{M}\sum_{j=1}^{M} \mu_j(n_j+1)P(\mathbf{n}-e_i+e_j)q_{ji} = \sum_{i=1}^{M}\sum_{j=1}^{M} \mu_i(n_i)P(\mathbf{n})q_{ij} \tag{3.4}$$

We again assume that the local balance holds, and verify our claim. However, finding the local balance equation is a bit more difficult here because we must express the arrival rate exclusively in terms of completion rate at other stations. So, we illustrate a somewhat different approach here. Since this system is quasi-reversible, we can remove the outer summation over stations in equation (3.4), and get the partial balance equations. Since all q_{ij}'s on the right-hand side must sum to 1, we thus get

$$\sum_{j=1}^{M} q_{ji}\mu_j(n_j+1)P(\mathbf{n}-e_i+e_j) = \mu_i(n_i)P(\mathbf{n}) \tag{3.5}$$

Let us now multiply both sides of (3.5) by the visit ratio v_i, and on the right-hand side use (3.3). Rearranging terms, this gives

$$\sum_{j=1}^{M} q_{ji}\left[v_i\mu_j(n_j+1)P(\mathbf{n}-e_i+e_j) - v_j\mu_i(n_i)P(\mathbf{n})\right] = 0 \tag{3.6}$$

which suggests the following local balance equation

$$v_j\mu_i(n_i)P(\mathbf{n}) = v_i\mu_j(n_j+1)P(\mathbf{n}-e_i+e_j) \tag{3.7}$$

We can now see that equation (3.7) indeed represents local balance, since the departure rate from station i is $\mu_i(n_i)$, and the effective arrival rate can be computed as v_j/v_i multiplied by the service rate of station j. We comment at this point that if we remove both summations from (3.4), we will get a set of detailed balance equations; however, since it is possible that $q_{ij} > 0$ but $q_{ji} = 0$, we know that detailed balance cannot hold here.

From our derivation, it is clear that all local balance equations for the present system are of the form (3.7) and satisfy the global balance equation. Therefore, they must yield the only and correct solution. Let $u_i = v_i s_i^\circ$ be the relative utilization of station i. Then by applying (3.7) n_i times, we can express $P(\mathbf{n})$ as follows:

$$P(\mathbf{n}) = \left(\frac{u_i}{u_j}\right)^{n_i} \times \frac{1}{V_i(n_i)} \prod_{k=1}^{n_i} C_j(n_j+k)P(\mathbf{n}-n_i e_i + n_i e_j)$$

Continuing this process over all stations other than j, we eventually get

$$P(\mathbf{n}) = \frac{1}{G(N,\Omega)} \prod_{i=1}^{M} \frac{u_i^{n_i}}{V_i(n_i)} \tag{3.8}$$

where $G(N,\Omega) = u_j^N/[V_j(N)P(N,0,\ldots,0)]$ denotes the normalization constant for the network Ω with population N.

Let $P_i^{(iso)}(n|N)$ denote the probability of finding n customers at station i in isolation under finite population N. Also let $X_i(n) = u_i^n/V_i(n)$. Since $P_i^{(iso)}(n|N) \propto X_i(n)$, we again see that the solution is in the form of a product of solutions for each station in isolation. Also, $X_i(n)$ can be interpreted as the *unnormalized probability* of finding n customers at station i. Let $\mathbf{S}$ denote the set of all feasible states of the network. Since $\sum_{\mathbf{S}} P(\mathbf{n}) = 1$, we have

$$G(N,\Omega) = \sum_{\mathbf{S}} \prod_{i=1}^{M} \frac{u_i^{n_i}}{V_i(n_i)} \tag{3.9}$$

Let $P_i(n|N)$ denote the marginal probability of finding n customers at station i when the entire network contains N customers. Unlike open networks, $P_i(n|N) \neq P_i^{(iso)}(n|N)$; instead, to get the former, we should sum state probabilities over all states such that station i contains n customers. That is,

$$P_i(n|N) = \sum_{n_i=n} P(\mathbf{n}) \tag{3.10}$$

which, in turn, can be used to compute the desired performance parameters.

6.3.2 Brute-Force Algorithm

Equations (3.8) through (3.10) can be used directly for solving closed product-form networks. This "brute force" method is expensive and unnecessary, but we present it here to illustrate the computations. As usual, our primary interest is in computing the average parameters, namely throughput (λ_i), utilization (U_i), queue length (Q_i), and response time (R_i). The steps are as follows:

1. Compute visit ratios for all stations as illustrated in Section 4.2.3, and then the relative utilizations u_i's.
2. Compute the normalization constant G using (3.9), and the marginal probabilities $P_i(n|N)$'s using (3.10).
3. Compute the queue lengths using $Q_i(N) = \sum_{n=1}^{N} nP_i(n|N)$, and the utilizations as

$$U_i(N) = \begin{cases} 1 - P_i(0|N) & \text{if station } i \text{ is load-independent} \\ Q_i(N) & \text{if station } i \text{ is a delay server} \\ \sum_{n=1}^{N} C_i(n)P_i(n|N) & \text{if station } i \text{ is load-dependent} \end{cases} \tag{3.11}$$

4. Find the throughputs and response time using

$$\lambda_i(N) = U_i(N)\mu_i^\circ \quad \text{and} \quad R_i = Q_i(N)/\lambda_i(N) \tag{3.12}$$

The complexity of this algorithm is dominated by step (2) because it requires $O(|\mathbf{S}|)$ operations. We illustrate the algorithm by an example.

Example 6.3 Consider the model shown in Fig. 6-6. The service times are $s_1(n) = 45(1 + 0.02n)$ ms, $s_2 = 25$ ms, $s_3 = 90$ ms, and the routing probability $q = 0.6$. Solve the model for populations of 1 and 2 and obtain the average performance parameters.

Solution We start by computing the visit ratios. Suppose that $v_1 = 1$. Then $v_2 = 0.6$ and $v_3 = 0.4$. Let $u_{ij} = v_i s_i(j)$. Here u_{i1}'s represent relative utilizations u_i's. We shall omit the subscript j for load-independent stations. The relevant values of u_{ij}'s are:

$$u_{11} = s_1(1) = 45(1 + 0.02) = 45.9$$

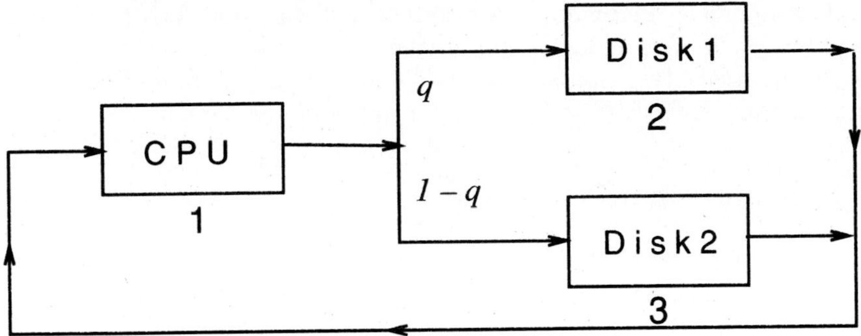

FIGURE 6-6: A closed model of a computer system.

$$u_{12} = s_1(2) = 45(1 + 0.04) = 46.8$$
$$u_2 = 0.6s_2 = 15, \qquad u_3 = 0.4s_3 = 36$$

At population 1, the only feasible states are (1,0,0), (0,1,0), and (0,0,1). From equation (3.9), $G(1) = u_{11} + u_2 + u_3 = 96.9$. Also, at unit population, $P(e_i) = u_i/G(1)$. Therefore,

$$P(1,0,0) = 0.4737 \qquad P(0,1,0) = 0.1548 \qquad P(0,0,1) = 0.3715$$

This means $U_1(1) = Q_1(1) = P(1,0,0) = 0.4737$ and $\lambda_1(1) = U_1/u_{11} = 0.01032$. Also, $R_1(1)$ = service time = u_{11}=45.9. Parameters for stations 2 and 3 can also be computed similarly.

Next consider the $N = 2$ case. The feasible states are (2,0,0), (1,1,0), (1,0,1), (0,2,0), (0,0,2), and (0,1,1). Therefore, from equation (3.9),

$$G(2) = u_{11}u_{12} + u_{11}(u_2 + u_3) + u_2^2 + u_3^2 + u_2u_3 = 6550$$

State Probabilities

$$P(2,0,0) = u_{11}u_{12}/G(2) = 0.3280 \qquad P(1,1,0) = u_{11}u_2/G(2) = 0.1051$$
$$P(0,2,0) = u_2^2/G(2) = 0.0343 \qquad P(1,0,1) = u_{11}u_3/G(2) = 0.2523$$
$$P(0,0,2) = u_3^2/G(2) = 0.1979 \qquad P(0,1,1) = u_2u_3/G(2) = 0.0824$$

Marginal Probabilities

$$P_1(1|2) = P(1,1,0) + P(1,0,1) = 0.1051 + 0.2523 = 0.3564$$
$$P_2(1|2) = P(1,1,0) + P(0,1,1) = 0.1051 + 0.0824 = 0.1875$$
$$P_3(1|2) = P(0,1,1) + P(1,0,1) = 0.2523 + 0.0824 = 0.3347$$

$P_i(2|2)$'s are the same as $P(2e_i)$'s, which are already available above.

Performance Measures

$$Q_1(2) = P_1(1|2) + 2P_1(2|2) = 0.3564 + 2 \times 3280 = 1.0124$$
$$\lambda_1(2) = P_1(1|2)/s_1(1) + P_1(2|2)/s_1(2) = 0.3564/45.9 + 0.3280/46.8 = 0.1477$$
$$R_1(2) = Q_1(2)/\lambda_1(2) = 1.0124/0.01477 = 68.53$$
$$U_1(2) = \lambda_1(2)s_1(1) = 0.01477 \times 45.9 = 0.6648$$

Similar calculations can be made for stations 2 and 3 as well. Let U_i^* denote the probability of finding at least one customer at station i. Then $U_1^*(2) = P_1(1|2) + P_1(2|2)$=0.6844. Note that U_1^* is different from U_1. Since stations 2 and 3 are load-independent, U and U^* will be the same for them. □

6.3.3 Multiple-Chain Networks

The notation and other details here are very similar to the ones for open multiple-chain networks, and we shall abbreviate them. Using a state diagram similar to the one in Fig. 6-5 we can write the following global balance equations

$$\sum_{r=1}^{K}\sum_{i=1}^{M}\sum_{j=1}^{M} q_{ijr}\mu_{ir}^*(\mathbf{n}_i)P(\vec{\mathbf{n}}) = \sum_{r=1}^{K}\sum_{i=1}^{M}\sum_{j=1}^{M} q_{jir}\mu_{jr}^*(\mathbf{n}_j+e_r)P(\vec{\mathbf{n}}-e_{ir}+e_{jr}) \quad (3.13)$$

where μ_{ir}^* denotes the effective service rate for chain r at station i. Notice that on the left-hand side, the summation over j gives 1. As in the single-chain case, we can exploit quasi reversibility and write the following partial balance equations

$$\mu_{ir}^*(\mathbf{n}_i)P(\vec{\mathbf{n}}) = \sum_{j=1}^{M} q_{jir}\mu_{jr}^*(\mathbf{n}_j + e_r)P(\vec{\mathbf{n}} - e_{ir} + e_{jr}) \quad (3.14)$$

Multiplying both sides by v_{ir} and using the relation

$$v_{ir} = \sum_{j=1}^{M} v_{jr}q_{jir} \quad (3.15)$$

on the left-hand side, we identify the following local balance equation

$$v_{jr}\mu_{ir}^*(\mathbf{n}_i)P(\vec{\mathbf{n}}) = v_{ir}\mu_{jr}^*(\mathbf{n}_j + e_r)P(\vec{\mathbf{n}} - e_{ir} + e_{jr}) \quad (3.16)$$

Using equation (3.16) recursively over all chains and all stations along with the definition in equation (2.14), we get the following solution (the details are similar to those for open networks).

$$P(\vec{\mathbf{n}}) = \frac{1}{G(\mathbf{N}, \Omega)} \prod_{i=1}^{M} X_i(\mathbf{n}_i) \quad (3.17)$$

where G is the normalization constant, and

$$X_i(\mathbf{n}_i) = \frac{n_i!}{V_i(n_i)} \prod_{r=1}^{K} \frac{u_{ir}^{n_{ir}}}{n_{ir}!} \quad (3.18)$$

Once again, we see the solution in the form of a product of solutions for individual stations in isolation. G can be computed by equating the sum of probabilities over the set of all feasible states $\mathbf{S}$ to 1. That is,

$$G(\mathbf{N}, \Omega) = \sum_{\mathbf{S}} \prod_{i=1}^{M} X_i(\mathbf{n}_i) \quad (3.19)$$

Similarly, by summing $P(\vec{\mathbf{n}})$ over all states such that $\mathbf{n}_i = \mathbf{k}$, we can get an expression for the marginal probability $P_i(\mathbf{k}|\mathbf{N})$, and from there the expressions for various performance measures.

It should now be obvious how to come up with a "brute force" algorithm, but we shall not discuss it. Closed multiple-chain networks could be very expensive to solve, and we shall review some approaches for handling them in Section 6.5.

6.4 Multiple-Class Models

In this section we consider open and closed models that have multiple classes. For simplicity in exposition, we shall consider only the single-chain case. However, except for the necessary change in notation, exactly *the same* results apply to each chain of a multiple-chain network. Suppose that we have a network with M stations and C classes. As usual, we shall assume that all capacities are independent of the classes. Let q_{jdic} denote the probability that a customer, after receiving service at station j as a member of class d, goes to station i to receive service as a member of class c. Let v_{ic} denote the visit ratio of class c at station i, and C the total number of classes. Then from Section 4.4.2 we have

$$v_{ic} = q_{sic} + \sum_{j=1}^{M} \sum_{d=1}^{C} v_{jd} q_{jdic} \tag{4.1}$$

where q_{sic} is the probability that an external arrival goes to station i as a member of class c. Of course, external arrivals can occur only in an open model. Let N denote the total number of customers in the network, irrespective of whether the network is open or closed. We shall assume that the source node has the visit ratio of 1, which means that the total class c arrival rate to station i in an open network becomes $v_{ic}\Lambda(N)$.

In Section 4.4.2, we learned that in an open network there is no distinction between chains and classes.[2] It is instructive to verify this claim for product-form networks directly from the equations. In particular, if in Section 6.2.3 we were dealing with classes instead of chains, we would find that *nothing at all changes in the analysis*. This observation has one further implication. In Section 6.2.3, we showed that the external arrival rate of chain r may depend on N_r without violating product-form. We call this a *chain-dependent arrival model*. If chains can be treated like classes, we can also have a somewhat different arrival model: Generate all arrivals at a single source, and then split them up probabilistically among K streams, one for each class. In this case, we could let the original stream (and hence the substreams) depend on N, the total number of customers in the network. We call this a *chain-independent arrival model*. The equations

[2]There is one small point to keep in mind, however. When computing visit ratios, we assign an arbitrary value to one station for each chain, but this is not the case with classes. We can avoid this problem by always working with actual throughputs (instead of visit ratios) in an open network.

for this model can be developed as for the chain-dependent model, and we omit the details. With visit ratios defined relative to the source, and X_i defined as in equation (3.18), the final result is

$$P(\vec{\mathbf{n}}) = P(\vec{\mathbf{0}}) \prod_{i=1}^{M} X_i(\mathbf{n}_i) \times \prod_{k=0}^{N-1} \Lambda(k) \quad \text{where } N = \sum_{r=1}^{K} \sum_{i=1}^{M} n_{ir} \tag{4.2}$$

With both types of state-dependent arrival models, the solution algorithms are similar to those for a closed network, and will be discussed later.

Let us now consider *closed* multiple-class networks. As with closed multiple-chain networks, the state of the network can be described by the matrix $\vec{\mathbf{n}} = (\mathbf{n}_1, \ldots, \mathbf{n}_M)$, but its components n_{ic}'s must now satisfy the following condition

$$\sum_{i=1}^{M} \sum_{c=1}^{C} n_{ic} = N \tag{4.3}$$

The global balance equations remain the same as in equation (3.13), and so does the solution. It can be rewritten as

$$P(\vec{\mathbf{n}}) = \frac{1}{G(N, \Omega)} \prod_{i=1}^{M} \frac{n_i!}{V_i(n_i)} \prod_{c=1}^{C} \frac{u_{ic}^{n_{ic}}}{n_{ic}!} \tag{4.4}$$

Now suppose that we do not distinguish customers based on their class membership. Let v_i denote the overall visit ratio of station i, and u_i its overall relative utilization. That is,

$$v_i = \sum_{c=1}^{C} v_{ic} \quad \text{and} \quad u_i = \sum_{c=1}^{C} u_{ic} \tag{4.5}$$

Notice that all v_{ic}'s and u_{ic}'s are defined relative to a single reference, and thus it makes sense to add them. (Such an addition would not make sense for the multiple-chain case, since each chain uses a different reference.) Let $P(n_1, \ldots, n_M)$ denote the probability that each station i contains a total of n_i customers. Then

$$\begin{aligned} P(n_1, \ldots, n_M) &= \frac{1}{G(N, \Omega)} \prod_{i=1}^{M} \frac{1}{V_i(n_i)} \left[\sum_{|\mathbf{n}_i| = n_i} n_i! \prod_{c=1}^{C} \frac{u_{ic}^{n_{ic}}}{n_{ic}!} \right] \\ &= \frac{1}{G(N, \Omega)} \prod_{i=1}^{M} \frac{u_i^{n_i}}{V_i(n_i)} \end{aligned} \tag{4.6}$$

where we have applied the multinomial theorem. Thus, the result is the same as for a single-class network with relative utilization of u_i at station i. This result is similar to the one we found for multiple-chain open networks. This suggests that to solve a closed multiple-class network $\mathcal{Z}$, we solve only an equivalent single-class network $\mathcal{Z}^*$. In network $\mathcal{Z}^*$, each station i has the relative utilization of u_i and visit ratio of v_i as defined in equation (4.5).

Let $P_i(\mathbf{n}_i|N)$ denote the marginal distribution at station i in $\mathcal{Z}$. We can get an expression for $P_i(\mathbf{n}_i|N)$ from equation (4.4) by summing over all feasible states in which station i contains $\mathbf{n}_i$ customers. Similarly, let $P_i(n_i|N)$ denote the marginal distribution at station i in $\mathcal{Z}^*$. We can get an expression for this from (4.6) by summing over all feasible states in which station i contains n_i customers. It is then easy to see that the two probabilities are related as follows:

$$P_i(n_{i1},\ldots,n_{iC}|N) = P_i(n_i|N)\; n_i! \prod_{c=1}^{C} \frac{\rho_{ic}^{n_{ic}}}{n_{ic}!} \qquad \text{where} \quad \rho_{ic} = \frac{u_{ic}}{u_i} \tag{4.7}$$

This result is identical to the one in (2.26), and yields an equation like (2.30). That is, if $P_{ic}(n|N)$ denotes the marginal distribution of class c at station i, then

$$Q_{ic}(N) = \sum_{n=1}^{N} nP_{ic}(n|N) = \frac{u_{ic}}{u_i} Q_i(N) \tag{4.8}$$

We leave the details of the proof as an exercise. Since throughputs are not precomputed in a closed network, we also need to relate class-dependent throughputs to the class-independent throughputs. For notational convenience, we show the proof for class 1 only. From the throughput theorem,

$$\lambda_{i1}(N) = \sum_{n_{i1}=1}^{N} \sum_{n_{i2}=0}^{k_{i2}} \cdots \sum_{n_{iC}=0}^{k_{iC}} \frac{n_{i1}}{n_i} \mu_{i1}^{\circ} C_i(n_i) P_i(n_{i1},\ldots,n_{iC}|N) \tag{4.9}$$

where for $i > 1$, $k_{ic} = N - n_{i1} - \cdots - n_{i(c-1)}$. These upper bounds result from the fact that $n_i = \sum_{c=1}^{C} n_{ic}$ cannot exceed the population N. The manipulations from this point onward are similar to those in obtaining equation (2.30), and we only indicate the steps verbally: Substitute (4.7) in the above equation, simplify, substitute $n_{i1}+1$ for n_{i1}, rearrange summations so that the outermost summation is over n_i, apply multinomial theorem, use the fact that all ρ_{ic}'s sum to 1, and recognize the summation over n_i as the definition of class-independent throughput. The final result (generalized to apply to any class) is

$$\lambda_{ic}(N) = \frac{v_{ic}}{v_i} \lambda_i(N) \tag{4.10}$$

The main conclusion of this section is that *multiple classes are trivial to handle in product-form networks if the stations have class-independent capacities.* Because of this, we shall assume a single class per chain in all our future discussions on solution algorithms.

6.5 Algorithms for Closed PF Networks

Closed, single-chain networks are relatively easy to solve, therefore, much of the work on the topic concerns multiple-chain networks. There are three general approaches to the problem, and the choice depends on the size, calibration accuracy, and the evaluation objectives of the model.

I. *Exact solution:* Useful for models where the number of stations and/or the number of chains is small, though moderately large but "sparse" models can also be handled. Space and time complexity is exponential as a function of the number of chains or the number of stations.

II. *Approximate solution:* Useful for large models or when high accuracy is unnecessary (possibly because of uncertainties in model calibration). Space and time complexity is polynomial as a function of the number of chains and stations.

III. *Performance bounds:* Useful when a large number of alternatives must be examined quickly or when input parameters are known only crudely. Complexity is lower than for the approximate algorithms.

In the following, we provide an overview of the best-known algorithms in each of these three categories. Complexities are quoted assuming that each chain has the same population $\overline{N}$. The number of chains is K and the number of stations is M.

6.5.1 Exact Algorithms

Exact algorithms can be further divided into two classes: (a) those that do not take advantage of network *sparseness*, and (b) those that do. A network is called sparse if most of the chains go through only a small fraction of the total number of stations in the network. Class (a) algorithms include:

1. Convolution (or Buzen's Algorithm).
2. MVA - Mean Value Analysis.
3. LBANC - Local Balance based computation of Normalization Constant.
4. RECAL - Recursion by Chain.
5. MVAC - Mean Value Analysis by Chain.
6. DAC - Distribution Analysis by Chain.

The time complexity of the first three algorithms is $O(M(\overline{N}+1)^K)$ and that of the last three is $O((4M-1)K^{M+1}/(M+1)!)$ for large K. Space complexity of all the algorithms is of about the same order as time complexity. Note that the first three algorithms take polynomial time and space as a function of M but exponential time and space as a function of K. The situation for the last three is just the opposite. Thus, the first three algorithms are more efficient with a large number of stations but small number of chains, whereas the last three are more efficient for the other extreme.

The algorithms in class (b) include: (1) tree-convolution, and (2) tree-MVA. The complexity of these algorithms depends on the sparseness of the network. If the network is dense, these algorithms may actually be slower than the corresponding non-tree versions.

In the overview that follows, only single-chain networks are considered whenever possible. Numerical problems are also pointed out briefly.

1. Convolution

This algorithm first computes the normalization constant G for the network by a sequence of convolutions of the normalization constants of the individual stations. It then computes performance parameters using the G values. For example, if station i is load-independent, we can show that

$$Q_i(N) = \sum_{n=1}^{N} u_i^n \frac{G(N-n,\Omega)}{G(N,\Omega)}$$

Notice that this computation requires $G(n,\Omega)$ for several values of n. Convolution requires proper choice of visit ratios to avoid overflow/underflow in the computation of G's.

2. MVA/LBANC Algorithms

MVA does not compute the normalization constant G; instead, it uses the marginal local balance theorem in equation (4.2.30) to recursively compute the performance parameters at population n, given those at population $n-1$. This algorithm is robust for load-independent stations, but not for load-dependent stations. In the latter case, at any given population n, it computes the marginal probability $P_i(0|n)$ using the following numerically unstable equation

$$P_i(0|n) = 1 - \sum_{k=1}^{n} P_i(k|n) \tag{5.1}$$

LBANC is a modified form of MVA that uses "unnormalized" versions of MVA equations. It is a little more efficient in computation time and storage than regular MVA. It not only computes G but also uses an equation like (5.1). Therefore, it suffers from the numerical problems of both convolution and MVA.

3. RECAL/MVAC/DAC Algorithms

These algorithms are designed especially for multiple-chain networks. They start out with no chains in the network and add one chain at a time until all chains have been introduced. Each time, RECAL computes G, but MVAC and DAC compute some performance parameters. For simplicity in implementation, every original chain with population N is split into N identical chains, each with population 1. Since RECAL computes the normalization constant, it has the same numerical problems as convolution. MVAC/DAC are numerically robust, even for load-dependent stations.

4. Tree Convolution/MVA Algorithms

These algorithms are extensions of the corresponding sequential Convolution and MVA algorithms and are designed for sparse networks. Both algorithms start with individual stations and recursively combine them into larger and larger subnetworks until the entire network is covered. This recursion can be naturally depicted as a tree with stations as leaves and the entire network as the root. Savings are achieved because at any level of recursion, the chains that are either uncovered (i.e., not involved) or are fully covered (i.e., all stations through which the chain passes are already in the subnetwork), do not contribute to time/space complexity. Tree-convolution has the same numerical properties as sequential convolution, but tree-MVA is numerically robust.

6.5.2 Approximate Algorithms

These could be further divided into two categories:

(1) *Approximate MVA:* This includes algorithms based on MVA. Two well-known candidates are (a) first-order heuristic (Schweitzer's algorithm), and (b) second-order heuristic (Linearizer). The time/space complexity of these algorithms is $O(MK)$ and $O(MK^2)$ respectively, independent of chain populations.

(2) *Asymptotic expansion:* Here the idea is to obtain Taylor series expansion for the performance parameters and use only the first few terms. This requires solving a few small queuing networks at low populations. The complexity depends on the number of terms used.

We now describe these briefly. These algorithms were originally developed for networks without load-dependent stations and are described as such in the following overview. All these algorithms are free from any significant numerical problems.

1. Schweitzer's Algorithm

The mean value theorem in equation (4.2.34), along with Little's law, is used in the regular MVA to compute $Q_i(N)$ from $Q_i(N-1)$. The idea now is to come up with a heuristic equation that lets us go from $Q_i(N)$ back to $Q_i(N-1)$, and thereby set up an iterative solution procedure whose complexity is independent of N. Such a relationship, known as *Schweitzer's heuristic*, is given below:

$$\frac{Q_i(N-1)}{N-1} = \frac{Q_i(N)}{N} \tag{5.2}$$

It can be shown that this equation is exact as $N \to \infty$ and that the iterative procedure always converges. Accuracies of the order of 10–20% are typical, but could be much worse in some cases.

2. Linearizer

This is an improvement over Schweitzer's algorithm. Instead of using (5.2), it assumes that the difference between the fractional queue lengths at populations

$N-1$ and N, denoted D_i, is independent of N. With this assumption, we have:

$$Q_i(N-1) = (N-1)[Q_i(N)/N + D_i] \tag{5.3}$$

The algorithm starts with $D_i = 0$ and improves it iteratively. The main steps are as follows:

1. Iterate between populations $N-1$ and N using (5.3), and obtain $Q_i(N)$. If convergence has been achieved, stop.
2. Iterate between populations $N-2$ and $N-1$ using (5.3), and obtain $Q_i(N-1)$.
3. Compute a better estimate of D_i as $Q_i(N-1)/(N-1) - Q_i(N)/N$ and go to step 1.

3. Asymptotic Expansion

This algorithm is intended for multiple-chain networks only. Consider a network with $M+1$ stations, of which station 0 is of delay type, and stations $1..M$ are load-independent. Then, equation (3.19) can be expressed as

$$G(N,\Omega) = \sum_{\sum_i n_{i1}=N_1} \cdots \sum_{\sum_i n_{iK}=N_K} \prod_{r=1}^{K} \frac{u_{0r}^{n_{0r}}}{n_{0r}!} \prod_{i=1}^{M} \left[n_i! \prod_{r=1}^{K} \frac{u_{ir}^{n_{ir}}}{n_{ir}!} \right] \tag{5.4}$$

Notice that if we can somehow remove $n_i!$ from this equation, we can separate out the terms corresponding to each chain. An application of the multinomial theorem on each term then yields a compact representation that does not involve any summations. The $n_i!$ term can be eliminated by using Euler's integral representation of the factorial function. The final result is a M-fold integral of a rather complicated function. The idea then is to do the Taylor series expansion of the integrand and integrate term by term. Each term could then be recognized as the normalization constant of a simple network. This network has the same M stations, but has only a few chains, each with a small population. Thus, the normalization constant (and hence the performance parameters) can be computed rather inexpensively. This representation also provides error bounds since successive terms have different signs.

6.5.3 Performance Bounds

Bounds can typically be obtained only on the overall throughput and cycle time, though some of the techniques allow computation of loose bounds on queue lengths as well. A large number of bounding techniques have been proposed in the literature. Here we mention only three.

Asymptotic Bound Analysis (ABA)

The upper bounds are obtained by assuming that all customers are queued at the node with largest relative utilization (i.e., the *bottleneck node*). The lower bounds are obtained by assuming that no queuing takes place anywhere. As expected, these bounds do not require the product-form property, but may be very loose.

Balanced Job Bounds (BJB)

Upper bounds are obtained by assuming that all nodes have the same load as the bottleneck node. Lower bounds are obtained by assuming that every node carries the "average" load.

Performance Bound Hierarchies (PBH)

The mean value theorem yields a recursive expression for the cycle time, which can be expanded down to a certain number of levels (l levels of expansion will give an expression for cycle time at population N as a function of the performance parameters at population $N - l$). At this point, we apply the BJB results and get the bounds. The complexity is determined by l. For $l = N$, we get the exact results.

6.6 Conditions for Product-Form Solution

In sections 6.2 and 6.3 we showed that ordinary networks of exponential servers with processor-sharing discipline have product-form solution. In this section we state the conditions under which the product-form solution is known to hold, assuming a single class per chain. Although the list below includes most of the features, it is by no means exhaustive.

(1) The interarrival-time distribution is exponential for every open chain. The average arrival rate of chain r may depend either on the number of chain r customers in the network or on the total number of customers.

(2) Every station is of one of the following three types:

   (a) Delay (infinite server) with general service-time distribution for each chain. Scheduling discipline, of course, is irrelevant for a delay station.

   (b) LBPS scheduling discipline and arbitrary service-time distribution for each chain. The station may be load-dependent; the restrictions on this aspect are specified in item (3) below.

   (c) Any SI scheduling discipline with the *same exponential service-time distribution for every chain.* (FCFS and random are two examples of such disciplines.) The station could be load-dependent, but this dependence must apply to all chains. In other words, the dependence can only be on the magnitude of the occupancy vector.

(3) Let $\mu^*_{ir}(\mathbf{n}_i)$ denote the effective service rate at station i for chain r customers when the occupancy vector is $\mathbf{n}_i$. Then for any two distinct chains r and k passing through station i, the following condition must hold

$$\frac{\mu^*_{ir}(\mathbf{n}_i)}{\mu^*_{ik}(\mathbf{n}_i)} = \frac{\mu^*_{ir}(\mathbf{n}_i - e_k)}{\mu^*_{ik}(\mathbf{n}_i - e_r)} \tag{6.1}$$

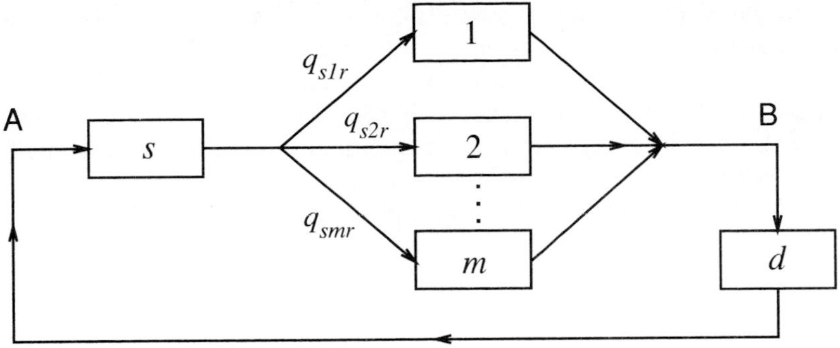

FIGURE 6-7: Network topology for state-dependent routing.

(4) Routing probabilities are either constant or depend only on the state of the destination station. In the latter case, we must have the topology shown in Fig. 6-7. Here the state-dependent routing occurs from a "source" station s to the components of a *parallel subnetwork*, and the customers exiting the parallel subnetwork go to a "destination" station d. (s and d need not be distinct stations, and each component of the parallel subnetwork could itself be an arbitrary single-entry, single-exit subnetwork.) Let n_{jr} denote the number of chain r customers in the jth branch of the subnetwork, and $n_r = \sum_{j=1}^{m} n_{jr}$ the total number of chain r customers in the parallel subnetwork. Then *at each level of nesting of parallel subnetworks*, the functional form of the routing probabilities $q_{sjr}(n_{jr})$'s is restricted to be the following:

$$q_{sjr}(n_{jr}) = \frac{a_r n_{jr} + b_{jr}}{a_r n_r + c_r} \qquad \text{where} \quad c_r = \sum_{k=1}^{m} b_{kr} \tag{6.2}$$

(5) A limited form of blocking may occur at any station. Suppose that a customer is routed from station i to station j. Then two types of blocking may occur at station j:

(a) The customer cannot be admitted into station j because of limited capacity and returns to station i for another round of service. The returned customer is treated like a normal customer at station i, and thus does not necessarily try to go to station j after finishing its service at station i. We call this *rejection blocking*.

(b) The customer belongs to one of, say C, classes, and station j is a multiserver with $b < C$ identical servers, each with exponentially distributed service time. At most one customer from each class may be in service at any time at station j. (This requirement makes the system non-conservative, since servers may remain idle even when there are customers waiting.) Other than this, the scheduling is nonpreemptive and does not pick customers according to their service demands. We call this *mutual blocking*.

We now make a few comments concerning conditions (2) and (3). Arbitrary service-time distribution is allowed at a delay station because a M/G/∞ queue behaves exactly like a M/M/∞ queue (see Section 5.5.3) and is thus quasi-reversible. Another way to show this is to verify that the behavior of a delay station can always be described adequately by a symmetric discipline. Since FCFS or random disciplines are not symmetric, they require that all customers be indistinguishable and have exponentially distributed service times. We also note the *insensitivity property* mentioned in Section 6.1.1; the form of the solution is not affected by the scheduling discipline or the service-time distribution. As a result, *the solutions that we obtained in Sections 6.2 and 6.3 remain valid under other scheduling disciplines and/or nonexponential service*. However, other assumptions about those solutions, namely chain-independent capacity functions, state-independent routing, and absence of blocking, are essential.

Let us now examine why the condition in equation (6.1) is essential for the product-form solution to hold. Fig. 6-8 illustrates *marginal local balance*, i.e., local balance when only the state of station i is considered. Here the arcs labeled with μ's represent transitions due to departures, and those labeled with λ's represent transitions due to arrivals. This representation will always have transitions in both directions between two adjacent states, and the effective transitions rates in the two directions must be the same. Thus, we can compute the probability of the state $\mathbf{n}_i$ in terms of the probability of state $(\mathbf{n}_i - e_r - e_k)$ by following either of the two paths – one via the state $(\mathbf{n}_i - e_r)$, and the other via $(\mathbf{n}_i - e_k)$. Obviously, if the local balance holds, both paths should give the same result. In an open network, the rates along the λ arcs are determined by the external arrival rate, which, according to condition (1) cannot depend on the state of an individual station. In a closed network, these rates are determined by the service rates, just like those of the μ arcs (see local balance equations in sections 6.2.3 and 6.3.3). It follows that in either case, local balance will hold if and only if the products of service rates along both paths from $\mathbf{n}_i$ to $(\mathbf{n}_i - e_r - e_k)$ are identical. Equation (6.1) specifies exactly this condition.

Since the final solution is the same in all cases where local balance holds, we can assume, without loss of generality, that the scheduling discipline is PS. We can thus express the effective service rate in terms of the occupancy vector-dependent capacity function using an equation like (2.14). That is, by substituting $\mu^*_{ir}(\mathbf{n}_i) = \frac{n_{ir}}{n_i}\mu^\circ_{ir}C_{ir}(\mathbf{n}_i)$ into (6.1), we get

$$\frac{C_{ir}(\mathbf{n}_i)}{C_{ik}(\mathbf{n}_i)} = \frac{C_{ir}(\mathbf{n}_i - e_k)}{C_{ik}(\mathbf{n}_i - e_r)} \tag{6.3}$$

We now see that if the capacity function depends only on n_i, instead of $\mathbf{n}_i$, equation (6.3) is always satisfied. In more general cases, it may be difficult or impossible to satisfy (6.3). For example, it is often desirable to "saturate" the capacity function beyond a certain load, i.e., $C_{ir}(\mathbf{n}) = C_{ir}(\mathbf{k})$ for all $\mathbf{n} \geq \mathbf{k}$. As shown in Exercise 6.8, most such capacity functions will fail to satisfy (6.3).

With chain-dependent capacities satisfying equation (6.3), the product-form solution can be obtained from equation (2.17) for open networks and from equation (3.16) for closed networks. For example, in a closed network, equation

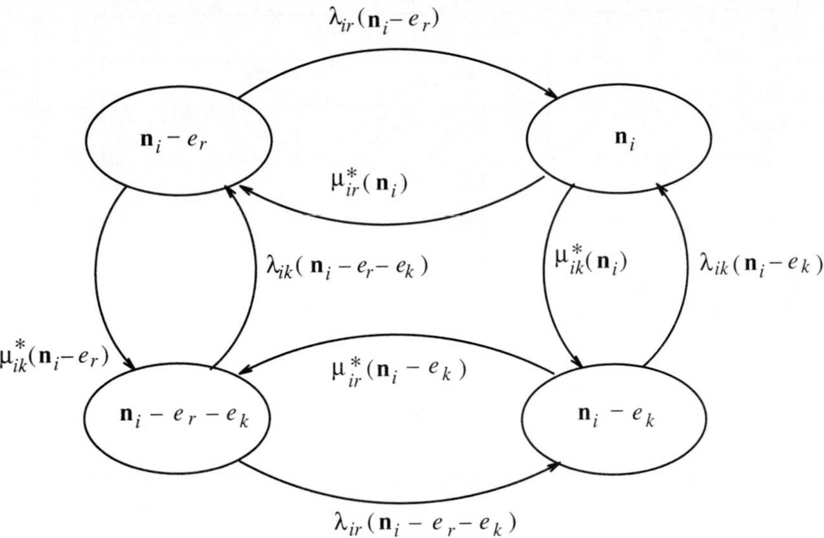

FIGURE 6-8: Illustration of conditions for marginal local balance.

(3.16) yields

$$P(\vec{\mathbf{n}}) = \frac{1}{G(\mathbf{N}, \Omega)} \prod_{i=1}^{M} \frac{n_i!}{V_i(\mathbf{n}_i)} \prod_{r=1}^{K} \frac{u_{ir}^{n_{ir}}}{n_{ir}!} \tag{6.4}$$

where the *occupancy vector-dependent* V_i *function* is given by

$$\begin{aligned} V_i(\mathbf{n}_i) &= \prod_{k_1=1}^{n_{i1}} C_{i1}(k_1, n_{i2}, \ldots, n_{iK}) \prod_{k_2=1}^{n_{i2}} C_{i2}(0, k_2, n_{i3}, \ldots, n_{iK}) \\ &\quad \times \cdots \times \prod_{k_K=1}^{n_{iK}} C_{iK}(0, \ldots, 0, k_K) \end{aligned} \tag{6.5}$$

These equations result from a reduction of equation (3.16) first over chain 1, then over chain 2, etc. Of course, the reduction order should not matter, and equation (6.3) can be interpreted as the condition that ensures this. Since the product in equation (6.5) contains exactly one term for each occupancy vector magnitude in the range $1 .. n_i$, it follows that if $C_{ir}(\mathbf{n}_i) = C_i(n_i)$ for all r, the product reduces to the familiar $V_i(n_i)$. Notice that equation (6.4) is identical to our regular solution in equation (3.17) except that $V_i(n_i)$ is replaced by $V_i(\mathbf{n}_i)$. Because of this close correspondence, most of the results hold in general, as we shall see in Chapter 7.

6.7 Exercises

1. A simple model of a distributed computer system consisting of three nodes is shown in Fig. 6-9. Jobs are always submitted and completed at node1, but

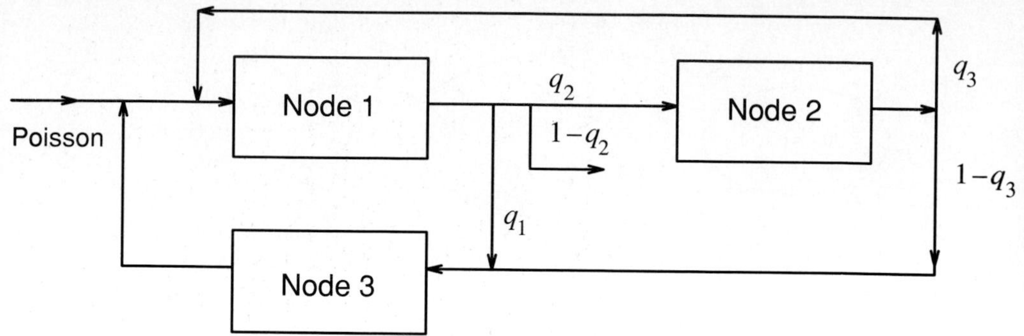

FIGURE 6-9: A model of a distributed system.

during the execution, a job may move from one node to another depending on its resource requirements. Arrivals can be assumed to be Poisson with a rate of 20/sec. The service-time distribution and scheduling disciplines are such that the product-form property holds. Node 1 has two processors, each with a rate of 10 mips (million instructions per second). Node 3 is a single-processor node with rate of 10 mips. Node 2 is a database node with a basic effective transfer rate of 4.5 Mbytes/sec (M= 10^6). Since it uses moving head disks, its effective transfer rate increases with load. The capacity function is $2n/(n+1)$. If scheduled at node 1 or node 3, a job will execute, on the average, 20,000 instructions, and if scheduled at node 2, will transfer 10,000 bytes of data. The routing probabilities are $q_1 = 0.25$, $q_2 = 0.8$, and $q_3 = 0.4$.

(a) Does this problem have a steady-state solution? Why? Find the steady-state distribution $P(n_1, n_2, n_3)$.

(b) Find queue length and response time at each node and over the entire system.

(c) Is any of the three nodes a bottleneck? To find out, increase the processing rate of each node by 5% in turn (not simultaneously) and recompute the percentage improvement in system response time for each case.

2. Show that the Q matrix of a reversible discrete parameter Markov chain can be written as $D^{-1}AD$ where D is a diagonal matrix and A is a symmetric matrix. Deduce from this that Q must have real eigenvalues.

3. Suppose that a Markov chain $X(t)$ with stationary distribution $\pi(i)$, $i \in A$ is truncated to the set $B \subset A$ to get chain $Y(t)$. Let $\pi_Y(i)$, $i \in B$, denote the stationary distribution of $Y(t)$. Show that $\pi_Y(i)$, $i \in B$, is proportional to $\pi(i)$, if and only if the following partial balance equations hold

$$\pi(i) \sum_{j \in B} q(i,j) = \sum_{j \in B} \pi(j) q(j,i) \tag{7.1}$$

Let $Z(t)$ denote the process obtained by truncating the reversed process $X(-t)$ to set B. Show that $Y(-t)$ and $Z(t)$ have the same transition rates if and only if equation (7.1) holds.

4. Consider a load-independent station fed with two Poisson arrival streams. Both types of customers have the same exponentially distributed service times. The server gives preemptive priority to class 1 customers over class 2 customers. Using the notion of quasi reversibility, show that the class 1 departure stream and the overall departure stream are Poisson, but the class 2 departure stream is not!

5. Define symmetric disciplines using an equation like (1.6) for multiple-class networks. Show that the LCFSPR discipline can be defined to satisfy this equation, but random selection cannot. How would you characterize the LBPS class of disciplines? Also show that if no customer has to wait (i.e., we have a multiserver station with at least as many servers as the number of customers present), we can always characterize the queue by the symmetry property.

6. Show that the local balance equation (2.7) satisfies the global balance equations (2.5) and (2.6). Do the same for the multiple-chain case using equation (2.17). Also derive equation (4.2) which gives solution for the alternate arrival model.

7. Show that equation (3.2) correctly gives the number of states in a closed multiple-chain network. (Hint: The number of possibilities for chain i is the number of ways of distributing N_i tokens among M bins.) Extend the result for multiple classes per chain.

8. Suppose that you want (6.3) to hold when the capacity is saturated beyond some vector $\mathbf{k}$. Characterize the types of dependencies that are ruled out by this requirement.

9. Derive equation (6.4) from equation (3.16). Show that $V_i(\mathbf{n}_i)$ in equation (6.5) is invariant under renumbering of chains.

Bibliographic Notes

The product-form solution for queuing networks is introduced in Jackson (1963), which considers open networks with exponential service-time distributions at each station. Gordon and Newell (1967) shows that closed queuing networks with load-dependent exponential service-time distributions also have a product-form solution. Baskett, Chandy, Muntz, and Palacios (1975) extends these results to multiple-chain networks. This result is popularly known as the *BCMP theorem.* Muntz in 1972 investigated the $M \Rightarrow M$ property, and showed that networks of such stations have product-form solution and exhibit the $M \Rightarrow M$ property themselves. Chandy, Howard and Towsley (1977) introduces the concept of station balance and proves the results that we mentioned in Section 6.1.1. Noetzel (1979) shows that under some restrictions, *LBPS scheduling discipline is necessary and sufficient for station balance to hold.* Chandy and Martin (1983) provides further characterization of product-form networks in terms of station balance. Product-form solution under the random scheduling discipline is shown in Spirn (1979).

Time-reversed Markov processes were first considered by Kolmogorov in 1936 and later by Reich, Kendall, Burke, Kelly, and others. Kelly (1976) studies quasi reversibility in single-chain and multiple-chain networks, and introduces symmetric queuing disciplines. Kelly proves that under such disciplines, the service-time distribution could be a mixture of Erlang distributions. The book by Kelly (1979) is an excellent source of results on reversible and quasi-reversible systems. Our discussion on the topic and some of the exercises have been taken from this book.

Notes regarding computational algorithms for closed networks appear in later chapters and are omitted here.

CHAPTER

7

Basic Algorithms for Product-Form Networks

In this chapter, we discuss the fundamental algorithms for single and multiple-chain closed product-form networks. We develop convolution and mean value analysis in detail and mention LBANC briefly. We then show how mixed networks can be analyzed using the closed network algorithms as a "subroutine". Finally, we discuss the approximate mean value analysis, which is useful for handling large models.

7.1 Single-Chain Convolution

This algorithm is based on the convolution property of the normalization constant and the relationships between the normalization constant and performance measures. Let Ω denote the set of stations forming the queuing network, and Ω_{LD} a subset of Ω containing all load-dependent stations. *Delay stations are not included in* Ω_{LD}. Let N denote the population of this network and $G(N, \Omega)$ the normalization constant. In the following, we use the notation $\mathbf{S}(\omega, n)$ to denote the set of all feasible states of a subnetwork ω at population n. Thus, $\mathbf{S}(\Omega, N)$ would represent the state space of the given network. We shall use the notation $\mathbf{S}(<\text{cond}>)$ to denote the subset of $\mathbf{S}(\Omega, N)$ that satisfies the boolean condition <cond>. Finally, we define $X_i(n)$ as $u_i^n/V_i(n)$.

7.1.1 Fundamental Relationships

In this section, we derive a number of interesting relationships that are needed in the convolution algorithm.

Lemma 7.1 (Convolution theorem). Let a network Ω be partitioned into two disjoint, nonempty subsets Ω_1 and Ω_2. Then,

$$G(N,\Omega) = \sum_{n=0}^{N} G(N-n,\Omega_1)G(n,\Omega_2) \tag{1.1}$$

That is, the G for the entire network is the convolution of the G's of its subnetworks.

Proof From the defining equation (6.3.9) for $G(N,\Omega)$, we have

$$\begin{aligned}
G(N,\Omega) &= \sum_{\mathbf{S}(\Omega,N)} \prod_{i\in\Omega} X_i(n_i) = \sum_{\mathbf{S}(\Omega,N)} \prod_{i\in\Omega_1} X_i(n_i) \prod_{i\in\Omega_2} X_i(n_i) \\
&= \sum_{n=0}^{N} \sum_{\mathbf{S}(\Omega_1,N-n)} \prod_{i\in\Omega_1} X_i(n_i) \sum_{\mathbf{S}(\Omega_2,n)} \prod_{i\in\Omega_2} X_i(n_i) \\
&= \sum_{n=0}^{N} G(N-n,\Omega_1)G(n,\Omega_2) = G(\cdot,\Omega_1) \bullet G(\cdot,\Omega_2)(N)
\end{aligned}$$

where "$\bullet$" is the convolution operator. □

Corollary 7.1 Let Ω_i denote the set of stations $\{1\,..\,i\}$ and n some population level. Then,

$$G(n,\Omega_i) = \sum_{k=0}^{n} G(n-k,\Omega_{i-1}) \frac{u_i^k}{V_i(k)} \tag{1.2}$$

Proof The unnormalized probability of finding k customers at station i, i.e., $G(k,\{i\})$, is $u_i^k/V_i(k)$. □

Corollary 7.2 Let i be a load-independent station. Then,

$$G(n,\Omega_i) = G(n,\Omega_{i-1}) + u_i G(n-1,\Omega_i) \tag{1.3}$$

Proof From Corollary 7.1 and the fact that $V_i(k) = 1$ for all k, we have

$$\begin{aligned}
G(n,\Omega_i) &= \sum_{k=0}^{n} u_i^k G(n-k,\Omega_{i-1}) = G(n,\Omega_{i-1}) + \sum_{k=1}^{n} u_i^k G(n-k,\Omega_{i-1}) \\
&= G(n,\Omega_{i-1}) + u_i \sum_{k=0}^{n-1} u_i^k G(n-1-k,\Omega_{i-1})
\end{aligned}$$

	1	2	3	...	i	...	M
1	u_1	$u_1 + u_2$					$\sum_{m=1}^{M} u_m$
2	$u_1^2/V_1(2)$						
...							
n					$G(n, \Omega_i)$		
...							
N	$u_1^N/V_1(N)$						

TABLE 7.1: Convolution algorithm represented in a tabular format.

which, by Corollary 7.1 again, gives equation (1.3). □

Using Corollaries (7.1) and (7.2) we can compute G systematically by starting with an empty subnetwork and adding one station at a time. Let ϕ denote the empty set. It is easy to see that the proper initializations are

$$\forall n > 0 \;\; G(n, \phi) = 0, \qquad \text{and} \qquad \forall i \;\; G(0, \Omega_i) = 1 \tag{1.4}$$

The computation can be arranged in a tabular form shown in Table 7.1. Here the ith column is intended to contain G's for the subnetwork Ω_i at populations from $1..N$. From Corollary 7.2, if station i is load-independent, the computation of value for the box (i, n) only needs values from boxes $(i, n-1)$ and $(i-1, n)$. For a load-dependent station, however, we need to use Corollary 7.1 that requires entries from all the boxes $(i-1, k), k \in 1..n$. Thus, the addition of a load-independent station to the network costs $O(N)$ operations whereas the addition of a load-dependent station costs $O(N^2)$ operations. As for the space complexity, though $G(N, \Omega)$ itself can be computed by storing only the current and previous columns, more columns may be needed for computing performance measures.

We now relate performance parameters to G values. It will be seen that we may need G values for various subnetworks at several population levels.

Lemma 7.2 The marginal distribution at a load-independent station i is given by the following equations

$$P_i(n_i \geq k|N) = u_i^k \frac{G(N-k, \Omega)}{G(N, \Omega)} \tag{1.5}$$

$$P_i(n_i = k|N) = \frac{u_i^k}{G(N, \Omega)}[G(N-k, \Omega) - u_i G(N-k-1, \Omega)] \tag{1.6}$$

Proof From the product-form property and the fact that $V_i(k) = 1$ for all k, we have

$$P_i(n_i \geq k|N) \;\; = \;\; \frac{1}{G(N, \Omega)} \sum_{\mathbf{S}(n_i \geq k)} u_i^{n_i} \prod_{\substack{m=1 \\ m \neq i}}^{M} X_m(n_m)$$

$$= \frac{u_i^k}{G(N,\Omega)} \sum_{\mathbf{S}(\Omega,N-k)} u_i^{n_i} \prod_{\substack{m=1 \\ m \neq i}}^{M} X_m(n_m)$$

$$= \frac{u_i^k}{G(N,\Omega)} \sum_{\mathbf{S}(\Omega,N-k)} \prod_{m=1}^{M} X_m(n_m) = u_i^k \frac{G(N-k,\Omega)}{G(N,\Omega)}$$

where, in the second line, we have used the observation that the set of states wherein station i has at least k customers are precisely those states where the remaining $N-k$ customers can be assigned to various stations in all possible ways. In other words, these are all the states of the closed network Ω with population $N-k$. Now, equation (1.6) results from the observation that

$$P_i(n_i = k|N) = P_i(n_i \geq k|N) - P_i(n_i \geq k+1|N) \tag{1.7}$$

□

Corollary 7.3 The queue length at a load-independent station is given by

$$Q_i(N) = \sum_{k=1}^{N} u_i^k \frac{G(N-k,\Omega)}{G(N,\Omega)} \tag{1.8}$$

Proof Follows from equations (1.5) and (B.1.30). □

Lemma 7.3 The marginal distribution for a general load-dependent station i is given by

$$P_i(n|N) = \frac{u_i^n}{V_i(n)} \frac{G(N-n,\Omega-\{i\})}{G(N,\Omega)} \tag{1.9}$$

Proof By definition,

$$P_i(n|N) = \frac{1}{G(N,\Omega)} \sum_{\mathbf{S}(n_i=n)} \prod_{m=1}^{M} X_m(n_m)$$

$$= \frac{1}{G(N,\Omega)} \frac{u_i^n}{V_i(n)} \sum_{\mathbf{S}(\Omega-\{i\},N-n)} \prod_{m \neq i} X_m(n_m)$$

where we have again used the observation that if we fix n customers at station i, we have all the states in which $N-n$ customers are spread arbitrarily over the rest of the network. Now by the definition of G, we get (1.9). □

Lemma 7.4 (Throughput theorem). The throughput of station i is given by

$$\lambda_i(N) = v_i \frac{G(N-1,\Omega)}{G(N,\Omega)} \tag{1.10}$$

Proof From the throughput law, we have

$$\lambda_i(N) = \sum_{n=1}^{N} \mu_i(n) P_i(n|N) = \sum_{n=1}^{N} \mu_i^\circ C_i(n) P_i(n|N)$$

Using equation (1.9) and simplifying, we get

$$= v_i \sum_{n=1}^{N} \frac{u_i^{n-1}}{V_i(n-1)} \frac{G(N-n, \Omega - \{i\})}{G(N, \Omega)}$$

$$= \frac{v_i}{G(N,\Omega)} \sum_{n=0}^{N-1} \frac{u_i^n}{V_i(n)} G((N-1)-n, \Omega - \{i\}) = v_i \frac{G(N-1,\Omega)}{G(N,\Omega)}$$

□

Multiplying both sides of equation (1.10) by s_i°, we get an alternate form of the throughput theorem

$$U_i(N) = u_i \frac{G(N-1,\Omega)}{G(N,\Omega)} \tag{1.11}$$

7.1.2 Algorithmic Considerations

The throughput theorem applies to any type of station and involves G values only at two adjacent population levels. However, queue lengths are more complicated to compute. In the following, we note a few important points concerning queue length and related computations for each of the three types of stations: delay, simple (or load-independent), and general load-dependent.

1. For a delay station, the average queue length is the same as utilization, and thus only the throughput theorem need be used. However, if higher moments of queue length or marginal probabilities are also needed as outputs, we have little choice but to treat the station like a general load-dependent station.
2. As seen from equations (1.5) through (1.8), for a load-independent station, we need G's only for the entire network. Thus, if all the stations in the network are simple, only the last column in the table of G's is needed for computing the performance measures. As for the computation of G's themselves, a single column of storage is enough since we can overwrite as we go. [This can be seen clearly from equation (1.3)].
3. The computation in equation (1.9) needs $G(n, \Omega - \{i\})$ for every load-dependent station i. Thus, if i is not the last station in our initial computation of the G table, we must renumber the stations and recompute such that this is the case. $G(n, \Omega - \{i\})$ is then available from the last-but-one column. For each such reordering, the last column will give G's for the entire network, and need not be recomputed. The storage requirements are at least two columns, but more storage can be used to reduce the computation time as discussed below.

1. Number the stations in the following order: first simple, then delay, and finally load-dependent. Initialize $G(0, \Omega_i) = 1$ for $i = 1..M$.
2. Compute visit ratios and relative utilizations of all stations. Scale relative utilizations to avoid numerical problems.
3. Calculate $G(n, \Omega_1)$ for $n = 1..N$ using $G(n, \Omega_1) = G(n-1, \Omega_1) \times u_1/C_1(n)$. Add stations $i = 2..M$ and compute G values using Corollary 7.1 or 7.2.
4. If there is more than one load-dependent station, reorder and compute G's for $\Omega - \{i\}$ for all $i \in \Omega_{LD}$.
5. Compute the performance parameters for station $i = 1..M$ using the relations in Section 7.1.1.

FIGURE 7-1: Single-chain convolution algorithm.

Let $L = |\Omega_{LD}|$, i.e., the number of load-dependent stations in the network. Then we can number the stations such that the $(M-L)$ simple/delay stations are at the low end, and compute $G(n, \Omega_{M-L})$ only once. We then take L orderings of the remaining L stations and start off the computation with the $(M-L)$th column each time. Assuming $L > 1$, this scheme requires the storage of three columns. If we can store more columns, we do not have to start at the $(M-L)$th column each time, and some computational savings can be achieved. However, the returns become progressively smaller as more columns are retained. If there are D delay stations and $S = M-L-D$ simple stations in the network, the worst-case time complexity for computing all required G's is $O(S\,N + N^2\,D + N^2\,L^2)$. The time needed to compute performance parameters from the G's is not a dominant part; therefore, the entire algorithm also has this complexity. The entire convolution algorithm is shown in Fig. 7-1.

Let us now look at the numerical aspects of the algorithm. Although the performance parameters are independent of the relative utilizations, the value of G is not. Therefore, an imprudent choice may lead to numerical problems of overflow, underflow, or poor precision. Furthermore, $G(n, \Omega_i)$ is not necessarily monotonic with n or Ω_i; thus overflow/underflow may occur at intermediate steps even if the final G is within the allowable range. Most of these problems can be alleviated by scaling the relative utilizations properly. In the following, we devise a scheme for computing the scaling factor.

Suppose that we convert the closed network into an open network by breaking the loop somewhere and choose the external arrival rate such that the network remains stable. This amounts to choosing the relative utilizations such that if they were to be the real utilizations, the open network would be stable. We denote these relative utilizations as u_i's. Let

$$G_\infty = \sum_{n=0}^{\infty} G(n, \Omega) \tag{1.12}$$

Since all $G(n,\Omega)$'s must be positive, it follows that $G(n,\Omega) < G_\infty$ for all n. Therefore, overflow can be avoided by ensuring that G_∞ is not too large. Notice that $G(n,\Omega)$ *can be interpreted as the unnormalized probability of having* n *customers in the network*. Thus, G_∞ gives the normalization constant of the open network (this is like viewing an open network as a network with all possible population values). Therefore, $P(0)$, the probability of finding the network empty, is given by

$$P(0) = G(0,\Omega)/G_\infty = 1/G_\infty \tag{1.13}$$

Thus, to ensure that G_∞ does not overflow, we only have to make sure that $P(0)$ does not underflow. Since $P(0)$ should always be less than 1, we also have the assurance that G_∞ will remain larger than 1 and cannot underflow. From equation (6.2.13), $P(0)$ can be obtained as a product of $P_i^{(\text{iso})}(0)$'s, i.e., by considering each station in isolation. From Section 5.5, we know that for a load-independent station, $P_i^{(\text{iso})}(0) = 1 - u_i$, and for a delay station, $P_i^{(\text{iso})}(0) = e^{-u_i}$. Also, for a general load-dependent station,

$$P_i^{(\text{iso})}(0) \triangleq f_i(u_i) = \left[1 + \sum_{k=1}^{\infty} \frac{u_i^k}{V_i(k)}\right]^{-1} \tag{1.14}$$

Let σ denote the scaling factor and u_i' the scaled relative utilization for station i; i.e., $u_i' = \sigma u_i$. Then the problem reduces to determining σ such that $P(0)$, computed using u_i''s, exceeds the smallest representable floating point number, say ε. We want $P(0)$ to be close to ε so that individual $G(n,\Omega)$'s do not become too small and cause the underflow problem. Suppose that we number simple stations as $1\,..\,S$, delay stations as $S+1\,..\,S+D$, and the rest as $S+D+1\,..\,M$. Then σ can be determined using the following inequality

$$\left[\prod_{i=1}^{S}(1-\sigma u_i) \prod_{i=S+1}^{S+D} e^{-\sigma u_i} \prod_{i=S+D+1}^{M} f_i(\sigma u_i)\right] > \varepsilon \tag{1.15}$$

Because of the complexity of the above equation, an iterative solution comes naturally. To ensure that this iteration converges and it itself does not cause overflow/underflow problems, we should always choose σ such that

$$\sigma < \min_{1\le i\le S} \frac{1-\varepsilon}{u_i}, \qquad \sigma < \min_{S<i\le S+D} \frac{-\ln(\varepsilon)}{u_i}, \qquad \min_{S+D<i\le M} f_i(\sigma u_i) > \varepsilon \tag{1.16}$$

Example 7.1 Consider a model of a computing system shown in Fig. 7-2. (Ignore the chain shown in broken lines for now.) The calibration parameters for the model are as follows: average think time = 1 sec, CPU service rate = 25/sec, CPU capacity function $C(n) = 1/(0.95 + 0.05n)$, disk service rate = 20/sec, and $q = 0.25$. The disk station is load-independent.

Solve the model for $N = 2$ active terminals and determine the mean queue length, response time, throughput and utilization of each station.

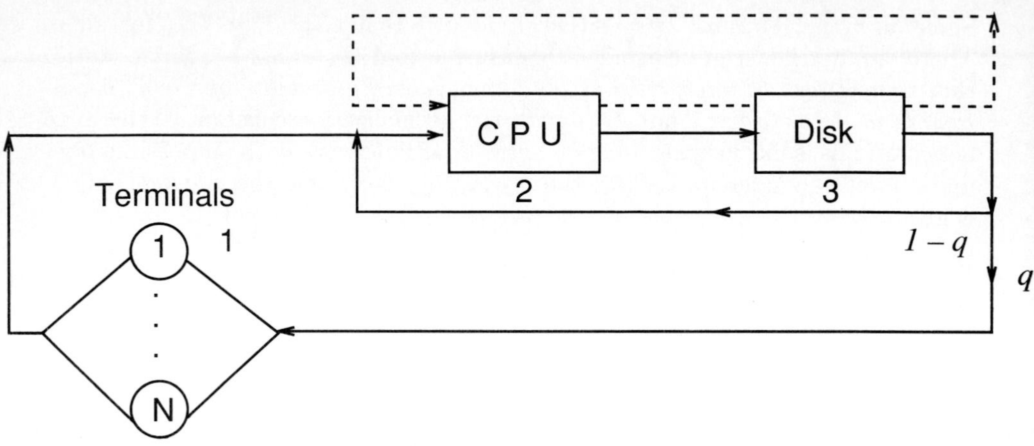

FIGURE 7-2: An example queuing network.

Solution We have $s_1 = 1000$ ms, $s_2 = 40$ ms, and $s_3 = 50$ ms. For the visit ratios, we have $v_2 = v_3 = v_1/q$. Let us arbitrarily choose $v_1 = 1$. Then $v_2 = v_3 = 4$. The corresponding relative utilizations are

$$u_1 = v_1 s_1 = 1000, \qquad u_2 = v_2 s_2 = 160, \qquad u_3 = v_3 s_3 = 200$$

Unfortunately, this choice of relative utilizations is poor since it will make the normalization constant large even for small populations. The reasons are easy to see: G is expressed as a sum of the products of relative utilizations; therefore, choosing u_i's much larger or smaller than 1 will surely lead to problems. Instead of doing a formal scaling, we shall simply divide relative utilizations by 100. Thus, $u_1 = 10$, $u_2 = 1.6$, and $u_3 = 2$.

We order the stations as suggested in Fig. 7-1. (To avoid confusion, we don't actually renumber the stations, but only add them in the order 3, 1, 2 for computing G). For $n = 1$,

$$G(n, \{3\}) = 2.0, \qquad G(n, \{3, 1\}) = 12.0, \qquad G(n, \{3, 1, 2\}) = 13.6$$

For $n = 2$, we start with $G(2, \{3\}) = u_3^2 = 4$. Now

$$G(2, \{3, 1\}) = \sum_{n=0}^{2} G(2 - n, \{3\}) \frac{u_1^n}{V_1(n)} = 74.0 \tag{1.17}$$

$$G(2, \{3, 1, 2\}) = \sum_{n=0}^{2} G(2 - n, \{3, 1\}) \frac{u_2^n}{V_2(n)} = 95.888 \tag{1.18}$$

Now we are ready to compute the performance parameters. By equation (1.11), $U_1(2) = u_1 G(1)/G(2) = 1.4183$. Since station 1 is of the delay type, $Q_1 = U_1$, and $R_1(2) = s_1 = 1000$ ms. By the utilization law, $\lambda_1(2) = U_1(2)/s_1 = 1.4183$/sec.

We can compute throughputs and utilizations of other stations by noting that they must be proportional to the visit ratios and relative utilizations, respectively. Since station 2 is load-dependent, we need to compute its marginal probabilities using equation (1.9). One of these probabilities can also be computed by the requirement that all probabilities sum to 1.

$$P_2(1|2) = \frac{u_2}{V_2(1)} \frac{G(1, \{3, 1\})}{G(2, \Omega)} = 0.200233$$

$$P_2(2|2) = \frac{u_2^2}{V_2(2)} \frac{G(0, \{3, 1\})}{G(2, \Omega)} = 0.028033$$

$$P_2(0|2) = 1 - P_2(1|2) - P_2(2|2) = 0.771733$$

$$Q_2(2) = P_2(1|2) + 2P_2(2|2) = 0.2563 \qquad \lambda_2(2) = (v_2/v_1)\lambda_1(2) = 5.6733/\text{sec}$$

Therefore, $U_2(2) = \lambda_2(2)s_2 = 0.226931$, and $R_2(2) = Q_2(2)/\lambda_2(2) = 45.176$ ms. Since station 3 is load-independent,

$$Q_3(2) = u_3 \frac{G(1)}{G(2)} + u_3^2 \frac{G(0)}{G(2)} = 0.325372$$

$$\lambda_3(2) = (v_3/v_1)\lambda_1(2) = 5.67329/\text{sec}$$

$$U_3(2) = \lambda_3(2)s_3 = 0.283664, \qquad R_3(2) = Q_3(2)/\lambda_3(2) = 57.3529 \text{ ms}$$

If needed, the marginal probabilities can be computed for station 3 using equation (1.6) in general. For the problem at hand, however, we can get $P_3(2|2)$ using equation (1.5), and then get $P_3(1|2)$ using the fact that the utilization is $P_3(1|2) + P_3(2|2)$. □

7.2 Single-Chain Mean Value Analysis

This algorithm is based on the marginal local balance (MLB) theorem proved using operational arguments in Section 4.2.5. We now prove this result using stochastic arguments.

Lemma 7.5 (Marginal local balance theorem). The marginal distribution of station i in a closed PF network is given by

$$P_i(n|N) = \frac{U_i(N)}{C_i(n)} P_i(n-1|N-1) \tag{2.1}$$

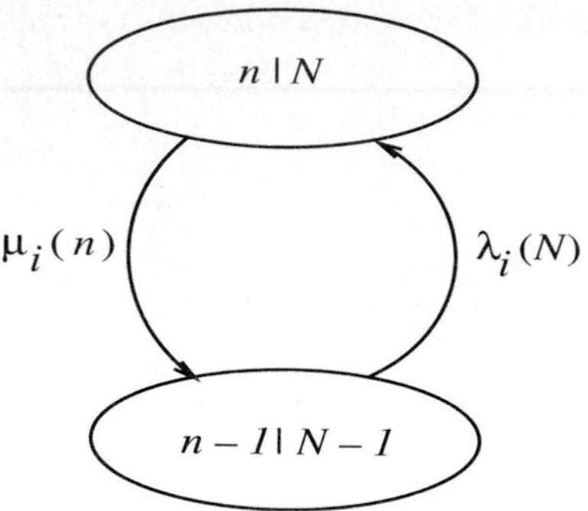

FIGURE 7-3: Marginal local balance for station i.

Proof From equation (1.9),

$$P_i(n-1|N-1) = \frac{u_i^{n-1}}{V_i(n-1)} \frac{G(N-n, \Omega - \{i\})}{G(N-1, \Omega)}$$

Also, using equation (1.9) for $P_i(n|N)$, we get

$$\frac{P_i(n|N)}{P_i(n-1|N-1)} = \frac{u_i}{C_i(n)} \frac{G(N-1, \Omega)}{G(N, \Omega)}$$

which, along with equation (1.11), reduces to equation (2.1). □

MLB theorem can be interpreted as a detailed balance between two adjacent "states" for station i as shown in Fig. 7-3. The rate of departure from state $(n|N)$ is $\mu_i(n)$, whereas the rate of entry into it from state $(n-1|N-1)$ is the throughput $\lambda_i(N)$.

The MLB equation can be used to derive several other relationships that are useful in computing performance measures recursively. For example, for a load-dependent station,

$$Q_i(N) = \sum_{n=1}^{N} nP_i(n|N) = U_i(N) \sum_{n=1}^{N} \frac{n}{C_i(n)} P_i(n-1|N-1) \tag{2.2}$$

which, along with Little's law, yields,

$$R_i(N) = s_i^\circ \sum_{n=1}^{N} \frac{n}{C_i(n)} P_i(n-1|N-1) \tag{2.3}$$

where s_i° is the basic service time for station i. If station i is load-independent,

$$R_i(N) = s_i \sum_{n=1}^{N} nP_i(n-1|N-1) = s_i[1 + Q_i(N-1)] \tag{2.4}$$

which is the familiar *mean value theorem* that was proved in Section 4.2.5. It can also be written in the following alternate form

$$Q_i(N) = U_i(N)[1 + Q_i(N-1)] \tag{2.5}$$

Equation (2.4) has a simple and intuitive interpretation. Consider the average response time experienced by a typical customer. The average number in the system following the arrival of this customer will be $1 + QA_i(N)$, where QA_i denotes the average queue length seen by the arriver. Since we can always assume the scheduling discipline to be PS in product-form networks, the server is equally shared among these customers. Therefore, to obtain s_i units of service, the arriving customer must spend $s_i[1 + QA_i(N)]$ time units at the station. From the arrival theorem (see Section 4.2.5), we know that $QA_i(N) = Q_i(N-1)$ in a closed product-form network, which gives the mean value theorem.

With the above intuitive explanation, it is easy to manufacture heuristic response time equations even for those cases where the product-form solution does not hold. Thus, MVA can be heuristically extended to handle complex scheduling disciplines, something that is not possible with Convolution and other algorithms. We shall study these extensions in Section 8.3.

Notice that the right-hand sides of equations (2.3) and (2.4) involve performance parameters only at population $N-1$. Thus, if we know these parameters, we can compute the response times for all stations at population N. Applying Little's law to the entire network, we could then compute the throughputs, as illustrated in equation (4.2.22). With throughputs known, we can use Little's law for each station to compute queue lengths at population N. The utilizations, of course, can be obtained by multiplying throughputs with basic service times. For a load-dependent station i, $P_i(n|N)$ for $n > 0$ could then be computed using equation (2.3). Finally, we can compute $P_i(0|N)$ as

$$P_i(0|N) = 1 - \sum_{n=1}^{M} P_i(n|N) \tag{2.6}$$

Thus, we have a complete step of the MVA algorithm. Now starting at population of zero (for which we know everything trivially), we can keep stepping through the populations until we reach the desired population N. The complete algorithm is given in Fig. 7-4. As illustrated, it is enough to compute the cycle time of only one station, which we have chosen as station 1.

The time and space complexities of the algorithm are $O(NM)$ and $O(M)$ respectively if there are no load-dependent stations, and increase to $O(N^2M)$ and $O(NM)$ respectively if all stations are load-dependent. It is interesting to compare these numbers against those for the convolution algorithm. It is seen that although the complexities are different for the two algorithms, the differences are not particularly significant. If most stations are load-dependent (a rare case), MVA takes less time but more space. Numerically, MVA is more robust than Convolution since it computes performance parameters directly. In fact, the equations dealing with load-independent and delay stations are free of any numerical problems. However, for load-dependent stations, the computation of $P_i(0|n)$ in equation (2.6) is unstable and may yield negative probabilities. Since $P_i(0|n)$ is needed for computing $P_i(1|n+1)$, its underestimation will underestimate $P_i(1|n+1)$ which in turn means that $P_i(0|n+1)$ may be overestimated. Thus, the errors propagate in a chaotic manner. Although it is possible to get

```
for i = 1 to M do
  if i ∈ Ω_LD then P_i(0|0) = 1 else Q_i(0) = 0;
for n = 1 to N do
  begin
    for i = 1 to M do
      begin
        case i of
          simple : R_i(n) = s_i[1 + Q_i(n − 1)]
          delay : R_i(n) = s_i
          load-dep. : R_i(n) = s_i Σ_{k=1}^{n} (k / C_i(k)) P_i(k − 1|n − 1)
      end ;
    CT_1(n) = 0;
    for i = 1 to M do CT_1(n) = CT_1(n) + v_i R_i(n)/v_1;
    λ_1(n) = n/CT_1(n);
    for i = 1 to M do
      begin
        Q_i(n) = R_i(n)λ_1(n)v_i/v_1;    U_i(n) = s_i λ_1(n)v_i/v_1;
      end ;
    for i ∈ Ω_LD do
      begin
        for k = 1 to n do P_i(k|n) = U_i(n)P_i(k − 1|n − 1)/C_i(k);
        P_i(0|n) = 1 − Σ_{k=1}^{n} P_i(k|n);
      end ;
  end ;
```

FIGURE 7-4: Mean value analysis for single-chain networks.

$P_i(0|n)$ without using subtraction, the refined algorithm is too expensive. Standard measures such as using extended precision arithmetic, sorting probabilities in an increasing order, etc., can be of some value in alleviating numerical problems.

Example 7.2 Solve the network of Example 7.1 using mean value analysis.

Solution Here the scaling is irrelevant, so we retain the original values of relative utilizations. We start with population 1. Since there is no queuing for unit population, the results can be obtained trivially as

$$R_1(1) = 1000 \text{ ms}, \qquad R_2(1) = 40 \text{ ms}, \qquad R_3(1) = 50 \text{ ms}$$

Therefore, the cycle time $CT_1(1) = 1000 + 4 \times (40 + 50) = 1360$. Hence by Little's law,

$$\lambda_1(1) = 1/1360 = 0.73529/\text{sec}, \qquad \lambda_2(1) = \lambda_3(1) = 4\lambda_1(1) = 2.9412/\text{sec}$$

Using the utilization law, we could then obtain utilizations as

$$U_1(1) = 0.73539, \quad U_2(1) = 0.11765, \quad U_3(1) = 0.14706$$

For unit population, these numbers represent the queue lengths as well. The marginal probabilities are required only for station 2. For unit population, however, we need not use equation (2.1) since the utilization is already known.

$$P_2(1|1) = U_2(1) = 0.11765, \quad P_2(0|1) = 1 - P_2(1|1) = 0.88235$$

We now show the computations for population 2. We start by computing response times using equation (2.3) for a load-dependent station, and equation (2.4) for a load-independent station.

$$\begin{aligned} R_1(2) &= 1000 \text{ ms} \\ R_2(2) &= s_2[P_2(0|1) + 2 \times 1.05 \times P_2(1|1)] = 45.176 \text{ ms} \\ R_3(2) &= s_3[1 + Q_3(1)] = 50(1 + 0.14706) = 57.353 \text{ ms} \end{aligned}$$

Therefore, $CT_1 = R_1 + 4R_2 + 4R_3 = 1410.1$, where we have dropped population indicator for simplicity. Now,

$$\lambda_1 = 2/CT_1 = 1.4183/\text{sec} \qquad \lambda_2 = \lambda_3 = 4\lambda_1 = 5.6732/\text{sec}$$

$$\begin{aligned} &Q_1 = R_1\lambda_1 = 1.4183 && Q_2 = R_2\lambda_2 = 0.25629 && Q_3 = R_3\lambda_3 = 0.3254 \\ &U_1 = s_1\lambda_1 = 1.4183 && U_2 = s_2\lambda_2 = 0.22692 && U_3 = s_3\lambda_3 = 0.28366 \end{aligned}$$

□

7.3 Multiple-Chain Convolution

The multiple-chain convolution algorithm is a straightforward multi-dimensional extension of its single-chain version. We start with the multiple-chain counterparts to the relations shown in Section 7.1.1. Although we are primarily interested in chain-independent capacity functions, many of the results hold in general and will be proved as such. In view of equation (6.6.4), the corresponding chain-independent results can be obtained by simply replacing $V_i(\mathbf{n}_i)$ by $V_i(n_i)$. We start with the Convolution theorem.

Lemma 7.6 (Convolution theorem). Let Ω_1 and Ω_2 be two nonempty partitions of Ω, and let $\mathbf{n}$ denote the vector $(n_1, n_2, \ldots, n_K)$. Then,

$$G(\mathbf{N}, \Omega) = \sum_{n_1=0}^{N_1} \sum_{n_2=0}^{N_2} \cdots \sum_{n_K=0}^{N_K} G(\mathbf{N} - \mathbf{n}, \Omega_1) G(\mathbf{n}, \Omega_2) \tag{3.1}$$

Proof The proof is almost identical to the one for the single-chain case and is omitted. (Notice that the proof has nothing to do with the nature of the capacity function.)

□

Corollary 7.4 Let Ω_i denote the set $\{1..i\}$. Then,

$$G(\mathbf{N}, \Omega_i) = \sum_{n_{i1}=0}^{N_1} \cdots \sum_{n_{iK}=0}^{N_K} G(\mathbf{N} - \mathbf{n}_i, \Omega_{i-1})\, X_i(\mathbf{n}_i) \tag{3.2}$$

where $X_i(\mathbf{n}_i)$ denotes the unnormalized probability for station i, i.e.,

$$X_i(\mathbf{n}_i) = \frac{n_i!}{V_i(\mathbf{n}_i)} \prod_{r=1}^{K} \frac{u_{ir}^{n_{ir}}}{n_{ir}!} \tag{3.3}$$

Proof Obvious. □

Corollary 7.5 Let i be a load-independent station. Then,

$$G(\mathbf{N}, \Omega_i) = G(\mathbf{N}, \Omega_{i-1}) + \sum_{r=1}^{K} u_{ir} G(\mathbf{N} - e_r, \Omega_i) \tag{3.4}$$

Proof Let $\mathbf{S}_i(\mathbf{N})$ denote the set of all states for station i at network population $\mathbf{N}$. Decompose $\mathbf{S}_i(\mathbf{N})$ as $\mathbf{S}_0 \cup \mathbf{S}'$ where $\mathbf{S}_0$ is the set of all those states where station i is empty, and $\mathbf{S}'$ is the set of all remaining states. Let $f(\mathbf{n}_i)$ be some function that depends on the occupancy of station i. Then,

$$\sum_{\mathbf{S}_i(\mathbf{N})} f(\mathbf{n}_i) = f(\mathbf{0}) + \sum_{\mathbf{S}'} f(\mathbf{n}_i) = f(\mathbf{0}) + \sum_{k=1}^{K} \sum_{\mathbf{S}'(n_{ik}>0)} \frac{n_{ik}}{n_i} f(\mathbf{n}_i) \tag{3.5}$$

where we have changed the order of summation and put in the additional condition $n_{ik} > 0$ (which does not change anything). Let $f(\mathbf{n}_i) = G(\mathbf{N} - \mathbf{n}_i, \Omega_{i-1}) X_i(\mathbf{n}_i)$. Since i is a load-independent station, from the definition of X_i, we have

$$n_{ik} X_i(\mathbf{n}_i)/n_i = u_{ik} X_i(\mathbf{n}_i - e_k) \tag{3.6}$$

Thus, from equation (3.5) and the definition of the G function, we have

$$\begin{aligned} G(\mathbf{N}, \Omega) &= G(\mathbf{N}, \Omega_{i-1}) + \sum_{k=1}^{K} \sum_{\mathbf{S}'(n_{ik}>0)} G(\mathbf{N} - \mathbf{n}_i, \Omega_{i-1}) u_{ik} X_i(\mathbf{n}_i - e_k) \\ &= G(\mathbf{N}, \Omega_{i-1}) + \sum_{k=1}^{K} u_{ik} \sum_{\mathbf{S}_i(\mathbf{N} - e_k)} G(\mathbf{N} - e_k - \mathbf{n}_i, \Omega_{i-1}) X_i(\mathbf{n}_i) \end{aligned}$$

where we have substituted $\mathbf{n}_i$ for $\mathbf{n}_i - e_k$ in the last step. The effect of this is to remove the condition $n_{ik} > 0$, since $\mathbf{n}_i$ can now take all values from $\mathbf{0}$ to $\mathbf{N} - e_k$. That is, the summation is now over $\mathbf{S}_i(\mathbf{N} - e_k)$, the set of all possible states from $\mathbf{0}$ to $\mathbf{N} - e_k$ for station i. Now by applying Corollary 7.4 to the inner summation, we get equation (3.4). □

As in single-chain networks, Corollaries (7.4) and (7.5) provide the necessary equations for efficient computation of G. The computations involved are merely K-dimensional analogues of the ones in the single-chain case. We can again arrange the computations in a tabular form as in Table 7.1, except that in each column we now have entries corresponding to all possible population vectors from $\mathbf{0}$ to $\mathbf{N}$. This means that the time and space complexity of Convolution depends on the product of chain populations. Let

$$H = \prod_{r=1}^{K} (N_r + 1) \tag{3.7}$$

Then, to add a load-independent station, we need $O(KH)$ operations, whereas to add a load-dependent station, we need $O(H^2)$ operations. (In case of a load-dependent station, we are assuming that $X_i(\mathbf{n}_i)$ is computed from a previous value in $O(1)$ operations; but this does require extra space.) Minimum space needed to compute G is two columns, each of size H. Thus, the space complexity is $O(H)$.

Lemma 7.7 The chain-dependent marginal distribution at station i is given by

$$P_i(\mathbf{n}_i|\mathbf{N}) = \frac{G(\mathbf{N}-\mathbf{n}_i, \Omega - \{i\})}{G(\mathbf{N}, \Omega)} X_i(\mathbf{n}_i) \tag{3.8}$$

Proof It follows from the simple observation that if $\mathbf{n}_i$ customers are fixed at station i, the remaining $\mathbf{N} - \mathbf{n}_i$ customers can be spread arbitrarily over the rest of the network. Again the proof has nothing to do with the nature of the capacity function. □

For load-independent stations, it is no longer possible to obtain an equation like (1.5). However, we can obtain a multiple-chain analogue of the equation (1.6). For this, let us assume that station i is the last numbered station, so that Ω_{i-1} is the same thing as $\Omega - \{i\}$. Now, substitute equation (3.4) in equation (3.8). This yields

$$P_i(\mathbf{n}_i|\mathbf{N}) = \frac{n_i!}{G(\mathbf{N}, \Omega)} \left[G(\mathbf{N}-\mathbf{n}_i, \Omega) - \sum_{r=1}^{K} u_{ir} G(\mathbf{N}-e_r - \mathbf{n}_i, \Omega) \right] \prod_{r=1}^{K} \frac{u_{ir}^{n_{ir}}}{n_{ir}!} \tag{3.9}$$

Note that equation (3.9) itself is independent of any ordering, and *applies to any station i.*

Lemma 7.8 (Throughput theorem).

$$\lambda_{ir}(\mathbf{N}) = v_{ir} \frac{G(\mathbf{N}-e_r, \Omega)}{G(\mathbf{N}, \Omega)} \tag{3.10}$$

Proof The proof is similar to the one for the single-chain case, so it is sketched only briefly. Let $\mathbf{k}$ denote the occupancy vector at station i and $k = |\mathbf{k}|$. From the definition of throughput

$$\lambda_{ir}(\mathbf{N}) = \sum_{\mathbf{k}=e_r}^{\mathbf{N}} \frac{k_r}{k} \mu_{ir}^{\circ} C_{ir}(\mathbf{k}) P_i(\mathbf{k}|\mathbf{N}) \tag{3.11}$$

Substituting for $P_i(\mathbf{k}|\mathbf{N})$ from equation (3.8) into the above equation, simplifying, and using Corollary 7.4, we get the desired result. □

By multiplying both sides with s_{ir}°, we can also get the alternate form of the throughput theorem

$$U_{ir}(\mathbf{N}) = u_{ir} \frac{G(\mathbf{N}-e_r, \Omega)}{G(\mathbf{N}, \Omega)} \tag{3.12}$$

Let us now consider algorithmic details of computing performance parameters. Throughputs (and hence utilizations) are easily computed using equation (3.10). For a delay station, the average queue length is the same as utilization; therefore, unless higher moments or marginal distribution is required, we are done. For a load-independent station, the marginal distribution can be computed using equation (3.9). The G values needed in this equation are those from the last column of G's, and thus already available. Notice that if only the first few queue-length moments are needed, there is no need to store $P_i(\mathbf{n}_i|\mathbf{N})$'s, but their implicit computation is still needed. Exercise 7.3 shows a way of computing total average queue length for a load-independent station, but that too has the same time complexity. For a load-dependent station, we must use equation (3.8) to compute marginal distributions (and from there the queue-length moments). If the network contains more than one load-dependent station, we need to reorder them exactly as in the single-chain case. At least three "columns" of space will be needed in this case, but more columns can be used to reduce computation time.

It is easy to see that even for a modest multiple-chain model, the space and time requirements could grow enormous. Even worse, the large number of floating point operations could make the algorithm particularly susceptible to problems of overflow, underflow, and round-off errors. Thus, proper scaling is crucial in multiple-chain networks. One simple way of extending the scaling technique discussed in Section 7.1 is as follows:

1. Restrict the choice of visit ratios such that the largest loading (i.e., largest relative utilization) for all chains is the same. With this restriction, we only need to find one scaling factor for all chains.
2. The scaling can again be done such that the open network corresponding to the given closed network is not saturated. Recall that in an open product-form network with chain-independent capacities, all chains can be merged into one by determining the total relative utilization at each station. Thus, we find the scaling factor by applying the method of Section 7.1 to the aggregated single-chain network.

The main motivation of step 1 of this method is to minimize imbalances between the contributions of various chains to the G values. However, the G values corresponding to population vectors that result in large powers of very small relative utilizations could still cause underflow. More sophisticated scaling techniques are available, but we shall not go into those.

Example 7.3 Consider both chains in Fig. 7-2. Chain 1 (solid line) is for interactive jobs and chain 2 (broken line) is for the batch jobs. The average think time is 1 second and $q = 0.25$. Other parameters are given below:

CPU: PS, chain-independent capacity: $C(n) = 1/(0.95 + 0.05n)$.
Basic service rates: chain 1: 25/sec, chain 2: 12.5/sec.

Disk: FCFS, load-independent, exponential service-time distribution,
Service rates: chain 1: 20/sec, chain 2: 20 /sec.

Let $N_1 = 2$ and $N_2 = 1$. Solve the model and obtain all mean performance measures.

Solution For chain 1, the service times are $s_{11} = 1000$ ms, $s_{21} = 40$ ms, and $s_{31} = 50$ ms. From Example 7.1, the visit ratios are $v_{11} = 1$, $v_{21} = 4$, and $v_{31} = 4$. For chain 2, $s_{12} = 0$, $s_{22} = 80$ ms, and $s_{32} = 50$ ms. The visit ratios are $v_{12} = 0$, $v_{22} = v_{32} = 1$. The relative utilizations, scaled by a factor of 100, are listed below:

$$\begin{array}{lll} u_{11} = 10, & u_{21} = 1.6, & u_{31} = 2.0 \\ u_{12} = 0.0, & u_{22} = 0.8, & u_{32} = 0.5 \end{array} \tag{3.13}$$

For any subnetwork ω, $G([0,0],\omega) = 1$, and $G(e_r,\omega)$ is the sum of chain r relative utilizations over the stations in ω. We compute the remaining G functions in the following. To reduce notational clutter, we shall write $G(\mathbf{n},\omega)$ as $G_\omega(\mathbf{n})$ instead. Following the recommendations of Section 7.1, the stations are added in the order 3, 1, 2. Using equation (3.2) for $\mathbf{n} = (1,1)$, we get

$$G_3(1,1) = X_3(1,1) = 2!/(1!1!)u_{31}u_{32} = 2 \times 0.5 \times 2 = 2$$

$$\begin{aligned} G_{31}(1,1) &= \sum_{n_1=0}^{1}\sum_{n_2=0}^{1} X_3([1,1]-[n_1,n_2])\, X_1(n_1,n_2) \\ &= X_3(1,1)X_1(0,0) + X_3(1,0)X_1(0,1) + X_3(0,1)X_1(1,0) \\ &\qquad + X_3(0,0)X_1(1,1) = 2 + 0 + 0.5 \times 10 + 0 = 7 \end{aligned}$$

$$\begin{aligned} G_{312}(1,1) &= G_{31}(1,1) + G_{31}(1,0)X_2(0,1) \\ &\qquad + G_{31}(0,1)X_2(1,0) + G_{31}(0,0)X_2(1,1) \\ &= 7 + (12 \times 0.8) + (0.5 \times 1.6) + (2 \times 1.05 \times 1.6 \times 0.8) = 20.088 \end{aligned}$$

Similarly, at population vector (2,1), $X_3(2,1) = \frac{3!}{2!1!}u_{31}^2 \times u_{32} = 6.0$, and

$$\begin{aligned} G_{31}(2,1) &= X_3(2,1) + X_3(2,0)X_1(0,1) + X_3(1,1)X_1(1,0) \\ &\quad + X_3(1,0)X_1(1,1) + X_3(0,1)X_1(2,0) + X_1(2,1) = 51.0 \\ G_{312}(2,1) &= G_{31}(2,1) + G_{31}(2,0)X_2(0,1) + G_{31}(1,1)X_2(1,0) \\ &\quad + G_{31}(1,0)X_2(1,1) + G_{31}(0,1)X_2(2,0) + X_2(2,1) = 162.1 \end{aligned}$$

network	Station 3	Station 1	Station 2
G(1,0)	2.0	12.0	13.6
G(2,0)	4.0	74.0	95.888
G(0,1)	0.5	0.5	1.3
G(1,1)	2.0	7.0	20.088
G(2,1)	6.0	51.0	162.1

TABLE 7.2: Table of G values for Example 7.3.

All the G values are shown in Table 7.2. Using the throughput theorem and relationships between throughputs, we get

$$\begin{array}{lll} \lambda_{11}(2,1) = 1.239/\text{sec}, & \lambda_{21}(2,1) = 4.957/\text{sec}, & \lambda_{31}(2,1) = 4.957/\text{sec} \\ \lambda_{12}(2,1) = 0/\text{sec}, & \lambda_{22}(2,1) = 5.915/\text{sec}, & \lambda_{32}(2,1) = 5.915/\text{sec} \end{array}$$

We could then obtain utilizations using the utilization law. Because for station 1, the queue length is the same as the utilization, the former need not be computed explicitly. For station 3, we first obtain $G_{12}(\mathbf{N})$ using equation (3.4). Thus,

$$\begin{aligned} G_{12}(2,1) &= G_{312}(2,1) - G_{312}(1,1)u_{31} - G_{312}(2,0)u_{32} = 73.976 \\ G_{12}(2,0) &= G_{312}(2,0) - G_{312}(1,0)u_{31} = 68.688 \\ G_{12}(1,1) &= G_{312}(1,1) - G_{312}(0,1)u_{31} - G_{312}(1,0)u_{32} = 10.688 \end{aligned}$$

Now, using equation (3.8), we can compute the marginal distribution $P_3(n_1, n_2)$. (As stated earlier, if only a few queue-length moments are needed, it is not necessary to store this distribution explicitly.)

$$\begin{aligned} P_3(0,0) &= G_{12}(2,1)/G_{312}(2,1) = 0.45637 \\ P_3(0,1) &= u_{32}G_{12}(2,0)/G_{312}(2,1) = 0.21187 \\ P_3(1,1) &= 2u_{32}u_{31}G_{12}(1,0)/G_{312}(2,1) = 0.14316 \\ P_3(1,0) &= u_{31}G_{12}(1,1)/G_{312}(2,1) = 0.13187 \\ P_3(2,0) &= u_{31}^2G_{12}(0,1)/G_{312}(2,1) = 0.019741 \\ P_3(2,1) &= 3u_{31}^2u_{32}G_{312}(0,0)/G_{312}(2,1) = 0.037015 \end{aligned}$$

Therefore, the marginal probability for chain 1 at station 3 can be obtained as $P_{31}(n_1) = P_3(n_1, 0) + P_3(n_1, 1)$ for $n_1 = 0..2$. This gives $P_{31}(0) = 0.66824$, $P_{31}(1) = 0.27503$, and $P_{31}(2) = 0.05675$. Thus, by the definition of queue length,

$Q_{31}(2,1) = 0.38851$. Similarly, we can compute $P_{32}(n_2)$, and thereby $Q_{32}(2,1)$, which turns out to be 0.39201. Hence by applying Little's law, $R_{31}(2,1) = Q_{31}/\lambda_{31} = 78.375$ ms, and $R_{32}(2,1) = Q_{32}/\lambda_{32} = 66.27$ ms.

Since $G_{31}(\mathbf{N})$ is available from the initial computation, we have

$$\begin{aligned}
P_2(0,0) &= G_{13}(2,1)/G_{312}(2,1) = 51/162.1 = 0.31463 \\
P_2(0,1) &= u_{22}G_{13}(2,0)/G_{312}(2,1) = 0.36521 \\
P_2(1,0) &= u_{21}G_{13}(1,1)/G_{312}(2,1) = 0.069095 \\
P_2(1,1) &= 2u_{21}u_{22}G_{13}(1,0)/[C_2(2)G_{312}(2,1)] = 0.19899 \\
P_2(2,0) &= u_{21}^2G_{13}(0,1)/[C_2(2)G_{312}(2,1)] = 0.0082914 \\
P_2(2,1) &= 3u_{21}^2u_{22}G_{13}(0,0)/[C_2(2)C_2(3)G_{312}(2,1)] = 0.043778
\end{aligned}$$

Using formulas similar to that for station 3, we thus get $Q_{21}(2,1) = 0.37227$, $Q_{22}(2,1) = 0.60799$, $R_{21}(2,1) = 75.10$ ms, and $R_{22}(2,1) = 102.79$ ms. □

7.4 Multiple-Chain Mean Value Analysis

This algorithm is a simple extension of the corresponding single-chain algorithm and will be discussed only briefly. We start by stating the multiple-chain version of the marginal local balance (MLB) theorem. In the following, $\mathbf{n}$ denotes the vector $(n_1, \ldots, n_K)$ where n_r gives the number of chain r customers at the station in question.

Lemma 7.9 The marginal distribution at station i is given by

$$P_i(\mathbf{n}|\mathbf{N}) = \frac{\lambda_{ir}(\mathbf{N})}{\mu^*_{ir}(\mathbf{n})} P_i(\mathbf{n}-e_r|\mathbf{N}-e_r) \tag{4.1}$$

Proof From the definition of $X_i(\mathbf{n})$,

$$X_i(\mathbf{n}) = \frac{nu_{ir}}{n_r C_i(\mathbf{n})} X_i(\mathbf{n} - e_r) \tag{4.2}$$

Substituting this into equation (3.8), we get

$$P_i(\mathbf{n}|\mathbf{N}) = \frac{nu_{ir}}{n_r C_i(\mathbf{n})} \frac{X_i(\mathbf{n}-e_r)}{G(\mathbf{N},\Omega)} G(\mathbf{N} - \mathbf{n}, \Omega - \{i\})$$

From the alternate form of the throughput theorem in equation (3.12), we have

$$P_i(\mathbf{n}|\mathbf{N}) = \frac{nU_{ir}(\mathbf{N})}{n_r C_i(\mathbf{n})} \frac{X_i(\mathbf{n}-e_r)G(\mathbf{N}-e_r - (\mathbf{n}-e_r), \Omega - \{i\})}{G(\mathbf{N}-e_r, \Omega)}$$

Now by applying equation (3.8) and using the definition of μ^*_{ir}, we get the result. □

As in the single-chain case, equation (4.1) balances the effective flow between the marginal states $(\mathbf{n}|\mathbf{N})$ and $(\mathbf{n}-e_r|\mathbf{N}-e_r)$. Henceforth, we assume that the capacities are chain-independent. For this case, equation (4.1) reduces to

$$P_i(\mathbf{n}_i|\mathbf{N}) = \frac{n_i U_{ir}(\mathbf{N})}{n_{ir} C_i(n_i)} P_i(\mathbf{n}_i - e_r|\mathbf{N}-e_r) \tag{4.3}$$

A further consequence of chain-independent capacity is that chain-dependent marginal probabilities are not needed for computing the average performance parameters. To show this, we start with an important result, known as the aggregate MLB theorem.

Lemma 7.10 (Aggregate MLB theorem). If station i has chain-independent capacity, its chain-independent marginal distribution is given by

$$P_i(n|\mathbf{N}) = \sum_{r=1}^{K} \frac{U_{ir}(\mathbf{N})}{C_i(n)} P_i(n-1|\mathbf{N}-e_r) \tag{4.4}$$

Proof By definition, $P_i(n-1|\mathbf{N}-e_r) = \sum_{|\mathbf{n}_i|=n-1} P_i(\mathbf{n}_i|\mathbf{N}-e_r)$. We note that in this summation, $\forall\ k\ n_{ik} \geq 0$, $n_{ir} \leq N_r - 1$, and $\forall\ k \neq r\ n_{ik} \leq N_k$. Now, by substituting $\mathbf{n}_i - e_r$ for $\mathbf{n}_i$ on the right-hand side, we get

$$P_i(n-1|\mathbf{N}-e_r) = \sum_{n_{ir}>0,\ |\mathbf{n}_i|=n} P_i(\mathbf{n}_i - e_r|\mathbf{N}-e_r) \tag{4.5}$$

By using equation (4.3) to replace $P_i(\mathbf{n}_i - e_r|\mathbf{N}-e_r)$ in equation (4.5), we get

$$\frac{U_{ir}(\mathbf{N})}{C_i(n)} P_i(n-1|\mathbf{N}-e_r) = \sum_{n_{ir}>0, |\mathbf{n}_i|=n} \frac{n_{ir}}{n} P_i(\mathbf{n}_i|\mathbf{N})$$

Now the condition $n_{ir} > 0$ can be removed from the left-hand side, and by summing over all the chains and changing the order of summation, we get

$$\sum_{r=1}^{K} \frac{U_{ir}(\mathbf{N})}{C_i(n)} P_i(n-1|\mathbf{N}-e_r) = \sum_{|\mathbf{n}_i|=n} \sum_{r=1}^{K} \frac{n_{ir}}{n} P_i(\mathbf{n}_i|\mathbf{N}) = P_i(n|\mathbf{N})$$

□

The main significance of equation (4.4) is that the aggregate marginal probabilities (and hence the aggregate performance measures) can be computed without involving chain-dependent marginal probabilities. We next show that *chain-dependent average parameters* can also be obtained by using *chain-independent* marginal probabilities.

Lemma 7.11 If station i has chain-independent capacity, then

$$R_{ir}(\mathbf{N}) = s_{ir}^{\circ} \sum_{n=1}^{N} \frac{n}{C_i(n)} P_i(n-1|\mathbf{N}-e_r) \tag{4.6}$$

Proof By definition,

$$
\begin{aligned}
Q_{ir}(\mathbf{N}) &= \sum_{k=1}^{N_r} k\,Pr(n_{ir}=k|\mathbf{N}) = \sum_{k=1}^{N_r} \sum_{\forall \mathbf{n}_i, n_{ir}=k} kP_i(\mathbf{n}_i|\mathbf{N}) \\
&= \sum_{k=1}^{N_r} \sum_{\forall \mathbf{n}_i:\, n_{ir}=k} U_{ir}(\mathbf{N}) \frac{n_i}{C_i(n_i)} P_i(\mathbf{n}_i - e_r|\mathbf{N}-e_r)
\end{aligned}
$$

where we have used equation (4.3). Notice that in the last equation, the two summations collectively cover all occupancy vectors where $n_{ir} > 0$. Therefore, by grouping together terms for each value of $|\mathbf{n}_i|$, we get,

$$
\begin{aligned}
Q_{ir}(\mathbf{N}) &= U_{ir}(\mathbf{N}) \sum_{n=1}^{N} \frac{n}{C_i(n)} \sum_{|\mathbf{n}_i|=n, n_{ir}>0} P_i(\mathbf{n}_i - e_r|\mathbf{N}-e_r) \\
&= U_{ir}(\mathbf{N}) \sum_{n=1}^{N} \frac{n}{C_i(n)} P_i(n-1|\mathbf{N}-e_r)
\end{aligned}
$$

where we have applied equation (4.5). Now by applying Little's law, we get the result. □

For the special case of a load-independent station, $C_i(n) = 1$ for all n; therefore, equation (4.6) can be put into the following closed form

$$
R_{ir}(\mathbf{N}) = s_{ir}[1 + Q_i(\mathbf{N}-e_r)] \tag{4.7}
$$

This equation is the same as (4.4.30), i.e., the mean value theorem for multiple-chain networks. It has the same intuitive interpretation as in the single-chain case. In particular, from the arrival theorem, $QA_i^{(r)}(\mathbf{N}) = Q_i(\mathbf{N}-e_r)$; therefore, $1 + Q_i(\mathbf{N}-e_r)$ gives the average number of customers that will share the server equally following the arrival of a typical chain r customer. Therefore, to receive s_{ir} units of service, this customer must spend $s_{ir}(1 + Q_i(\mathbf{N}-e_r))$ units of time in the system.

Multiplying by $\lambda_{ir}(\mathbf{N})$ on both sides of equation (4.7), we get the queue-length version of mean value theorem, which is useful in some of the algorithms.

$$
Q_{ir}(\mathbf{N}) = U_{ir}(\mathbf{N})[1 + Q_i(\mathbf{N}-e_r)] \tag{4.8}
$$

The complete MVA algorithm is shown in Fig. 7-5. For convenience in expressing it, we assume that all quantities are zero at negative populations. The body of the for-loop over $\mathbf{n}$ forms the single step of the MVA algorithm. The computations in the single step *for each chain* are similar to the ones for the single-chain MVA; i.e., we first compute the response times, then apply Little's law to the entire network to obtain throughputs, and finally compute the utilizations, queue lengths, and marginal distributions. The single MVA step must be executed for all population vectors from $\mathbf{0}$ to $\mathbf{N}$; therefore, the dominant factor

for $i = 1$ **to** M **do**
  begin
    if $i \in \Omega_{LD}$ **then** $P_i(0|\mathbf{0}) = 1$;
    for $r = 1$ **to** K **do** $Q_{ir}(\mathbf{0}) = 0$;
  end ;
for n $=$ **0 to N do**
  begin
    for $r = 1$ **to** K **do**
      begin
        for $i = 1$ **to** M **do**
          case station-type[i] of
            delay-server : $R_{ir}(\mathbf{n}) = s_{ir}$
            load-independent: $R_{ir}(\mathbf{n}) = s_{ir}(1 + Q_i(\mathbf{n} - e_r))$
            load-dependent : $R_{ir}(\mathbf{n}) = s_{ir} \sum_{k=1}^{n} \frac{k}{C_i(k)} P_i(k-1|\mathbf{n} - e_r)$
          end ;
        $CT_{jr} = 0$; {Pick some station j with nonzero v_{jr}}
        for $i = 1$ **to** M **do** $CT_{jr} = CT_{jr} + \frac{v_{ir}}{v_{jr}} R_{ir}(\mathbf{n})$;
        for $i = 1$ **to** M **do**
          begin
            $\lambda_{ir}(\mathbf{n}) = (v_{ir}/v_{jr})(N_r/CT_{jr})$;
            $U_{ir}(\mathbf{n}) = s_{ir}\lambda_{ir}(\mathbf{n})$; $Q_{ir}(\mathbf{n}) = R_{ir}(\mathbf{n})\lambda_{ir}(\mathbf{n})$;
          end ;
      end ;
    for $i \in \Omega_{LD}$ **do**
      begin
        for $k = 1$ **to** n **do**
          begin
            $P_i(k|\mathbf{n}) = 0$;
            for $r = 1$ **to** K **do** $P_i(k|\mathbf{n}) = P_i(k|\mathbf{n}) + \frac{U_{ir}(\mathbf{n})}{C_i(k)} P_i(k-1|\mathbf{n} - e_r)$;
          end ;
        $P_i(0|\mathbf{n}) = 1$;
        for $k = 1$ **to** n **do** $P_i(0|\mathbf{n}) = P_i(0|\mathbf{n}) - P_i(k|\mathbf{n})$;
      end ;
  end ;

FIGURE 7-5: Mean value analysis algorithm for multiple-chain networks.

in the time complexity is H, as defined in equation (3.7). It is clear that the time complexity of the entire algorithm per station is $O(KNH)$ for a load-dependent station, and $O(KH)$ otherwise. The space complexity is also of the same order, i.e., $O((K + N)H)$ for a load-dependent station, and $O(KH)$ otherwise. It is instructive to compare these numbers against those for Convolution. For a load-independent station, the time complexity is the same for both algorithms, but convolution is much more expensive for a load-dependent station. In particular, Convolution requires $O(H^2)$ operations for adding such a station, which is much larger than $O(KNH)$. The difference comes because *Convolution really does not take advantage of chain-independent capacities.*

Even though the space complexity of MVA is similar to its time complexity, significant space savings could be achieved by careful coding. Since all performance parameters depend on the population vector, a simple-minded data structure for storing them is a K-dimensional array indexed by chain populations. A fixed-size multi-dimensional array will not use space efficiently; therefore, one should either use dynamic arrays (if available), or carve out the desired multi-dimensional array from a single fixed-size, one-dimensional array. The simplest implementation of the loop over $\mathbf{n}$ in Fig. 7-5 is to use K nested loops, one over each chain. In such an implementation, we only need values at the previous population level for the outermost chain. Thus, if we choose the outermost chain to be the one with the largest population, significant storage savings are achieved. However, the nested loop implementation "hard wires" the maximum number of chains, which is undesirable. It would also do several unnecessary index expression evaluations whenever the number of chains in the model is smaller than the maximum allowed. A better approach is to organize the algorithm such that it has a loop only for the total population n, and for each value of n, it explicitly generates all feasible population vectors $\mathbf{n}$ and computes performance parameters for them. Since the computations at population $\mathbf{n}$ only need results at population vector $\mathbf{n}-e_r$, any results computed in earlier passes can be discarded. As a final note, it is unnecessary to store U_{ir}'s and R_{ir}'s, since these can be computed from queue lengths and throughputs.

Although the computation of $P_i(0|\mathbf{n})$ is unstable, it involves only n terms (as it would in the single-chain case). If, however, we were dealing with chain-dependent capacity functions, the numerical problems will be further exacerbated.

Example 7.4 Solve the network of Example 7.3 using mean value analysis.

Solution For notational simplicity, we shall omit population vectors from the parameters except when necessary. Results for population vectors (1,0) and (2,0) are already available from Example 7.2. The results for population (0,1) are trivial to compute (since there is no queuing), and are listed below:

$$R_{12} = 0, \qquad R_{22} = 80 \text{ ms}, \qquad R_{32} = 50 \text{ ms}$$

$$\begin{aligned} P_2(1|0,1) &= Q_{22} = U_{22} = u_{22}/(u_{22}+u_{32}) = 0.61539 \\ P_2(0|0,1) &= Q_{32} = U_{32} = u_{32}/(u_{22}+u_{32}) = 0.38461 \end{aligned}$$

<u>Population (1,1):</u> Of course, $R_{11} = 1000$ ms and $R_{12} = 0$.

$$R_{21} = 40\left[P_2(0|0,1) + \frac{2}{C_2(2)}P_2(1|0,1)\right] = 67.077 \text{ ms}$$

$$
\begin{aligned}
R_{31} &= 50[1 + Q_3(0,1)] = 69.231 \text{ ms} \\
\lambda_{11} &= \frac{1}{R_{11} + 4(R_{21} + R_{31})} = 0.64172/\text{sec} \\
\lambda_{21} &= \lambda_{31} = 4\lambda_{11} = 2.5886/\text{sec} \\
R_{22} &= 80\left[P_2(0|1,0) + \frac{2}{C_2(2)} P_2(1|1,0)\right] = 90.353 \text{ ms} \\
R_{32} &= 50[1 + Q_3(1,0)] = 57.353 \text{ ms} \\
\lambda_{12} &= 0, \quad \lambda_{22} = \lambda_{32} = 1/(R_{22} + R_{32}) = 6.7702/\text{sec} \\
Q_{31} &= R_{31}\lambda_{31} = 0.17921, \quad Q_{32} = R_{32}\lambda_{32} = 0.38829 \\
U_{21} &= s_{21}\lambda_{21} = 0.10355, \quad U_{22} = s_{22}\lambda_{22} = 0.54162 \\
P_2(1|1,1) &= U_{21}P_2(0|0,1) + U_{22}P_2(0|1,0) = 0.51772 \\
P_2(2|1,1) &= 1.05\left[U_{21}P_2(1|0,1) + U_{22}P_2(1|1,0)\right] = 0.13381 \\
P_2(0|1,1) &= 1 - P_2(1|1,1) - P_2(2|1,1) = 0.34847
\end{aligned}
$$

Population (2,1): Again, $R_{11} = 1000$ ms and $R_{12} = 0$. By equation (4.6) we get $R_{21} = 75.09$ ms and $R_{22} = 102.78$ ms. By equation (4.7), $R_{31} = 78.375$ ms and $R_{32})] = 66.27$ ms. Therefore,

$$
\begin{aligned}
\lambda_{11} &= 2/[R_{11} + 4(R_{21} + R_{31})] = 1.2393/\text{sec} \\
\lambda_{21} &= 4\lambda_{11} = 4.957/\text{sec}, \quad \lambda_{31} = \lambda_{21} = 4.957/\text{sec} \\
\lambda_{12} &= 0, \quad \lambda_{22} = \lambda_{32} = 1/(R_{22} + R_{32}) = 5.9155/\text{sec}
\end{aligned}
$$

Therefore, by utilization and Little's laws, we have

$$
\begin{array}{lll}
U_{11} = 1.23926, & U_{21} = 0.19828, & U_{31} = 0.2479 \\
U_{12} = 0, & U_{22} = 0.4732, & U_{32} = 0.2958 \\
Q_{11} = 1.23926, & Q_{21} = 0.3722, & Q_{31} = 0.3885 \\
Q_{12} = 0, & Q_{22} = 0.6079, & Q_{32} = 0.3920
\end{array}
$$

□

7.5 The LBANC Algorithm

This algorithm is merely a simple modification of the mean value analysis, and we shall only indicate its major steps for the multiple-chain case. In one step of the MVA algorithm, we first compute the response times, then the throughputs, and finally the queue lengths and marginal probabilities. This somewhat roundabout computation is necessary because the equations (4.8) and (4.4) involve utilizations at population $\mathbf{N}$ and cannot be used directly. The LBANC algorithm avoids this problem by using *unnormalized* versions of the parameters, and thus can save a bit of computation. Unlike MVA, however, it needs to compute the normalization constant G.

We define unnormalized queue lengths and marginal probabilities by simply multiplying them with G and denote them using lower-case letters. Thus, for example, the unnormalized queue-length $q_{ir}(\mathbf{N})$ can be defined as $Q_{ir}(\mathbf{N})G(\mathbf{N})$. Using the throughput theorem, it is easy to verify that the unnormalization of equation (4.1) yields,

$$p_i(\mathbf{n}|\mathbf{N}) = \frac{nu_{ir}}{n_r C_i(\mathbf{n})} p_i(\mathbf{n}-e_r|\mathbf{N}-e_r) \tag{5.1}$$

Assuming chain-independent capacities, we only need the unnormalized version of equation (4.4), which is

$$p_i(n|\mathbf{N}) = \sum_{r=1}^{K} \frac{u_{ir}}{C_i(n)} p_i(n-1|\mathbf{N}-e_r) \tag{5.2}$$

This, in turn, yields the following expression for chain-dependent queue lengths

$$q_{ir}(\mathbf{N}) = u_{ir} \sum_{n=1}^{N} \frac{n}{C_i(n)} p_i(n-1|\mathbf{N}-e_r) \tag{5.3}$$

For a load-independent station, the mean value theorem yields

$$q_{ir}(\mathbf{N}) = u_{ir}\left[G(\mathbf{N}-e_r) + q_i(\mathbf{N}-e_r)\right] \tag{5.4}$$

For a delay station, queue length equals utilization; therefore, by the alternate form of the throughput theorem, we have

$$q_{ir}(\mathbf{N}) = u_{ir} G(\mathbf{N}-e_r) \tag{5.5}$$

Given the unnormalized performance parameters at population $\mathbf{N}-e_r$ for all r, the last three equations can be used to compute unnormalized queue lengths at population $\mathbf{N}$. We could then determine $G(\mathbf{N})$ using the fact that all unnormalized queue lengths for any chain r must sum to $N_r G(\mathbf{N})$. However, a numerically better method is to use the total queue lengths, i.e., $\sum_{i=1}^{M} q_i(\mathbf{N}) = NG(\mathbf{N})$. Finally, we can compute $p_i(n|\mathbf{N})$ using equation (5.2) for $n > 0$, and $p_i(0|\mathbf{N})$ as $G(\mathbf{N}) - \sum_{n=1}^{N} p_i(n|\mathbf{N})$. Thus, all performance parameters at population $\mathbf{N}$ can be computed. The complete algorithm should now be obvious and will not be presented.

7.6 Algorithms for Mixed Networks

Mixed models can be solved by modifying the service rates of various stations to account for the service capacity consumed by the open chains and then considering only the closed chains. Open chain parameters could then be computed using the closed chain parameters. Thus, *the complexity of solving a mixed model is governed primarily by the number of closed chains*. For mixed models, we need to make sure that the steady-state solution exists. This is done by considering only the open chains, since closed chains cannot cause instability.

A major application of mixed models is in the approximate solution of large closed networks. Recall that the complexity of solving closed models depends on the product of chain populations; therefore, if some chains have a large population, the solution may be expensive. Large populations may also cause the bottleneck phenomenon at certain stations. Let b denote a bottleneck station, and B the set of chains passing through b. Then, we can make all these chains open with Λ_r, $r \in B$ set to $\mu_{br}(\infty)f_r$, where f_r is the fraction of service capacity dedicated to serving chain r customers *under the bottleneck phenomenon*. It is essential to estimate f_r by some independent means, the details of which are not important here.

It was shown in Section 6.2.3 that open chains behave like classes, and if the capacities are chain-independent, we can merge them all into one before attempting the solution. Throughout this section, we assume chain-independent capacities; hence, it suffices to consider only one open chain in the network. We will number the open chain as "0". Chains $1..K$ will be closed, as usual, with the population vector $\mathbf{N} = (N_1, \ldots, N_K)$.

In the following, we denote the original mixed network as $\mathcal{Z}_M$ and the corresponding closed network as $\mathcal{Z}_C$. The "corresponding closed network" refers to the original network without the open chain, *but with the effect of open chain accounted for indirectly*. We shall denote parameters for $\mathcal{Z}_C$ by appending a "C" (or "c") to the notation for the parameters of the original network. In particular, we use the symbol PC for the normalized probabilities of $\mathcal{Z}_C$, XC for its unnormalized probabilities, etc. Also, if in $\mathcal{Z}_M$, $\mathbf{n}_i = (n_{i0}, n_{i1}, \ldots, n_{iK})$ is the occupancy vector at station i, we denote the corresponding quantity for $\mathcal{Z}_C$ as $\mathbf{nc}_i = (n_{i1}, \ldots, n_{iK})$. As usual, we use the symbol n_i for $|\mathbf{n}_i|$ and nc_i for $|\mathbf{nc}_i|$. Obviously, $n_i = n_{i0} + nc_i$. Now from the product-form solution of $\mathcal{Z}_M$, we have

$$P(\mathbf{n}_1, \mathbf{n}_2, \ldots, \mathbf{n}_M) = \frac{1}{G(\mathbf{N}, \Omega)} \prod_{i=1}^{M} X_i(\mathbf{n}_i) \tag{6.1}$$

where $\mathbf{n}_i = (n_{i0}, n_{i1}, \ldots, n_{iK})$ and

$$X_i(\mathbf{n}_i) = \frac{n_i!}{V_i(n_i)} \prod_{r=0}^{K} \frac{u_{ir}^{n_{ir}}}{n_{ir}!} \tag{6.2}$$

Notice the lower bound of $r = 0$ in the above equation. In the following, we shall abbreviate $G(\mathbf{N}, \Omega)$ as G. Since the real utilization can be precomputed for the open chain, we shall choose u_{i0} as simply U_{i0}. Now if we sum equation (6.1) over all possible values of $n_{i0}, i \in 1..M$, we get the state probability involving only closed chains. That is,

$$\begin{aligned} PC(\mathbf{nc}_1, \ldots, \mathbf{nc}_M) &= \frac{1}{G} \sum_{n_{10}=0}^{\infty} \cdots \sum_{n_{M0}=0}^{\infty} \prod_{i=1}^{M} X_i(\mathbf{n}_i) = \frac{1}{G} \prod_{i=1}^{M} \sum_{n_{i0}=0}^{\infty} X_i(\mathbf{n}_i) \\ &= \frac{1}{G} \prod_{i=1}^{M} \sum_{n_{i0}=0}^{\infty} \left[\frac{(n_{i0} + nc_i)!}{V_i(n_{i0} + nc_i)} \frac{U_{i0}^{n_{i0}}}{n_{i0}!} \right] \prod_{r=1}^{K} \frac{u_{ir}^{n_{ir}}}{n_{ir}!} \end{aligned}$$

$$\triangleq \quad \frac{1}{G}\prod_{i=1}^{M}\frac{nc_i!}{VC_i(nc_i)}\prod_{r=1}^{K}\frac{u_{ir}^{n_{ir}}}{n_{ir}!} \tag{6.3}$$

where we have introduced a new function VC_i, defined as

$$\frac{1}{VC_i(nc_i)} = \sum_{n_{i0}=0}^{\infty}\binom{n_{i0}+nc_i}{n_{i0}}\frac{U_{i0}^{n_{i0}}}{V_i(n_{i0}+nc_i)} \tag{6.4}$$

This allows us to write (6.3) in the following compact form

$$PC(\mathbf{nc}_1,\ldots,\mathbf{nc}_M) = \frac{1}{G}\prod_{i=1}^{M} XC_i(\mathbf{nc}_i) \tag{6.5}$$

where

$$XC_i(\mathbf{nc}_i) = \frac{nc_i!}{VC_i(nc_i)}\prod_{r=1}^{K}\frac{u_{ir}^{n_{ir}}}{n_{ir}!} \tag{6.6}$$

This equation is interesting, because it shows that the solution for the closed chains is exactly as in a closed network provided that we replace the V_i function with VC_i. Now, just as V_i is a product of given capacities, we can interpret VC_i as the product of *effective capacities*, denoted as CC_i. That is,

$$CC_i(k) = \frac{VC_i(k)}{VC_i(k-1)} = C_i(k)\frac{VR_i(k-1)}{VR_i(k)} \tag{6.7}$$

where we have introduced a new function VR_i that expresses the ratio of original and modified V_i functions. That is, $VR_i(n) = V_i(n)/VC_i(n)$. Thus, we can write equation (6.4) as follows:

$$VR_i(nc_i) = \sum_{n=0}^{\infty}\binom{nc_i+n}{n}\prod_{l=nc_i+1}^{nc_i+n}\frac{U_{i0}}{C_i(l)} \tag{6.8}$$

To summarize, *if we use the capacity function CC_i, instead of C_i, we can ignore the open chain as far as the performance parameters of the closed chains are concerned.* The resulting closed network $\mathcal{Z}_C$ can be solved using any of the algorithms mentioned in Section 6.5. The only difficulty arises in the evaluation of equation (6.8) since it involves infinite summation. Fortunately, in most models of real systems, it is reasonable to assume that the capacity saturates at some point. In such cases, we can obtain a simple expression for the VR_i function. Let w_i denote the saturation point. Then for $k \geq w_i - 1$, equation (6.8) yields

$$VR_i(k) = \sum_{n=0}^{\infty}\binom{k+n}{n}\left[\frac{U_{i0}}{C_i(w_i)}\right]^n = \frac{1}{[1-U_{i0}/C_i(w_i)]^{k+1}} \tag{6.9}$$

Let $\eta(l) = U_{i0}/C_i(l)$ and $\phi_k(m) = \prod_{l=k+1}^{m} C_i(w_i)/C_i(l)$. Then for $k < w_i - 1$, some simple manipulation of equation (6.8) gives

$$VR_i(k) = \sum_{n=0}^{w_i-2}\binom{k+n}{n}\frac{\phi_k(k+n)-\phi_k(w_i-1)}{[\eta(w_i)]^n} + \frac{\phi_k(w_i-1)}{[1-\eta(w_i)]^{k+1}} \tag{6.10}$$

Next, we show how to compute the performance measures for the open chain. The starting point for this is the expression for the marginal probability $P_i(\mathbf{n}_i|\mathbf{N})$ in equation (3.8). Equation (6.5) shows that the state probabilities for the network $\mathcal{Z}_C$ have the same form as those for the original network $\mathcal{Z}_M$; therefore, we can also write

$$PC_i(\mathbf{n}_i|\mathbf{N}) = XC_i(\mathbf{n}_i)\frac{G(\mathbf{N}-\mathbf{n}_i, \Omega - \{i\})}{G(\mathbf{N}, \Omega)} \tag{6.11}$$

where we specifically note that the G functions for $\mathcal{Z}_C$ are the same as those for $\mathcal{Z}_M$, since the former is just a different way of viewing $\mathcal{Z}_M$. It thus follows that

$$P_i(\mathbf{n}_i|\mathbf{N}) = \frac{X_i(\mathbf{n}_i)}{XC_i(\mathbf{nc}_i)} PC_i(\mathbf{nc}_i|\mathbf{N}) \tag{6.12}$$

Now by substituting the definitions of X_i and XC_i from equations (6.2) and (6.6) in this equation, we get

$$P_i(\mathbf{n}_i|\mathbf{N}) = U_{i0}^{n_{i0}} \binom{n_i + n_{i0}}{n_{i0}} \left[VR_i(nc_i) \prod_{l=nc_i+1}^{n_i+n_{i0}} C_i(l) \right]^{-1} PC_i(\mathbf{nc}_i|\mathbf{N}) \tag{6.13}$$

Let $P_{i0}(n|\mathbf{N})$ denote the marginal probability that station i contains n chain 0 customers. We can obtain this by summing the last equation over all possible vectors $\mathbf{nc}_i$. We can group these vectors into $N+1$ subsets, one for each possible value of nc_i. The summation then yields

$$P_{i0}(n|\mathbf{N}) = U_{i0}^{n} \sum_{nc=0}^{N} \binom{nc + n}{n} \left[VR_i(nc) \prod_{l=nc+1}^{nc+n} C_i(l) \right]^{-1} PC_i(nc|\mathbf{N}) \tag{6.14}$$

where nc is a shorthand for nc_i. This equation says that $P_{i0}(n|\mathbf{N})$ can be computed from $PC_i(nc|\mathbf{N})$, the aggregate marginal distribution for the closed chains. Note that if we use MVA to solve the closed network, $PC_i(nc|\mathbf{N})$ will be computed automatically in the course of the algorithm. Of course, here we are speaking of load-dependent stations; for load-independent and delay stations, there is no need to compute marginal distributions, unless such distributions are needed themselves. We shall show this shortly, but first we show that if only the mean performance measures are needed, some simplifications are possible even for load-dependent stations. Using equation (6.14) and the definition of mean queue length, we have

$$Q_{i0}(\mathbf{N}) = \sum_{n=1}^{\infty} n P_{i0}(n|\mathbf{N}) = \sum_{nc=0}^{N} f(nc) PC_i(nc|\mathbf{N}) \tag{6.15}$$

where

$$\begin{aligned} f(nc) &= \frac{1}{VR_i(nc)} \sum_{n=1}^{\infty} n \binom{nc+n}{n} U_{i0}^{n} \left[\prod_{l=nc+1}^{nc+n} C_i(l) \right]^{-1} \\ &= \frac{(nc+1)U_{i0}}{C_i(nc+1)} \frac{VR_i(nc+1)}{VR_i(nc)} = U_{i0} \frac{nc+1}{CC_i(nc+1)} \end{aligned} \tag{6.16}$$

where in the last line we changed the summation index and used the definition of VR_i from equation (6.8). Thus, the open chain queue length can be computed from

$$Q_{i0}(\mathbf{N}) = U_{i0} \sum_{nc=0}^{N} \frac{(nc+1)}{CC_i(nc+1)} PC_i(nc|\mathbf{N}) \tag{6.17}$$

Note the resemblance of this equation to equation (4.6). With queue lengths known, the response times for the open chain can be obtained using Little's law.

We now specialize the results for load-independent and delay stations. For a load-independent station, from equation (6.9) and the definition of VR_i, we get

$$VC_i(k) = 1/VR_i(k) = (1 - U_{i0})^{k+1} \tag{6.18}$$

for all k. Although this can be used directly in equation (6.6), it is worth making a simple observation. Let sc_{ir} denote the service time for chain r at station i in the network $\mathcal{Z}_C$, and uc_{ir} the corresponding relative utilization. Let

$$sc_{ir} = s_{ir}/(1 - U_{i0}) \tag{6.19}$$

where s_{ir} is the original service time of chain r at station i. Then,

$$XC_i(\mathbf{nc}_i) = nc_i! \prod_{r=1}^{K} \frac{uc_{ir}^{n_{ir}}}{n_{ir}!} = \frac{nc_i!}{[1 - U_{i0}]^{nc_i}} \prod_{r=1}^{K} \frac{u_{ir}^{n_{ir}}}{n_{ir}!} \tag{6.20}$$

Thus, using $VC_i(k)$ from (6.18) in (6.6) has the same effect as bloating the service time by the factor $(1 - U_{i0})$.[1] Also, equation (6.17) reduces to

$$Q_{i0}(\mathbf{N}) = U_{i0} \sum_{nc=0}^{N} \frac{(nc+1)}{1 - U_{i0}} PC_i(nc|\mathbf{N}) = \frac{U_{i0}}{1 - U_{i0}} [1 + QC_i(\mathbf{N})] \tag{6.21}$$

In view of equation (5.5.3), this equation has an interesting interpretation: *Open chain queue length at a load-independent station in the presence of closed chains is the open chain queue length in isolation multiplied by the "slow-down" factor arising from the presence of closed chains.*

Next, we turn to the special case of a delay station. Since there is no contention at a delay station, we should be able to consider closed chains without regard to open chains, and vice versa. To confirm this intuition, note that equation (6.8) reduces to

$$VR_i(nc_i) = \sum_{n=0}^{\infty} \binom{nc_i + n}{n} U_{i0}^{n} \frac{nc_i!}{(nc_i + n)!} = e^{U_{i0}} \tag{6.22}$$

That is, $VR_i(k)$ is independent of k. Using equation (6.7), this implies that $CC_i(nc) = nc$, i.e., *a delay station behaves like a delay station even in the network* $\mathcal{Z}_C$. Also, it is easy to verify that $Q_{i0}(\mathbf{N}) = U_{i0}$, as expected. The entire algorithm for dealing with mixed networks is summarized in Fig. 7-6.

[1]Actually, the two expressions differ by a constant, but the constant can be absorbed into the normalization constant.

1. Aggregate all open chains into one by using equation (6.2.25).
2. Modify the station parameters to take into account the effect of the open chain: If the station is of delay type, there is no change. If the station is load-independent, increase its service time using (6.19). If the station is load-dependent, compute its effective capacity function using equations (6.9), (6.10), and (6.7).
3. Ignore the (aggregated) open chain, and solve the closed network (with modified parameters). Obtain performance parameters for the closed chains.
4. Use equations (6.17) or (6.21) to compute queue length (and hence the response time) for the open chain. These measures can be split to apply to original open chains as discussed in Section 6.2.3.

FIGURE 7-6: Algorithm for solving mixed networks.

7.7 Approximate Mean Value Analysis

The exact mean value analysis of Section 7.4 steps through all population vectors from **0** to **N**, which makes it very expensive. In this section we describe an approximate version of the algorithm that does away with this expense because it iterates only between populations **N** and $\mathbf{N}-e_r$ (for all r). Section 6.5.2 introduced the first and second-order heuristic for this in the context of single-chain networks; here, we concentrate on multiple-chain extensions of these. Henceforth we shall call the exact algorithm *unidirectional MVA* (UMVA) and the heuristic algorithm as *bidirectional MVA* (BMVA). To start with, we assume that the model contains only load-independent and delay stations. The heuristic is then as follows:

$$Q_{ik}(\mathbf{N}-e_r) = \begin{cases} Q_{ik}(\mathbf{N}) & \text{if } k \neq r \\ \dfrac{N_r - 1}{N_r} Q_{ir}(\mathbf{N}) & \text{if } k = r \end{cases} \tag{7.1}$$

This equation assumes that the removal of a customer from chain r does not affect any other chain, and the proportion in which chain r customers are distributed across the network remains unchanged. (Of course, neither of these assumptions is theoretically correct.) Equation (7.1), along with the standard equations for one step of UMVA algorithm, can be used to iterate between population levels **N** and $\mathbf{N}-e_r$ until all $Q_{ir}(\mathbf{N})$'s converge. This is then the multiple-chain version of Schweitzer's algorithm. The multiple-chain Linearizer is based on this and is discussed next.

7.7.1 Multiple-Chain Linearizer

Let $F_{ik}(\mathbf{n})$ denote the fraction of chain k jobs in station i at population $\mathbf{n} = (n_1, \ldots, n_K)$, i.e., $F_{ik}(\mathbf{n}) = Q_{ik}(\mathbf{n})/n_k$. Let D_{ikj} denote the change in F_{ik} when a chain j job is removed. That is,

$$D_{ikj}(\mathbf{n}) = F_{ik}(\mathbf{n} - e_j) - F_{ik}(\mathbf{n}) \tag{7.2}$$

Let $(\mathbf{n} - e_j)_k$ denote the kth component of the vector $\mathbf{n} - e_j$. Then,

$$Q_{ik}(\mathbf{n} - e_j) = (\mathbf{n} - e_j)_k \left[F_{ik}(\mathbf{n}) + D_{ikj}(\mathbf{n})\right] \tag{7.3}$$

With $\mathbf{n}$ chosen as $\mathbf{N}$, this equation is identical to (7.1) except for the correction term $D_{ikj}(\mathbf{N})$. Thus, given the estimates of $D_{ikj}(\mathbf{N})$'s, we can iterate between population levels $\mathbf{N}$ and $\mathbf{N} - e_j$ exactly as in Schweitzer's heuristic. The so-called *core algorithm* for doing this is given in Fig. 7-7. It takes the population vector $\mathbf{n}$ as a parameter. The superscripts *curr* and *prev* indicate, respectively, the queue lengths from the current and previous iterations. The termination test requires all Q_{ik}'s to converge. The error threshold ε should decrease with the total population $n = |\mathbf{n}|$ to avoid premature termination, because as n increases, the effect of removing one customer will decrease. The chosen value of ε is as suggested in the original paper on the subject.

Let us now see how D_{ikj}'s can be estimated. To avoid confusion, let us speak of D_{ikr}'s instead (where r also ranges over all chains). By definition,

$$D_{ikr}(\mathbf{n}) = F_{ik}(\mathbf{n}-e_r) - F_{ik}(\mathbf{n}) \tag{7.4}$$

To use this equation for computing $D_{ikr}(\mathbf{n})$'s, we need to invoke the CORE algorithm $(K + 1)$ times, with $\mathbf{n}$ set to $\mathbf{N}$, and $\mathbf{N} - e_r$, $r \in 1..K$. Now, each of these invocations would itself require D_{ikj}. There is no circularity here, since the algorithm is iterative in nature. Thus, the core algorithm will use existing estimates of D_{ikj} and provide us with F_{ik}'s which can be used to obtain better estimates of D_{ikj}'s. However, one problem still needs to be resolved. Invoking the core algorithm at populations $\mathbf{N}$ and $\mathbf{N}-e_r$ means that we need estimates of both $D_{ikj}(\mathbf{N})$ and $D_{ikj}(\mathbf{N}-e_r)$. Notice that equation (7.4) produces only $D_{ikr}(\mathbf{N})$'s. Thus, we need some further assumptions. Linearizer assumes that $D_{ikj}(\mathbf{N}-e_r) = D_{ikj}(\mathbf{N})$, i.e., independent of the population level. From equation (7.2), this is equivalent to assuming that F_{ik} is a linear function of chain populations, hence the name *linearizer*. In contrast, Schweitzer's heuristic assumes that F_{ik}'s are constant. This means that we can view Schweitzer's algorithm as first order, and Linearizer as second order. We can also design higher-order algorithms. For example, if we assume that $D_{ikj}(\mathbf{N}) - D_{ikj}(\mathbf{N}-e_r)$ is constant and estimate it by going down one further level, we would have a third order algorithm. Of course, the time complexity of the algorithm increases by a factor of K each time we go to the next higher-order heuristic.

The top level of the Linearizer algorithm is shown in Fig. 7-8. The use of $L = 3$ as the stopping criterion is based on the empirical evidence that more top-level iterations produce negligible accuracy improvements. Since Linearizer assumes $D_{ikj}(\mathbf{N}-e_r) = D_{ikj}(\mathbf{N})$, only one array is needed to hold D_{ikj}'s for all invocations of CORE.

procedure CORE($\mathbf{n}$);

Initialization: Set $I = 1$; $\varepsilon = 1/(4000 + 16n)$;

Step 1: Using the latest estimates of $Q_{ik}(\mathbf{n})$ and $D_{ikj}(\mathbf{n})$, compute $Q_{ik}(\mathbf{n} - e_j)$ for $i \in 1..M$, and $k, j \in 1..K$ using (7.3).

Step 2: Compute new estimates of $Q_{ik}(\mathbf{n})$ from $Q_{ik}(\mathbf{n} - e_j)$. For this, first compute response times using $Q_i(\mathbf{n} - e_j)$, and then throughputs and queue lengths, exactly as in ordinary MVA.

Termination Test: Let $error = \max_i \max_k \frac{1}{n} |Q_{ik}^{(curr)}(\mathbf{n}) - Q_{ik}^{(prev)}(\mathbf{n})|$.
If $error > \varepsilon$, set $I = I + 1$ and go to Step 1, else stop.

end CORE;

FIGURE 7-7: The core routine of the Linearizer algorithm.

Initialization: Let $\mathcal{V}(k)$ denote the set of stations visited by chain k. Initially, assume that for all i, $Q_{ik}(\mathbf{N}) = N_k/|\mathcal{V}(k)|$. Set $D_{ikj}(\mathbf{N}) = 0$ for all i, k, j. Set Linearizer iteration index $L = 1$.

Step 1: Invoke CORE($\mathbf{N}$) using the most recent estimates of $Q_{ik}(\mathbf{N})$'s and $D_{ikj}(\mathbf{N})$'s. The output will be an improved estimate of $Q_{ik}(\mathbf{N})$'s.

Termination Test: If $L = 3$ then stop, otherwise continue with Step 2.

Step 2: For each chain r invoke CORE($\mathbf{N}-e_r$). As discussed in the text, we let $D_{ikj}(\mathbf{N}-e_r) = D_{ikj}(\mathbf{N})$ for this purpose. Since Step 1 also produces estimates of $Q_{ik}(\mathbf{N}-e_r)$, they could be used as starting values in the iteration.

Step 3: Compute new estimates of $D_{ikr}(\mathbf{N})$ for all i, k, r using equation (7.4). Set $L = L + 1$ and go to Step 1.

FIGURE 7-8: Top-level structure of the Linearizer algorithm.

7.7.2 Extensions for Load-Dependent Stations

In this section we discuss modifications to the Linearizer algorithm to handle load-dependent servers with chain-independent capacities. As we shall see, the modifications are confined to the CORE algorithm; therefore, we shall assume that we are dealing with parameters at population $\mathbf{n}$. We use the heuristic that the removal of a single customer from a chain does not change the marginal probability distribution significantly, i.e., $P_i(\ell|\mathbf{n}-e_r) \approx P_i(\ell|\mathbf{n})$ for $\ell = 0..n-1$. Substituting this on the right-hand side of the aggregate marginal local balance equation, we get

$$P_i(\ell|\mathbf{n}) = \frac{U_i(\mathbf{n})}{C_i(n)} P_i(\ell - 1|\mathbf{n}) \quad \text{for } \ell = 1 \mathinner{..} n \tag{7.5}$$

where $U_i(\mathbf{n}) = \sum_{r=1}^{K} U_{ir}(\mathbf{n})$ is the total utilization of station i. Now, given an estimate of $U_i(\mathbf{n})$, we can evaluate $P_i(\ell|\mathbf{n})$'s for $\ell > 0$. Finally, we can determine $P_i(0|\mathbf{n})$ by using the requirement that all probabilities sum to 1. This numerically unstable computation can be avoided if the capacity function saturates beyond some value, denoted w. Let $\rho_i = U_i(\mathbf{n})/C_i(w)$. It is then easy to verify from equation (7.5) that

$$P_i(0|\mathbf{n}) = \left[1 + \sum_{\ell=1}^{w-1} \frac{[U_i(\mathbf{n})]^\ell}{V_i(\ell)} + \frac{[U_i(\mathbf{n})]^w (1 - \rho_i^{n-w+1})}{V_i(w)(1 - \rho_i)}\right]^{-1} \tag{7.6}$$

which is numerically stable. For load-dependent stations, the correction term D_{ikj} is not used; therefore, the only modification comes in the CORE algorithm. In step 1 of CORE, we approximate $P_i(\ell|\mathbf{n} - e_j)$ by $P_i(\ell|\mathbf{n})$. In step 2 of CORE, we use equation (4.6) to compute the response time (and from there the throughputs, utilizations, and queue lengths) at population $\mathbf{n}$, exactly as in the regular MVA. With $U_i(\mathbf{n})$'s known, we can compute better estimates of $P_i(\ell|\mathbf{n})$ using (7.5). (This is really an application of equation (4.4), as in the regular MVA). Other details of CORE remain unchanged.

The above heuristics does not ensure that the resulting $P_i(\ell|\mathbf{n} - e_j)$'s sum to 1. We can correct this problem by instead using

$$P_i(\ell|\mathbf{n} - e_j) = P_i(\ell|\mathbf{n})/(1 - P_i(n|\mathbf{n})) \tag{7.7}$$

To start the algorithm, we would need initial estimates of $P_i(\ell|\mathbf{n})$'s. One possibility here is to assume a *truncated geometric distribution* with the same mean as the assumed queue length value $Q_i(\mathbf{n})$. That is, $P_i(\ell|\mathbf{n}) = (1 - \rho)\rho^\ell/(1 - \rho^{n+1})$, where ρ can be computed using the following equation

$$\frac{\rho}{1-\rho} + \frac{(n+1)\rho^{n+1}}{1 - \rho^{n+1}} = \sum_{\forall k:\, i \in \mathcal{V}(k)} \frac{n_k}{|\mathcal{V}(k)|} \tag{7.8}$$

Finally, we note that unlike the exact algorithms, the basic Linearizer algorithm would work just fine with non-integer chain populations. With some care, the extension for load-dependent stations can also handle non-integer populations. This is important in approximate modeling, as we shall see in Section 8.2.

7.7.3 Cost and Accuracy

The CORE algorithm is the fundamental unit of Linearizer, but its expense is difficult to characterize. One might expect more CORE iterations for larger populations and for worse initial guesses; but this is not always true. Usually CORE converges fast (e.g., 10 or so iterations). The number of core iterations for the second top-level iteration are typically even smaller because the starting values are very close to the final values. For a given total population, additional chains do not seem to require more CORE iterations. Thus, in stating the complexity results, we shall assume that the number of iterations is constant. Since the approximation for load-dependent stations is rather simple minded, it costs only $O(L(N+K))$ for a model with L load-dependent stations. For load-independent stations, we compute $Q_{ik}(\mathbf{n}-e_j)$ for all k and j, which results in time complexity of $O((M-L)K^2)$. Linearizer invokes the CORE algorithm $3+2K$ times, thus yielding the total cost that increases as the third power of K. The storage requirements are $O(NL+MK^2)$. In contrast, the time and space complexity of exact MVA is exponential with respect to K.

It is interesting to note that by a slight modification to the computations for load-independent stations, the time complexity of CORE can be reduced to $O(MK)$, thereby lowering the complexity of Linearizer to $O(MK^2)$. The basic observation is that step 2 of CORE (which is the same as one step UMVA) needs only $Q_i(\mathbf{n}-e_j)$ rather than $Q_{ik}(\mathbf{n}-e_j)$. Thus, instead of computing Q_{ik}'s separately in step 1, we can develop an expression for $Q_i = \sum_{k=1}^{K} Q_{ik}$ using equation (7.3). This is trivial and is explored in Exercise 7.18. We have avoided making this change in our earlier presentation because one may wish to use CORE-like algorithms in the context of heuristic modeling of nonproduct-form scheduling disciplines as well. As we shall see in Section 8.3, the response time equations would need individual Q_{ik}'s in such cases.

Before considering the accuracy aspect, let us define appropriate error measures. The usual fractional error measure may not always be suitable since a large fractional error in a small quantity is often quite acceptable. This is because the object of performance modeling is typically to identify trouble spots, e.g., stations with significant congestion; being unable to accurately predict response times and queue lengths at lightly loaded stations does not lessen the usefulness of modeling or of the solution technique. For this reason, we define *tolerance errors*. We use the notation $TE(\alpha)$ to denote the tolerance error in the performance parameter α, where α could be R (response time), Q (queue length), U (utilization), or P (marginal probability). Let

$$\eta_i = \max_{1 \le n \le N} C_i(n) \tag{7.9}$$

Then the tolerance errors can be defined as follows:

$$TE(U_{ir}) = \frac{N \times \text{abs}(U_{ir}[\text{exact}] - U_{ir}[\text{approx}])}{N_r \eta_i} \tag{7.10}$$

$$TE(P_i(n)) = \text{abs}(P_i(n)[\text{exact}] - P_i(n)[\text{approx}]) \tag{7.11}$$

$$TE(R_{ir}) = \frac{\text{abs}(R_{ir}[\text{exact}] - R_{ir}[\text{approx}])}{CT_{ir}[\text{exact}]} \tag{7.12}$$

$$TE(Q_{ir}) = \frac{\text{abs}(Q_{ir}[\text{exact}] - Q_{ir}[\text{approx}])}{N_r} \tag{7.13}$$

where CT_{ir} denotes the cycle time for chain r at station i. For *a given network*,

Parameter	Error type	Magnitude (%)
Response Time	Avg MTE	0.4
	Max MTE	2.3
	Std. dev.	0.5
Queue Length	Avg MTE	0.3
	Max MTE	1.6
	Std. dev.	0.3
Marginal Probs	Avg MTE	0.8
	Max MTE	6.1
	Std. dev.	1.4

TABLE 7.3: Tolerance errors for the generalized Linearizer algorithm.

one typically uses the maximum tolerance error (MTE) computed over all its stations and chains. For a given set of test networks, it is useful to compute both the average and maximum of individual MTE's.

To see the usefulness of these measures, consider $TE(R_{ir})$, which indicates how well the approximate algorithm estimates the contribution of station i toward the cycle time of chain r. If station i has only a small contribution, $TE(R_{ir})$ will remain small in spite of a large fractional error in the estimation. Similar comments can be made regarding other tolerance error measures.

Approximate methods typically predict throughputs and utilizations accurately, so it is adequate to consider only response time, queue length, and marginal probability MTE's. Typically, response times have larger errors as compared to queue lengths, and so queue length MTE's can also be ignored. For networks with only load-independent and delay stations, the average and maximum response time MTE's given by Linearizer are 0.33% and 0.88% respectively. If the experiments are restricted to only "stress networks", i.e., networks where the heuristic is expected to perform poorly, the average and maximum response time MTE's are 0.48% and 2.34% respectively. Table 7.3 shows the average and maximum MTE's, and their standard deviation, for networks with load-dependent stations. It can be seen that Linearizer does an excellent job of estimating average performance measures, and is reasonable for marginal probabilities.

Before closing this section, we briefly discuss some of the basic questions concerning the solution obtained by the BMVA technique. We start with single-chain networks. It is easy to show (see Exercise 7.16) that the equations resulting from Schweitzer's heuristic have a unique solution, such that the resulting cycle time is an upper bound on the exact cycle time. With proper initialization, it can also be shown that the iteration converges monotonically to this solution. Existence and uniqueness can also be shown for Linearizer (see Exercise 7.17), but only preliminary results are available concerning the relationship between Linearizer cycle time and exact cycle time. Generally, the Linearizer cycle time is an underestimation of the true cycle time at low populations, but the situation reverses at high populations. Similar results have also been obtained on networks with load-dependent stations having monotonically nondecreasing capacity functions. Existence, uniqueness, and asymptotic convergence have also been established for multiple-chain versions of these algorithms, but many other problems remain open.

7.8 Exercises

1. Show that all delay stations in a (single-chain or multiple-chain) product-form network can be merged into one before attempting solution.

2. Give expressions for the number of multiplications and divisions needed to compute mean performance measures using the convolution algorithm in a network with K chains, each of which passes through all M stations. The network has L load-dependent stations, D delay stations and the rest are load-independent. Use the result of Exercise 7.1.

3. Let Q_i denote the total queue length at station i in a multiple-chain network. Using equation (3.9) show that if station i is load-independent,

$$Q_i(\mathbf{N}) = \sum_{\forall\,\mathbf{n}>\mathbf{0}} \frac{G(\mathbf{N}-\mathbf{n},\Omega)}{G(\mathbf{N},\Omega)} n! \prod_{r=1}^{K} \frac{u_{ir}^{n_r}}{n_r!} \tag{8.1}$$

4. Consider a multiple-chain network consisting of only load-independent stations. Using equation (8.1) show that $G(\mathbf{N},\Omega)$ can be computed recursively using the following

$$G(\mathbf{N},\Omega) = \sum_{\forall\,\mathbf{n}>\mathbf{0}} \frac{G(\mathbf{N}-\mathbf{n},\Omega)}{N_1+\cdots+N_K} n! \sum_{i=1}^{M} \prod_{r=1}^{K} \frac{u_{ir}^{n_r}}{n_r!} \tag{8.2}$$

   Using the result of Exercise 7.1, modify the above equation to handle delay stations as well.

   Hint: Let j be the delay station. Then $Q_j(\mathbf{N})$ is the same as $U_j(\mathbf{N})$, which in turn can be expressed using the alternate form of the throughput theorem. Using this and equation (8.1), you can express the summation of all queue lengths in the form (8.2) by altering the definition slightly for $\mathbf{n} = e_r$.

5. Using the results of Exercise 7.4, devise a "new" convolution algorithm for networks with only load-independent and delay stations. How do the space and time complexity of this method compare against the one discussed in Section 7.3? (Note: This algorithm is not new; it is called CCNC).

6. Let S_{ir} denote the second moment of queue length at station i for chain r customers. Assume that the capacities are chain-independent. Using the marginal local balance theorem, show that

$$S_{ir}(\mathbf{N}) = Q_{ir}(\mathbf{N}) + U_{ir}(\mathbf{N})U_{ir}(\mathbf{N}-e_r)\sum_{n=2}^{N} \frac{n(n-1)P_i(n-2|\mathbf{N}-2e_r)}{C_i(n)C_i(n-1)} \tag{8.3}$$

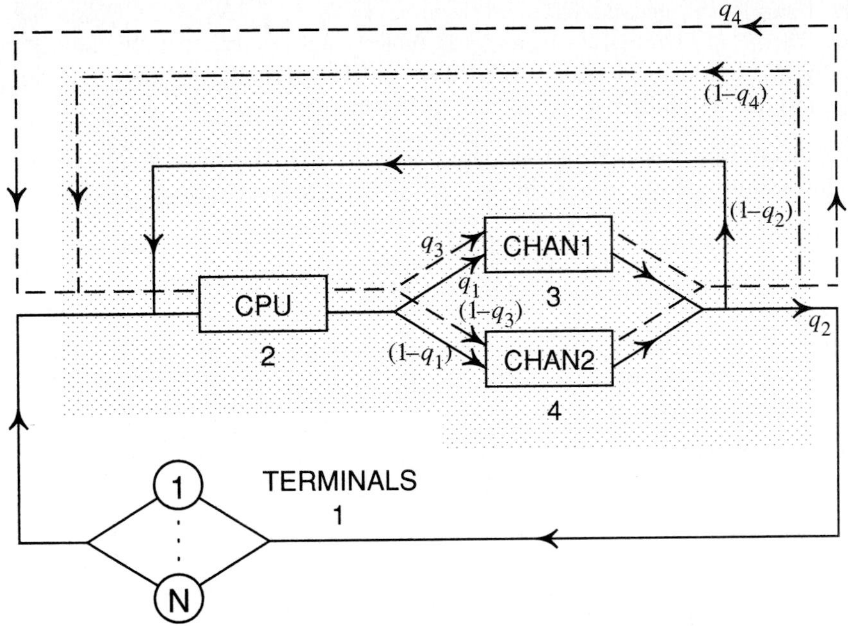

FIGURE 7-9: A two-chain model of a computer system.

Specialize this equation for simple and delay servers. How would you use these results to compute second moments as well in the multiple-chain MVA algorithm?

7. Consider the two-chain closed network shown in Fig. 7-9. Chain 1 (solid lines) is for interactive jobs, and chain 2 (broken lines) is for batch jobs. All the fixed parameters are given below:

Chain 1

Terminal: Average think time = 1 sec, Number denoted as N_1.
CPU: PS, Basic service rate = 40/sec, $C(n) = 1/(0.95 + 0.05n)$
CHAN1: FCFS, exponential, load-independent, rate = 20/sec
CHAN2: FCFS, exponential, load-independent, rate = 25/sec
Routing: $q_1 = 0.75$, $q_2 = 0.25$.

Chain 2

CPU: PS, Basic service rate = 25 /sec.
Channels: Same as for chain 1.
Routing: $q_3 = 0.6$, $q_4 = 0.15$.

Ignore chain 2 in the above model and let N_1=2. Solve the single-chain model using (1) Convolution, (2) mean value analysis, and (3) LBANC. The results should include queue length, utilization, throughput, and response time for each station.

8. Now include the second chain also and let $N_1 = 2$, $N_2 = 1$. Solve the model using (1) Convolution, and (2) mean value analysis. Note that the results at population vectors (10), (20), and (01) are either known or can be computed trivially.

9. Using equation (3.4) show that the queue length at a load-independent station i can be computed using

$$Q_{ir}(\mathbf{N}) = u_{ir}\frac{G(\mathbf{N}-e_r, \Omega + \{i\})}{G(\mathbf{N}, \Omega)} \tag{8.4}$$

where $\Omega + \{i\}$ denotes a network with a second copy of station i added, i.e.,

$$G(\mathbf{N}, \Omega + \{i\}) = \sum_{\mathbf{n}=\mathbf{0}}^{\mathbf{N}} G(\mathbf{N} - \mathbf{n}, \Omega) X_i(\mathbf{n}) \tag{8.5}$$

10. Consider the convolution algorithm for networks containing only simple and delay stations. Suppose that we use equation (8.4) for simple stations. What is the resulting space/time complexity of the algorithm? Would the complexity change if the convolutions are arranged in the form of a tree?

11. Consider a network of M simple stations where every station has the same relative utilization u.

    (a) Using the relationship between G and performance parameters, show that all stations must have identical queue lengths and *residence* times.

    (b) Give explicit expressions for $Q(N)$, $G(N)$ and $\lambda_i(N)$ for $i = 1..M$.

    (c) Now suppose that we add a delay station, with relative utilization of u_0, to our network. Using the results from part (b), obtain explicit expressions for $G(N)$ and $\lambda_i(N)$.

12. Prove equations (6.9) and (6.10). Derive an efficient recursive expression for computing $VR_i(k)$. Specialize the equation for the case of a multiserver station.

13. Derive expressions for time and space complexity of solving a mixed network with K_c closed chains and K_o open chains. Assume that the network has L load-dependent servers with capacities saturating at or below the value w. All other stations are load-independent. Assume that the MVA algorithm is used for solving the closed network $\mathcal{Z}_C$.

14. Consider the network of Fig. 7-9. Suppose that the batch chain is opened with external arrival rate of 2.5 jobs per second. Show that this network has a steady-state solution. Let $N_1 = 3$. Solve the network and obtain all mean performance measures.

15. Consider a single-chain closed network with population N and let $S_i(N)$ denote the second moment of the queue length at station i. By using the identity $n^2 = 1 + 3 + 5 + \cdots + 2n - 1$, show that

$$S_i(N) = 2\sum_{k=1}^{N} kP_i(n_i \geq k) - Q_i(N) \tag{8.6}$$

Show how this relationship can be used in the convolution algorithm to compute the second moment of queue length efficiently at a load-independent station i.

16. Consider a single-chain closed network with only simple and delay stations. Using the mean value theorem and Schweitzer's heuristic, obtain an expression for the cycle time. (Assume that the visit ratio of station 1 is 1, and cycle time is with respect to this station.) Your cycle time expression will be implicit, i.e., of the form $C(N) = f(C(N))$ where f is the function that you have to come up with. Show that this equation has a solution and that the solution is unique. (Hint: For existence, consider the solution as the intersection point of two curves $y = x$ and $y = f(x)$. For uniqueness, assume that there are two solutions C_1, C_2 such that $C_1 < C_2$, and derive a contradiction.)

17. How will the cycle time expression of Exercise 7.16 change if we employ the heuristic used by Linearizer? You may consider only the first pass of the Linearizer. Show that a solution still exists and is unique. Also show that the cycle time computed by this algorithm is always smaller than that given by Schweitzer's heuristics.

18. Show that by avoiding the computation of individual $Q_{ik}(\mathbf{n} - e_j)$'s and of $D_{ikj}(\mathbf{n})$'s in the CORE algorithm, the complexity of the Linearizer can be reduced from $O(MK^3)$ to $O(MK^2)$. [This result is shown in Silva and Muntz (1990)].

Bibliographic Notes

The convolution algorithm was first introduced in Buzen (1973) for closed single-chain networks, and is often referred to as *Buzen's algorithm*. It has subsequently been extended to multiple-chain networks by Bruell and Balbo in 1980. The mean value analysis is developed in Reiser and Lavenberg (1980) for both single and multiple-chain networks. Many further results on computational algorithms, including LBANC, are developed in Sauer and Chandy (1981). Chandy and Sauer have also developed the CCNC (computation of normalization constant) algorithm (which was mentioned in Exercise 7.5), for solving networks with only simple and delay servers. Discussions on various computational algorithms may be found in Lavenberg (1983) and Sauer and Chandy (1981). Bruell, Balbo, and Afshari (1984) provides a comprehensive solution technique for mixed networks and our discussion is based upon this work.

One topic that we have not addressed is the computation of joint queue length distributions in a closed product-form network. We shall discuss this briefly in Section 10.2.3.

The bidirectional MVA (BMVA) approach was developed by Schweitzer and Bard in 1979. The Linearizer algorithm (and an earlier version called SCAT) are developed in Chandy and Neuse (1982). These BMVA algorithms either did not deal with load-dependent stations or took a very crude approach. Krzesinski and Greyling (1984) extends these algorithms to cover load-dependent stations as well. Detailed validation of these algorithms may be found in the original papers. Akyildiz and Sieber (1988), and Agre and Tripathi (1985) discuss other approximate approaches for analyzing networks with load-dependent servers. Analysis of existence, uniqueness, and other properties of Schweitzer's algorithm appear in Eager and Sevcik (1984). Some further work, including examination of properties of a simplified version of the Linearizer algorithm, appears in Srinivasan and Kant (1986). Pattipati, Kostreva, and Teele (1990) shows several further results on both Schweitzer's algorithm and Linearizer.

CHAPTER

8

Aggregation and Approximate Modeling

In this chapter we shall study several techniques that form the basis for solving complex queuing network models. The techniques give exact solution in some cases; in others, they are merely an approximation. The topics that we discuss here in detail are flow-equivalent aggregation, contention for passive resources, a MVA-based approach for handling complex scheduling disciplines, and the decomposition approximation.

8.1 Flow-Equivalent Aggregation

This technique allows us to replace a subnetwork of a queuing network by a single station with appropriately chosen service rate function. The replacement is exact for product-form (PF) networks, and an acceptable approximation for many others. Aggregation finds uses in hierarchical modeling, parametric studies, iterative solution, and modeling of resource constraints.

To see the motivation for the technique, consider a *single-chain network* Ω shown in Fig. 8-1. Suppose that we wish to study its behavior by varying parameters corresponding to the subnetwork Ω_u, but leaving the remaining portion, denoted Ω_a, the same throughout. It is then computationally advantageous to

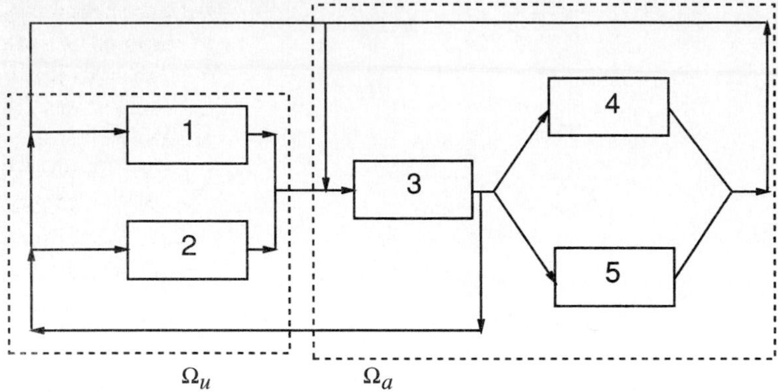

FIGURE 8-1: The original model.

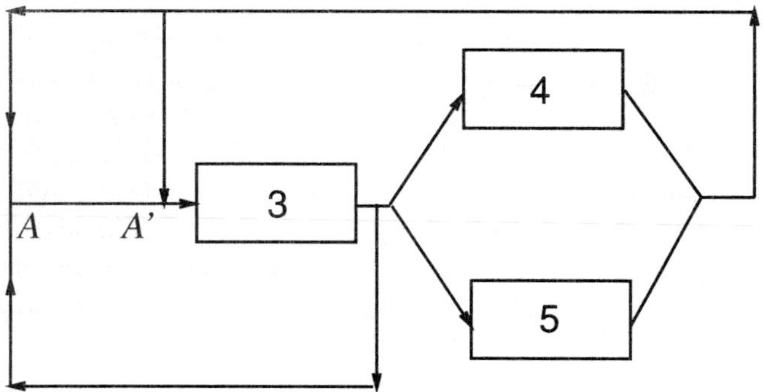

FIGURE 8-2: Subnetwork to be aggregated.

replace Ω_a by a single aggregate station that shows the same behavior as Ω_a, thereby obtaining a model like in Fig. 8-3.[1] In general, this is not possible, since a single station may not be able to exhibit the spectrum of behavior that is possible from several stations connected together. However, the class of networks with product-form solution does have this property. The aggregate station "a" turns out to be *flow-equivalent* to the subnetwork Ω_a; i.e., the service rate of a is the same as the processing rate of Ω_a in isolation. In this section we show several results concerning such aggregation.

8.1.1 Characterization of Aggregate Station

To characterize the aggregate station a that mimics the behavior of Ω_a, we need to specify two parameters: (1) service rate, denoted as $\mu_a(n)$, where n is the load, and (2) the scheduling discipline. Since all admissible scheduling disciplines for product-form networks lead to the same state probabilities, the scheduling discipline could well be assumed to be PS. The service rate $\mu_a(n)$

[1] The subscript u in Ω_u indicates that this is the unaggregated portion of the network.

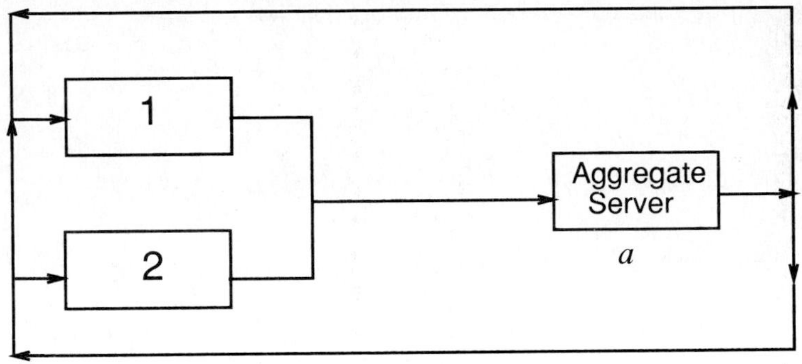

FIGURE 8-3: Aggregated model.

is the throughput of Ω_a operating in isolation with a population of n. This situation is similar to the one in electrical circuits where a subnetwork can be replaced by an equivalent impedance (possibly with a current source in parallel) so that the current (or flow-rate) through this impedance is the same as in the original subnetwork in isolation. Therefore, this result is often known as *Norton's theorem*.

Without loss of generality, we can let $\Omega_u = 1\mathinner{..}L$ and $\Omega_a = L+1\mathinner{..}M$ for some $1 \leq L \leq M-2$. We first isolate Ω_a by "shorting out" all the stations belonging to Ω_u. This is shown in Fig. 8-2 where the arc AA' represents the portion corresponding to Ω_u. Let Ω^* denote the original network with the Ω_a part replaced by the aggregate station a. The replacement will go as follows: all the outputs directed from Ω_u to Ω_a will be directed to station a. Similarly, all outputs from Ω_a to Ω_u will come out of station a. See Fig. 8-3. Let $\mathcal{F}$ denote the set of stations in Ω_u whose output goes to some station in Ω_a. Then, the visit ratio of the aggregate, denoted v_a, is given by

$$v_a = \sum_{i \in \mathcal{F}} v_i \sum_{j \in \Omega_a} q_{ij} \tag{1.1}$$

The next step in the aggregation is to solve the subnetwork Ω_a for populations $n \in 1\mathinner{..}N$ and determine the throughput through the arc $A\,A'$, denoted $\Lambda_a(n)$. Then we have the following result:

Lemma 8.1 (Norton's theorem). If we set $\mu_a(n) = \Lambda_a(n)$ for $n \in 1\mathinner{..}N$ in Ω^*, then Ω and Ω^* are equivalent.

Proof: We first show that Ω and Ω^* have the same normalization constant at any population n. From the convolution theorem we get

$$G(n, \Omega^*) = \sum_{i=0}^{n} G(n-i, \Omega_u) \prod_{j=1}^{i} \frac{v_a}{\mu_a(j)} \tag{1.2}$$

Applying the throughput theorem to the subnetwork Ω_a, we get

$$\mu_a(j) = \Lambda_a(j) = v_a \frac{G(j-1, \Omega_a)}{G(j, \Omega_a)} \tag{1.3}$$

Substituting (1.3) into (1.2) and using the fact that $G(0, \Omega_a) = 1$, we get

$$G(n, \Omega^*) = \sum_{i=0}^{n} G(n-i, \Omega_u) G(i, \Omega_a)$$

which, by the convolution theorem, is the same as $G(n, \Omega)$. Since all performance parameters of stations in Ω_u (and of the aggregate station) are determined by these normalization constants, the two networks must be equivalent. □

Notice that the proof is independent of how the subnetworks Ω_u and Ω_a are chosen; for example, there is no requirement that their stations be directly connected to one another. From equation (1.3), we can interpret $\Lambda_a(j)$ as the throughput of a (possibly hypothetical) station in Ω_a that has v_a as its visit ratio. Then if we let station a in Ω^* have the visit ratio v_a and service rate of $\Lambda_a(j)$, the equivalence is achieved. Also, the proof depends only on $\Lambda_a(j)/v_a$. Let ℓ be some (real) station belonging to Ω_a. Since $\Lambda_\ell(j)/v_\ell = \Lambda_a(j)/v_a$ for all j, it follows that we could as well use the parameters of station ℓ in applying Norton's theorem. In other words, *the definition of v_a given by equation (1.1) is not needed for performing aggregation.* This is not surprising because the queue length distribution depends only on the relative utilizations.

8.1.2 Analysis of the Aggregate Station

Norton's theorem allows us to collapse uninteresting portions of the network into a single station and thereby save computational effort. The solution to the aggregated network Ω^* gives performance parameters for all its stations, including station a, but this still leaves the problem of finding performance measures for the individual stations within the subnetwork Ω_a. Let i denote such a station. Obviously,

$$\lambda_i(N) = \frac{v_i}{v_a} \lambda_a(N) \tag{1.4}$$

Marginal probabilities (and hence the queue-length moments) for station i can be obtained by a weighted summation (or superposition) of the marginal probabilities for i as a part of Ω_a. This is similar to the Superposition theorem of electrical networks if we view each population level as a different "source" that drives the system.

Lemma 8.2 (Superposition theorem). Let $P_i(k|n, \Omega_a)$ denote the probability of finding k customers at station i when considered as a part of the network Ω_a with population n. Let $P_a(n|N)$ denote the probability of having n customers in the aggregate Ω_a. Then,

$$P_i(k|N) = \sum_{n=k}^{N} P_i(k|n, \Omega_a) P_a(n|N) \tag{1.5}$$

Proof Let $X_i(n) = u_i^n / V_i(n)$. From equation (7.1.9), we have

$$\begin{aligned} P_i(k|N) &= \frac{X_i(k) G(N-k, \Omega - \{i\})}{G(N, \Omega)} \\ &= \frac{X_i(k)}{G(N,\Omega)} \sum_{n=0}^{N-k} G(N-k-n, \Omega_u) G(n, \Omega_a - \{i\}) \\ &= \sum_{n=k}^{N} G(N-n, \Omega_u) \frac{X_i(k)}{G(N,\Omega)} G(n-k, \Omega_a - \{i\}) \\ &= \sum_{n=k}^{N} G(N-n, \Omega_u) \frac{G(n, \Omega_a)}{G(N,\Omega)} P_i(k|n, \Omega_a) \end{aligned}$$

where in the last step, we used the definition of $P_i(k|n, \Omega_a)$ from equation (7.1.9). Now, from the definition of product-form solution, it is easy to show that

$$Pr(n \text{ customers in } \Omega_a) = G(N-n, \Omega_u) \frac{G(n, \Omega_a)}{G(N, \Omega)} \tag{1.6}$$

From which, the result follows. □

Corollary 8.1 Let $Q_i(n, \Omega_a)$ denote the average queue length at station i when considered as a part of Ω_a with population n. Then,

$$Q_i(N) = \sum_{n=1}^{N} Q_i(n, \Omega_a) P_a(n|N) \tag{1.7}$$

Proof: The proof follows from the definition of queue length and the superposition theorem. □

With both throughput and queue lengths known, other average parameters can be obtained in a standard way. Note that if the entire network is to be solved only for one set of input parameters, no computational advantage is obtained by first aggregating a portion of it and finally applying the superposition theorem.

8.1.3 Aggregation in Multiple-Chain Networks

Both Norton's theorem and the superposition theorem extend to multiple-chain networks in a straightforward manner. For Norton equivalence, the subnetwork Ω_a must be solved for all possible population vectors $\mathbf{n} \in \mathbf{0} .. \mathbf{N}$ to obtain the throughputs $\Lambda_{ar}(\mathbf{n})$, $r \in 1 .. K$. Then, if the effective service rate at the aggregate station a, denoted as $\mu_{ar}^*(\mathbf{n})$ for chain r, is chosen to be $\Lambda_{ar}(\mathbf{n})$, the original network Ω is equivalent to the aggregated network Ω^*. The proof of this equivalence again involves showing that the two networks have identical G function at all population vectors, and it is left as an exercise. The superposition theorem takes the following form

$$P_i(\mathbf{k}|\mathbf{N}) = \sum_{\mathbf{n}=\mathbf{k}}^{\mathbf{N}} P_i(\mathbf{k}|\mathbf{n}, \Omega_a) P_a(\mathbf{n}|\mathbf{N}) \tag{1.8}$$

Which further implies that

$$Q_{ir}(\mathbf{N}) = \sum_{n_1=1}^{N_1} \cdots \sum_{n_K=1}^{N_K} Q_{ir}(\mathbf{n}, \Omega_a) P_a(\mathbf{n}|\mathbf{N}) \tag{1.9}$$

Proofs of these results proceed along the same lines as in the single-chain case and are omitted. We can define the visit ratio at station a for each chain by using an equation like (1.1), but this is again unnecessary. Instead, for each chain r, we pick some station $j \in \Omega_a$ visited by chain r, and let $v_{ar} = v_{jr}$ and $\mu^*_{ar}(\mathbf{n}) = \Lambda_{jr}(\mathbf{n})$. As in the single-chain case, the results will be independent of which stations we pick.

Although the above extensions are conceptually straightforward, exact aggregation in multiple-chain networks is only of limited value. To see this, let us consider the inherent service rate $\mu_{ar}(\mathbf{n})$ of the aggregate station. From equation (4.4.9) and Norton's theorem, we have

$$\mu_{ar}(\mathbf{n}) = n\Lambda_{ar}(\mathbf{n})/n_r \qquad \text{where} \quad n = |\mathbf{n}| \tag{1.10}$$

It is clear that, in general, μ_{ar} will depend on $\mathbf{n}$, rather than just n. In fact, it is easy to verify that the only nontrivial situation in which μ_r depends only on n is where Ω_a consists of a balanced set of load-independent stations. These occupancy vector dependent service rates are not only expensive to handle, but also undesirable for another reason. Often, the purpose of aggregation is to indirectly model some non-PF feature by appropriately modifying the service rate of the aggregate station. Unfortunately, simple modifications to an occupancy-dependent service rate (e.g., saturating the service rate beyond a threshold) will violate the necessary condition for product-form solution given by (6.6.1). It is important to note that in a single-chain network, the service rate function can be modified arbitrarily without losing the product-form property.

8.2 Applications Of Aggregation

Apart from parametric studies, the main use of aggregation is in simplifying the model so that it is possible to efficiently model nonstandard features such as contention for passive resources, parallelism, and complex scheduling disciplines. For example, if we wish to analyze a model that uses a non-PF scheduling discipline at the CPU, but otherwise satisfies product-form restrictions, we can aggregate

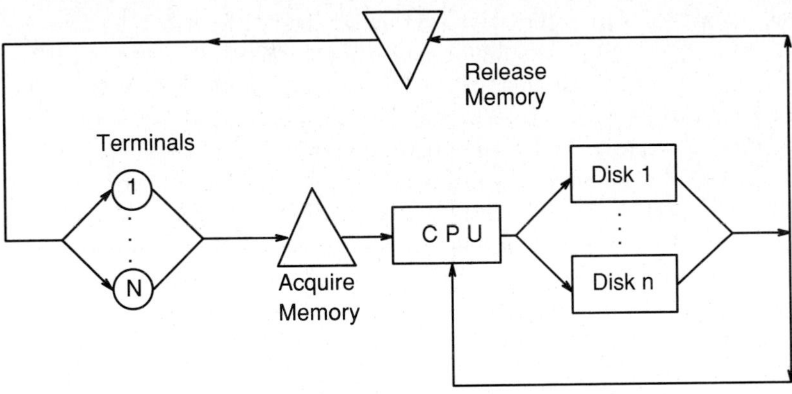

FIGURE 8-4: Model of a multiprogramming system.

everything except the CPU into a single station. Typically, the resulting two-station model is easy enough even for global balance equation–based solution, and thus an accurate solution can be obtained. It is important to note here that a single non-PF feature is enough to invalidate Norton's theorem and related results; therefore, this technique will only give approximate results even if the two-station aggregate model is solved exactly. Nevertheless, the method usually gives acceptable results.

Aggregation can be used recursively to deal with nested submodels and nested resource constraints. It is thus useful in hierarchical modeling. When several disjoint portions of a model contain non-PF features, we can also use it iteratively to get accurate results. The main idea is to consider only one non-PF feature at a time, analyze its impact, and then modify some input parameter of the model so as to reflect it in the analysis of other non-PF features. Because of the cyclic dependencies between the results of various submodels involved in such an approach, iteration comes naturally. Unfortunately, mathematical analysis of important issues such as convergence, accuracy, and so on, is typically intractable and extensive experimental validation becomes essential.

In the following we discuss some important modeling problems that can exploit aggregation. All these problems involve *simultaneous resource possession* in some form, i.e., situations where a customer may occupy two or more resources simultaneously. Although it may be possible to construct a Markovian model of this situation, the complexity considerations lead us to consider techniques that are based on the solution of a simple queuing model.

8.2.1 Resource Constraints in Single-Chain Networks

Here we consider the problem of modeling contention for serially reusable passive resources (e.g., main memory, buffers, I/O channels, tape devices, printers, etc.). in single-chain networks. We shall illustrate the ideas by considering the modeling of memory constraints, but the same technique applies in other situations as well.

Consider the model of an interactive system shown in Fig. 8-4. Each process (or customer) requests main memory before entering the central subsystem (CS). In the real system, this corresponds to the allocation of sufficient memory for loading the program to be run as a result of the command issued by a terminal user. The memory is released when the customer exits the CS (i.e., when the command is finished). This model does not satisfy product-form solution because of the blocking caused by the memory limitation. Since the internal details of the CS are not relevant for memory allocation/deallocation, we first aggregate the CS into a single station. The resulting two-station model is simple enough to be solved by global balance techniques; however, we can do even better. Notice that in doing aggregation, we would use the throughput of CS in isolation, denoted $\Lambda_a(n)$, as the service rate of the aggregate station, i.e., $\mu_a(n) = \Lambda_a(n)$. Suppose that the average program size is ρ and the available memory is $\mathcal{M}$. Then, on the average, we can have only $L = \mathcal{M}/\rho$ programs resident in the main memory. (Assume for now that L is an integer.) This also means that, on the average, no more than L customers could be active inside the central subsystem. In other words, the average rate at which the central subsystem can turn out jobs will saturate if the degree of multiprogramming exceeds L. Therefore, we can model the memory constraint by choosing the service rate of the aggregate station in the following way

$$\mu_a(n) = \begin{cases} \Lambda_a(n) & \text{if } n \leq L \\ \Lambda_a(L) & \text{if } n > L \end{cases} \tag{2.1}$$

With this choice of μ_a, the aggregated model becomes an ordinary two-station PF network and can be solved easily. The solution will give, among other things, $Q_a(N)$, the average queue length at the aggregate station. This queue length includes those customers actually inside the CS and those waiting to get in. Let these quantities be denoted as $Q_{cs}(N)$ and $Q_{mem}(N)$ respectively. By the superposition theorem, we can obtain the former as

$$Q_{cs}(N) = \sum_{n=1}^{L-1} nP_a(n|N) + L\sum_{n=L}^{N} P_a(n|N) \tag{2.2}$$

This equation comes from the simple observation that for $n \geq L$, only L customers can reside in the CS. We could then determine $Q_{mem}(N)$ as $Q_a(N) - Q_{cs}(N)$. The queue lengths at stations of the CS can also be determined using the superposition theorem. For example

$$Q_{cpu}(N) = \sum_{n=1}^{L-1} Q_{cpu}(n, \Omega_a)P_a(n|N) + Q_{cpu}(L, \Omega_a)\sum_{n=L}^{N} P_a(n|N) \tag{2.3}$$

We emphasize, however, that *the application of Norton's theorem and superposition theorem in this problem is only an approximation.*

Note that equation (2.1) does not consider any details of memory management. In particular, with dynamic partitioned memory management, some storage will be wasted due to fragmentation, and the effective L may be lower than $\mathcal{M}/\rho$. If the fraction of memory lost due to fragmentation can be estimated (by analysis or simulation), we can get a better estimate of L. Finally, if L is a fractional number, we can compute the results for both $\lfloor L \rfloor$ and $\lceil L \rceil$ and then do linear interpolation on throughputs and queue lengths.

The above technique can also be applied when several disjoint portions of the model have independent resource constraints or when the constraints are nested. As an example of the former, suppose that we have resource constraints in both subnetworks Ω' and Ω_a in Fig. 8-1. In such a case we would aggregate both subnetworks and thereby get a two-station aggregated model. The service rates of these two stations could then be saturated appropriately to reflect the resource limitations. In the case of nesting, we simply apply the technique recursively starting from the innermost level. For example, suppose that in Fig. 8-4 the system uses dynamic buffer allocation to handle disk I/O. That is, each process must get the desired number of buffers from the common pool before proceeding to the disk. In this case we have a population limitation for the I/O subsystem (in addition to the one for the entire central subsystem). Thus, we cannot solve the CS model directly; instead we must do the following: (a) solve the I/O subsystem in isolation and obtain its throughput, (b) replace the I/O subsystem by a single station with properly chosen service rate, and (c) solve the resulting two-station CS model, and proceed as before. It should also be clear how to handle multiple, nested subnetworks with resource constraints.

The modeling above implicitly assumed that the customers, who are unable to enter a subnetwork because of the resource limitations, do not affect the system behavior in any way. However, if the requested resource is needed to hold the customers themselves, this assumption must be changed. For example, in a communication network each waiting packet occupies a buffer and if all available buffers are full, an incoming packet must be sent somewhere. A common approach is to simply drop the packet and let the source retransmit it (which means that the source node must retain the packet in its input queue even after the packet has been transmitted). This leads to the rejection blocking that we mentioned in Section 5.5.4. In a manufacturing environment, a processed part will typically stay at its source server (and thus prevent that machine from processing other parts), until a slot becomes available in the input queue of the next downstream machine. This leads to the production blocking of Section 5.5.4. The effect of such blocking is not covered by the throughput saturation technique discussed above, and should be modeled separately.

Example 8.1 Consider only chain 1 in the model of Exercise 7.7 and let $N_1 = 12$. Suppose that the system has 2 MB of available memory and the average program size is 0.4 MB. Each command issued from the terminal requires the allocation of memory before it can get into the central subsystem. The memory is released when the command completes. Solve the model and estimate the average number of jobs blocked for memory.

Solution Let Ω denote the full model and Ω_a its central subsystem. Let $v_1 = 1$. It is easy to see that $v_2 = 4$, $v_3 = 3$, and $v_4 = 1$. We first short out the terminal

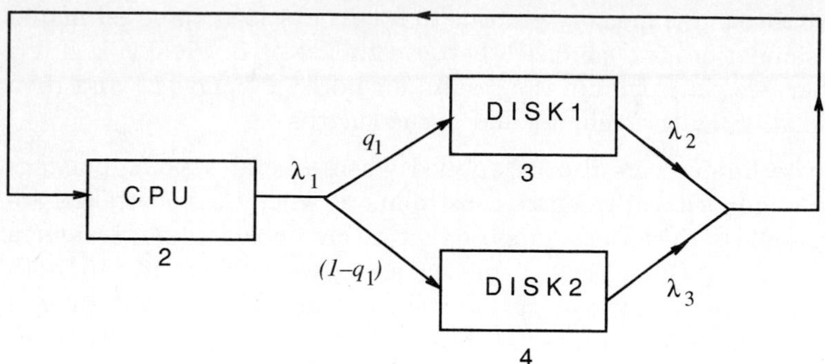

FIGURE 8-5: Central subsystem of Fig. 7-9 in isolation.

to get Ω_a network shown in Fig. 8-5.

Let us choose station 4 as the reference station ℓ for aggregation. The throughput for station 4 (in jobs/sec) obtained from this model is shown in Table 8.1. Next we construct the high-level model Ω^*, consisting of terminal and aggregate stations, *numbered as 1 and 2 respectively*. In Ω^*, $v_1 = 1$, $v_2 \triangleq v_\ell = 1$, $s_1 = 1000$ ms, and $s_2 = 1/3.44828 = 290$ ms. Obviously, $L = 2/0.4 = 5$, therefore, the capacity of station 2 will saturate beyond load of 5. The capacity values are

$$1.0000, \quad 1.4230, \quad 1.6340, \quad 1.7499, \quad 1.8176$$

By solving the aggregated model Ω^* at population 12, we obtain the following results. (The superscript $*$ indicates that we are speaking of Ω^*).

$$\lambda_1^* = \lambda_2^* = 6.040/\text{sec}, \qquad Q_1^* = 6.0401, \qquad Q_2^* = 5.9599$$

The marginal probabilities at the aggregate station, denoted $P_a(n|N)$, are listed in Table 8.2.

pop	thruput	pop	thruput
1.0	3.44828	7.0	6.49985
2.0	4.90694	8.0	6.55724
3.0	5.63447	9.0	6.59449
4.0	6.03402	10.0	6.61889
5.0	6.26768	11.0	6.63497
6.0	6.41028	12.0	6.64560

TABLE 8.1: Population versus throughput for Example 8.1.

Now going back to the original model Ω, equation (1.4) gives $\lambda_4(12) = 6.04$/sec, $\lambda_2(12) = 24.16$/sec, etc. From equation (2.2), we get $Q_{cs}(12) = 4.4878$. This means that on the average $5.9599 - 4.4878 = 1.4721$ jobs are blocked for memory while 4.4878 are executing inside the CS. □

n	$P_a(n\|N)$	n	$P_a(n\|N)$
1.0	0.019662	7.0	0.159222
2.0	0.044076	8.0	0.127018
3.0	0.078226	9.0	0.081062
4.0	0.116677	10.0	0.038800
5.0	0.148925	11.0	0.012381
6.0	0.166326	12.0	0.001975

TABLE 8.2: Load versus marginal probabilities for the aggregated model.

8.2.2 Swapping and Partial Allocation

In the previous section, we implicitly assumed that a resource request is accepted only when there are enough free units to satisfy it, and there is no preemption of the allocated resources. In some situations, these assumptions do not hold. For example, the allocation may be done piecemeal to achieve better resource utilization. (Piecemeal allocation may result in deadlocks, but we are not concerned with that aspect here.) Note that demand-paged or segmented memory allocation can be regarded as a special kind of piecemeal allocation. Also, after a resource has been allocated to a process, it may be taken away from it before the process is finished. This happens in the case of swapping and demand paging. Resource allocation/deallocation may also involve some associated activities that cause significant overhead, for example, disk I/O involved in program loading, swapping, and paging. Usually, the allocation/deallocation itself takes negligible time.

As in the last subsection, we shall specifically deal with memory management here, but the techniques apply to other types of resources as well. We start with swapping without piecemeal allocation. The most important aspect here is the overhead of writing a program image to the disk and reading it back. The swapping device may be dedicated or used for normal I/O as well. In either case we need to estimate the service demand related to swapping. This service demand can be thought of as the product of two factors: $S(swap)$, the average time needed to save or load a program, and $F(swap)$, the frequency of swaps. We can think of $S(swap)$ as the service time of the swap device and $F(swap)$ as its visit ratio. Thus, if visit ratios are defined relative to the lifetime of a program, $F(swap)$ gives the average number of swaps experienced by the program over its lifetime. $S(swap)$ can be easily computed from the average program size and disk transfer characteristics. However, $F(swap)$ is under the control of the operating system and is determined by several parameters such as the number of active processes, their memory requirements, and possibly their CPU time requirements. Thus, if the performance study involves changes in these parameters, swapping frequency must be estimated separately as a function of these model parameters, so that the effect of changes can be reflected accurately.

Let us consider the situation in Fig. 8-4, assuming that there is a separate swapping device. Here a new program must be loaded from the swapping device for each command. Obviously, $S(swap)$ here is the loading time and $F(swap)$ is 1 if visit ratios are relative to the terminal. Now suppose that we introduce the following swapping mechanism: Whenever a process is blocked for normal I/O, we consider swapping it out if another process is waiting to get into the central subsystem.[2] This waiting process may either be a new one or one that was swapped out earlier because it was blocked for I/O. To estimate the effect of this policy on $F(swap)$, we assume that all programs are identical in size. Let v_b denote the visit ratio associated with all those devices that cause the visiting process to be blocked, and thus become eligible for swap-out. (In Fig. 8-4, $v_b = v_{cpu}$ since the visit ratio of the CPU is the sum of the visit ratios of all I/O devices that block the process.) Let $P(swap)$ denote the probability that a swap-out is need when a process visits an I/O device. Since each program is swapped in initially, we can express $F(swap)$ as

$$F(swap) = 1 + 2v_b P(swap) \tag{2.4}$$

where the factor "2" comes from the fact that a swapped-out process must be swapped back in sometime later. Let us now see how we can estimate $P(swap)$ for the model in Fig. 8-4. Let N denote the network population, L the maximum number of programs that can be held in main memory, Q_t the average number of thinking users, and Q_{cpu} the average number of ready processes. We assume that $L < N - Q_t$, because otherwise the memory is not a limiting factor. On the average, there are $N - Q_t - Q_{cpu}$ blocked processes, but the memory can hold only $L - Q_{cpu}$ of these. Therefore, we can estimate $P(swap)$ as follows:

$$P(swap) = 1 - \frac{L - Q_{cpu}}{N - Q_t - Q_{cpu}} \tag{2.5}$$

Since Q_t and Q_{cpu} are the output parameters of the model, iteration is necessary for solving this model. The technique applies even if the swapping device is not distinct, since we can represent swapping activity by a different class. We emphasize here that the equations just developed are rather crude and may not give very good results if the effect of swapping is substantial. It is crucial to validate such approximate models before using them for further study. Another approach is to calibrate the base system by direct measurement, and then consider approximate ways of modeling changes to swapping frequency as a result of system modifications. For example, we can assume that the swapping frequency increases linearly with the number of processes waiting to be allocated.

Next we briefly look at demand paged memory allocation. In a simple model, paging I/O may be lumped with other I/O, but if we wish to study the memory management aspect carefully, we must consider paging separately. A simple-minded view of the situation is that each time a page-fault occurs, a page must be fetched. Thus, the visit ratio of the paging device is determined by the *life-time curve* (see Section 4.5.6) and the service time is simply the time needed to fetch one page. (If the device is also being used for normal I/O, this is the

[2]Here we are assuming that a process does not do any terminal I/O until it is finished. If this were not the case, it would be more sensible to swap out a process blocked for terminal I/O.

additional load placed by paging.) In reality, however, we need to consider many details of the paging mechanism. First, any useful system would cache discarded pages in memory; thus, a "page-fault" should really mean a page-fault such that a swap in is needed. Second, pages are typically read in clusters, so the service time corresponds to the time for reading a cluster. Third, the writing of dirty pages is typically done in large clusters and its effect should be taken into account. These aspects can be taken into account using the relevant measurement data such as the probability of a page read when a page-fault occurs, average read cluster size, average write cluster size, etc. Fortunately, such data are reported by most monitors.

8.2.3 Multiple-Resource Types

Here we consider the same problem as in Section 8.2.1, except that we now allow multiple resource types, one or more of which may be needed in different portions of the network. More specifically, we have J resource types, denoted $\Delta_1, \ldots, \Delta_J$, with available units $A_1, \ldots, A_J$. The network, denoted $\mathcal{Z}$, is divided into ns subnetworks, denoted $V_1, \ldots, V_{ns}$. For tractability, we assume that all subnetworks are disjoint and every resource type is requested in only one subnetwork. Thus, we can define a function $\alpha(j)$ for resource type j that gives the subnetwork requesting this resource. This function does not have a unique inverse since several resource types may be requested in one subnetwork. Note that it is adequate to index relevant quantities with just the resource type, since the corresponding subnetwork number is unique. Suppose that on the average, a customer needs ρ_j units of resource Δ_j. Let L_s denote the resource constraint in terms of the number of allowed customers in subnetwork s. Obviously,

$$L_s = \min_{\forall j:\alpha(j)=s} [A_j/\rho_j] \tag{2.6}$$

The above equation uses the fact that if more than one resource type is needed in subnetwork s, the most scarce resource determines the number of allowed customers. That is, we are assuming that either the customer gets all resource types that it needs and enters the subnetwork, or it waits outside. It is convenient to assume here that L_s is *not* an integer. The solution algorithm is a simple extension of the one for the single-resource case, and is stated below:

1. Consider each subnetwork s ($s \in 1\,..\,ns$) in isolation. Solve the subnetwork to obtain its throughput, denoted $\Lambda_s(n)$ for $n \in 1\,..\,\lceil L_s \rceil$.
2. Construct the aggregated model $\mathcal{Z}_a$ by using a load-dependent station s' for each subnetwork V_s. Let $l = \lfloor L_s \rfloor$. The service rate of s', denoted $\mu'_s(n)$, is given by

$$\mu_{s'}(n) = \begin{cases} \Lambda_s(n) & \text{if } n \le l \\ \Lambda_s(l) + (L_s - l)[\Lambda_s(l+1) - \Lambda_s(l)] & \text{if } n > l \end{cases} \tag{2.7}$$

   Solve the network to obtain marginal distribution at each aggregate station, denoted $P_{s'}(n|N)$ for $n = 1\,..\,N$.

3. Let $Q_s^{(u)}(N)$ denote the number of unblocked (or active) customers in subnetwork s. We can compute this quantity using a relationship similar to equation (2.2), i.e.,

$$Q_s^{(u)}(N) = \sum_{n=1}^{\lfloor L_s \rfloor} nP_{s'}(n|N) + L_s \sum_{n=\lceil L_s \rceil}^{N} P_{s'}(n|N) \tag{2.8}$$

The average number of customers waiting to get into subnetwork s, denoted $Q_s^{(w)}(N)$, could then be computed as $Q_{s'}(N) - Q_s^{(u)}(N)$ where $Q_{s'}(N)$ is the average queue length for station s' in $\mathcal{Z}_a$.

This algorithm can also handle properly nested resource constrained subnetworks. Allowing a resource to be used in more than one subnetwork is, however, more difficult (but can be approached like the shared memory constraints discussed in the next section).

8.2.4 Resource Constraints in Multiple-Chain Models

Here we extend the algorithm of the last subsection to multiple-chain networks. We continue to use the notation from the last section, except that some parameters become chain-dependent. In particular, we use ρ_{jr} to denote the average number of units of resource Δ_j requested by a chain r customer. The division of the total number of available units of type j, denoted as A_j, among different chains can be done in one of the following two ways:

1. Dedicate a certain number of units to each chain. We denote chain r's share of resource type j as A_{jr}, where $\sum_{r=1}^{K} A_{jr} = A_j$. This is called the *independent resource constraint* (IRC).
2. All chains obtain required units from a common pool containing A_j units of type j. We call this the *shared resource constraint* (SRC). In the case of SRC, we can still define the parameters A_{jr}, but they are not known a priori.

These two policies correspond, respectively, to static and dynamic allocation on a per-chain basis. For example, in the context of memory management, IRC policy corresponds to fixed partitions and SRC policy to dynamic partitioned allocation. It is possible to consider a more general case encompassing both IRC and SRC. This is done by defining several "domains", each of which is shared by a distinct set of chains. For simplicity, we shall not do so, but all the algorithms for SRC extend easily to this more general situation. We also assume that there is no piecemeal allocation and resources are never released prematurely. We shall develop an algorithm that applies to both IRC and SRC.

To start with, suppose that we directly extend the technique of Section 8.2.3 to deal with multiple chains. Consider a subnetwork s of a two-chain IRC system with population constraints of $L1$ and $L2$ respectively. Then the service rate for chain r at the aggregate station s' can be chosen as

$$\mu_{s'r}(n_1, n_2) = \Lambda_{sr}[\min(L1, n_1), \min(L2, n_2)] \tag{2.9}$$

Unfortunately, this form of service rate does not satisfy the product-form condition in (6.6.1). Therefore, we consider some further approximations that require solving only single-chain models. The basic idea is to construct an aggregated model, say $\mathcal{Z}_a(r)$, with respect to each chain r. This model will have a load-dependent station for each subnetwork through which chain r passes, and the service rate at such a station will be a function of only the number of chain r customers in the corresponding subnetwork. Thus, the set of steps in the algorithm of Section 8.2.3 will be repeated for each chain r. In aggregating a subnetwork s with respect to chain r, we vary the population of only chain r, and fix the populations of the other chains at their "average values". The underlying assumption in doing this is that chain r throughput varies linearly with the number of customers in other chains. Under this assumption, it is easy to show that the service rate of the aggregate depends only on the mean number of customers of other chains. (See Exercise 8.2). It is difficult to justify this assumption analytically; therefore, we shall later comment on the accuracy of the algorithm based on empirical evidence. One difficulty in using this heuristic is that the mean number of customers is an output parameter of the model and is not known initially. Thus, the algorithm starts with an initial estimate and refines it iteratively. The complete algorithm is as follows:

1. Ignore all resource constraints and solve the network. Compute the average number of chain r customers in subnetwork s, denoted $Q_{sr}(\mathbf{N})$.

2. Let D_{jr} denote the average number of units of type j demanded by chain r in the absence of any resource constraints. Obviously,

$$D_{jr} = Q_{\alpha(j)\,r}\ \rho_{jr} \tag{2.10}$$

where $\alpha(j)$ is the (unique) subnetwork that uses resource of type j. Define $D_j = \sum_{r=1}^{K} D_{jr}$. For SRC, we now estimate A_{jr} as the "proportional share" of the available units. That is,

$$A_{jr} = A_j D_{jr}/D_j \tag{2.11}$$

For IRC, A_{jr} is, of course, given. If $D_{jr} \leq A_{jr}$, it means that chain r has enough units of resource j, and we need to dedicate only D_{jr} units to chain r. If however $D_{jr} > A_{jr}$, we can dedicate all A_{jr} units to chain r. Therefore, the number of units allocated to chain r is $\min(D_{jr}, A_{jr})$. Now to get an initial estimate of Q_{sr} for a subnetwork s under resource constrains, we have to consider the constraint placed by the most scarce resource. This yields:

$$Q_{sr} = \min_{\forall j:\alpha(j)=s} [\min(D_{jr}, A_{jr})/\rho_{jr}] \tag{2.12}$$

3. Let L_{sr} denote the *maximum feasible population* of chain r in subnetwork s in the "average environment" of other chains. Under IRC, A_{jr} is given, which makes L_{sr} independent of other chains. That is,

$$L_{sr} = \min_{\forall j:\alpha(j)=s} [A_{jr}/\rho_{jr}] \tag{2.13}$$

For SRC however, let $\theta_{jr} = A_j - \sum_{k \neq r} Q_{\alpha(j)\,k}\ \rho_{jk}$. Obviously, θ_{jr} gives the available resource units of type j for chain r in the average environment of other chains. However, if we use θ_{jr}'s directly, it is possible that their sum, taken over all chains, does not match the resource constraint A_j. Therefore, we scale θ_{jr}'s to meet this requirement. Let $\theta'_{jr} = A_j\theta_{jr}/\sum_{k=1}^{K}\theta_{jk}$. Therefore, for SRC,

$$L_{sr} = \min_{\forall j:\alpha(j)=s} [\theta'_{jr}/\rho_{jr}] \tag{2.14}$$

4. For each chain r, construct a *single-chain aggregated model* $\mathcal{Z}_a(r)$ and solve it to get a better estimate of Q_{sr} (for all s). This is done as follows:

   (a) Consider each subnetwork s, $(s \in 1\mathinner{..}ns)$ in isolation. Set its population vector to $(Q_{s1}, \ldots, Q_{s(r-1)}, n, Q_{s(r+1)}, \ldots, Q_{sK})$ where n takes all values in the range $1\mathinner{..}\lceil L_{sr}\rceil$. Solve the subnetwork to obtain throughput of chain r, denoted $\Lambda_{sr}(n)$.

   (b) Construct the single-chain model $\mathcal{Z}_a(r)$ by using a load-dependent aggregate station s' for each subnetwork s. [The subnetworks through which chain r does not pass, do not appear in $\mathcal{Z}_a(r)$]. Set the service rate of s', denoted $\mu_{s'r}(n)$, using equation (2.7). (Our notation now carries the subscript r, but that does not change anything.) The population of this network is N_r. The visit ratio of station s' can be chosen as discussed in Section 8.1.1; i.e., by picking a station in the subnetwork s and using its throughput and visit ratio.

   (c) Solve $\mathcal{Z}_a(r)$ to obtain the marginal distribution at each aggregate station s', denoted $P_{s'r}(n|N_r)$, for $n = 1\mathinner{..}N_r$.

   (d) Find a better estimate of Q_{sr} for all s using equation (2.8). That is,

$$Q_{sr} = \sum_{n=1}^{\lfloor L_{sr}\rfloor} nP_{s'r}(n|N_r) + L_{sr} \sum_{n=\lceil L_{sr}\rceil}^{N_r} P_{s'r}(n|N_r) \tag{2.15}$$

5. Check for the convergence of Q_{sr}'s for all s and r. If convergence has not been achieved, go to step 4 for IRC and step 3 for SRC. Otherwise, compute performance parameters for individual stations. (One can also find the average number of blocked customers exactly as in Section 8.2.3).

Note that steps 1 and 2 are only for initialization, and the estimate A_{jr} for SRC is neither modified, nor used in later steps. Equation (2.12), in effect, multiplies Q_{sr} obtained in step 1 by $\min(1, A_j/D_j)$ where the index j corresponds to the most scarce resource in the subnetwork s. Finally, L_{sr} does not change in the case of IRC; therefore, the purpose of iteration is only to achieve convergence of Q_{sr}'s. Also, step 4a in the algorithm requires solution of a network with fractional chain populations. The obvious technique is to use a $K-1$ way linear interpolation, but that may be expensive. A judicious rounding of populations can often avoid the need for interpolation. A different approach is to use the Linearizer algorithm since it can handle fractional populations, but that would introduce additional errors.

We now comment on the accuracy of the algorithm. Experimental results show that the algorithm generally performs very well for IRC and reasonably well for SRC. However, under highly imbalanced situations or when the resource constraints are very tight, the algorithm may cause substantial errors. As with our previous algorithms, this one can also handle properly nested resource constrained subnetworks.

8.2.5 Modeling Channel Contention

Explicit modeling of channels becomes important when the system has fewer channels than the number of disk drives. In this case, a channel must be dynamically connected to a disk drive to do I/O. The channel must remain connected to the disk for the entire duration of data transfer, but is not needed during the seek operation. Since seek typically takes a substantial amount of time, it is possible to obtain good performance without dedicating one channel per disk drive. In such systems, the typical sequence of events for doing an I/O operation on disk D on behalf of process P will go as follows:

(a) Allocate disk D to process P.

(b) Obtain a free channel C that has a physical path to disk D.

(c) Issue a seek command to disk D (if necessary) via channel C. If the drive has rotational position sensing (RPS) capability, also supply the desired sector number (in addition to the desired cylinder number). Release C.

(d) Wait until the seek operation is complete and an interrupt is posted to the processor (this does not require a channel as an intermediary). If the drive has RPS capability, the interrupt is posted only when the head is within one sector of the desired sector number.

(e) Obtain a free channel C' that has a physical path to disk D and allocate it to process P. Start the I/O operation.

(f) When the I/O is finished, release channel C' and disk D, unblock process P, etc.

Like memory contention, channel contention also involves simultaneous resource possession, but the situation is more complex. First, the channels are needed only for part of the I/O operation. Second, a given disk drive can connect only to certain channels depending on the physical configuration of the I/O subsystem. Third, if the drive has RPS capability, there is only one sector rotation worth of time to connect to a channel; if a free channel cannot be found in this time, no transfer can occur for an entire rotation (even if a channel becomes available shortly after the desired sector is missed). Thus, the modeling must consider the number of tries needed for a successful connect. A fourth problem arises when disk controllers are also shared; that is, a channel is shared by several controllers, each of which in turn is shared by several drives. This complicates the topology further.

We start our analysis with a very simple case. Suppose that we have k disjoint pools of channels, each of which is used by a distinct pool of disks. Any disk in the ith disk pool can be connected to any channel in the ith channel pool but to no others. Also suppose that the channel remains connected to a disk even during the seek. Then we can apply the technique of Section 8.2.3 directly. In particular, the k disk pools would form k disjoint subnetworks with channel pools treated as k different passive resource types. If we relax the assumption that channels are held during seek, it is still possible to use memory constraint-based modeling, as shown in Fig. 8-6. This Fig. shows only one disk pool (or subnetwork), denoted s, but all comments apply in general. For simplicity, the use of the channel for issuing the seek command is ignored. The model involves two classes where class 1 activity through the disks corresponds to seek operation and class 2 activity to data transfer. Upon entering subnetwork s, a customer first goes through as a member of class 1 (default) to do the seek. It then unconditionally changes over to class 2, obtains a channel, performs data transfer, releases the channel, and changes back to class 1. The solution of this model would involve aggregating the I/O subsystem and saturating the service rate for class 2. The resulting higher-level multiple-chain model will not satisfy product-form conditions, but we can use a technique similar to the one in Section 8.2.4. Note that the situation here fits the IRC model with L_{s1} chosen as the network population and L_{s2} as the number of available channels. The difference is that we are dealing with two classes, instead of chains, but the technique can be easily adapted for this situation as well.

An alternate method to solve the above problem involves *iterative aggregation*. The idea is to construct a model, denoted $\mathcal{Z}$, where every channel pool is represented by a delay station (but all disks that can connect to these channels are included explicitly). Let c' denote the delay station corresponding to the channel pool c. The service time at c' is intended to represent the channel contention time. This time can be estimated by aggregating all other stations into one using Norton's theorem and solving the simplified model using global balance techniques. This procedure is applied cyclically to each pool, each time using the latest contention delays, until convergence is achieved. We could then solve the fully calibrated network $\mathcal{Z}$ to get the final results. Clearly, the method would be impractical except for very small systems because of the state space explosion.

In the following we consider a MVA-based heuristic approach that applies to tree-like I/O structures with *only one channel per pool*. The main advantages of the method are its intuitive appeal and low solution expense. The technique may

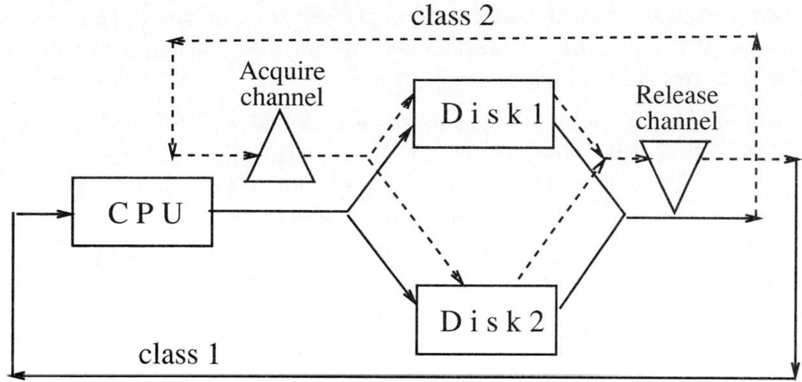

FIGURE 8-6: Modeling channel contention using passive resources.

not yield accurate results if the channel contention is very high. In this approach the model includes only the disks explicitly; the effect of channel contention is accounted for by modifying the response time equation for the disks. For the system shown in Fig. 8-11, we would short out the two channel stations and then write modified response time equations for each of the four disks.

Consider a channel that controls d disks embedded in a single-chain network with population N. Let $S_i(seek)$, $S_i(rotation)$, and $S_i(transfer)$ denote the average seek, rotation, and transfer time for disk i. Then the average service time at disk i, denoted S_i, is given by

$$S_i = S_i(seek) + S_i(rotation) + S_i(transfer) \tag{2.16}$$

Let $QA_j(N)$ denote the average number of requests seen at disk j ($j \in 1..d$) by a "typical" I/O request $\mathcal{A}$ made for disk i. In view of the arrival theorem, we shall approximate $QA_j(N)$ as simply $Q_j(N-1)$. Let $CT_i(N)$ denote the channel contention time for $\mathcal{A}$. Let us assume that the disks do not have RPS capability, and the *channel scheduling* is FCFS. Then $\mathcal{A}$ must wait for all others in front, each of which holds the channel for the latency and transfer time. Therefore,

$$CT_i(N) = \sum_{j=1}^{d}[S_j(rotation) + S_j(transfer)]Q_j(N-1) \tag{2.17}$$

Let $R_i(N)$ denote the average response time for $\mathcal{A}$. $R_i(N)$ includes the service time of $\mathcal{A}$, the seek time of all the requests for disk i ahead of $\mathcal{A}$, and the channel contention time. Notice that $CT_i(N)$ already includes the time spent by the requests ahead of $\mathcal{A}$ in rotational delay and data transfer. Therefore,

$$R_i(N) = S_i + S_i(seek)Q_i(N-1) + CT_i(N) \tag{2.18}$$

Thus, by using this response time equation instead of the mean value theorem for the disks, we can solve the entire model using MVA.

Although we illustrated the method in the context of single-chain networks, equations (2.17) and (2.18), and hence the entire algorithm, extend to the multiple-chain case in an obvious way.

Let us now note a few points regarding the assumed FCFS scheduling. In practice, the scheduling of the channel among the requests going to different disks would probably be FCFS, but the selection among requests headed for a given disk would follow a disk scheduling discipline such as SCAN, C-SCAN, or SSTF. As shown in Appendix C, a simple way to handle complex disk scheduling is to make the seek time load-dependent, but to assume the scheduling to be FCFS. In this sense, our FCFS scheduling assumption for the channel is satisfactory. The load-dependence and non-FCFS disciplines can be handled approximately by using the techniques of Section 8.3.6.

Let us now extend the above algorithm for the case when the disks have RPS capability. In this case the channel contention time must be computed differently. Let Rot_i denote the rotation time for disk i and $r_i(N)$ the average number of *unsuccessful* connection attempts made by disk i. Then the channel contention time, now denoted as $CT'_i(N)$ is simply $Rot_i \times r_i(N)$. For computing $r_i(N)$, we can assume that the probability of missing the connection, denoted $P_i(N)$, remains constant over all retries. Then the distribution of the number of retries is geometric, and $r_i(N)$ is given by

$$r_i(N) = \frac{P_i(N)}{1 - P_i(N)} \tag{2.19}$$

(We note here that in practice, it is found that $P_i(N)$ increases slightly with the number of tries.) The probability $P_i(N)$ is the same as the probability of finding the channel busy given that disk i is not transferring. Let $U_{ch}(j, N)$ denote the channel utilization due to disk j. We can interpret this quantity as the probability of finding the channel busy due to transfers by disk j. Therefore, by the definition of the conditional probability, we have

$$P_i(N) = \frac{U_{ch}(N) - U_{ch}(i, N)}{1 - U_{ch}(i, N)} \quad \text{where } U_{ch}(N) = \sum_{j=1}^{d} U_{ch}(j, N) \tag{2.20}$$

With RPS mechanism, the channel is occupied for the duration of the transfer time only, thus if $\lambda_i(N)$ is the throughput of disk i, we have $U_{ch}(i, N) = \lambda_i(N) S_i(transfer)$. Since only the transfer time is included in $CT'_i(N)$, the response time expression for a request arriving at disk i becomes

$$R_i(N) = S_i + [S_i(seek) + S_i(rotation)]Q_i(N - 1) + CT'_i(N) \tag{2.21}$$

Thus, we can again apply the MVA algorithm; the only difficulty being that $CT'_i(N)$ involves λ_i at population N. This problem can be handled easily by an iterative procedure. As with the non-RPS case the equations here also extend to the multiple-chain case and non-FCFS scheduling disciplines.

When a device is connected to multiple channels, the modeling depends on how the redundant connections are used. If the redundant links are used only when a fault develops in the primary links or channels, the redundancy does not affect performance modeling. If the channels are chosen probabilistically, it is still possible to develop appropriate MVA equations by using a weighted summation over all relevant channels. If the device simply grabs the first channel that it finds free, there is no easy way of writing down an expression for the contention time. The bibliographic notes at the end of the chapter provide pointers to some further work on the modeling of such systems.

8.3 Modeling Non-PF Scheduling Disciplines

As mentioned in Section 7.2, the mean value theorem lends itself to heuristic extensions to handle rather complex scheduling disciplines *at load-independent stations*. The crucial parameter required in writing down corresponding response time expressions is the average queue length seen by an arriving customer. In a PF network, we can exploit the arrival theorem for this purpose; however, in general, the arriver's distribution is difficult to characterize. In heuristic extensions of MVA to other scheduling disciplines, one typically assumes that the arrival theorem still holds, though the accuracy of this assumption deteriorates as the discipline becomes less and less like a PF discipline. With priority-based scheduling and moderate to heavy loading, the assumption will typically yield unacceptable results. In such cases, one uses some ad hoc ways of improving the accuracy.

In this section we present MVA-based modeling of several scheduling disciplines. Although the primary interest here is in closed networks, all equations apply to open networks by simply removing the population dependence. In particular, this amounts to assuming that the arriver's distribution is the same as that of a random observer. If the arrivals are Poisson, this assumption is indeed true (see Section 9.2.1), irrespective of the service-time distribution or the scheduling discipline. As a result, many of the results become exact in the context of an ordinary M/G/1 queuing system.

The scheduling disciplines included in the following sections are chosen based partly on their importance and partly to illustrate the technique. It should be clear from this discussion that heuristic response time equations can be manufactured for almost any type of scheduling discipline for which average parameters are adequate; however, it is not advisable to use them without careful validation.

8.3.1 FCFS Scheduling Discipline

Consider a load-independent station i in a single-chain closed network with population N. Suppose that the station has nonexponential service-time distribution but FCFS scheduling discipline (thus violating the PF requirement). Let $\mathcal{A}$ denote an arriving customer. The response time of $\mathcal{A}$ includes the following components: (1) remaining service time (or the *residual life*) of the customer found in service, if any, (2) time needed to serve all other customers ahead of $\mathcal{A}$, and (3) $\mathcal{A}$'s own service time. Assuming that the arrival theorem holds, $\mathcal{A}$ will find, on the average, $Q_i(N-1)$ customers at the station on arrival, of which $U_i(N-1)$ will be busy receiving service from the server. We shall show in Section 9.2.1 that the average residual life of a customer, denoted γ_i, is given by:

$$\gamma_i = s_i \frac{(CV_i^2 + 1)}{2} \tag{3.1}$$

and CV_i is the coefficient of variation of the service time. Therefore, component (1) of the average response time is $U_i(N-1)\gamma_i$. The average time needed to serve other customers ahead of $\mathcal{A}$ is $s_i[Q_i(N-1) - U_i(N-1)]$. Therefore, by adding the three components together, we get

$$R_i(N) = s_i[1 + Q_i(N-1)] + U_i(N-1)(\gamma_i - s_i) \tag{3.2}$$

We could now use this expression instead of (7.2.3) in the MVA algorithm; all other steps remain the same. One could even use this expression in a *bidirectional MVA* algorithm to avoid exponential complexity; however, this will surely introduce additional errors.

The above equation can be extended in a straightforward manner to multiple-chain networks. Let the mean and coefficient of variation of service time for chain r customers be denoted as s_{ir} and CV_{ir} respectively. Assuming the arrival theorem again, an arriver $\mathcal{A}$ belonging to chain r will find, on the average, $Q_{ik}(\mathbf{N}-e_r)$ customers of chain k at station i, of which $U_{ik}(\mathbf{N}-e_r)$ would be in service. Thus, by accounting for all the delays experienced by $\mathcal{A}$, the response time expression becomes

$$R_{ir}(\mathbf{N}) = s_{ir} + \sum_{k=1}^{K} s_{ik} Q_{ik}(\mathbf{N}-e_r) + \sum_{k=1}^{K} U_{ik}(\mathbf{N}-e_r)(\gamma_{ik} - s_{ik}) \tag{3.3}$$

where γ_{ik} is the average residual life for chain k customers, i.e.,

$$\gamma_{ik} = s_{ik}(CV_{ik}^2 + 1)/2 \tag{3.4}$$

These multiple-chain equations (and all others in this section) can be used for the multiple-class situation as well; the only change being that $\mathbf{N}$ and $\mathbf{N}-e_r$ will be replaced by N and $N-1$ respectively. We can also specialize any closed network equation to an open network by simply removing the population indicator. For example, equation (3.2) reduces to

$$R_i = s_i(1 + \lambda_i R_i) + U_i(\gamma_i - s_i)$$

where we have used Little's law. Simplifying further, we get the following explicit expression for the average waiting time W_i

$$W_i = \frac{U_i \gamma_i}{1 - U_i} \tag{3.5}$$

This equation is identical to (9.3.8), which gives the average waiting time for a M/G/1/FCFS/∞/∞ system. Thus, equation (3.2) is asymptotically exact (i.e., as $N \to \infty$) *provided that the arrivals are Poisson*. However, it should be kept in mind that the flows in a network are mostly non-Poisson even under PF conditions, as discussed in Section 5.5.6.

For an open network, equation (3.3), along with Little's law, gives the following expression for the average waiting time W_{ir}:

$$W_{ir} = \sum_{k=1}^{K} U_{ik} W_{ik} + \sum_{k=1}^{K} U_{ik} \gamma_{ik} \tag{3.6}$$

Let $\mathcal{V}_i = \sum_{k=1}^{K} U_{ik} W_{ik}$. Multiplying both sides of equation (3.6) by U_{ir}, summing over all r, and simplifying, we get

$$\mathcal{V}_i = \frac{U_i}{1 - U_i} \sum_{k=1}^{K} U_{ik} \gamma_{ik} \tag{3.7}$$

where $U_i = \sum_{k=1}^{K} U_{ik}$ is the total utilization of station i. Substituting equation (3.7) back in equation (3.6), we get the following explicit expression for W_{ir}.

$$W_{ir} = \frac{1}{1 - U_i} \sum_{k=1}^{K} U_{ik} \gamma_{ik} \tag{3.8}$$

This is an exact waiting time expression for a multiple chain M/G/1/FCFS/∞/∞ system. Notice that the right-hand side of (3.8) is independent of r because the FCFS discipline does not favor customers based on their chain membership.

It is interesting to compare this expression with the one for the PS discipline. Since the product-form solution holds for the PS discipline, and the chains can be treated like classes in an open network, by Little's law and equations (6.2.30) and (5.5.5), we have

$$W_{ir}^{(PS)} = \frac{1}{\lambda_{ir}} \frac{U_{ir}}{U_i} \frac{U_i^2}{(1 - U_i)} = \frac{U_i}{(1 - U_i)} s_{ir} \tag{3.9}$$

which depends on s_{ir}, and actually increases linearly with it. This is because under PS discipline, the server is shared equally among all jobs, which effectively gives a priority that decreases linearly with the service time requirement. As expected from the conditions given in Section 6.6, equations (3.8) and (3.9) match when all chains have exponential service-time distribution *with the same mean*.

In spite of the asymptotic exactness of heuristic equations (3.2) and (3.3), they should not be used without due regard to errors. Although they generally give good results, unacceptable errors may result when the coefficient of variation is large (> 2) or when the parameters of different chains are substantially different.

8.3.2 Priority Scheduling Discipline

Consider a station i in a closed network where the customers can be classified into K categories such that category k has higher priority than category r if $k > r$. If this categorization holds only at station i or if the customers can change between categories, we model the situation by considering these categories as classes; otherwise, each category would define a separate chain. As mentioned in the last subsection, the equations would be identical in the two cases except for the population indicators; therefore, we shall choose the more general chain-based categorization. That is, we have K chains, and a chain k customer has higher priority than a chain r customer, if $k > r$. The priority scheduling could be preemptive or nonpreemptive. In the preemptive case it is convenient to write down the expression for the response time directly; for the nonpreemptive case we first write down the expression for the waiting time and then get the response time. The difference arises because in the preemptive case we must consider higher priority arrivals during the service time of our tagged arriver $\mathcal{A}$, but in the nonpreemptive case such arrivals are of no concern.

The scheduling of customers belonging to the same chain may follow another policy. As an example, consider the FCFS discipline within a chain and preemptive priority across chains. The response time of a tagged customer $\mathcal{A}$ belonging to chain r consists of the following: (1) its own service time, (2) remaining service time of a customer found by $\mathcal{A}$ having the same or higher priority, (3) time required to service customers of the same or higher priority found waiting by $\mathcal{A}$, and (4) time required to serve any higher-priority arrivals during the response time of $\mathcal{A}$. Thus, assuming the arrival theorem, we get the following expression for the average response time:

$$\begin{aligned} R_{ir}(\mathbf{N}) &= s_{ir} + \sum_{k=r}^{K} [\gamma_{ik} U_{ik}(\mathbf{N}-e_r) + s_{ik}[Q_{ik}(\mathbf{N}-e_r) - U_{ik}(\mathbf{N}-e_r)]] \\ &\quad + \sum_{k=r+1}^{K} \lambda_{ik}(\mathbf{N}-e_r) R_{ir}(\mathbf{N}) s_{ik} \end{aligned} \tag{3.10}$$

where the last term comes from the fact that the number of chain k arrivals during $\mathcal{A}$'s response time is $\lambda_{ik}(\mathbf{N}-e_r)R_{ir}(\mathbf{N})$. The equation simplifies to

$$R_{ir}(\mathbf{N}) = \frac{s_{ir} + \sum_{k=r}^{K} [\gamma_{ik} U_{ik}(\mathbf{N}-e_r) + s_{ik}[Q_{ik}(\mathbf{N}-e_r) - U_{ik}(\mathbf{N}-e_r)]]}{1 - \sigma_{i(r+1)}(\mathbf{N}-e_r)} \tag{3.11}$$

where the σ function is defined by

$$\sigma_{ir}(\mathbf{n}) = \sum_{k=r}^{K} U_{ik}(\mathbf{n}) \tag{3.12}$$

With nonpreemptive scheduling, we can use a similar argument and obtain the following expression for the average *waiting time*

$$W_{ir}(\mathbf{N}) = \frac{\sum_{k=1}^{K} \gamma_{ik} U_{ik}(\mathbf{N}-e_r) + \sum_{k=r}^{K} s_{ik}[Q_{ik}(\mathbf{N}-e_r) - U_{ik}(\mathbf{N}-e_r)]}{1 - \sigma_{i(r+1)}(\mathbf{N}-e_r)} \quad (3.13)$$

Note that unlike the preemptive case, $\mathcal{A}$ must now wait for the customer in service, if any, irrespective of its chain affiliation. This explains the summation over the range $1..K$ for the residual life term.

The infinite population version of equation (3.13) becomes exact if the arrivals are Poisson. In particular, removing the population dependence turns it into a triangular system of linear equations, which can be solved recursively to yield the following explicit expression for W_{ir}:

$$W_{ir} = \frac{\sum_{k=1}^{K} U_{ik}\gamma_{ik}}{(1 - \sigma_{ir})(1 - \sigma_{i(r+1)})} \quad (3.14)$$

Unfortunately, equation (3.11) does not yield the exact result, which is

$$R_{ir} = \frac{s_{ir}(1 - \sigma_{ir}) + \sum_{k=r}^{K} U_{ik}\gamma_{ik}}{(1 - \sigma_{ir})(1 - \sigma_{i(r+1)})} \quad (3.15)$$

Note that under preemptive priority, chain r response time is entirely independent of the parameters of chains $j < r$. But for the residual-life term in the numerator, this is also true of the nonpreemptive priority case. Also note that under priority scheduling, it is possible that $\sigma_p < 1$ but $\sigma_{p-1} \geq 1$ for some p. This means that chains $p, \ldots, K$ will experience bounded delays, whereas others will face an unstable situation.

Let us now examine the accuracy of equations (3.11) and (3.13). Unfortunately, the priority structure makes the distribution seen by a low priority job considerably different from what the arrival theorem would predict. The effect generally worsens with decreasing priority. This is best seen intuitively with preemptive scheduling (though one would expect similar arguments to apply for the nonpreemptive case as well). Consider those times when a chain r job is receiving service. In this situation, no jobs of higher priority could be present at the station. Clearly, the conditions prevailing at this time are far from "typical", but this aspect is ignored in equation (3.11). There we estimated the number of chain k arrivals during the service time of chain r by using the arrival rate $\lambda_{ik}(\mathbf{N}-e_r)$, which is incorrect. In fact, we can even see the direction of the error, since we would expect chain r customers to fill "holes" left by the higher-priority customers. That is, the probability of arrival of a chain $k > r$ customer during the service time of a chain r customer will be lower than in a "typical" interval of the same length. The same is also true during the waiting time of a chain r customer, since this customer is being passed over by the higher-priority customers. Thus, we would expect equations (3.11) and (3.13) to overestimate the response time, and this overestimate to worsen with lower and lower priority. This is precisely the behavior one finds in practice. Thus, the response times obtained from equation (3.11) and (3.13) for the lowest priority chain will be grossly overestimated if the total load placed by higher-priority chains (i.e., σ_{i2}) is close to 1.

Since priority scheduling is practically important, several attempts have been made to improve the accuracy of MVA approximations. One such method is called the *shadow approximation*. It evaluates the effect of higher-priority customers on chain r by considering the service to those customers as a "breakdown" as far as chain r is concerned. Because of this breakdown, chain r customers get only $1 - \sigma_{i(r+1)}(\mathbf{N})$ units of service per unit time. Under preemptive priority, this slowdown factor will affect the entire response time of a chain r customer, but lower-priority customers will have no effect at all. Therefore,

$$R_{ir}(\mathbf{N}) = \frac{s_{ir}[1 + Q_{ir}(\mathbf{N} - e_r)] + U_{ir}(\mathbf{N} - e_r)(\gamma_{ir} - s_{ir})}{1 - \sigma_{i(r+1)}(\mathbf{N})} \tag{3.16}$$

where the numerator considers only chain r and is thus the same as equation (3.2).

Notice that equation (3.16) and (3.11) have similar (but not the same) denominators, but the summation over higher-priority chains is missing from the numerator of equation (3.16). Thus, equation (3.16) will give lower response times than equation (3.11). Generally, this approximation works better for low priority chains, but may still give unacceptable results when the loading by high priority chains is high. Also, since equation (3.16) involves utilization at population $\mathbf{N}$ in the denominator, it will require iteration in the MVA algorithm.

A significantly better approximation can be obtained if we abandon the arrival theorem. Let $\vec{Q}_i = [Q_{i1}(\mathbf{N}), \ldots, Q_{iK}(\mathbf{N})]$. The idea is to assume that the arrival rate during the response time of $\mathcal{A}$ should be evaluated at population of $\mathbf{N} - \vec{Q}_i$, instead of $\mathbf{N} - e_r$, since the $\vec{Q}_i$ customers are present at station i and cannot contribute to the arrivals. This would lead to expressions like (3.11) and (3.13), except that the denominator becomes $[1 - \sigma_{i(r+1)}(\mathbf{N} - \vec{Q}_i)]$. Needless to say, this assumption is only a heuristic with no theoretical justification; but it appears to work quite well. (The estimates could now be either underestimates or overestimates depending on the parameter combinations.) The disadvantages are that the results at fractional population levels are needed and the BMVA approach can no longer be used.

8.3.3 Biased Processor Sharing Discipline

Ordinary round-robin discipline with a small time slice (which can be approximated as the PS discipline) shares the server equally among all the customers. It may sometimes be desirable to provide a different share of the station to customers of different categories. Two of the several possible ways to implement this are (1) to use a different time-slice for each category, and (2) to pick higher-priority customers several times during each "cycle". Assuming that the total time devoted to each category per cycle is still much smaller than the average service time of that category, we can approximate such disciplines by a *biased processor sharing* (BPS) discipline, which can be described as follows: Suppose that we have customers of K categories and assign a finite, positive real number τ_k to category $k = 1..K$. The interpretation of τ_k is that during the time category r customers get τ_r units of service, category k customers will get τ_k units of service. As in the ordinary PS discipline, each customer still gets an infinitesimal amount of service each time it is scheduled for service. Thus, the fraction of the server devoted to chain r is $\tau_r / \sum_{k=1}^{K} \tau_k$.

As in other sections, we assume that the categories represent chains (although similar equations would apply to classes). Assuming the arrival theorem, a chain r arriver $\mathcal{A}$ will find $Q_{ik}(\mathbf{N} - e_r)$ chain k customers present at station i on the average. Thus, the "slowdown" experienced by chain r due to chain k customers would be $\tau_k Q_{ik}(\mathbf{N} - e_r)/\tau_r$. Thus, to get 1 unit of service, $\mathcal{A}$ must spend $1 + \sum_{k=1}^{K} \tau_k Q_{ik}(\mathbf{N} - e_r)/\tau_r$ units of time in the system. It then follows that

$$R_{ir}(\mathbf{N}) = s_{ir} \left[1 + \sum_{k=1}^{K} \frac{\tau_k}{\tau_r} Q_{ik}(\mathbf{N} - e_r) \right] \tag{3.17}$$

So long as the largest time slice remains small compared with the smallest $s_{ir}, r \in 1..K$, this approximation works very well. It can be used for modeling the *multilevel round-robin* discipline that is a popular short-term process scheduling strategy in many contemporary operating systems. For the limiting case of $N \to \infty$, equation (3.17) gives the following explicit waiting time expression:

$$W_{ir} = \frac{s_{ir}}{1 - U_i} \sum_{k=1}^{K} \frac{\tau_k}{\tau_r} U_{ik} \tag{3.18}$$

This expression is obtained much like equation (3.8). It is an exact expression for a M/G/1 queue under biased processor sharing discipline.

8.3.4 Shortest Job Next Scheduling

Shortest job next (SJN) discipline is useful when the service demand is known in advance. Two examples of situations where this discipline is useful are printing where the job size is the number of lines to be printed out, and disk seek where the job size is the number of cylinders to be skipped. The main purpose of this section is to illustrate how complex disciplines such as SJN can be modeled in the MVA setting.

We start with the single-chain case. Suppose that a tagged customer $\mathcal{A}$ arrives at a SJN station (say, i) with the service time requirement of x. We can consider $\mathcal{A}$ as belonging to class x while it is at station i. This gives an uncountable number of classes and the probability of a customer belonging to a class in the range $(x, x + dx)$ is given by $f_i(x)dx$ where f_i is the service time density. Let $W_i(x, N)$ denote the average waiting time of $\mathcal{A}$ at network population N. It consists of the following components: (a) remaining service time of the customer in service, if any, (b) service time of all waiting customers found by $\mathcal{A}$

with service time requirement of less than or equal to x, and (c) the service time of all customers with requirement of less than x who arrive during $\mathcal{A}$'s waiting time. We denote these as RL_i, QD_i, and AD_i respectively. It is easy to see that

$$RL_i(N) = (1 + CV_i^2)s_iU_i(N-1)/2 \tag{3.19}$$

$$QD_i(x,N) = \lambda(N-1)\int_0^x W_i(\tau, N-1)\tau f_i(\tau)\,d\tau \tag{3.20}$$

$$AD_i(x,N) = \lambda(N-1)\int_0^{x^-} W_i(x,N)\tau f_i(\tau)\,d\tau \tag{3.21}$$

where x^- denotes the left limit of x. The expression for QD_i can be explained as follows: Since we are speaking of the situation as seen by $\mathcal{A}$, we exclude it in estimating various quantities. The throughput of customers with service time requirement in the range $(\tau, \tau + d\tau)$ is $\lambda(N-1)f_i(\tau)\,d\tau$. By Little's law, the average number of waiting customers with service time requirement of τ is this throughput multiplied by $W_i(\tau, N-1)$. Each of these customers delays $\mathcal{A}$ by the time τ. The expression for AD_i follows a similar logic.

Now, $W_i(x,N) = RL_i(N) + QD_i(x,N) + AD_i(x,N)$. To put this in a compact form, let

$$\psi_i(x) = \int_0^x \tau f_i(\tau)\,d\tau \tag{3.22}$$

$$\phi_i(x,N) = \int_0^x W_i(\tau,N)\tau f_i(\tau)\,d\tau \tag{3.23}$$

Then we get the following integral equation for $W_i(x,N)$

$$W_i(x,N) = \frac{(1 + CV_i^2)s_iU_i(N-1)/2 + \lambda_i(N-1)\phi_i(x,N-1)}{1 - \lambda_i(N-1)\psi_i(x^-)} \tag{3.24}$$

Let $R_i(x,N)$ denote the *conditional response time*, i.e., the average response time for customers with service time of x. Then $R_i(x,N) = W_i(x,N) + x$, and

$$R_i(N) = \int_0^\infty W_i(x,N)f_i(x)\,dx + s_i \tag{3.25}$$

Thus, we have the necessary response time equation. Exercise 8.8 shows that with $N \to \infty$, equation (3.24) reduces to the exact equation for an isolated SJN station, which when solved gives the following explicit expression:

$$W_i(x) = \frac{(1 + CV_i^2)s_iU_i/2}{[1 - \lambda_i\psi_i(x)]^2} \tag{3.26}$$

Also, if the service time is deterministic; i.e., $f_i(x) = 1$ for $x = s_i$ and zero otherwise, it gives the same result as equation (3.2).

The use of equation (3.24) in the MVA algorithm would require evaluating equation (3.23) numerically for each population level $n \in 1..N$. An added difficulty here is that we need ϕ_i as a function of x, with x ranging from 0 to ∞. This rules out the use of quadrature methods for numerical integration; instead we need to use a method that uses fixed subdivisions. The problem of infinite range can be tackled in two ways: (a) by a transformation such as $z = 1 - e^{-x/\alpha}$, which makes the range $0 \mathinner{..} 1$, or (b) by using the analytic approximation $a - be^{-c(x-L)}$ for $x > L$, where L is the cutoff point for numerical integration. With $f_i(x)$ approximated by a branching Erlang distribution, it is found that $L = 8s_i$ and numerical integration via Simpson's rule with 32 subdivisions, is adequate. The advantage of branching Erlang representation is that the ψ_i function can be evaluated symbolically, and does not need numerical integration.

Overall, the SJN heuristics provides excellent accuracy. With utilizations limited to 97%, the maximum tolerance error in response times is found to be only 3%.

The equations above can be easily extended to the multiple-chain case. It is also possible to model situations involving SJN discipline for customers within each chain, and some other (e.g., nonpreemptive priority) across chains. The details are straightforward and left as an exercise.

8.3.5 Comparison of Scheduling Disciplines

In this section we make some comments regarding the performance of various scheduling disciplines. Equation (3.2) indicates that for the FCFS discipline, as CV_i increases, so does the average response time, because small jobs could get "stuck" behind a large job. In contrast, under PS discipline, we have only the first term on the right-hand side of equation (3.2), and the coefficient of variation does not play any role in the response time equation. For the round-robin discipline, the effect of the coefficient of variation will be expected to decrease with the time slice duration. From the conservation laws (discussed later in Section 9.2.2), it can be concluded that under priority disciplines, a good service can be provided to higher-priority customers only at the expense of low priority customers. Yet, the overall response time may depend on the discipline. For example, it can be shown that the *SJN discipline gives the smallest average response time of all the nonpreemptive priority disciplines.*

One useful measure of the performance of a scheduling discipline is the *conditional waiting time*, denoted $W(x)$. It is defined as the average waiting time of all those customers whose service time requirement is x. Recall that in Section 8.3.4, the conditional waiting time was computed as a by-product of the modeling technique. A related measure is the *penalty function*, defined as $PF(x) = W(x)/x$. $PF(x)$ can be interpreted as the average time "wasted" by customers having service requirement of x to get one unit of service. It is a measure of the discriminatory power of the scheduling discipline with respect to the service time requirement. In the following we compare a few disciplines with respect to these measures. The reported characteristics are easy to see for the infinite population case but the same should hold for the finite population case as well.

It can be seen from equation (3.26) that for the SJN discipline, both $W(x)$

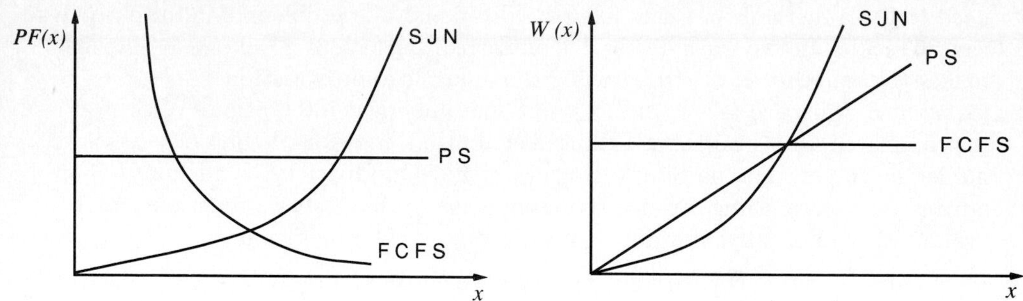

FIGURE 8-7: Conditional waiting time and penalty function for some disciplines.

and $PF(x)$ increase with x; thus SJN favors small jobs to the extent that breaking up a large job into small pieces would be beneficial. In contrast, under the FCFS discipline, $W(x)$ is independent of x, since the waiting time of a customer is not affected by its service time. This means that $PF(x) \propto \frac{1}{x}$. That is, FCFS actually favors large jobs, and it is advantageous to combine several small jobs into one large one. For the PS discipline, the conditional waiting time is given by

$$W_i^{(PS)}(x) = \frac{xU_i}{(1 - U_i)} \tag{3.27}$$

Thus, $W_i(x)$ increases with x linearly. This, in turn, means that $PF(x)$ is independent of x. That is, *under PS discipline, a customer must spend a fixed amount of time in the system to get one unit of service*; therefore, combining several small jobs into one or splitting a large job into several smaller ones does not affect the waiting time. Fig. 8-7 shows the relative performance of various scheduling disciplines. We can also see how the biased processor sharing discipline would behave. If the relative priority decreases as the service time requirement increases, we would essentially increase the discriminatory power beyond that for the PS discipline, thereby getting a behavior similar to that for the SJN discipline.

It is instructive to see how we get (3.27), because it illustrates the important concept of *attained service*. With a preemptive scheduling discipline such as PS, each customer starts accumulating service gradually, until it is done. Let X denote the random variable for the attained service of a customer under PS discipline, and let $\alpha(x)\Delta x$ be the number of customers who have attained service in the range $(x, x + \Delta x)$. Irrespective of the nature of the arrival and service processes, we can write the following equation for $\alpha(x)$.

$$\alpha(x)\Delta x = \lambda[1 - F_{\mathcal{S}}(x)] \times [R(x + \Delta x) - R(x)] \tag{3.28}$$

Here λ denotes the arrival rate, $\mathcal{S}$ the random variable for the service time, and $R(x)$ the *conditional response time*. This equation is basically an application of Little's law. The rate at which customers, having attained service of x, come back for more is $\lambda Pr(\mathcal{S} > x)$. Since the server is being shared equally and continuously among all customers, the time spent in the system to progress from the attained service of x to that of $x + \Delta x$ is the same as $[R(x + \Delta x) - R(x)]$. Multiplying the two, we get the average number that have attained service in the range $(x, x + \Delta x)$. Dividing by Δx and taking the limit as $\Delta x \rightarrow \infty$, we get the following relationship

$$\alpha(x) = \lambda[1 - F_{\mathcal{S}}(x)]\frac{d\,R(x)}{d\,x} \tag{3.29}$$

We can write another equation for $\alpha(x)$ by considering the rate at which customers with an attained service of x increase it further. The relationship turns out to be

$$\frac{d\,\alpha(x)}{d\,x} = -\frac{f_{\mathcal{S}}(x)}{1 - F_{\mathcal{S}}(x)}\alpha(x) \tag{3.30}$$

This equation has the solution $\alpha(x) = \alpha(0)[1 - F_{\mathcal{S}}(x)]$ where $\alpha(0)$ can be shown to be $\lambda/(1 - U)$. Therefore, from equation (3.29), we get (3.27).

8.3.6 Load-Dependent Stations

One major weakness of the approximations discussed until now is that they apply only to load-independent stations. In general, response time equations for load-dependent stations require marginal probabilities, which are difficult to estimate accurately. If the station capacity changes very slowly with the load, we can replace the load-dependent station by a load-independent station with an appropriately chosen service rate. In other cases, we can only handle capacities of a special form. For example, consider the following model of the capacity

$$C_i(n) = 1/[\alpha + (1 - \alpha)/n] \quad \text{where} \quad \alpha \geq 0 \tag{3.31}$$

By Norton's theorem, it is easy to show that a subnetwork of $1/\alpha$ identically loaded single-servers, each with service rate of μ, is equivalent to a single station with basic service rate of μ and capacity function in equation (3.31). (If $1/\alpha$ is not an integer, we cannot form a meaningful mental picture of this equivalence, but the computations still go through unaffected.) We shall denote the original load-dependent station with capacity as in equation (3.31) by S, and the corresponding subnetwork as SS-net. The approximation now is to replace S by SS-net even if the given scheduling discipline, say $\mathcal{D}$, is of non-PF type. Thus, if we have heuristic MVA equations for simple stations operating under $\mathcal{D}$, we can also allow stations with capacity of the type (3.31). It is important to note that the replacement of S by SS-net does not increase the solution complexity in any way. We just assume S to be load-independent (i.e., have one "representative" station of SS-net physically present in the network), but modify its performance parameters to reflect the effect of having $1/\alpha$ of them.

The above technique is interesting in many ways. First, except when the station is heavily loaded, it works extremely well.[3] Second, it applies to multiple-chain networks as well. (In general, the aggregation of a subnetwork will give

[3] That is, the technique works extremely well if the real capacity is of the form (3.31). Errors caused in approximating the real capacity by (3.31) would be additional.

chain-dependent capacities; however, a balanced network of single-servers gives chain-independent capacity, as mentioned in Section 8.1.3). Third, we can even choose $\alpha > 1$ and thereby model decreasing capacity functions, though the accuracy tends to deteriorate as α increases (because the decrease in capacity function effectively increases the load).

The main problem with equation (3.31) is that it cannot accurately model the rather common situation of a multiserver station. To this end, we replace the original station with a parallel subnetwork of two stations, one of which is a load-independent and the other is of delay type. Both stations have identical basic service time, but an incoming customer goes to the load-independent station with probability q and to the delay station with probability $1 - q$. We call this representation a SD-net. The SD-net model can also be used with any scheduling discipline, since we need to develop a heuristic response time equation only at the load-independent station. As such, this model underestimates the capacity function of a multiserver station with $1/q$ servers, which means that it will only provide an upper bound on the response time. However, we can also get a lower bound by regarding a multiserver station as a delay station if the average queue length is below a threshold Q', and as a load-independent station with capacity $1/q$ if it is above Q'. The threshold Q' can be chosen as the average queue length at the station obtained from the SD-net approximation. With the lower and upper bounds at hand, we can obtain an approximation by simply computing their average. This gives very good results generally. Unfortunately, the SD-net model does not apply to multiple-chain networks.

8.4 Decomposition Approximation

In sections 8.1 and 8.2, we studied Norton's (or aggregation) theorem for product-form networks and showed how it can be used to obtain a simpler higher-level model which can be solved easily. In this section we shall study how to decompose a complex model into several simpler models by exploiting weak coupling between subsystems. Unlike aggregation, decomposition does not require product-form property, and thus provides another important method for tackling complex systems.

8.4.1 Physical and Logical Decomposition

In solving large problems, it is desirable to decompose the model into several submodels and solve them independently. A *physical decomposition* into submodels (that correspond to subsystems) is possible if the subsystems interact weakly. For example, consider a model of a pipelined computer system that includes detailed modeling of (1) overall job execution and (2) pipelining behavior. It is clear that once a job is scheduled on the CPU, it will typically make several "visits" to the stations within the pipeline model before it is finished. In other words, a pipeline element interacts with other elements within the pipeline much more frequently than with those outside the pipeline. Thus, it is possible to solve the pipelining

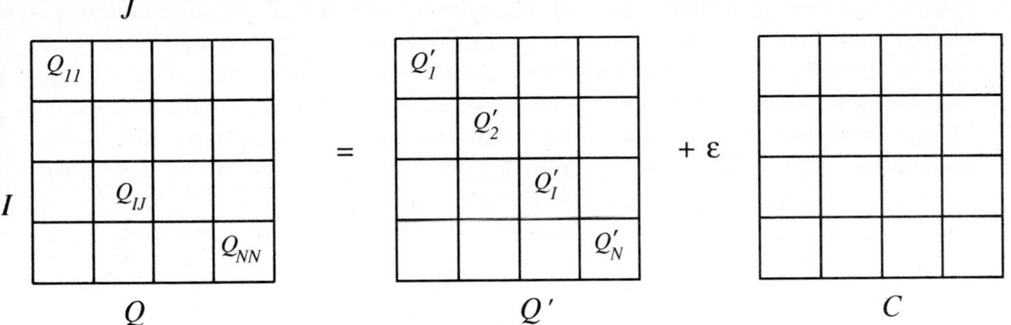

FIGURE 8-8: Decomposition of a nearly-completely decomposable matrix.

model in isolation. Similarly, if other parts of the overall model show locality of interactions, we can solve them separately and thereby simplify the higher-level model, which would include only the external behavior of the lower-level models.

If the model involves several classes of weakly interacting random processes, it may be possible to do a *logical decomposition* which considers these classes separately. As an example, consider the model of a gracefully degrading multiprocessor system. There are two classes of random processes in such a model: (a) job arrival and service, and (b) processor failure and repair. The two sets of processes are not independent, since the service rate depends on the number of operational processors. However, if failures and repairs occur infrequently compared with arrivals and service, as normally expected, and some minimum level of service is always available, decomposition becomes possible. The assumption is that between successive failures/repairs, the system operates in a steady state with respect to the traffic handling aspect.

In both physical and logical decomposition, we eventually have to solve a higher-level model that incorporates the results of the lower level models. This process is similar to that needed with respect to aggregation. In the pipelining example introduced above, the higher-level model may represent the entire pipeline by a single station having the same service rate as the throughput of the pipeline in isolation. This is precisely what we do when applying the aggregation theorem, *even though the justification is no longer based on the product-form property*. In this sense, there is a close relationship between the flow-equivalent aggregation and decomposition.

8.4.2 Nearly Completely Decomposable Systems

Although the notion of decomposability applies to any type of stochastic system, its formal characterization is difficult in general. We henceforth assume that the system can be described by a Markov chain $\mathcal{Z}$. Because of the equivalence between continuous and discrete parameter chains shown in equation (5.2.18), it suffices to consider only the discrete parameter case. For generality, we assume that the system under consideration has a finite number of states, denoted n. Since we are interested in only steady-state solutions, we shall assume that $\mathcal{Z}$ is ergodic. It is thus described by a $n \times n$ stochastic matrix $Q = [q_{ij}]$, with steady solution given by $\Pi = \Pi Q$. How the states of $\mathcal{Z}$ are numbered is crucial for what follows; however, we shall defer commenting on that aspect until we have seen the solution technique. Given a numbering scheme, we can partition the states into N sets as follows: the first $n(1)$ states belong to partition 1, next $n(2)$ to partition 2, etc. The choice of $n(i)$'s is also crucial, but we defer commenting on it as well. With this partitioning, we can express the state probability vector Π as follows:

$$\Pi = (\Pi_1, \ldots, \Pi_N) \qquad \text{where} \quad \Pi_I = (\pi_{I,1}, \ldots, \pi_{I,n(I)}) \tag{4.1}$$

That is, $\pi_{I,i}$ gives the stationary probability of the ith state of the Ith partition. We shall henceforth denote the Ith set of states as $\mathcal{S}_I$. The matrix Q can also be similarly partitioned into N^2 submatrices, as shown in Fig. 8-8. We shall use I and J as row and column indices for the partitions, and i and j as indices within a partition. We denote the (I, J)th submatrix of Q as Q_{IJ}. Obviously, Q_{IJ} is a $n(I) \times n(J)$ matrix. We shall denote the (i, j)th element of Q_{IJ} as $q_{ij}(I, J)$. Now let Q' denote a stochastic, *block diagonal matrix* represented as

$$Q' = \text{diag}(Q'_1, Q'_2, \ldots, Q'_N) \tag{4.2}$$

where the submatrices Q'_I are $n(I) \times n(I)$; i.e., of the same size as Q_{II}. (Block diagonal means that $Q'_{IJ} = \mathbf{0}$ for $I \neq J$). We call Q' *completely decomposable*, because a Markov chain described by Q' represents N disjoint subchains, one for each Q'_I. Now let C denote a $n \times n$ matrix and ε a real, positive constant such that

$$Q = Q' + \varepsilon C \tag{4.3}$$

Since Q and Q' are stochastic, all elements in each row of C must sum to zero. Notice that the submatrices Q_{II} are *substochastic*; i.e., their rows sum to less than 1. Since Q' must be stochastic, we cannot simply choose $Q'_I = Q_{II}$. However, a good strategy is to start with $Q'_I = Q_{II}$ and increase its row elements so that it becomes stochastic. One way of viewing this process is to say that to construct the ith row of Q'_I, we take the sum of all elements in the (I, i)th row of Q belonging to nondiagonal blocks, and distribute this sum over the row i elements of Q_{II}. This means that C should be such that all elements of its diagonal submatrices C_{II}'s are nonpositive and others are nonnegative. We shall return to this topic in Section 8.4.3.

The term εC is supposed to represent how far the matrix Q is from the completely decomposable matrix Q'. We shall choose ε such that the largest element of C has magnitude 1. Since the elements of Q and Q' are probabilities, it is easy to see that $0 \leq \varepsilon < 1$. However, this condition by itself is inadequate to make ε a meaningful measure of decomposability. The problem is that if $\Pi Q = \Pi$, then for any $\alpha > 0$, if we let

$$\mathcal{Q} = \alpha.Q + (1 - \alpha).I \tag{4.4}$$

then $\Pi\mathcal{Q} = \Pi$. Also, if Q is stochastic, so is $\mathcal{Q}$. Now suppose that in (4.3), ε is chosen such that the largest element of C is 1. Substituting (4.3) into (4.4), we get

$$\mathcal{Q} = \mathcal{Q}' + \alpha\varepsilon C \quad \text{where} \quad \mathcal{Q}' = \alpha.Q' + (1-\alpha).I \tag{4.5}$$

That is, by choosing a small α, one can get an artificially small multiplier of the matrix C. To plug this loophole, we actually do the opposite – we choose α as large as possible. It is clear that the choice

$$\alpha = 1\Big/\left(1 - \min_i q_{ii}\right) \tag{4.6}$$

will make the smallest diagonal element of $\mathcal{Q}$ zero; therefore, α could be no larger. We henceforth assume this transformation has already been applied, and therefore (a) $\min_i q_{ii} = 0$ and (b) ε is the proper decomposability measure. Thus, if $\varepsilon \ll 1$, we can call matrix Q *nearly completely decomposable* or NCD. It is clear from equation (4.3) that Q in this case represents N subsystems corresponding to Q', which interact only weakly. The parameter ε then represents the *degree of coupling* between these subsystems.

It should be clear from the discussion above that proper numbering of states and appropriate choice of partition sizes are crucial in obtaining the decomposition in equation (4.3) with a small ε. Normally, one would identify the weakly interacting subsystems by exploiting the intuitive understanding of how the system works, which makes the above issues easy. However, to get a significant advantage out of the decomposition, the sizes of the individual submatrices (i.e., $n(I)$'s) must be of the same order.

We assume that Q'_I's are ergodic, so that each subsystem has a unique stationary distribution. We denote this distribution as $Y'(I) = (y'_{I,1}, \ldots, y'_{I,n(I)})$. It is obtained by solving the system

$$Y'(I)Q'_I = Y'(I) \quad \text{and} \quad Y'(I)\cdot\mathbf{e} = 1 \tag{4.7}$$

It can be shown that *in a nearly completely decomposable system, each subsystem I is able to achieve a short-term equilibrium characterized by the probability vector $Y'(I)$*. Therefore, we call these probabilities *micro probabilities*. The *long-term equilibrium* is defined by interactions between subsystems. To characterize it, we define an aggregated Markov chain $\mathcal{Z}^*$ that has N states, whose Ith state corresponds to subsystem I. Let $A = [a_{IJ}]$ denote the transition probability matrix for $\mathcal{Z}^*$. We can define a_{IJ} as the probability of going to some state of subsystem J in the next transition, given that we are currently in some state of subsystem I. That is,

$$a_{IJ} = \sum_{i=1}^{n(I)} y'_{I,i} \sum_{j=1}^{n(J)} q_{ij}(I,J) \tag{4.8}$$

Notice that equation (4.8) is exact if $y'_{I,i}$ is the actual probability that $\mathcal{Z}$ is in state (I,i), given that it is somewhere in subsystem I. However, we obtained

$y'_{I,i}$ from equation (4.7) by solving subsystem I in isolation, and this makes equation (4.8) merely an approximation (unless the system is indeed completely decomposable). Let $X' = (x'_1, \ldots, x'_N)$ denote the steady-state probability vector for $\mathcal{Z}^*$. As usual, we can compute X' using the equations

$$X' = X'A \quad \text{and} \quad X' \cdot \mathbf{e} = 1 \tag{4.9}$$

We call these probabilities *macro probabilities*. Then, we can estimate the state probabilities for $\mathcal{Z}$ as

$$\pi_{I,i} \approx x'_I \, y'_{I,i} \tag{4.10}$$

This completes the solution by decomposition. Obviously, the main advantage of the approach is that instead of dealing with a large matrix Q, we only deal with smaller matrices Q'_I's and A. It is clear that to achieve maximum savings, we should have all submatrices of the same size, which in turn means that $N = \sqrt{n}$. In this case we reduce the problem of solving one linear system of N^2 variables to that of $N+1$ linear systems, each of size N. The savings achieved depend on how sparse Q is to begin with. If decomposition is a viable technique, Q would most likely be sparse, and one has to weigh the additional error introduced against the computational savings. Note that even though the construction of the A matrix could theoretically take $O(N^4)$ time, this is unlikely in view of the sparsity of Q. Finally, if partition sizes are substantially different from $O(\sqrt{n})$, the decomposition may not be worthwhile.

Apart from computational savings, solution by decomposition has another advantage over direct solution that is worth noting. By definition, in a nearly completely decomposable matrix, the elements of the Q_{IJ} submatrices, $I \neq J$, will be small compared with those of Q_{II} matrices. This difference in magnitudes makes the matrix Q ill-conditioned, thereby leading to numerical problems. The solution using decomposition will deal only with individual Q_{II} matrices and thus will be much more robust. Of course, decomposition only gives an approximate answer, so we have to weigh inaccuracy against numerical problems.

The solution method described above can be used in a hierarchical manner. That is, the matrices Q'_I's obtained from the first level decomposition may themselves be considered as nearly completely decomposable, and thus subject to further decomposition. The solution in this case proceeds recursively starting from the innermost level. Note that one can always flatten out this hierarchy, but that may be undesirable owing to cost considerations. Since the optimal size of an aggregate is $\sqrt{n}$, multilevel decomposition may be worth considering if the "natural" aggregate size is much smaller than $\sqrt{n}$.

Example 8.2 Consider a continuous parameter Markov chain with 5 states, whose transition rate matrix is given below. Find the steady-state distribution directly and by decomposition, and compare the results.

$$Q = \begin{bmatrix} -4.2 & 4.0 & 0 & 0.1 & 0.1 \\ 0 & -6.0 & 6.0 & 0 & 0 \\ 6.0 & 0 & -6.2 & 0 & 0.2 \\ 0.05 & 0 & 0 & -2.05 & 2.0 \\ 0.05 & 0.1 & 0 & 4.0 & -4.15 \end{bmatrix} \tag{4.11}$$

Solution Even though we can convert this matrix to a transition probability matrix of a discrete parameter chain before proceeding, this is really not necessary, so long as we take care of the minor differences between the discrete and continuous parameter cases. We also don't have to adjust the Q matrix in the continuous parameter case (for making ε a meaningful measure of coupling between subsystems). We start by noting that Q as given is irreducible and all its rows sum to zero, as desired. It is clear from its structure that this system consists of two weakly interacting subsystems with $\mathcal{S}_1 = \{1,2,3\}$ and $\mathcal{S}_2 = \{4,5\}$. We first identify the matrices Q'_1 and Q'_2. There are several ways to do this, here we choose to do the following: in the first four rows, we shall add the off diagonal block weight to the diagonal element and in the fifth row distribute it over the elements of the diagonal block according to the vector $(0.1, 0.05)$. This gives

$$Q'_1 = \begin{bmatrix} -4.0 & 4.0 & 0 \\ 0 & -6.0 & 6.0 \\ 6.0 & 0 & -6.0 \end{bmatrix} \quad \text{and} \quad Q'_2 = \begin{bmatrix} -2.0 & 2.0 \\ 4.1 & -4.1 \end{bmatrix}$$

Let $D = [d_{ij}]$ denote the corresponding error matrix, i.e., $Q = Q' + D$. We have

$$D = \begin{bmatrix} -0.2 & 0 & 0 & 0.1 & 0.1 \\ 0 & 0 & 0 & 0 & 0 \\ 0 & 0 & -0.2 & 0 & 0.2 \\ 0.05 & 0 & 0 & -0.05 & 0 \\ 0.05 & 0.1 & 0 & -0.1 & -0.05 \end{bmatrix}$$

As shown in Exercise 8.13, the correct characterization of the coupling parameter ε is now given by

$$\varepsilon = \max_{i,j} |d_{ij}| / \max_i |q_{ii}| \tag{4.12}$$

Thus, for our numerical problem, $\varepsilon = 0.2/6.2 = 0.032$. Let us now proceed with the solution. The two subsystems of this system are easy to solve, and the equations $Y'(I)Q'(I) = \mathbf{0}$, $Y'(I) \cdot \mathbf{e} = 1$ for $I = 1, 2$, give the following solutions

$$\begin{array}{lll} y'_{1,1} = 0.42857, & y'_{1,2} = 0.28571, & y'_{1,3} = 0.28571 \\ y'_{2,1} = 0.67213, & y'_{2,2} = 0.32787 & \end{array}$$

Therefore,

$$\begin{aligned} a_{12} &= 0.42857 \times 0.2 + 0.28571 \times 0.2 = 0.14286, \\ a_{21} &= 0.67213 \times 0.05 + 0.32787 \times 0.15 = 0.082787 \end{aligned}$$

Obviously, $a_{11} = -a_{12}$ and $a_{22} = -a_{21}$, and we have the complete A matrix. The equations $X'A = \mathbf{0}$, $X' \cdot \mathbf{e} = 1$ have the solution: $x'_1 = 0.36689$ and $x'_2 = 0.63311$. The final solution is $x'_I\, y'_{I,i}$ and is given by (the primes on π_i's indicate that these probabilities are approximate)

$$\pi'_1 = 0.157239, \quad \pi'_2 = 0.104826, \quad \pi'_3 = 0.104826,$$
$$\pi'_4 = 0.425533, \quad \pi'_5 = 0.207577$$

The exact probabilities can be obtained by solving the system $\Pi.Q = \mathbf{0}$, $\Pi \cdot \mathbf{e} = 1$, and are given by

$$\pi_1 = 0.157500, \quad \pi_2 = 0.108508, \quad \pi_3 = 0.105008,$$
$$\pi_4 = 0.418460, \quad \pi_5 = 0.210523$$

It can be seen that the errors are much smaller than ε. □.

8.4.3 Decomposability Criteria and Error Estimation

In the last section we justified decomposition in terms of short-term and long-term equilibrium, characterized, respectively by stationary distributions in equations (4.7) and (4.9). With this view, it is clear that the accuracy of the solution by decomposition depends on two aspects (a) coupling between subsystems characterized by the parameter ε, and (b) how quickly any given subsystem approaches equilibrium operation. In the following we first discuss the effect of these factors separately and then examine the combined effect.

We start with aspect (a). It is clear that the solution in equation (4.10) is approximate because we use the approximate micro probabilities $y'_{I,i}$'s instead of the true conditional probability of being in state i, given that we are in subsystem I. We denote the latter as $y_{I,i}$. Thus, the accuracy of the approximation with respect to the Ith subsystem, denoted δ_I, is given by

$$\delta_I = \max_{i \in \mathcal{S}_I} |y'_{I,i} - y_{I,i}| \tag{4.13}$$

From equations (4.3) and (4.7) one can show that δ_I must be $O(\varepsilon)$. It then follows that the error in $\pi_{I,i}$, as estimated using equation (4.10), is also $O(\varepsilon)$. This means that the error can be made arbitrarily small by making ε arbitrarily small. Also, if the eigenvalues of the aggregate matrix A can be computed, we can improve the accuracy of the estimation from $O(\varepsilon)$ to $O(\varepsilon^2)$. The details are omitted here, and may be found in the literature. Also, it is typically found that even with our simple estimation procedure above, the error is actually smaller than ε. We have already seen this in Example 8.2. Let us define a new parameter ε_{eff} as follows:

$$\varepsilon_{eff} = \max_{\forall I} \max_{\forall i \in \mathcal{S}_I} y'_{I,i} \sum_{J=1, J \neq I}^{N} \sum_{j=1}^{n(J)} q_{ij}(I,J) \tag{4.14}$$

This can be interpreted as an approximation of the maximum unconditional probability of leaving an aggregate, given that the system is in that aggregate. It can be shown that $\varepsilon_{eff} < \varepsilon$, and is a better estimate of the error.

Let us now consider aspect (b). We shall see in Section 9.6.2 that the rate of approach of a Markovian system to equilibrium depends on how different the subdominant eigenvalue of its transition probability matrix Q is from the dominant eigenvalue. Because Q is a stochastic matrix, the latter is always 1. Let $\lambda(2_I)$ denote the subdominant eigenvalue of the matrix Q'_I. It follows that the rate of approach of subsystem I to short-term equilibrium, and hence the error in estimating $(\pi_{I,1}, \ldots, \pi_{I,n(I)})$ using equation (4.10) will depend on $\eta_I = 1 - |\lambda(2_I)|$. Therefore, we refer to η_I as the *indecomposability* of the Q'_I matrix. Note that for an irreducible matrix, $0 < \eta_I \leq 1$. Bounds are available in the literature on the subdominant eigenvalue of stochastic matrices, and thus a lower bound on indecomposability can be obtained. This, in turn, gives us some guidelines for choosing the Q'_I matrices, to achieve maximum indecomposability. We stated in the previous section that we get Q'_I by starting with Q_{II} and adding to each row the remaining probability, denoted $\alpha(I, i)$, in order to make the matrix stochastic. However, it is still unspecified how $\alpha(I, i)$ should be distributed over the $n(I)$ elements of the ith row of Q_{II}. It turns out that a good strategy is to minimize the difference between the smallest and largest element value in the row.[4]

A detailed error analysis, which we omit here, indicates that the dominant term of the error is proportional to $\theta_I = \varepsilon/\eta_I$. Thus, while our claim of $O(\varepsilon)$ is correct, the true magnitude of the error depends on η_I as well. Since the ability to achieve short-term equilibrium at the subsystem level (between successive switches across subsystems) is key to solution by decomposition, it is useful to define the NCD property relative to this requirement. It can be shown that short-term equilibrium is possible if $\theta_I < \frac{1}{2}$ for all subsystems. It follows that the largest value of ε, beyond which Q cannot be considered to be a NCD matrix, is given by:

$$\varepsilon < \min_I \eta_I/2 \qquad (4.15)$$

This means that if all Q'_I's are totally indecomposable (i.e., $\eta_I = 1$), ε can be as large as 0.5, and yet short-term equilibrium will be possible. However, if η_I's are small, only a small value of ε can be allowed. Again, the available lower bounds on $\lambda(2_I)$ will be useful here.

8.4.4 Lumpable and Other Special Matrices

In this section we consider a special class of NCD matrices that possess a number of interesting properties. These are so-called *block stochastic* and *near block*

[4]The reader should not lose sight of the fact that we are still talking about a discrete parameter case though one can easily translate these comments to the continuous parameter case via equation (5.2.18).

stochastic matrices. A transition probability matrix Q is called *row block stochastic* (RBS) if all rows in a submatrix Q_{IJ} have identical sums. It is called *column block stochastic* (CBS) if a similar property holds with respect to the columns. More precisely, Q is row block stochastic if there exist numbers w_{IJ} such that

$$\forall i, 1 \leq i \leq n(I) \left[\sum_{j=1}^{n(J)} q_{ij}(I,J) = w_{IJ} \right] \tag{4.16}$$

Since Q is stochastic, we also expect that

$$\forall i, 1 \leq I \leq N \left[\sum_{J=1}^{N} w_{IJ} = 1 \right] \tag{4.17}$$

Substituting (4.16) into (4.8), and using the fact that all $y'_{I,i}$'s must sum to 1, we get $a_{IJ} = w_{IJ}$; that is, the matrix A is the same as $[w_{IJ}]$. From this, we can prove the following properties about such matrices.

1. The eigenvalues of matrix A are also the eigenvalues of matrix Q. To show this, we start with the eigenvalue equation for A; (i.e., $XA = \delta X$) and use equation (4.16).
2. The solution x'_I gives the *exact* probability of being in subsystem I, i.e., $x'_I = x_I$. One way to see this is to note that equation (4.8) would imply $a_{IJ} = w_{IJ}$ even with the exact micro probabilities $y_{I,i}$'s.

The last property implies that the original Markov chain $\mathcal{Z}$ is *lumpable*; i.e., the probability of being in one of the aggregates (or subsystems) is computed exactly. It is important to note that this result holds irrespective of the value of ε; thus the *NCD property is not needed here*. However, we still cannot claim that the individual state probabilities $\pi_{I,i}$ are computed exactly. The error arises because in equation (4.10), the micro probabilities $y'_{I,i}$ are still computed using the modified matrix Q'_I. Since Q'_I differs from the real matrix by $O(\varepsilon)$, the error is still of the same order (but probably has a much smaller constant).

Let us now examine column block stochastic (CBS) matrices. For such matrices, there are constants v_{IJ}'s such that

$$\forall j, 1 \leq j \leq n(J) \left[\sum_{i=1}^{n(I)} q_{ij}(I,J) = v_{IJ} \right] \tag{4.18}$$

We can show an interesting property regarding such matrices, that allows us to solve the corresponding system very easily.

Lemma 8.3 Suppose that we construct each Q'_I matrix by distributing the off-diagonal weight equally across all elements in a row of Q_{II}. Then Q'_I is *doubly stochastic*, i.e., its rows and columns sum to 1.

Proof Let $q'_{ij}(I)$ denote the (i,j)th element of Q'_I and $\alpha(I,i)$ the total off-diagonal weight. Then $q'_{ij}(I) = q_{ij}(I,I) + \alpha(I,i)/n(I)$. Obviously, this makes Q'_I stochastic. Now to show that the columns of Q'_I also sum to 1, note that

$$\begin{aligned}\sum_{i=1}^{n(I)} q'_{ij}(I) &= \sum_{i=1}^{n(I)} q_{ij}(I,I) + \frac{1}{n(I)} \sum_{J=1,J\neq I}^{N} \sum_{j=1}^{n(J)} \sum_{i=1}^{n(I)} q_{ij}(I,J) \\ &= v_{II} + \frac{1}{n(I)} \sum_{J=1,J\neq I}^{N} n(J)v_{IJ} = \frac{1}{n(I)} \sum_{J=1}^{N} n(J)v_{IJ} = 1\end{aligned}$$

where in the last step, using the CBS property, we note that $n(J)v_{IJ}$ is the sum of all elements of the submatrix Q_{IJ}. Since Q is stochastic, the summation over all J then gives us $n(I)$. □

Note that if a matrix B is doubly stochastic then $\mathbf{e}^T B = \mathbf{e}^T$ (where $\mathbf{e}^T$ is a row vector of all 1's). Since an irreducible stochastic matrix has a unique stationary distribution, it follows that all states of such a system must be equiprobable. Thus, $y'_{I,i} = 1/n(I)$ for all i. Thus, the solution by decomposition only amounts to solving the aggregated chain $\mathcal{Z}^*$. Furthermore, we can show that the error in the approximation is now $O(\varepsilon^2)$ instead of $O(\varepsilon)$. Unfortunately, CBS matrices do not occur frequently in practice, and we shall not discuss them further.

Let us now reexamine the concept of lumpability to understand it better. Consider a Markov chain $\mathcal{Z}$ whose states have been partitioned into sets $\mathcal{S}_1, \ldots, \mathcal{S}_N$. Suppose that we want to find out if all states in each of the $\mathcal{S}_I$'s can be lumped together so as to give an aggregated Markov chain $\mathcal{Z}^*$ with macrostate s_I representing the set $\mathcal{S}_I$. To this end, let us write the global balance equation for the macrostate s_I by choosing the boundary around the set $\mathcal{S}_I$. This equation will look as follows:

$$\sum_{m\in\mathcal{S}_I} \sum_{J\neq I} \sum_{l\in\mathcal{S}_J} P(m) q_{ml} = \sum_{J\neq I} \sum_{m\in\mathcal{S}_J} P(m) \sum_{l\in\mathcal{S}_I} q_{ml} \tag{4.19}$$

This equation involves the micro probability $P(m)$ on both sides, but if aggregation is feasible, we should be able to express it using macro probabilities only. It is clear that if the last summation term on the right-hand side of (4.19) is independent of m, we can express summation over $P(m)$ as $P(s_J)$ and get the desired form. The same is true of the left-hand side. It is also clear that if this condition does not hold, we cannot do aggregation in general. Thus, a necessary and sufficient condition for aggregation is given by

$$\forall I\ \forall J \neq I \left[\forall m \in \mathcal{S}_J \sum_{l\in\mathcal{S}_I} q_{ml} = w_{JI} \right] \tag{4.20}$$

where we have used the subscript JI on w to indicate its dependence on the "from" and "to" sets $\mathcal{S}_J$ and $\mathcal{S}_I$. Using this, we can rewrite equation (4.19) as

$$P(s_I) \sum_{J\neq I} w_{IJ} = \sum_{J\neq I} P(s_J) w_{JI} \tag{4.21}$$

Expressed in terms of our matrix partitioning, equation (4.20) says that each row in the submatrix Q_{JI}, $J \neq I$, should have an identical sum. Since every row in Q must sum to 1, this further implies that all rows in Q_{JJ} should also have identical sums. In other words, Q should be a row block stochastic matrix. A different way to say the same thing is that *if $\mathcal{Z}$ is lumpable, the interactions between the subsystems are independent of the interactions within a subsystem, and therefore the macrolevel behavior can be considered in terms of subsystems only*. It is again important to remember that lumpability does not imply that the microlevel behavior can be characterized exactly by considering subsystems in isolation.

Lumpability can occur along with the NCD property and induces equivalence classes over the subsystems defined by the NCD property. Consider, for example, a NCD matrix of which the first L submatrices are of the same size M. Suppose that the part of the system covered by these first L submatrices can be lumped in the following way: There are M macrostates, such that the ith macrostate consists of the ith microstate of each of the L subsystems. Viewed in terms of the lumpability characterization, consider the set S_i which contains the states (I, i) for $I = 1 \mathinner{..} L$, i.e., the microstate i from each of the first L subsystems. Similarly, let S_i contain the states (J, j) for $J = 1 \mathinner{..} L$. Then for any microstate in S_i, the sum of the transition probabilities to the microstates of S_j must be the same for all I. In other words,

$$\sum_{J=1}^{L} q_{ij}(I, J) = b_{ij} \qquad \forall I \in 1 \mathinner{..} L \tag{4.22}$$

In such a case the first L subsystems form an equivalence class and thus only one member of this class need be considered in further analysis. One way to think about this is to assume that the first $L-1$ rows and columns from Q have been "chopped-off", thereby giving a NCD matrix with only $N - L + 1$ subsystems. Fig. 8-9 shows this situation, where the resulting matrix is represented by Q^*. Of course, the elements of the submatrix Q'_L in Q^* will change to the values b_{ij}'s given in equation (4.22). Note that for the lumping to be exact, all upper rectangular matrices UR_i's in Fig. 8-9 should be identical. Similarly, all lower rectangular matrices LR_j's should be identical. These properties are essential so that it does not matter which one of the L subsystems in the equivalence class we use. If this is not so, the error introduced will be only $O(\varepsilon)$ because the elements of all these matrices must be $O(\varepsilon)$ according to the NCD assumption. Nevertheless, it may be worthwhile to alter the elements of UR_L and LR_L of Q^* in a way that brings us closer to the requirement of exact lumpability. Computing the (i, j)th element as an average of (i, j)th elements from all L matrices is one such idea, but its efficacy is difficult to show formally.

Following the lumping, we can solve the smaller NCD system (represented by Q^*) using decomposition. The results will include, among other things, the probability that the system is in ith state of the first subsystem of Q^*. This represents the macrostate probability with respect to the lumping that we did. If we are interested in the probabilities of the microstates as well, we need to

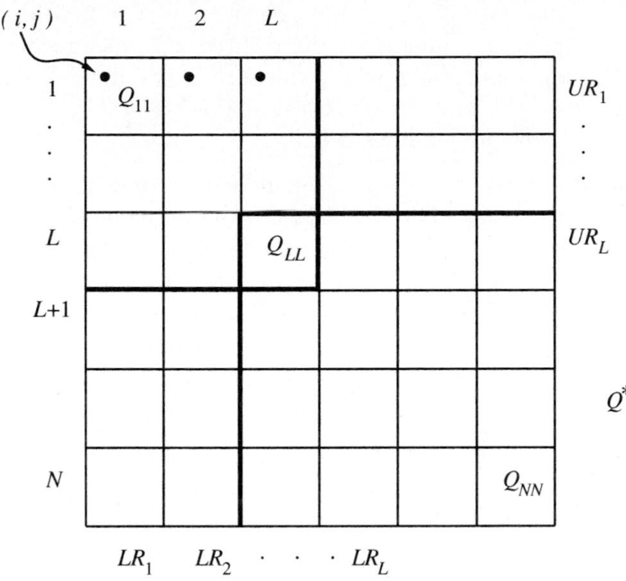

FIGURE 8-9: A lumpable, nearly-completely decomposable matrix.

solve the Markov chain that describes the behavior of all microstates belonging to a given macrostate. (This is like solving a subsystem of a row block stochastic system discussed above.)

Although we illustrated the combination of lumpability and NCD properties in a special setting, it is clear that the same procedure applies if the submatrices identified by the NCD property were grouped in some arbitrary way into a set of equivalence classes. Yet another point to note is that in the above we considered only complete lumpability. Now, just as we dealt with NCD, we could analyze situations involving *near complete lumpability*. That is, if all rows of a submatrix do not sum to the same value, we could extract the difference in an error matrix C as in equation (4.3). The rest of the method remains the same; i.e., we do the lumping on matrix Q' and get the probabilities for macrostates and microstates within macrostates. If both lumpability and decomposition cause $O(\varepsilon)$ error, the final result will still have $O(\varepsilon)$ accuracy.

8.4.5 Modeling Degradable Multiserver Systems

In this section we discuss, in some detail, the steady-state performance modeling of a multiserver queuing system subject to breakdowns and repairs. We mentioned this example earlier in Section 8.4.1 in the context of logical decomposition. We shall consider both finite and infinite population versions of the problem and assume that the failure/repair rates are much smaller than the arrival/service rates. We shall look at the problem in several different ways and compare the approaches. The problem is characterized by four random variables:

interarrival time, service time, interfailure time, and repair time. We shall assume that these random variables are exponentially distributed with mean rates of λ, μ (per server), $f(c)$, and $r(c)$ respectively, where the argument c indicates a possible dependence of f and r on the number of operational servers. The total number of servers at the station will be denoted as C.

We start with an approach based on a simple decomposition that does not exploit the theory that we have developed so far. Let $U(c)$ denote the system utilization with c operational servers, and let k be a number such that $U(k) > 0.9k$ and $P_f = Pr(c < k)$. We assume that P_f is negligible, i.e., the system rarely goes into saturation. Then the system can achieve short-term equilibrium between successive failures and repairs. Let us also assume that the failure and repair rates are independent of the number of customers queued for service. In this case solution by decomposition can be done in a very intuitive way, and would go as follows:

1. Consider only the failure/repair model. The Markov chain for this model is described by a birth-death process where the state is represented by the number of operational servers, and the forward and backward transitions in state c are $r(c)$ and $f(c)$ respectively. Therefore, the distribution of the number of operational processors, denoted $P_{op}(c|C)$, is given by equation (5.4.7).

2. Consider only the arrival/service process while keeping the number of operational processors fixed at c (for $c \in k \mathinner{..} C$). Determine the performance parameters of interest in each case.

3. Let $X(c)$ denote some performance parameter (e.g., queue length) when c processors are operational. We could then obtain the overall value of this parameter, denoted X, by a weighted summation over $X(c)$, i.e., $X = \sum_{c=k}^{C} X(c) P_{op}(c|C)$.

Notice that the decomposition in this problem applies in general has nothing to do with the nature of distributions of various parameters. For example, the failure/repair model may not be a birth-death process, but this would only complicate the estimation of P_{op}.

Next, we shall apply the formal decomposition approach (assuming that all distributions are exponential). This exercise has three purposes: (a) to justify the informal procedure, (b) to note some difficulties in tackling this system by decomposition, and (c) to show how the assumptions made here can be weakened.

With exponential distributions, the state of the overall system can be represented by the pair (c, n), where $c \in 0 \mathinner{..} C$ is the number of operational servers, and n is the number of customers at the station. Then we can create a separate partition for each value of c. Fig. 8-10 shows a part of the transition rate matrix. (The diagonal element in each row is left unspecified since it must equal the negative of the sum of all others.) Since we have assumed that r and f are much smaller than λ and μ, the elements of the nondiagonal blocks are much smaller than those in diagonal blocks, and solution by decomposition is worth

$$
\begin{array}{c} \\ \cdot \\ 20 \\ 21 \\ 22 \\ \cdot \\ \cdot \\ 30 \\ 31 \\ 32 \\ \cdot \end{array}
\left[\begin{array}{cccccccccccc}
\cdot & 20 & 21 & 22 & \cdot & \cdot & 30 & 31 & 32 & \cdot & \cdot \\
\cdot & \cdot & \cdot & \cdot & \cdot & \cdot & \cdot & \cdot & \cdot & \cdot & \cdot \\
\cdot & - & \lambda & 0 & \cdot & \cdot & r & 0 & 0 & \cdot & \cdot \\
\cdot & \mu & - & \lambda & \cdot & \cdot & 0 & r & 0 & \cdot & \cdot \\
\cdot & 0 & 2\mu & - & \cdot & \cdot & 0 & 0 & r & \cdot & \cdot \\
\cdot & \cdot & \cdot & \cdot & \cdot & \cdot & \cdot & \cdot & \cdot & \cdot & \cdot \\
\cdot & \cdot & \cdot & \cdot & \cdot & \cdot & \cdot & \cdot & \cdot & \cdot & \cdot \\
\cdot & f & 0 & 0 & \cdot & \cdot & - & \lambda & 0 & \cdot & \cdot \\
\cdot & 0 & f & 0 & \cdot & \cdot & \mu & - & \lambda & \cdot & \cdot \\
\cdot & 0 & 0 & f & \cdot & \cdot & 0 & 2\mu & - & \cdot & \cdot \\
\cdot & \cdot & \cdot & \cdot & \cdot & \cdot & \cdot & \cdot & \cdot & \cdot & \cdot
\end{array}\right]
$$

FIGURE 8-10: Transition rate matrix for a degradable system.

pursuing. However, we immediately run into some difficulties. In the finite population case the submatrix Q'_{00} will be reducible (and hence decomposable), and in the infinite population case, the system will become unstable if c falls below some threshold. Decomposition does not apply in such cases, because the short-term equilibrium is impossible for certain subsystems. In the above, we avoided this problem by assuming that P_f is negligible, which allows us to truncate the Markov chain by ignoring states for which $c < k$. Another approach is to include all states with $c \leq k$ in the first submatrix itself. However, such a decomposition is unlikely to be useful in the infinite population case because a system with up to k servers may be no easier to solve than one with up to C servers.

Let us suppose that P_f is negligible and look at other aspects of the problem. The decomposition applies even if f and r depend on n, the number of customers in the system. However, if there is no such dependence, as we have implicitly assumed until now, the system enjoys some further properties. It is clear from Fig. 8-10 that the Q matrix for such a system (or more accurately for the corresponding discrete parameter system) is row block stochastic. Therefore, step 1 of our informal algorithm performs an exact aggregation to get the subsystem probabilities x_I's. Step 2 solves the individual subsystems to get $Y'(I)$'s. It obtains submatrices Q'_I by adding the weight $\alpha(I, i)$ to the diagonal element $q_{ii}(I, I)$. The superposition in step 3 follows from equation (4.10).

It is interesting to note that the problem at hand can be solved nicely using the matrix-geometric techniques of Section 9.5 since our system is simply a M/M/c queue operating in a random environment.[5] Thus, if we abstract out the c part of the state (c, n), we get a standard quasi birth and death process like the one in equation (9.5.31), which can be solved as illustrated there. For example, let $C = 2$, $I_1 = \text{diag}(0, 1, 1)$, and $I_2 = \text{diag}(0, 1, 2)$. Then the Q matrix

[5] We include the details of this technique here for the sake of completeness. Readers unfamiliar with the contents of Section 9.5.3 may skip to the next paragraph without loss of continuity.

can be expressed as

$$\begin{bmatrix} A-\lambda I & \lambda I & 0 & 0 & \cdots \\ \mu I_1 & A-\lambda I-\mu I_1 & \lambda I & 0 & \cdots \\ 0 & \mu I_2 & A-\lambda I-\mu I_2 & \lambda I & \cdots \\ 0 & 0 & \mu I_2 & A-\lambda I-\mu I_2 & \cdots \\ 0 & 0 & 0 & \mu I_2 & \cdots \\ . & . & . & . & \cdots \end{bmatrix} \tag{4.23}$$

where I is the identity matrix, and

$$A = \begin{bmatrix} -r(0) & f(1) & 0 \\ r(0) & -f(1)-r(1) & f(2) \\ 0 & r(1) & -f(2) \end{bmatrix} \tag{4.24}$$

To summarize, we can make the following observations regarding our problem.

1. Decomposition requires that the failure/repair rates be small compared to arrival/service rates, but the matrix-geometric solution does not. Also, whenever applicable, matrix-geometric solution is exact, whereas decomposition is not.
2. Matrix-geometric solution can handle temporary instabilities, but decomposition generally gives very poor results if any of the subsystems (represented by Q_I''s) even begins to approach saturation. (That is why we assumed that $U(k) < 0.9k$ earlier, instead of $U(k) < k$).
3. Matrix-geometric solution will fail if the failure/repair rate depends on the load, or if the arrival/service rates show state dependence beyond the boundary states. Decomposition is not affected by these.
4. Decomposition applies to a system of any complexity, whereas a matrix-geometric solution has a much more limited scope.

8.5 Exercises

1. Prove Norton's theorem and the superposition theorem for closed multiple-chain product-form networks. Also prove equations (1.8) and (1.9).
2. Let $\mu_{ar}^*(\mathbf{n})$ denote the effective service rate for chain r for the aggregate station a at occupancy vector $\mathbf{n} = (n_1, \ldots, n_K)$. Assume that μ_{ar}^* is a linear function of n_k, $k \neq r$. By a weighted summation over all other chains (with state probabilities as weights), show that the marginal service rate for chain r, denoted $\mu_{ar}(n_r)$, depends only on the average queue length Q_{ak} for $k \neq r$.
3. Consider the two-chain model in Exercise 7.7, and let $N_1 = 8$ and $N_2 = 4$. Suppose that the system has a total of 6 MB memory available for user programs, and the average user program size is 1 MB. Thus, on the average, only six (out of a total of 12) jobs could be in the central subsystem (shown by the shaded area in Fig. 7-9). Every job must request memory before going into the central subsystem and release it before coming out.

(a) Suppose that both chains share the available memory. Use the algorithm in Section 8.2.4 to solve this memory constrained two-chain system.

(b) Now suppose that we reserve 4 MB memory for chain 1, and 2 MB for chain 2. Would you expect this scheme to perform better or worse than the shared scheme? Verify your predictions.

4. Write a program for simulating the model of the previous problem. Assume (pure) paged memory management with page size of 4 KB. The number of pages required by a job is uniformly distributed in the range 100 .. 400 pages. Compare the results against analytic results and relate the discrepancies to the aspects neglected in analytic modeling.

   Notes on simulation: Memory pages can be represented by "tokens" that are provided in most simulation languages. Run the model for 1000 command completions, clear the statistics, and then run for an additional 5000 completions, dumping statistics after every 1000 completions. Assuming that the sample means of each of the five subruns are normally distributed, construct a 95% confidence interval for the average response time, average number of jobs waiting to get memory, and average throughput. Check whether the analytic values lie within the confidence intervals.

5. Consider the model shown in Appendix C. Ignore output spooling and print functions and regard input spooling as normal I/O (i.e., there is no class 3 in chain 1; instead, class 2 customers go to Disk1 with probability $1 - p_2$). Also assume that the scheduling discipline at each device is such that the product-form solution holds.

   (a) Solve the model without taking into account the memory constraint. (As discussed in Section 6.4, this would involve first merging all classes of a chain into one class.)

   (b) Next bring in the memory constraints. For this, you can start with the single-class model obtained above. You can also ignore all details of memory management and only consider the average parameters.

   (c) Next suppose that the O/S attempts to squeeze in one more process in the main memory by using explicit swapping. It is observed that this results in swapping for 5% of the normal disk I/O operations. A program is swapped to the same disk from which it originally came. Solve this modified model and comment on whether the swapping improves the performance.

6. Consider the model shown in Fig. 8-11, which includes two channels, each of which controls two different disks. The model parameters are given below:

   Terminals: Think time = 2.00 sec, Number of terminals = 15.
   CPU: Load-independent. Basic service time = 50 ms.
   Disk 1: S(seek) = 15 ms, S(rotation) = 08 ms, S(transfer) = 10 ms.
   Disk 2: S(seek) = 20 ms, S(rotation) = 10 ms, S(transfer) = 10 ms.

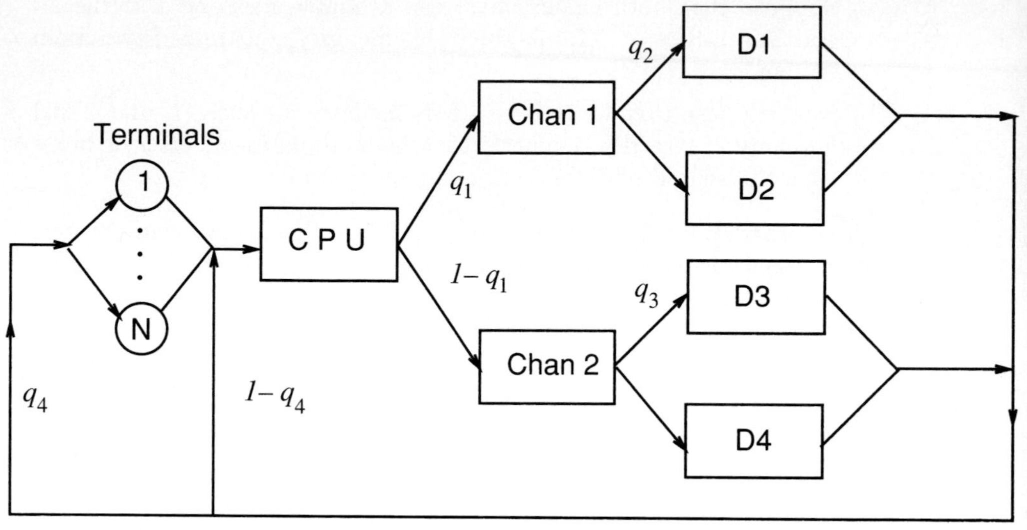

FIGURE 8-11: A computer system model with multiple channels.

Disk 3: S(seek) = 20 ms, S(rotation) = 10 ms, S(transfer) = 15 ms.
Disk 4: S(seek) = 30 ms, S(rotation) = 15 ms, S(transfer) = 18 ms.
Routing: $q_1 = 0.6$, $q_2 = 0.5$, $q_3 = 0.4$, $q_4 = 0.2$

Simulate and analytically solve this model for the following channel characteristics: (a) neither of the two channels has RPS capability, (b) both channels have RPS capability, and (c) channel 1 has RPS capability, but channel 2 does not. Comment on the relative performance of the three cases. Also compare simulation and analytic results and explain the discrepancies.

7. Obtain the "shadow approximation" for modeling nonpreemptive priority discipline among chains. Also show the expression and implementation details for the priority modeling technique mentioned in Section 8.3.2 that does not assume the arrival theorem. In particular, explain what intermediate results need to be stored and how the fractional populations can be handled efficiently.

8. Show that if $f_i(x)$ is continuous, as $N \to \infty$, equation (3.24) reduces to the following differential equation

$$[1 - \lambda_i \psi_i(x)] \frac{dW_i(x)}{dx} = 2\lambda_i x f_i(x)$$

which has the unique solution given in equation (3.26).

9. The SCAN disk scheduling policy works by making passes across the disk from cylinder 0 to cylinder $C - 1$ (the highest numbered cylinder) and back, serving requests for each cylinder as it encounters them. Let the

stepping time across one cylinder be α and the service time for a request (latency plus transfer) be exponentially distributed with mean β. Suppose that the disk is a part of a single-chain closed network with population N and is numbered as station i. Let $W_{ij}(l, N)$ denote the waiting time for a request for cylinder j, given that the head is at cylinder l when the request arrives. Assuming the arrival theorem, obtain a heuristic expression for $W_{ij}(l, N)$. Further assume that all the cylinders are equally likely to be requested. Using this, obtain an expression for $W_{ij}(N)$; i.e., the average waiting time for requests to cylinder j. Now by treating requests targeted for each cylinder as defining a different class, give the necessary equations to solve the model using MVA.

10. Show, by induction, that the solution given in equation (3.14) satisfies (3.13) as $N \to \infty$. Also derive equations (3.15) and (3.14) directly for an open M/G/1 priority system.

11. Using the approach of Sections 8.3.4 and 8.3.2, derive response time equations for the case where the scheduling discipline is SJN within a chain, and nonpreemptive priority across chains.

12. Consider a computer system model like the one in Fig. 8-4 except that the memory allocation scheme is paging. Assume, for simplicity, that there are $M < N$ pages of memory, and each customer wants exactly one page to enter the central subsystem. Assuming that the interactions within the central subsystem are much more frequent than those outside, show how the problem can be solved using decomposition.

13. Prove equation (4.12). For this, let $\delta = -\max_i q_{ii}$ and use (5.2.18) to convert Q to a transition probability matrix, say Q_d. Show that the smallest element of Q_d is zero and then write an expression for ε.

14. Consider the following transition rate matrix Q for a continuous time Markov chain. Indicate how this matrix could be decomposed. Solve the system both directly and using decomposition, and verify that the errors are $O(\varepsilon_{\mathit{eff}})$.

$$Q = \begin{bmatrix} -5.35 & 5.0 & 0 & 0.1 & 0.1 & 0.15 \\ 0 & -7.1 & 7.0 & 0 & 0 & 0.1 \\ 6.0 & 0 & -6.3 & 0.1 & 0.2 & 0 \\ 0.05 & 0 & 0.05 & -5.6 & 2.0 & 3.5 \\ 0.15 & 0.05 & 0 & 4.0 & -5.7 & 1.5 \\ 0 & 0.1 & 0 & 0 & 4.5 & -4.6 \end{bmatrix} \tag{5.1}$$

Bibliographic Notes

The aggregation theorem was first proposed for single-chain networks in Chandy, Herzog, and Woo (1975), and is also called the *CHW theorem*. It has subsequently been generalized to multiple-chain networks by Chandy and others [See Sauer and Chandy (1981)]. Further generalizations that cover mixed networks and occupancy vector-dependent capacities are reported in Kritzinger, Van-Wyk, and Krzesinski (1982).

Approximate modeling of memory constraints in single-chain networks is proposed by Sauer and is contained in Sauer and Chandy (1981). Its extension to multiple-chain networks is proposed in Lazowska and Zahorjan (1982) and is also discussed in Lazowska, Zahorjan, Graham, and Sevcik (1984). This method does not give very good results for the shared memory case. The technique has been improved and extended for multiple memory constrained subnetworks in Krzesinski and Teunissen (1985). Our discussion in Section 8.2.4 is based on this work. All these approaches involve solving models with noninteger populations. Silva and Muntz (1987) presents a somewhat different approach, which retains integer populations and simplifies aggregation. To illustrate it in a simple setting, suppose that the network consists of two subnetworks $\mathcal{S}_1$ and $\mathcal{S}_2$, at least one of which has a resource constraint. Then we construct two models, in one $\mathcal{S}_2$ is aggregated, and in the other $\mathcal{S}_1$ is aggregated. The aggregate station is chosen to be a multiserver FCFS station where the number of servers is the same as the resource constraint. The service rates of these stations are chosen such that the performance parameters of the two networks match up. The solution thus involves dealing with a multiserver FCFS station with different service rates for different chains. The authors develop an approximation for dealing with such a station in the context of the MVA algorithm. Brandwajn (1982, 1984) discusses another approach for modeling shared memory constraints.

Iterative methods for the approximate analysis of queuing networks with various non-PF features have been examined by several researchers. Some of the relevant work is reported in Neuse and Chandy (1982), Silva, Lavenberg, and Muntz (1984), Agrawal (1985), Marsan and Marie (1979), and Akyildiz and Sieber (1988).

A large number of papers have dealt with the modeling of channel contention. Some of the early work, on which our presentation is based, appears in Wilhelm (1977), Zahorjan, Hume and Sevcik (1978), Bard (1980, 1982), and Brandwajn (1983, 1984). Of these, Bard (1980, 1982) and Brandwajn (1983) consider the contention problem when multiple paths exist between channels, control units, and disks. Buzen and Shum (1987) presents a detailed operational analysis of reconnect delays in RPS systems with single and multiple paths.

Simultaneous resource possession also arises in the modeling of delays caused by serialized access to shared software resources such as critical sections. The situation here is similar to the one in Fig. 8-6, because the processes access the critical section only part of the time. Agrawal and Buzen (1983) proposes an approximate iterative solution technique that introduces delay stations to account for serialization delays, like the one suggested in Section 8.2.5. Jacobson and Lazowska (1983) presents another technique for the same problem.

Modeling of non-PF scheduling disciplines in the context of an isolated M/G/1 queue is discussed in Kleinrock (1976) and to a limited extent in Coffman and Denning (1973). The results reported there for mean performance measures and distributions are exact. In contrast, only approximate modeling of non-PF disciplines is available in the context of closed networks. Two general approaches have been examined here. One is based on iterative aggregation, and the work of Marsan and Marie (1979), Akyildiz and Sieber (1988), and others applies here. These approaches can handle general load-dependence. The second approach is based on heuristic response time equations in the MVA setting and is limited to load-independent stations and stations with limited load-dependence. This is discussed in Sauer and Chandy (1981), and in Lazowska, Zahorjan, Graham, and Sevcik (1984). Bryant, Krzesinski, Lakshmi, and Chandy (1984) discusses various approximations for priority scheduling which we mentioned in Section 8.3.2. Bondi and Chuang (1988) proposes an approximation for preemptive priorities that uses modified response time equations at other stations as well in order to account for the effect of priority scheduling on other stations of the network. This method provides good accuracy, but is difficult to use in general. Modeling of shortest job next discipline is discussed in Kant (1991, Perf Eval). This paper also includes the approximations for limited forms of load-dependence discussed in Section 8.3.6. The method of Silva and Muntz (1987) can handle multiserver stations with FCFS discipline. Bondi (1984) discusses an approximation of an isolated M/G/m queue operating with preemptive priority discipline. A detailed analysis of the SCAN scheduling disciplines for moving head disks is contained in Oney (1975).

Suri (1983) examines the question of robustness of results obtained under product-form assumption. This issue is important because in practice many of the product-form assumptions may be violated, and it is important to know how far the network characteristics could drift away from product-form before we have to consider special purpose modeling techniques.

One topic that we have omitted concerns the computation of flow time (i.e., response time across a subnetwork) distributions in product-form networks. Kelly and Pollett (1983) discusses the computation of flow-time distributions in closed overtake-free networks. (The overtake-free condition makes the response times of individual stations independent, but rules out having multiple servers at any station.) Morrison and Mitra (1985) discusses waiting time approximations in queuing networks with PS discipline under heavy traffic. Boxma, Kelly, and Konheim (1984) discusses product-form for the flow-time distribution in a cyclic network of exponential queues. Rege and Sengupta (1988) discusses approximations for response-time distribution by exploiting Norton's theorem. This is an approximation, since the replacement only preserves marginal distributions, not flow-time distributions. Raatikainen (1989) presents another approximation that computes flow time as a random sum of the response times of individual stations in isolation.

The idea of "near complete decomposability" was originally proposed by Simon and Ando in 1961 in the context of economic analysis. The idea is applied to Markovian models in Courtois (1977). Our discussion in Section 8.4 is based on this. Courtois also discusses several further results on the decomposability of specific types of queuing network models, a topic we have omitted. Stewart (1983), and Courtois and Semuel (1985) discuss computation of error bounds in aggregating Markov chains. Conway and Georganas (1986,TSE) discusses the exact analysis of closed, product-form multiple-chain networks of FCFS load-independent stations by decomposing the transition rate matrix with respect to each chain. Such an approach may be useful in parametric studies involving changes to the parameters of a chain (as opposed to those of a station).

Part II

Advanced Topics

CHAPTER

9

Advanced Stochastic Analysis

This chapter builds further on the discussion in Chapter 5. We first analyze one more system using z-transforms primarily to show the difficulties with that approach. We then discuss a number of concepts, including conservation laws and semi-Markov processes, that are useful for analyzing complex queuing systems. This discussion prepares us for the detailed analysis of a M/G/1 queuing system, which has numerous practical applications. Next we discuss phase-type distributions and matrix-geometric methods for solving advanced queuing systems. Finally we discuss representation of arrival/service processes arising in real-life applications, and the direct methods of solving global balance equations for Markovian systems.

9.1 Solution Using Generating Functions

In Section 5.6, we analyzed a number of queuing systems using z-transforms (or probability generating functions). Although transform methods are indispensable for solving infinite-state queuing systems, their use is not always as straightforward as our previous encounter with them might suggest. The main purpose of this section is to illustrate these difficulties and to present the techniques for coping with them. We shall consider only one-dimensional z-transforms in this

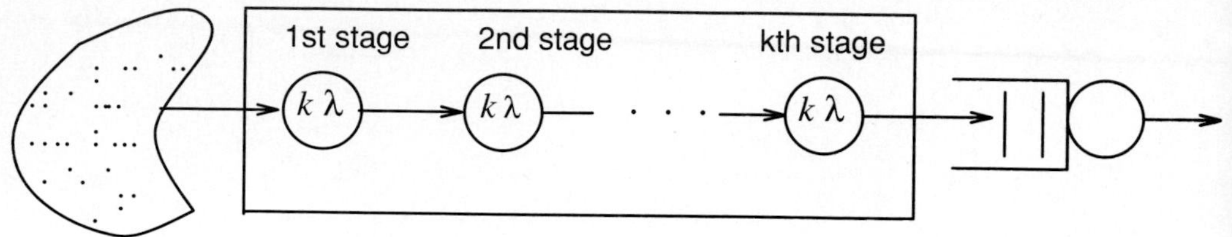

FIGURE 9-1: Representation of the $E_k/M/1$ queuing system.

discussion, since dealing with multi-dimensional transforms is generally exceedingly difficult. In order to keep the discussion from being too abstract, we shall use an $E_k/M/1/FCFS/\infty/\infty$ system as a running example. Actually, this system itself is not that difficult to analyze, but it serves to provide a context for discussing the difficulties in general.

To start with, let us obtain the global balance equations and the probability generating function for our $E_k/M/1$ system. Fig. 9-1 shows this model pictorially. To the left of the "arrival box", we have an infinite number of customers available. A customer that enters the arrival box "begins arriving". It has to pass through k stages and exit the box before it can enter the queue at the service station. Thus, the state of the system can be described by the pair (n, j), where n and j have the following interpretation: n represents the number of already arrived customers, i.e., those that are to the right of the arrival box. Exactly one customer could be inside the box at any time, and j represents its current stage. As soon as a customer exits the arrival box and joins the queue at the station, another one enters the box from the other end.

Since there are exactly k stages for each value of n, we can get a one-dimensional representation of the state by making the substitution $m = nk+j-1$. Then m ranges from 0 to ∞. Let $k\lambda$ denote the rate for each arrival stage, μ the service rate of the station, and $\rho = \lambda/\mu$. If the system is in state m, the flow out occurs due to service completion (with rate μ) and the advance of a customer to the next stage (with rate $k\lambda$). The flow in occurs due to service completion in state $m+k$ or an advance of a customer to the next stage, while in state $m-1$.[1] Therefore, the global balance equations are

$$\begin{aligned} k\rho P(0) &= P(k) \\ k\rho P(m) &= k\rho P(m-1) + P(m+k) \quad \text{for } 1 \leq m \leq k-1 \\ (k\rho+1)P(m) &= k\rho P(m-1) + P(m+k) \quad \text{for } m \geq k \end{aligned} \tag{1.1}$$

From these equations, we get the following expression for the z-transform of the queue length distribution

$$\Phi(z) = \frac{(1-z^k)\sum_{m=0}^{k-1} P(m)z^m}{k\rho z^{k+1} - (1+k\rho)z^k + 1} \tag{1.2}$$

[1]Service completion reduces n by 1, and thus takes us from state $m+k$ to m.

Unlike our previous encounters with z-transforms, $\Phi(z)$ here involves the initial probabilities $P(0), \ldots, P(k-1)$, for which we do not have any independent equations. The reader may wish to verify that we have indeed used up all equations in (1.1). As usual, we can get one more equation by requiring that all probabilities sum to 1, but this still leaves $k-1$ unknown probabilities. This situation arises frequently and is the main source of difficulties in solving a queuing system via z-transforms. To resolve this problem, note that $\Phi(z)$ is defined as a power series with probabilities (i.e., real numbers in the range $0 \mathinner{..} 1$) for the coefficients. Therefore,

$$|\Phi(z)| \leq \Phi(1) = 1 \qquad \text{for } \ |z| \leq 1 \tag{1.3}$$

It follows that if the Markov chain is positive recurrent (i.e., the system is stable), $\Phi(z)$ must be *analytic* (i.e., continuous and finite) for $|z| \leq 1$. Therefore, $\Phi(z)$ cannot have any *poles* with magnitude smaller than or equal to 1. Since z is a complex-valued variable, $|z| \leq 1$ defines a *unit disk* centered on the origin of the complex plane. It follows that *any zeros of the denominator of* $\Phi(z)$ *inside or on the unit disk should also be the zeros of its numerator*. Another way to come to the same conclusion is by examining the partial-fraction expansion of $\Phi(z)$. This expansion will involve terms with $(z-r)^i$, $i = 1, 2, \ldots$ in the denominator; therefore, if we invert $\Phi(z)$ to get the state probability $P(m)$, we shall get a sum of terms, each of which will have r^{-m} as its dominant part. Now if the Markov chain is positive recurrent, the state probabilities $P(m)$ must decay as $m \to \infty$, which requires that $|r| > 1$. Thus, *if a root* r *of the denominator of* $\Phi(z)$ *is such that* $|r| \leq 1$, *the numerator should also vanish at* $z = r$. If everything is right, this should give us exactly as many additional equations as we need to complete the solution.

Let $D(z)$ denote the denominator of (1.2). Since $D(z)$ is a polynomial of degree $k+1$, it has $k+1$ roots. One of these roots is easily seen to be 1. In fact, $z = 1$ is often a root and is easy to check for. Since $z = 1$ is also a root of the $1 - z^k$ term in the numerator, we can dismiss it. Taking the $z - 1$ factor out of the denominator, we are left with the following polynomial, denoted $D_1(z)$

$$D_1(z) = k\rho z^k - z^{k-1} - z^{k-2} - \cdots - z - 1 \tag{1.4}$$

We thus need to show that, of the k zeros of $D_1(z)$, exactly $k-1$ lie *inside or on the unit disk*. For proving something like this, we often need a simple but powerful result from the complex variable theory known as Rouche's theorem.

Rouche's theorem: Let $f(z)$ and $g(z)$ be two functions of z that are analytic on and inside a closed contour C, and $|g(z)| < |f(z)|$ *on* C. Then $f(z)$ and $f(z) \pm g(z)$ have the same number of zeros *inside* C.

This theorem is useful because it lets us deal with a simpler function $f(z)$ instead of the original function $f(z) + g(z)$. That is, if we want to show that there are k zeros of $f(z) + g(z)$ inside C, we choose $f(z)$ such that it is easy to prove that $f(z)$ has k zeros inside C. (Sometimes, it may be necessary to apply Rouche's theorem a few times to get a sufficiently simple function.) To apply Rouche's theorem to a queuing problem, we choose C as the circle $|z| = 1$, $D(z) = f(z) + g(z)$, and the inequality $|g(z)| < |f(z)|$ need hold only when the system is stable. In our E$_k$/M/1 system, the stability condition is simply $\rho < 1$. In a conservative system, the stability condition is usually obvious, and the corresponding restriction can be exploited in proving $|f(z)| > |g(z)|$; but in others, we may have to actually derive the stability condition by determining the range of the loading parameter ρ such that the poles that could not be the zeros as well, stay outside the unit disk.

Let us note a few important points regarding the use of Rouche's theorem for our purposes.

1. One could very well let $D(z) = f(z) - g(z)$, instead of $D(z) = f(z) + g(z)$, without changing anything. This is because $|g(z)| = |-g(z)|$.
2. The condition $|f(z)| > |g(z)|$ is needed *only on the unit circle, and not inside*. That is, the condition should hold for every complex number $z = a + ib$ such that $a^2 + b^2 = 1$.
3. Since we are dealing with polynomials, two points can be noted. First, the analyticity of $f(z)$ or $g(z)$ is not a problem. Second, $f(z)$ must include at least one term z^n with $n \geq k - 1$. (If $n = k - 1$, we know that $f(z)$ has only $k - 1$ zeros, and so we only have to show that they all lie inside the unit disk.)
4. Rouche's theorem *does not* say that $f(z)$ and $f(z) \pm g(z)$ have the same set of zeros inside C; they most often don't. (Only the number of zeros is the same.)
5. The theorem only tells us how many zeros exist inside the unit disk, and does not say anything about how many lie *on* the unit disk.

The proper choice of functions $f(z)$ and $g(z)$ often requires trial and error, and can be tedious. In any case, given a choice, the verification of $|f(z)| > |g(z)|$ requires the properties of the modulus operator. For easy reference, let us note some simple properties. Let z be a complex number. We can represent it either in the cartesian form $a+ib$ or the polar form $r.e^{i\theta}$ where $i = \sqrt{-1}$. Let $\bar{z} = a - ib = r.e^{-i\theta}$ denote the *complex conjugate* of z. By definition, $|z| = |-z| = |iz| = |\bar{z}| = \sqrt{z \cdot \bar{z}}$. Since we can view a complex number as a vector in the complex plane, the following properties are easy to demonstrate for any two functions ϕ_1 and ϕ_2.

$$\begin{aligned}
|\phi_1(z_1) + \phi_2(z_2)| &\leq |\phi_1(z_1)| + |\phi_2(z_2)| \\
|\phi_1(z_1) - \phi_2(z_2)| &\geq |\phi_1(z_1)| - |\phi_2(z_2)| \qquad \text{assuming } |\phi_1(z_1)| \geq |\phi_2(z_2)| \\
|\phi_1(z_1) * \phi_2(z_2)| &= |\phi_1(z_1)| * |\phi_2(z_2)| \\
|\phi_1(z_1)/\phi_2(z_2)| &= |\phi_1(z_1)|/|\phi_2(z_2)| \qquad \text{assuming } \phi_2(z_2) \neq 0 \\
\overline{\phi_1(z_1) \cdot \phi_2(z_2)} &= \overline{\phi_1(z_1)} \cdot \overline{\phi_2(z_2)}
\end{aligned} \tag{1.5}$$

In most cases, these relationships must be used in conjunction with other constraints such as the fact that $|f(z)| > |g(z)|$ has to hold only on the unit circle (i.e., $|z| = 1$) and when the system is stable.

Before proceeding, let us make a few comments regarding the zeros lying *on* the unit disk. Since $\Phi(z)$ cannot have a pole on the unit disk either, it appears that Rouche's theorem only gives us a partial solution. However, this is really not a problem. First, when dealing with a model with traffic parameters (such as the intensity ρ) retained symbolically, such zeros should either depend on those parameters, or they could not be instrumental in obtaining the initial unknown probabilities. Thus, in our $E_K/M/1$ problem, the zero at $z = 1$ is independent of ρ and not needed for determining the unknown probabilities. Second, one could always include the unit circle by applying Rouche's theorem to $\mathcal{U}(1+\delta)$, i.e., a unit disk of radius $1+\delta$, where δ is an arbitrarily small but positive number.

In our $E_K/M/1$ problem, it is easier to work with $D(z)$ instead of $D_1(z)$. Let $f(z) = 1 - (1 + k\rho)z^k$ and $g(z) = k\rho z^{k+1}$. A convenient way to show the desired result is to let $|z| = 1+\delta$ where δ is an arbitrarily small positive number. Then by using the results in (1.5), we get

$$\begin{aligned} |g(z)| &= k\rho(1+\delta)^{k+1} = k\rho[1+(k+1)\delta] + o(\delta) \\ |f(z)| &\geq (k\rho+1)|z|^k - 1 = k\rho(1+k\delta) + k\delta + o(\delta) \end{aligned}$$

which means that so long as $\rho < 1$, $|g(z)| < |f(z)|$ remains true for a nonzero δ. Since $f(z)$ has k roots, all of which lie *inside* $\mathcal{U}(1+\delta)$, the same must be true of $D(z)$. Now as $\delta \to 0$, we can conclude that $D(z)$ must have k roots inside or on $\mathcal{U}(1)$. We have already shown that one root of $D(z)$ lies on $\mathcal{U}(1)$, and it is easy to show that there couldn't be any more on $\mathcal{U}(1)$. Therefore, $D(z)$ must have $k-1$ roots inside $\mathcal{U}(1)$.

Let z_0 denote the root of $D(z)$ that is outside the unit disk. Then we can express $D_1(z)$ as $(z - z_0)D_2(z)$. Therefore,

$$\Phi(z) = \frac{(1-z^k)\sum_{m=0}^{k-1} P(m)z^m}{(z-1)(z-z_0)D_2(z)} \tag{1.6}$$

It is clear from equation (1.6) that $D_2(z)$ must be proportional to the summation term in the numerator because the roots of $1 - z^k$ all lie on the unit circle, but those of $D_2(z)$ lie inside. We now get a simplified expression for $\Phi(z)$.

$$\Phi(z) = \frac{c(1-z^k)}{(z-1)(z-z_0)} \tag{1.7}$$

where c is the proportionality constant. The appearance of the unknown parameter c is not surprising, since we still have not used the requirement $\Phi(1) = 1$. Using this requirement, we finally get

$$\Phi(z) = \frac{(z_0-1)(1-z^k)}{k(z-1)(z-z_0)} \tag{1.8}$$

Before proceeding with (1.8), let us note a few difficulties that we rather cleverly avoided in this example. In general, we cannot dispose the unknown terms from the numerator quite so easily. For example, if the numerator in (1.2) had an additive term, we could not claim that all roots of $D_2(z)$ should come out of the summation term. The only general method in such cases is to explicitly compute all zeros of $D(z)$ inside $\mathcal{U}(1)$ using an appropriate numerical technique. Since $D(z)$ is a real polynomial, its roots must be either real or complex conjugate. There are several results in classical complex number theory that are helpful in finding the number of real roots, the number of real, positive roots, etc. Methods also exist for locating roots in a particular region, such as those inside the unit disk. In our current example, we only have to find z_0, which is supposed to be outside the unit disk.

Consider a general problem, and suppose that find that r distinct roots $z_1, \ldots, z_r$ lie inside the unit disk. Let $N(z)$ denote the numerator of $\Phi(z)$. Then we get the following system of linear equations for the unknown initial probabilities.

$$\Re[N(z_i)] = 0 \text{ and } \Im[N(z_i)] = 0 \quad \text{for } 1 \le i \le r \tag{1.9}$$

where $\Re$ and $\Im$ denote the real and imaginary parts respectively. Because the roots are either real or complex-conjugate, the number of nontrivial and linearly independent equations in equation (1.9) should be r. Let k denote the number of unknown initial probabilities. If all roots are distinct, we expect $r = k - 1$, and thus all unknowns can be determined. (We say $k - 1$ because we also have the constraint $\Phi(1) = 1$ to satisfy.) If, however, there are multiple roots, r will be less than $k - 1$, and we are still not done. This also raises two side questions: Can we tell if $D(z)$ has only distinct roots? If not, how do we determine the multiplicity of each root? One has to use further results from complex variable theory to approach these questions. Usually, determining the multiplicity of roots is itself a challenging task. Now to get additional equations, suppose that $D(z)$ has a root α of multiplicity i. This means that

$$\lim_{z \to \alpha} \left[N(z)/(z - \alpha)^j\right] = 0 \quad \text{for } 0 \le j \le i - 1 \tag{1.10}$$

However, this equation is not convenient to work with. By induction on j and the basis $N(\alpha) = 0$, it is easy to show that an equivalent condition is as follows:

$$\left.\frac{d^j N(z)}{dz^j}\right|_{z=\alpha} = 0 \quad \text{for } 0 \le j \le i - 1 \tag{1.11}$$

Thus, we have all the necessary equations to compute the k unknown probabilities.

Let us now get back to equation (1.8). $\Phi(z)$ cannot be inverted here directly because the degree of the numerator is larger than that of the denominator. However, from the property in equation (B.3.9), we know how to handle multiplication by z^k in the transform domain. Therefore, by ignoring the $1 - z^k$ term, we can invert the rest to get a function $f(m)$. It is easy to verify that

$$f(m) = (1 - z_0^{-m-1})/k \quad \text{for } m = 0, 1, 2, \ldots \tag{1.12}$$

This implies that $P(m) = f(m) - f(m-k)$. Since $f(m) = 0$ for $m < 0$, we have

$$P(m) = \begin{cases} (1 - z_0^{-m-1})/k & \text{for } 0 \le m < k \\ z_0^{k-m-1}(1 - z_0^{-k})/k & \text{for } m \ge k \end{cases} \tag{1.13}$$

Let $\pi(n)$ denote the probability of finding n customers at the station. Obviously,

$$\pi(n) = \sum_{j=1}^{k} P(nk + j - 1) \tag{1.14}$$

Because by definition, $D(z_0) = 0$, from equation (1.4) it follows that $(1 - z_0^{-k}) = k\rho(z_0 - 1)$. Using this property and equation (1.13), we get the following expression for $\pi(n)$.

$$\pi(n) = \begin{cases} 1 - \rho & \text{for } n = 0 \\ \rho(z_0^k - 1)z_0^{-nk} & \text{for } n > 0 \end{cases} \tag{1.15}$$

Thus, the queue length distribution is basically geometric with root z_0 appearing as the parameter of the geometric distribution. It is also interesting to note that by letting $\sigma = z_0^{-k}$, (1.15) reduces to the general solution for a GI/M/1 system given later in equation (2.43).

9.2 Some Results on General Queuing Systems

In this section we study several results on isolated queuing stations under various assumptions. In particular, we discuss consequences of Poisson arrivals, use of semi-Markov processes in analyzing complex systems, and certain invariant relationships known as conservation laws.

9.2.1 Properties of Systems with Poisson Arrivals

In this section, we derive two important results concerning systems where the arrivals are Poisson. The first result is often known as the PASTA property, which stands for *poisson arrivals see time averages*. It refers to the fact that under Poisson arrivals, the arriver's distribution is same as the random observer's. To show this, we start with the stochastic definition of the arriver's distribution. Let t denote an arbitrarily chosen time instant. Then,

$$\begin{aligned} PA(n) &= \lim_{\Delta t \to 0} Pr[n \text{ in system at } t \mid \text{arrival occurs in } (t, t + \Delta t)] \\ &= \lim_{\Delta t \to 0} \frac{Pr[n \text{ in system at } t \;\&\; \text{arrival occurs in } (t, t + \Delta t)]}{Pr[\text{arrival occurs in } (t, t + \Delta t)]} \\ &= \lim_{\Delta t \to 0} \frac{Pr[\text{arrival in } (t, t + \Delta t) \mid n \text{ in system at } t] Pr[n \text{ in system at } t]}{Pr[\text{arrival occurs in } (t, t + \Delta t)]} \\ &= Pr[n \text{ in the system at } t] = P(n) \end{aligned}$$

where the last step follows from the fact that the probability of an arrival is independent of the number of customers already in the system. It may appear at first that the entire proof will go through whenever the arrival rate is state-independent, irrespective of whether the arrival process is Poisson. This, however, is not true. With non-Poisson arrivals, the probability of an arrival depends on how long it has been since the last arrival. Therefore, it is not very meaningful to speak of an arrival during an interval $(t, t + \Delta t)$ without specifying the time since the last arrival. If instead we average this probability over all possible values of time since the last arrival, the last step will not go through. To see this, consider the situation when the system is empty. In this case, we know that the last arrived customer must have been served already, i.e., we know that a time greater than or equal to the service time of the last customer served has elapsed since the last arrival! That is, the probability of an arrival given that the system is empty, cannot, in general, be the same as the overall probability. Here again we see the subtle differences between operational and stochastic arguments. We saw in Section 4.2.5 that in an open system, if the arrivals are homogeneous, the arriver's distribution must be the same as that of the random observer. The difference is that our current arguments concern all possible behavior sequences and thus are dependent on distributional characteristics. We made a similar point in Section 4.2.6.

In Section 4.2.5, we saw that in an open network under one-step behavior and flow balance, the distributions seen by an arriver and departer are the same. This result holds in a stochastic sense under steady state whenever the arrivals and departures are restricted to occur singly (i.e., no batch arrivals or service). This is proved as follows. Using the notation of Section 4.2, we have

$$PA_i(n) = \frac{A_i(n)}{A_i} = \frac{A_i(n) - D_i(n+1) + D_i(n+1)}{A_i - D_i + D_i} \tag{2.1}$$

where all quantities are over the observation period 0 through T. From equation (4.2.23), we have $|A_i(n) - D_i(n+1)| \leq 1$. Also, $A_i - D_i = X(T)$ gives the net increase in backlog over the period 0 through T. Now if we increase T without limit, both $D_i(n+1)$ and D_i will increase without bound; but so long as the system is stable, $X(T)$ will remain finite. Therefore, in the limit as $T \to \infty$, the right-hand side of the above equation becomes $D_i(n+1)/D_i$, which by definition is $PD_i(n)$. Thus, the *arriver's and departer's distributions are identical for any GI/G/1 type of queue with single arrivals and services*. It is important to note that this result does not hold under batch services or arrivals, even if we have a finite upper bound on batch sizes. To see this, suppose that arrivals occur singly but services are always in a batch of size 2. Thus, if the system is in state 1, the server must stay idle and no departure can occur. In terms of our proof, as $T \to \infty$, $A_i(0)$ will increase without bound, but $D_i(1)$ will stay at zero.

This equivalence between arriver's and departer's distributions continues to hold in a finite capacity system with rejection blocking. If the arrivals are Poisson, we can also relate the arriver's and random observer's distributions. Let K denote the system capacity. The arrival rate may depend on the system state and is denoted as $\lambda(n)$. By following the reasoning similar to that used for showing the PASTA property, it is easy to see that

$$PA(n) = \frac{\lambda(n)P(n)}{\sum_{k=0}^{K-1} \lambda(k)P(k)} \tag{2.2}$$

As a special case, if λ is state-independent, we get the stochastic counterpart of equation (4.2.31). That is,

$$PA_i(n|N) = P_i(n|N)/[1 - P_i(N|N)] \tag{2.3}$$

As an interesting application of these results, consider the classical M/G/1 queuing system. Combining the GI/G/1 result with the PASTA property, we conclude that *in a M/G/1 system, the departer's distribution is the same as that of the random observer.* We shall use this property in Section 9.3 to analyze the M/G/1 queue. Similarly, we can conclude that in a finite capacity M/G/1 queue, the arriver's and departer's distributions are simple renormalizations of the random observer's distribution.

Next we consider the *residual life* of a customer in service. This is the amount of remaining service time of a customer in service from the point of view of a random observer. Often, we are interested in the remaining service time from the point of view of an arriving customer as well, since under any nonpreemptive scheduling discipline, the arriver must wait for at least this duration to start its service. In general, the two definitions are different; however, if the arrivals are Poisson, they are the same. This results from the PASTA property; *there is no difference between the outlook of a random observer and that of a Poisson arriver.* More formally, this means that *with Poisson arrivals, the joint distribution of the arrival instants is uniform.* This is easy to prove, but we shall not do so here.

Consider a time interval wherein a sequence of services are performed at station i, and let x_k be the kth service duration. Because of the uniform distribution of the arrival instants, the probability that an arrival occurs during the kth service interval will be proportional to x_k, the length of the service interval. Since this probability is independent of the index k, it is the same for any interval of length x_k. Therefore, the probability that the arrival occurs in a service interval of length between t and $t + \delta t$ is proportional to $tf_{\mathcal{S}}(t)\delta t$ where $f_{\mathcal{S}}(t)$ is the density function of the service time $\mathcal{S}$. The proportionality constant is the mean service time, because

$$\int_0^\infty tf_{\mathcal{S}}(t)\, dt = s_i$$

Now consider a random arrival during a service time of length t. Because of uniform distribution of arrival instants, the remaining service time for this arriver is $t/2$. Therefore, the average remaining service time of a customer in service, denoted γ, can be obtained as

$$\gamma = \int_0^\infty \frac{t}{2} \frac{tf_{\mathcal{S}}(t)}{s_i}\, dt = \frac{E[\mathcal{S}^2]}{2s_i} = \frac{CV_i^2 + 1}{2} s_i \tag{2.4}$$

where CV_i is the coefficient of variation of the service time. Note that γ is always larger than one-half of the mean service time and increases rapidly with the coefficient of variation, because the probability of an arrival is greater during larger service intervals. For exponentially distributed service times $CV_i = 1$, and hence the expected remaining service time is the same as the full service time! Also note that the average remaining service time without assuming that a customer is indeed in service would be γ multiplied by U_i, the station utilization.

Let $F_S(t)$ denote the distribution function of the service time. It can be shown that the density function of the remaining service time, denoted $f_\Gamma(t)$ is given by

$$f_\Gamma(t) = (1 - F_S(t))/s_i \tag{2.5}$$

Note that with exponentially distributed service times, $f_\Gamma(t) = f_S(t)$. This again shows the memoryless property of the exponential distribution. A related quantity of interest is the *attained service*, i.e., the amount of service that a customer being served would have received at the time of a new arrival. Because of the uniform distribution of arrival instants, the density function of the attained service must be the same as that of the residual service time and is given by equation (2.5).

9.2.2 Virtual Load and Conservation Laws

In this section we study certain relationships or *laws* that hold under very general circumstances. These laws not only illustrate some fundamental tradeoffs but are also sometimes useful in solving queuing systems. They could be used either as additional equations in an exact solution algorithm or as consistency constraints in an approximate solution algorithm. We start the discussion by noting that our analysis of M/M systems did not specify any particular scheduling discipline. Indeed a careful consideration of the problem would reveal that the results hold for any scheduling discipline that satisfies the following properties:

1. There is no artificial creation or loss of work in the system; i.e., the server never stays idle while there are customers present, a preempted customer does not have to start over, services are not aborted, etc.
2. Scheduling is not based on the service time requirements of the customers. For example, a scheduling discipline like "shortest-job-next" does not satisfy this requirement.

We denoted such scheduling disciplines as SI in Section 5.5. Scheduling disciplines that satisfy *only* condition (1) are known as *work conserving*, since under such disciplines, the expected *unfinished work* remains the same, irrespective of how the customers are picked up for service. This simple observation can be used to derive *conservation laws* for general queues. Let us start by formalizing the notion of unfinished work, often known as *virtual load*. Viewed as a random variable, the virtual load at time t, denoted $\mathcal{V}(t)$, is defined as the total number of seconds of service that would have to be imparted to serve all the customers already present at time t, given that no more customers arrive. If the scheduling discipline is FCFS, the customers arriving after time t do not interfere with the service of those present at time t, therefore, we do not need the latter assumption. Note that *the concept of virtual load measures how much* backlog *exists in the system and not how long it would take to clear that backlog.* If the system has only one load-independent station, the virtual load indeed equals the time that this server would need to clear the backlog. However, if the system has multiple servers, they can collectively clear the same backlog faster, but that does not change the virtual load measure itself. Obviously, $\mathcal{V}(t)$ will be independent of the order of service so long as condition (1) is satisfied. Normally, we are only interested in steady-state conditions, and the time origin t is irrelevant.

Consider a system with K classes (or chains, the distinction being irrelevant for now). We assume that K is countable and finite, but other cases can also be handled easily. (See Exercise 9.3). Suppose that we schedule customers based on their class affiliation (e.g., priority scheduling where the priority level is a function of the class number). Let $V(r)$ denote the expected virtual load corresponding to the customers of class r. Then, work conservation implies that there exists a constant V_0, independent of how the customers of various classes are scheduled, such that

$$\sum_{r=1}^{K} V(r) = V_0 \tag{2.6}$$

That is, *thc backlog attributed to various classes may depend on the scheduling discipline, but the total backlog does not.* This relationship can be made more specific under further assumptions. Let λ_r denote the arrival rate, and μ_r the service rate of each server for chain r. Let $U_r = \lambda_r/\mu_r$ be the utilization of class r and U the total utilization (i.e., the sum of all U_r's). Suppose that the service times are exponentially distributed. Then,

$$V(r) = Q_r/\mu_r = U_r R_r \tag{2.7}$$

This result follows from that fact that Q_r gives the average number of unprocessed customers (from a random observer's point of view), each with the average service time requirement of $1/\mu_r$. The exponential service time assumption is needed so that we can pretend that the customer in service is also "unprocessed". Now, if the arrivals are Poisson, we can find V_0 by picking any work-conserving scheduling discipline for which R_r is easy to compute. We shall see in Section 6.4 that under PS discipline, a multiple-class system is almost as easy to solve as a single-class system, and the results can be obtained from those in Section 5.5.2. For example in the case of a load-independent station, the class-specific response time is given by

$$R_r^{(PS)} = 1/[\mu_r(1-U)] \tag{2.8}$$

Thereforc,

$$\sum_{r=1}^{K} V(r) = \sum_{r=1}^{K} U_r R_r = \sum_{r=1}^{K} U_r R_r^{(PS)} = \frac{1}{1-U} \sum_{r=1}^{K} \frac{U_r}{\mu_r}$$

That is, for an open M/M/1 type of system under any work-conserving scheduling discipline, we have

$$\sum_{r=1}^{K} U_r R_r = \frac{1}{1-U} \sum_{r=1}^{K} \frac{U_r}{\mu_r} \tag{2.9}$$

Since everything on the right-hand side of this equation is known, this equation says that *the achievable response time vector* $[R_1, \ldots, R_K]$ *must lie on the same hyperplane irrespective of the scheduling discipline*. We can obtain similar results for the multiserver case as well.

For another special case, we consider only nonpreemptive scheduling disciplines. For such disciplines, the average remaining service time for a class r customer (from the point of view of a random observer) is its average residual life $\gamma_r = (CV_r^2 + 1)/(2\mu_r)$. Since, on the average, U_r customers from class r (out of a total of Q_r customers) are in service and the rest are waiting, we can obtain $V(r)$ as follows:

$$V(r) = (Q_r - U_r)/\mu_r + U_r\gamma_r = U_r R_r - U_r(1/\mu_r - \gamma_r) \tag{2.10}$$

Substituting (2.10) in (2.6), we get

$$\sum_{r=1}^{K} U_r R_r = V_0 + \sum_{r=1}^{K} U_r \left(\frac{1}{\mu_r} - \gamma_r \right)$$

Since $R_r = W_r + 1/\mu_r$ for a multiserver station, *for any GI/G/c queue under nonpreemptive scheduling*, we have

$$\sum_{r=1}^{K} U_r W_r = V_0 - \sum_{r=1}^{K} U_r \gamma_r \tag{2.11}$$

If the arrivals are Poisson and the station is load-independent, we can find an expression for V_0. FCFS discipline is the obvious choice here for two reasons. First, under FCFS discipline, arriving customers do not interfere with those already present at the station. Therefore, *for a load-independent station FCFS station,* V_0 *must be the same as the average waiting time* W_{fcfs}. Second, a M/G/1/FCFS system is easy to analyze for expected performance measures even when each class has a different service-time distribution as we saw in Section 8.3.1. From equation (8.3.8), we have

$$V_0 = \frac{W_0}{(1-U)} \qquad \text{where } W_0 = \sum_{r=1}^{K} U_r \gamma_r \tag{2.12}$$

Therefore for any M/G/1 queue under nonpreemptive scheduling, we have

$$\sum_{r=1}^{K} U_r W_r = \frac{U}{1-U} \sum_{r=1}^{K} U_r \gamma_r \tag{2.13}$$

This equation also says that the waiting time vector must lie on an appropriate hyperplane. Informally, both (2.9) and (2.13) say that if some customers are given preferential treatment (resulting in smaller waiting times), the others will suffer. This effect is best seen in shortest-job-next (SJN) discipline where better service to short jobs may result in starvation of the long ones. Note that SJN is one example of a discipline with an uncountably infinite number of priorities.

In addition to the equality constraints above, one could also derive certain inequalities. Suppose that we consider only those customers that belong to a specific subset, say ω, of the set of all classes. Obviously then, the backlog of customers belonging to the set ω (in the presence of other classes) can be no less than the backlog if no other classes were present. Therefore, if in equations (2.9) and (2.13) we restrict r to range only over ω, we should replace equality with the $\geq$ sign. Let $U_\omega = \sum_{r\in\omega} U_r$. Then for a M/M/1 queue, we have

$$\sum_{r\in\omega} U_r R_r \geq \frac{1}{1-U_\omega} \sum_{r\in\omega} \frac{U_r}{\mu_r} \tag{2.14}$$

And for a M/G/1 queue with nonpreemptive scheduling,

$$\sum_{r\in\omega} U_r W_r \geq \frac{U_\omega}{1-U_\omega} \sum_{r\in\omega} U_r \gamma_r \tag{2.15}$$

Note carefully that R_r *and* W_r *in these equations are evaluated in the presence of classes other than* ω, and this is what results in $\geq$ relation. The significance of these inequalities is that they provide lower bounds on the weighted response times of the set of classes to which we wish to give favored treatment.

9.2.3 Properties of Renewal Processes

Renewal processes were introduced in Section 5.1.3. In this section we derive a few fundamental results for renewal processes and use them to analyze semi-Markov chains. Let $\{X_i\}$ denote a renewal process and $N(t)$ the number of renewals during the time interval $(0, t]$. From equation (5.1.4), the density function of $N(t)$, the number of renewals by time t, is given by

$$Pr[N(t) = n] = F_{(n)}(t) - F_{(n+1)}(t) \tag{2.16}$$

The quantity of main interest about renewal processes is the average number of renewals in time t, henceforth denoted as $M(t)$. From equation (B.1.30), we know that the expected value of a discrete, nonnegative random variable is simply the summation over its complementary distribution function. Therefore,

$$M(t) = \sum_{n=1}^{\infty} F_{(n)}(t) = \sum_{n=1}^{\infty} Pr[N(t) = n] + \sum_{n=1}^{\infty} F_{(n+1)}(t) \tag{2.17}$$

The first term in the last equation is simply $Pr[N(t) > 0]$, which is the same as the probability that the interevent time is no more than t. This, by definition, is

$F_X(t)$. Also, since $S_{n+1} = S_n + X_{n+1}$, we can view $F_{(n+1)}(t)$ as the convolution of $F_{(n)}(t)$ and $F_X(t)$. Therefore,

$$M(t) = F_X(t) + \sum_{n=1}^{\infty} \int_0^t F_{(n)}(t-x) f_X(x)\, dx \tag{2.18}$$

Taking the summation inside the integral, and again using equation (B.1.30), we finally get

$$M(t) = F_X(t) + \int_0^t M(t-x) f_X(x)\, dx \tag{2.19}$$

Thus, we get an integral equation for $M(t)$, often known as the *fundamental renewal equation*. We can write a similar equation for the *renewal density*, denoted $m(t)$. Renewal density is simply the instantaneous renewal rate, i.e., $m(t) = M'(t)$. From equation (2.19), we have

$$m(t) = f_X(t) + \int_0^t m(t-x) f_X(x)\, dx \tag{2.20}$$

Either of these equations is best solved using Laplace transforms. In fact, we can tackle a somewhat more general equation, known as the *renewal type equation*. Let $h(t)$ be an arbitrary but known function. Then the renewal type equation has the following form

$$g(t) = h(t) + \int_0^t g(t-x) f_X(x)\, dx \tag{2.21}$$

To solve this equation, we take Laplace transform on both sides. Let Ψ_g, Ψ_h, and Ψ_X denote Laplace transforms of $g(t)$, $h(t)$, and $f_X(t)$ respectively. By using the convolution property of Laplace transforms (see Appendix B), we get $\Psi_g(s) = \Psi_h(s) + \Psi_g(s)\Psi_X(s)$, which simplifies to

$$\Psi_g(s) = \Psi_h(s)/[1 - \Psi_X(s)] \tag{2.22}$$

Thus, $g(t)$ can be obtained by inverting the RHS of equation (2.22). It is, however, interesting to obtain an explicit expression for $g(t)$ in terms of $m(t)$, the renewal density. To this end, we first let $h(t) = f_X(t)$ in (2.22) to get the Laplace transform of the renewal density, i.e.,

$$\Psi_m(s) = \Psi_X(s)/[1 - \Psi_X(s)] \tag{2.23}$$

By inverting this, we can determine $m(t)$. As an example, consider the Poisson process for which $f_X(x) = \lambda e^{-\lambda x}$. Therefore, $\Psi_X(s) = \lambda/(\lambda + s)$ and $\Psi_m(s) = \lambda/s$, which means that $m(t) = \lambda$. That is, the renewal rate is λ and thus independent of time. Note that the interval $(0, t]$ may begin and end some arbitrary time after a renewal, yet the renewal rate remains constant, independent of t. This is basically a result of the memorylessness property of the exponential distribution.

From equation (2.23), $[1 - \Psi_X(s)]^{-1} = 1 + \Psi_m(s)$. Substituting this in equation (2.22), we have

$$\Psi_g(s) = \Psi_h(s) + \Psi_h(s)\Psi_m(s) \tag{2.24}$$

By inverting this, we get the desired solution

$$g(t) = h(t) + \int_0^t h(t-x)m(x)\,dx \tag{2.25}$$

We now mention two limit theorems without proof. First, from the law of large numbers, it is to be expected that the *time-averaged* renewal rate over a large time interval should approach the *expected* renewal rate. That is

$$\lim_{t\to\infty} \frac{M(t)}{t} = \frac{1}{E[X_i]} \tag{2.26}$$

where $E[X_i]$ is the expected renewal time. This result is known as the *elementary renewal theorem*. The second result gives us the behavior of $g(t)$ in equation (2.25) as $t \to \infty$. The result is

$$\lim_{t\to\infty} \int_0^t h(t-x)m(x)\,dx = \frac{1}{E[X_i]} \int_0^\infty h(z)\,dz \tag{2.27}$$

This is a fundamental result, known as the *key renewal theorem*. To illustrate its use, let us consider an erogodic semi-Markov chain. The successive entries to any given state i of this chain can be considered as its renewal points. Let C_i denote the length of the *renewal cycle* starting at state i. The parameter $\theta_{ii} = E[C_i]$ is known as the *mean recurrence time* for state i. We can write $C_i = X_i + Y_i$, where X_i is the time spent in state i and Y_i is the time spent elsewhere. By definition, the state i is visited only once during the renewal cycle and Y_i is independent of X_i. Let $E[X_i] = \theta_i$, and let $\mathcal{F}_i$ denote the fraction of time spent in state i. Obviously, $\mathcal{F}_i = X_i/(X_i + Y_i)$, and by definition, the state probability π_i is simply $E[\mathcal{F}_i]$. The next lemma shows that the expectation operator can be applied separately to the numerator and the denominator.

Lemma 9.1 The expected fraction of time spent in state i is given by:

$$\pi_i = E[X_i]/(E[X_i] + E[Y_i]) = \theta_i/\theta_{ii} \tag{2.28}$$

Proof Suppose that the process enters state i at time 0, and let $P_i(t)$ denote the probability that it is in state i at time t. Then,

$$P_i(t) = \int_0^\infty Pr[\text{in state } i \text{ at time } t | C_i = x] f_{C_i}(x)\,dx \tag{2.29}$$

Now if $x > t$, it means that the cycle time is longer than the observation time t; that is, the process never left state i since time 0, and hence $X_i > t$. However, if $x \le t$, it means that the process has gone through some previous cycles. Since all cycles are statistically identical, the situation in this case is the same as at time $t - x$. Therefore, we get the following recursion

$$Pr[\text{in state } i \text{ at time } t|C_i = x] = \begin{cases} P_i(t-x) & \text{if } x \le t \\ P(X_i > t|C_i = x) & \text{if } x > t \end{cases} \tag{2.30}$$

Substituting back in equation (2.29), we get

$$P_i(t) = \int_0^t P_i(t-x) f_{C_i}(x)\,dx + \int_t^\infty P(X_i > t|C_i = x) f_{C_i}(x)\,dx \tag{2.31}$$

By the definition of conditional probability, the second term in the above equation is simply $P(X_i > t)$. Thus, we get the following renewal type of equation

$$P_i(t) = 1 - F_{X_i}(t) + \int_0^t P_i(t-x) f_{C_i}(x)\,dx \tag{2.32}$$

which has an explicit solution as in (2.25). That is,

$$P_i(t) = 1 - F_{X_i}(t) + \int_0^t [1 - F_{X_i}(t-x)] m(x)\,dx \tag{2.33}$$

Now, $\pi_i = \lim_{t\to\infty} P_i(t)$ and by the definition of the distribution function, $F_{X_i}(\infty) = 1$. Therefore, by taking the limit as $t \to \infty$ and using the key renewal theorem, we get

$$\pi_i = \frac{1}{E[C_i]} \int_0^\infty [1 - F_{X_i}(x)]\,dx = \frac{E[X_i]}{E[C_i]} = \frac{\theta_i}{\theta_{ii}} \tag{2.34}$$

where we have used equation (B.1.29). □

We can specialize equation (2.28) for discrete and continuous parameter semi-Markov chains to get more explicit results. Let X_j denote the time spent in state j for each visit to state i and $E[X_j] = \theta_j$. Now in the discrete parameter case, θ_j's are measured as the number of visits to state j (for each visit to state i). Thus, $\theta_i = 1$ and θ_{ii} is given by equation (5.3.2). Therefore,

$$\pi_i = 1/\theta_{ii} \tag{2.35}$$

For a continuous parameter chain $\mathcal{Z}$, let r_j denote the mean *residence time* in state j, i.e., the time spent in state j on each visit. (If the chain is fully Markovian, $r_j = -1/q_{jj}$.) Then $\theta_i = r_i$. To characterize the number of visits to each state, we consider a discrete parameter chain $\mathcal{Z}^*$ embedded at the transition points of $\mathcal{Z}$. We could then show that:

Lemma 9.2 Let $[\pi_0', \pi_1', \ldots]$ and $Q' = [q_{ij}']$ denote, respectively, the state probability vector and the transition probability matrix of $\mathcal{Z}^*$. Then,

$$\pi_i = \pi_i' r_i \Big/ \sum_{j=0}^{\infty} \pi_j' r_j \tag{2.36}$$

Proof Let θ_{ji} denote the mean time taken by the chain $\mathcal{Z}$ to transit from state j to another state i. This quantity is often known as the *first passage time*. Obviously, θ_{ji} is r_j plus the passage time from state k to i if the chain transits to state k first, i.e.,

$$\theta_{ji} = r_j + \sum_{\forall k \neq i} q'_{jk}\theta_{ki} \tag{2.37}$$

Multiplying both sides by π'_j, summing over all j, and changing the order of the double summation, we get

$$\sum_{j=0}^{\infty} \pi'_j \theta_{ji} = \sum_{j=0}^{\infty} \pi'_j r_j + \sum_{k \neq i} \theta_{ki} \sum_{j=0}^{\infty} \pi'_j q'_{jk} \tag{2.38}$$

Now, by definition, the last summation on the right-hand side is simply π'_k. Therefore, by adding $\pi'_i\theta_{ii}$ on both sides and cancelling the common summation term, we get

$$\pi'_i \theta_{ii} = \sum_{j=0}^{\infty} \pi'_j r_j \tag{2.39}$$

Now by equation (2.28), $\pi_i = r_i/\theta_{ii}$, and we get the result. □

Since the embedded chain $\mathcal{Z}^*$ only captures visits to various states (but not the time spent in each state), we can interpret π'_j/π'_i as the number of visits to state j for each visit to state i. Thus, equation (2.36) could have been obtained directly as a result of (2.28). Equation (2.36) is useful whenever it is easier to compute Π' and mean state residence time of $X(t)$, instead of computing Π directly. We shall see an example of this in Section 12.3.1.

9.2.4 Solution Using Embedded Markov Chains

It is often the case that a continuous-time non-Markovian random process that we wish to analyze has a Markov chain embedded at certain points. Such a chain can be exploited in analyzing the system easily. In this section, we shall use this technique to analyze M/G/1, GI/M/c, and GI/G/1 type of queuing systems.

To start with, let us identify an embedded Markov chain in a M/M type of system itself. Let $\mathcal{Z}$ denote the continuous-time Markov chain for this system, and $\mathcal{Z}^*$ the discrete-parameter chain embedded at its transition points. Surely, $\mathcal{Z}^*$ is Markovian (for the simple reason that $\mathcal{Z}$ is Markovian). Let $Q' = [q'_{ij}]$ denote the transition probability matrix of $\mathcal{Z}^*$. Suppose that $\mathcal{Z}^*$ is in a state $n > 0$. At the next transition point, it can go to only one of the two states: $n+1$ (because of an arrival) or $n-1$ (because of a departure). The transition will be made depending on which of the two events (arrival or departure) occurs first. Let $X_a(n)$ and $X_s(n)$ denote, respectively, the interarrival and service times in state n. Since both $X_a(n)$ and $X_s(n)$ are exponentially distributed, it is easy to verify that for $n > 0$[2]

$$q'_{n,n+1} = Pr[X_a(n) < X_s(n)] = \frac{\lambda_n}{\lambda_n + \mu_n}$$
$$q'_{n,n-1} = Pr[X_s(n) < X_a(n)] = \frac{\mu_n}{\lambda_n + \mu_n} \tag{2.40}$$

Of course, $q'_{01} = 1$ since only an arrival can occur in this situation. We can now obtain the limiting distribution, say Π', for $\mathcal{Z}^*$ by solving the equation $\Pi' = \Pi' Q'$. Obviously, Π' will be different from Π, the limiting distribution for $\mathcal{Z}$, and the two are related via equation (2.36).

We now look at the M/G/1/FCFS/∞/∞ system. Here we can identify an embedded Markov chain $\mathcal{Z}^*$ at *departure points* of the original chain $\mathcal{Z}$. The state of $\mathcal{Z}^*$ is described by the number of customers left behind by a departing customer. Suppose that we start numbering the customers at some point. Let

$\mathcal{N}_k$: Number of customers left behind by the kth departing customer.

X_k: Number of arrivals during the service time of the kth customer.

Then

$$\mathcal{N}_k = \begin{cases} \mathcal{N}_{k-1} + X_k - 1 & \text{if } \mathcal{N}_{k-1} > 0 \\ X_k & \text{if } \mathcal{N}_{k-1} = 0 \end{cases} \tag{2.41}$$

In words, the first equation says that the number of customers left behind by the kth departer are those left behind by the $(k-1)$st departer, plus those that arrive during the service time of the kth customer, minus the kth customer itself. The second equation comes from the fact that if the $(k-1)$st customer left the system empty, nothing happens until the kth customer arrives and is put into service. So, the number left behind by the kth customer is X_k (rather than $X_k - 1$). This equation describes a semi-Markov chain because:

1. $\mathcal{N}_k$ depends only on $\mathcal{N}_{k-1}$ and *not* $\mathcal{N}_{k-2}, \mathcal{N}_{k-3}, \ldots$, etc.
2. The state residence times of $\mathcal{Z}^*$ (i.e., the interdeparture times in $\mathcal{Z}$) are arbitrarily distributed.[3]
3. The number of arrivals during a service time (X_k) is independent of any past history.

It appears that equation (2.41) does not require Poisson arrivals, and thus should hold for a GI/G/1 queue also. Whereas there is nothing in equation (2.41) itself that limits it to a M/G/1 queue, property (3) does not hold in general. To see this, suppose that the $(k-1)$st customer leaves at time t_d and the last

[2] Because of the memoryless property of the exponential distribution, at any point in time, the time until the next arrival (departure) has the same distribution as $X_a(n)$ ($X_s(n)$).

[3] When the system is nonempty, the interdeparture time equals service time; otherwise, it is a sum of the residual interarrival time and the service time. Because the arrivals are Poisson, the residual interarrival time has the same distribution as the full interarrival time.

arrival occurred at some time t_a before that. Then, in general, the probability of an arrival during the service time of the kth customer will depend on $(t_d - t_a)$. In other words, the number of arrivals during the service time of the kth customer will depend on what happened during the service time of the $(k-1)$st customer. This problem disappears if (and only if) the arrival process is Poisson, since in that case the remaining interarrival time has the same distribution as the full interarrival time.

Equation (2.41) can be used to analyze a M/G/1 system, but we shall defer the details until Section 9.3. This analysis only gives the departer's distribution, but from Section 9.2.1 we know that the random observer's distribution is also the same. Unfortunately, the above analysis does not apply to a M/G/c/FCFS case with $c > 1$ because the sequence $\{\mathcal{N}_k\}$ does not form a semi-Markov chain. The reason is that with more than one server, the $(k-1)$st and kth departers may come from two different servers, which means that we need to speak of the number of arrivals during the *remaining service time* of the kth departer. Since the service-time distribution is not memoryless, past history gets involved.

Next we consider a GI/M/1/FCFS/∞/∞ type of system. Here we can identify an embedded Markov chain at arrival instants. Again, we start numbering customers at some point. Let $\mathcal{N}_k$ denote the number of customers seen by the kth arrival, and Y_k the number of customers served during the interarrival time between kth and $(k+1)$st arrival. The $(k+1)$st arriver will see $\mathcal{N}_k$ customers, plus the kth arriver, minus the number that have been served during the interarrival time. Therefore,

$$\mathcal{N}_{k+1} = \begin{cases} \mathcal{N}_k + 1 - Y_k & \text{if } Y_k \leq \mathcal{N}_k + 1 \\ 0 & \text{otherwise} \end{cases} \tag{2.42}$$

This equation defines a Semi-Markov chain because $\mathcal{N}_{k+1}$ depends only on $\mathcal{N}_k$, the state residence times (i.e., interarrival times) are arbitrarily distributed, and Y_k is independent of the past history. We could write (2.42) even for a GI/G/1 queue, but Y_k would involve past history because the number of service completions between the kth and $(k+1)$st arrivals would depend on the *attained service* of the customer in service at the time of kth arrival. We can use equation (2.42) to find arriver's distribution in essentially the same way as we would proceed with (2.41) to find a departer's distribution. The arriver's distribution here is *not* the same as the random observer's distribution. However, the latter can be obtained easily. Let $\Psi_{\mathcal{A}}(s)$ denote the Laplace transform of the interarrival time density, and let σ be a positive root of the equation $x = \Psi_{\mathcal{A}}(\mu - \mu x)$ where $\mu = 1/E[\mathcal{S}]$ is the average service rate. It can be shown that such a root exists and is unique. Also, let $\rho = \lambda/\mu$ where $\lambda = 1/E[\mathcal{A}]$ is the average arrival rate. Then, it can be shown that

$$P(n) = \begin{cases} 1 - \rho & \text{if } n = 0 \\ \rho(1-\sigma)\sigma^{n-1} & \text{if } n > 0 \end{cases} \tag{2.43}$$

Since the distribution in (2.43) is basically geometric, all M/M/1 results apply almost directly. For example, the response-time distribution is easy to find and turns out to be exponential. Furthermore, *the analysis applies even for the GI/M/c/FCFS case with some minor changes*, because the time between successive arrivals is not affected by having multiple servers. In contrast, *in a M/G system, the time between successive departures is affected by having multiple servers*, and so the analysis does not apply to the multiserver case. Unfortunately, a GI/M system is practically not very useful, and we shall not study it in detail.

Next, we consider the GI/G/1/FCFS/∞/∞ system. Here we cannot identify an embedded Markov chain at either arrival or departure instants, and thus no direct solution method is known for the state probabilities. However, it is possible to identify an embedded *Markov process* for the waiting times. Let $\mathcal{W}_k$ denote the waiting time of kth customer, $\mathcal{A}_k$ the interarrival time between kth and $(k+1)$st customer, and $\mathcal{S}_k$ the service time of kth customer. Then,

$$\mathcal{W}_{k+1} = \begin{cases} \mathcal{W}_k + \mathcal{S}_k - \mathcal{A}_k & \text{if } \mathcal{W}_k + \mathcal{S}_k - \mathcal{A}_k > 0 \\ 0 & \text{if } \mathcal{W}_k + \mathcal{S}_k - \mathcal{A}_k \leq 0 \end{cases} \tag{2.44}$$

The sequence $\{\mathcal{W}_k\}$ is Markovian because $\mathcal{S}_k$ and $\mathcal{A}_k$ do not depend on any past history; in fact, they are independent of even the current state. (The "current state" here is the waiting time of the kth customer.) Let $\delta_k = \mathcal{S}_k - \mathcal{A}_k$. Then since δ_k is independent of $\mathcal{W}_k$, under steady state, the density function of the waiting time $\mathcal{W}$ is the convolution of itself with the density of δ. This gives the following equation for the density function of $\mathcal{W}$

$$f_{\mathcal{W}}(t) = \int_{-\infty}^{t} f_{\mathcal{W}}(t-x) f_{\delta}(x)\, dx \qquad \text{for } \; 0 \leq t < \infty \tag{2.45}$$

and $f_{\mathcal{W}}(t) = 0$ for $t < 0$. This is known as *Lindley's integral equation*. Note that this equation is different from a simple convolution equation because of the condition $f_{\mathcal{W}}(t) = 0$ for $t < 0$. This equation is difficult to solve in general, but if we express both interarrival and service-time distributions as branching Erlang distributions, it can be shown that the waiting-time distribution is *mixed exponential*, i.e., a weighted summation of several exponential distributions. Several other approximations have also been proposed for GI/G/1 queues. Here we quote one such approximation for the mean waiting time

$$W \approx \frac{CV_a^2 + \rho^2 CV_s^2}{1 + \rho^2 CV_s^2} \frac{\rho(1 + CV_s^2)}{2\mu(1-\rho)} \tag{2.46}$$

where $\rho = \lambda/\mu$ is the utilization, and CV_a, CV_s are the coefficient of variations of the interarrival and service times. This result is exact for M/G/1, good for GI/M/1, and fair for GI/G/1. It improves with ρ since it is derived from an upper bound for the heavy traffic case. Under heavy traffic, one can also use the *diffusion approximation* to get waiting time and queue length distributions. This approximation considers the system state $X(t)$ as a continuous variable. That is, each arrival causes an infinitesimal forward jump in $X(t)$ and a departure causes an infinitesimal backward jump. Thus, $X(t)$ essentially describes the current position of a particle subject to both backward and forward random displacements. The resulting partial differential equation is exactly the diffusion equation, and hence the name. This equation is solved with a reflecting boundary at zero so that $X(t)$ takes only nonnegative values. The details are somewhat involved and have been omitted. The queue length distribution turns out to be geometric, and is given by

$$P(n) = \begin{cases} 1-\rho & \text{if } n=0 \\ \rho(1-\sigma)\sigma^{n-1} & \text{if } n \geq 1 \end{cases} \tag{2.47}$$

where

$$\sigma = \exp\left[-2(1-\rho)/(\rho CV_a^2 + CV_s^2)\right] \tag{2.48}$$

Note that equation (2.47) is identical to (2.43), except that σ is defined differently. The geometric distribution is not surprising because the diffusion model claims that the future behavior of $X(t)$ depends only on the present. This, in a sense, is like assuming memorylessness, and hence the geometric distribution. This approximation is good when CV_s is small and ρ is large.

For completeness, we also briefly discuss some results for multiserver GI/G queues. Unfortunately, the recurrence equation (2.44) no longer holds because the $(k+1)$st customer may go to a server other than the one to which the kth customer went. Thus, the $(k+1)$st customer is not always delayed by the additional amount $\max(0, \mathcal{S}_k - \mathcal{A}_k)$. However, several approximations are available. One approximation is based on the upper bound for a GI/G/1 queue and the exact formula for M/M/c queue, and is given by

$$W = \frac{\mathcal{C}(\rho, c)}{c\mu(1-\rho)} \frac{CV_a^2 + CV_s^2}{2} \tag{2.49}$$

where $\mathcal{C}(\rho, c)$ is Erlang's C formula in equation (5.5.13). This formula is exact for M/M/c and M/G/1 queues, and reasonable otherwise. Generally, the error increases with both CV_a and CV_s, as expected.

A different way of approaching any kind of multiserver queue (e.g., GI/G/c or M/G/c) is to consider bounds in terms of "comparable" single-server queues. For the upper bound, we consider c single-server queues, with customers distributed cyclically to them. That is, the ith customer is sent to the $(\text{mod}(i, c) + 1)$st queue. Since all these queues would have identical performance parameters, we consider only one of them, denoted Z. Let $f_a(t)$ denote the interarrival time density in the original system. Then the interarrival time density for Z is a c-fold convolution of $f_a(t)$. The service-time distribution remains the same. Z can now be solved using the methods for single-server queues. Notice that the systematic assignment of customers restricts load sharing between servers; therefore, the waiting time computed for Z will be an upper bound on the waiting time in the original system.

For a lower bound, we replace the c servers with a single-server having the rate $c\mu$. Let us denote the parameters for the original multiserver by the subscript ms and for the single-server by ss. Let us consider the virtual delays V_{ms} and V_{ss} for the two systems. In the ss system, no service capacity ever goes idle, whereas in a ms system, not all the servers could be busy whenever the backlog drops below c. Therefore $V_{ss} \leq V_{ms}$. Now V_{ms} is the total service requirement of all waiting customers plus those in service. Using equation (5.5.12), we have

$$V_{ms} = L/\mu + c\rho E[\Gamma] \tag{2.50}$$

where Γ denotes the residual life given by equation (2.4) and $\rho = \lambda/(c\mu)$. Applying Little's law, this yields

$$V_{ms} = c\rho W_{ms} + \frac{c\rho(CV_s^2 + 1)}{2\mu} \tag{2.51}$$

In the single-server case, $Q = L + \rho$; therefore, by the same reasoning, the virtual wait for the single-server turns out to be

$$V_{ss} = c\rho W_{ss} + \frac{\rho(CV_s^2 + 1)}{2\mu} \tag{2.52}$$

In writing the last two equations, it is important to remember that only the work-capacity of the station changes; the work-requirement of the customers remains the same. (See Section 4.1.2). Therefore, in both the multiserver and single-server cases, we have to use the same work-requirement measure, which we can choose to be $1/\mu$. Now, the inequality $V_{ms} \geq V_{ss}$ yields

$$W_{ms} \geq W_{ss} - \frac{c-1}{c}\frac{CV_s^2 + 1}{2\mu} \tag{2.53}$$

In terms of response times, this relationship becomes

$$R_{ms} \geq R_{ss} - \frac{(c-1)(CV_s^2 - 1)}{2c\mu} \tag{2.54}$$

It is interesting to note that if $CV_s = 1$, $R_{ms} \geq R_{ss}$. This result was mentioned in Section 5.5.2. If $CV_s < 1$, the multiserver performs even worse. It improves with increasing CV_s.

These bounds can be applied to both M/G/c and GI/G/c queues. Even in the former case, the upper bound will be an approximation or a bound since we need to solve a E_c/G/1 queue.

9.3 The M/G/1 Queuing System

The M/G/1 queuing system arises in a great variety of applications; therefore, we shall study it in some detail. We shall assume FCFS discipline for now, but later show that *the resulting queue-length distribution holds for any nonpreemptive SI discipline*. The starting point of the analysis is equation (2.41). Since the random observer's distribution is the same as that of the departer, we shall henceforth work with the latter only. Let $\delta(x)$ be the *unit step function*, i.e., if $x \leq 0$ then $\delta(x) = 0$, else $\delta(x) = 1$. Then we can write (2.41) in the following compact form

$$\mathcal{N}_k = \mathcal{N}_{k-1} - \delta(\mathcal{N}_{k-1}) + X_k \tag{3.1}$$

Let λ denote the average arrival rate, and $\mathcal{S}$ the random variable for the service time. By the utilization law, $\rho = \lambda E[\mathcal{S}]$ is the steady-state utilization, and we can show that the Markov chain is ergodic for $\rho < 1$. Under steady state, the subscript k does not play any role in the distributions, and will be omitted.

9.3.1 Queue-Length Moments

There are three ways of proceeding from equation (3.1) to get queue-length moments, and it is instructive to briefly look at all of them, since these three methods can be used for *any* embedded Markov chain. The first method is to start working with expected values right away. This is most useful if we are only interested in the average queue length $Q = E[\mathcal{N}_k]$. Taking expected values of both sides of equation (3.1), we get $E[\delta(\mathcal{N})] = E[X]$ where we have dropped the subscripts from $\mathcal{N}$ and X. By its very definition, $E[\delta(\mathcal{N})] = \rho$, which means that $E[X] = \rho$. Next, squaring both sides of (3.1) and taking expected values we get

$$E[\mathcal{N}^2] = E[(\mathcal{N} - \delta(\mathcal{N}))^2] + E[X^2] + 2E[X]E[\mathcal{N} - \delta(\mathcal{N})] \tag{3.2}$$

Since,

$$E[(\mathcal{N} - \delta(\mathcal{N}))^k] = \sum_{n=0}^{\infty}[n - \delta(n)]^k P(\mathcal{N} = n) = \sum_{n=1}^{\infty}(n-1)^k P(\mathcal{N} = n) \tag{3.3}$$

for any k, expanding (3.2) and substituting Q for $E[\mathcal{N}]$ we get $-2Q+\rho+E[X^2]+2\rho Q - 2\rho^2 = 0$, which simplifies to

$$Q = [\rho - 2\rho^2 + E[X^2]]/[2(1-\rho)] \tag{3.4}$$

Since the arrivals are Poisson, $E[X^2|\mathcal{S} = t] = (\lambda t)^2 + \lambda t$ (the second moment of the Poisson distribution). Unconditioning over $\mathcal{S}$, we get

$$E[X^2] = \lambda^2 E[\mathcal{S}^2] + \lambda E[\mathcal{S}] = \rho^2(1 + CV_s^2) + \rho \tag{3.5}$$

where CV_s is the coefficient of variation of the service time. Thus, we get the final result

$$Q = \frac{\rho}{1-\rho} + \frac{\rho^2(CV_s^2 - 1)}{2(1-\rho)} \tag{3.6}$$

This equation is known as the *Pollaczek-Khinchine formula*. Note that the first term on the RHS of this equation is Q_{exp}, the average queue length for a comparable M/M/1 system. The second term increases rapidly with CV_s^2; therefore, the assumption of exponential service time is poor when CV_s is large. At the other extreme, i.e., for a M/D/1 system,

$$Q_{\text{det}} = \frac{\rho(1-\rho/2)}{1-\rho} = \left(1 - \frac{\rho}{2}\right) Q_{\text{exp}} \tag{3.7}$$

which shows that under heavy traffic, the queue length with deterministic service is only about one-half of that for the exponential case. One final point to note about the M/G/1 queue is that the average waiting time is very simply related to the average remaining service time. By Little's law $W = L/\lambda = (Q - \rho)/\lambda$ and can be expressed as

$$W = \frac{\rho}{1-\rho}\gamma \quad \text{where } \gamma = \frac{(1 + CV_s^2)}{2} E[\mathcal{S}] \tag{3.8}$$

Obviously, γ is the expected residual life. Thus, $W = Q_{\text{exp}}\gamma$. Since $W = Q_{\text{exp}}.s$ for a M/M/1 queue, it is interesting to note that by simply replacing full service time with the residual service time, we get results for a M/G/1 queue! Another point to note is that the asymptotic behavior of a M/G/1 queue as $\rho \to 1$ is similar to that of a M/M/1 queue; i.e., the queue length and waiting time increase as $1/(1-\rho)$. Even the GI/G/1 queue shows a similar asymptotic behavior.

The next method is based on z-transforms and yields the queue length distribution. Let $\Phi(z)$ denote the z-transform of $\mathcal{N}$. Since by definition $\Phi(z) = E[z^{\mathcal{N}}]$, and X_k is independent of $\mathcal{N}_{k-1}$, equation (3.1) yields

$$\Phi(z) = E\left[z^{\mathcal{N}_{k-1}-\delta(\mathcal{N}_{k-1})}\right] E[z^{X_k}] \tag{3.9}$$

Dropping the subscript k, the first term on the right-hand side evaluates to

$$\begin{aligned} E\left[z^{\mathcal{N}-\delta(\mathcal{N})}\right] &= \sum_{n=0}^{\infty} z^{[n-\delta(n)]} P(\mathcal{N}=n) = P(0) + \sum_{n=1}^{\infty} z^{n-1} P(\mathcal{N}=n) \\ &= P(0) + \frac{\Phi(z) - P(0)}{z} \end{aligned} \tag{3.10}$$

The second term in (3.9) is easy to evaluate, since the arrival process is Poisson with rate λ. Let a_n denote the probability of n arrivals during the service time of a customer, i.e., $a_n = Pr(X = n)$. Then,

$$a_n = \int_0^{\infty} P(X = n|\mathcal{S} = t) f_{\mathcal{S}}(t)\,dt = \int_0^{\infty} \frac{e^{-\lambda t}(\lambda t)^n}{n!} f_{\mathcal{S}}(t)\,dt \tag{3.11}$$

Let $\Psi_{\mathcal{S}}$ denote the Laplace transform of the service time density. Then,

$$E[z^X] = \sum_{n=0}^{\infty} a_n z^n = \int_0^{\infty} e^{-\lambda t}\left(\sum_{n=0}^{\infty} \frac{(\lambda z t)^n}{n!}\right) f_{\mathcal{S}}(t)\,dt \tag{3.12}$$

$$= \int_0^{\infty} e^{-\lambda t(1-z)} f_{\mathcal{S}}(t)\,dt = \Psi_{\mathcal{S}}(\lambda - \lambda z) \tag{3.13}$$

Therefore, from equations (3.9), (3.10), and (3.13), we get

$$\Phi(z) = \frac{(z-1)\Psi_{\mathcal{S}}(\lambda - \lambda z)(1-\rho)}{z - \Psi_{\mathcal{S}}(\lambda - \lambda z)} \tag{3.14}$$

where we have replaced $P(0)$ by $1-\rho$. The queue length could then be obtained as $\Phi'(1)$, and gives the same result as equation (3.6).

The last method is to use equation (5.2.8), which gives solution to any discrete parameter Markov chain under steady state. For this, we need to determine the transition probability matrix $\hat{Q}$ for the embedded Markov chain. Let q_{ij} be the (i, j)th element of $\hat{Q}$. Then using equation (2.41) we can define the nonzero elements of q_{ij}'s as follows:

$$q_{ij} = \begin{cases} a_{j-i+1} & \text{if } i > 0,\ j \geq i-1 \\ a_j & \text{if } i = 0 \end{cases}$$

where a_n is again given by equation (3.11). That is,

$$\hat{Q} = \begin{bmatrix} a_0 & a_1 & a_2 & a_3 & \cdots \\ a_0 & a_1 & a_2 & a_3 & \cdots \\ 0 & a_0 & a_1 & a_2 & \cdots \\ 0 & 0 & a_0 & a_1 & \cdots \\ . & . & . & . & \cdots \\ . & . & . & . & \cdots \end{bmatrix} \tag{3.15}$$

Unfortunately, the equation $\Pi = \Pi\hat{Q}$ cannot be solved explicitly here, so we still have to resort to taking z-transform of this equation (by multiplying it with $[1\ z\ z^2\ z^3\ \ldots]^T$ on both sides). However, the method is still important because it shows how to analyze a number of variants of the basic M/G/1 queue, such as the M/G/1/FCFS/N/N queue, M/G/1 queue with batch arrivals, and the M/G/1 queue where the mean service rate can change at departure points. For example, in a M/G/1/FCFS/N/N system, everything remains the same except that Π and Q become finite. Also, as discussed in Section 9.2.1, the departer's distribution is now a renormalization of the random observer's distribution, rather than being equal to it. Similarly, to analyze a M/G/1 system with batch arrivals, we only have to modify equation (3.11) to take batch arrivals into account (though this does not directly give us the random observer's distribution). Finally, if the service rate can change at departure points, the only change is that the transition probabilities q_{ij}'s depend not only on $j - i$ but also on i.

The analysis above applies to any nonpreemptive SI discipline, since (2.41) only concerns the kth *departing* customer, irrespective of the exact order of service. Obviously, preemption will invalidate this equation; and in fact we have already seen that under the PS discipline, CV_s is not involved in the queue length expression. It is also important to realize that if we consider a priority discipline, where different priority classes have different average service time requirements, the results again do not hold, since the customers *are* being distinguished based on their service time requirements.

9.3.2 Response-Time and Busy-Period Distribution

For a M/G/1/FCFS system, response-time distribution is easy to compute because of the following observation: the customers left behind by a departer are exactly those that arrived during its response time. That is, the probability that a customer leaves behind n in the system is the same as the probability of n

arrivals during its response time. Since the arrivals are Poisson, this yields the following relationship

$$P(n) = \int_0^\infty \frac{(\lambda t)^n e^{-\lambda t}}{n!} f_{\mathcal{R}}(t)\, dt \tag{3.16}$$

where $f_{\mathcal{R}}(t)$ is the density function of the response time. Notice that $P(n)$ is really the departer's distribution, but is the same as that of a random observer for a M/G/1 queue. By taking z-transform of both sides of (3.16), we get [see equation (3.12)]

$$\Phi(z) = \sum_{n=0}^{\infty} z^n P(n) = \int_0^\infty e^{-\lambda t(1-z)} f_{\mathcal{R}}(t)\, dt \tag{3.17}$$

Let $\Psi_{\mathcal{R}}$ denote the Laplace transform of the response time density function. Then, the last equation can be written as follows:

$$\Phi(z) = \Psi_{\mathcal{R}}[\lambda(1-z)] \tag{3.18}$$

We can derive two results from this. Let $FQ^{(k)}$ denote the kth *factorial moment* of queue length, i.e.,

$$FQ^{(k)} = E[\mathcal{N}(\mathcal{N}-1)\cdots(\mathcal{N}-k+1)] \tag{3.19}$$

By the basic property of z-transforms, $FQ^{(k)}$ is simply the kth order derivative of $\Phi(z)$ evaluated at $z = 1$. Thus, by differentiating (3.18) k times and evaluating at $z = 1$, we get the following generalization of Little's Law

$$FQ^{(k)} = \lambda^k R^{(k)} \qquad \text{for } k \geq 1 \tag{3.20}$$

where $R^{(k)}$ is the *regular* kth order moment of response time, and comes from the moment generation property of Laplace transforms. This result says that the response time moments can be computed trivially from the queue-length moments for a M/G/1/FCFS queue. This is not true with other disciplines (including other nonpreemptive SI disciplines). A similar result can also be obtained for waiting times, and it applies even to a M/G/c/FCFS queue. Note that in a M/G/c/FCFS queue, the probability of n arrivals during the waiting time of a customer must be the same as the probability that a customer leaves behind n customers *waiting in the queue*. Therefore, equation (3.16) applies if n represents the number of waiting customers (left behind by a departer) and $\mathcal{R}$ is the waiting time. It follows that for a M/G/c/FCFS queue, we have

$$FL^{(k)} = \lambda^k W^{(k)}, \qquad k \geq 1 \tag{3.21}$$

where $FL^{(k)}$ is the kth factorial moment of waiting line length and $W^{(k)}$ is the ordinary kth moment of waiting time. Equations (3.20) and (3.21) are often known as *distributional forms of Little's Law*.

For the second result, we substitute (3.14) into (3.18) and change the variable from $\lambda(1-z)$ to s. This gives us an equation for $\Psi_{\mathcal{R}}(s)$, the Laplace transform of the response time density

$$\Psi_{\mathcal{R}}(s) = \frac{(1-\rho)s\Psi_{\mathcal{S}}(s)}{s-\lambda[1-\Psi_{\mathcal{S}}(s)]} \tag{3.22}$$

which provides another way of computing response time moments. This equation can also be derived by accounting for the delays suffered by a tagged customer, as in Section 5.5.7. In fact, it is possible to obtain response-time distribution for many other scheduling disciplines, and the interested reader may wish to consult Kleinrock (1976). If we are only interested in average performance parameters, even complex disciplines can be handled easily, as we saw in Section 8.3.

In some applications of the M/G/1 queue (e.g., token ring with exhaustive service), it is desirable to find the moments of the *busy period*, i.e., the duration of time for which the queue remains nonempty. Let $\mathcal{B}$ denote the busy period, $f_{\mathcal{B}}(x)$ its density function, and $\Psi_{\mathcal{B}}(s)$ the Laplace transform of this density. Each busy period starts when a customer arrives to an idle system. Let us denote this first customer as $\mathcal{F}$, and its service time as $\mathcal{S}$. During this service time, more customers may arrive, each of which starts its own busy period. Let $\mathcal{C}$ denote the sum of all these secondary busy periods. Then, $\mathcal{B} = \mathcal{S} + \mathcal{C}$, and hence by the convolution property, we have

$$f_{\mathcal{B}}(x) = \int_0^x f_{\mathcal{C}}(x-t) f_{\mathcal{S}}(t)\, dt \tag{3.23}$$

Now by conditioning on the number of arrivals during t, we get

$$f_{\mathcal{B}}(x) = \int_0^x \sum_{n=0}^{\infty} f_{\mathcal{B}}^{(n)}(x-t) \frac{(\lambda t)^n e^{-\lambda t}}{n!} f_{\mathcal{S}}(t)\, dt \tag{3.24}$$

where $f_{\mathcal{B}}^{(n)}$ is the n-fold convolution of $f_{\mathcal{B}}$ and gives the density of the secondary busy period $\mathcal{C}$ under the condition that exactly n arrivals occur during the service time of $\mathcal{F}$. For conciseness, let $\alpha_n(t) = (\lambda t)^n e^{-\lambda t} f_{\mathcal{S}}(t)/n!$. By taking the Laplace transform of both sides, we get

$$\begin{aligned}
\Psi_{\mathcal{B}}(s) &= \int_{x=0}^{\infty} \int_{t=0}^{x} \sum_{n=0}^{\infty} e^{-sx} f_{\mathcal{B}}^{(n)}(x-t)\alpha_n(t)\, dt\, dx \\
&= \int_{t=0}^{\infty} \int_{x=t}^{\infty} \sum_{n=0}^{\infty} e^{-sx} f_{\mathcal{B}}^{(n)}(x-t)\alpha_n(t)\, dx\, dt \\
&= \int_{t=0}^{\infty} \sum_{n=0}^{\infty} e^{-st}[\Psi_{\mathcal{B}}(s)]^n \alpha_n(t)\, dt = \int_0^{\infty} e^{-(s+\lambda)t} \exp[\lambda t \Psi_{\mathcal{B}}(s)] f_{\mathcal{S}}(t)\, dt
\end{aligned}$$

where the last step is obtained by noting that $\sum_{n=0}^{\infty} x^n/n! = e^x$. Now, the integral in the above equation is the Laplace transform of the service time density evaluated at $s + \lambda - \lambda\Psi_{\mathcal{B}}(s)$. Thus, we get the following implicit equation for the Laplace transform of the busy period

$$\Psi_{\mathcal{B}}(s) = \Psi_{\mathcal{S}}[s + \lambda - \lambda\Psi_{\mathcal{B}}(s)] \tag{3.25}$$

The mean and variance of the busy period could then be computed from (3.25), and are reported below:

$$E[\mathcal{B}] = \frac{E[\mathcal{S}]}{(1-\rho)}, \qquad \text{Var}[\mathcal{B}] = \frac{(CV_s^2 + \rho)(E[\mathcal{S}])^2}{(1-\rho)^3} \tag{3.26}$$

where, as usual, $\rho = \lambda E[\mathcal{S}]$ is the utilization. It is interesting to note that the mean busy period depends only on the mean of service-time distribution, and in fact is the same as the response time of a comparable M/M/1 queue!

9.4 Phase-Type Distributions

In this section, we briefly study a special class of probability distributions that are defined via a finite Markov chain. These distributions can be thought of as generalizations of the stage type distributions discussed in Section B.2.2. These distributions are fundamental to the matrix analytic solution techniques discussed in Section 9.5.

9.4.1 Continuous Phase-Type Distributions

Consider a continuous parameter Markov chain $\mathcal{Z}$ with $k+1$ states, of which states $1..k$ are transient and state $k+1$ is *absorbing*; i.e., a process in state $k+1$ must stay there forever. Suppose that the chain is started with initial distribution $\Pi(0) = [\alpha_1, \ldots, \alpha_k, 0]$. Let X denote the random variable that gives the time until absorption. Then we say that X has a *phase-type distribution*. More specifically, we say that X is $PH(A, \boldsymbol{\alpha})$ where the parameters A and $\boldsymbol{\alpha}$ are defined as follows:

- Let A^* denote the transition rate matrix of $\mathcal{Z}$. Since state $k+1$ is an absorbing state, we can write A^* as

  $$A^* = \begin{bmatrix} A & \boldsymbol{\eta} \\ 0 & 0 \end{bmatrix} \tag{4.1}$$

  Thus, A is the portion of the transition rate matrix having to do with the first k states, and $\boldsymbol{\eta}$ is a *column vector* giving the rate of absorption while in states $1..k$. Since the matrix A^* must be c-stochastic, we have $\boldsymbol{\eta} = -A \cdot \mathbf{e}$, where $\mathbf{e}$ denotes a *column vector* of all 1's. In the following, we shall use $-A \cdot \mathbf{e}$ and $\boldsymbol{\eta}$ interchangeably.

- $\boldsymbol{\alpha}$ essentially specifies $\Pi(0)$. That is, we assume that $\mathcal{Z}$ is not in state $k+1$ initially, and let $\Pi(0) = [\boldsymbol{\alpha}, 0]$. (In rare cases, one cannot assume that $\alpha_{k+1} = 0$, and it should be specified explicitly.)

To obtain the distribution of X, note that the probability of the absorption occurring by time t is the same as $\pi_{k+1}(t)$, i.e., the probability that the system is (or has arrived) in state $k+1$ by time t. From equation (5.2.15), the transient solution of $\mathcal{Z}$ is $\Pi(t) = \Pi(0)\exp(A^*t)$. This can be rewritten as

$$\Pi(t) = [\alpha_1 \ \cdots \ \alpha_k \ \ 0]\begin{bmatrix} e^{At} & \mathbf{e} - e^{At}\cdot\mathbf{e} \\ 0 & 1 \end{bmatrix} \tag{4.2}$$

Thus, we get the following expression for the distribution function of X

$$F_X(t) = \pi_{k+1}(t) = 1 - \boldsymbol{\alpha} e^{At}\cdot\mathbf{e} \tag{4.3}$$

where we have used the fact that $\sum_{i=1}^{k}\alpha_i = 1$. Differentiating equation (4.3) and using $-A\cdot\mathbf{e} = \boldsymbol{\eta}$, we get the density function of X

$$f_X(t) = \boldsymbol{\alpha} e^{At}\boldsymbol{\eta} \tag{4.4}$$

From this equation, the Laplace transform of the density can be obtained as (see Exercise 9.8)

$$\Psi_X(s) = \int_0^\infty e^{-st} f_X(t)\,dt = \boldsymbol{\alpha}(sI - A)^{-1}\boldsymbol{\eta} \tag{4.5}$$

Using the moment generation property of Laplace transforms and $\boldsymbol{\eta} = -A\cdot\mathbf{e}$, we get the following expression for the moments of the phase-type distribution

$$E[X^n] = (-1)^n\, n!\,\boldsymbol{\alpha}\, A^{-n}\cdot\mathbf{e} \tag{4.6}$$

In the above, we implicitly assumed that the system is absorbed (i.e., reaches state $k+1$) with probability 1. This can be guaranteed *irrespective of the value of* $\boldsymbol{\alpha}$ if state $k+1$ is reachable from every other state. Using this and the basic properties of the $A = [a_{ij}]$ matrix (i.e., $a_{ii} < 0$, $a_{ij} \geq 0$ for $i \neq j$, and $|a_{ii}| \geq \sum_{j\neq i} a_{ij}$) we can show that A must be nonsingular, and thus A^{-1} exists. This further means that all eigenvalues of A must be nonpositive. [See discussion following equation (5.2.16)].

Phase-type distributions are closely related to the stage type distributions studied in Appendix B. In particular, the behavior of $\mathcal{Z}$ can be mimicked by a generalized stage-type distribution, denoted $\mathcal{Z}^*$, whose stages are simply the states of $\mathcal{Z}$. The routing probabilities among the stages can be obtained as the transition probabilities of the Markov chain embedded at the transition points of $\mathcal{Z}$. Because of the Markovian property, we know that the residence time of each state of $\mathcal{Z}$ (and hence the service time of each stage of $\mathcal{Z}^*$) must be exponential. Let γ_i denote the average service time in stage i. From the discussion in Section 5.3, it follows that γ_i is the inverse of the total rate at which the system moves out of state i. The initial distribution $\boldsymbol{\alpha}$ of $\mathcal{Z}$ is represented in $\mathcal{Z}^*$ by having an entry point and regarding α_i as the routing probability from the entry point to stage i. Fig. 9-2 shows an example of $\mathcal{Z}$ and the corresponding $\mathcal{Z}^*$. Here $\mathcal{Z}$ contains three states, of which states 1 and 2 are transient and state 3 is absorbing. The transition probabilities of the embedded chain can be computed following the

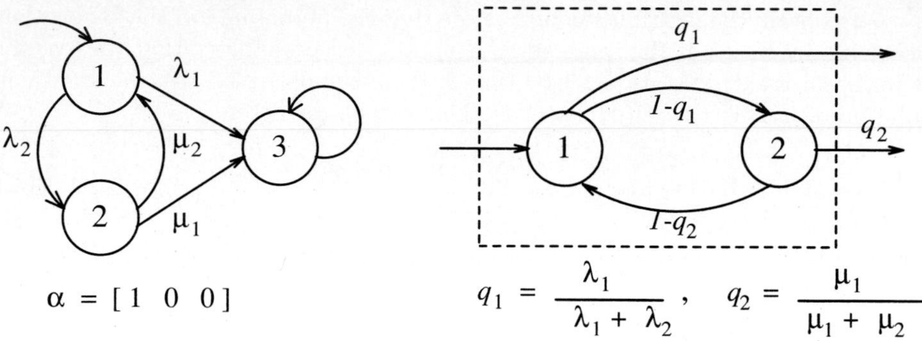

FIGURE 9-2: (a) A Markov chain $\mathcal{Z}$ and (b) Its stage representation.

discussion in Section 9.2.4 and are as shown. The mean state-residence times (or the mean service times of corresponding stages) are obviously $\gamma_1 = 1/(\lambda_1 + \lambda_2)$ and $\gamma_2 = 1/(\mu_1 + \mu_2)$. It is clear that the absorption-time distribution of $\mathcal{Z}$ is identical to the service-time distribution of $\mathcal{Z}^*$.

We can now see that the stage type distributions discussed in Appendix B are merely special cases of general phase-type distributions. In particular, a k-stage Erlang distribution is represented by a Markov chain where state i can only lead to state $i+1$ with rate $k\mu$, and the system is in state 1 initially. Similarly, the hyperexponential distribution corresponds to a Markov chain where each state i leads directly to state $k+1$ (with rate μ_i) and $\alpha_i = q_i$. The branching Erlang distribution (defined with only real-valued parameters) can also be easily seen as a special case of phase-type distributions.

Phase-type distributions have several other advantages. Note that equations (4.3) through (4.6) have a striking resemblance to the corresponding expressions for the exponential distribution. In fact, for $k = 1$ we get the regular exponential distribution with rate η. Thus, *we can consider phase-type distributions as matrix generalizations of the exponential distribution*, which makes them desirable for numeric computations. They are also attractive in recursive computations, because they are closed under many operations. Here we state only two closure properties. Let X and Y be two independent random variables with $X \sim PH(A, \boldsymbol{\alpha})$ (meaning that X has $PH(A, \boldsymbol{\alpha})$ distribution), and $Y \sim PH(B, \boldsymbol{\beta})$. Then the closure holds under the following operations:

Convolution: Let $Z = X+Y$. Then the density of Z is the convolution of densities of X and Y, and $\Psi_Z(s) = \Psi_X(s)\Psi_Y(s)$. Using equation (4.5), it is then easy to show that $Z \sim PH(C, \boldsymbol{\alpha})$, where

$$C = \begin{bmatrix} A & -A \cdot \mathbf{e}\boldsymbol{\beta} \\ 0 & B \end{bmatrix} \tag{4.7}$$

Mixture: Suppose that Z takes the values of X with probability q and those of Y with probability $1-q$. From equation (4.3) it is easy to show that $Z \sim PH(C, \boldsymbol{\gamma})$

where

$$\gamma = [q\boldsymbol{\alpha} \;\; (1-q)\boldsymbol{\beta}], \qquad C = \begin{bmatrix} A & 0 \\ 0 & B \end{bmatrix} \tag{4.8}$$

More details on the closure properties may be found in Neuts (1981, chapter 2). In particular, the integral $\int_0^x (1 - F_X(t))dt$ also has a phase-type representation, and so do $Z = \max(X, Y)$ and $Z = \min(X, Y)$. Unfortunately, in the last two cases, the size of the resulting matrices is the product of the sizes of constituent matrices, thereby severely limiting their usefulness.

9.4.2 Discrete Phase-Type Distributions

The development of discrete phase-type distributions is almost identical to the continuous case. In particular, we define such distributions as the time of absorption of a $k+1$ state discrete parameter Markov chain with transition probability matrix A^* given by

$$A^* = \begin{bmatrix} A & \boldsymbol{\eta} \\ 0 & 1 \end{bmatrix} \tag{4.9}$$

Since A^* must be a d-stochastic matrix, $\boldsymbol{\eta} = \mathbf{e} - A \cdot \mathbf{e}$ is a column vector that gives the probability of absorption in states $1..k$. We denote this distribution as $PH(A, \boldsymbol{\alpha})$ where $\boldsymbol{\alpha}$ specifies $\Pi(0)$. We again assume that state $k+1$ is reachable from every other state. In this case, the matrix $I - A$ will always have an inverse. We now denote the random variable for time until absorption as N. Again, $F_N(n) = \pi_{k+1}(n)$ where $\pi_{k+1}(n)$ can be obtained from the transient solution $\Pi(n) = \Pi(0)[A^*]^n$. This gives the following expression for $F_N(n)$.

$$F_N(n) = \boldsymbol{\alpha}(I - A^n) \cdot \mathbf{e} \qquad n = 1, 2, 3, \ldots \tag{4.10}$$

Since $f_N(n) = F_N(n) - F_N(n-1)$ and $(I - A) \cdot \mathbf{e} = \boldsymbol{\eta}$, we get the following expression for the mass function

$$f_N(n) = \boldsymbol{\alpha} A^{n-1} \boldsymbol{\eta} \qquad n = 1, 2, 3, \ldots \tag{4.11}$$

We could have obtained (4.11) directly as well, by noting that to fall into state $k+1$ in the nth transition, the system must go to some state, say j, after the first $n-1$ transitions and then transit to state $k+1$. The z-transform of the mass function can be obtained as

$$\Phi(z) = \sum_{n=1}^{\infty} z^n f_N(n) = z\boldsymbol{\alpha}(I - zA)^{-1}\boldsymbol{\eta} \tag{4.12}$$

and by differentiation, the factorial moments as

$$E[N(N-1)\cdots(N-k+1)] = n!\boldsymbol{\alpha} A^{n-1}(I - A)^{-n} \cdot \mathbf{e} \tag{4.13}$$

Discrete PH distributions also have a number of interesting properties, most of which parallel the corresponding properties of the continuous PH distributions. As we saw in Section 5.1, the geometric distribution plays the same role in the discrete case as the exponential distribution does in the continuous case. Thus, *discrete PH distributions appear as matrix generalizations of the geometric distribution*. In particular, equations (4.10) through (4.13) closely resemble the equations for the geometric distribution and reduce to them when $k = 1$. Discrete PH distributions are also closed under the operations mentioned above, i.e., (discrete) convolution, probabilistic selection, summation, max and min with representations similar to the ones for the continuous case. In addition, they possess the following two properties that are not true of their continuous counterparts.

1. A time shift retains the phase-type nature. That is, if $f_X(n)$ is of phase-type, then so will $f_X(n+m)$, for both $m > 0$ and $m < 0$.
2. Any discrete density that is nonzero only over a finite number of points can be considered to be of phase-type by associating a state with each such point.

Finally, it is easy to show that an infinite mixture of continuous PH densities in proportions defined by a discrete PH density is itself of phase-type.

9.5 Matrix-Analytic Methods

In this section, we study a special class of nonexponential queuing systems that can be solved using matrix techniques (as opposed to the transform techniques of the previous sections). In particular, we shall analyze a rather broad class of systems, whose solution resembles that of G/M systems except that the scalar operations are replaced by matrix operations. That is, the form σ^n for a G/M/1 queue is replaced by R^n, where R is a matrix.[4] These *matrix-geometric* techniques are a special case of the more general *matrix analytic* techniques that we will mention only briefly. The main advantage of such methods is computational convenience, as we shall see shortly.

Matrix analytic methods are useful in a variety of situations including analysis of queuing systems using phase-type distributions, analysis of degradable systems and systems with blocking, studying pseudotransient behavior of queuing systems, and as finite approximations to infinite-state systems.

9.5.1 Analysis of M/PH/1 Queue

The close resemblance between PH (phase-type) distributions and the corresponding scalar distributions is not limited to distributions alone and carries over to the solution of a large variety of queuing systems using phase-type distributions. In particular, the solutions to PH/M/1, M/PH/1, and PH/PH/1 queues become geometric in terms of matrices. From a computational standpoint there is little reason to expand the matrices symbolically and get scalar expressions

[4]This notation conflicts with our usual notation for response time; we did not change it in order to retain compatibility with much of the literature on matrix-geometric solutions.

(and surely, such expressions would be as complex as those obtained by the techniques of Section 5.6). Thus, in effect, we can handle distributions more general than branching Erlang and yet obtain results that are almost identical in form to those obtained assuming exponential distribution!

In this section, we shall illustrate how matrix-geometric solutions come about by considering a rather simple example of a M/PH/1/FCFS/∞/∞ queuing system. In this system, arrivals are Poisson, say with rate λ, and the service time $\mathcal{S}$ has a phase-type distribution, denoted as $PH(A, \boldsymbol{\alpha})$. The state of this system can be represented by the pair (n, i), where n is the total number of customers in the system and i is the phase of the customer in service. (For $n = 0$, we have only one state, however.) Let π_{ni} denote the steady-state probability of state (n, i) and let Π be a vector of these. Let Q denote the transition rate matrix. Let us order the states as 0, $(1,1), (1,2), \ldots, (1,k)$, $(2,1), (2,2), \ldots, (2,k)$, etc. We shall express Π as $[\pi_0,\ \Pi_1,\ \Pi_2,\ \ldots\ ]$ where $\Pi_n = [\pi_{n1}, \ldots, \pi_{nk}]$. We call n as a *macrostate*, and (n, i) as a *microstate*. This partitioning of Π induces a similar partitioning of the transition rate matrix Q. For ease of reference, we shall denote the partitioned matrix as $\tilde{Q}$ (even though it is still the same matrix). We have,

$$\tilde{Q} = \begin{array}{c} \\ 0 \\ 1 \\ 2 \\ 3 \\ 4 \\ \cdot \\ \cdot \end{array} \left[\begin{array}{cccccc} 0 & 1 & 2 & 3 & 4 & 5 \\ -\lambda & \lambda\boldsymbol{\alpha} & 0 & 0 & \cdot & \cdot \\ \boldsymbol{\eta} & A - \lambda I & \lambda I & 0 & \cdot & \cdot \\ 0 & \boldsymbol{\eta\alpha} & A - \lambda I & \lambda I & \cdot & \cdot \\ 0 & 0 & \boldsymbol{\eta\alpha} & A - \lambda I & \lambda I & \cdot \\ 0 & 0 & 0 & \boldsymbol{\eta\alpha} & A - \lambda I & \cdot \\ \cdot & \cdot & \cdot & \cdot & \cdot & \cdot \\ \cdot & \cdot & \cdot & \cdot & \cdot & \cdot \end{array} \right] \tag{5.1}$$

Here the row/column numbers correspond to the values of n. That is, with the exception of the first row and first column, each entry in the matrix is itself a matrix of size $k \times k$. Obviously, the element in position (0,0) is a scalar ($= -\lambda$). Other elements in row 0 are $1 \times k$ vectors, and those in column 0 are $k \times 1$ vectors.

To see how this structure arises, let us consider the elements of Q. If the system is in microstate (n, i), an arrival will take it to the microstate $(n+1, i)$ with rate λ. This means that in $\tilde{Q}$, the element in position $(n, n+1)$ will be the matrix λI, where I is the identity matrix. A departure will leave $n-1$ customers, and the next customer to be served can start in some phase j with probability α_j. Since the departure (or absorption) rate in phase i is η_i, the system will move to microstate $(n-1, j)$ with probability $\eta_i\alpha_j$. This gives rise to the $\boldsymbol{\eta\alpha}$ matrix. (Recall that $\boldsymbol{\eta}$ is a *column vector*, whereas $\boldsymbol{\alpha}$ is a *row vector*, which means that $\boldsymbol{\eta\alpha}$ is a $k \times k$ matrix.) Since the interarrival and service phase times are exponentially distributed, the only other event is the change in phase from i to, say, $j \neq i$. Since, $\mathcal{S} \sim PH(A, \boldsymbol{\alpha})$, this occurs at the rate a_{ij}. Since Q must be c-stochastic, the element $q_{ni,ni}$ must equal the negative of the total rate at which the system moves out of microstate (n, i). The magnitude of this element is given by

$$-\lambda_i - \eta_i \sum_{\forall j} \alpha_j - \sum_{j \neq i} a_{ij} = -\lambda_i - \eta_i + (a_{ii} + \eta_i) = a_{ii} - \lambda_i$$

Thus, for transitions from microstate (n,i) to (n,j), the transition rate is a_{ij} for $i \neq j$, and $a_{ii} - \lambda_i$ otherwise. This gives rise to the matrix $A - \lambda I$ along the diagonal. The reason for $\boldsymbol{\eta}$ in position (1,0) is that a departure in this case does not leave any customer who could start immediately. The reason for $\lambda\boldsymbol{\alpha}$ in position (0,1) should be obvious.

We can now obtain the solution using the equation $\Pi\tilde{Q} = 0$. Notice that the form of $\tilde{Q}$ in equation (5.1) is much like the one for an M/M/1 queue in equation (5.2.20), and so a matrix-geometric solution should not be surprising. To solve $\Pi\tilde{Q} = 0$, we can consider one equation at a time, just as we did for (5.2.20). The first equation gives

$$\Pi_1 \boldsymbol{\eta} = \lambda \pi_0 \tag{5.2}$$

where π_0 can be obtained from the utilization law. That is, $U = \lambda E[\mathcal{S}]$, which we call ρ to keep the correspondence with the M/M/1 queue. Therefore, $\pi_0 = 1 - \rho$. The other equations can be written as

$$\pi_0 \lambda \boldsymbol{\alpha} + \Pi_1(A - \lambda I) + \Pi_2 \boldsymbol{\eta\alpha} = [0] \tag{5.3}$$

$$\Pi_{n-1}\lambda I + \Pi_n(A - \lambda I) + \Pi_{n+1}\boldsymbol{\eta\alpha} = [0] \quad \text{for } n \geq 2 \tag{5.4}$$

The solution technique is now similar to the one for a local balance system. That is, we equate the flow into a *macrostate* caused by an arrival to the flow out of the *macrostate* due to service completion. For macrostate n, such an equation can be identified as

$$\Pi_n \boldsymbol{\eta} = \lambda \Pi_{n-1} \cdot \mathbf{e} \quad \text{for } n \geq 2 \tag{5.5}$$

Now by replacing $\Pi_{n+1}\boldsymbol{\eta}$ by $\lambda\Pi_n \cdot \mathbf{e}$ in equation (5.4), we immediately get the following simple recursion for $n \geq 2$

$$\Pi_n = \Pi_{n-1} R \quad \text{where } R = (I - \mathbf{e}\boldsymbol{\alpha} - \lambda^{-1} A)^{-1} \tag{5.6}$$

It is easy to verify that the above decomposition does not cause any inconsistencies, and hence the solution given by it must be correct. By using equation (5.6) recursively, we get $\Pi_n = \Pi_1 R^{n-1}$. Now, by substituting equation (5.5) in (5.3), we get $\Pi_1 = \pi_0 \boldsymbol{\alpha} R$. Since $\pi_0 = (1 - \rho)$, we have the following complete solution

$$\Pi_n = (1 - \rho)\boldsymbol{\alpha} R^n \quad \text{for } n \geq 1 \tag{5.7}$$

Notice that we are only interested in $\Pi_n \cdot \mathbf{e}$, the probability of finding n customers at the station, rather than in Π_n. If only queue-length moments are needed, we can find the z-transform of $\Pi_n \cdot \mathbf{e}$, which works out to be

$$\Psi(z) = \pi_0 + \sum_{n=1}^{\infty} z^n \Pi_n \cdot \mathbf{e} = (1 - \rho)\boldsymbol{\alpha}(I - zR)^{-1} \cdot \mathbf{e} \tag{5.8}$$

This, in turn, gives the mth *factorial moment* as

$$E[X(X-1)\cdots(X-m+1)] = m!(1-\rho)\boldsymbol{\alpha}(I-R)^{-m-1}R^m \cdot \mathbf{e} \tag{5.9}$$

We can see that equation (5.9) is well suited for recursive numerical computation, and there is no need to get scalar symbolic expressions. Also, comparing this analysis against the one for the M/E$_k$/1 queue in Section 5.6.2, we notice the comparative ease of analysis and generality (because the analysis applies to any phase-type service-time distribution).

9.5.2 Matrix-Geometric Solutions

In this section, we provide a general treatment of systems having matrix-geometric solutions. Consider an ergodic Markov chain whose state is represented by a m-tuple $(n_1, \ldots, n_m)$ such that n_2 through n_m take only a finite set of values. Then we can put the transition probability (or rate) matrix Q in a matrix of matrix form, as we did in equation (5.1), with n_1 as the row and column index of $\tilde{Q}$. In general, this $\tilde{Q}$ may not have the special structure in equation (5.1), and an explicit solution may not be possible. Thus, *the structure of matrix $\tilde{Q}$ is crucial for a matrix analytic solution.* In Section 9.2.4, we showed how M/G/1 and GI/M/1 queues can be analyzed by considering embedded Markov chains at departure and arrivals points respectively. Interestingly, the *form* of the transition probability matrix for these two embedded Markov chains is suitable for getting matrix analytic solutions. That is, if we replace the elements of these matrices by $k \times k$ matrices (for some k), we get two desirable forms for $\tilde{Q}$. We start with $\tilde{Q}$ in the *canonical GI/M/1 form*

$$\tilde{Q} = \begin{bmatrix} B_0 & A_0 & 0 & 0 & \cdots \\ B_1 & A_1 & A_0 & 0 & \cdots \\ B_2 & A_2 & A_1 & A_0 & \cdots \\ B_3 & A_3 & A_2 & A_1 & \cdots \\ \cdot & \cdot & \cdot & \cdot & \cdots \\ \cdot & \cdot & \cdot & \cdot & \cdots \end{bmatrix} \tag{5.10}$$

where all the elements are $k \times k$ matrices. Let Π denote the state probability vector for the Markov chain, say $\mathcal{Z}$, described by this $\tilde{Q}$. We shall partition Π also in accordance with $\tilde{Q}$. That is, we let $\Pi = (\Pi_0, \Pi_1, \ldots)$ where $\Pi_i = (\pi_{i1}, \ldots, \pi_{ik})$. We assume that $\mathcal{Z}$ is ergodic, so that Π can be determined uniquely, and satisfies $\Pi = \Pi\tilde{Q}$ (for discrete parameter case) or $\Pi\tilde{Q} = 0$ (for continuous parameter case). From this point onwards, we shall discuss these two cases separately.

1. Discrete Parameter Case

Consider the following matrix equation for a $k \times k$ matrix X of all *nonnegative elements*

$$X = \sum_{n=0}^{\infty} X^n A_n \tag{5.11}$$

It can also be shown that if the chain is ergodic, the minimal nonnegative solution to equation (5.11) is unique. We can obtain this solution iteratively as follows: Let $X[0] = A_0$, and successively substitute $X[i-1]$ on the right-hand side to get $X[i]$. It can be shown that this iteration creates a monotonic sequence, i.e., any entry of the matrix $X[i]$ is no less than the corresponding entry of the matrix $X[i-1]$. Therefore, the iterative method will converge to the unique solution, henceforth denoted as R.

The next step is to assume that the recurrence relation $\Pi_n = \Pi_{n-1}R$ holds for all $n \geq 1$. This, of course, yields the following matrix-geometric solution

$$\Pi_n = \Pi_0 R^n \quad \text{for} \;\; n \geq 1 \tag{5.12}$$

Now to check the validity of the solution, let us write the global balance equations for Π_n, $n > 0$.

$$\Pi_n = \sum_{j=0}^{\infty} \Pi_{j+n-1} A_j \tag{5.13}$$

Substituting equation (5.12) into (5.13) and using the fact that all elements of both Π_0 and R are nonnegative, we get equation (5.11). Thus, our solution must be correct. For Π_0, the global balance equation is $\Pi_0 = \sum_{n=0}^{\infty} \Pi_n B_n$. Using (5.12), we can express this equation as $\Pi_0 = \Pi_0 B[R]$, where

$$B[R] = \sum_{n=0}^{\infty} R^n B_n \tag{5.14}$$

Also, $\sum_{n=0}^{\infty} \Pi_n = \Pi_0 \sum_{n=0}^{\infty} R^n = \Pi_0(I-R)^{-1}$. Therefore, Π_0 is the unique positive solution of the system

$$\Pi_0 B[R] = \Pi_0 \quad \text{and} \quad \Pi_0(I-R)^{-1} \cdot \mathbf{e} = 1 \tag{5.15}$$

Thus, we have the complete matrix-geometric solution. We now say a few words about the ergodicity of $\tilde{Q}$ (i.e., that of the Markov chain $\mathcal{Z}$). As mentioned in Section 5.3, irreducibility is generally obvious, but difficult to characterize. However, because of the special structure of $\tilde{Q}$, positive recurrence can be characterized easily as shown in the next two lemmas, which we state without proof.

Lemma 9.3 If $\tilde{Q}$ is irreducible, it is positive recurrent if and only if (a) the spectral radius of R, denoted η, is strictly less than 1, and (b) the system of equations for Π_0 has a positive solution.

□

Let $\mathcal{A} = \sum_{n=0}^{\infty} A_n$. In almost all practical situations (including our M/PH/1 queue) the $\mathcal{A}$ matrix is irreducible. It is clear from equation (5.10) that $\mathcal{A}$ is also substochastic. (If $\lambda_{n\to\infty} B_n = [0]$, as is often the case, then $\mathcal{A}$ will be fully stochastic). Let ξ denote the spectral radius of $\mathcal{A}$. It follows that $0 < \xi \leq 1$ where the equality applies if $\mathcal{A}$ is (fully) stochastic. As shown in Exercise 9.10, $\eta \leq \xi$. This immediately implies that if $\mathcal{A}$ is only irreducible (but not stochastic), $\eta < 1$. For the stochastic case, we have the following result.

Lemma 9.4 Suppose that $\mathcal{A}$ is irreducible and d-stochastic and let ν denote its unique steady-state probability vector. That is, $\nu\mathcal{A} = \nu$ and $\nu \cdot \mathbf{e} = 1$. Then the eigenvalues of R lie inside the unit circle if

$$\nu \cdot \sum_{n=1}^{\infty} nA_n \cdot \mathbf{e} > 1 \tag{5.16}$$

□

If $\mathcal{A}$ is irreducible, we can also say a bit more about the R matrix. It turns out that in this case R is irreducible if and only if every row of A_0 has at least one positive element. Finally, if $\mathcal{A}$ is stochastic (but not necessarily irreducible), we have the following result.

Lemma 9.5 Suppose that $\mathcal{A}$ is d-stochastic. Then

$$A_0 \cdot \mathbf{e} = \sum_{j=1}^{\infty} R^j \sum_{n=j+1}^{\infty} A_n \cdot \mathbf{e} \tag{5.17}$$

Proof Since R satisfies equation (5.11), by substituting $\mathcal{A} - A_0 - \sum_{n=2}^{\infty} A_n$ for A_1, we get

$$R = (I - R)A_0 + R \cdot \mathcal{A} - \sum_{n=2}^{\infty} R(I - R^{n-1})A_n$$

If $\mathcal{A}$ is d-stochastic, then $\mathcal{A} \cdot \mathbf{e} = \mathbf{e}$; therefore, by postmultiplying both sides by $\mathbf{e}$ we see that $R \cdot \mathbf{e}$ cancels from both sides. Now, $(R - R^n)$ can be factored as $(I - R)(R + R^2 + \cdots + R^{n-1})$ and since $(I - R)$ is nonsingular, we can cancel it from both sides. This yields

$$A_0 \cdot \mathbf{e} = \sum_{n=2}^{\infty} \sum_{j=1}^{n-1} R^j A_n \cdot \mathbf{e} = \sum_{j=1}^{\infty} R^j \sum_{n=j+1}^{\infty} A_n \cdot \mathbf{e}$$

where in the last step, we have changed the order of the summations. □

Until now we have assumed that all matrices in $\tilde{Q}$ are $k \times k$. In most situations, the states on the boundary may show a somewhat different behavior than a general state, thereby causing the first few rows and columns to be of a different size. The $\tilde{Q}$ in equation (5.1) is one such example. It is clear that if we allow the first row and first column to have an arbitrary width, say k_1, we can handle any *complex boundary behavior*. This indeed can be done, except for a minor problem: The element in position $(0, 1)$ can no longer be A_0 because A_0 is $k \times k$. Assume for the moment, that $k_1 > k$. Then, the matrix in position $(0, 1)$ should have first $k_1 - k$ rows as zeros, whereas as the rest form A_0. That is, by splitting the first row and column into two, we get the following structure

$$\tilde{Q} = \begin{bmatrix} B_{00} & B_{01} & 0 & 0 & 0 & \cdots \\ B_{10} & B_{11} & A_0 & 0 & 0 & \cdots \\ B_{20} & B_{21} & A_1 & A_0 & 0 & \cdots \\ B_{30} & B_{31} & A_2 & A_1 & A_0 & \cdots \\ B_{40} & B_{41} & A_3 & A_2 & A_1 & \cdots \\ \cdot & \cdot & \cdot & \cdot & \cdot & \cdots \\ \cdot & \cdot & \cdot & \cdot & \cdot & \cdots \end{bmatrix} \tag{5.18}$$

where the width of the first two columns (and also rows) is $k_1 - k$ and k respectively. Now to solve this system, we define the R as before, and get $\Pi_2, \Pi_3, \ldots$ using the familiar recurrence

$$\Pi_n = \Pi_1 R^{n-1} \qquad \text{for} \quad n \geq 2 \tag{5.19}$$

However, Π_0 and Π_1 will now change, as one might expect. To obtain them, we write the first two global balance equations and use equation (5.19). This, along with the condition that all probabilities sum to 1, yields the following system

$$[\Pi_0 \;\; \Pi_1] B[R] = [\Pi_0 \;\; \Pi_1] \qquad \text{and} \qquad \Pi_0 \cdot \mathbf{e} + \Pi_1 (I - R)^{-1} \cdot \mathbf{e} = 1 \tag{5.20}$$

where the matrix $B[R]$ is now given by

$$B[R] = \begin{bmatrix} B_{00} & B_{01} \\ C_0 & C_1 \end{bmatrix} \qquad \text{where} \;\; C_i = \sum_{n=1}^{\infty} R^{n-1} B_{ni} \tag{5.21}$$

Note that the vector Π_0 is now of size $k_1 - k$ (but all others are still of size k). The conditions for positive recurrence given in Lemmas 9.3 and 9.4 remain the same.

If $k_1 < k$, we can consider the second row and second column as a part of the boundary and get back to the $k_1 > k$ case. In some cases, one may find that the matrix $\tilde{Q}$ is not in the desired form, because the "natural" partitioning suggested by the structure of the state space may be inappropriate from a computational point of view. In such cases, repartitioning with a different block size may be helpful. Renumbering of states may also be of value. In any case, if there is more than one way to put the original matrix in the canonical GI/M/1 form, the partitioning with the smallest possible block size would be the most desirable one.

2. Continuous Parameter Case

Since we are dealing with steady-state solutions, all the results for the discrete parameter case can be converted easily to those for the continuous parameter case. One way to do this is to first convert the given c-stochastic matrix $\tilde{Q}$ to a d-stochastic matrix, say $\tilde{Q}'$, by using the relationship (5.2.18) and then use the results for the discrete case. For the canonical GI/M/1 form, the solution is still given by $\Pi_n = \Pi_0 R^n$, where R is the minimal nonnegative solution of the equation

$$\sum_{n=0}^{\infty} X^n A_n = 0 \tag{5.22}$$

and Π_0 is the unique positive solution of the system

$$\Pi_0 B[R] = 0 \quad \text{and} \quad \Pi_0 (I - R)^{-1} \cdot \mathbf{e} = 1 \tag{5.23}$$

where $B[R]$ is still defined as $\sum_{n=0}^{\infty} R^n B_n$. Lemma 9.3 still holds unchanged. Lemma 9.4 can now be restated as follows:

Lemma 9.6 Suppose that $\mathcal{A} = \sum_{n=0}^{\infty} A_n$ is irreducible and c-stochastic. Let ν denote the unique steady-state probability vector of $\mathcal{A}$, i.e., $\nu\mathcal{A} = 0$ and $\nu \cdot \mathbf{e} = 1$. Then the eigenvalues of R lie inside the unit circle if

$$\nu \cdot \sum_{n=1}^{\infty} (n-1) A_n \cdot \mathbf{e} > \nu A_0 \cdot \mathbf{e} \tag{5.24}$$

□

Lemma 9.5 holds unchanged. Other results also remain the same except for some minor changes arising from the forms (5.2.8) and (5.2.17). For example, in the case of complex boundary behavior, equation (5.21) holds with R defined above, but equation (5.20) changes to

$$[\Pi_0 \;\; \Pi_1] B[R] = [0] \quad \text{and} \quad \Pi_0 \cdot \mathbf{e} + \Pi_1 (I - R)^{-1} \cdot \mathbf{e} = 1 \tag{5.25}$$

We could now point out that in our M/PH/1 example, with any reasonable phase-type service representation (including branching Erlang or hyperexponential), the matrix $\mathcal{A} = A + \boldsymbol{\eta\alpha}$ will be irreducible, *even though A is reducible*. Basically, the addition of $\boldsymbol{\eta\alpha}$ to A turns all transitions to the $(k+1)$st state back to the first k states in the Markov chain defining the PH distribution. $\mathcal{A}$ is also stochastic because $\mathcal{A} \cdot \mathbf{e} = A \cdot \mathbf{e} + \boldsymbol{\eta\alpha} \cdot \mathbf{e} = 0$.

3. Quasi Birth and Death Processes

In a large number of practical cases, including the M/PH/1 queue discussed in the last section, the matrix $\tilde{Q}$ turns out to be tri-diagonal. The general form is given below:

$$\tilde{Q} = \begin{bmatrix} B_0 & A_0 & 0 & 0 & \cdots \\ B_1 & A_1 & A_0 & 0 & \cdots \\ 0 & A_2 & A_1 & A_0 & \cdots \\ 0 & 0 & A_2 & A_1 & \cdots \\ \cdot & \cdot & \cdot & \cdot & \cdots \\ \cdot & \cdot & \cdot & \cdot & \cdots \end{bmatrix} \tag{5.26}$$

This form is very special, and can be called the M/M/1 canonical form, since it resembles in form to equation (5.2.20). Markov processes characterized by this form have also been called *Quasi Birth and Death* (QBD) processes. For QBD processes, the results above simplify considerably; and in some cases, such as the M/PH/1 queue above, the matrix R can be obtained explicitly. For this discussion, let us assume that we are dealing with a continuous parameter Markov chain. The results can be translated to the discrete parameter case by using (5.2.18). The general solution, given earlier, now reduces to the following: $\Pi_n = \Pi_0 R^n$ where the matrix R is the unique minimal positive solution to the equation

$$R^2 A_2 + RA_1 + A_0 = 0 \tag{5.27}$$

and Π_0 is the unique positive solution to

$$\Pi_0(B_0 + RB_1) = 0 \quad \text{and} \quad \Pi_0(I - R)^{-1} \cdot \mathbf{e} = 1 \tag{5.28}$$

The condition for stability (or positive recurrence) in equation (5.24) reduces to

$$\nu A_2 \cdot \mathbf{e} > \nu A_0 \cdot \mathbf{e} \tag{5.29}$$

Since the matrix $\mathcal{A}$ is always c-stochastic here, equation (5.17) yields the following simple relationship

$$A_0 \cdot \mathbf{e} = R\, A_2 \cdot \mathbf{e} \tag{5.30}$$

We could similarly specialize the results for complex boundary behavior. For example, systems with M/M/c canonical form can be modeled as QBD processes with complex boundary behavior. (The M/PH/1 queue also shows the complex boundary behavior, even though the final solution is very simple.)

Let us consider a few other examples of systems that can be modeled as QBD processes. The PH/M/1 queue is one such example. We can define its state as (n, i) where i is the phase of an arriving customer. The solution method is very similar to that for the M/PH/1 case, but R cannot be obtained explicitly. The analysis extends to the PH/M/c case by using results on complex boundary behavior. The PH/PH/1 can also be analyzed as a QBD process by considering the state as a triplet (n, i, j) where n is the number of customers, i is the arrival phase, and j is the service phase. If the arrival process has k_a phases and the service process has k_s phases, the element matrices of $\tilde{Q}$ are of order $k_a \times k_s$, which could make the solution expensive. A different way of dealing with the same problem is to consider it as a special case of the GI/PH/1 queue, but then we have to contend with the full GI/M/1 canonical form. QBD processes can also be used to study two queue systems where the second queue has a limited storage capacity. For example, consider the modeling of production blocking (see Section 5.5). Here we have two stations, such that the second one has only finite storage capacity. If the waiting room at the second station is full, the first server gets blocked. Several policies can be defined for blocking and unblocking the first server. If we represent the system state as (n_1, n_2) and abstract out the second part of the state, we again get a QBD process.

Since a finite population M/M/1 queue has a truncated geometric distribution, it is natural to ask if a finite-state QBD process has a truncated matrix-geometric distribution. Unfortunately, the answer is generally negative – in fact, in most cases, there is no simple matrix-analytic solution available. However, the finite state M/PH/1 queue is a significant exception, and does yield a truncated matrix-geometric solution.

9.5.3 Queues in a Random Environment

An interesting application of matrix-geometric methods is in analyzing queuing systems operating in a *random environment*. This random environment may affect the arrivals and/or the service. For example, if the servers are subject to breakdowns and repairs, the service rate fluctuates depending on the number of operational servers. If the queue under consideration is of the M/M/c type, we get a QBD process, which can be analyzed easily. Henceforth we shall consider only this special case. For such a system, the state can be defined as (n, j), where n is the number of customers in the system and j is the number of operational servers. By abstracting out the second part of the state, we get the standard QBD representation. The $\tilde{Q}$ here is similar to the one that appears in equation (5.31) later in this section. The matrix A in this case represents a Markov chain $\mathcal{Z}$ whose states are the number of operational servers and the transition rates are the failure and repair rates. Note that the service rate changes instantaneously as a result of failure or repair in this model. The service rate could well change while a customer is being served; but because the service-time distribution is exponential, this does not cause any difficulty (i.e., it is as if we forget about the service already provided to the customer and restart it with a new rate). In job shop modeling, the random environment can be used to model the effect of tool wear (which reduces service rate) and tool replacement (which may increase service rate).

Although for tractability reasons, much of the queuing analysis assumes that the Markov chain is homogeneous and operating in steady state, most real systems show considerable fluctuations in the workload. For example, the arrival rate to a bank may show a considerable upsurge during the lunch hour (or other special times). Such fluctuations are not random variations and should really be regarded as fluctuations in the expected value. Consequently, the homogeneity assumption may yield poor results. In fact, it is well known that sharp increases in workload over short intervals of time may affect the overall performance adversely. The idea of operation in a random environment can be used to study such phenomena *without leaving the realm of steady-state solutions*. We shall illustrate this with an example.

Suppose that we are modeling the performance of a call-processing system in a telephone network and want to characterize the call-attempt process. In a simplified model, we can assume that the average call-attempt rate has a 24-hour cycle; i.e., the statistical characteristics do not vary from day to day. However, during a 24-hour period, significant variations are expected. Suppose that we divide this 24-hour period into k "phases", and determine the average calling rate during those as $\lambda_1, \ldots, \lambda_k$.[5] Then we can model the system as a M/M/1 queue (or a M/PH/1 queue, if necessary) operating in a random environment. We shall assume a M/M/1 case here, but allow the service rate μ to also depend on the phase. (This may make sense practically, since the system could alter connection strategy during periods of heavy load.) The state can be represented by the pair (n, i) where n is the number of pending or active connection requests, and $i \in 1..k$ is the "arrival phase". By abstracting out the phase part, we get a $\tilde{Q}$ matrix shown in equation (5.31) where the matrix A represents a Markov chain $\mathcal{Z}$ that characterizes transitions between phases. Although it seems natural to let $\mathcal{Z}$ cycle through k phases sequentially, this is not necessary and may not even be the best model. For example, if the incoming traffic goes through several peaks throughout the day, it may be desirable to construct a $\mathcal{Z}$ that has fewer than k states and decide on transitions among the states such that the multiple-peak behavior is well represented. Since the details of such an exercise are irrelevant to the present discussion, we shall ignore them, but assume that $\mathcal{Z}$ is an arbitrary ergodic Markov chain with k states.

It is important to note the differences between the chain $\mathcal{Z}$ for the last example and the chain, say $\mathcal{Z}'$, that represents the phase-type distribution in a M/PH/1 or PH/M/1 type of queue. In chain $\mathcal{Z}'$, we have an absorbing state, numbered $k+1$, such that the transition rate from state i to state $k+1$ represents a change in the n part of the state (n, i). In contrast, the chain $\mathcal{Z}$ has only k states, is ergodic, and only specifies how we switch between the k phases. To each phase i we can independently assign an arrival rate λ_i and a service rate μ_i. Thus, if the system is currently in state (n, i), three types of transitions are possible: (a) to state $(n+1, i)$ with rate λ_i, (b) to state $(n-1, i)$ with rate μ_i, and (c) to state (n, j) with rate a_{ij}. (Presumably, a_{ij}'s are much smaller than λ_i's and μ_i's, but this is not a requirement.) Therefore, the $\tilde{Q}$ matrix for these systems is given by

$$\tilde{Q} = \begin{bmatrix} A - \Delta\lambda & \Delta\lambda & 0 & 0 & \cdots \\ \Delta\mu & A - \Delta\lambda - \Delta\mu & \Delta\lambda & 0 & \cdots \\ 0 & \Delta\mu & A - \Delta\lambda - \Delta\mu & \Delta\lambda & \cdots \\ 0 & 0 & \Delta\mu & A - \Delta\lambda - \Delta\mu & \cdots \\ \cdot & \cdot & \cdot & \cdot & \cdots \\ \cdot & \cdot & \cdot & \cdot & \cdots \end{bmatrix} \tag{5.31}$$

where $\boldsymbol{\lambda} = [\lambda_1, \ldots, \lambda_k]$ and $\boldsymbol{\mu} = [\mu_1, \ldots, \mu_k]$ are *column vectors*, and $\Delta\lambda$ and $\Delta\mu$ represent $k \times k$ diagonal matrices constructed from them, i.e.,

$$\Delta\lambda = \begin{bmatrix} \lambda_1 & & & \\ & \lambda_2 & & \\ & & \ddots & \\ & & & \lambda_k \end{bmatrix}, \qquad \Delta\mu = \begin{bmatrix} \mu_1 & & & \\ & \mu_2 & & \\ & & \ddots & \\ & & & \mu_k \end{bmatrix} \tag{5.32}$$

[5] Deciding how many phases are adequate, their duration, when they begin, etc., are interesting problems, but not relevant to the discussion here.

Because of the special form of $\tilde{Q}$ and A, the solution is even more explicit here than for a general QBD process. Since A is ergodic, $\mathcal{Z}$ has a unique steady-state distribution given by equation (5.2.17), which we denote by the row vector $\mathbf{x} = [x_1, \ldots, x_k]$. Now, equation (5.30) yields the simple relationship $\boldsymbol{\lambda} = R\boldsymbol{\mu}$. The expected arrival rate is $\mathbf{x}\boldsymbol{\lambda}$ and the expected service rate is $\mathbf{x}\boldsymbol{\mu}$. The overall traffic intensity (different from overall station utilization), denoted as ρ, is given by

$$\rho = \mathbf{x}\boldsymbol{\lambda}/\mathbf{x}\boldsymbol{\mu} \tag{5.33}$$

From equation (5.29), the stability condition can be seen to be $\rho < 1$. Using equation (5.27) it is easy to verify that $\Pi_0 = \mathbf{x}(I - R)^{-1}$ satisfies equation (5.28). Therefore, the solution is given by

$$\Pi_n = \mathbf{x}(I - R)^{-1}R^n \tag{5.34}$$

It is easy to see that $\sum_{n=0}^{\infty} \Pi_n = \mathbf{x}$, as expected. [Using the terminology of Section 8.4.4, this means that the overall Markov chain is lumpable with respect to the n part of the state (n, i)]. Also, we may have $\lambda_i \geq \mu_i$ for several phases, and yet ρ could be less than 1. This is interesting as it allows us to study the effect of transients without leaving the domain of steady-state solutions. As already indicated, the results in such cases could be drastically different from those for an ordinary M/M/1 station with arrival rate of $\mathbf{x}\boldsymbol{\lambda}$ and service rate of $\mathbf{x}\boldsymbol{\mu}$. Neuts (1981) considers an example with eight phases, where the chain $\mathcal{Z}$ cycles through all states sequentially with rate 1. The service rate in each phase is fixed at 6.25, but the arrival rate vector $\boldsymbol{\lambda}$ is $[30, 2, 2, 2, 1, 1, 1, 1]$. That is, the arrival rate is very high in phase 1 and then drops off to a very low value and remains low. The ρ works out to be 0.8. The average queue length Q is found to be 41.43. In contrast, a simple M/M/1 queue with $\rho = 0.8$ has $Q = 4$. That is, a temporary surge in the arrival rate causes a ten-fold increase in the mean queue length! A closer examination reveals that even though the queue length builds up quickly in phase 1, it dissipates very slowly. (The mean queue length of 53.81 in phase 1 reduces to only 29.96 by phase 8). This is a familiar phenomenon in real-life situations (e.g., traffic buildup on a highway) and is captured very well by the phase-type model.

9.5.4 Queues of M/G/1 Type

In the above, we only considered the canonical GI/M/1 form. We could also consider $\tilde{Q}$ in the *canonical M/G/1 form.* In fact, we can consider a $\tilde{Q}$ that is somewhat more general than the one obtained from the Q matrix for an M/G/1 queue [see equation (3.15)] and is described below:

$$\tilde{Q} = \begin{bmatrix} B_0 & B_1 & B_2 & B_3 & \cdots \\ C_0 & A_1 & A_2 & A_3 & \cdots \\ 0 & A_0 & A_1 & A_2 & \cdots \\ 0 & 0 & A_0 & A_1 & \cdots \\ \cdot & \cdot & \cdot & \cdot & \cdots \\ \cdot & \cdot & \cdot & \cdot & \cdots \end{bmatrix} \tag{5.35}$$

As in the GI/M/1 canonical form, the boundary matrices may be of size other than $k \times k$. It can be shown that such a system can also be solved using matrix techniques; however, *the solution is not matrix-geometric*, and usually much more difficult. One of the fundamental ideas here is to set up a matrix equation for the z-transform of the probability of transit from "level" $n+1$ to level n [where n is the first part of the state (n, i)]. This equation can be used to compute probabilities Π_n's and moment vectors $\sum_{\forall n} n^m \Pi_n$ for $m = 1, 2, \ldots$. Unfortunately, the expressions quickly become exceedingly complex and one may have to resort to more traditional methods to complete the solution. For example, to obtain Π_n for $n > 2$, one may have to go back to standard methods for solving systems of linear equations. The interested reader is referred to the book by Neuts (1990) on the solution of M/G/1 type of systems.

9.6 Additional Topics

In this section we discuss two additional topics of practical interest. These are the modeling of arrival processes in a real system and the direct solution of global balance equations in cases where special purpose techniques described above fail.

9.6.1 Representation of Arrival Processes

In modeling real systems, one has to choose realistic but analytically tractable models for the arrival and service processes at each queuing facility. As we have already seen, general interarrival or service times can often be handled, but a combination of the two is very difficult to analyze. In this section, we take a more careful look at various types of representations and their applications. In practice, these representations are most often used for characterizing the arrival process, and we shall discuss them in that context. However, much of the discussion applies to the service process as well.

Poisson arrival process is very attractive in analytic modeling because of its numerous properties discussed in sections 5.1.3 and 9.2.1. However, many practical situations demand more general models. Several models of varying generality have been proposed depending on the application needs. One simple model that we have seen in Section 5.6.1 is to allow the arrivals to occur in batches, but to keep the process Poisson in terms of batches. Such a process is an instance of a *compound Poisson process*, which can be characterized as follows: Let $C_1, C_2, \ldots$ denote a set of positive integer-valued iid random variables, and let $N(t)$ be a Poisson process. Then

$$X(t) = \sum_{i=0}^{N(t)} C_i \tag{6.1}$$

is called a compound Poisson process. For the case of batch Poisson process, C_i is the size of the ith batch and $N(t)$ is the number of batches arriving during the time t. Thus, $X(t)$ represents the total number of arrivals during time t. Other than modeling situations where the arrivals are really batchy, the batch model can also be used when the traffic is bursty, i.e., when the process exhibits several arrivals close together and long pauses. For example, if we use the geometric batch size model of Section 5.6.1 to model burstiness, we have only one parameter (α) to estimate. This can be done by measuring the average queue length and using equation (5.6.7) to compute α.

In some cases, the arrival process may be a Poisson process operating in a random environment; i.e., the rate parameter changes depending on some external effect. As we saw in Section 9.5.3, we can model this situation by defining a discrete or continuous parameter Markov chain, say $\mathcal{Z}$, and generate Poisson arrivals with rate λ_i in state i of $\mathcal{Z}$. The arrival process, so defined, is usually known as the *Markov Modulated Poisson Process* or MMPP. This model is attractive because the queues using it can be analyzed using matrix-geometric techniques. Notice that the transitions in $\mathcal{Z}$ can occur at any point in time with respect to the arrival process. This does not cause any problems because of the memorylessness property of the Poisson process. If the arrivals in a state were non-Poisson, we would have to keep track of the time since last arrival, and the modeling scheme will fail.

The MMPP model can often be used for modeling the effect of flow or congestion control mechanisms. For example, consider a M/M/c/SI/K/∞ queue with arrival rate of λ. Whenever there are K customers at the station, any new arrivals are rejected. Thus, if the station is in state K, the *overflow process* is Poisson with rate λ; otherwise it is shut off. We would need to characterize this overflow process if the rejected customers are routed to another service facility (e.g., to another node in a distributed system). This yields a binary (i.e., two-state) MMPP. Notice that the capacity limitation may well be deliberate, introduced as a control mechanism. This type of control can be called *hard* (often also known as *bang-bang control*). A *soft control* may increase the rejection ratio gradually as the queue length at the station crosses some preset thresholds. In this case, the overflow process operates in several states and can again be modeled as MMPP.

The processes described above can be referred to as *perturbed Poisson processes*, since they are all derived from a simple Poisson process. In some applications, it may be more appropriate to model the arrivals as a general renewal process. If a general interarrival-time distribution is difficult to handle, we can use a phase-type representation for it (which may allow the use of matrix analytic techniques). Such processes are called *PH renewal processes*.

General or PH renewal processes can be generalized further, much as we generalized the Poisson process. For example, we could bring in batch arrivals and thereby get a process that is a special case of *reward renewal process*. Reward renewal processes can be defined as in equation (6.1), except that $N(t)$ becomes a general renewal process. (The name results from the fact that C_i can be considered as the "reward" earned at the time of the ith renewal.) Another generalization is often referred to as *semi-Markov process* or SMP. The idea is to use a general continuous-time random process $\mathcal{Z}$ that has a Markov chain, say $\mathcal{Z}'$, embedded at its transition points. We then assume that an arrival occurs whenever $\mathcal{Z}$ makes a transition. Since the residence time in each state of $\mathcal{Z}$ could have a different and arbitrary distribution, the arrival process becomes a mixture of several renewal processes. As an example of its application, consider a situation involving rejection blocking, where the rejected customers try again (possibly after some delay). Assume that the new-arrival and feedback processes are of renewal type. Then the combined arrival process will be a mixture of two renewal processes.

Notice that a SMP can be considered as a generalization of MMPP, except that we have cleverly avoided the problem of remaining interarrival time. However, the SMP model has one limitation: successive interarrival times correspond to different states. That is, if we use only as many states as the number of renewal processes that we want to mix, any two successive interarrival times will have different distributions. This is unrealistic in most applications, so we may have to use several states with identical distributions in order to get a desired mixture. Thus, in the rejection blocking example above, we would need at least two states for each of the two types of arrival streams in order to get a realistic representation of the combined arrival process. Obviously, the solution expense would increase with the number of states. The analysis of systems using SMP arrivals is also generally quite involved; however, if the residence time of each state is represented by a PH distribution, it may be possible to use matrix-analytic techniques. As a special case, we may assume the residence-time distribution as exponential, thereby resulting in a *mixed Poisson process*. This special case can still model interarrival-time distributions with coefficient of variation greater than 1. To see this, note that a hyperexponential distribution is basically a selection among two or more exponential distributions with different rates.

In some applications (e.g., modeling of telecommunication systems handling packetized voice), there may be significant correlation between successive arrivals, and thus we have to move away from a pure renewal type of arrival model. It is generally very difficult to work with nonrenewal arrival processes, and some indirect modeling is required. The SMP arrival process is one such indirect model where the transition to a different state after the arrival provides a way of modeling dependencies between successive arrivals. For example, if we use two states in a SMP representation, one with a small residence time and the other with a large one, successive arrivals will be negatively correlated. Since general SMP is difficult to deal with, a special case known as *Markovian Arrival Process* (MAP) has also been considered in the literature. This process can be viewed as a slight generalization of the PH renewal process. The difference is that the $\boldsymbol{\alpha}$ in $PH(A, \boldsymbol{\alpha})$ is not fixed; instead, it depends on the state from which the absorption occurred last time. This makes successive arrivals interdependent.

In reality, the arrival process is often nonstationary; i.e., the mean arrival rate varies with time. If the mean arrival rate appears to be going through several clearly identifiable phases, a MMPP model may be appropriate. On the other hand, if the mean rate changes slowly, we can regard the arrival process to be a renewal process with a changing mean rate λ. If this change has very little randomness, we can describe it by making λ a deterministic function of time. This gives a *nonhomogeneous process approximation* (in the sense of Section

5.2) to the original process. Note that a nonhomogeneous process, by definition, is nonstationary. If the change appears random, we could regard λ itself as a random variable and estimate its density function, say $f_\lambda(x)$. This is a *stationary point process* approximation to the real process. In either case, we compute the desired output parameter of a queuing system, say the response time R, as usual. If λ is considered a function of time, we thus get R also as a function of time, henceforth denoted as $R(t)$. If instead λ is considered as a random variable, R can be regarded as the conditional output parameter, denoted as $R(\lambda)$. In practice, $f_\lambda(x)$ will be estimated as a discrete density; therefore, the unconditional value of R can be computed as

$$R = \sum_{i=1}^{n} R(\lambda = x_i) f_\lambda(x_i) \tag{6.2}$$

where n is the number of values at which the density function is specified. Notice that the approximation here is basically a logical decomposition where the slow process is the change in the mean arrival rate. Thus, the accuracy of the approximation depends on whether a short-term equilibrium in terms of traffic handling can be achieved (relative to the changes in the mean rate). It follows that if the mean rate changes rapidly or if $\max(x_i)$ approaches the service rate, the approximation will be poor.

9.6.2 Direct Solution of Global Balance Equations

Direct solution to global balance equations in (5.2.8) or (5.2.17) is needed if the problem at hand cannot be tackled by the specialized techniques discussed until now. The direct solution discussed here applies only to finite (i.e., closed) systems, although one can often truncate an infinite system to get a finite system without introducing significant errors. (The truncation would still ensure that all probabilities sum to 1, since this is one of the equations.) In either case, often the number of states is large, and the solution may become very expensive. Typically, as Q grows in size, it becomes more and more sparse, thus sparse matrix methods can be used.

Let n denote the number of states in the Markov chain. Then Q is singular with rank $n-1$. By equation (5.2.18), the system $\Pi Q = 0$ for the continuous parameter case can also be written as $\Pi W = \Pi$ where $W = \delta Q + I$. Therefore, it suffices to consider only the discrete parameter case. Let $\alpha_1 \geq \cdots \geq \alpha_n$ denote the eigenvalues of W and $\mathbf{x}_1, \ldots, \mathbf{x}_n$ the corresponding *eigenvectors*; i.e., for $1 \leq i \leq n$, $\mathbf{x}_i W = \alpha_i \mathbf{x}_i$. Since the Markov chain is irreducible and W is a d-stochastic matrix, we know that (a) $\alpha_1 = 1$, and (b) all other eigenvalues are positive and strictly less than 1.

There are two methods for solving a system of linear equations $A\mathbf{x} = \mathbf{b}$: direct and iterative. Direct methods, such as Gaussian elimination, modify the matrix A as they go along, and may cause "fill-in"; therefore, they are not suitable for the large sparse systems at hand. Iterative methods, however, leave A alone;

they start out with an approximation for $\mathbf{x}$, and improve on it successively. In the following, we mention some iterative methods briefly.

The *power method* iteratively solves the equation $\Pi W = \Pi$ using the schema $\Pi(i+1) = \Pi(i)W$ with $\Pi(0)$ arbitrarily chosen. Using the spectral representation of W, it is easy to show that *the rate of convergence depends on the ratio of dominant and subdominant eigenvalues*. That is, if α_2 is close to 1, the convergence will be slow. Since the transient solution of a discrete parameter chain is also given by the schema $\Pi(i+1) = \Pi(i)W$, this result also applies when we consider the approach of such a chain to steady-state operation. In fact, as we shall see in Section 13.4.4, even a continuous parameter Markov chain will have the same behavior.

The *simultaneous iteration method* is similar to the power method, except that it attempts to determine eigenvectors corresponding to $k > 1$ largest eigenvalues by starting out with k trial vectors. The convergence rate for the ith eigenvector is controlled by α_{k+1}/α_i, which means that good convergence can be obtained for the first eigenvector (which is the desired solution) even if some of the subdominant eigenvalues are close to 1.

The most popular iterative techniques for solving the $A\mathbf{x} = \mathbf{b}$ type of systems are (a) Jacobi, (b) Gauss-Seidel, and (c) successive over-relaxation (SOR). To describe these, let us decompose A as $L + D + U$ where L is lower triangular, U is upper triangular, and D is diagonal. Let $\mathbf{x}(i)$ denote the approximation to vector $\mathbf{x}$ after the ith iteration. Then the Jacobi method uses the schema

$$D\mathbf{x}(i+1) = \mathbf{b} - (L+U)\mathbf{x}(i) \tag{6.3}$$

and the Gauss-Seidel method uses the schema

$$(D+L)\mathbf{x}(i+1) = \mathbf{b} - U\mathbf{x}(i) \tag{6.4}$$

where $\mathbf{x}(0)$ is chosen arbitrarily. The Gauss-Seidel method is similar to the Jacobi method except that in computing x_j, the already computed values of $x_1(i+1), \ldots, x_{j-1}(i+1)$ are used on the right-hand side. (We define $\mathbf{x}$ as $[x_1, \ldots, x_n]$.) The Gauss-Seidel method usually requires half the steps of the Jacobi method. The SOR method modifies the Gauss-Seidel method by a *relaxation factor* ω, as follows:

$$[D + \omega L]\mathbf{x}(i+1) = [(1-\omega)D - \omega U]\mathbf{x}(i) + \omega\mathbf{b} \tag{6.5}$$

The purpose of the relaxation factor is to improve convergence. $\omega = 1$ corresponds to the Gauss-Seidel method, and generally ω is chosen close to 2, but never larger.

Unfortunately, none of these methods is directly suited for our problem, since the convergence of these methods requires that all eigenvalues be strictly less than 1. To overcome this problem, we "shift" the matrices. For example, the *shifted Gauss-Seidel* method iteratively computes two vectors $\mathbf{x}$ and $\mathbf{y}$ as follows. Let τ be the "shift" and $\mathbf{y}(0) = (D+L)\mathbf{x}(0)$ where $\mathbf{x}(0)$ is chosen arbitrarily. Then

$$\mathbf{y}(i+1) = (1-\tau)\mathbf{y}(i) - \tau U\mathbf{x}(i) \quad \text{and} \quad (D+L)\mathbf{x}(i+1) = \mathbf{y}(i+1) \tag{6.6}$$

It is easy to see that when convergence is achieved, **x** is the desired solution. Methods exist to choose τ for fast convergence. The shifted SOR method can also be defined similarly, but is not recommended because of difficulties in choosing ω.

9.7 Exercises

1. Construct the state transition diagram for an infinite population M/M/1 system with two classes of customers such that class 1 has nonpreemptive priority over class 2. (The exact discipline within a class does not matter, so long as it is of SI type.) Class i customers arrive with rate λ_i but have a common mean service rate of μ. Define the state of the system as (n_1, n_2, j) where n_i is the number of customers of class i at the station, and j is the class of currently served customer. Write down the global balance equations and define the two-dimensional partial generating functions $H_j(z_1, z_2)$ for $j = 1, 2$. In defining H_j, choose 1 as the lower limit for n_j, and 0 for the other variable. (This choice is motivated by the fact that the states $(0, n_2, 1)$, $n_2 = 0, 1, \ldots$ and $(n_1, 0, 2)$, $n_1 = 0, 1, \ldots$ are infeasible.) Then the overall transform $H(z_1, z_2)$ is given by

$$H(z_1, z_2) = H_1(z_1, z_2) + H_2(z_1, z_2) + P(0)$$

The resulting expressions will have three unknown probabilities. To determine these, note that $H_i(1, 1)$ gives the probability that the customer from class i is in service. That is, $H_i(1, 1) = U_i = \lambda_i/\mu$. Also, $H(1, 1) = 1$. Find expressions for the expected queue lengths $Q_1 = \frac{dH(z_1,1)}{dz_1}|_{z_1=1}$ and $Q_2 = \frac{dH(1,z_2)}{dz_2}|_{z_2=1}$.

2. Prove equation (2.2). If instead of stochastic quantities, we were considering operational quantities, what assumptions do we need to obtain this relationship?

3. Specialize the conservation equations for situations where the number of classes are uncountably infinite. (Obviously, the summations will turn into integrals in this case.) Apply these equations to the case of shortest-job-next scheduling discipline.

4. Show that the elementary renewal theorem is a special case of the key renewal theorem.

5. In Section 9.3 we analyzed the M/G/1 queue using three different methods starting with equation (3.1). Do the same for a GI/M/1 queue starting with equation (2.42).

6. Starting with equation (3.15), find the departer's distribution for a M/G/1/-FCFS/3/∞ system. From this, obtain the random observer's distribution.

7. Apply Lindley's integral equation to an $E_2/E_2/1$/FCFS/∞/∞ queue, and obtain the Laplace transform of the waiting time density.

8. Let $\Psi(t) = e^{At}$. Convert this equation to a first-order matrix differential equation and then find its Laplace transform. Using this, derive equations (4.5) and (4.6).

9. Complete derivation of equations (4.7) and (4.8). Give a probabilistic interpretation to these equations in terms of the transitions within each chain and between different chains.

10. Let π denote the left eigenvector corresponding to the largest eigenvalue of $\mathcal{A}$ (which is ξ itself). That is, $\pi\mathcal{A} = \xi\pi$. Consider the iterative solution to equation (5.11) starting with $X[i] = 0$ for $i = 0$, and by induction on i show that $\pi R \leq \xi\pi$, i.e., the spectral radius of R is less than ξ. [Hint: One of the inequalities needed in the proof is $\sum_{n=0}^{\infty} \xi^n A_n \leq \mathcal{A}$.]

11. Represent a PH/M/c queuing system as a QBD process with complex boundary behavior. Characterize its solution. Show that when the interarrival time distribution is Erlang, only one row of matrix R is nonzero, and an explicit expression can be found for it.

12. Consider a M/M/1 queue in random environment where the arrival can be viewed as a three-phase process that cycles through the three phases systematically and spends equal time in each phase. Let $\lambda_1 = \lambda_3 = \mu/2$ and λ_2 ranging from $\mu/2$ to 1.85μ. This corresponds to the overall station utilization varying from 0.5 to 0.95. Find numerical values of the mean and variance of the queue length. Compare them against those from a simple M/M/1 system with the same utilization.

13. Consider a M/E_2/1/FCFS/5/5 system with $\lambda = 4$/sec and $\mu = 5$/sec. Using the results of Section 5.6.2, obtain global balance equations and put them in the matrix form. Solve the resulting system by the techniques of Section 9.6.2.

Bibliographic Notes

As with the material in Chapter 5, most of the material in this chapter is also classical and can be found in Kleinrock (1975), Gross and Harris (1985), Kleinrock (1976), Ross (1970, 1983), etc. Our discussion in Section 9.1 is partly based on Kleinrock (1975). Henrici (1988) is an acknowledged classic on the theory of complex variables, and Volume 1 of that book contains most of the results alluded to in Section 9.1. The mixed exponential representation of response-time distribution for GI/G/1 is derived in Gross and Harris (1985). Some of our discussion in Section 9.2 and 9.3 is based on this. Kleinrock (1976) discusses several results for GI/G/1 queues under heavy traffic, and contains detailed derivations of results under diffusion approximation. Our discussion on conservation laws is partly based on Gelenbe and Mitrani (1980), which contains a detailed treatment on the design of optimal scheduling strategies. Trivedi (1982) provides a lucid treatment of renewal theory and discusses several applications of renewal type equations. Keilson and Servi (1988) shows that for many systems that satisfy

Little's law, a distributional form (i.e., relationships involving higher moments) is also valid.

The discussion on matrix-geometric techniques is based on Neuts (1981), which is a comprehensive reference on the subject. Our discussion also greatly benefited from a chapter from a book by D. M. Lucantoni and V. Ramaswamy (not yet published). Neuts (1984) provides a brief survey of matrix-analytic techniques in general. The recent book by Neuts (1990) contains a comprehensive treatment of matrix analytic methods for systems of the M/G/1 type. The MMPP process is used in Heffes and Lucantoni (1986) for analyzing multiplexer behavior in packetized voice environments. The MAP process is introduced in Lucantoni, Meier-Hellstern and Neuts (1990), which considers the analysis of a MAP/G/1 queuing system. They have further generalized this process by allowing the arrivals to occur in batches. The resulting process is called batch MAP or BMAP. This process, including the analysis of the BMAP/G/1 queue, may be found in Lucantoni (1990). Neuts (1979) defines a very general class of point processes. Several researchers have analyzed queues driven by such a process, usually called N/G/1 queues [e.g., see Blondia (1989)]. It turns out that the BMAP process is equivalent to this arrival process. Solution methods for sparse linear systems may be found in most numerical analysis books, such as George and Liu (1981). Stewart (1978) provides a survey of several numerical techniques for solving Markov chains.

CHAPTER

10

Algorithms for Networks with Specialized Features

In this chapter, we discuss a number of algorithms that allow us to handle a larger class of networks than those in Chapter 7. In Section 6.6, we mentioned a number of advanced features such as chain-dependent capacities, variable populations, state-dependent routing and blocking that retain the product-form property. Thus, one objective of this chapter is to explore the product-form solution and the algorithms when these features are present. We have also seen that large, closed models could be very expensive to solve; therefore, we also discuss algorithms that exploit certain features of the model. In particular, we discuss (a) algorithms that introduce one chain at a time and are well suited for networks with a small number of stations and many chains, (b) tree algorithms that exploit sparsity, and (c) an asymptotic expansion based algorithm that assumes that the loading of the load-independent stations compared to that of the delay stations, is small.

10.1 Networks with Advanced Features

In this section, we discuss product-form solutions for networks with advanced features, namely chain-dependent capacities, variable chain populations, state-dependent routing, rejection blocking, and mutual blocking. The solutions in these cases are somewhat different from what we have seen until now and deserve special treatment. We also show how convolution and MVA algorithms can be adapted for such networks. Since the algorithmic extensions are mostly straightforward, our discussion will be rather brief.

10.1.1 Chain-Dependent Capacities

We have already seen the product-form solution for this case in Section 6.6, and it is identical to our regular solution except that $V_i(n_i)$ is replaced by the $V_i(\mathbf{n}_i)$ function. Furthermore, as shown in Section 7.3, the basic equations needed in the convolution algorithm [namely (7.3.2), (7.3.8), (7.3.10), and (7.3.12)] hold for the most general form of capacities. Therefore, the nature of capacity function does not significantly affect the convolution algorithm or its complexity. As for the MVA algorithm, the marginal local balance equation in equation (7.4.1) also holds in general. Recall that $\mu^*_{ir}(\mathbf{n}) = \frac{n_{ir}}{n_i}\mu^\circ_{ir}C_i(\mathbf{n})$; therefore, by definition,

$$\begin{aligned}
Q_{ir}(\mathbf{N}) &= \sum_{k=1}^{N_r} \sum_{\forall\, \mathbf{n}_i, n_{ir}=k} kP_i(\mathbf{n}_i|\mathbf{N}) \\
&= U_{ir}(\mathbf{N}) \sum_{k=1}^{N_r} \sum_{\forall\, \mathbf{n}_i, n_{ir}=k} \frac{n_i}{C_i(\mathbf{n}_i)} P_i(\mathbf{n}_i - e_r|\mathbf{N}-e_r) \\
&= U_{ir}(\mathbf{N}) \sum_{\mathbf{n}_i=e_r}^{\mathbf{N}} \frac{n_i}{C_i(\mathbf{n}_i)} P_i(\mathbf{n}_i - e_r|\mathbf{N}-e_r) \qquad (1.1)
\end{aligned}$$

Therefore, by Little's law, we get the following response time equation

$$R_{ir}(\mathbf{N}) = s^\circ_{ir} \sum_{\mathbf{n}_i=e_r}^{\mathbf{N}} \frac{n_i}{C_i(\mathbf{n}_i)} P_i(\mathbf{n}_i - e_r|\mathbf{N}-e_r) \qquad (1.2)$$

Apart from this modified response time equation, the MVA algorithm remains unchanged. That is, after computing response times, we obtain throughputs by applying Little's law to the entire network, and then go back and compute the marginal probabilities $P_i(\mathbf{n}_i|\mathbf{N})$ for $\mathbf{n}_i > \mathbf{0}$. Finally, we get $P_i(0|\mathbf{N})$ using

$$P_i(0|\mathbf{N}) = 1 - \sum_{\forall\, \mathbf{n}>\mathbf{0}} P_i(\mathbf{n}|\mathbf{N}) \qquad (1.3)$$

This last equation could be very problematic numerically, because a large number of probabilities must be summed before the subtraction. In contrast, the convolution algorithm does not alter its numerical characteristics very much. In terms of the time complexity, it is clear from equation (1.2) that general capacities increase the time complexity of MVA from $O(KNH)$ to $O(KH^2)$ per station, but convolution retains its $O(H^2)$ time complexity per station. On the other hand, while convolution always needs only $O(H)$ space, MVA needs $O(H^2)$ space for each station with chain-dependent capacity. Thus, *with general capacities, convolution is the better algorithm.*

Until now, we have discussed only two extremes — chain-independent capacity model and the general chain-dependent capacity model. It is, of course, possible to use a model that lies somewhere between these two extremes. For example, consider the form

$$C_{ir}(\mathbf{n}_i) = \alpha_i(n_i)\beta_{ir}(n_{ir}) \tag{1.4}$$

where α_i and β_{ir} are arbitrary functions. It is easy to verify that this form satisfies the product-form condition (6.6.3). It may be more desirable than either of the two extremes. It is possible to adapt both convolution and MVA for this case as well, as explored in Exercises 10.1 and 10.2. It may be noted that the restricted form improves MVA on all accounts (i.e., time complexity, space complexity, and numerical instability), but convolution is not affected significantly.

10.1.2 Networks with Variable Populations

In this section, we consider networks in which the population of each chain varies between some lower and upper bounds. Such networks are interesting because they allow a direct modeling of the variable degree of multiprogramming in computer systems, variable window size in computer networks, etc. The population change in such networks can be modeled by *loss* and *trigger* mechanisms. That is, after exiting a regular station, a customer may drop into a "control" node and disappear. Independently, the control node may spawn a new customer (with exponentially distributed spawn time). The loss and trigger rates for a chain may either depend on the total network population or on the population of that particular chain. This dependence allows us to control the way the population changes (and to enforce lower and upper bounds on chain populations).

We have already encountered a special case of such models: namely, open models where the external arrival rate depends on the network state. In such models, the exit of a customer from the system can be considered a "loss", and the arrival a "trigger". Variable population models are more general than these because they allow the set of feasible populations to be chosen arbitrarily. Thus, the algorithms of this section can be easily adapted to solve open models with state-dependent arrival rates.

Let us define each feasible population $\mathbf{N}$ as a *macrostate* of the network. Recall that in Section 6.2.3 we required the following concerning the arrival rates: for each chain r, if $\Lambda_r(k) = 0$ for any k then $\Lambda_r(n) = 0$ for all $n > k$. This is needed for the irreducibility of the Markov chain. Let L_r denote the largest population of chain r such that $\Lambda_r(L_r - 1) > 0$, and let $\mathbf{L} = (L_1, \ldots, L_K)$. In Section 6.2.3, every population $\mathbf{N} < \mathbf{L}$ was feasible, whereas now any *irreducible subset* of macrostates is permitted. Let us denote this subset as S_{mac}. Since we are considering a network of quasi-reversible queues and the inter-trigger time is exponentially distributed, it follows that the lost customers should form an independent Poisson stream. Thus, we can describe changes to the macrostate by a Markov chain, denoted $\mathcal{Z}_{\text{mac}}$. We shall assume that this Markov chain is reversible. Therefore, for any pair of states $\mathbf{N}$ and $\mathbf{N} - e_r$, either there should be

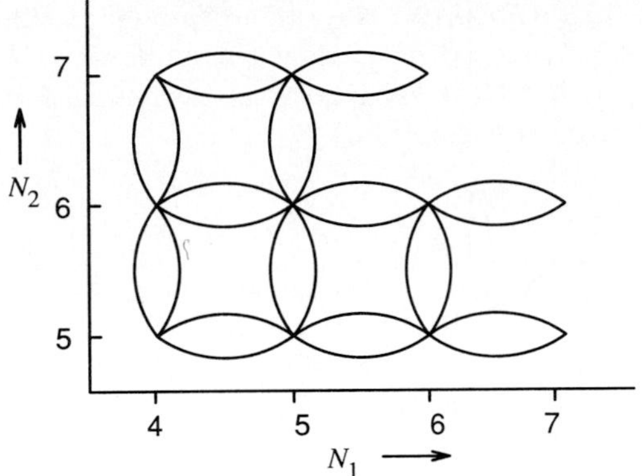

FIGURE 10-1: An example macrochain for networks with variable population.

no transition in either direction or in both directions, and the detailed balance must hold. Fig. 10-1 shows an example of $\mathcal{Z}_{\text{mac}}$ that is irreducible and reversible.

We assume that the trigger (or arrival) rate depends on the populations of individual chains. Similar statements can also be made for dependence on the total network population. Let $S_{\text{mic}}(\mathbf{N})$ denote the set of microstates of the queuing network model under population vector $\mathbf{N}$. An element of $S_{\text{mic}}(\mathbf{N})$ is given by $\vec{\mathbf{n}} = (\mathbf{n}_1, \ldots, \mathbf{n}_M)$ along with the restriction (6.3.1). Then S, the set of all states, is given by

$$S = \bigcup_{\mathbf{N} \in S_{\text{mac}}} S_{\text{mic}}(\mathbf{N}) \tag{1.5}$$

Since a transition at the macro level represents an arrival or departure of a customer at the micro level, and all queues are quasi-reversible, local balance should hold at the micro level. That is, the equations (6.2.17) and (6.2.19) still hold, except for the following differences:

1. Corresponding to each network state $\vec{\mathbf{n}}$, we can define the population vector $\mathbf{N} = (N_1, \ldots, N_K)$, which gives the number of customers of each chain in the network. This $\mathbf{N}$ must belong to the set of macrostates S_{mac}.
2. The proportionality constant is not $P(\mathbf{0})$, but instead some other number, which we denote by $1/G$. This results from the fact that not all possible macrostates are feasible.

Thus, the product-form solution in (6.2.19) can be expressed as

$$P(\vec{\mathbf{n}}) = \frac{\sigma(\mathbf{N})}{G} \prod_{i=1}^{M} X_i(\mathbf{n}_i|\mathbf{N}) \tag{1.6}$$

where

$$\sigma(\mathbf{N}) = \prod_{r=1}^{K} \prod_{k=0}^{N_r-1} \Lambda_r(k) \tag{1.7}$$

and $X_i(\mathbf{n}_i|\mathbf{N})$ is given by equation (6.3.18). $X_i(\mathbf{n}_i|\mathbf{N})$ can be interpreted as the *unnormalized probability* for station i in a closed network with population $\mathbf{N}$ having relative utilization u_{ir} for chain r. Let $G(\mathbf{N},\Omega)$ denote the normalization constant of this closed network. Then from equation (1.5),

$$G = \sum_{\forall \mathbf{N} \in S_{\text{mac}}} \sigma(\mathbf{N}) \sum_{\forall \vec{\mathbf{n}} \in S_{\text{mic}}(\mathbf{N})} \prod_{i=1}^{M} X_i(\mathbf{n}_i|\mathbf{N}) \tag{1.8}$$

which can be rewritten as

$$G = \sum_{\forall \mathbf{N} \in S_{\text{mac}}} \sigma(\mathbf{N}) G(\mathbf{N},\Omega) \tag{1.9}$$

We are now ready to discuss the computational algorithms. Let us start with the convolution algorithm. It is clear that we can compute $G(\mathbf{N},\Omega)$ in equation (1.9) efficiently using the regular convolution algorithm. Let $\mathcal{P}(\mathbf{N})$ denote the probability that the network has population $\mathbf{N}$. From equation (1.6), we have

$$\mathcal{P}(\mathbf{N}) \triangleq \sum_{\forall\, \vec{\mathbf{n}} \in S_{\text{mic}}(\mathbf{N})} P(\vec{\mathbf{n}}) = \frac{\sigma(\mathbf{N})G(\mathbf{N},\Omega)}{G} \tag{1.10}$$

Let $P_i(\mathbf{n}_i|\mathbf{N})$ denote the marginal distribution of station i, given that the network has population $\mathbf{N}$. By definition then,

$$P_i(\mathbf{n}_i) = \sum_{\forall\, \mathbf{N} \geq \mathbf{n}_i} P_i(\mathbf{n}_i|\mathbf{N})\mathcal{P}(\mathbf{N}) \tag{1.11}$$

Here $P_i(\mathbf{n}_i|\mathbf{N})$ can be computed using equation (7.3.8) or (7.3.9), depending on whether station i is load-dependent or load-independent. Thus, the marginal distribution $P_i(\mathbf{n}_i)$ can be obtained. [If only the average queue lengths are needed, we can instead use equation (1.14) derived later in this section.] For the throughput, we can obtain the following interesting relationship.

Lemma 10.1 The throughput of chain r at station i is given by

$$\lambda_{ir} = \frac{v_{ir}}{G} \sum_{\forall\, \mathbf{N} \in S_{\text{mic}},\ N_r > 0} G(\mathbf{N}-e_r,\Omega)\sigma(\mathbf{N}) \tag{1.12}$$

Proof Let $\mathbf{L}$ denote the largest population vector in the set S_{mic}. By the throughput law and equation (1.11), we have

$$\begin{aligned}
\lambda_{ir} &= \sum_{\mathbf{n}_i = e_r}^{\mathbf{L}} \mu_{ir}^{*}(\mathbf{n}_i) \sum_{\forall\, \mathbf{N} \geq \mathbf{n}_i} P_i(\mathbf{n}_i|\mathbf{N})\mathcal{P}(\mathbf{N}) \\
&= \sum_{\mathbf{n}_i = e_r}^{\mathbf{L}} \frac{n_{ir}}{n_i} \mu_{ir}^{\circ} C_{ir}(\mathbf{n}_i) \sum_{\forall\, \mathbf{N} \geq \mathbf{n}_i} \frac{G(\mathbf{N}-\mathbf{n}_i, \Omega - \{i\})}{G(\mathbf{N},\Omega)} X_i(\mathbf{n}_i) \frac{G(\mathbf{N},\Omega)\sigma(\mathbf{N})}{G}
\end{aligned}$$

Using equation (7.4.2) and simplifying, we get

$$\lambda_{ir} = \frac{v_{ir}}{G} \sum_{\mathbf{n}_i = e_r}^{\mathbf{L}} \sum_{\forall\, \mathbf{N} \geq \mathbf{n}_i} \sigma(\mathbf{N}) G(\mathbf{N} - \mathbf{n}_i, \Omega - \{i\}) X_i(\mathbf{n}_i - e_r)$$

The crucial step now is the change in the order of summation, which gives

$$\lambda_{ir} = \frac{v_{ir}}{G} \sum_{\forall\, \mathbf{N},\ N_r > 0} \sigma(\mathbf{N}) \sum_{\mathbf{n}_i = e_r}^{\mathbf{N}} G(\mathbf{N} - \mathbf{n}_i, \Omega - \{i\}) X_i(\mathbf{n}_i - e_r)$$

Since $\mathbf{N} - \mathbf{n}_i$ can be expressed as $\mathbf{N} - e_r - (\mathbf{n}_i - e_r)$, by applying equation (7.3.2) to the inner summation, we get the final result. □

With G defined in equation (1.9), it is easy to see that equation (1.12) is a straightforward extension of the throughput theorem in equation (7.3.10). We can put this equation in an even more intuitive form. Using the throughput theorem and equation (1.10) in (1.12), we get

$$\lambda_{ir} = \sum_{\forall\, \mathbf{N} \in S_{\text{mic}}} \lambda_{ir}(\mathbf{N}) \mathcal{P}(\mathbf{N}) \tag{1.13}$$

where we have removed the condition $N_r > 0$ with the understanding that $\lambda_{ir}(\mathbf{N})$ is zero whenever chain r is empty. With marginal distribution and throughputs known, other parameters can be obtained in a standard way. From equations (1.11) and (1.13) we see that *the results for variable population networks can be obtained by a mere superimposition of results for closed networks*. It should also be clear that equations (1.11) and (1.13) hold irrespective of other features such as chain-dependent capacities, state-dependent routing, blocking, etc. Also, *the complexity of the algorithm is comparable to that of solving a closed network with population equal to the largest population vector* $\mathbf{L}$. This is because the most expensive part of the algorithm is the computation of G values, and the computation of $G(\mathbf{L})$ automatically yields G at all smaller population vectors. Unfortunately, this also means that the structure of S_{mac} cannot be exploited for reducing the complexity.

Next, let us consider the MVA algorithm. Here again, we basically superimpose the results for individual population vectors. Thus, once $\lambda_{ir}(\mathbf{N})$ is obtained via the regular MVA, we can get the overall λ_{ir} from equation (1.13). Similarly, we can use (1.11) to compute the general marginal distribution, after computing $P_i(\mathbf{n}_i|\mathbf{N})$ using the regular MVA. However, if only the average performance parameters are needed, we can get a similar expression for the queue length. By definition, $Q_{ir} = \sum_{\forall\, \mathbf{n}_i} n_{ir} P_i(\mathbf{n}_i)$. Using equation (1.11), changing the order of summation as we did above, and simplifying, we get the following intuitive result

$$Q_{ir} = \sum_{\forall\, \mathbf{N} \in S_{\text{mic}}} Q_{ir}(\mathbf{N}) \mathcal{P}(\mathbf{N}) \tag{1.14}$$

where $Q_{ir}(\mathbf{N})$ is the queue length in a closed network with population $\mathbf{N}$. Thus, the only thing remaining is the computation of $\mathcal{P}(\mathbf{N})$. Unfortunately, it is not possible to compute this in a pure MVA setting because we cannot consider the macromodel independent of the micromodel. However, we can also compute the G's recursively in the MVA algorithm by using the throughput theorem. That is, after $\lambda_{ir}(\mathbf{n})$ has been computed, we can compute $G(\mathbf{n})$ as

$$G(\mathbf{n}, \Omega) = \frac{v_{ir}}{\lambda_{ir}(\mathbf{n})} G(\mathbf{n} - e_r, \Omega) \tag{1.15}$$

where $G(\mathbf{0}, \Omega)$ is initialized as 1. This completes the MVA algorithm. As with convolution, at the macrolevel the complexity depends primarily on the largest population vector in the set S_{mic}, rather than on the size of S_{mic}. However, as discussed in Section 7.4, the use of MVA at the microlevel would exploit chain-independent capacities, but convolution would not.

10.1.3 State-Dependent Routing

We start with the practical significance of state-dependent routing. It is intuitively clear and in many cases provable that whenever we have a set of resources with similar functionality, loading them equally (i.e., achieving the same utilization) will yield better performance than if the loads were uneven. Therefore, *adaptive routing* is often used in real systems to achieve balanced loads. The adaptive routing may either be deterministic (e.g., routing to the station with the shortest queue) or probabilistic (e.g., varying the probability of routing according to the queue length). State-dependent routing, as it applies to product-form networks, is a probabilistic model, but can also approximate deterministic routing by using multiple, nested levels with different thresholds.

The conditions stated in Section 6.6 for product-form solution under state-dependent routing concerned only the current level. If the subnetwork such as the one shown in Fig. 6-7 lies on a branch of a higher-level subnetwork, we would have a routing probability associated with this branch as well. This higher-level subnetwork could itself have state-dependent routing. Thus, in general, at nesting level l, the effective routing probability could be a l-fold product of terms like those in equation (6.6.2). Fortunately, the nesting can be handled by a recursive solution technique, and thus the characterization in (6.6.2) is adequate. The recursive solution is made possible by Norton's theorem, discussed in Section 8.1, which allows us to replace any arbitrary subnetwork of a product-form network by a single station. Thus, at any level of nesting we can assume that each component of the "parallel subnetwork" is a single station. Therefore, from this point onward, we assume that of the M stations that consist of the network, stations $1\,..\,m$ form the parallel subnetwork and the rest have state-independent routing. The "source" station s could be any one of the stations $m+1\,..\,M$.

Let us now examine equation (6.6.2) more closely. Basically, $q_{sjr}(n_{jr})$ need only be of the following form

$$q_{sjr}(n_{jr}) = h_{jr}(n_{jr}) / h_r(n_r) \tag{1.16}$$

where h_{jr} and h_r are functions of n_{jr} and n_r respectively. (The first function can be different for each station j, hence the subscript j in h_{jr}.) Since all the routing probabilities must sum to 1, the function h_r must be a sum of h_{jr}'s. This requires that h_{jr}'s be linear and of the form

$$h_{jr}(n) = a_r n + b_{jr} \tag{1.17}$$

which implies that

$$h_r(n_r) = \sum_{k=1}^{m} h_{kr}(n_{kr}) = a_r n_r + \sum_{k=1}^{m} b_{kr} \tag{1.18}$$

and we get the form in equation (6.6.2). The state dependence also requires a redefinition of the concept of "visit ratios". Obviously, the true visit ratios will now be state-dependent and cannot be computed in advance. For this reason, we shall exclude the state-dependent aspect from the visit ratios. That is, in Fig. 6-7, we let $v_{jr} = v_{sr}$ for all $j \in 1..m$ and account for the state-dependent part explicitly. Let X_i be defined as in equation (6.3.18), and

$$f_{jr}(n) = \prod_{k=0}^{n-1} h_{jr}(k) \qquad g_r(n) = \prod_{k=0}^{n-1} h_r(k) \tag{1.19}$$

For generality, we shall consider a closed network with state-dependent routing. The global balance equations are easy to write and we omit them. Let j be a station in the subnetwork and i outside it. We could then write a local balance equation expressing $P(\vec{\mathbf{n}})$ in terms of $P(\vec{\mathbf{n}} - e_{jr} + e_{ir})$ almost by inspection. By equation (1.16), the true visit ratio of chain r at station j in the network state $\vec{\mathbf{n}}$ is $v_{jr}h_{jr}(n_{jr}-1)/h_r(n_r-1)$. Therefore, in analogy with equation (6.3.16), we can write the following local balance equation:

$$\mu^*_{jr}(\mathbf{n}_j)P(\vec{\mathbf{n}}) = \frac{v_{jr}}{v_{ir}} \frac{h_{jr}(n_{jr}-1)}{h_r(n_r-1)} \mu^*_{ir}(\mathbf{n}_i + e_r) \times P(\vec{\mathbf{n}} - e_{jr} + e_{ir}) \tag{1.20}$$

It can be shown that this is a correct local balance equation. By using it repeatedly over all components of $\mathbf{n}_j = (n_{j1}, \ldots, n_{jK})$ we get $\prod_{r=1}^{K} f_{jr}(n_{jr})$ in the numerator and $\prod_{r=1}^{K} h_r(n_r-1)h_r(n_r-2)\cdots h_r(n_r-n_{jr})$ in the denominator. A similar reduction for all other stations eventually gives the following solution

$$P(\vec{\mathbf{n}}) = \frac{1}{G(\mathbf{N},\Omega)} \prod_{i=1}^{M} X_i(\mathbf{n}_i) \prod_{r=1}^{K} \frac{1}{g_r(n_r)} \prod_{j=1}^{m} f_{jr}(n_{jr}) \tag{1.21}$$

where $X_i(\mathbf{n}_i)$ is again defined by (6.3.18). It is easy to verify that if we let $h_r(k) = 1$ and $h_{jr}(k) = q_{sjr}$ for all $j \in 1..m$ and $r \in 1..K$, we get back the solution for the state-independent case.[1] Thus, the solution in equation (1.21)

[1] Because of the modified definition of the visit ratios, the $\prod_{r=1}^{K} q_{sjr}^{n_{jr}}$ term must be absorbed into the $X_j(\mathbf{n}_j)$ term.

can be used in general. Now, suppose that we define f_{ir} as identically 1 for all stations outside the parallel subnetwork, and let

$$X_i'(\mathbf{n}_i) = X_i(\mathbf{n}_i)\prod_{r=1}^{K} f_{ir}(n_{ir}) \triangleq \frac{n_i!}{V_i(\mathbf{n}_i)}\prod_{r=1}^{K}\frac{f_{ir}(n_{ir})u_{ir}^{n_{ir}}}{n_{ir}!} \tag{1.22}$$

Then we can rewrite equation (1.21) in the following more compact form

$$P(\vec{\mathbf{n}}) = \frac{1}{G(\mathbf{N},\Omega)}\prod_{i=1}^{M} X_i'(\mathbf{n}_i)\prod_{r=1}^{K}\frac{1}{g_r(n_r)} \tag{1.23}$$

We note at this point that state-dependent routing can be extended further somewhat, and the extension provides a limited form of rejection blocking. With reference to Fig. 6-7, the extension is to have a nonzero state-dependent routing probability from station s to station d. This branch can, in effect, be used to route customers if no more can be admitted into the parallel subnetwork. However, since we can handle general rejection blocking, we shall not pursue this possibility.

We now show how the convolution algorithm can be extended to handle state-dependent routing. Let $\Omega_p = \{1\,..\,m\}$ and $\Omega' = \Omega - \Omega_p$. Obviously, $G(\mathbf{n}, \Omega')$ can be obtained by the regular convolution algorithm. Let

$$G^*(\mathbf{n}, \Omega_p) = \sum_{\forall S(\Omega_p,\mathbf{n})}\prod_{i=1}^{m} X_i'(\mathbf{n}_i) \tag{1.24}$$

This can also be computed by the standard convolution algorithm, except that the function f_{ir} in X_i' rules out efficient computation even if station i is load-independent, and a straight convolution of X_i''s must be performed. Let $\mathbf{k} = (k_1, \ldots, k_r)$ denote a vector such that k_r gives the number of chain r customers in the subnetwork Ω_p. Also, let

$$\zeta(\mathbf{k}) = \prod_{r=1}^{K} g_r^{-1}(k_r) \tag{1.25}$$

Then by equation (1.23), we have

$$\begin{aligned} G(\mathbf{N},\Omega) &= \sum_{\forall\,\mathbf{S}}\left[\prod_{i=1}^{m} X_i'(\mathbf{n}_i)\zeta(\mathbf{k})\prod_{i=m+1}^{M} X_i(\mathbf{n}_i)\right] \\ &= \sum_{\mathbf{k}=\mathbf{0}}^{\mathbf{N}}\left[\sum_{\mathbf{S}(\Omega_p,\mathbf{k})}\prod_{i=1}^{m} X_i'(\mathbf{n}_i)\zeta(\mathbf{k})\right]\left[\sum_{\mathbf{S}(\Omega',\mathbf{N}-\mathbf{k})}\prod_{i=m+1}^{M} X_i(\mathbf{n}_i)\right] \\ &= \sum_{\mathbf{k}=\mathbf{0}}^{\mathbf{N}} G^*(\mathbf{k},\Omega_p)\zeta(\mathbf{k})G(\mathbf{N}-\mathbf{k},\Omega') \end{aligned} \tag{1.26}$$

Thus, apart from the $\zeta(\mathbf{k})$ term, equation (1.26) is exactly the convolution theorem, and can be used to compute the G's. The only remaining problem is to relate performance measures to G's. Of course, nothing changes for stations $m+1 \mathinner{..} M$, so let us only consider a station j belonging to Ω_p. The marginal distribution can be determined using the following equation

$$P_j(\mathbf{n}|\mathbf{N}) = \frac{X_j'(\mathbf{n})}{G(\mathbf{N},\Omega)} \sum_{\mathbf{k}=\mathbf{n}}^{\mathbf{N}} G^*(\mathbf{k}-\mathbf{n},\Omega_p - \{j\})\zeta(\mathbf{k})G(\mathbf{N}-\mathbf{k},\Omega') \tag{1.27}$$

This equation is a straightforward extension of equation (7.3.8). It results from the observation that if $\mathbf{n}$ customers are fixed at station j, then (a) the parallel subnetwork must contain $\mathbf{k} \geq \mathbf{n}$ customers, of which $\mathbf{k}-\mathbf{n}$ are distributed over other stations of the subnetwork, and (b) the remaining network should contain $\mathbf{N}-\mathbf{k}$ customers. Using this marginal distribution we can determine the queue-length moments. We can also determine the throughputs using the throughput *law* in equation (4.4.13). Note that the throughput theorem no longer holds.

We can also develop the MVA algorithm, but it is cumbersome to describe. For simplicity, we first solve the subnetworks Ω_p and Ω' in isolation to obtain their flow-equivalent stations, and then solve the resulting two-station network (see Section 8.1). Therefore, it suffices to consider a station j *inside the isolated subnetwork* Ω_p. For this case, by equation (1.26) $G(\mathbf{N},\Omega_p) = G^*(\mathbf{N},\Omega_p)\zeta(\mathbf{N})$, and equation (1.27) simplifies to

$$P_j(\mathbf{n}|\mathbf{N}) = \frac{X_j'(\mathbf{n})}{G(\mathbf{N},\Omega_p)} G^*(\mathbf{N}-\mathbf{n},\Omega_p - \{j\})\zeta(\mathbf{N}) \tag{1.28}$$

Let us now define a quantity θ_{jr} as

$$\theta_{jr}(\mathbf{N}) = \frac{1}{h_r(N_r-1)} \sum_{n=0}^{N_r-1} h_{jr}(n)P_{jr}(n|\mathbf{N}-e_r) \tag{1.29}$$

where P_{jr} gives the chain-dependent marginal distribution. We could then express throughput via a relationship that looks much like the throughput theorem, i.e.,

$$\lambda_{jr}(\mathbf{N}) = v_{jr}\theta_{jr}(\mathbf{N})\frac{G(\mathbf{N}-e_r,\Omega_p)}{G(\mathbf{N},\Omega_p)} \tag{1.30}$$

The proof of this relationship is sketched in Exercise 10.3. We can also derive the following marginal local balance-like equation

$$P_j(\mathbf{n}_j|\mathbf{N}) = \frac{h_{jr}(n_{jr}-1)}{\mu_{jr}^*(\mathbf{n}_j)h_r(N_r-1)\theta_{jr}(\mathbf{N})}\lambda_{jr}(\mathbf{N})P_j(\mathbf{n}_j - e_r|\mathbf{N}-e_r) \tag{1.31}$$

The proof of this is sketched in Exercise 10.4. We can use these two equations in the MVA algorithm in the usual manner. That is, using (1.31) we can write down an expression for the response time that involves parameters only at population $\mathbf{N}-e_r$.

$$R_{jr}(\mathbf{N}) = s^{\circ}_{jr} \sum_{\forall \mathbf{n}_j, n_{jr}>0} \frac{n_j h_{jr}(n_{jr}-1)}{C_{jr}(\mathbf{n}_j) h_r(N_r-1)\theta_{jr}(\mathbf{N})} P_j(\mathbf{n}_j - e_r|\mathbf{N}-e_r) \quad (1.32)$$

Unfortunately, because of the h_{jr} function in equation (1.31), even if the station has load-independent capacity, we cannot work with only aggregate marginal probabilities as in equation (7.4.6). However, we can use the same techniques as those for dealing with capacities of the form (1.4), and this would avoid a direct summation over all vectors in equation (1.32). Basically, we only need to maintain probabilities of finding a total of n_j customers at the station, of which n_{jr} belong to chain r. Exercise 10.2 explores the MVA algorithm for this case. Other details of the MVA algorithm are straightforward and are omitted.

10.1.4 Rejection Blocking

Rejection blocking, as it applies to product-form networks, requires the rejected customer to return to the source for another round of service. This is realistic in telecommunication applications, where rejection corresponds to a dropped packet which must be retransmitted by the source. However, the product-form solution also requires two further restrictions:

1. On the next try, a rejected customer must once again choose its destination in a probabilistic manner. This is unrealistic in most applications, though situations involving random rerouting along alternate paths do arise occasionally.
2. The topology of the subnetwork involving rejection blocking is similar to the one shown in Fig. 6-7. That is, station s is of the nonblocking type, and blocking occurs only with regard to the routing from station s to stations $1..m$.

Rejection blocking can be specified by a *blocking function*, which gives the probability that an incoming customer will be accepted into the station. We denote the blocking function for station i and chain r as $b_{ir}(\mathbf{n}_i)$, where, as usual, $\mathbf{n}_i$ gives the state of station i. We express this function as follows:

$$b_{ir}(\mathbf{n}_i) = h_{ir}(n_{ir})/h_i(n_i) \quad (1.33)$$

where the functions h_{ir} and h_i are arbitrary as long as $0 \le b_{ir}(\mathbf{n}_i) \le 1$, and the Markov chain remains irreducible. Irreducibility is ensured if h_{ir} is such that if $h_{ir}(k) = 0$ for some k, then it remains zero for all $n > k$. Since b_{ir} will appear as a multiplicative coefficient to u_{ir} in the local balance equation, the product-form solution takes the following form

$$P(\vec{\mathbf{n}}) = \frac{1}{G(\mathbf{N},\Omega)} \prod_{i=1}^{M} \left[X_i(\mathbf{n}_i) \prod_{k=1}^{n_i} h_i^{-1}(k-1) \times \prod_{r=1}^{K} \prod_{k=1}^{n_{ir}} h_{ir}(k-1) \right] \quad (1.34)$$

We can express this solution in a much more compact form. First, the h_i term can be absorbed into the capacity function even when the original capacity is chain-independent by defining:

$$C_i'(k) = C_i(k)h_i(k-1) \quad \text{and} \quad V_i'(n) = \prod_{k=1}^{n} C_i'(k) \tag{1.35}$$

Of course, similar equations apply for the general case as well, and hence we shall use $V_i'(\mathbf{n}_i)$ in the following for the modified V function. The conclusion is that the h_i function does not buy us any modeling power; we could as well choose the capacity function appropriately. Furthermore, let

$$f_{ir}'(n_{ir}) = \prod_{k=1}^{n_{ir}} h_{ir}(k-1) \tag{1.36}$$

$$X_i'(\mathbf{n}_i) = \frac{n_i!}{V_i'(n_i)} \prod_{r=1}^{K} \frac{f_{ir}'(n_{ir})u_{ir}^{n_{ir}}}{n_{ir}!} \tag{1.37}$$

Then we get the following expression for the product-form solution

$$P(\vec{\mathbf{n}}) = \frac{1}{G} \prod_{i=1}^{M} X_i'(\mathbf{n}_i) \tag{1.38}$$

which is identical in form to equation (6.3.17). This form also shows the similarities and differences between state-dependent routing and blocking. Note that equation (1.23) is somewhat more involved than equation (1.38) because of the g_r function. On the other hand, while in equation (1.19) h_{jr} must be linear, h_{ir} in equation (1.36) can be arbitrary. Thus, the two features are incomparable.

Let us now turn to the computational algorithms. It is clear from equations (1.37) and (1.38) that the only difference between rejection-blocking networks and the regular ones is in the definition of the X_i function. Suppose that instead of using the regular V_i function, we use

$$V_i^*(\mathbf{n}_i) = V_i(\mathbf{n}_i) \frac{\prod_{k=1}^{n_i} h_i(k-1)}{\prod_{r=1}^{K} \prod_{k=1}^{n_{ir}} h_{ir}(k-1)} \tag{1.39}$$

Then the network can be analyzed like an ordinary product-form network. Now *if the station has a capacity of the form (1.4), the* V_i^* *function can also be characterized by a similar capacity function*. As a special case, if station i has chain-independent capacity, to characterize V_i^*, we can choose the following values for α_i and β_{ir} in the form (1.4):

$$\alpha_i(n) = h_i(n-1)C_i(n) \quad \text{and} \quad \beta_{ir}(n_r) = 1/h_{ir}(n_r - 1) \tag{1.40}$$

This observation has two consequences. First, the solution method of Exercise 10.2 can be applied to this problem, and second, rejection blocking does not add any more raw modeling power than capacities of the form (1.4).

We note here that the various features discussed in this and previous subsections can be mixed freely. For example, we have already retained the $V_i(\mathbf{n}_i)$ function in the equations above to allow for chain-dependent capacities. Similarly, if we have both state-dependent routing and rejection blocking, we can identify the solution easily. Let $f''_{ir} = f'_{ir} f_{ir}$. Then the product-form solution is as in equation (1.23), with X''_i given by

$$X''_i(\mathbf{n}_i) = \frac{n_i!}{V'_i(\mathbf{n}_i)} \prod_{r=1}^{K} \frac{f''_{ir}(n_{ir}) u_{ir}^{n_{ir}}}{n_{ir}!} \tag{1.41}$$

Note that equation (1.41) is computationally similar to equation (1.37) since if f'_{ir} is arbitrary, so is f''_{ir}.

It is important to note that in all cases of product-form solution, each station (or a station group in the case of state-dependent routing) contributes to a distinct term. This has two consequences: (a) it is trivial to identify the product-form solution where different stations have different characteristics, and (b) the convolution algorithm, which proceeds to compute G station by station, remains applicable in all cases. The MVA algorithm also applies; but because the nature of X_i's changes substantially, the details are more complex.

10.1.5 Mutual Blocking

Rejection blocking occurs because the needed passive resources (buffers, memory modules, devices, etc.) are in short supply. In some situations, a pool of passive resources may be accessible only via a limited number of agents (or servers). Thus, a request may not be granted either because all agents are busy or because the desired passive resource is in use. Here we assume that the requesting customer simply waits until its request can be granted. Formally, we can model the situation as follows. The resource pool consists of resources of type $1\,..\,C$. The customers that request resource of type $c \in 1\,..\,C$ can be identified as members of class c. There are b identical agents, and they can be viewed as the servers of a multiserver station i. The customers arrive at station i and wait until they can be served (in FCFS order). The service time is the resource access time and could be different for each class. Assume, for simplicity, that each of the C resource types contains but one unit. Then the correct modeling of the situation requires that station i serve at most one customer from each class. Note that if $b = 1$, this constraint is automatically satisfied; hence the problem is interesting only when i is a multiserver station. Also, if $b \geq c$, we could represent the situation by having C single-server stations corresponding to C passive resources and ignore the agents completely. Similarly, b must be smaller than the network population in order for the problem to be interesting. We call the resulting situation as *mutual blocking* because the customers of a given class block one another.

An example of mutual blocking is the bus contention problem in multiprocessor systems. Here the customers are processors, the resources are memory modules, and the servers are the busses. A processor wants to access a specific memory module, and to do that it needs a bus. The bus service time in this case represents the memory access time. Obviously, only one processor can access a given memory module at a time, even if other processors have a free bus available. That is, at most one customer from each class may be in service, even if there are free servers available. A different example is where the customers are processes, resources are critical sections, and the servers are CPU's.

It can be shown that mutual blocking also yields product-form solution, though the form of the solution is now much more complicated. Nevertheless, in view of the comments made above, the complexity is limited only to mutual-blocking stations, and the solution is completely specified if we give an expression for the X_i term corresponding to a station i that has mutual blocking. Let b_i denote the number of servers at station i, and $m_i > b_i$ the number of classes. That is, whenever a customer arrives at station i, it is assigned to one of m_i classes according to some probabilities. The state of the station can be described by the tuple $(\mathcal{A}_i, \mathbf{n}_{i1}, \ldots, \mathbf{n}_{iK})$ where $\mathcal{A}_i$ denotes the set of active classes and $\mathbf{n}_{ir}$ for $r \in 1..K$ is a vector of length m_i giving the number of customers of each class belonging to chain r that are present at station i. The component $\mathcal{A}_i$ is needed because whenever customers from more than b_i classes are present at the station, we need to know which b_i classes are currently active (or being served). We can consider $\mathcal{A}_i$ as a set of pairs (r, c), one for each active customer, where r denotes the chain and c denotes the class within the chain. Note that at the mutual blocking station, class c of any chain r has the same purpose, which is to access a particular resource. However, the probabilities used in assigning classes may vary from chain to chain. The X_i term for station i then takes the following form

$$X_i(\mathcal{A}_i, \mathbf{n}_{i1}, \ldots, \mathbf{n}_{iK}) = \prod_{r=1}^{K} n_{ir}! \left[\prod_{c=1}^{m_i} \frac{u_{irc}^{n_{irc}}}{n_{irc}!} \right] \psi(\mathcal{A}_i, \mathbf{n}_i) \prod_{(r,c)\in\mathcal{A}_i} u_{irc} \tag{1.42}$$

where n_{ir} represents the magnitude of the vector $\mathbf{n}_{ir}$ and following our usual notation, $\mathbf{n}_i$ is the vector of n_{ir}'s. The function ψ is defined recursively as follows:

$$\psi(\mathcal{A}_i, \mathbf{n}_i) = \begin{cases} b_i^{-1} \sum_{\forall r, n_{ir}>0} \psi(\mathcal{A}_i, \mathbf{n}_i - e_r) & \text{if } \exists (r,c) \notin \mathcal{A}_i, n_{ir} > 0 \\ 1 & \text{otherwise} \end{cases} \tag{1.43}$$

Once the marginal probability $P_i(\mathcal{A}_i, \mathbf{n}_i)$ is known, we can compute various performance measures of interest, such as average number of customers waiting to access a given resource, probability that a given resource is being accessed, server utilization, waiting time due to unavailability of server, and the mutual blocking delay. In terms of the computational algorithms, it is still possible to use convolution over different stations, but because of equation (1.43) no further simplifications can be made.

10.2 Chain-Based Recursion Algorithms

In this section we discuss RECAL and MVAC, the two algorithms mentioned in Section 6.5.1. Both of these algorithms set up recursion on the number of chains in the network, and are well suited for networks with a small number of stations and many chains. RECAL, like convolution, computes the normalization constant, but MVAC deals with the performance parameters directly. *Both of these algorithms require chain-independent capacities, and we shall assume this to be the case.*

10.2.1 Recursion-By-Chain Algorithm

RECAL computes the normalization constant by a recursive algorithm that introduces one chain at a time. Since all chains share the service station through which they pass, we cannot simply ignore not-yet-introduced chains. Instead, the customers of some chains are included in the normal way, whereas the others are *fixed*, i.e., allocated to various stations in some way. The idea is then to start with all *fixed chains*, and gradually start including them in a normal way. At any stage, let w_i denote the number of *fixed* customers at station i, and n_i the *normal* customers. Then, the effective capacity of station i from the point of view of the normal customers, denoted θ_i, is given by

$$\theta_i(n_i, w_i) = \frac{n_i}{n_i + w_i} C_i(n_i + w_i) \tag{2.1}$$

We can think of the fixed customers as cycling around at station i in a closed chain and consuming the fraction $w_i/(n_i+w_i)$ of the server capacity. Let $G_k(\mathbf{w}_k)$ denote the normalization constant of a network with chains $1..k$ included in the normal way, and the customers of the rest of the $K-k$ chains distributed according to the vector $\mathbf{w}_k = (w_{1k}, \ldots, w_{Mk})$. Henceforth we shall denote the set of all feasible values of $\mathbf{w}_k$ as W_k. We then recursively compute G_k for all $\mathbf{w}_k \in W_k$ using appropriate G_{k-1}'s. When $k = K$, we have already accounted for customers of all K chains in the normal way; therefore, $G_K(\mathbf{0})$ is the desired normalization constant of the entire network.

To simplify computations, we replace each chain k with N_k chains, each with population 1. Let $\mathcal{Z}$ denote the original network, and $\mathcal{Z}^\circ$ the modified network. In the following, the quantities with the degree sign will denote those pertaining to $\mathcal{Z}^\circ$ instead of $\mathcal{Z}$. Obviously, $N^\circ = K^\circ = N$. Let us enumerate the customers in $\mathcal{Z}^\circ$ as $1, \ldots, N$, and let $\sigma(k)$ denote the chain in $\mathcal{Z}$ to which the kth customer belongs. Then the basic recursion for computing G's can be stated as follows:

$$G_k^\circ(\mathbf{w}_k) = \sum_{i=1}^{M} \frac{(1 + w_{ik}) u_{i\sigma(k)} G_{k-1}^\circ(\mathbf{w}_k + e_i)}{C_i(1 + w_{ik})} \tag{2.2}$$

with the initial condition $G_0^\circ(\mathbf{w}_0) = 1$ for all $\mathbf{w}_0 \in W_0$. Obviously, W_0 is the set of all possible ways of distributing $N = |\mathbf{N}|$ customers over all the stations. This equation has a simple intuitive interpretation: In the situation being considered, the customers of chains $k+1..K$ remain allocated to various stations according to the vector $\mathbf{w}_k$. Now, in the previous step, the chain k customer would also have been allocated in this way. Thus, $G_{k-1}(\mathbf{w}_k + e_i)$ represents the unnormalized probability of that allocation, assuming that the chain k customer was placed at station i. The probability of placing the chain k customer at station i must be proportional to its effective relative utilization[2], which is $u_{i\sigma(k)}$ divided by the capacity available to this customer. The latter is obviously $C_i(1+w_{ik})/(1+w_{ik})$.

The recursion in equation (2.2) will start with $G_0^\circ(\mathbf{w}_0)$'s, and eventually yield $G_N^\circ(\mathbf{0})$ and $G_{N-1}^\circ(e_i)$ for $i \in 1..M$. In turn, these can be used to compute various performance measure of *the last numbered chain* (i.e., chain N or K° of $\mathcal{Z}^\circ$). Since all customers belonging to a chain of $\mathcal{Z}$ are statistically identical, we can immediately get the performance measures for chain $\sigma(K^\circ)$ as

$$\begin{aligned} \lambda_{i\sigma(K^\circ)}(\mathbf{N}) &= N_{\sigma(K^\circ)}\lambda^\circ{}_{iK^\circ}(\mathbf{N}) \\ R_{i\sigma(K^\circ)}(\mathbf{N}) &= R^\circ{}_{iK^\circ}(\mathbf{N}) \end{aligned} \tag{2.3}$$

which also implies that $U_{i\sigma(K^\circ)}(\mathbf{N})$ and $Q_{i\sigma(K^\circ)}(\mathbf{N})$ can be obtained by multiplying those for chain K° by $N_{\sigma(K^\circ)}$.

Now, to calculate performance measures for other chains, we can renumber the customers in $\mathcal{Z}^\circ$ such that the chain $\sigma(K^\circ)$ is changed to another chain. To minimize the recomputation needed in equation (2.2) because of this change, we initially number the chains of $\mathcal{Z}^\circ$ such that the last K chains in $\mathcal{Z}^\circ$ include all the K chains of $\mathcal{Z}$. Let $\eta(i) = \sum_{k=1}^{i}(N_k - 1)$ with $\eta(0) = 0$. Note that $\eta(K) = N - K$. Let $\sigma^{(1)}$ denote the initial numbering function. By definition, $\sigma^{(1)}(k)$ gives the chain of $\mathcal{Z}$ to which chain k of $\mathcal{Z}^\circ$ corresponds. It can be characterized as follows:

$$\sigma^{(1)}(k) = \begin{cases} i & \text{if } 1 + \eta(i-1) \le k \le \eta(i) \quad 1 \le i \le K \\ N - k + 1 & \text{if } 1 + \eta(K) \le k \le N \end{cases} \tag{2.4}$$

As an example, suppose that $\mathcal{Z}$ has three chains and the population vector $\mathbf{N} = (3,4,2)$. Then $\sigma^{(1)}$ arranges these nine customers into 9 chains as follows: 1,1,2,2,2,3,3,2,1. That is, chains 1, 2, and 9 of $\mathcal{Z}^\circ$ correspond to the original chain 1.

Let us now consider the renumbering function $\sigma^{(s+1)}$ for computing parameters for chain $s+1$ (after computing those for chain s). This function simply rotates the last $K - s + 1$ chains by one position to make chain $s+1$ the last chain. Formally,

$$\sigma^{(s+1)}(k) = \begin{cases} \sigma^{(s)}(k) & \text{for } 1 \le k \le s - 1 + \eta(K) \\ s & \text{for } k = s + \eta(K) \\ \sigma^{(s)}(k) + 1 & \text{for } s + 1 + \eta(K) \le k \le N \end{cases} \tag{2.5}$$

This re-enumeration ensures that in the $(s+1)$th iteration the first $n(s) = \eta(K) + s - 1$ chains of Z° are not affected; therefore, we only need to have $G_{n(s)}^\circ(\mathbf{w}_{n(s)})$ available for all feasible $\mathbf{w}_{n(s)}$, and can start the computation from there. (These optimizations are similar in spirit to those in ordinary convolution for load-dependent stations.)

---

[2] Recall that in a single-chain network with one customer, the state probabilities are proportional to the relative utilizations of the stations.

We now derive a few relationships between the performance parameters and G_k functions of $\mathcal{Z}°$. These results only require the last numbered chain to have unit population; therefore, in stating them we shall speak of the original network $\mathcal{Z}$.

Lemma 10.2 If chain K has unit population, then

$$\lambda_{iK}(\mathbf{N}) = v_{iK}\frac{G_{K-1}(\mathbf{0})}{G_K(\mathbf{0})} \tag{2.6}$$

$$Q_{iK}(\mathbf{N}) = u_{iK}\frac{G_{K-1}(e_i)}{G_K(\mathbf{0})} \tag{2.7}$$

Proof If N_K=1, the removal of a chain K customer amounts to the removal of chain K itself. Therefore, equation (2.6) follows from the throughput theorem. Also, the average queue length of chain K at station i is simply $Pr(\mathbf{n}_K = e_i)$. To see why this must equal the RHS in equation (2.7), note that if we use $w_K = \mathbf{0}$ in equation (2.2), the ith term on the right-hand side gives the unnormalized probability of having the sole chain K customer allocated to station i in a normal way. Dividing this by the normalization constant, we get $Pr(\mathbf{n}_K = e_i)$. □

Lemma 10.3 Suppose that chain K has unit population. If there is a delay station, say j, in the network, then $G_{K-1}(\mathbf{0}) = G_{K-1}(e_j)$. Otherwise, if all stations are load-independent, then

$$G_{K-1}(\mathbf{0}) = \sum_{j=1}^{M}\frac{G_{K-1}(e_j)}{(M+N-1)} \tag{2.8}$$

Proof If j is a delay station, $Q_{jk}(\mathbf{N}) = U_{jk}(\mathbf{N})$, and the result follows from equations (2.6) and (2.7). If there are no delay stations, equation (2.7) yields

$$\begin{aligned}\sum_{j=1}^{M} G_{K-1}(e_j) &= G_K(\mathbf{0})\sum_{j=1}^{M}\frac{U_{jK}(\mathbf{N})}{u_{jK}}(1+Q_j(\mathbf{N}-e_K)) \\ &= G_{K-1}(\mathbf{0})(M+N-1)\end{aligned}$$

where we have used the mean value theorem and equation (2.6). □

It would be noted from equation (2.2) that by the time we have computed $G_K(\mathbf{0})$, we would also have $G_{K-1}(e_i)$'s. However, to use equation (2.6), we need $G_{K-1}(\mathbf{0})$, which must be computed separately. Thus, the significance of Lemma 10.3 is that if the network has at least one delay station, or all stations are load-independent, we only need to follow the steps needed for computing $G_K(\mathbf{0})$.

The complete algorithm should now be obvious. The time and space complexity expressions for the algorithm are somewhat involved, therefore, we only mention some asymptotic results. Let us suppose that each chain has the same population $\overline{N} > 1$, which means that $N = \overline{N}K$. Then, if K is large, we get

$$\text{Time}: \quad \frac{(5M-1)}{(M+1)!}K^{M+1} \qquad \text{Space}: \quad \frac{\overline{N}^{M-1}+1}{(M-1)!}K^{M-1} \tag{2.9}$$

And if M is large

$$\text{Time}: \quad \frac{10M^N}{(N-1)!} \qquad \text{Space}: \quad \frac{2M^N}{N!} \tag{2.10}$$

It is clear that the algorithm is polynomial in the number of chains when K is large, and would perform well if M is small. On the other hand, if M is large, it may perform poorly even for moderate populations. This is indeed borne out in practice. As a final note, RECAL can take advantage of sparsity in routing much like tree-convolution discussed later in this section. Like convolution, RECAL suffers from the problem of overflow/underflow of G values, and proper scaling of relative utilizations is essential.

10.2.2 Mean Value Analysis by Chain

Mean value analysis by chain (MVAC) is related to RECAL in much the same way as ordinary MVA is related to convolution. Like RECAL, MVAC works by introducing one chain at a time, but it computes the performance parameters directly. Our description of the algorithm will be rather brief. It would be helpful for the reader to read Sections 10.2.1 and 7.4 before proceeding further with this section.

Like RECAL, we shall assume that the original network $\mathcal{Z}$ has been converted to the network $\mathcal{Z}^\circ$ where every chain has but one customer. Since equation (2.3) can be used to get parameters for $\mathcal{Z}$, we shall only consider computing parameters for $\mathcal{Z}^\circ$. For simplicity, we shall describe the version of the algorithm that applies to networks *without load-dependent stations*. In this case, equation (2.2) simplifies to the following

$$G_k(\mathbf{w}) = \sum_{m=1}^{M}(1 + w_m\delta_m)u_{mk}G_{k-1}(\mathbf{w} + e_m) \tag{2.11}$$

where δ_m is defined as 1 if station m is load-independent and as 0 if it is a delay station. We have also eliminated the subscript k from w_{mk} and $\mathbf{w}_k$. For $r \in \{1..N\}$, let $Q^k_{ir}(\mathbf{w})$ denote the mean number of chain r customers at station i for the network that has normalizing constant $G_k(\mathbf{w})$. It can be shown that the mean number of chain r customers at station i in a product-form queuing network is related to the derivative of the normalizing constant with respect to the relative utilization u_{ir}. (See Exercise 10.7). Applying this result to the network with normalizing constant $G_k(\mathbf{w})$ yields

$$\frac{dG_k(\mathbf{w})}{du_{ir}} = \frac{G_k(\mathbf{w})}{u_{ir}}Q^k_{ir}(\mathbf{w}) \tag{2.12}$$

Therefore, by differentiating equation (2.11) with respect to u_{ik} and using (2.12) on both sides, we get

$$Q_{ik}^{k}(\mathbf{w}) = (1 + w_i\delta_i)u_{ik}\frac{G_{k-1}(\mathbf{w} + e_i)}{G_k(\mathbf{w})} \tag{2.13}$$

Here we have used the fact that G_{k-1} does not involve chain k and thus is independent of u_{ik}. Next, differentiating equation (2.11) with respect to u_{ir}, $r = 1\,..\,k-1$, and using equation (2.12) yields

$$Q_{ir}^{k}(\mathbf{w}) = \sum_{m=1}^{M}(1 + w_m\delta_m)u_{mk}\frac{G_{k-1}(\mathbf{w} + e_m)}{G_k(\mathbf{w})}Q_{ir}^{k-1}(\mathbf{w} + e_m) \tag{2.14}$$

By substituting equation (2.13) into (2.14), we get

$$Q_{ir}^{k}(\mathbf{w}) = \sum_{m=1}^{M} Q_{mk}^{k}(\mathbf{w})Q_{ir}^{k-1}(\mathbf{w} + e_m) \qquad \text{for} \quad r = 1\,..\,k-1 \tag{2.15}$$

Summing equation (2.15) over $r = 1\,..\,k$ we get

$$Q_{i}^{k}(\mathbf{w}) = \sum_{m=1}^{M} Q_{mk}^{k}(\mathbf{w})Q_{i}^{k-1}(\mathbf{w} + e_m) + Q_{ik}^{k}(\mathbf{w}) \tag{2.16}$$

where $Q_i^k(\mathbf{w})$ is the mean number of "normal" (i.e., nonfixed) customers at station i for the network that has the normalizing constant $G_k(\mathbf{w})$.

We now invoke the key recursion from standard MVA. For $r = 1\,..\,k$ let $R_{ir}^k(\mathbf{w})$ denote the mean response time for chain r at station i for the network that has normalizing constant $G_k(\mathbf{w})$. Also let $\lambda_r^k(\mathbf{w})$ denote the chain r throughput at some specified station visited by chain r. (We choose visit ratios for chain r relative to this station.) Then if station i is load-independent, we have

$$R_{ik}^{k}(\mathbf{w}) = s_{ik}[1 + Q_i^{k-1}(\mathbf{w}) + w_i] \tag{2.17}$$

This equation should be obvious because the last two terms on the RHS give, respectively, the number of normal and fixed customers at station i when the lone chain k customer is removed from the network that has normalizing constant $G_k(\mathbf{w})$. By Little's law then, we have

$$Q_{ik}^{k}(\mathbf{w}) = \lambda_k^k(\mathbf{w})u_{ik}\left[1 + Q_i^{k-1}(\mathbf{w}) + w_i\right] \tag{2.18}$$

And for a delay station, we have

$$Q_{ik}^{k}(\mathbf{w}) = \lambda_k^k(\mathbf{w})u_{ik} \tag{2.19}$$

For simplicity, we number the stations so that stations $1\,..\,M_1$ are load-independent and stations $M_1 + 1\,..\,M$ are delay type. We assume $M_1 \geq 1$ since otherwise the network has a trivial solution. Since chain k has a single customer, by summing (2.18) and (2.19) over all stations, it follows that

$$\lambda_k^k(\mathbf{w}) = \left[\sum_{m=1}^{M} u_{mk} + \sum_{m=1}^{M_1} u_{mk}(Q_m^{k-1}(\mathbf{w}) + w_m)\right]^{-1} \tag{2.20}$$

Using these equations, we can thus execute one step of the MVAC algorithm, as shown in the procedure one-step in Fig. 10-2. The lower bound of the **for**-loop, denoted k_0, denotes the starting chain for the computation. Initially, we start with $k_0 = 1$. The ensuing computation will give results for chain N. Now to get performance parameters for another chain, all we have to do is renumber chains and recompute. For this, we can follow exactly the same approach as in RECAL. That is, after the initial computation we start off with $k_0 = N - K + 1$, and use the $\sigma^{(s)}$ function for renumbering in further iterations. It turns out that the renumbering is required only for those chains that do not pass through any delay station; however, we shall not go into the details of this optimization.

We shall now briefly comment on the computational cost of MVAC. Again, the actual cost expressions are rather involved, so we only consider asymptotic values. Let $\overline{N}$ be the population of each chain in the original network $\mathcal{Z}$. Then the time and space complexity of MVAC can be summarized as follows:

$$\begin{array}{ll} O(K^{M+2}) & \text{if } \overline{N} \text{ and } M \text{ fixed, } K \text{ large} \\ O(\overline{N}^{M+1}) & \text{if } K \text{ and } M \text{ fixed, } \overline{N} \text{ large} \\ O(M^{N+1}) & \text{if } \overline{N} \text{ and } K \text{ fixed, } M \text{ large} \end{array} \tag{2.21}$$

These costs are similar to the ones for RECAL (though a bit larger).

10.2.3 The DAC Algorithm

In some applications, it is desirable to compute joint queue length distributions (or their first few moments). Typically, this information is of concern if we want to study correlation between the congestion levels of two or more stations. In all the algorithms that we have described, we did not consider this computation. Any normalization constant based algorithm (e.g., convolution and RECAL) can be adapted trivially to obtain this information, since $P(\mathbf{n})$ [or $P(\vec{\mathbf{n}})$ in the multiple-chain case] itself is the joint distribution involving all stations and all chains. Starting from equation (7.4.3), it is easy to obtain necessary equations for the recursive computation of joint queue length distribution *at a given station* (e.g., the probability that there are n_{ir} chain r and n_{ik} chain k customers at station i) as explored in Exercise 10.8. The recursive computation of joint distributions involving *multiple stations* is also possible. One algorithm for doing this is called *distribution analysis by chain* or DAC and is similar in spirit to MVAC. That is, it works with single-customer chains and introduces them one by one. However, unlike RECAL and MVAC, chains $k+1..N$ are truly absent now, so the computations are much like ordinary MVA.

```
procedure one-step(k_0: integer);
begin
  for k := k_0 to N do
    begin
      for w ∈ {W_k ∪ ··· ∪ W_N} do
        begin
          Compute λ_k^k(w) using equation (2.20);
          for i := 1 to M do Compute Q_ik^k(w) using (2.18) and (2.19);
          for i := 1 to M do Compute Q_i^k(w) using (2.16);
        end ;
    end ;
end ;

begin        {beginning of the main program}
  Compute relative utilizations for all m ∈ 1..M, r ∈ 1..K.
  Initialize Q°_m(w) = 0 for m ∈ 1..M and w ∈ {W_0 ∪ ··· ∪ W_N}.
  Number chains of Z° according to σ^(1) function.
  call one-step(1);
  for s := 1 to K − 1 do
    begin
      Rotate last K − s + 1 chains according to σ^(s+1);
      call one-step(N − K + s);
    end ;
  Compute response time and utilization for all chains;
end ;
```

FIGURE 10-2: Mean value analysis by chain algorithm.

In the following, we provide a brief overview of DAC. Although this algorithm can compute regular performance parameters in addition to joint distributions, we shall concentrate here only on the latter. Also, we shall ignore chain membership and only examine the computation of joint distribution of total number of customers at a set of stations. Let $\mathbf{n} = (n_1, \ldots, n_M)$ denote the network state (ignoring chain memberships) and $\mathcal{P}(\mathbf{n})$ the state probability. Let us use the superscript k to indicate that only chains $1..k$ have been included. We still assume that the capacity functions are chain-independent. Using the product-form property, it is then easy to show the following recursion (see Exercise 10.9)

$$\mathcal{P}^k(\mathbf{n}) = \lambda_k^k(\mathbf{n}) \sum_{i=1}^{M} u_{ik} \frac{n_i}{\mu_i(n_i)} \mathcal{P}^{k-1}(\mathbf{n} - e_i) \tag{2.22}$$

where λ_k is the throughput of chain k (specified as the throughput of some station visited by chain k for which we assume a unit visit ratio). This equation can be used recursively for $k = 2..N$. For $k = 1$, we have only one customer in the network (since each chain contains only one customer). Therefore, $\mathbf{n}$ can only take the values e_i, $i \in 1..M$. Obviously,

$$\mathcal{P}^1(e_i) = u_{i1} / \sum_{m=1}^{M} u_{m1} \quad \text{for } i = 1..M \tag{2.23}$$

Now, in each step, we need to first compute λ_k^k. This is done as in the ordinary MVA. That is, given $\mathcal{P}^{k-1}(\mathbf{n} - e_i)$, we obtain $\mathcal{P}_i^{k-1}(n_i - 1)$, the marginal distribution for station i, by a simple summation over other stations. Then we apply equation (7.4.6) to get chain-dependent response time $R_{ik}^k(\mathbf{n})$'s, and finally use Little's Law over the entire network to get $\lambda_k^k(\mathbf{n})$. When the recursion ends, we would have the overall joint distribution over all stations, and the standard performance parameters (average response time, throughput, etc.) *for chain* N. It is also possible to get performance parameters of other chains by a renumbering scheme much like the one for RECAL/MVAC, but we shall omit the details. It turns out that DAC is not only somewhat simpler than MVAC, but also a bit more efficient.

Let us now compare the algorithms that we have seen thus far. The convolution algorithm works by introducing one station at a time, MVA by stepping through the population vectors, and RECAL/MVAC/DAC by stepping through the chains. These differences translate into a number of differences between the performance of these algorithms with respect to various characteristics of the problem.

Since both convolution and MVA must step through all population vectors in some way, their complexity is governed primarily by the product of chain populations. With chain-based recursion algorithms, the dominant factor is the number of ways of distributing the fixed customers (i.e., the number of states of a closed single-chain network). When M is small and K is large, this number does not grow very rapidly; therefore, chain-based recursions would be the preferred. But as M increases, the advantage of these algorithms is lost. In terms of generality, if the capacity function is chain-dependent, a scheme based on systematic chain addition must fail, but others still apply.

With convolution, if we wish to study the performance with station M deleted or modified (or with a new station added), the operation is computationally inexpensive. This is not true with other algorithms, since all stations must be considered throughout the computation. On the other hand, if we wish to study the performance at population $N + 1$, given the results for population N, MVA can handle the change most naturally (convolution is also easy to use, but requires the storage of the entire row for population N). Unfortunately, both RECAL and MVAC are unable to handle any changes easily. If we wish to study the network with the last chain deleted/modified or one more chain added, the only viable algorithm is DAC, since the computations here are truly independent of the not-yet-added chains.

10.3 Algorithms Exploiting Sparsity

Models of distributed systems and communication networks typically exhibit *sparsity*, which refers to the following two properties: (1) Most chains, on the average, visit only a fraction of the network, and (2) Chains are clustered in certain parts of the network. It is possible to exploit these properties and obtain an algorithm that would be much more efficient on typical problems arising in practice. In this section we shall see how this is done in the context of the convolution and MVA algorithms.

10.3.1 Tree-Convolution

The convolution algorithm of Section 7.3 convolves the G's of the individual stations sequentially in some order. However, since the convolution operator is associative and commutative, we can organize the convolutions in form of a tree that exploits the sparsity.

Let $\mathcal{V}(k)$ be the set of stations visited by chain k and let $\omega \subseteq \Omega$ be a subnetwork of the entire network Ω. With respect to ω, chain k is said to be *fully covered* if $\mathcal{V}(k) \subseteq \omega$; i.e., if all stations visited by chain k are included in ω. Similarly, chain k is said to be *noncovered* if $\mathcal{V}(k) \cap \omega = \phi$; i.e., none of the stations of ω are visited by chain k. In other cases, chain k is said to be *partially covered*. Thus, we can divide the set of all K chains into the subsets $\sigma_{pc}(\omega)$, $\sigma_{fc}(\omega)$, and $\sigma_{nc}(\omega)$, where pc, fc, and nc refer to partially covered, fully covered and noncovered conditions respectively.

Let $G(\cdot, \omega)$ denote the vector $[G(\mathbf{0}, \omega), \ldots, G(\mathbf{N}, \omega)]$, and suppose that we have already computed $G(\cdot, \Omega_0)$ for some subnetwork Ω_0. Let $\mathbf{c} = (c_1, \ldots, c_K)$ denote a vector where c_r represents the number of chain r customers in Ω_0. If chain r is fully covered by Ω_0, we only need $c_r = N_r$ in $G(\mathbf{c}, \Omega_0)$ for further computations of the G values. If it is uncovered, we only need $c_r = 0$ in $G(\mathbf{c}, \Omega_0)$. However, if chain r is partially covered by Ω_0, we need all values of c_r in the range $0 \mathinner{..} N_r$ for further computations. Thus, *it is adequate to store* $G(\cdot, \Omega_0)$ *as an array with as many dimensions as the number of partially covered chains*. It is clear that for networks with sparsity and locality property, the space savings could be considerable.

Sparsity yields savings in time also. To see this, let us partition the subnetwork Ω_0 into two disjoint subnets Ω_1 and Ω_2. Chain r is said to be *overlapped* if it is partially covered with respect to both Ω_1 and Ω_2. We can partition the set of K chains into the following four subsets based on their status with respect to Ω_0 (partially covered or not) and its subnets (overlapped or not overlapped):

- σ_{00} nonoverlapped and partially uncovered
- σ_{01} nonoverlapped and partially covered
- σ_{10} overlapped and partially uncovered
- σ_{11} overlapped and partially covered

Consider the time needed in convolving subnets Ω_1 and Ω_2 with respect to chains in these four sets. By definition,

$$G(\cdot,\Omega_1) \bullet G(\cdot,\Omega_2)(\mathbf{c}) = \sum_{\tau_1=0}^{c_1} \cdots \sum_{\tau_K=0}^{c_K} G(\mathbf{c}-\boldsymbol{\tau},\Omega_1)G(\boldsymbol{\tau},\Omega_2) \tag{3.1}$$

Consider a chain r. If $r \in \sigma_{00}$, it is either uncovered by both Ω_1 and Ω_2, or fully covered by exactly one of them. In the first case, we must choose $c_r = 0$, which also implies that $\tau_r = 0$. Similarly, in the second case, we must choose $c_r = N_r$, which further means that τ_r must be 0 or N_r, depending on whether chain r is fully covered by Ω_1 or Ω_2. Thus, in both cases, the summation over chain r does not contribute any extra terms. Now suppose that $k \in \sigma_{01}$. Then chain r must be partially covered by either Ω_1 or by Ω_2 but not both; thus, although all values of c_k in the range $0 \mathinner{..} N_r$ must be considered, only one value of τ_r (0 or c_r) is feasible in each case. Next suppose that $r \in \sigma_{10}$. Then since chain r must be fully covered by Ω_0, we only need to consider $c_r = N_r$ (but τ_r can range from $0 \mathinner{..} c_r$). Finally, if $r \in \sigma_{11}$, we must consider all values of c_r, and for each such value, consider all values of τ_r in the range $0 \mathinner{..} c_r$. Therefore, the entire process takes time proportional to

$$\prod_{r\in\sigma_{10}\cup\sigma_{01}} (N_r+1) + \frac{1}{2} \prod_{r\in\sigma_{11}} (N_r+1)(N_r+2) \tag{3.2}$$

It is easy to see that if the routing is sparse and the stations are merged so as to minimize the number of partially covered chains, considerable savings can be achieved. The subnet mergers can be depicted by a binary tree whose leaves are the individual stations and the root is the entire network. This tree, henceforth called a *convolution tree*, defines the order of mergers and its proper construction is crucial to the success of the algorithm. To see this, consider the network shown in Fig. 10-3. Here the optimal tree would first merge stations 1,2 and 3,4 respectively. These mergers would make chains 1 and 3 fully covered at level 1 of the tree. Thus, at level 2, we have only one partially covered chain, namely chain 2. The resulting tree is shown in Fig. 10-4. If however, we merged stations 1,3 and 2,4 at level 1, none of the chains 1-3 will get fully covered. As a result, no advantage will be taken of the sparsity in routing.

Unfortunately, the problem of determining the optimal convolution-tree is NP-hard. A heuristic approach that works very well in practice is discussed in Lam and Lien (1983). We shall not go into its details here, but only discuss the basic ideas. Let us say that $u \sqsupseteq v$, if all partially covered chains of v are contained in the set of partially covered chains of u. If $u \sqsupseteq v$, then u and v are merged first to quickly cover any chains that pass only through u and v. This itself is adequate to obtain the complete tree shown in Fig. 10-4 for the network in Fig. 10-3. If no mergers are possible according to this criterion, we perform mergers based on a weight-factor, which is chosen to assign higher weight to subnets whose partially covered chains visit many stations outside the subnet. That is, for a subnet ω,

$$weight(\omega) = \sum_{r\in\sigma_{pc}(\omega)} |\mathcal{V}(r) - \omega| \tag{3.3}$$

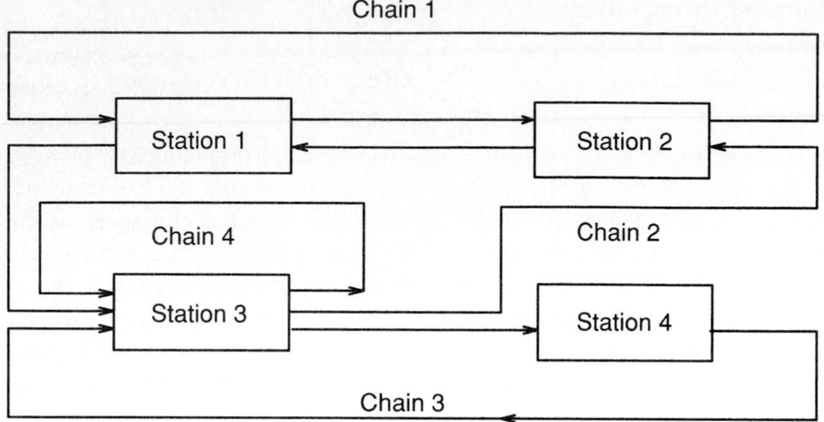

FIGURE 10-3: A network with sparse routing.

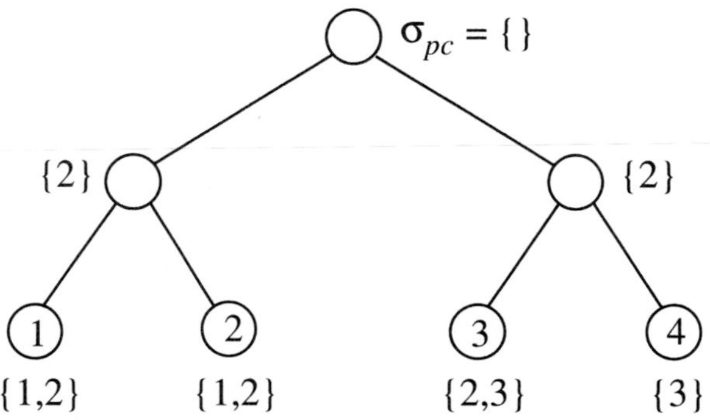

FIGURE 10-4: Optimal convolution-tree for Fig. 10-3.

Thus, in deciding which subnets, denoted u and v, to merge next, we pick u such that $weight(u)$ is the largest. We then pick a v such that its merger with u will result in the fewest possible partially covered chains.

At each node of the convolution tree, we store the *G-array* (i.e., $G(\cdot, \omega)$ where ω is the subnetwork represented by that node). The algorithm visits the tree in post-order and for each node visited, computes its G-array from those of its children. The G-arrays for the leaves are X_i's as defined in (6.3.18). When the traversal ends, we would have computed $G(\mathbf{N}, \Omega)$ for the entire network Ω, henceforth abbreviated as $G(\mathbf{N})$.

As in sequential convolution, once the G's have been computed, all performance parameters can be obtained easily. We compute throughputs using the throughput theorem in (7.3.10) and marginal probabilities for load-dependent stations using (7.3.8). However, for load-independent stations, we use equation (7.8.4). With throughputs and queue lengths known, other parameters can be determined as usual.

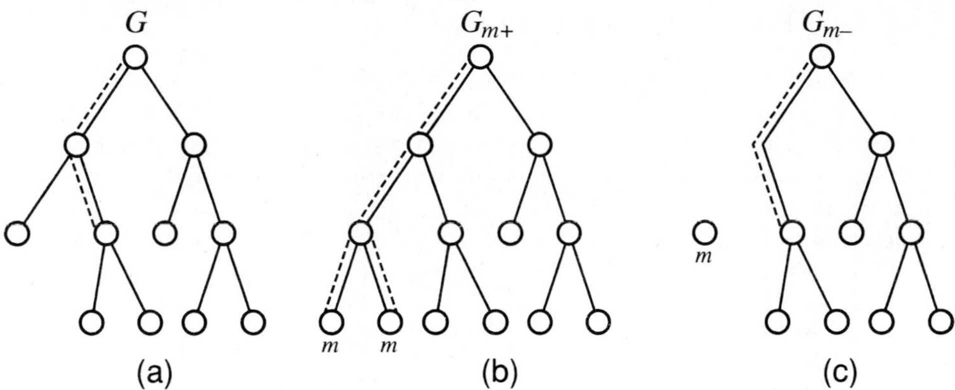

FIGURE 10-5: Computation of various G values.

Let us abbreviate $G(\mathbf{n}, \Omega - \{m\})$ as $G_{m-}(\mathbf{n})$ and $G(\mathbf{n}, \Omega \cup \{m\})$ as $G_{m+}(\mathbf{N})$. Then to compute the mean performance measures, we need $G(\mathbf{N}-e_r)$, $G_{m+}(\mathbf{N}-e_r)$, and $G_{m-}(\mathbf{N}-\mathbf{n})$, in addition to $G(\mathbf{N})$ itself.

Consider the computation of $G(\mathbf{N}-e_r)$. Let $\mathcal{F}(r)$ denote the node at which chain r becomes fully covered. According to our algorithm for computing $G(\mathbf{N})$, we would have G value only for $c_r = N_r$ at this node, but for all chain r populations at its descendent nodes. Thus, we do an array convolution at $\mathcal{F}(r)$ with index value $c_r = N_r - 1$ (since all the information needed for this is already available). Following this, we redo convolutions along the path from $\mathcal{F}(r)$ to the root. The resulting normalization constant at the root node is $G(\mathbf{N}-e_r)$. This is pictorially shown in Fig. 10-5(a).

To compute G_{m+}, we first replace the node corresponding to station m with a subnet node containing two copies of m. This would require convolution over all partially covered chains of station m. Next, we recompute the G-arrays along the path from this subnet to the root. This is shown in Fig. 10-5(b). Finally, to compute G_{m-}, we delete node m and redo the convolutions along the path between station m and the root, as shown in Fig. 10-5(c). Note that equation (7.3.8) needs G_{m-} at all possible populations of the partially covered chains of station m; therefore, we must have all these G values even at the root level.

Since the computation of some of the modified G values requires starting at the leaf level, we cannot simply discard any portion of the "G-tree". (This is unlike sequential convolution where only the last G-array corresponding to the subnet of simple and delay stations needs to be maintained.) If space is a problem, we can recompute the portion of the tree close to the root each time. Assuming that the complete G-tree is stored, the expense of computing various G's is primarily governed by the depth of the tree. For a balanced tree, the number of convolutions required to get G_{m-}, G_{m+}, and $G(\mathbf{N}-e_r)$ is $O(\log_2 M)$. In reality, $O(M)$ convolutions may sometimes be required, since the tree-planting procedure sketched above is not designed to build a balanced tree.

10.3.2 Tree Mean Value Analysis

The standard MVA algorithm cannot exploit sparsity very well because it needs to consider all stations at each step.[3] Therefore, the tree-MVA algorithm takes a different approach: it recursively replaces two-station subnets by a single flow equivalent station using Norton's theorem. This leads to a tree structure exactly like the one for the tree-convolution, and in fact, the savings are achieved for exactly the same reasons as in tree-convolution. Therefore, all the discussion concerning coverage of chains and tree planting in the context of tree-convolution applies here as well.

Given the tree, we can do a postorder traversal and merge subnets until we reach the root. Let Ω_1 and Ω_2 be two sibling subnets, and let Ω_0 be the subnet obtained by their merger. Except when Ω_1 and Ω_2 are leaf nodes, they will have occupancy vector dependent service rates. We denote the *effective service time* for chain r in subnet Ω_1 at the occupancy vector of $\mathbf{k} = (k_1, \ldots, k_K)$ as $S_r^*(\Omega_1, \mathbf{k})$. (This is the reciprocal of the effective service rate μ^*.) Since the subnets Ω_1 and Ω_2 have been solved by now, the service times $S_r^*(\Omega_1, \mathbf{k})$ and $S_r^*(\Omega_2, \mathbf{k})$ are known. Let $P_{\Omega_1}(\mathbf{k}|\mathbf{n})$ and $P_{\Omega_2}(\mathbf{k}|\mathbf{n})$ denote the marginal distribution for the composite stations (or subnets) Ω_1 and Ω_2. Next we must solve subnet Ω_0, which is a network containing stations Ω_1 and Ω_2 with equal visit ratios. We do this using MVA. That is, at any population level $\mathbf{n}-e_r$, we use $S_r^*(\Omega_1, \mathbf{k})$ and $S_r^*(\Omega_2, \mathbf{k})$ to get the response times for subnets Ω_1 and Ω_2 at population $\mathbf{n}$. From equation (1.2), we have

$$R_r(\Omega_1, \mathbf{n}) = \sum_{\mathbf{k}=e_r}^{\mathbf{n}} k_r S_r^*(\Omega_1, \mathbf{k}) P_{\Omega_1}(\mathbf{k} - e_r|\mathbf{n}-e_r) \tag{3.4}$$

A similar equation holds for $R_r(\Omega_2, \mathbf{n})$ as well. However, since the subnet Ω_0 contains only stations Ω_1 and Ω_2, it follows that

$$P_{\Omega_2}(\mathbf{k}|\mathbf{n}) = P_{\Omega_1}(\mathbf{n} - \mathbf{k}|\mathbf{n}) \tag{3.5}$$

for any $\mathbf{k}$ and $\mathbf{n}$. That is, we only need to compute and store P_{Ω_1}; P_{Ω_2} is then known trivially. With response times known, we can compute the throughput of subnet Ω_0 by Little's law

$$\lambda_r(\Omega_0, \mathbf{n}) = \frac{n_r}{R_r(\Omega_1, \mathbf{n}) + R_r(\Omega_2, \mathbf{n})} \tag{3.6}$$

As in the regular MVA, we can now go back and compute the marginal probabilities at population $\mathbf{n}$. That is, for any $\mathbf{k} > \mathbf{0}$, we have

$$P_{\Omega_1}(\mathbf{k}|\mathbf{n}) = P_{\Omega_1}(\mathbf{k} - e_r|\mathbf{n}-e_r)\lambda_r(\Omega_0, \mathbf{n}) S_r^*(\Omega_1, \mathbf{k}) \tag{3.7}$$

$P_{\Omega_1}(0|\mathbf{n})$ can be computed by the requirement that all probabilities sum to 1, but this computation will be numerically unstable. So we exploit the fact that

[3] When computing parameters for a chain, we could surely avoid going over the stations that the chain does not visit, but there is no concept of a fully-covered chain — instead, the parameters of all chains must be updated at each step.

the network contains only two stations. From the MLB equation for station Ω_2 at $\mathbf{k} = \mathbf{n}$, the relation (3.5), and the fact that both stations have the same throughput, it follows that

$$P_{\Omega_1}(0|\mathbf{n}) = \lambda_r(\Omega_0, \mathbf{n}) S_r^*(\Omega_2, \mathbf{n}) P_{\Omega_1}(0|\mathbf{n}-e_r) \tag{3.8}$$

This equation is free of any numerical problems. Again, because of equation (3.5), *there is no need to do similar computations for subnet* Ω_2.

Thus, we have a complete step of the MVA algorithm at a given tree level. This computation needs to be done iteratively for all populations, starting from **0** and proceeding through **N**. By Norton's theorem (see Section 8.1.1), a byproduct of these computations is $S_r^*(\Omega_0, \mathbf{n}) = 1/\lambda_r(\Omega_0, \mathbf{n})$, which will be needed as we move up to the next level of the tree.

With the above procedure, when we arrive at the root of the tree, we would have the throughput of the entire network. Note that if we assign a visit ratio of 1 to some station $j(r)$ for each chain r, the "network throughput" for chain r is the throughput of station $j(r)$. We could then obtain throughputs of other stations, since all throughputs must be proportional to visit ratios. However, the queue lengths at individual stations are not available directly. To get the queue lengths, we need to apply the superposition theorem in Section 8.1.2 at each step of the aggregation. So let us again consider the situation during the merger of subnets Ω_1 and Ω_2 into Ω_0. Let $Q_{ir}(\Omega_1, \mathbf{n})$ denote the average queue length of chain r at station i when this station is considered as a part of subnet Ω_1. This quantity will be available, because subnet Ω_1 has already been solved. Then by the superposition theorem, we have

$$Q_{ir}(\Omega_0, \mathbf{n}) = \sum_{\mathbf{k}=e_r}^{\mathbf{n}} P_{\Omega_1}(\mathbf{k}|\mathbf{n}) Q_{ir}(\Omega_1, \mathbf{k}) \tag{3.9}$$

We can similarly compute queue lengths at stations belonging to subnet Ω_2 when those stations are considered a part of subnet Ω_0. It is clear that when we arrive at the root, we would have the correct queue lengths for all the stations in the network. This technique applies even to higher moments of the queue length (and to the marginal distribution itself).

In the usual case where the leaf nodes of the tree have chain-independent capacities, the merger at this level can follow the regular MVA algorithm shown in Fig. 7-5, which is much less expensive. Also note that in equation (3.4), we are really computing the *residence time* (since we assume a visit ratio of 1 for both stations in a subnet). Therefore, we should compute the residence times at the leaf level as well (by multiplying the response times with the visit ratios).

Finally, let us note a few computational issues regarding the algorithm. The algorithm involves climbing up the tree and running the MVA-steps from populations **0** through **N** at each level. For example, in Fig. 10-4, the algorithm will proceed as follows:

1. Run the regular MVA algorithm on subnet Ω_1. It is important that the performance parameters at all intermediate population levels are retained

in this application of MVA, since they will be needed for computing the effective service times $S_r^*(\Omega_1, \mathbf{k}) = 1/\lambda_r(\Omega_1, \mathbf{k})$, and for computing queue lengths $Q_{ir}(\Omega_0, \mathbf{n})$, $r = 1, 2$, $i = 1, 2$ using equation (3.9).

2. Run the regular MVA on subnet S_2, and save all its parameters too.
3. Run the specialized MVA discussed above on subnet Ω_0, and apply the superposition theorem.

Note that we could discard all performance parameters of Ω_1 and Ω_2, after those of Ω_0 have been computed. This observation would be useful in minimizing storage requirements if Ω_0 were a part of a larger tree. Another point to note is that although we could arrange the computation slightly differently (i.e., go all the way up to the root of the tree for each population level), this scheme is not storage-efficient.

Although the above description did not make it explicit, the vectors $\mathbf{k}$ and $\mathbf{n}$ vary over their full range only for the partially covered chains. This is what leads to time and space savings. The details are similar to that for tree-convolution; i.e., in equation (3.4), if chain r is fully covered, $k_r = n_r$, and if it is uncovered then $k_r = 0$. This means that the number of dimensions needed in the array for storing the vector $\mathbf{k}$ is simply the number of partially covered chains. The computational complexity of tree-MVA is of the same order as that of the tree-convolution; however, because of repeated use of the superposition theorem, it is somewhat more expensive in terms of the actual operation count.

10.4 Asymptotic Expansions

As mentioned in Section 6.5.2, this technique is based on Taylor series expansion of $G(\mathbf{N}, \Omega)$, or more generally of some performance parameter, since all performance parameters can be related to the normalization constant. Obviously, the expansion must be convergent, and to be useful, should converge rather rapidly. This requirement places restrictions on how the expansion is done and what type of networks can be handled. Here we only consider the so-called *normal usage networks*, which can be characterized as follows:

1. Every chain passes through at least one delay station.
2. The total load at any nondelay station i is small compared to the sum of the loads at all delay stations.

We defer a precise statement of the second condition until later. For now, we only note that the ratio of the load at a load-independent and a delay station, henceforth denoted as x, is the crucial parameter in the expansion. This is because the kth term in the expansion is of the form $A_k x^k$. Thus, if x is small, the series will decay fast and a few terms would be adequate to get good accuracy. In general, one could expect a smaller x for networks with more stations; therefore, the technique is intended primarily for networks with many stations.

To start with, we assume that the network has no load-dependent stations. It suffices to assume that there is only one delay station, since all delay stations in a PF network can be lumped into one (see Exercise 7.1). Thus, we consider a network with $M+1$ stations, of which station 0 is of delay type and the rest are load-independent. The starting point is equation (6.5.4). Consider Euler's integral representation of the factorial function, i.e.,

$$n_i! = \int_0^\infty e^{-\theta_i}\theta_i^{n_i}\,d\theta_i = \int_0^\infty e^{-\theta_i}\prod_{r=1}^{K}\theta_i^{n_{ir}}\,d\theta_i \tag{4.1}$$

where the last step follows from the relation $\sum_{r=1}^{K} n_{ir} = n_i$. Substituting this into (6.5.4), simplifying, and applying the multinomial theorem for each chain, we get

$$G(\mathbf{N}) = \prod_{r=1}^{K}\frac{1}{N_r!}\int_0^\infty\cdots\int_0^\infty\prod_{i=1}^{M}e^{-\theta_i}\prod_{r=1}^{K}\left[u_{0r}+\sum_{i=1}^{M}u_{ir}\theta_i\right]^{N_r} d\theta_1\cdots d\theta_M \tag{4.2}$$

Let $\boldsymbol{\theta}$ denote the row vector $(\theta_1,\ldots,\theta_M)$, $\mathbf{e}$ a column vector of all 1's, and $\mathbf{u}_r$ as the column vector $(u_{1r},\ldots,u_{Mr})$. Then equation (4.2) can be rewritten in the following compact form

$$G(\mathbf{N}) = \prod_{r=1}^{K}\frac{u_{0r}^{N_r}}{N_r!}\int_{Q^+}e^{-\boldsymbol{\theta}\cdot\mathbf{e}}\prod_{r=1}^{K}\left[1+\frac{\boldsymbol{\theta}\,\mathbf{u}_r}{u_{0r}}\right]^{N_r} d\boldsymbol{\theta} \tag{4.3}$$

where Q^+ denotes the M-dimensional space of vectors $\boldsymbol{\theta}$ having nonnegative real-valued components. It is convenient to choose $u_{0r} = 1$ for each chain r (which amounts to replacing all other u_{ir}'s by u_{ir}/u_{0r}). Also, the term outside the integral in equation (4.3) is a constant, which we denote as simply C_1. Thus, equation (4.3) can be further rewritten as

$$G(\mathbf{N}) = C_1\int_{Q^+}\exp\left[-\boldsymbol{\theta}\cdot\mathbf{e}+\sum_{r=1}^{K}N_r\ln[1+\boldsymbol{\theta}\mathbf{u}_r]\right] d\boldsymbol{\theta} \tag{4.4}$$

The idea now is to expand the integrand. It can be shown that to make this expansion convergent, the α_i's defined below should be *strictly greater than zero.*

$$\alpha_i = 1-\sum_{r=1}^{K}N_r u_{ir} \qquad \text{for} \quad 1\le i\le M \tag{4.5}$$

Note that u_{ir}'s here are defined relative to the loading of the delay station; therefore, (4.5) implies that u_{ir}'s must decrease as the number of chains or their populations increase. For example, if all chains place approximately equal load on station i, convergence requires that u_{ir}'s be less than $1/N$th of the loading of the delay station.

Now, to actually do the asymptotic expansion, let us introduce the parameter x in the equations. This parameter should be chosen such that $\beta_r = N_r x$

and u_{ir}/x are $O(1)$. One possibility is to let it be the average of all u_{ir}'s. Now we make the substitutions $v_i = \alpha_i \theta_i$, and $\eta_{ir} = u_{ir}/(x\alpha_i)$ in equation (4.4). It is then easy to show that

$$G(\mathbf{N}) = \left[\prod_{j=1}^{K} \frac{1}{N_j!} \Big/ \prod_{i=1}^{M} \alpha_i \right] \int_{Q+} \exp(-\mathbf{c} \cdot \mathbf{e}) H(x, \mathbf{c})\, d\mathbf{c} \tag{4.6}$$

where $\boldsymbol{\eta}_r = (\eta_{1r}, \ldots, \eta_{Mr})$, $\mathbf{c} = (v_1, \ldots, v_M)$, and

$$H(x, \mathbf{c}) = \exp \left[-\sum_{r=1}^{K} \beta_r [\boldsymbol{\eta}_r \mathbf{c} - x^{-1} \ln(1 + \boldsymbol{\eta}_r \mathbf{c} x)] \right] \tag{4.7}$$

Henceforth we shall denote the integral on the RHS of equation (4.6) as $I(x)$. We now represent $H(x, \mathbf{c})$ as Taylor series around the origin, i.e., $H(x, \mathbf{c}) = \sum_{k=0}^{\infty} h_k(\mathbf{c}) x^k$, where

$$h_k(\mathbf{c}) = \frac{1}{k!} \frac{\partial^k H(x, \mathbf{c})}{\partial x^k} |_{x=0} \tag{4.8}$$

which yields $I(x) = \sum_{k=0}^{\infty} A_k x^k$, where

$$A_k = \int_{Q+} \exp(-\mathbf{c} \cdot \mathbf{e}) h_k(\mathbf{c})\, d\mathbf{c} \tag{4.9}$$

With some algebra, we find that $h_0(\mathbf{c}) = 1$, and for $k = 1, 2, \ldots$

$$h_k(\mathbf{c}) = -\frac{1}{k} \sum_{m=1}^{k} m g_{m+1}(\mathbf{c}) h_{k-m}(\mathbf{c}) \quad \text{and} \quad g_m(\mathbf{c}) = \frac{(-1)^m}{m} \sum_{r=1}^{K} \beta_r [\boldsymbol{\eta}_r \mathbf{c}]^m \tag{4.10}$$

Now if we distribute the integral in equation (4.9) over its summation terms, it turns out that each integral can be interpreted as the normalization constant of a closed queuing network, called the *pseudonetwork*, and could be obtained by the ordinary convolution algorithm. Each pseudonetwork has only the load-independent stations of the original network with relative utilizations of η_{ir}'s. It has only a few chains at small populations, depending on the term. For example, $A_0 = 1$, $A_1 = -\sum_{r=1}^{K} \beta_r G^*(2e_r)$, and

$$A_2 = \sum_{r=1}^{K} \beta_r \left[2G^*(3e_r) + 3\beta_r G^*(4e_r) + \frac{1}{2} \sum_{k=1, k \neq r}^{K} \beta_k G^*(2e_r + 2e_k) \right] \tag{4.11}$$

where a notation like $G^*(2e_r)$ refers to the normalization constant of the pseudo-network with only chain r at population of 2. Let $p = \min(M, k)$. Then it can be shown that the kth term in the expansion will involve $\binom{M}{p}$ pseudonetworks, each with M load-independent stations, at most p chains, and a total population of $2k$ distributed over the chains involved. In practice $k = 4$ is usually sufficient, thereby resulting in a small cost, independent of the number of chains and their populations in the original network.

Until now we have considered only the computation of the normalization constant. Since the performance parameters are directly related to G's, it is possible to do a Taylor series expansion for those as well. This is explored briefly in Exercises 10.14 and 10.15.

Unlike the Linearizer and other approximate solution algorithms, the current method can also obtain error bounds. It can be shown that the Taylor series expansion has terms with alternating signs; moreover, each term bounds the error involved in neglecting the remaining terms. This immediately leads to upper and lower bounds on the values. Also, the method can easily obtain higher and even joint moments of queue lengths quite easily, something that is not possible with the Linearizer. However, although Linearizer applies to arbitrary networks, this is not so with the current algorithm, as already discussed. Unlike Linearizer, the current algorithm is also unable to handle non-PF scheduling disciplines heuristically.

Let us now briefly consider the extension of the algorithm to networks containing load-dependent stations. Let i be such a station. The convergence condition is still $\alpha_i > 0$, except that α_i is now defined as follows:

$$\alpha_i = 1 - \gamma_i \sum_{r=1}^{K} N_r u_{ir} \qquad \text{where } \gamma_i = \lim_{n\to\infty} \frac{1}{C_i(n)} \tag{4.12}$$

The final expression again looks like equation (4.6) except that the integral term $I(x)$ is different. If we expand this integral as in equation (4.9), the coefficients A_k's again turn out to be sums of terms involving normalization constants of certain pseudonetworks. In fact, *the expressions for* A_k*'s are exactly the same as before*. The only difference comes in the pseudonetworks, and it only relates to the capacity of the stations. That is, station i in the pseudonetwork must have a capacity function $C_i'(n)$ such that

$$V_i'(n) \triangleq \prod_{k=1}^{n} C_i'(k) = \sum_{m=0}^{\infty} \frac{(n+m)!}{m!} \frac{(1-\alpha_i)^m}{V_i(n+m)} \tag{4.13}$$

Although this definition requires the capacity function at all values of the load, only the values for $n \leq N$ affect the normalization constant expressions. Thus, we are free to choose any arbitrary capacity values for $n > N$. Since we only use the first few terms in the asymptotic expansion, the final result still depends on how we choose the capacity values for $n > N$. Quite interestingly, it can be shown that $C_i(n) = 0$ for $n > N$ would give the most accurate results; however, such a choice precludes a closed form for V_i' even for a simple multiserver station.

All other properties, including the fact that the kth term in the expansion bounds the magnitude of the sum of the remaining terms, still hold. It is also possible to develop expansions that give queue-length moments, as before. The details may be found in Mitra and McKenna (1986).

10.5 Exercises

1. Extend the convolution algorithm to the case where the capacities are of the form (1.4) and discuss its time and space complexities.
2. Suppose that station i has a capacity of the form (1.4). Let $P_i(n, n_r|\mathbf{N})$ denote the joint marginal probability of finding a total of n customers at station i, of which n_r belong to chain r. Using the MLB equation, show the following

$$P_i(n|\mathbf{N}) = \sum_{r=1}^{K} \sum_{n_r=1}^{\min(n,N_r)} \frac{U_{ir}(\mathbf{N})}{\alpha_i(n)\beta_{ir}(n_r)} P_i(n-1, n_r - 1|\mathbf{N}-e_r) \tag{5.1}$$

$$R_{ir}(\mathbf{N}) = s_{ir}^{\circ} \sum_{n_r=1}^{N_r} \sum_{n=n_r}^{N-N_r+n_r} \frac{nP_i(n-1, n_r - 1|\mathbf{N}-e_r)}{\alpha_i(n)\beta_{ir}(n_r)} \tag{5.2}$$

   Using these relations, develop the mean value analysis algorithm for this case. State the time and space complexity of the algorithm. What techniques would you use to minimize the space requirements?
3. Using equations (1.22), show that for networks with state-dependent routing,

$$\mu_{jr}^{*}(\mathbf{n}_j)X_j'(\mathbf{n}_j) = v_{jr}h_{jr}(n_{jr} - 1)X_j'(\mathbf{n}_j - e_r) \tag{5.3}$$

   Now derive equation (1.30). The major steps are as follows: Start with the throughput law and use equations (1.28) and (5.3), simplify, and finally apply equation (1.28) at population vector $\mathbf{N}-e_r$.
4. Derive equation (1.31). For this, substitute equation (5.3) into (1.28), and use equation (1.30) to eliminate G's.
5. Consider a single-chain closed network with state-dependent routing. As in Section 10.1.3, assume that there is but one parallel subnetwork of individual stations. Assuming exponential service-time distributions, write down global balance equations. Identify partial balance equations, and from there the local balance equations. Find the product-form solution and check it against equation (1.21).
6. Devise an implementation of the RECAL algorithm that computes marginal distributions and minimizes space requirements. Are there any space/time tradeoffs to consider?
7. Starting from the definition of the normalization constant in equation (6.3.19), show that in a closed product-form network with chain-independent capacities, the following relationship holds

$$\frac{1}{G(\mathbf{N})}\frac{dG(\mathbf{N})}{du_{jk}} = \frac{Q_{jk}(\mathbf{N})}{u_{jk}} \tag{5.4}$$

8. Starting with the marginal local balance theorem in equation (7.4.3) for multiple chains, derive equations that can be used to compute joint and individual moments of chain-dependent queue lengths at a given station.
9. Let $\mathcal{P}^k(\mathbf{n})$, $\mathbf{n} = (n_1, \ldots, n_M)$ denote the aggregate state probability for a closed k-chain product-form network with chain-independent capacities and one customer per chain. Using equation (6.3.17), write down an expression for $\mathcal{P}^k(\mathbf{n})$. By rearranging summations and using the throughput theorem, prove equation (2.22).
10. Devise suitable data structures for the tree-convolution algorithm that can operate in a given amount of storage. (Assume that the given storage is between the minimum and maximum limits.)
11. Show that if every chain passes through every station, tree-MVA is more expensive than the sequential MVA.
12. Consider an arbitrarily large network where every chain has the same population $\overline{N}$, every chain passes through a fraction f of stations, and no station has more than two chains passing through it. How would you construct the tree for this situation? With this tree, how small does f have to be to make tree-MVA more efficient than sequential MVA?
13. Derive equation (4.3) starting from equation (6.5.4).
14. Let $G(\mathbf{N}-e_r) = \sum_{k=0}^{\infty} A_k x^k$ and $G(\mathbf{N}) = \sum_{k=0}^{\infty} B_k x^k$. Show that the coefficients in the ratio $G(\mathbf{N}-e_r)/G(\mathbf{N})$, denoted C_k, satisfy the following triangular system of equations:

$$A_k = \sum_{r=0}^{k} B_r C_{k-r} \tag{5.5}$$

Hence, by using the throughput theorem get an expansion for the throughput.
15. Suppose that we define a modified form of the normalization constant, denoted G', by introducing a θ_i as a multiplicand to the integrand in equation (4.4). Show that

$$Q_{ik}(\mathbf{N}) = u_{ik}\frac{G'(\mathbf{N}-e_k)}{G(\mathbf{N})} \tag{5.6}$$

Hence, by using the result of Exercise 10.14, obtain an asymptotic expansion for Q_{ik}.
16. Discuss how RECAL and MVAC can take advantage of the sparsity in routing. What storage structures will you use to realize the savings? Give expressions for time and space complexities, as was done for tree-convolution.

Bibliographic Notes

Product-form solution in networks with variable population is shown in Lam (1977); therefore, such networks are often referred to as *Lam-type networks*.

Single-chain product-form networks with state-dependent routing are examined in Towsley (1980), and computational algorithms for these networks are provided in Sauer (1983). Multiple-chain extensions to these results are contained in Krzesinski (1987). Networks with rejection blocking have been examined in several works including Pittel (1979), Hordijk and Vandijk (1981), and Akyildiz and Von Brand (1989). The convolution algorithm for networks with rejection blocking has been examined in Akyildiz (1989), and the mean value analysis algorithm is given in Akyildiz (April 1988). Akyildiz (Jan 1988, 1989) examines some approximations for networks with rejection blocking. Unfortunately, no efficient exact algorithms are known for handling more realistic forms of rejection blocking or production blocking. Onvural (1990) contains an up to date survey of the work on various forms of blocking and shows equivalence between several of them. Mutual blocking is explored in its full generality in Le Boudec (1986), though more restricted results were discovered earlier in Irani and Onyuksel (1984). Related work appears in Chiola, Marsan and Balbo (1988).

The RECAL algorithm is developed in Conway and Georganas (1986, JACM). The authors also discuss the application of the dynamic scaling algorithm of Lam (1982) to avoid problems of overflow/underflow. Greenberg and McKenna (1989) discusses the implementation of RECAL and its tree version on a shared memory multiprocessor machine. The MVAC algorithm is reported in Conway, Silva, and Lavenberg (1989). The derivations of the governing equations of MVAC by purely probabilistic arguments and some implementation issues may be found in this paper. Silva and Muntz (1988) derives relationships between the derivatives of the normalization constant and queue-length moments. Extension of the mean value analysis to get higher moments (individual and joint) of queue length at a given station is described in Strelen (1986). The DAC algorithm appears in Silva and Lavenberg (1989) and includes many details that we have omitted in our brief overview.

The tree-convolution algorithm is developed in Lam and Lien (1983). This paper solves a model of a store and forward communication network with 26 nodes, 64 unidirectional communication links, and 32 virtual circuits, each represented as a separate chain. This example would be infeasible using sequential convolution/MVA algorithms. The tree-MVA algorithm was motivated by tree-convolution, and was developed independently by two groups of researchers: Tucci and Sauer (1985), and Hoyme, Bruell, Afshari, and Kain (1986).

Initial work on asymptotic expansions appears in McKenna, Mitra, and Ramakrishnan (1981) and McKenna and Mitra (1982). The second paper considers general closed multiple-chain networks under normal usage and shows expansions for the normalization constant. Our presentation is based primarily on this paper. A later paper, McKenna and Mitra (1984), discusses expansions for the modified G function that are useful in computing queue-length moments. Finally, the extensions to handle load-dependent stations are reported in Mitra and McKenna (1986). Morrison and Mitra (1985) considers asymptotic expansion of waiting times in networks with heavy usage. McKenna (1987) considers asymptotic expansions of sojourn times over overtake-free paths of multiserver FCFS stations in product-form networks.

CHAPTER

11

Bounds On Performance

During the design phase of a system, many of the system parameters are not known accurately. Furthermore, the number of alternative designs that need to be considered may be very large. In such cases, the computational expense involved in obtaining the exact solution for a model of such a system may not be justifiable. We would like to be able to quickly evaluate several alternatives and reject those that are clearly bad. Performance bounds become useful in these instances, since they usually require much less computation as compared to the exact (or even approximate) solution.

A large number of bounding techniques have been proposed for the performance measures of queuing networks. These techniques are usually for product-form networks, and are typically for single-chain networks without load-dependent stations (nodes). In fact, with some techniques, even the introduction of delay stations complicates the expressions considerably. For the most part, these techniques obtain bounds on the system throughput (or the cycle time, since the two are related by Little's law), although some bounds have also been obtained on mean queue lengths and response times.

In this chapter we study some of the techniques which obtain bounds on the throughput and cycle time for single-chain product-form networks with load-independent and delay stations. Following that, we obtain the bounds for single-chain networks with multiple-server stations. Next, we consider bounds on the mean queue lengths for single-chain networks. Finally, we consider bounds on networks with multiple chains.

11.1 Bounds on Single-Chain Networks

In this section we assume that all stations in the network under consideration are either load-independent or of delay type. As shown in Exercise 7.1, all delay stations can be merged into a single delay station. Therefore, it suffices to consider only one delay station. We index this as station 0 and denote the load (or relative utilization) there by Z. We index the load-independent stations as $1 \,..\, M$, with u_i being the load at station i. Without loss of generality, we assume that $u_1 \leq \ldots \leq u_M$. Hence, from equation (7.1.8), we have $Q_1(N) \leq \ldots \leq Q_M(N)$ for any population N. We also assume that the visit ratio at some load-independent station in the network is 1. The throughput and cycle time of the network will then be determined with reference to this station.

Let L be the sum of the loads on the load-independent stations, i.e., $L = \sum_{i=1}^{M} u_i$. Let L' denote the total load in the network, i.e., $L' = L + Z$. We use b to denote the index of the "bottleneck" node, i.e., a load-independent station with a load greater than or equal to any other load-independent station. With our assumption that $u_1 \leq \ldots \leq u_M$, we can set $b = M$, although we will continue to let b denote the index for the bottleneck node. The "average" load, u_a, is defined as $u_a = L/M$. Notice that u_a is the average load only over the load-independent stations. Finally, *we use $R_i(N)$ to denote the residence time at station i, rather than the response time.*

11.1.1 Asymptotic Bound Analysis

The *asymptotic bound analysis* (ABA) does not require the product-form (PF) property to hold. The bounds are obtained by considering two extreme situations: (1) no queuing takes place at any node, and (2) at least one node is saturated. Without any queuing, the cycle time is obviously L'; therefore, by Little's formula $\lambda(N) \leq N/L'$. However, this bound may not satisfy the restriction that the utilization of a load-independent station cannot exceed 1. Thus, we have the additional constraint that $\lambda(N) \leq 1/u_b$. Consequently, the upper bound on throughput is given by

$$\lambda(N) \leq \min(N/L', 1/u_b) \tag{1.1}$$

Using Little's law, this also gives a lower bound on the cycle time. Now to get the lower bound, note that the throughput will be minimum if every customer has to wait behind the remaining $N-1$ other customers *at every load-independent station in the network*. Clearly then

$$\lambda(N) \geq N/(N\,L + Z) \tag{1.2}$$

Notice that we did not use the product-form assumption in deriving these bounds. The bounds could, however, be rather loose. Subsequent bounds in this chapter are tighter but do require the product-form assumption.

11.1.2 Balanced Job Bounds

The *balanced job bound* (BJB) analysis uses the mean value theorem to obtain an upper bound on the cycle time. From the mean value theorem for load-independent stations, we have

$$R_i(N) = u_i(1 + Q_i(N-1)) \tag{1.3}$$

Assuming that there are no delay stations, and summing over all stations, we get

$$CT(N) = L + \sum_{i=1}^{M} u_i Q_i(N-1) \tag{1.4}$$

Since $u_b \geq u_i$ for all i, we have

$$CT(N) \leq L + u_b(N-1) \tag{1.5}$$

Note that this bound essentially assumes that all stations are loaded as heavily as the bottleneck node; hence the name "balanced job bound". A lower bound can be obtained by again assuming that all stations are equally loaded. For this we first prove the following property.

Lemma 11.1 Consider two sequences $x_i, y_i, i = 1..n$ such that $x_1 \leq \ldots \leq x_n$ and $y_1 \leq \ldots \leq y_n$. Then,

$$\sum_{i=1}^{n} x_i y_i \geq \frac{1}{n} \sum_{i=1}^{n} x_i \sum_{j=1}^{n} y_j \tag{1.6}$$

Proof By induction. The result holds trivially for $n = 1$. Assume that it holds for $n-1$. Then,

$$\begin{aligned}
\sum_{i=1}^{n}\sum_{j=1}^{n} x_i y_j &= \sum_{i=1}^{n-1} x_i \left(\sum_{j=1}^{n-1} y_j + y_n \right) + x_n \sum_{j=1}^{n} y_j \\
&\leq (n-1)\sum_{i=1}^{n-1} x_i y_i + y_n \sum_{i=1}^{n-1} x_i + x_n \sum_{j=1}^{n} y_j \\
&= n\sum_{i=1}^{n} x_i y_i + \sum_{i=1}^{n-1} (x_i - x_n)(y_n - y_i) - x_n y_n \;\leq\; n \sum_{i=1}^{n} x_i y_i
\end{aligned}$$

where the last step follows from the fact that every term in the second summation of the previous step is nonpositive. □

From Lemma 11.1, setting $x_i = u_i$, and $y_i = Q_i(N-1)$, we obtain

$$\sum_{i=1}^{M} u_i Q_i(N-1) \geq u_a \sum_{i=1}^{M} Q_i(N-1) \tag{1.7}$$

Hence, from equation (1.4) we get,

$$CT(N) \geq L + (N-1)u_a \tag{1.8}$$

As with ABA, we again have to make sure that no station has a utilization greater than 1. This requires that $CT(N)$ be at least Nu_b. Therefore,

$$CT(N) \geq \max[Nu_b, L + (N-1)u_a] \tag{1.9}$$

Corresponding bounds on throughput can be obtained using Little's law. Apart from the initial computation of L, both upper and lower bounds can be evaluated in $O(1)$ time. In contrast, the exact solution would require $O(MN)$ operations.

Now consider the case where the delay station is also present. For notational compactness, we shall denote $N-1$ as N^-. The bounds are still achieved by assuming balanced loads at all the load-independent stations. As before, from Lemma 11.1 and equation (1.4), we get

$$CT(N) \geq Z + L + u_a \sum_{i=1}^{M} Q_i(N^-) = L' + u_a[N^- - Q_0(N^-)] \tag{1.10}$$

In a similar manner, we can get

$$CT(N) \leq L' + u_b[N^- - Q_0(N^-)] \tag{1.11}$$

For the lower bound, we again have to make sure that no load-independent station has utilization greater than 1.

In equations (1.10) and (1.11), we can set $Q_0(N^-) = Z\lambda(N^-)$. Note that an upper bound on $\lambda(N^-)$ would yield a lower bound on $CT(N)$ in equation (1.10). Similarly, a lower bound on $\lambda(N^-)$ would yield an upper bound on $CT(N)$. Proceeding inductively, it is clear that an upper bound on $\lambda(N^-)$ is given by $\lambda_a(N^-)$, where $\lambda_a(N^-)$ represents the system throughput assuming that each load-independent station has average load. Similarly, a lower bound on $\lambda(N^-)$ is provided by $\lambda_b(N^-)$, where $\lambda_b(N^-)$ represents the system throughput assuming that each load-independent station has the same load as the bottleneck node. This yields

$$\max(Nu_b - Z, L' + \eta_a) \leq CT(N) \leq L' + \eta_b \tag{1.12}$$

where $\eta_a = u_a[N^- - Z\lambda_a(N^-)]$ and $\eta_b = u_b[N^- - Z\lambda_b(N^-)]$. Still remaining is to determine the throughputs $\lambda_a(N^-)$ and $\lambda_b(N^-)$. For this, note that for networks with delay stations, it is possible to get an explicit expression for $G(N)$ when all load-independent stations are equally loaded. (See Exercise 7.11.) Then by using the throughput theorem, we can get expressions for these two throughputs. Let u be the load on each load-independent station. Then,

$$G(N) = \sum_{n=0}^{N} \frac{(n+M-1)!}{n!(M-1)!} u^n \frac{Z^{N-n}}{(N-n)!} \tag{1.13}$$

The evaluation of this expression, however, does require $O(N)$ time, which makes the bounds more expensive to obtain. An alternate approach is to use the ABA lower and upper bounds for these throughputs [see equations (1.1) and (1.2)].

11.1.3 Performance Bound Hierarchies

The BJB analysis only provides one set of bounds, which at times may be too loose to be useful. A number of bounding techniques have recently been proposed that can provide increasingly tighter bounds at the expense of increasing computation. One such technique is the performance bound hierarchies (PBH) algorithm, which uses the mean value theorem to obtain bounds with increasing levels of accuracy. The basis for the PBH bounds are the ABA lower and upper bounds, which are termed here as the "level-0" bounds. The PBH technique applies the mean value theorem ℓ times for some $\ell \leq N$ in order to get "level-ℓ" bounds. For any $\ell < N$, the level-$(\ell+1)$ bounds can be shown to be tighter than the level-ℓ bounds. The PBH bounds are based on the following equation, which is obtained from equation (1.3) together with a simple application of Little's law

$$R_i(n) = u_i \left[1 + \frac{(n-1)R_i(n-1)}{Z + CT^*(n-1)}\right] \tag{1.14}$$

where $CT^*(n) = \sum_{i=1}^{M} R_i(n)$ for all n.

Let $R_i^{(\ell)}(n)$ denote the residence time at station i with network population n, evaluated at level-ℓ, and let $CT^{*(\ell)}(n) = \sum_{i=1}^{M} R_i^{(\ell)}(n)$. Then, from equation (1.14), we can write

$$R_i^{(\ell)}(n) = u_i \left[1 + \frac{(n-1)R_i^{(\ell-1)}(n-1)}{Z + CT^{*(\ell-1)}(n-1)}\right] \tag{1.15}$$

The significance of this equation is that, given a lower or an upper bound on $CT^{*(\ell-1)}(n-1)$, with proper choice of values for $R_i^{(\ell-1)}(n-1)$, we can obtain a similar bound on $CT^{*(\ell)}(n)$. It must be noted that the values of $R_i^{(\ell-1)}(n-1)$ are not necessarily lower/upper bounds, but the corresponding values for $CT^{*(\ell-1)}(n-1)$ are. Similarly, although the resulting values of $R_i^{(\ell)}(n)$ are not necessarily bounds, the corresponding values of $CT^{*(\ell)}(n)$ are. The suggested choices for initialization are

$$R_i^{(0)}(n) = \max(nu_b - Z, L)/M \tag{1.16}$$

for obtaining the lower bound on $CT^*(n)$, and

$$R_i^{(0)}(n) = nL\delta(i,b) \tag{1.17}$$

for obtaining the upper bound on $CT^*(n)$. In equation (1.17), $\delta(k,j)$ is the selector function, which is 1 for $k = j$ and 1 otherwise. It is easy to see that the value of $CT^{*(0)}(n)$ resulting from this initialization is simply the ABA bound on the cycle time discussed in Section 11.1.1. The proof that these initializations indeed give lower/upper bounds is omitted. Now to achieve the bound hierarchy, we use equation (1.15) recursively. That is, in order to get the level-ℓ bounds on $CT^*(N)$, we start with the initialization of the form given by equations (1.16) and (1.17) for $R_i^{(0)}(N-\ell)$ and recursively substitute the results back in equation

(1.15) until we obtain $CT^{*(\ell)}(N)$. It can be shown that each step in the recursion maintains the bounding property of cycle times, and that the bounds become tighter for increasing levels. In particular, if we let $\ell = N$ and define $R_i^{(0)}(0) = 0$, this implies that we start the recursion with the exact values for $R_i^{(1)}(1)$ in equation (1.15). This, in turn, implies that the final values will be the exact solution.

To illustrate the PBH bounds, denote the level-ℓ lower and upper bounds on $CT^*(N)$ as $\underline{CT}^{*(\ell)}(N)$ and $\overline{CT}^{*(\ell)}(N)$ respectively, and let

$$\sigma_k = \sum_{i=1}^{M} u_i^k, \qquad a(n) = \max[nu_b - Z, L] \tag{1.18}$$

and

$$\phi_1(n) = \frac{1}{M}\frac{a(n)}{Z + a(n)}, \qquad \phi_2(n) = \frac{nL}{Z + nL} \tag{1.19}$$

Again, we shall denote $N - 1$ as N^-. Therefore, the level-1 PBH bounds on $CT^*(N)$ are: $\underline{CT}^{*(1)}(N) = L + N^- L\phi_1(N^-)$, and $\overline{CT}^{*(1)}(N) = L + N^- u_b\phi_2(N^-)$.

It may be observed that, *for networks without delay stations, the level-1 PBH bounds are just the balanced job bounds*. The level-2 PBH bounds on $CT^*(N)$ are

$$\underline{CT}^{*(2)}(N) = L + N^-\sigma_2\left[\frac{1 + (N-2)\phi_1(N-2)}{L' + (N-2)L\phi_1(N-2)}\right] \tag{1.20}$$

and

$$\overline{CT}^{*(2)}(N) = L + N^-\left[\frac{\sigma_2 + (N-2)u_b^2\phi_2(N-2)}{L' + (N-2)u_b\phi_2(N-2)}\right] \tag{1.21}$$

From a computational point of view, the PBH bounds can be evaluated efficiently by not performing any MVA-like iterations at all. To get the level-ℓ bounds, we first calculate σ_k for $k = 1..\ell$. Then, the level-ℓ member of the PBH evaluated at N, denoted $PB(\ell, 1, N)$, is given by the following recursion:

$$PB(j, k, N) = \sigma_k + N^-\frac{PB(j-1, k+1, N^-)}{Z + PB(j-1, 1, N^-)} \tag{1.22}$$

The boundary conditions in this recursion are as follows: For the upper bound on the cycle time, we let $PB(0, k, n) = nu_b^{k-1}$ for all n, and for the lower bound we let $PB(0, k, n) = \frac{\sigma_{k-1}}{M}a(n)$.

It is clear that each additional level of PBH requires $4M$ operations; therefore, to obtain bounds at level ℓ, the technique requires $O(\ell M)$ operations. The time complexity of computing level-N PBH bounds is identical to that of the exact MVA algorithm.

11.1.4 Successively Improving Bounds

The *successively improving bounds* (SIB) technique is based on the MVA algorithm and is applicable to single-chain networks with load-independent and delay stations. Some extensions for handling load-dependent stations are discussed in Section 11.2. To obtain a level-ℓ bound on the cycle time (or system throughput) at population N, an equation is first developed for $CT(N)$ in terms of $\lambda(n)$, for n ranging from $N-\ell$ up to $N-1$. The values for $\lambda(n)$ in this equation are replaced by their upper (lower) bounds, thereby generating a corresponding lower (upper) bound on $CT(N)$. It can be shown that the SIB technique gives better bounds than the PBH technique with comparable computational effort for small ℓ; but unlike the PBH technique, the bounds produced by the SIB technique do not converge to the exact solution in the limit.

To motivate the technique, let $\theta_i = u_i/L'$, and define the function $f_i^{(\ell)}(n)$ recursively as

$$f_i^{(\ell)}(n) = \theta_i[f_i^{(\ell-1)}(n) - \sum_{p=1}^{M} \theta_p f_p^{(\ell-1)}(n)] \quad \text{for } \ell > 0 \tag{1.23}$$

with $f_i^{(0)}(n) = Q_i(n)$. Also, let $\alpha_\ell = Y^{(\ell)}(1)$ and

$$Y^{(\ell)}(n) = \sum_{i=1}^{M} \theta_i f_i^{(\ell)}(n) \quad \text{for } \ell \geq 0 \tag{1.24}$$

From our earlier definition of σ_k [see equation (1.18)], and noting that $Q_i(1) = \theta_i$, we can observe that $\alpha_0 = \sum_{i=1}^{M} \theta_i^2 = \sigma_2/(L')^2$. Setting $\ell = 1$ in the equation for $Y^{(\ell)}(n)$, we get

$$Y^{(1)}(n) = \sum_{i=1}^{M} \theta_i f_i^{(1)}(n) = \sum_{i=1}^{M} \theta_i^2 Q_i(n) - \alpha_0 Y^{(0)}(n) \tag{1.25}$$

and

$$\alpha_1 = \sum_{i=1}^{M} \theta_i f_i^{(1)}(1) = \sum_{i=1}^{M} \theta_i^3 - \alpha_0^2 \tag{1.26}$$

and so on. Note that α_ℓ's involve only the relative utilizations, whereas $Y^{(\ell)}(n)$'s involve the mean queue lengths. Define

$$\Lambda_{n,k} = \begin{cases} \prod_{j=0}^{k}[L'\lambda(n-j)] & \text{if } n \geq k \geq 0 \\ 1 & \text{if } k < 0 \end{cases} \tag{1.27}$$

The SIB technique is based on the following result that we state without proof. Here again, we denote $N-1$ as N^-.

Lemma 11.2 For $N > \ell \geq 0$, we have

$$CT(N) = L'\left[1 + \sum_{k=0}^{\ell-1}(N^- - k)\alpha_k \Lambda_{N^-,k-1} + Y^{(\ell)}(N^- - \ell)\Lambda_{N^-,\ell-1}\right] \tag{1.28}$$

□

We now develop a level-1 upper bound on the cycle time. The bounds at higher levels are obtained in a similar manner. Setting $\ell = 1$ in the preceding equation, and using equation (1.25), we have

$$CT(N) = L'\left\{1 + N^-\alpha_0 + [\psi(n) - \alpha_0 Y^{(0)}(N-2)]\, L'\lambda(N^-)\right\} \tag{1.29}$$

where $\psi(n) = \sum_{i=1}^{M} \theta_i^2 Q_i(n)$. It is clear that

$$\psi(N-2) \leq \theta_b \sum_{i=1}^{M} \theta_i Q_i(N-2) = \theta_b Y^{(0)}(N-2) \tag{1.30}$$

Hence, using Little's law to set $\lambda(N^-) = N^-/CT(N^-)$, we obtain the following inequality

$$CT(N) \leq L'\left[1 + N^-\alpha_0 + L'\frac{N^-}{CT(N^-)}(\theta_b - \alpha_0)Y^{(0)}(N-2)\right]$$

Note from equation (1.28) that $CT(n) = L'[1 + Y^{(0)}(n-1)]$. Let

$$\eta(n) = (\theta_b - \alpha_0)Y^{(0)}(n)/[1 + Y^{(0)}(n)] \tag{1.31}$$

Then the above inequality can be rewritten as

$$\begin{aligned} L'(1 + Y^{(0)}(N^-)) &\leq L'[1 + N^-(\alpha_0 + \eta(N-2))] \\ &\leq L'[1 + N^-(\alpha_0 + \eta(N^-))] \end{aligned} \tag{1.32}$$

where the second inequality follows from the fact that $\theta_b - \alpha_0 \geq 0$, and that $Y^{(0)}(n)$ is increasing in n. This is a quadratic in $Y^{(0)}(N^-)$, which can be easily solved, thereby obtaining the desired level-1 upper bound on $CT(N)$. The upper bounds of higher levels on $CT(N)$ are obtained by including more and more terms in the above expression for $CT(N)$. The corresponding lower bounds on $\lambda(N)$ are then easily obtained using Little's law. The higher-level bounds require the development of some additional properties, and are omitted here.

It can easily be shown that $Y^{(\ell)}(n) \geq 0$ for $n \geq 0$. Hence, in order to obtain the lower bounds, we can ignore the term involving $Y^{(\ell)}(n)$ altogether to get

$$CT(N) \geq L'\left[1 + \sum_{i=0}^{k-1}(N^- - i)\alpha_i \Lambda_{N^-,i-1}\right] \tag{1.33}$$

For a given $\ell > 0$, a level-ℓ lower bound on the cycle time can be obtained by using suitably chosen lower bounds on $\Lambda_{N^-,k-1}$ for $k < \ell$ in the above equation.

We present the level-1 and level-2 lower bounds on $CT(N)$. Setting $\ell = 1$, the level-1 bound is easily seen to be

$$\underline{CT}^{(1)}(N) = L'[1 + N^{-}\alpha_0] \tag{1.34}$$

Note the similarity between the above level-1 bound and the level-2 PBH bound. In fact, if the delay station was absent, then $\phi_1 = 1/M$, $\phi_2 = 1$, and $\alpha_0 = \sigma_2/L^2$. Thus, for networks without delay stations, the level-1 SIB lower bound on $CT(N)$ is identical to the level-2 PBH lower bound. For the level-2 lower SIB bound on $CT(N)$, we write equation (1.33) for $\ell = 2$ as

$$CT(N) \geq L'\left[1 + N^{-}\alpha_0 + (N-2)\alpha_1\lambda(N^{-})\right] \tag{1.35}$$

Now, a suitably chosen lower bound on $\lambda(N^{-})$ [for example, the level-1 lower bound on $\lambda(N^{-})$] gives the desired lower bound on $CT(N)$. As in the ABA bound, we again have to make sure that no station has a utilization larger than 1. It can be shown that these bounds are strictly nested; thus a level-$(\ell + 1)$ bound is tighter that a level-ℓ bound, and so on. The computational complexity here is of a similar order as for the PBH bounds.

11.2 Networks with Load-Dependent Stations

Relatively little work has been done on obtaining bounds for networks with load-dependent stations. Almost all the results obtained for these networks are for single-chain networks. The addition of load-dependent stations increases the computational complexity of the exact solution to $O(MN^2)$ operations. Hence, the bounding techniques are even more useful here. We restrict our attention to networks where the only form of load-dependent behavior is due to stations with multiple servers (MS stations). The bibliographic notes contain references to work on obtaining bounds for networks exhibiting other forms of load-dependent behavior. The approach taken to obtain bounds for a network with MS stations is as follows: suppose it is desired to obtain an upper bound on the throughput of such a network. We then consider an alternate network consisting only of load-independent and delay stations, whose throughput is guaranteed to be at least that of the original network, for all customer populations. Then, an upper bound on the throughput of this latter network gives the desired upper bound on the throughput of the original network. A similar approach leads to a lower throughput bound. We first require the following result.

Lemma 11.3 Consider two closed queuing networks Ω and Ω', each having M stations and network population N, where every station has a nondecreasing capacity function. The two networks are identical except for the capacity functions at station M, denoted $C_M(n)$ and $C'_M(n)$ for Ω and Ω' respectively. Then if $C'_M(n) \leq C_M(n)$ for all n then $\lambda'(N) \leq \lambda(N)$.

□

The proof of Lemma 11.3 follows from the results on the monotonicity of throughputs in product-form networks, and is omitted here. We use this result as follows: suppose that Ω has exactly one MS station with c identical servers, with the other stations being load-independent or delay types. Without loss of generality, let this MS station be station M, and let its load be u_M. To obtain an upper bound on the throughput for this network, we instead consider the throughput of another network Ω', which is identical to network Ω, except that station M is a load-independent station having load u_M/c. It is then obvious from Lemma 11.3 that an upper bound on the throughput of network Ω', which can be obtained using any of the bounding techniques presented earlier, gives the desired bound. In general, if Ω has more than one MS station, each corresponding station in Ω' is a load-independent station with the load chosen as above. Of course, when there are many MS stations such a technique could result in a very loose bound, even if an exact algorithm is used to obtain the throughput of the resulting network.

To obtain the lower throughput bound for networks with MS stations, we again consider, for ease of discussion, a network Ω with only a single MS station, which is assumed to be station M. In network Ω', this station is replaced by a flow equivalent server, which consists of one load-independent station and one delay station with suitably chosen loads. We could then show the following:

Lemma 11.4 Consider two closed subsystems, each having n customers. The first subsystem consists of a single station M with load u_M having c identical servers. The second subsystem consists of one flow-equivalent server $M1$, which represents the aggregation of a load-independent station with load u_M/c, and a delay station with load $u_M(c-1)/c$. Let $\lambda^M(n)$ and $\lambda^{M1}(n)$ denote the throughput of these two subsystems. Then

$$\lambda^M(n) \geq \lambda^{M1}(n) \tag{2.1}$$

Proof Consider the second subsystem $M1$. From equation (1.1), an upper bound on the throughput of this subsystem at population n, denoted $\overline{\lambda}^{M1}(n)$, is given by

$$\overline{\lambda}^{M1}(n) = \min\left[\frac{c}{u_M}, \frac{n}{[u_M/c + u_M(c-1)/c]}\right] = \min\left[\frac{c}{u_M}, \frac{n}{u_M}\right] \tag{2.2}$$

Now, consider the throughput of the subsystem with the multiserver station. This is given by

$$\lambda^M(n) = \begin{cases} n/u_M & \text{if } n \leq c \\ c/u_M & \text{if } n \geq c. \end{cases} \tag{2.3}$$

Comparing equations (2.2) and (2.3), the result follows. □

Example 11.1 Consider a network with 11 stations. Stations 1 through 8 are MS stations with 6, 5, 5, 4, 4, 3, 3, and 2 multiservers respectively. Stations 9 through 11 are load-independent stations. The loads on the 11 stations are 120, 160, 140, 100, 100, 90, 72, 30, 20, 16, and 15, respectively. Obtain a level-1 SIB lower bound on the throughput of this network at population of 50.

Solution We construct the alternate network Ω' as specified in Lemma 11.4. Since all the delay stations can be combined into one, the resulting Ω' has 11 load-independent stations with loads 20, 32, 28, 25, 25, 30, 24, 15, 20, 16, and 15, and a delay station with load $Z = 613$. For this network, $L' = 863$. The bottleneck station in this network has a load $u_b = 32$, with $\theta_b = 0.03708$ and $\alpha_0 = 0.008110$. Using the SIB technique, the level-1 upper bound on the cycle time at population 50 is obtained from the quadratic given by equation (1.32). Solving for this, we get the upper bound on $Y^{(0)}(49)$ as 1.1596. Thus, the level-1 upper bound on the cycle time = 1863.73, and the corresponding lower bound on the throughput = 0.02683. For comparison, the exact value for the throughput is 0.030. □

11.3 Bounds on Mean Queue Lengths

The techniques discussed above obtain bounds only on the throughput (or the cycle time) of the network. In this section, we develop some simple upper and lower bounds on mean queue lengths. First, we present some bounds that are easy to evaluate once the bounds on the throughput (or equivalently, on the utilization) have been obtained. Let $\overline{U}_i(N)$ ($\underline{U}_i(N)$) denote an upper (lower) bound on the utilization at station i. We first note that $\lambda(n) \leq \lambda(n+1)$ for all n. By definition,

$$Q_i(N) = \sum_{n=1}^{N} u_i^n \frac{G(N-n)}{G(N)} = \sum_{n=1}^{N} u_i^n \prod_{k=N-n+1}^{N} \lambda_i(k) \leq \sum_{n=1}^{N} U_i(N)^n \tag{3.1}$$

Since $U_i(N) \leq 1$, it follows that

$$Q_i(N) \leq \overline{U}_i(N) \frac{1 - [\overline{U}_i(N)]^{N+1}}{1 - \overline{U}_i(N)} \tag{3.2}$$

For the lower bound, we start with equation (3.1), but now use the fact that $CT(n) \leq CT(n+1)$ for all n. Since $\lambda(n) = n/CT(n)$ for all n, we have

$$Q_i(N) = \sum_{n=1}^{N} u_i^n \prod_{k=N-n+1}^{N} \frac{k}{CT(k)} \geq \sum_{n=1}^{N} \frac{N!}{(N-n)!} \left(\frac{U_i(N)}{N}\right)^n \tag{3.3}$$

Equation (3.3) can be simplified (after some algebra) to give

$$Q_i(N) \geq \underline{U}_i(N) \frac{(N-1)[1 - \underline{U}_i(N)] + 1}{(N-1)[1 - \underline{U}_i(N)]^2 + 1} \tag{3.4}$$

Although these bounds require very little computation, they can be quite loose for stations with high utilizations because equations (3.2) and (3.4) involve bounds on utilizations. To obtain tighter bounds on the mean queue length at station i, we consider an alternate network $\Omega^{(i)}$, which has all the stations that are present in Ω. In addition, network Ω' has one extra station, which is identical to station i in network Ω. Let $\lambda^{(i)}(N)$ denote the throughput of $\Omega^{(i)}$. Then from the single-chain version of equations (7.8.4) and (7.1.11), we immediately have the following result

$$Q_i(N) = \frac{\lambda^{(i)}(N)u_i}{1 - \lambda^{(i)}(N)u_i} \tag{3.5}$$

It may be noted in passing that equation (3.5) bears a striking similarity to the equation for the mean queue length at a station in an open product-form queuing network. We can exploit equation (3.5) to get upper and lower queue length bounds by simply substituting the upper and lower bounds on $\lambda^{(i)}(N)$, obtained through any bounding technique. For ABA and BJB, each augmented network can be evaluated with only a constant number of additional operations, but the situation becomes more complex for higher-order PBH or SIB bounds. As a final note, the multiple-chain PBH discussed next provides lower bounds on the mean queue lengths as a by-product, but does not provide upper bounds.

11.4 Bounds for Multiple-Chain Networks

Although a number of techniques have been proposed for single-chain networks, relatively few techniques exist for networks with multiple chains. We review some of these techniques in this section, restricting our attention to networks having only load-independent and delay stations. To discuss these bounds, we need to modify some of our notation. To this end, let L_r denote the sum of the loads on the load-independent stations for chain r, and Z_r the load at the delay station. Define $L'_r = L_r + Z_r$, and u_{br} as the load at the bottleneck station for chain r. The performance measures of interest are the cycle time and throughput of chain r, denoted CT_r and λ_r respectively. The ABA and BJB bounds are very similar to those for single-chain case but could be much more loose. The multiple-chain PBH bounds are very different from the corresponding single-chain bounds.

11.4.1 Asymptotic and Balanced Job Bounds

Consider first an *asymptotic upper bound* on the throughput for chain r. Assuming that a chain r customer does not wait at any station and using the restriction that the chain r utilization cannot exceed 1 at any station, we have

$$\lambda_r(\mathbf{N}) \leq \min(N_r/L'_r, 1/u_{br}) \tag{4.1}$$

The corresponding lower bound can be obtained by assuming that a chain r customer waits behind the $N-1$ remaining customers at every load-independent station in the network. That is,

$$\lambda_r(\mathbf{N}) \geq \frac{N_r}{Z_r + \sum_{k=1}^{K} N_k L_k} \tag{4.2}$$

From the mean value theorem for multiple-chain networks, we immediately get the following *balanced lower bound* on chain r throughput

$$\lambda_r(\mathbf{N}) \geq \frac{N_r}{L'_r + (N-1)u_{br}} \tag{4.3}$$

Note, however, that an analogous upper bound on $\lambda_r(\mathbf{N})$ cannot be obtained using the average loading u_{ar} for chain r.

An alternate asymptotic upper bound on the throughput for chain r is obtained by considering the lower bounds on the throughputs for all chains $k, k \neq r$, as obtained from, say, equation (4.3). For simplicity, we consider networks consisting only of load-independent stations. We now present these upper bounds, termed *composite upper bounds*. An extension of this approach to consider networks with delay stations is straightforward, and is omitted here.

Lemma 11.5 Let $\underline{\lambda}_k(\mathbf{N})$ denote any lower bound on the throughput of chain k. Then the composite upper bound on the throughput of chain $r, \overline{\lambda}_r^{cub}(\mathbf{N})$, is given by

$$\overline{\lambda}_r^{cub}(\mathbf{N}) = \min_i \frac{1 - \sum_{k \neq r} \underline{\lambda}_k(\mathbf{N}) u_{ik}}{u_{ir}} \tag{4.4}$$

Proof Since each station must have utilization less than 1, $U_{ir}(\mathbf{N}) \leq 1 - \sum_{k \neq r} U_{ik}(\mathbf{N})$. Therefore, by using the definition of utilization, we get the desired result. □

11.4.2 Performance Bound Hierarchies

Like the single-chain version, the multiple-chain PBH (MC-PBH) technique develops a sequence of increasingly tighter bounds using the mean value theorem. To get level-ℓ bounds in a multiple-chain network, the basic idea is to start with appropriate estimates of performance measures for all feasible population vectors $\mathbf{n}$ such that $|\mathbf{n}| = N - \ell$ and then apply appropriate recursion equations that are based on the MVA algorithm for multiple chains until the population vector $\mathbf{N}$ is reached. If $\ell = N$, the computation is equivalent to that of the mean value algorithm and the bounds are exact.

The MC-PBH technique, however, is quite different in approach from the single-chain PBH (SC-PBH) technique, because the MC-PBH uses a modification of the MVA equations. Furthermore, though we required two different estimates for the upper and lower bounds in SC-PBH, the MC-PBH works with a single set of initial estimates. In fact, the MC-PBH equations do not reduce to SC-PBH equations if we let $K = 1$.

Let $\overline{\lambda}_r^{(\ell)}(\mathbf{N})$ and $\underline{\lambda}_r^{(\ell)}(\mathbf{N})$ represent the level-ℓ upper and lower bounds on the throughput for chain r. Also let $CT_r(\mathbf{N}) = Z_r + CT_r^*(\mathbf{N})$, and let $\overline{CT}_r^{*(\ell)}(\mathbf{N})$ and $\underline{CT}_r^{*(\ell)}(\mathbf{N})$ represent the level-ℓ upper and lower bounds on $CT_r^*(\mathbf{N})$. These bounds are, of course, related by Little's law as given below.

$$\underline{\lambda}_r^{(\ell)}(\mathbf{N}) = \frac{N_r}{Z_r + \overline{CT}_r^{*(\ell)}(\mathbf{N})} \tag{4.5}$$

and

$$\overline{\lambda}_r^{(\ell)}(\mathbf{N}) = \frac{N_r}{Z_r + \underline{CT}_r^{*(\ell)}(\mathbf{N})} \tag{4.6}$$

Let $\underline{Q}_{ir}^{(\ell)}(\mathbf{n})$ denote the level-ℓ lower bound on the mean queue length at station i for chain r customers, at population vector $\mathbf{n}$. Given the level-$(\ell - 1)$ bounds for the mean queue lengths, the level-ℓ lower bound on the residence time at station i for a chain-r customer is obtained directly from the MVA theorem as

$$\underline{R}_{ir}^{(\ell)}(\mathbf{n}) = u_{ir}\left[1 + \sum_{r=1}^{K} \underline{Q}_{ir}^{(\ell-1)}(\mathbf{n} - e_r)\right] \tag{4.7}$$

A level-ℓ lower bound on $CT_r^*(\mathbf{N})$ can be obtained by summing up these lower bounds on the residence times for chain r. However, the PBH technique improves on this obvious lower bound by considering the "congestion" that was not accounted for by the level-$(\ell - 1)$ mean queue length lower bounds. In fact, the PBH technique obtains a level-ℓ upper bound on $CT_r^*(\mathbf{N})$, using the residence time lower bounds and this unaccounted network congestion.

This measure of network congestion is the difference between the exact value for the mean number of chain r customers summed over all the load-independent stations, and the estimate of this total provided by the lower bounds on the mean queue lengths. The PBH technique works with upper and lower bounds on this congestion measure, henceforth referred to as *pessimistic* and *optimistic heaps*. For chain r at population $\mathbf{n}$, we denote the level-ℓ optimistic and pessimistic heaps as $\underline{\Theta}_r^{(\ell)}(\mathbf{n})$ and $\overline{\Theta}_r^{(\ell)}(\mathbf{n})$ respectively. The use of these heaps in the PBH recursion basically represents the modification to the MVA equations that was mentioned earlier. The following equations clarify the concept of these heaps

$$\overline{\Theta}_r^{(\ell)}(\mathbf{N}) = \overline{CT}_r^{*(\ell)}(\mathbf{N})\underline{\lambda}_r^{(\ell)}(\mathbf{N}) - \sum_{i=1}^{M} \underline{Q}_{ir}^{(\ell)}(\mathbf{n}) \tag{4.8}$$

and

$$\underline{\Theta}_r^{(\ell)}(\mathbf{n}) = \underline{CT}_r^{*(\ell)}(\mathbf{N})\overline{\lambda}_r^{(\ell)}(\mathbf{N}) - \sum_{i=1}^{M} \underline{Q}_{ir}^{(\ell)}(\mathbf{n}) \tag{4.9}$$

We can observe the following from these equations: if the network has only load-independent stations, both heaps for chain r are equal to N_r less the sum of the mean queue length lower bounds at all stations. However, if delay stations are present, the pessimistic heap will exceed the optimistic heap by some amount.

As noted earlier, the heap for each chain represents the customers in that chain who are not accounted for by the mean queue length lower bounds. It is convenient to consider all these customers as being allocated to a fictitious load-independent station. To get an upper bound on $CT^*_r(\mathbf{N})$, we consider an upper bound on the average time a chain r customer spends at this fictitious node. To this end, let $\overline{\chi}_{rk}$ denote the maximum of the chain r loadings, over all load-independent stations visited by a chain k. Then an upper bound on the time spent at this station by chain r customers because of the congestion from chain k is $\overline{\chi}_{rk} \cdot \overline{\Theta}_r^{(\ell)}(\mathbf{N})$. Similarly, a lower bound on this time would be $\underline{\chi}_{rk} \cdot \underline{\Theta}_r^{(\ell)}(\mathbf{N})$, with $\underline{\chi}_{rk}$ defined as the minimum of the chain r loadings over all load-independent stations visited by chain k. Thus, the upper bound on $CT^*_r(\mathbf{N})$ is given by

$$\overline{CT}_r^{*(\ell)}(\mathbf{N}) = \sum_{i=1}^{M} \underline{R}_{ir}^{(\ell)}(\mathbf{N}) + \sum_{k=1}^{K} \overline{\chi}_{rk} \overline{\Theta}_r^{(\ell-1)}(\mathbf{N} - e_r) \tag{4.10}$$

Similarly, we can consider a lower bound on $CT^*_r(\mathbf{N})$ as

$$\underline{CT}_r^{*(\ell)}(\mathbf{N}) = \sum_{i=1}^{M} \underline{R}_{ir}^{(\ell)}(\mathbf{N}) + \sum_{k=1}^{K} \underline{\chi}_{rk} \underline{\Theta}_r^{(\ell-1)}(\mathbf{N} - e_r) \tag{4.11}$$

The asymptotic lower bound on $CT^*_r(\mathbf{N})$ for chain r, denoted $A_r^{(\ell)}(\mathbf{N})$, can be obtained using equation (4.4), as

$$A_r^{(\ell)}(\mathbf{N}) = \max_i \frac{N_r u_{ir}}{1 - \sum_{k \neq r} \underline{\lambda}_k(\mathbf{N}) u_{ik}} - Z_r \tag{4.12}$$

The lower bound on $CT^*_r(\mathbf{N})$ is the larger of the values obtained from equations (4.11) and (4.12). Note that in equations (4.10) and (4.11) there is a component in the second summation for the case where $k = r$. This accounts for the congestion caused to a chain r customer at the fictitious node owing to the other customers from chain r that are "allocated" to this station.

We are now ready to describe the MC-PBH algorithm. For ease of discussion, we consider networks consisting only of load-independent stations. The technique can be extended easily to networks with delay stations and stations with limited load-dependent behavior. Suppose that the level-$(\ell - 1)$ bounds on the mean queue lengths and the corresponding optimistic and pessimistic heaps have been calculated. Then the MC-PBH algorithm uses the modified MVA equations to calculate the performance bounds for chain r as follows: The level-ℓ lower bound on the residence time at each station i is first obtained using equation (4.7). Following this, the upper bound on $CT^*_r(\mathbf{N})$ is obtained by equation (4.10). The lower bound on the throughput for the chain can then be obtained using Little's law, as given by equation (4.5). Now, the level-ℓ lower bound on the mean queue length for chain r customers at station i is obtained by another application of Little's law:

$$\underline{Q}_{ir}^{(\ell)}(\mathbf{N}) = \underline{R}_{ir}^{(\ell)}(\mathbf{N}) \times \underline{\lambda}_r^{(\ell)}(\mathbf{N}) \tag{4.13}$$

Once all the mean queue length lower bounds are obtained in this manner, then a level-ℓ pessimistic heap for each chain can be calculated using equation (4.8). We can now use equation (4.11) in conjunction with equation (4.12) to obtain a lower bound on $CT_r^*(\mathbf{N})$. Following this, the upper bound on the throughput for chain r can be obtained from equation (4.6). Finally the level-ℓ iterations can be completed by calculating the optimistic level-ℓ heap using equation (4.9).

The basis for the MC-PBH algorithm is provided by the level-0 bounds. In order to obtain the level-ℓ bounds on the performance measures at some network population $\mathbf{N}$, the algorithm starts with a level-0 lower bound on the mean queue lengths at each load-independent station i for all population vectors $\mathbf{n}$ such that $n = N - \ell$. These level-0 lower bounds are chosen to be zero for each station and chain. This implies that the initial values for the pessimistic and optimistic heaps are equal to their corresponding chain population. The iterations are then done as indicated above. It can be shown that the iterations produce a sequence of increasingly tighter bounds on all the performance measures, when they are carried out in conjunction with the asymptotic bounds. This implies that the heaps get smaller and smaller at increasingly higher levels. In particular, if the level-N bounds are to be determined, then the iterations are started at a network population equal to 0. At this starting point, the heaps are all equal to 0 and remain so throughout the iterations. Thus, in obtaining the level-N bounds we are in fact using the exact MVA equations for multiple chains, and hence this produces the exact values for the performance measures.

11.5 Exercises

1. Consider a network with four load-independent stations having loads 10, 10, 9, and 8. Obtain the upper and lower balanced job bounds on the cycle time and the throughput at network populations of 10, 20, 30, and 40. Compare your results to the exact values obtained using the MVA algorithm.

2. Let $\mathbf{x} = \{x_i\}, \mathbf{z} = \{z_i\}$ be two sequences of numbers defined for $i = 1 \,..\, M$, and suppose that $x_M \geq x_{M-1} \geq \ldots \geq x_1 \geq 0$. Then we say that the sequence $\mathbf{z}$ has a *partial correspondence* with $\mathbf{x}$, denoted as $\mathbf{z}(PC)\mathbf{x}$ if for some j, $1 \leq j \leq M$, we have $z_M \geq \ldots \geq z_j \geq 0$ and $z_{j-1}, \ldots, z_1 \leq 0$. Using the definitions in Section 11.1.4, let $\mathbf{f}^{(\ell)}(n) = \{f_i^{(\ell)}(n)\}$, and $\boldsymbol{\theta} = \{\theta_i\}, m = 1 \,..\, M$. By induction on ℓ show that for $n \geq 0$ $\mathbf{f}^{(\ell)}(n)(PC)\boldsymbol{\theta}$ and $Y^{(\ell)}(n) = \sum_{i=1}^{M} \theta_i f_i^{(\ell)}(n) \geq 0$.

3. Obtain the level-1 upper SIB bound on $CT(N)$ from equation (1.28). Indicate how you would proceed to obtain the level-2 SIB upper bound on $CT(N)$.

4. Obtain the level-1 throughput bounds for the network with multiserver stations given in Exercise 11.1 at network populations of 10, 20, 30, and 40.

5. Consider the network given in Exercise 11.1. Suppose this network also has a delay station with load $Z = 100$. Develop the upper and lower bounds on the cycle time at network populations of 10, 20, 30 and 40 using (a) level-2 PBH bounds, and (b) level-1 SIB Bounds. Compare your results with the values obtained by exact analysis.
6. Indicate why it is not possible to use the expression $CT_j(\mathbf{N}) \geq L_j + (N - 1)u_{ar}$ to obtain a lower bound on $CT_r^*(\mathbf{N})$.
7. Consider the MC-PBH algorithm for a network having two load-independent stations and two chains passing through them. Suppose that $N_1 = 2$, $N_2 = 3$, $u_{11} = 0.4$, $u_{12} = 0.8$, $u_{21} = 0.6$, and $u_{22} = 0.2$. Obtain the level-3 MC-P2H bounds on the system residence time for both chains and compare them to the values obtained by exact analysis.

Bibliographic Notes

The asymptotic bound analysis for single-chain networks was introduced by Muntz and Wong in 1974. It is discussed in Kleinrock (1976) and in Denning and Buzen (1978). The balanced job bounds for single-chain networks are given in Zahorjan et al. (1982). The BJB analysis has subsequently been extended in Kriz (1984) to produce better bounds for networks with delay stations. The performance bound hierarchies are developed in Eager and Sevcik (1983). The successively improving bounds are developed in Srinivasan (1987). Suri (1984) introduces *generalized quick bounds* which also produce a hierarchy of improving bounds. All of these techniques are based on the MVA algorithm. Stephens and Dowdy (1984) obtains the *convolutional bound hierarchies* based on the convolution algorithm. These bounding schemes, which construct a hierarchy of bounds, are basically recursive in nature. A recursive scheme for producing a hierarchy of improving bounds, based on an initialization with queue lengths proportional to the loads, is introduced in Hsieh and Lam (1987). The authors also show the optimal population sequence over which the recursions are to be executed.

Networks with limited load-dependent behavior have also been considered by several authors. Dallery and Suri (1986) considers networks with multiple-server stations. Srinivasan (1988) obtains bounds for networks with multiserver stations, as well as stations that have a special capacity function. Shanthikumar and Yao (1988) shows a radically different approach to obtain bounds for networks with load-dependent behavior, which are effective under some situations.

The composite upper bounds introduced in Section 11.4 are from Kerola (1986), which follows up on the results presented in Kriz (1984). Hsieh and Lam (1987) also extend their bounding scheme to consider networks with multiple chains. The performance bound hierarchy for multiple chains is from Eager and Sevcik (1986), and is probably the most comprehensive among the bounding techniques presented here. This technique also considers stations with limited load-dependent behavior and produces a hierarchy of bounds that converge to the exact values. It also produces lower bounds on mean queue lengths.

CHAPTER

12

Petri Net-based Performance Modeling

In modeling the performance of computer systems, we have to consider two important aspects: (1) contention for resources and (2) synchronization between various concurrent activities. The former aspect can be adequately represented by queuing network modeling, but the latter cannot. Petri nets have long been used for modeling synchronization behavior of concurrent systems. By adding the concept of time to Petri nets, we can make them suitable for performance studies as well. In this chapter, we shall study several such proposals, both for discrete and continuous time cases. We shall also see how timed Petri net models can be solved using Markovian techniques. As an example of their application, we shall show how several variations on the problem of bus contention in multiprocessor systems can be modeled using timed Petri nets. Finally, we shall briefly discuss the subclass of timed Petri nets that have been found to possess product-form solution.

12.1 Classical Petri Nets

In this section, we provide an overview of classical Petri nets and discuss some analysis techniques. Most of the concepts apply directly to timed Petri nets discussed in later sections.

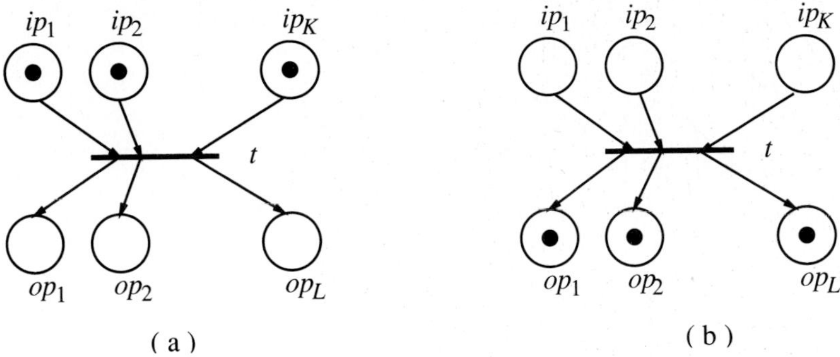

FIGURE 12-1: A Petri net (a) before firing and (b) after firing.

12.1.1 Basic Definitions and Motivation

A Petri net (PN) is a 5-tuple $(\mathcal{P}, \mathcal{T}, \mathcal{I}, \mathcal{O}, \mathcal{M})$ where $\mathcal{P}$ is the set of *places*, $\mathcal{T}$ is the set of *transitions*, $\mathcal{I} \subset \mathcal{P} \times \mathcal{T}$ is the *input function*, $\mathcal{O} \subset \mathcal{T} \times \mathcal{P}$ is the *output function*, and $\mathcal{M} \subset \mathcal{P} \times Z^+$ is a *marking*. (Here, Z^+ denotes the set of all nonnegative integers.) Petri nets are usually represented graphically according to the following conventions: Places are represented by circles, transitions by bars, input function by arcs directed from places to transitions, output function by arcs directed from transitions to places, and markings by small filled circles called *tokens*. A *marking* defines the number of tokens in each of the places of the Petri net. The dynamic behavior of a Petri net is described by the sequence of transition *firings*. The firing rules are as follows: Let t be a transition with incoming arcs from places $ip_1, \ldots, ip_K$ and outgoing arcs to places $op_1, \ldots, op_L$ for some $K, L \geq 1$. Then t can fire if and only if each of the K input places contains at least one token. As a result of firing, one token will be removed from each of the K input places, and one token will be added to each one of L output places. Fig. 12-1 shows this pictorially.

A transition that can fire is known as *enabled*. When several transitions are enabled simultaneously, we have *nondeterminism* in the sense that any one of these transitions may fire next. Also, a firing may disable some of the originally enabled transitions; therefore, if several transitions are enabled, each one of the possible firing choices could lead to an entirely different behavior in the future. Fig. 12-2 shows such a situation where the transitions t_1 and t_2 share the same input place p_2. We say that these transitions *conflict*, because the firing of one disables the other. In classical Petri nets, the selection in case of a conflict situation is purely nondeterministic, but in some extended versions, a different rule might apply. For example, the decision might be based on routing probabilities, priorities, or firing rates associated with t_1 and t_2.

Often, it is convenient to allow a transition to remove more than one token from its input places and deposit more than one token into its output places. Pictorially, this can be represented by putting *weights* on the input and output arcs of each transition. To deal with this capability mathematically, we introduce

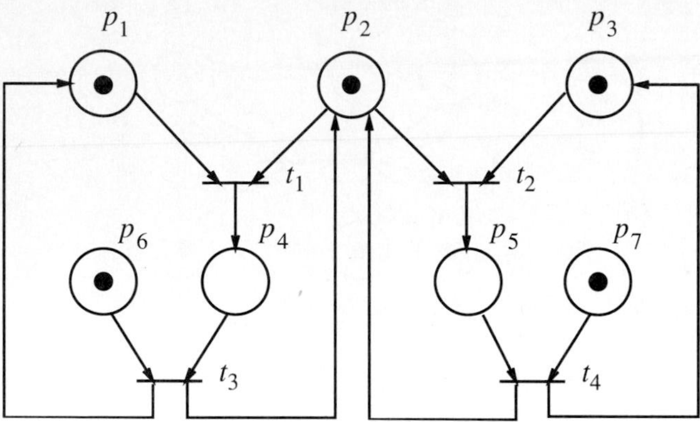

FIGURE 12-2: Firings leading to multiple behavior sequences.

the concept of a *bag* or *multiset*. A bag is a set with duplication of elements allowed; that is, for each set element, we also keep track of its "occurrence count". Thus, with each transition t we can associate an *input bag*, denoted $\mathcal{I}(t)$, and an *output bag*, denoted $\mathcal{O}(t)$. The input bag $\mathcal{I}(t)$ gives the number of tokens removed from each of the input places of t when t fires. Similarly, the output bag $\mathcal{O}(t)$ gives the number of tokens placed in each of the output places of transition t when t fires. Because of the context in which we use bags here, a convenient representation of a bag is by a vector $(b_1, \ldots, b_{|\mathcal{P}|})$ where b_i is an integer specifying the number of tokens removed from (or placed into) place p_i. For example, assuming the arc weights of 1 in Fig. 12-2, we have $\mathcal{I}(t_1) = (1,1,0,0,0,0,0)$, $\mathcal{O}(t_1) = (0,0,0,1,0,0,0)$, etc. Unless stated otherwise, we shall henceforth assume that all arc weights are 1, which means that $\mathcal{I}(t)$ and $\mathcal{O}(t)$ can be regarded as ordinary sets.

We now show why Petri nets are appropriate models for concurrent activities. Without loss of generality, we can restrict our attention to concurrent programs. In studying the concurrency-related issues for such programs, we must precisely represent all interactions between various processes; the sequential portions of the computations being somewhat irrelevant. We could then speak of the *state* of each process in terms of whether it is ready to interact with others in a particular way. At any given time instant, the set consisting of the current state of each process of the system defines the global state. In the Petri net representation, *each feasible marking represents such a global state*. The places then represent the holders of state information, and transitions are the "events" that can happen in various global states. The evolution of the concurrent program is represented by the sequence of transition firings (or occurrence of events). For example, in Fig. 12-2, a token in places p_1 and p_3 may represent, respectively, that two processes, say P and Q, are ready to enter a *critical section*. Place p_2 may be used to indicate whether the critical section is free or occupied—the presence of a token meaning that it is free. The firing of t_1 (respectively t_2) then represents the fact that process P (respectively Q) is able to get into the critical section. Thus, a token in place p_4 (p_5) means that P (Q) is inside the critical sec-

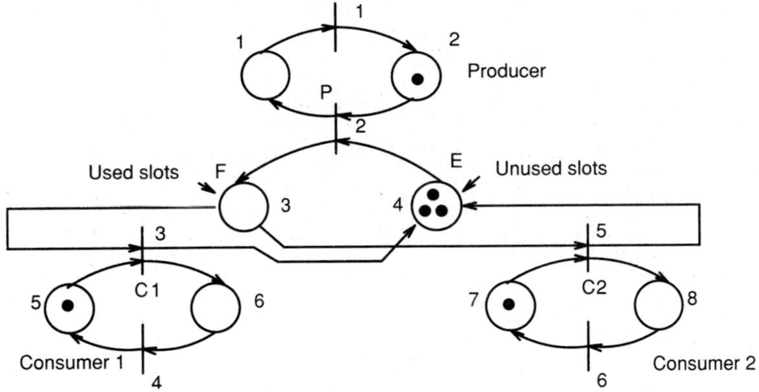

FIGURE 12-3: Bounded-buffer problem with one producer and two consumers.

tion. The firing of t_3 (t_4) means that P (Q) has come out of the critical section. Places p_6 and p_7 may represent some other relevant conditions in the system. The state of the system as shown is {1,1,1,0,0,1,1}, and the firing of t_1 will take it to state {0,0,1,1,0,0,0}, etc.

With the above interpretation, it is possible to directly represent several aspects of concurrent programs using Petri nets and check for desirable properties. It is well known that "fork" and "join" constructs can represent arbitrary execution precedences. These constructs have direct counterparts in Petri nets in the form of multiple output and input arcs for a transition. Nondeterministic selection and mutual exclusion can be represented by introducing conflicts, as in Fig. 12-2. Resource constraints can be represented by providing a limited number of tokens. For example, in Fig. 12-2 the number of tokens in place p_2 can be interpreted as the number of available resource units. Other types of synchronization can also be represented easily. Fig. 12-3 shows the representation of the classical bounded-buffer problem with one producer and two consumer processes. The number of tokens in place $F(E)$ indicates the number of full (empty) slots in the buffer. Therefore, the consumer transitions $C1$ and $C2$ can fire only if place F has a token and the producer transition P can fire only if place E has a token. Fig. 12-4 shows a model of a simple communication protocol where the sender *window-size* is 3 (i.e., the sender can have at most three unacknowledged messages). The receiver gets one message at a time and acknowledges each. By introducing more places and transitions one can represent more complex protocols as well. Exercise 12.1 explores the representation of the classical reader-writer problem using Petri nets.

The Petri net representation of concurrent activities can be used for checking if the system has the desired synchronization properties. To this end, we shall define a number of properties of general Petri nets. It turns out that the verification of many of these properties is infeasible or very expensive in general; therefore, we shall define a number of restricted classes of Petri nets where the verification is easier.

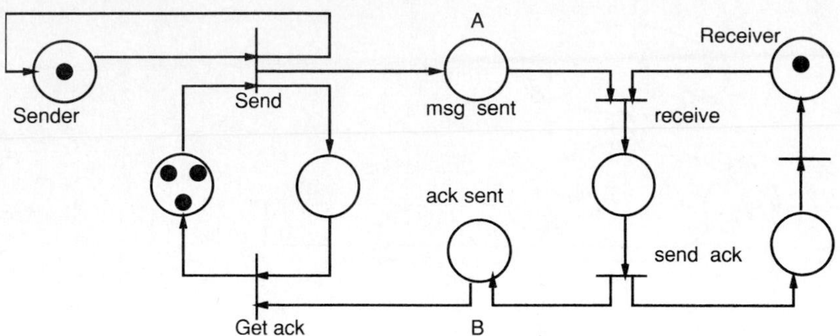

FIGURE 12-4: A communication protocol with sender window size of 3.

Since the markings of a Petri net can be considered as "states", we can view a Petri net as an automaton that computes a function in the same sense as a finite state machine or a Turing machine does. It is most natural to think of this computation as a language recognition problem. For this, we associate a symbol with each transition, such that the firing of the transition generates that symbol. We also pick certain markings as *starting states*, and certain others as *goal states*. Thus, we can define the language generated by a Petri net as the set of all strings that can be generated in transiting from a starting state to a goal state. We can also characterize the class of languages generated by Petri nets under various assumptions. Such a characterization allows us to compare the modeling power of Petri nets against those of other well-known models such as Turing machines or push-down automata.

Petri nets, as described above, are usually referred to as *classical Petri nets*. In spite of their ability to specify complex synchronization, they are inadequate to represent arbitrary computations. That is, they cannot generate recursively enumerable sets, which is the language generated by Turing machines. What is lacking is the "not" operation: It is impossible to specify that a transition should fire if something does *not* happen. This weakness can be removed by adding *inhibitor arcs* to Petri nets. These arcs go from places to transitions and are denoted by a small circle on the transition end. The semantics is that in order for the transition to fire, the originating place of the inhibitor arc should not have any token. Petri nets with inhibitor arcs have the full power of Turing machines and thus can represent arbitrary computations. In practice, one often needs the ability to count; i.e., to fire a transition after a certain number of events have occurred. It is easy convince oneself that if a potentially unbounded number of events can occur, counting by a Petri net is impossible without inhibitor arcs (or some other features of similar modeling power). Exercise 12.2 shows a concrete example of this.

Several other extensions to classical Petri nets have also been proposed in the literature, but most of them are only for representational convenience. For example, classical Petri nets coupled with firing priorities have the same raw modeling power as those with inhibitor arcs, but are much more convenient to work with. Similarly, having multiple arcs between a given place-transition pair is more convenient, but does not increase the modeling power.

The modeling power of classical Petri nets does not fit the Chomsky hierarchy, which is commonly used to characterize languages. It is easy to see that such nets are more powerful than *finite state machines*, and thus can generate non-regular languages; however, they generate some (but not all) context-free and some context-sensitive languages. The details depend on the following two aspects:

1. The goal states may either be limited to the given finite set of states, or specified as any superset of such a set. These lead to the so-called G and L type of languages, respectively.
2. The λ-*transitions*, i.e., transition firings that do not generate any string, may or may not be allowed. In the former case, we get the G_λ and L_λ languages.

These languages satisfy several *closure properties*, which are often useful in proving results regarding their modeling power. For example, the union of two Petri-net languages of any type is also a Petri-net language of the same type.

12.1.2 Properties and Analysis Problems

The tokens in a Petri net play the same role as the customers in a queuing network. Therefore, we shall use our familiar notation $\mathbf{n} = (n_1, \ldots, n_m)$ with $m = |\mathcal{P}|$, to denote a marking. Thus, n_i gives the number of tokens in place p_i. Since a system must start in some valid initial state if it is to behave correctly, we need to assume a set of all valid initial markings, henceforth denoted as $\mathcal{M}_0$. In the following, we shall define various properties relative to a $\mathbf{n}^{(0)} \in \mathcal{M}_0$.

We say that a marking $\mathbf{n}'$ *covers* another marking $\mathbf{n}$ if $\forall i\,(n_i \geq n_i)$. We shall denote this relationship as $\mathbf{n}' \succeq \mathbf{n}$. In this situation, if $\mathbf{n}' \neq \mathbf{n}$, i.e., at least one place has more tokens under $\mathbf{n}'$ than under $\mathbf{n}$, then we say that $\mathbf{n}'$ *strictly covers* $\mathbf{n}$. We shall denote this situation as $\mathbf{n}' \succ \mathbf{n}$.

The *reachability set* $RS(\mathbf{n}^{(0)})$ of the Petri net is defined as the set of all markings that can be reached in zero or more firings from $\mathbf{n}^{(0)}$. The temporal relationships between these markings can be represented by a graph known as the *reachability graph*. In the reachability graph, if the firing of some enabled transition in marking $\mathbf{n}$ results in marking $\mathbf{n}'$, then we draw an arc from $\mathbf{n}$ to $\mathbf{n}'$. If the reachability graph is finite, we can construct it systematically by starting with the initial marking $\mathbf{n}^{(0)}$ and considering all possible transition firings in each marking. In the infinite case, it is often useful to consider a finite representation of the reachability graph known as the *coverability tree*. In this representation, we ignore any already-encountered markings during the construction (thereby obtaining a tree, as opposed to a general graph), and also use the symbol ω to indicate places having an arbitrary number of tokens (which makes the representation finite).

To see when ω is used in the coverability tree, suppose that a marking $\mathbf{n}$ already exists in the tree, and we encounter another one, say $\mathbf{n}'$, which strictly covers $\mathbf{n}$, but exactly the same set of transitions are enabled in $\mathbf{n}$ and $\mathbf{n}'$. Let $\mathcal{P}^* \subseteq \mathcal{P}$ be the set of places that contain strictly more tokens under $\mathbf{n}'$ than under $\mathbf{n}$, such that any further increase in tokens in these places does not change the set of enabled transitions. Then we alter $\mathbf{n}'$ as follows: for every place $p_i \in \mathcal{P}^*$ we change the n_i' component of $\mathbf{n}'$ to ω. We then continue on with the construction. In dealing with the ω values in the construction, we use the following rules: (a) for any finite integer n, $n < \omega$, $\omega + n = \omega - n = \omega$ and (b) $\omega \leq \omega$. It can be shown that the use of ω always results in a finite coverability tree. However, the coverability tree does not contain all the information in the reachability graph, its use may only provide bounds, rather than the exact results.

It turns out that most of the interesting questions regarding Petri nets are related to the following *reachability problem*: Given a marking (or a set of markings), could they be reached from the initial marking $\mathbf{n}^{(0)}$? For classical Petri nets, the reachability problem is decidable, but has been shown to be exponential space-hard. With inhibitor arcs, it is basically the halting problem for a Turing machine, and thus undecidable. Often, in applications, the net is bounded, and therefore, the theoretical results are not important; however, we still must contend with the fact that the number of reachable markings can be exponential as a function of the number of places and transitions.

Let us now introduce a number of useful properties. A marking $\mathbf{n}$ is called *coverable* if there exists a marking $\mathbf{n}' \in RS(\mathbf{n}^{(0)})$ such that $\mathbf{n}' \succ \mathbf{n}$. If in every marking $\mathbf{n} \in RS(\mathbf{n}^{(0)})$ no place contains more than k tokens, we say that the net is *k-bounded*. For example, the net in Fig. 12-5 is 2-bounded. If the net is k-bounded for some finite $k \geq 1$, it is called bounded, otherwise it is called *unbounded*. A Petri net is called *structurally bounded* if it is bounded for every finite initial marking. Since the tokens in a Petri net model represent resources or customers, a bounded net corresponds to the situation where none of the entities could grow indefinitely. A 1-bounded net is also known as *safe*. Safeness is a useful concept when the physical system cannot have any pending activities. For example, if the firing of a transition that puts a token in place p represents an interrupt generation, safeness with respect to place p means that no new interrupts can arrive while one interrupt is in service.

A Petri net is called *strictly conservative* if the total number of tokens in the net is conserved by every transition firing. It is called *conservative* if this condition holds with respect to a given positive weight vector, i.e., if

$$\exists [w_1 > 0, \ldots, w_m > 0] \; \forall \mathbf{n} \in RS(\mathbf{n}^{(0)}) \left[\sum_{i=1}^{m} w_i n_i = \text{const} \right] \tag{1.1}$$

As an example, a closed queuing network model with population N can be represented by a strictly conservative, N-bounded Petri net.

A Petri net is called *persistent* if in any marking $\mathbf{n}$, an enabled transition t can get disabled only after it has itself fired (i.e., the firing of any other concurrently enabled transition will not disable t). Persistence essentially implies

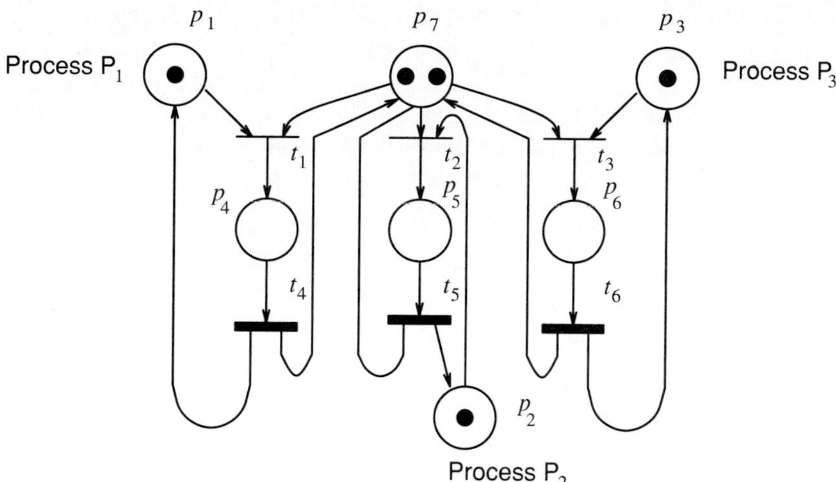

FIGURE 12-5: Two resources shared among three processes.

that the condition under which t is enabled cannot be invalidated by other activities in the system. A Petri net is called *irreducible* if its reachability graph is *strongly connected*, i.e., if for every pair of markings $\mathbf{n}$ and $\mathbf{n}' \in RS(\mathbf{n})$, we have $\mathbf{n} \in RS(\mathbf{n}')$. Informally, irreducibility means that all states in $RS(\mathbf{n}^{(0)})$ are important for the long-term behavior of the system. A Petri net is called *recurrent* if every marking can occur infinitely often.

In any reachable marking $\mathbf{n} \in RS(\mathbf{n}^{(0)})$, zero or more transitions may be enabled. If no transitions are enabled, the system represented by the Petri net model cannot evolve any further. The situation at this point may be one of either termination or deadlock. At the level of a Petri net model, however, there is little distinction between these two situations, and we shall refer to both situations as "deadlock". For example, the net of Fig. 12-2 would deadlock (or terminate) after three or five transition firings because tokens are never put back in places p_6 and p_7. A transition t is said to be *live* if for any marking $\mathbf{n} \in RS(\mathbf{n}^{(0)})$, there exists a marking $\mathbf{n}' \in RS(\mathbf{n})$ in which t is enabled. Informally, a transition is live if in any marking, there is a finite sequence of firings that will enable it. Note carefully that our liveness definition is not equivalent to the following: There exists a marking $\mathbf{n}' \in RS(\mathbf{n}^{(0)})$ such that t is enabled. The difference comes if $\mathbf{n}^{(0)}$ is not reachable from all other markings.

If all transitions of the net are live, we say that the net is live. For example, Fig. 12-5 shows the problem of sharing two units of a serially reusable resource among three processes P_1, P_2, and P_3. Place p_7 has two tokens initially, and indicates the free resource units. The transitions $t_1 \mathinner{..} t_3$ represent resource allocation, and $t_4 \mathinner{..} t_6$ represent its use. This net is live because every transition can keep firing indefinitely. Note that *a live net is deadlock-free, but not vice versa*. This is because some of the transitions in a net may "go dead" while the rest of the network keeps functioning normally. For example, in Fig. 12-2, if the arc from t_4 to

p_3 was instead directed to place p_7 and place p_6 did not exist, transitions t_1 and t_3 can keep firing, but others will go dead eventually. Some work on Petri nets distinguishes between several levels of liveness. Our definitions of liveness and deadlock-freedom correspond to the highest and lowest levels of liveness in this terminology. An example of an intermediate level is found where each transition can fire eventually, but not necessarily in a finite number of steps.

As shown in Exercise 12.3, most of the above-mentioned properties, including boundedness, liveness, safety, and coverability, can be reduced to the reachability problem. Thus, the difficulty in solving the reachability problem also implies similar difficulty with other problems. Because of this, we consider proper subsets of Petri nets. If each transition can have at most one input and one output arc, we can eliminate transitions from the representation and get the restricted model called *state machine*. Clearly, a state machine cannot create/destroy tokens or represent synchronization between various activities. A state machine is basically a finite state automaton and thus the corresponding complexity results apply. An example of a state machine is an ordinary closed queuing network. Therefore, if a state machine is well-formed (in the sense of queuing networks), then every state is reachable from every other. Since we are looking for models more general than queuing networks, state machines are not very interesting.

If each place can have at most one input and one output arc, we call such Petri nets *marked graphs*. We can eliminate places from marked graph representation and get a model that looks like a *classical task graph*, i.e., a task graph with only fork and join operations. Obviously, such models cannot represent branch (i.e., nondeterministic or probabilistic choice) operation, and thus cannot model the "conflict" situation. For this reason, such models are also known as *decision-free nets*. This property further means that the firing of a transition cannot disable other enabled transitions; i.e., such nets are always persistent. Marked graphs are also unable to represent the merge operation (i.e., starting a given activity when any one of a set of other activities is finished). It can be shown that *the number of tokens on a cycle in a marked graph does not change as a result of transition firing*. This leads to two simple results: (1) a marking is live if and only if the number of tokens on each cycle is at least one, and (2) a live marking is safe if and only if every place in the graph is on a cycle with exactly one token. In turn, this results in a simple polynomial algorithm for the reachability problem.

Free-choice nets are a generalization of marked graphs where places can have multiple input and output arcs, but any transition receiving input from a multi-output place cannot have any other input arcs. This limits the conflict in that a token in a conflict place has a "free choice" to go to any one of the conflicting transitions. In free choice nets, the conflict and join synchronization are uncoupled, which makes them easier to analyze than general Petri nets. Free-choice nets can be viewed as *extended task graphs*, i.e., task graphs with "branch" and "merge" operations in addition to the "fork" and "join" operations. (See Section 13.3.1.) Unfortunately, the reachability and liveness problems become NP-complete in free-choice nets. Nevertheless, it is possible to get some results

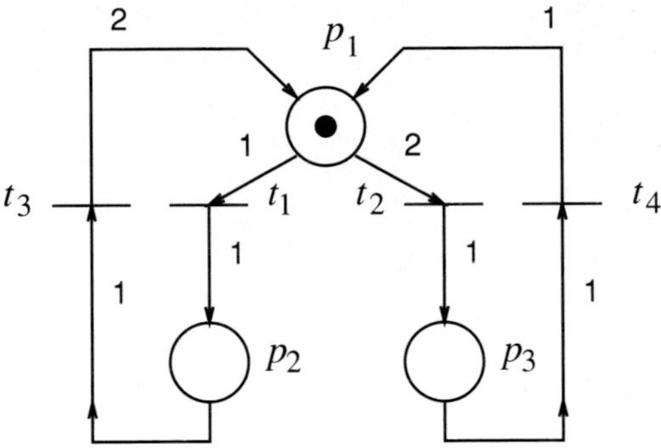

FIGURE 12-6: Petri net model for Example 12.1.

based on structural analysis which is generally more efficient than the reachability analysis. As a final note, one can place further restrictions on marked graphs, free-choice nets, and classical Petri nets that ensure properties like boundedness and safeness, and thereby get special classes that may be easier to analyze. We shall see some of these in the next section.

Example 12.1 Consider the Petri net model shown in Fig. 12-6. The labels on the arcs specify their multiplicity. Assuming that $\mathbf{n}^{(0)} = [1, 0, 0]$, construct the reachability graph and coverability tree and identify the subclass to which the net belongs.

Solution This net is free-choice because the only inputs to transitions t_1 and t_2 are from the conflict place p_1. Because of its simplicity, we can easily see that this net is unbounded (and hence nonconservative and unsafe) but live. A part of the reachability graph is shown in Fig. 12-7(a) and the coverability tree in Fig. 12-7(b). To see how ω transitions arise, consider the markings $\mathbf{n} = (2, 0, 0)$ and $\mathbf{n}' = (3, 0, 0)$. Then $\mathbf{n}' \succ \mathbf{n}$ and the same set of transitions are enabled in both markings. The set $\mathcal{P}^*$ is $\{p_1\}$, and any further increase in p_1 does not change the set of enabled transitions. Therefore, we change $\mathbf{n}'$ to $(\omega, 0, 0)$ and continue. Similarly, we can change $(0, 2, 0)$ to $(0, \omega, 0)$. Note that except for the back arcs, the graphs in the two figures are identical up to this point. In Fig. 12-7(a), we can go directly to marking $(2, 1, 0)$ from both $(3, 0, 0)$ and $(0, 2, 0)$. However, by replacing definite integers with ω, we have lost the ability to count, and therefore the next states in Fig.12-7(b) are different (but generic in nature). This clearly shows that the coverability tree does not have all the information contained in the reachability graph. □

12.1.3 Structural Analysis of Petri Nets

Although reachability analysis is essential for answering detailed questions regarding the behavior of an arbitrary Petri net, it is possible to obtain valuable behavioral information by examining only the structure of the Petri net. For

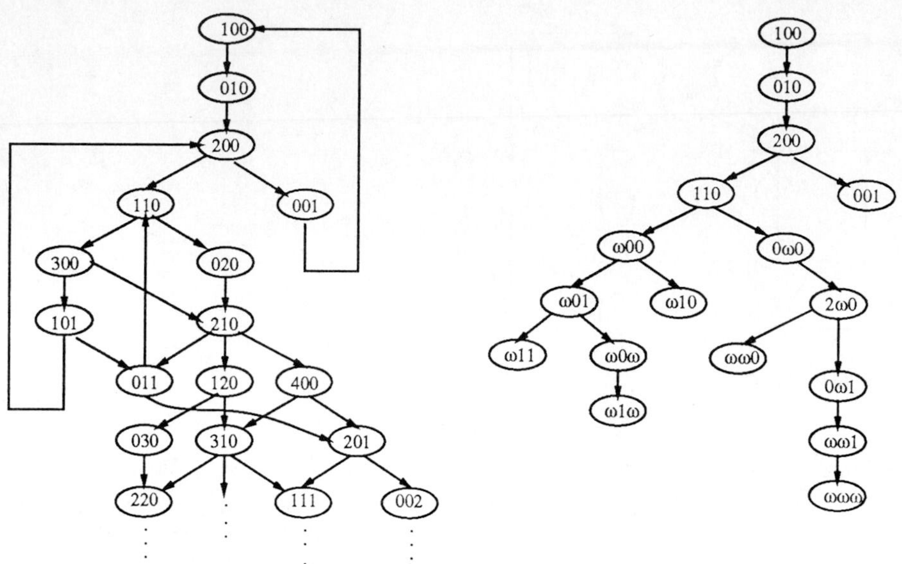

FIGURE 12-7: Reachability graph and coverability tree for Example 12.1.

example, we may be able to identify a set of structural restrictions that ensure that the Petri net is live. Then if we design the system such that it satisfies these restrictions, liveness would be ensured automatically.

To examine the structural properties, we shall represent the behavior of a *classical* Petri net by a set of matrix equations. Let a^+_{tp} denote the number of arcs from a transition $t \in \mathcal{T}$ to a place $p \in \mathcal{P}$ and a^-_{tp} the number of arcs in the opposite direction. Let

$$a_{tp} = a^+_{tp} - a^-_{tp} \tag{1.2}$$

It is clear that a_{tp} represents the change in the number of tokens in place p when transition t fires. Let $m = |\mathcal{P}|$ and $M = |\mathcal{T}|$. We define the *incidence matrix* of the Petri net, denoted A, as the $M \times m$ matrix of a_{tp}'s. Given a marking $\mathbf{n}$, transition t will be enabled if and only if $a^-_{tp} \leq n_p$ for all p; i.e., there are at least as many tokens in place p as needed for firing transition t. Let $\mathbf{n}^{(k)}$ denote a *column* vector of size m representing the marking after the kth firing and U_k another column vector of size M with a 1 in some position and zeros elsewhere. If U_k has a 1 in tth position, the $m \times 1$ vector $A^T U_k$ gives the change in the number of tokens in each place because of the firing of transition t. Therefore, the dynamics of the Petri net is described by the following recursive equation[1]

$$\mathbf{n}^{(k)} = \mathbf{n}^{(k-1)} + A^T U_k \tag{1.3}$$

Note that the above equation only gives the result of transition t firing; it says nothing of whether the transition can fire in the marking $\mathbf{n}^{(k-1)}$. However, if U_k is always defined such that it corresponds to an enabled transition in marking $\mathbf{n}^{(k)}$, the firing, and hence the resulting $\mathbf{n}^{(k)}$, will remain valid.

Now we can make a number of interesting observations. Suppose that the marking $\mathbf{n}^{(d)}$ is reachable from the initial marking $\mathbf{n}^{(0)}$ by the firing sequence $U_1, \ldots, U_d$. Then from equation (1.3) we have

$$\mathbf{n}^{(d)} = \mathbf{n}^{(0)} + \sum_{k=1}^{d} A^T U_k \tag{1.4}$$

Let $\Delta\mathbf{n} = \mathbf{n}^{(d)} - \mathbf{n}^{(0)}$. Also let $\sigma = \sum_{k=1}^{d} U_k$ denote the *firing count vector*. The tth element of σ represents the number of times transition t fires in the entire sequence. Equation (1.4) now becomes

$$A^T \sigma = \Delta\mathbf{n} \tag{1.5}$$

Consider a column vector $X = (x_1, \ldots, x_M)$ of nonnegative integers satisfying the equation

$$A^T X = [0] \tag{1.6}$$

From equation (1.5), we can see that X represents a firing count vector that leaves the Petri net in its initial state. We call X a *T-invariant*. If there exists an X with strictly positive elements, the net is said to be *consistent*. Consistency means that a scenario exists in which every transition fires at least once before the net returns to its initial state; i.e., there exists a finite cycle to which every transition contributes.

The net in Fig. 12-5 has three linearly-independent T-invariant vectors: $T_1 = [1,0,0,1,0,0]$, $T_2 = [0,1,0,0,1,0]$, and $T_3 = [0,0,1,0,0,1]$. These correspond, respectively, to processes P_1, P_2, and P_3 grabbing the resource, using it, and returning it back. Note that none of these T-invariants has all positive elements, but that does not mean that the net is inconsistent. This is because any linear combination of T_1, T_2, and T_3 should also be a T-invariant. One such combination is $T_1 + T_2 + T_3 = [1,1,1,1,1,1]$, which is enough to show that the net is consistent. As mentioned earlier, this net is live and bounded.

It turns out that *a live and bounded net always has a T-invariant with all positive elements (i.e., is consistent)*. Unfortunately, the opposite is not true. Here one can see the main weakness of the structural analysis. The existence of a positive vector X only means that if tth transition fired $X[t]$ times, the

[1]It is unnecessary to explicitly include t in the notation U_k, since t is uniquely determined by the index k.

Petri net can be returned to its initial state. There is nothing to guarantee that such a firing vector is indeed realizable. This is the reason why T-invariant does not imply liveness or boundedness. It is also clear that, in general, only the reachability analysis can reveal which firing sequences are valid and which are not. Nevertheless, structural analysis gives us some very useful results in special cases as we shall see shortly.

Consider a column vector $Y = (Y_1, \ldots, Y_m)$ such that

$$AY = [0] \tag{1.7}$$

Such a vector is called an *S-invariant* of the Petri net. Since the tth row of A gives the changes in marking when transition t fires, the condition (1.7) implies invariance of weighted summations of changes. In other words, *the existence of an S-invariant with all positive components is a necessary and sufficient condition for the net to be conservative.* If $Y = [1\ 1\ \cdots\ 1]$ is an S-invariant, then the net must be strictly conservative.

We can determine T and S invariants by obtaining all possible solutions to equations (1.6) and (1.7). The number of solutions depends on the rank of A matrix, denoted r. Let us partition A into four submatrices such that A_{12} (see below) is a $r \times r$ nonsingular matrix. Let $Y = [Y_1\ Y_2]$ be a decomposition of Y compatible with that of A. Then equation (1.7) can be written as follows:

$$\begin{array}{c|c|c|} & m-r & r \\ r & A_{11} & A_{12} \\ M-r & A_{21} & A_{22} \end{array} \quad \begin{array}{|c|c} 1 & \\ Y_1 & m-r \\ Y_2 & r \end{array} \quad = \quad \begin{array}{|c|} \\ 0 \\ 0 \end{array} \tag{1.8}$$

The first part of this equation yields $Y_2 = -A_{12}^{-1}A_{11}Y_1$. Combining it with the identity $Y_1 = Y_1$, we can write

$$[Y_1\ \ Y_2]^T = [I_{m-r}\ \ -A_{12}^{-1}A_{11}]^T Y_1 \tag{1.9}$$

where the matrix on the right-hand side, henceforth denoted as B, is obtained by vertically stacking I_{m-r} (an identity matrix of order $m-r$) and $-A_{12}^{-1}A_{11}$. This gives us all possible S-invariants. Multiplying both sides of equation (1.4) by B^T and simplifying, it can be shown that if $\mathbf{n}^{(d)}$ is reachable from $\mathbf{n}^{(0)}$, then

$$B^T \Delta\mathbf{n} = 0 \tag{1.10}$$

We can also show that a Petri net is structurally bounded if and only if there exists a vector Y of positive integers such that $AY \leq 0$. A number of other properties can be formulated in terms of the concepts introduced thus far. Also note that if the net has an S-invariant with all positive components, then it must be structurally bounded (but the opposite is not true). Practical applications often lead to Petri nets that are structurally bounded. It can be shown that *a Petri net without any subnets that consume all tokens is structurally bounded if and only if it has both a T-invariant and an S-invariant with all positive components.*

The matrix-based analysis introduced above is particularly useful for restricted subclasses of Petri nets. For example, in the case of marked graphs, each column of A can have at most one positive entry and at most one negative entry. Such a matrix can be viewed as the weighted incidence matrix of a graph (or circuit) where the transitions are nodes and places are arcs that connect a pair of nodes. For free-choice nets, there are two additional concepts, namely, siphons and traps. We shall define them here without referring to matrices. A *trap* $\mathcal{R}$ is a set of places and can be defined recursively as follows:

1. All places that are marked in $\mathbf{n}^{(0)}$ belong to $\mathcal{R}$.
2. If a place x belongs to $\mathcal{R}$, then so does at least one output place of each of the transitions for which the place x is an input.

A *siphon*, also known as a *deadlock*, denoted $\mathcal{D}$, is also a set of places and can be defined as follows:

1. All places that do not feed any transition are in $\mathcal{D}$.
2. If a place x belongs to $\mathcal{D}$, then so does at least one of the input places of each of the transitions that feed into the place x.

It is easy to see that a trap acts like a "trap" for tokens; i.e., a marked trap remains marked forever. Similarly, a siphon acts like a "token avoider"; if a siphon $\mathcal{D}$ becomes blank, it will stay so. We call a trap (siphon) *minimal* if no subset of it is a trap (siphon). We now state the following results without proof:

Lemma 12.1 A free-choice Petri net is live if and only if every siphon contains a trap.

Lemma 12.2 Hack's Theorem A free-choice Petri net is live and safe if and only if every minimal siphon is a minimal trap.

□

These results allow us to check for liveness and safeness of free-choice Petri nets. Although the number of possible traps and siphons in a Petri net is exponential in the worst case, usually the number is small. Because of this, liveness and safety analysis using these concepts is typically less expensive than the one via reachability analysis.

Example 12.2 Consider the bounded-buffer example in Fig. 12-3 with only one consumer, say $C1$, retained. Find the A matrix, and from there the T and S invariants. Identify the type of the net.

Solution The A matrix can be written down directly from Fig. 12-3.

$$A = \begin{array}{c} \\ t_1 \\ t_2 \\ t_3 \\ t_4 \end{array} \left[\begin{array}{cccccc} p_1 & p_2 & p_3 & p_4 & p_5 & p_6 \\ -1 & 1 & 0 & 0 & 0 & 0 \\ 1 & -1 & 1 & -1 & 0 & 0 \\ 0 & 0 & -1 & 1 & -1 & 1 \\ 0 & 0 & 0 & 0 & 1 & -1 \end{array} \right]$$

Instead of solving equations (1.6) and (1.7) directly to get the invariants, let us note some interesting properties of our A matrix that immediately lead to the results. First, we note that every column of A has one $+1$ and one -1 entry. This means that if we choose $X = [1\ 1\ 1\ 1]^T$, equation (1.6) is satisfied. In other words, given any marking, if each transition is fired once, the net returns to that marking. This should also be obvious from Fig. 12-3, because the firing of all transitions once amounts to depositing a message in the buffer and taking it out. It should also be obvious that this is the only way to bring the system back to the initial state; therefore, [1 1 1 1] is the only *minimal T-invariant*. To conclude this result formally, let $r(A)$ denote the rank of matrix A and $\mathcal{N}(A)$ its *null-space*.[2] A fundamental result in linear algebra states that the rank of A plus the dimension of A^T must equal the number of rows of A. Since $r(A) = 3$ for our A matrix, it follows that $|\mathcal{N}(A^T)| = 1$, which means that $A^T X = 0$ can have only one minimal solution. Also, since all components of the T-invariant are positive, the net must be consistent.

We note that in the rows of A, $+1$ and -1 come in the pairs (1,2), (3,4), and (5,6). Therefore, if we choose $Y = [n_1\ n_1\ n_2\ n_2\ n_3\ n_3]$ for any integers n_1, n_2, and n_3, equation (1.7) is satisfied. That is, we have three linearly-independent S-invariant vectors: $S_1 = [1,1,0,0,0,0]$, $S_2 = [0,0,1,1,0,0]$, and $S_3 = [0,0,0,0,1,1]$. Another way to see that our A matrix has three linearly-independent S-invariants is by noting that $|\mathcal{N}(A)| + r(A)$ must equal the number of columns. Since $S_1 + S_2 + S_3$ is a vector of all 1's, this net is strictly conservative.

In fact, the given net is a marked graph with 1, 3, and 1 tokens on the three loops involving the producer, the buffer, and the consumer, respectively. As expected, a transition firing preserves the number of tokens on each loop. □

12.2 Timed Petri Nets

The Petri net models discussed above assume that each activity takes zero time. Thus, a transition, once enabled, fires instantaneously and deposits tokens in its output places. This is adequate if the objective of the model is only to verify the correctness of synchronization between various activities. However, for answering any performance-related questions, we need to associate a finite time duration with transitions and/or places. Usually, it is adequate to make only the transitions timed, and we shall assume this to be the case. Timed transitions are usually represented by thick bars, and we shall also use this convention. The *firing time* of a transition represents the time taken by the activity represented by the transition. For example, in Fig. 12-3, the firing times of transitions t_1 and t_2 represent, respectively, the time taken to produce the next item and to actually place the item in the buffer. In the next two subsections, we discuss some general issues related to timed Petri nets.

[2]The null-space of a matrix A, denoted $\mathcal{N}(A)$, is defined as the vector-space spanned by all the solutions of the system $AX = 0$. We shall denote the dimensionality of this vector-space by $|\mathcal{N}(A)|$.

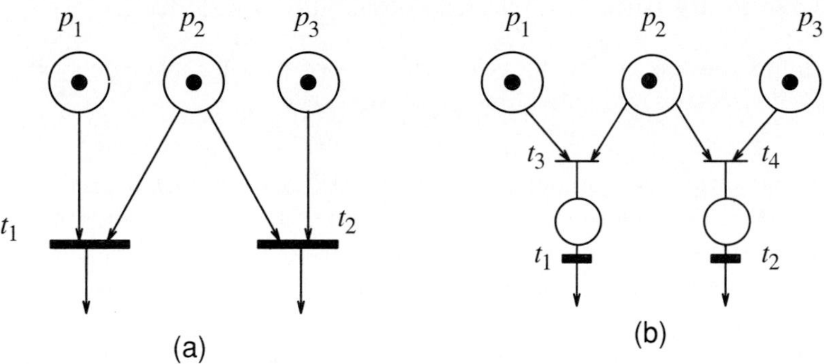

FIGURE 12-8: Illustration of AF and NF semantics.

12.2.1 Timing Semantics

The semantics of time in a Petri net is not as simple as might appear at first. In particular, we can consider the following two possibilities:

1. After a transition t is enabled, its firing is delayed by the time equal to its firing time. At the end of this period, if t is still enabled, it fires exactly like an ordinary Petri net; i.e., it removes tokens from all its input places and deposits tokens in all its output places in a single atomic operation. We shall call this *atomic firing* (AF) semantics.

2. As soon as the transition t is enabled, it removes its enabling tokens from the input places. This can be identified as the "start-firing" event. The transition then remains in the firing state for its firing time, and then it deposits tokens in its output places. This can be identified as the "end-firing" event. We call this *nonatomic firing* (NF) semantics.

It is also possible to consider a general semantics that covers both of these possibilities. The idea is to let a transition remain enabled for some *enabling time* before it absorbs tokens from its input places. The transition then spends some *firing time* before depositing tokens into its output places. We shall call this *generalized NF-semantics*. In much of our discussion, we shall ignore this general semantics because it can always be mimicked by introducing extra transitions.

There are important differences between the AF and NF semantics. With AF semantics, an enabled transition may be disabled before it has a chance to fire, but this cannot happen with NF semantics. Consider, for example, two conflicting transitions t_1 and t_2 shown in Fig. 12-8(a). If p_1 and p_2 initially have a token, and p_3 receives a token before t_1 fires, both t_1 and t_2 will be competing to fire from then on. Thus, if either one of them fires, the other will get disabled. In terms of its physical interpretation, this means that if one of the two competing activities finishes first, the other one is aborted. This has two consequences:

(a) The conflict is resolved entirely by the race condition, rather than by some independent means (such as a selection probability or priority).

(b) If the firing times are not memoryless, the abortion will make the system non work-conserving and thus difficult to analyze.

With NF semantics, the conflict is resolved at the time of start-firing event, and no abortion is needed. Thus, in the scenario presented above, t_1 will grab its input tokens immediately, and t_2 will never get enabled. Let us now consider a different scenario where a token is present in both p_1 and p_3, but there is none in p_2. When a token arrives in p_2, both t_1 and t_2 become enabled simultaneously. With AF semantics, nothing changes; i.e., both t_1 and t_2 will still compete to fire. However, with NF semantics, the conflict should now be resolved by some external means (e.g., by probabilistic selection or priorities).

It may appear that NF semantics is better than AF semantics, but this is not necessarily the case. With NF semantics, we need to distinguish between *start-firing* and *end-firing* situations. That is, in the Markovian model, we *might* need two distinct states to represent what is represented by a single state under AF semantics. (In some cases, the end-firing event of one transition can be combined with the start-firing event of another, so we don't necessarily double the number of states over the AF semantics.) Also, there *are* situations when we have a race condition in the real system — a classical example being a timer running in parallel with some system activity. This is represented naturally by the AF model, but *cannot be represented by the NF model.* On the other hand, when the real system does not have a race condition and we really want to make a probabilistic or priority-based selection, this aspect can be represented in the AF model by introducing additional untimed transitions. Fig. 12-8(b) shows how the Petri net in Fig. 12-8(a) can be modified to avoid the race condition. Here the conflict between the untimed transitions t_3 and t_4 can be resolved probabilistically, as we shall see in Section 12.3. The addition of untimed transitions surely increases the complexity of the model (and thus AF semantics doesn't always yield a smaller model than the NF semantics).

There is yet another aspect to consider, and this has to do with situations involving multiple enablings of a transition. For example, consider transition t_1 in Fig. 12-8(a). If both p_1 and p_2 contain at least two tokens, t_1 can fire twice. The two enablings represent two different activities (e.g., service times of two different jobs). Now, two interpretations are possible:

1. Only one activity occurs at a time. In the queuing network terminology, we can think of activities as customers, only one of which could be in service. Because of this analogy, we shall call this interpretation *single-server semantics* (or SS semantics).

2. Both activities proceed in parallel. In queuing terminology, we can think of the transition acting as a delay server, so we call this interpretation *delay server semantics* (or DS semantics).

Notice that this distinction is irrelevant for an untimed transition, so the difference is another side effect of introducing time in Petri nets. With discrete time, the DS semantics may lead to fewer states, since several activities may end simultaneously. Note that SS/DS classification is orthogonal to the AF/NF classification, so all four combinations are allowed. It is possible to further generalize SS/DS classification by making the firing duration of a transition an arbitrary function of the number of enablings. This is like treating the transition as a general load-dependent server, which obviously covers the SS and DS cases.

12.2.2 Issues in Analysis

The firing times associated with transitions may be either integer or real-valued; we shall study both in later sections.[3] Real-valued firing times are most useful for modeling behavior at a higher level (e.g., synchronization among tasks). Integer-valued firing times find applications at lower levels, particularly in synchronous systems. The earliest proposals considered *deterministic Petri nets* (DPN's), i.e., timed Petri nets where the firing times are fixed. A more general model is to let the firing times be random variables, thereby leading to *stochastic Petri net* (SPN) models. We shall study SPN's first and view DPN's as a special case of SPN's.

It is tempting to let the firing times in a SPN have an arbitrary distribution, but this causes problems whenever repetitive behavior is to be modeled. Repetition can be modeled by having cycles in the Petri net model, but the following problem arises. Suppose that a transition t_1 is enabled at some time, but before it fires, another transition, say t_2, also gets enabled. Now to study the evolution of the net, we need to compute the probability that transition t_1 (or t_2) will fire first. This depends on the remaining firing time of t_1 when t_2 is enabled. This remaining time could depend on the entire past evolution of the net, thereby making the analysis impossible. Because of this difficulty, most proposals on timed Petri nets either assume memoryless distributions of firing times or impose some further restrictions (e.g., only one transition is enabled at a time) to simplify the analysis.

The time-independent properties of an SPN (reachability, liveness, coverability, safeness, etc.) can still be characterized by considering the underlying untimed Petri net, except that we have to be careful about one aspect: The details of the timing behavior may make certain markings (or "states") infeasible. For example, with deterministic firing times, some transitions may always fire before certain others, thereby making certain situations impossible. Thus, the SPN may have a smaller reachability graph than the corresponding untimed Petri net. For the timing analysis itself, we first identify an appropriate (possibly embedded) Markov chain. For example, suppose that the firing-time distribution is memoryless (i.e., exponential for the continuous time case and geometric for the discrete time case). Then the marking itself adequately describes the "state"

[3]We shall also use the word *discrete* to refer to *integer-valued* firing times, even though this is strictly not correct.

of the system, and the reachability graph itself can be viewed as the transition diagram of the corresponding Markov chain. In a more general situation, we can model firing times by a stage-type or phase-type distribution, and thus get a Markovian model by including the stage or phase as a part of the state. In still other cases, we may have to depend on an embedded Markov chain at transition points. In any event, the close correspondence between the reachability graph and the Markov chain is valuable. For example, if the Markov chain of an SPN is ergodic, the underlying Petri net must be live and recurrent, etc. It is also worth noting that SPN's properly contain Markovian queuing network models.

In the next two sections, we shall see how we can construct Markovian models for continuous time and discrete time Petri nets. The state description for this Markovian model includes at least the marking, thus a solution to the model provides us with the stationary probability of each marking. Unfortunately, this information alone may be inadequate to compute the performance measures of interest. This is unlike the situation in ordinary queuing networks where the state probabilities provide all the necessary information. The problem arises because some of the places may contain *data tokens*, whereas others contain only *control tokens*. For example, in Fig. 12-4, tokens in places A and B only represent the condition that the message has been sent or received. Another problem is that two different places may hold tokens that trigger the activity of interest (as in the "join" operation), which means that the total token count is not necessarily a useful measure.

A general method to specify the information necessary for computing performance measures is to associate a set of *resources* with each transition. The idea is that the transition firing involves the use of those resources. Precisely what a resource means depends on what the transition firing represents. For example, suppose that Fig. 12-5 represents the sharing of two CPU's among three processes. Then the resources associated with the timed transitions t_4, t_5, and t_6 are the CPU's. A CPU will be in use whenever there is a token in places p_4, p_5, or p_6. Thus, given the state probabilities, it is easy to find the fraction of time the CPU's are in use by each process. As another example, consider the bounded-buffer problem in Fig. 12-3 assuming that all six transitions are timed and the "buffer" is actually located on the disk. Then the firing time of transitions t_2, t_3, and t_5 represents disk I/O time and we could associate the disk resource with them. Similarly, the firing time of t_1, t_4, and t_6 represents CPU time, and we could associate the CPU resource with them. It is then easy to compute the CPU and disk utilizations. Average queue lengths can be obtained directly from the marking probabilities provided that we count only the relevant tokens. Other parameters could then be obtained in a standard way (e.g., by using Little's law).

It is important to note that the interpretation of resource usage depends on the timing semantics. With NF semantics, the resources associated with a transition are considered to be in use in all states *where the transition is in the process of firing*. With AF semantics, the resources are in use in all states *where the transition is enabled*. Since an enabled transition does not necessarily fire in the AF case, one has to be careful about counting resource usage. For example, in the bounded-buffer problem discussed above, we have a conflict between the two consumers with respect to place p_3. Thus, to compute the disk utilization contributed by $C1$ in all the states in which both t_3 and t_5 are enabled, we need to compute the probability that t_3 will fire first. This may become involved if the firing-time distribution is of stage type (as opposed to exponential). The SS/DS aspect of the semantics is also relevant. In particular, with DS semantics, each enabling should be counted toward the resource usage.

12.3 Generalized Stochastic Petri Nets

The generalized stochastic Petri net (GSPN) is a specific proposal for continuous time stochastic Petri nets that allows both timed and untimed transitions. It assumes the firing time to be exponentially distributed, uses atomic firing semantics, and allows the firing rate to depend on the current marking. The analysis that we present in the following can also be applied *without any change* to situations having stage-type firing distributions. This is done by including additional transitions in the model, each having an exponential firing distribution. For example, if the firing-time distribution of a transition t is k-stage Erlang with rate μ, we can replace t by k transitions connected in tandem, each having exponential firing-time distribution with rate $k\mu$. Similar replacements can be done for any distribution that can be represented as a network of stages. Thus, there is no need to specifically address stage-type distributions in the analysis itself.

There are two main reasons for retaining untimed (or *immediate*) transitions in a timed Petri net model. First, such transitions are needed for representing various kinds of synchronization (e.g., transitions t_1, t_2, and t_3 in Fig. 12-5). Second, even if we consider only timed transitions, we are likely to find a wide variation in their firing times. For example, the time required to actually allocate or release a passive resource (memory, bus, buffer, etc.) is usually much smaller than the time for which the resource is held. Thus, if we make all transitions timed and solve the SPN model, we will encounter serious numerical problems. Moreover, the model will be fairly large even for a small system. These problems can be avoided by making short transitions immediate (and possibly adding their duration to the firing times of some other suitably chosen timed transitions).

12.3.1 Analysis Details

In a GSPN model, it is possible that both immediate and timed transitions are enabled at the same time. In that case, only an immediate transition can fire. The main consequence of this restriction is that *the reachability set of a GSPN is only a subset of the reachability set of the underlying untimed Petri net*. When several immediate transitions are enabled simultaneously, it is also essential (for the purposes of answering performance questions) to assign appropriate *firing probabilities* to them. A set of simultaneously enabled immediate transitions along with the firing probabilities is known as a *random switch*. The states of a GSPN can be classified as *tangible* or *vanishing*. A tangible state is the one in which only the timed transitions are enabled. All other states are vanishing (since they can occur only momentarily).

We now present a solution technique for GSPN models. Because of the presence of immediate transitions, we cannot consider the continuous time Markov chain for the model, say $\mathcal{Z}$, directly. Instead, we first solve $\mathcal{Z}'$, which is the embedded discrete parameter MC at the transition points of $\mathcal{Z}$. (The reader may wish to refer to the discussion at the beginning of Section 9.2.4.) Let $Q' = [q'_{ij}]$ denote the transition probability matrix for the embedded MC $\mathcal{Z}'$. Let $\mathcal{V}$ denote the set of vanishing states and $\mathcal{T}$ the set of tangible states. Also let $N_V = |\mathcal{V}|$ and $N_T = |\mathcal{T}|$. Then Q' is a $(N_V + N_T) \times (N_V + N_T)$ matrix, as shown below:

$$Q' = \begin{array}{c} \begin{matrix} N_V & \quad N_T \end{matrix} \\ \left[\begin{array}{c|c} Q'_{VV} & Q'_{VT} \\ \hline Q'_{TV} & Q'_{TT} \end{array}\right] \begin{matrix} N_V \\ N_T \end{matrix} \end{array} \tag{3.1}$$

The top half of this matrix concerns the firing of only immediate transitions and is fully known from the random switch specifications. (Whether the firing leads to a tangible state or another vanishing state is irrelevant.) The bottom half corresponds to a tangible current state which means that no immediate transitions could be enabled. Let i denote some tangible state, and H_i the set of *timed* transitions enabled in this state. Let $T_j(i)$ denote the mean firing time of transition t_j in state i and $r_j(i) \triangleq 1/E[T_j(i)]$ the mean firing rate. Let f_{ik} denote the probability that in state i transition t_k will fire first. Since the firing times are exponentially distributed, at any point in time after t_j is enabled, its remaining firing time has the same distribution as $T_j(i)$. It is then easy to verify that

$$f_{ik} = r_k(i) \Big/ \sum_{j \in H_i} r_j(i) \tag{3.2}$$

Now, if the firing of t_k takes the system to state n, then q'_{in} [the (i,n)th element of matrix Q'] is simply f_{ik}. In general, more than one enabled transition in state i may be such that its firing takes the system to state n. In such cases, q'_{in} will a sum of all the corresponding f_{ik}'s. Thus, by repeating this argument for all $i \in \mathcal{T}$, we can obtain the lower-half of the Q' matrix as well.

Let $N = N_V + N_T$ and let $\Pi' = (\pi'_1, \pi'_2, \ldots, \pi'_N)$ denote the stationary distribution of the embedded chain $\mathcal{Z}'$. We can compute Π' by solving the balance equations $\Pi' = \Pi' Q'$. Let $\Pi = (\pi_1, \pi_2, \ldots, \pi_{N_T})$ denote the state probabilities for the tangible states of the original Markov chain $\mathcal{Z}$. We can compute π_i's using equation (9.2.36). That is, let η_i denote the time spent in a tangible state i. Since the minimum of a set of exponentially distributed random variables has exponential distribution with rate as the sum of individual rates, we have

$$\eta_i = 1 \Big/ \sum_{j\in H_i} r_j(i) \qquad \text{for } \ i \in \mathcal{T} \tag{3.3}$$

Then equation (9.2.36) gives the following expression for π_i.

$$\pi_i = \frac{\pi'_i \eta_i}{\sum_{k\in\mathcal{T}} \pi'_k \eta_k} \qquad \text{for } \ i \in \mathcal{T} \tag{3.4}$$

It is worth noting that the above equation would hold even if η_i's were not exponentially distributed, since (9.2.36) holds for any semi-Markov chain.

Since the system can transit through immediate states in zero time, it is possible to define a modified embedded Markov chain, say $\mathcal{Z}^*$, that only involves the tangible states. Thus, instead of solving $\mathcal{Z}'$, we can solve the much smaller chain $\mathcal{Z}^*$, and then use equation (3.4). Whether this is a desirable approach, depends on several factors:

1. Desired performance measures. If we are interested in performance measures that concern immediate transitions, the compaction may lose the required information. For example, if a resource is requested for two different reasons, and the choice is represented in the model by a random switch, the elimination of the vanishing states may make it impossible to estimate the resource utilization for each situation.
2. Relative values of N_V and N_T. If $N_V \gg N_T$, as often is the case, the compaction may not help, since the effort in compaction may be of the same order as in solving the uncompacted system. Similarly, if $N_V \ll N_T$, there is little point in compacting.
3. Structure of the state space. As we shall see shortly, if the state transition diagram has cycles consisting of only immediate states, the compaction becomes expensive. Similarly, if the Q'_{TT} submatrix is close to being banded or triangular, but the compaction results in an irregular nonzero structure, the compaction may actually increase the solution cost.

Let $\mathcal{A} = [a_{it}]$ denote the $N_T \times N_T$ transition probability matrix of $\mathcal{Z}^*$. To obtain a_{it}, we must consider transitions through all intervening vanishing states. That is,

$$a_{it} = q'_{it} + \sum_{v\in\mathcal{V}} q'_{iv} Pr(v,t) \tag{3.5}$$

where $Pr(v,t)$ is the effective probability of transiting from the vanishing state v to the tangible state t in some number of steps. Let G denote the $N_V \times N_T$ matrix of $Pr(v,t)$'s. Then we can write the above equation in the following matrix form

$$\mathcal{A} = Q'_{TT} + Q'_{TV} G \tag{3.6}$$

Let us now get an expression for G. To this end, let $P_{VV}(v,w,k)$ denote the probability of going from a vanishing state v to another vanishing state w in exactly k steps. This probability is simply the (v, w)th element of the matrix $[Q'_{VV}]^k$ (i.e., matrix Q'_{VV} multiplied with itself k times). Obviously then,

$$Pr(v,t) = \sum_{k=0}^{\infty}\sum_{w=0}^{\infty} P_{VV}(v,w,k)q'_{wt} \tag{3.7}$$

Written in matrix form, this gives us an expression for G

$$G = \sum_{k=0}^{\infty}[Q'_{VV}]^k Q'_{VT} \tag{3.8}$$

where $[Q'_{VV}]^0$ is defined as the identity matrix I. From the irreducibility of the Markov chain, it follows that $\lim_{k\to\infty}[Q'_{VV}]^k = 0$ and the summation in equation (3.8) exists. Therefore,

$$G = [I - Q'_{VV}]^{-1}Q'_{VT} \tag{3.9}$$

Thus, $\mathcal{A}$ can be computed easily. We could then determine Π' using $\Pi'\mathcal{A} = \Pi'$, and finally Π using (3.4). (The Π' vector is now of size N_T instead of $N_T + N_V$.) Notice that the computation of G essentially amounts to finding the transitive closure of a graph. Since the transitive closure, matrix inversion, and matrix multiplication all have $O(n^3)$ time complexity, this method reduces the time complexity from $O(N^3)$ to $O[N(N_V^2 + N_T^2)]$ in the worst case. This is only a gain by a constant factor of 1/2 even in the best case, i.e., when $N_V \approx N_T$. In practice, however, Q' is rather sparse, which further diminishes the advantage of the refined method. In any case, to take advantage of the sparsity, we should use iterative methods for solving the balance equations ($\Pi'Q' = \Pi'$ or $\Pi'\mathcal{A} = \Pi'$). The G matrix can also be computed efficiently by putting (3.9) in the following form

$$[I - Q'_{VV}]G = Q'_{VT} \tag{3.10}$$

Although we can solve this linear system in G using iterative methods, a direct method based upon LU decomposition is probably preferable. To see this, let us examine the graph corresponding to the matrix Q'_{VV}. This graph is basically the state transition diagram with all the tangible states and transitions to them removed. In practice, this graph would have very few, if any, cycles. To start with, let us suppose that the graph is acyclic. Then we can define a partial order on the nodes and renumber states according to a scheme consistent with this partial order. This would make $[I - Q'_{VV}]$ a triangular matrix. Thus, the solution can be obtained by a series of back substitutions. Now if a few cycles do exist, it is possible to devise a technique for doing the triangulation (same as LU decomposition) quickly, particularly because all entries in the $[I - Q'_{VV}]$ matrix are nonnegative. (The relevant techniques may be found in any linear algebra text.)

The switch assignment and the solution method given above can be made more efficient by exploiting a simple observation. Since timed transitions cannot

state	marking	type	description
0	1110002	v	All processes idle
1	0111001	v	P_1 using resource
2	1010101	v	P_2 using resource
3	1100011	v	P_3 using resource
12	0011100	t	P_1 & P_2 using resource
13	0101010	t	P_1 & P_3 using resource
23	1000110	t	P_2 & P_3 using resource

TABLE 12.1: State description for Example 12.3.

fire if any immediate transitions are enabled, they form a "barrier" between immediate transitions. That is, as far as the evolution of immediate transitions is concerned, we can eliminate all timed transitions and then separately consider each connected component of the remaining net. Typically, there will be several connected components, thereby making the approach useful. Obviously, the switch assignment within each connected component can be done independently. More important, there is no need to compute the entire Q' matrix, since all we need is the $\mathcal{A}$ matrix. Suppose that we are given two tangible states t_1 and t_2. Then $a_{t_1 t_2}$ is the effective probability of transiting from t_1 to t_2 via the firing of all possible intermediate transitions. Since the transitions in each connected component can evolve independently, we can compute $a_{t_1 t_2}$ by a simple superimposition of the contribution of each component. That is, we examine each component separately, and thereby reduce the storage to what would be needed by the most complex component. The time requirement is also reduced, since we no longer examine the cartesian product of the state spaces of individual components. The contribution of each connected component is computed exactly as in the above; e.g., by using equations (3.10) and (3.6). If $N_V \gg N_T$, this simple trick could reduce the solution complexity considerably.

Example 12.3 Consider the resource allocation problem of Fig. 12-5.[4] The resource holding times for processes $P_1 .. P_3$ are exponentially distributed with rates $r_1 = 30$, $r_2 = 20$, and $r_3 = 10$, respectively. Determine the Q' matrix for this system by choosing random switches in some way that favors process P_1. Solve the system using the efficient method of this section.

Solution The first step in the analysis is to identify all reachable markings (or states). These are listed in Table 12.1. The leftmost column gives the state designations, and the peculiar choice is for ease of reference. The letters "v" and "t" mean vanishing and transient respectively. The corresponding Q' matrix is shown in Fig. 12-9, where

$$\rho_1 = \frac{r_1}{r_1 + r_2} = 0.60 \qquad \rho_2 = \frac{r_2}{r_2 + r_3} = 0.667 \qquad \rho_3 = \frac{r_3}{r_1 + r_3} = 0.25$$

[4]Since the transitions $t_1 .. t_3$ are untimed here, each process comes back with the next request immediately after releasing the resource. This is unrealistic, but is chosen to keep the model small.

	0	1	2	3	12	13	23
0	0	0.6	0.2	0.2	0	0	0
1	0	0	0	0	0.5	0.5	0
2	0	0	0	0	0.8	0	0.2
3	0	0	0	0	0	0.8	0.2
12	0	$1-\rho_1$	ρ_1	0	0	0	0
13	0	ρ_3	0	$1-\rho_3$	0	0	0
23	0	0	$1-\rho_2$	ρ_2	0	0	0

FIGURE 12-9: Q' matrix for Example 12.3.

The lower-half of the matrix is computed using the method given in the text. For example, in the tangible state 12, a race condition exists between transitions t_4 and t_5. Therefore, t_4 will fire first with probability ρ_1, and this firing will take the system to the vanishing state 2. Hence $q'_{12,2} = \rho_1$. Similar arguments can be made regarding transitions in other tangible states. Note that the Q'_{TT} part of the matrix is zero, because each timed transition firing takes the system to a vanishing state momentarily. The nonzero probabilities in the upper half of the matrix are chosen arbitrarily, but to strongly favor process P_1. For example, in the initial state, P_1 has a 60% probability of grabbing the first resource unit, whereas the others have only a 20% chance each. (We could have also given P_1 absolute priority over others, if desired, by choosing $q'_{0,1} = q'_{2,12} = q'_{3,13} = 1$.) We also assume that the resource units are allocated one at a time. Notice that the use of immediate transitions is essential for implementing arbitrary policy decisions in resource allocation. If instead we considered a simpler model of the problem where transitions t_1, t_2, and t_3 are timed, and others do not exist, the allocation policy will be completely determined by the rate parameters r_1, r_2, and r_3.

Clearly, there are no loops among the vanishing states of this model; therefore, G can be computed efficiently. In fact, since we can make at most one "hop" without visiting a tangible state, we know that $[Q'_{VV}]^2 = 0$. Thus, from equation (3.8), $G = (I + Q'_{VV})Q'_{VT}$ and can be computed easily. Equation (3.6) then gives the $\mathcal{A}$ matrix. Both G and $\mathcal{A}$ are as follows:

$$G = \begin{bmatrix} 0.46 & 0.46 & 0.08 \\ 0.5 & 0.5 & 0 \\ 0.8 & 0 & 0.2 \\ 0 & 0.8 & 0.2 \end{bmatrix}$$

$$\mathcal{A} = \begin{bmatrix} 0.5+0.3\rho_1 & 0.5-0.5\rho_1 & 0.2\rho_1 \\ 0.5\rho_3 & 0.8-0.3\rho_3 & 0.2-0.2\rho_3 \\ 0.8-0.8\rho_2 & 0.8\rho_2 & 0.2 \end{bmatrix} = \begin{bmatrix} .680 & .200 & .120 \\ .125 & .725 & .015 \\ .267 & .533 & .200 \end{bmatrix}$$

Now solving the $\Pi'\mathcal{A} = \Pi'$ system, we get $\Pi' = [0.299\ 0.644\ 0.057]$. These are, of course, transition point probabilities for states 12, 13, and 23, respectively. From equation (3.3),

$$\eta_{12} = 1/50 = 0.02 \qquad \eta_{13} = 1/40 = 0.025 \qquad \eta_{23} = 1/30 = 0.0333$$

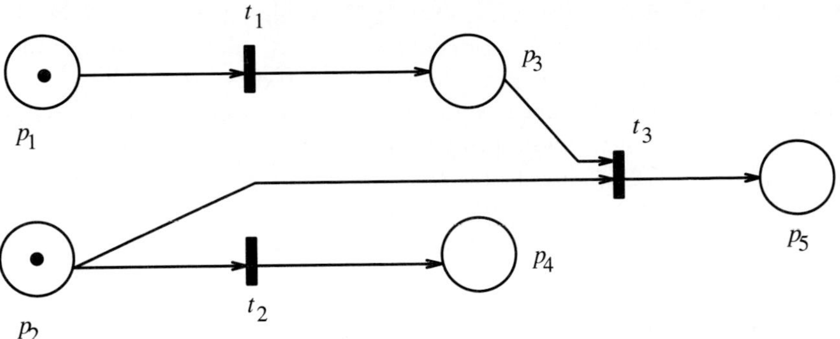

FIGURE 12-10: Illustration of confusion in a Petri net model.

Therefore, by applying equation (3.4), we get $\pi_{12} = 0.2494$, $\pi_{13} = 0.6714$, and $\pi_{23} = 0.07915$. Qualitatively, the results are as expected. Because process P_1 is strongly favored, the probability of P_2 and P_3 occupying the resource, i.e., π_{23} should be very low. Of the other two probabilities, we expect π_{13} to be higher, because while processes P_2 and P_3 get equal treatment, process P_3 holds the resource much longer. □

12.3.2 Refinements to the GSPN Model

The main problem with the GSPN model arises in specifying the random switches because we have to assign an appropriate probability in every vanishing marking in which more than one immediate transition is enabled. Thus, the modeler may have to examine a large portion of the state space. Ideally, the modeler should only specify the network and leave the task of dealing with the state space to the solution package (as is the case in the context of queuing network modeling). Although this ideal may not always be achievable, the GSPN model forces the user to specify even those random switches that have no effect on the overall behavior of the Petri net. For example, suppose that in Fig. 12-5, the processes do not immediately re-request the resource after using it and consider the situation where both units are available and only processes P_1 and P_2 are requesting them. Then it is totally irrelevant in what order the allocations are done to P_1 and P_2. Yet, the GSPN model would require the specification of a random switch to resolve this situation. A modified version of the GSPN model, dubbed GSPN2, attempts to automate the choice of irrelevant random switches. It places certain restrictions on the Petri nets but introduces priorities to make the restrictions easier to work with.

The key concept in explaining the modification is one of *confusion*. Confusion refers to the situation where two transitions, say t_2 and t_3, conflict structurally, but it is not possible to control the behavioral pattern resulting from this conflict without examining other possible conflicts as well. This is illustrated in Fig. 12-10 where the order of firing of t_1 and t_2 is important. If t_1 fires first, t_2 and t_3 conflict, but otherwise they do not. To see the problem with this scenario, note that this net requires the specification of two random switches, say A and B. Switch A corresponds to the situation where both t_1 and t_2 are simultaneously enabled, and switch B to the case where both t_2 and t_3 are simultaneously enabled. Clearly, the conflict between t_2 and t_3 represents some underlying characteristic of the system being modeled, and the modeler should be prepared to specify the random switch B. However, since t_1 and t_2 do not conflict directly, we may not realize the need to specify the switch A. Moreover, even if we realize this need, we cannot assign switching probability for A by examining the behavior of transitions t_1 and t_2 alone. Stated more generally, in the presence of confusion, we cannot assign switching probabilities without knowing the global states. It follows that if we wish to do this assignment by structural analysis only, confusion must be avoided. The opposite is also true; i.e., if confusion is avoided, reachability analysis is not necessary for switch assignments. So, the absence of confusion is desirable, but it raises the following crucial questions:

1. Are confusion-free nets powerful enough to model most of the practical situations?
2. If the answer is no, how do we enhance their power and yet retain confusion freedom?
3. How do we check whether a net is confusion-free without doing the reachability analysis?

We note that here we are using the word "power" in a pragmatic sense, rather than in the theoretical sense. Thus, although it is possible to live with confusion-free nets, the specification of complex synchronization constraints may become cumbersome. The problem can be mitigated to a large extent by introducing priorities among immediate transitions. Let the immediate transitions be given some priority > 0 and the timed transitions a priority of 0 (lowest). This still retains the semantics that a timed transition can fire only if no immediate transitions are enabled. As discussed in Section 12.1, although the addition of priorities alters decidability results, that aspect is not very important in performance modeling. Judicious choice of priorities can ensure that undesired transitions do not fire, thereby allowing the use of more complex synchronization patterns easily. Priority specification may even be preferable from a user's perspective, since the priority is a static feature and the user can examine its impact more easily than that of marking-dependent switching probabilities.

Without knowing the physical problem that the net in Fig. 12-10 is trying to solve, we cannot go on to discuss whether it is possible to get a confusion-free representation for this case by using priorities, so we shall not pursue that line of thought. It is, however, instructive to see how the situation will change if not all three transitions were at the same priority. If $prio(t_1) > prio(t_2)$, t_2 and t_3 will always conflict and only switch B remains important. If $prio(t_1) < prio(t_2)$, neither of the switches A and B is relevant. In either case, the net is confusion-free. If $prio(t_3) > prio(t_1) = prio(t_2)$, switch B becomes irrelevant, but switch A is still important. In this case, we have an *indirect conflict* between transitions t_1 and t_2, because these transitions do not conflict structurally. An indirect conflict is different from confusion in that the resolution of this conflict is not governed by the firing of other transitions. Thus, in all cases, *the effect of priorities is to break coupling between different switches and thereby allow switching probability determination without reachability analysis.*

Let us now address the third issue, i.e., whether freedom from confusion can be checked without doing reachability analysis. In general the answer here is no, since it is not possible to ensure that a conflict resolution is not affected by other transitions without examining all possible markings in which that conflict can occur. It is also difficult to characterize a sufficiently powerful subclass of Petri nets that are unconditionally confusion-free. (In fact, free-choice net is the only such class.) We can, however, define a set of *sufficient* conditions based on net invariants and other structural properties that can be checked without doing reachability analysis. The details are a bit involved and we shall omit them.

Let us now examine the problem of random switch assignment. The intention is to have the user specify a small set of parameters, from which all switch probabilities can be computed automatically. Suppose that the net has n *immediate* transitions. In the simplest case, we only ask the user for one weight for each of the n transitions. These weights reflect the relative importance or priority of various transitions whenever conflicts arise. For example, if $w(t_1) = 1$, $w(t_2) = 3$, and $w(t_3) = 4$, then if a three-way conflict arises between t_1, t_2, and t_3, we would fire t_1 with probability $1/(1+3+4) = 0.125$. Similarly, if a conflict arose only between t_1 and t_2, we would fire t_1 with probability $1/(1+3) = 0.25$. Thus, given the weights, the analysis tool can compute the switch probabilities for all possible markings and thereby fill out the upper half of the Q' matrix.

Although this technique can be used for an arbitrary GSPN, the resulting model may not faithfully represent the system that is being modeled. The problem is that the desired switch probabilities may depend on the entire state vector in a marking, instead of just the portion that has to do with conflicting transitions. Thus, any assignment that only considers conflicting transitions could be potentially wrong. From the user's perspective, n parameters are not enough in this situation to effect the fine control that a general net may demand. However, if the net is confusion free, such a coupling between conflicting and nonconflicting transitions does not exist, and the simple approach becomes feasible.

In a given current state, several distinct sets of enabled immediate transitions may conflict, each of which would define a distinct random switch. That is, in each marking, we can divide the set of all n immediate transitions, denoted Θ, into a set of equivalence classes with respect to the conflict relationship. Now, in the absence of coupling, it is possible to statically divide Θ into a number of subsets, say $\Theta_1, \ldots, \Theta_k$ for some k, such that in any marking each Θ_i contains at most one set of mutually conflicting transitions. The Θ_i's are called *effective conflict sets* or ECS's. They can be obtained by considering structural conflicts (as between t_2 and t_3 in Fig. 12-10), indirect conflicts (as between t_1 and t_2 when t_3 has a higher priority), and the causality relationship between transitions (e.g., t_3 cannot fire until t_1 does). The assignment of random switches can be done independently for each ECS, and within an ECS, there could be at most one set of transitions that mutually conflict. Also, because of priorities, in any given marking only the transitions with same priority can conflict. These properties not only speed up assignment, but also give a better idea to the user how the specified weights would be used to compute switching probabilities. For simplicity, we shall omit the construction details of ECS's, but the importance of the concept should be obvious.

The ideas developed above can be incorporated in an interactive tool for constructing the Q' matrix of the given Petri net. The first step is to determine if the given net suffers from structural confusion. If so, the tool can indicate the problem spots to the user, who would then do the priority assignments to eliminate the confusion. Next the tool can do the reachability analysis to construct the Markovian model and identify its $\mathcal{A}$ matrix. This phase would exploit connected components of immediate transitions, as discussed in the last subsection.

12.4 Discrete Time Petri Nets

In some applications, such as bus contention or cache coherence in synchronous machines, slotted communication protocols, etc., the time parameter is integer-valued (or discrete). With discrete time, it is possible to have both geometrically distributed and deterministic firing times. Since geometric distribution is the discrete counterpart of the exponential distribution, it is easier to handle than deterministic time. We shall study both in the following.

12.4.1 Geometric Firing Times

We start with the situation where all transitions are timed. Let ρ_i denote the unconditional probability of an enabled transition t_i firing in a unit time-slot. That is, the probability that t_i will fire after remaining enabled for the next n time slots, is given by

$$P(N_i = n) = (1 - \rho_i)^{n-1}\rho_i \tag{4.1}$$

The crucial property of this distribution is that it does not matter for how long transition t_i has been enabled in the past. Therefore, we can model the behavior of the system by a discrete time Markov chain whose states are the markings. Let $\mathcal{D} = [d_{ij}]$ denote the transition probability matrix for this Markov chain. To quantify this matrix, we need to consider all possible firings in each marking. Unlike the continuous time case, it is now possible for several transitions to fire simultaneously, subject to the restrictions imposed by conflicts. This complicates the computation of the elements of $\mathcal{D}$. Let $\mathcal{F}(m)$ denote the set of transitions enabled in marking m, and $2^{\mathcal{F}(m)}$ its power set. Because of the possibility of conflicts, not all subsets of $\mathcal{F}(m)$ may be eligible for simultaneous firing. Let $\Phi(m) \in 2^{\mathcal{F}(m)}$ denote the set of all subsets that can fire simultaneously in marking m. Let f be a member of $\Phi(m)$, and $FP(f)$ the probability that only the transitions in f fire, given that only the transitions in the set $\Phi(m)$ are eligible to fire. Let m' denote the new marking resulting from the firing of f. Then the element $d_{mm'}$ of matrix $\mathcal{D}$ is simply $FP(f)$. Typically, if f and f' are two distinct members of $\Phi(m)$, they will lead to different markings, but this is not necessary. In general, if every member in the set $\{f_1, \ldots, f_k\}$ yields the same marking m', then we compute $d_{mm'}$ as simply $\sum_{i=1}^{k} FP(f_i)$.

$FP(f)$ can be computed easily from its definition given above. To illustrate this computation, let us consider two extreme cases. Let $\mathcal{F}(m) = \{t_1, \ldots, t_k\}$. One extreme case arises when the firing of a transition $t_i \in \mathcal{F}(m)$ does not disable any other transition in $\mathcal{F}(m)$. Then $\Phi(m) = 2^{\mathcal{F}(m)}$, and for any subset of transitions $f \in \Phi(m)$, we have

$$FP(f) = \prod_{j \in f} \rho_j \prod_{j \in \mathcal{F}(m)-f} (1 - \rho_j) \tag{4.2}$$

For the other extreme, suppose that $t_1, \ldots, t_k$ are mutually exclusive; i.e., the firing of any one of them disables all others. Then $\Phi(m) = \{\{\ \}, \{t_1\}, \ldots, \{t_k\}\}$ since the only situations of interest are where no transition fires or only one fires. Obviously,

$$FP(\{t_i\}) = Pr(t_i \text{ fires} \mid \leq 1 \text{ transitions fire}) = \frac{Pr(\text{only } t_i \text{ fires})}{Pr(\leq 1 \text{ transitions fire})} \tag{4.3}$$

Obviously, $Pr(\text{only } t_j \text{ fires}) = \rho_j \prod_{\ell \neq j} (1 - \rho_\ell)$. Substituting this into equation (4.3), and simplifying, we get

$$FP(\{t_i\}) = \left[\frac{\rho_i}{1 - \rho_i}\right] \Big/ \left[1 + \sum_{j=1}^{k} \frac{\rho_j}{1 - \rho_j}\right] \tag{4.4}$$

Similar computations can be carried out for other situations as well. With matrix $\mathcal{D}$ known, we can get the steady-state distribution, if one exists, using the equation $\Pi = \Pi\mathcal{D}$.

As in the continuous time case, it is desirable to have both timed and immediate transitions here as well. This can be handled in essentially the same way as in GSPN's. Note that the probabilities $d_{mm'}$ apply at all (discrete) time instants, whereas the switching probabilities in the vanishing states are meaningful only at transition points. Thus, to deal with both tangible and vanishing states uniformly, we consider the Markov chain embedded at transition points. Let Q' denote the transition probability matrix for this embedded chain. This matrix can be partitioned exactly as in equation (3.1) and its upper half is again obtained from random switches. (The diagonal elements in this part must be zero, since we are considering the situation only at transition points.) In the lower part, however, an element $q'_{mm'}$ should be obtained as follows:

$$q'_{mm'} = \begin{cases} d_{mm'}/(1 - d_{mm}) & \text{if } m \neq m' \\ 0 & \text{if } m = m' \end{cases} \tag{4.5}$$

Obviously, $q'_{mm'}$, $m \neq m'$, gives the probability of going to state m', given that the MC moves out of state m. Therefore, $Q' = [q'_{mm'}]$ yields the transition probability matrix for the embedded Markov chain. Now to get the state probabilities for the original MC, we still use equation (3.4), except that the residence time in state m is now geometrically distributed with retention probability d_{mm}. Therefore,

$$\eta_m = 1/(1 - d_{mm}) \tag{4.6}$$

Since the Q' matrix here has the same interpretation as in Section 12.3, it follows that everything about the elimination of the vanishing states remains the same.

Example 12.4 Consider Example 12.3 again, but this time assume that transitions $t_4 \,..\, t_6$ have geometrically distributed firing times with parameters $\rho_1 = 0.4$, $\rho_2 = 0.25$, and $\rho_3 = 0.2$ respectively. Determine the Q' matrix for this system.

Solution The set of states, of course, remains the same and so does the upper half of the Q' matrix. The lower-half has a different nonzero structure (in addition to having different values) because in a given time-slot, both or neither resource units may be released. We start with the $\mathcal{D}$ matrix. To illustrate the computation, consider the state 12. Obviously, $\Phi(12) = 2^{\mathcal{F}(12)} = \{\{\ \}, \{4\}, \{5\}, \{4,5\}\}$, which is another way of saying that the enabled transitions t_4 and t_5 do not conflict. Thus, we can obtain FP's from equation (4.2). For example, for $f = \{4, 5\}$, we have $FP(f) = \rho_1\rho_2 = 0.1$. Since this firing takes the system to state 0, we have $d_{12,0} = 0.1$. Similarly,

$$\begin{aligned} d_{12,1} &= \rho_2(1-\rho_1) = 0.15 \qquad d_{12,2} = \rho_1(1-\rho_2) = 0.30 \\ d_{12,12} &= (1-\rho_1)(1-\rho_2) = 0.45 \end{aligned}$$

Other entries can be computed similarly. The complete lower part of the $\mathcal{D}$ matrix, say $\mathcal{D}_l$, is given here:

	0	1	2	3	12	13	23
12	0.10	0.15	0.30	0	0.45	0	0
13	0.08	0.12	0	0.32	0	0.48	0
23	0.05	0	0.15	0.20	0	0	0.60

Using equation (4.5), we get the lower part of the Q' matrix from the $\mathcal{D}_l$ matrix. We could then proceed to find the G matrix and thereby the $\mathcal{A}$ matrix, exactly as for the continuous time case. This in turn can be used to get Π'. The mean time spent in state i is given by $\eta_1 = 1/0.45 = 2.222$, $\eta_2 = 1/0.48 = 2.083$, and $\eta_3 = 1/0.60 = 1.667$. Then Π can be obtained using equation (3.4). □

12.4.2 Deterministic Firing Times

Deterministic firing times are important in many applications, either because the activity periods are truly deterministic or have a small coefficient of variation. Unfortunately, the lack of memorylessness makes the Markovian analysis of such models very difficult. Under certain restrictions, it is possible to easily obtain measures like maximum throughput, maximum cycle time, and critical path delay; however, to accurately evaluate the effect of contention and synchronization, Markovian analysis is essential.

Let us start by making a simple observation. Let Δ denote the duration of the basic unit of discrete time. Then deterministic firing times of duration Δ can be obtained by choosing the parameter ρ_i as 1 in the geometric distribution given in equation (4.1). To get a firing time of $n\Delta$ for some $n > 1$, one possibility is to replace the original transition with a series network of n transitions, each having a firing time of Δ. Fortunately, we can do considerably better than this by simply keeping track of the *remaining firing delay* (RFD) of each enabled transition. In the following, we explore such a model further.

We shall assume that the Petri net is bounded and recurrent, thereby leading to a finite irreducible Markov chain model. Let us first assume an AF/SS type of semantics. Then the state of the MC is given by a pair of vectors $(\mathbf{n}, D)$ where n_i, $i = 1 \mathinner{..} |\mathcal{P}|$, gives the marking of place p_i, and $D[j]$, $j = 1 \mathinner{..} |\mathcal{T}|$, gives the RFD of transition t_j. (Because of the SS semantics, only one RFD is needed for each transition.) At each time instant, one or more transitions whose RFD has reduced to zero can fire. As a result, any newly enabled transitions will get a fresh RFD equal to their firing time, and others will have them reduced by 1. If two enabled transitions mutually exclude each other, they will both have their RFD's reduced successively until the one with smaller RFD fires. The resulting change in marking would disable the other transition, thereby making its RFD irrelevant. (If both transitions have the same RFD, the tie must be resolved by some further specification.) It is clear that if none of the enabled transitions will fire at the next time instant, we need not represent the corresponding next state explicitly in the embedded chain $\mathcal{Z}'$. That is, we can always advance time to the point of next firing, i.e., by the minimum of the RFD's of all enabled transitions. This would help reduce state space without affecting the modeling. It is surely possible to have geometrically distributed firing times for some transitions, and deterministic times for others. In the former case, RFD is irrelevant and can be set to 1, but the transition only fires with some probability ρ. Obviously, the state space will increase rapidly with the number and firing duration of deterministic transitions, so such transitions should be used only when necessary.

Next, let us consider the NF/SS semantics. Here the state of the Markov chain (MC) can still be represented by the same pair, but it may be necessary to distinguish between an "end-firing" state and the next "start-firing" state. In this case, the "end-firing" state would be vanishing, and a random switch specification will be needed. The use of AF/DS or NF/DS semantics requires a more complex state representation, since several simultaneous enablings may exist for each transition. For each such enabling, we need to keep track of RFD's. Since the number of simultaneous enablings depend on the marking, so does the number of RFD vectors needed. This not only increases the state space size, but also causes implementation difficulties.

Let us now briefly examine the continuous (or real-valued) time case. The RFD based approach is still applicable, but the number of possible RFD's becomes uncountable. However, *if we use the technique of advancing time to the next firing instant, some problems may still have a finite state space*. For example, if the system behavior is characterized by a finite set of phases such that all activities within a phase complete before the next phase begins, and there are no cycles within a phase, arbitrary firing durations will yield finite state space. Similarly, if at most one transition can be enabled at any time (i.e., there is no concurrency), arbitrary, real-valued firing durations are acceptable. In most other situations, this extension is of little practical value, because the finite state space is likely to be incidental.

One concrete proposal for timed Petri nets with deterministic time is known as the *generalized timed Petri net* (GTPN) model. In a GTPN model, with each transition we associate a firing duration, firing frequency, and the set of resources used. The firing duration is a real-valued constant; however, by using a conflicting transition in a self-loop, it is possible to model geometric firing times. GTPN uses the NF/DS semantics, which requires switching probabilities for conflict resolution. These are specified by "firing frequencies" (which are really probabilities). There is actually one more attribute, called "combination flag", but its explanation is a bit involved, and we shall not go into it.

12.5 Modeling Multiprocessor Systems

Consider a multiprocessor system with n_p processors, n_m shared memory modules, and n_b busses. Each processor has a local cache memory that it uses until there is a cache miss. We assume that the cache usage time is exponentially distributed with mean $1/\lambda$. We also assume that in case of a miss, the processor retrieves a large chunk of information from the shared memory so as to minimize accesses to the shared memory. We further assume that the shared memory access time is exponentially distributed with mean $1/\mu$. Let $n_p = 5$, $n_m = 3$, and $n_b = 2$. Fig. 12-11 shows the GSPN model assuming that the time taken for bus acquisition and release is negligible. The model contains 12 places, 4 timed transitions, and 15 immediate transitions. Tokens in place p_1 represent the processors that are executing from their local caches. Tokens in place p_2 represent busses available for use. Each processor may issue shared memory access requests at the rate λ; so the transition t_1 fires at the rate $m_1\lambda$. (Here m_1 is the marking of the place p_1). A token in place p_3 represents a processor that needs to select a shared memory for access. The ith box ($i \in 1\,..\,3$) in the figure represents the actions involved in accessing the ith shared memory. The transitions and places in each box are named identically—they can be further distinguished by the box number. A processor selects the desired memory module by firing the immediate transition t_2, and the selection probabilities must be specified by a random switch. Note that the model assumes that every processor behaves in a statistically identical way. If this was not the case, we would need a more elaborate model.

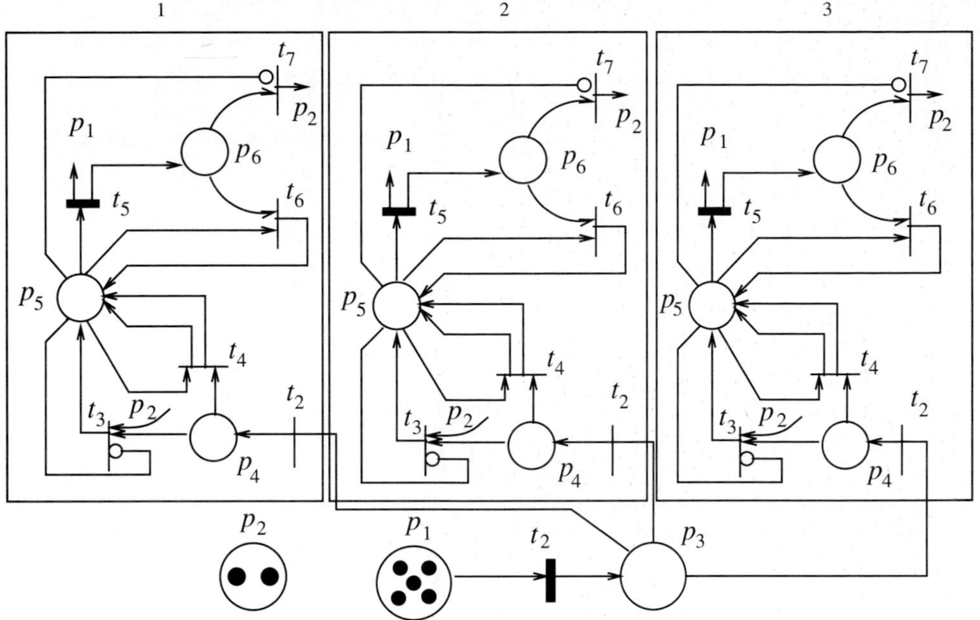

FIGURE 12-11: GSPN model of a multiprocessor system.

The bus access policy used in Fig. 12-11 is as follows: A processor first acquires the desired memory module, say i, and then requests a bus to access it. The firing of transition t_3 represents that this request has been granted. The bus so allocated is also used for accessing ith memory module by all other processors that make an access attempt during the "busy period" started by the first processor. Such a policy minimizes bus arbitration and switching times, and may be desirable when the bus contention is moderate. (Under high bus contention, it could cause starvation or unacceptably long delays in accessing infrequently used memory modules.) The apparent complexity of each box results because of this arbitration policy. All processors wishing to access memory module i reside in place p_5, but only one of them could be using the allocated bus, because transition t_5 has a marking-independent firing rate. When transition t_5 fires, the executing processor returns to place p_1. If place p_5 contains another processor, this processor starts accessing memory module i immediately using the same bus. If there is no such processor, transition t_7 fires, and the bus is released. The only purpose of transition t_6 is to make sure that the extra token generated by transition t_5 will be annihilated if some token is present in place p_5. This is essential to avoid unnecessary accumulation of tokens in p_6.

The reachability set of this GSPN model consists of 64 tangible states and 199 vanishing states. Although this is not so large a model, it is clear that a brute-force approach of assigning random switches to each vanishing state could be very tedious, particularly since most such switches are irrelevant from a modeling point of view.

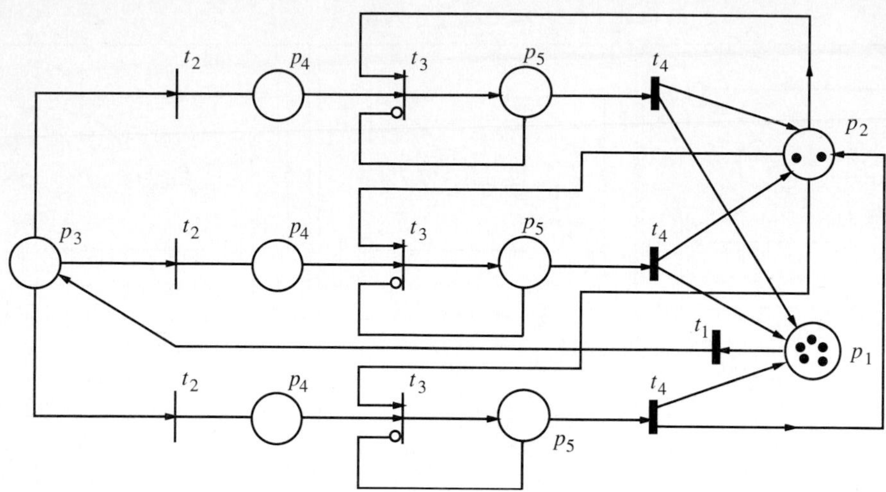

FIGURE 12-12: Simplified model for one-at-a-time bus arbitration.

If the bus arbitration policy is changed so that a bus is held only for the duration of one memory access, each box of Fig. 12-11 can be simplified to the model shown in Fig. 12-12. The main difference here is that at most one processor can advance to place p_5 and start using the memory. When it finishes, it releases the bus, and a processor waiting in place p_4 can enter if either another free bus is available or the bus that was just released is not grabbed for access to other memory modules. Other policies can also be represented similarly. If bus arbitration overhead is significant, we can make transition t_3 also timed.

The models shown above represent processors and busses by tokens but memories by subnets. Thus, increasing the number of processors or busses is trivial, but increasing the number of memories is not. A different subnet is required for each memory module, because we need to explicitly keep track of which memories are in use and which are not. If each memory module is equally likely to be accessed, we can compact the model further; however, it is still not possible to come up with a model whose structure is independent of the number of processors, memories, and busses. The problem arises because even with a uniform access pattern, a processor must get the memory module it requests, and not whichever happens to be free!

In the above, we assumed that the inter-request and access times are exponentially distributed. In reality, it may be reasonable to model time between successive cache misses as exponential, but the shared memory access time is likely to be almost deterministic. Also, it is probably more reasonable to consider these times as discrete, with the underlying time unit being one memory cycle. These considerations lead to a discrete time SPN model. No changes are necessary to the model in this case; only the solution details will change. If deterministic times are used only for shared memory access (and other times are geometrically distributed), it is still possible to solve reasonably large models efficiently. Note that all our example models used AF semantics. If other possibilities are considered, the model must be changed accordingly, as explored in Exercise 12.9.

12.6 Extensions to Stochastic Petri Nets

As with classical Petri nets, SPN's do not possess full modeling power without inhibitor arcs or firing priorities. We have already seen priorities in the context of GSPN's. Similar extensions are possible for discrete time SPN's. Such extensions have no bearing on modeling so long as we are dealing with finite reachability graphs. Another possible extension is the use of *colored tokens*, that is, tokens belonging to different categories and showing different types of behavior. The concept of colored tokens is similar to the concept of chains or classes in a queuing network model. Several other concepts have also been introduced in various versions of *high-level Petri net* (HLPN) models. While these extensions make the reachability and related problems even harder to tackle, they are still desirable if they allow a user to easily represent the real system without overly complicating the identification of the Q matrix of the Markov chain for the model. As an example of a HLPN model, consider Petri nets where each token carries an attribute (or tag), and the places are associated with predicates that take token attributes as arguments. The transition will fire if the predicate of each of its input places evaluates to true. An example of a predicate for place p is $nt(p, n) > 3$ where $nt(p, n)$ gives the number of tokens in place p having tag n.

It is easy to see that timed Petri nets properly contain queuing network models, but because a wide variety of solution techniques are available for queuing network models, it may still be desirable to use Petri net based analysis for only those parts of a system that cannot be handled using queuing networks (e.g., synchronization and simultaneous resource possession). This requires a hierarchical modeling approach mentioned in Section 8.1. For example, we can separate weakly interacting parts of the system and replace queuing subnetworks with flow-equivalent aggregates. The resulting compact Petri net could then be solved using the methods of this chapter. The results could then be propagated to individual elements of queuing subnetworks by the methods of Section 8.1.2.

12.7 Product-Form Solutions

The Markov chain of a stochastic Petri net model generally must be solved using global balance techniques because the synchronization precludes specialized solution techniques. However, product-form and matrix analytic solutions have recently been found to hold for certain subclasses of stochastic Petri nets. It turns out that these classes do not fit the usual hierarchy of Petri-nets (marked graphs, free-choice nets, classical Petri nets, and Petri nets with inhibitor arcs). For example, not all marked graphs can be analyzed this way. In terms of basic properties, the Petri nets must be live, but not necessarily safe, conservative, or bounded. Also, features such as generalized NF semantics, colored tokens, arbitrary initial markings, probabilistic routing, and marking-dependent firing rates can be handled. In fact, since the solution technique deals with an embedded Markov chain, two additional generalizations are possible in many cases: (a) generally distributed firing times can be handled, and (b) subnets that do not satisfy the product-form requirement stated below can be aggregated into one place or transition without affecting the results. However, the product-form solutions are now very different from what we are accustomed to in queuing networks. In the following we shall briefly summarize the main results without any proofs.

Consider a timed Petri net with $m = |\mathcal{P}|$ places and $M = |\mathcal{T}|$ transitions. We assume that this Petri net does not have any inhibitor arcs or priorities among transitions. For generality, we shall allow arc weights larger than one, which means that we must speak in terms of input and output bags of a transition. We also need the concept of a *collective bag* of a set of transitions. We denote the collective input (output) bag of a set of transitions T as $\mathcal{I}(T)$ ($\mathcal{O}(T)$). With the bag representation suggested in Section 12.1.1, we have

$$\mathcal{I}(T) = \sum_{t \in T} \mathcal{I}(t) \tag{7.1}$$

A similar definition applies to $\mathcal{O}(T)$. We shall also assume a generalized NF-semantics here to cover both AF and NF cases. That is, we associate both an enabling time (denoted E_i) and a firing time (denoted F_i) with each transition t_i. We assume that E_i and F_i have exponential distribution with means e_i and f_i respectively. Obviously, if $f_i = 0$, we get the regular AF semantics, and if $e_i = 0$, we get the NF semantics. It is possible to allow the tokens to come from one of C colors in the discussion that follows. This is similar in spirit to having multiple chains/classes in a product-form queuing network. The results remain essentially identical, except that we have to speak of the number of tokens of each color. For simplicity, however, we shall not do so. Thus, we can describe the marking of the Petri net by the vector $\mathbf{n} = (n_1, \ldots, n_m)$ where n_i gives the number of tokens in place p_i.

The analysis method works with an embedded Markov chain $\mathcal{Z}'$ at the enabling and firing points of the original random chain $\mathcal{Z}$ (which need not be Markovian). We define an *enabling point* as the time when the transition is enabled and a *firing point* as the time when it absorbs its tokens. Thus, we can describe the state of $\mathcal{Z}'$ by the pair $(\mathbf{n}', \mathbf{n})$ where $\mathbf{n}'$ gives the marking when some transition gets enabled, and $\mathbf{n}$ is the marking at the next firing point. We assume that $\mathcal{Z}'$ is irreducible and positive recurrent. We could then speak of the equilibrium probability $P(\mathbf{n}', \mathbf{n})$. We can also define marginal probabilities at enabling and firing points, denoted $P_e(\mathbf{n})$ and $P_f(\mathbf{n})$, respectively. It turns out that the product-form solution applies to all these probabilities. The equilibrium probabilities for the original system (which may not even be Markovian) can be obtained by an equation similar to (3.4).

Now we are ready to state the condition for product-form solution to hold.

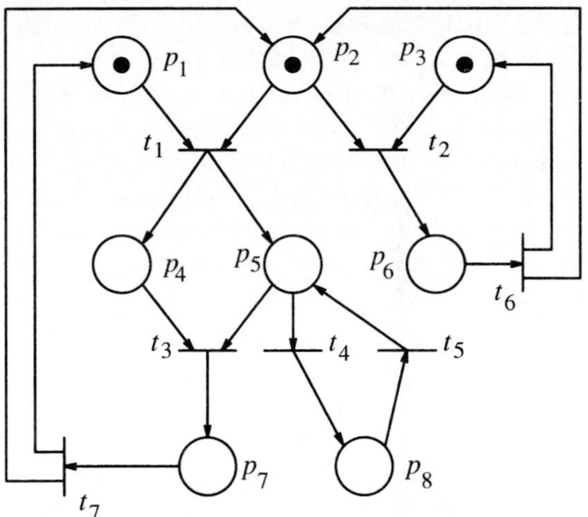

FIGURE 12-13: A timed Petri net satisfying product-form conditions.

Throughout this section, *we shall state everything so that it is applicable to both continuous time and discrete time models*. Basically, the difference is that in the discrete time case, several events can occur in a single time unit, whereas this is not possible in the continuous time case (under memoryless distributions). Thus, we shall consistently speak of a set of transitions simultaneously finishing their enabling or firing phases. When applying these results to the continuous time case, we merely assume that each such "set" contains but one transition. In light of this, the general statement of the product-form condition is as follows:

> **Product-Form Condition** For every transition set T, there is a unique transition set X such that $\mathcal{O}(T) = \mathcal{I}(X)$.

The whole point of this restriction is to be able to follow the evolution of the net in terms of how the bag $\mathcal{O}(T)$ "transforms" into the bag $\mathcal{I}(X)$ when the transitions in T finish firing. In other words, if in marking $\mathbf{n}$, the firing of the set T leaves the *residual marking* $\mathbf{n} - \mathcal{O}(T)$, it should be possible to have a sequence of firings that will recreate the marking $\mathbf{n}$ without moving any of the tokens from $\mathbf{n} - \mathcal{O}(T)$. Such a restriction is satisfied trivially in queuing networks since any given customer can move around through its chain without affecting others. In the special case of continuous time SPN's, both T and X must consist of a single transition. That is, *the output bag of every transition must be the input bag of another unique transition.*

Fig. 12-13 shows a continuous time Petri net that satisfies these requirements. For example, $\mathcal{O}(t_1) = (0,0,0,1,1,0,0,0)$, which is same as $\mathcal{I}(t_3)$. Notice that the firing of t_1 does enable another transition t_4, but that is not included in this *bag transformation*.

Let us now see a few situations where the PF condition would not hold. One such case arises if we remove the arc from p_5 to t_3. In this case, both t_3

and t_4 are still enabled, but neither's input bag is same as the output bag of t_1. Another case arises if we add an arc from p_4 to t_4. Here the problem is the lack of uniqueness. It is important to remember that such cases do not automatically rule out product-form solution of the underlying system, since it is often possible to alter the Petri net representation so that the PF condition is satisfied. We shall comment on this aspect later. It is also interesting to note that even if we cannot alter the net appropriately, it is still possible to get partial results. That is, if certain transitions in the net do not satisfy the PF condition, we can replace subnets containing them by a single (composite) place or transition such that the resulting net satisfies the PF condition. For example, in Fig. 12-13, place p_8 and/or transition t_6 could very well represent entire subnets that have been abstracted out because they did not satisfy product-form requirements. The solution to this higher-level net then gives *exact* results for the explicitly represented parts. An intuitive explanation of this phenomenon is that we are dealing with embedded Markov chain only; therefore, the behavior of the system between successive transition points could be arbitrary. Thus, *the product-form solution will hold so long as the PF condition holds with respect to the observable set of enabling and firing points*. In fact, a similar argument can be used to show that even the memorylessness of enabling and firing-time distributions is not required, so long as we can correctly identify the embedded Markov chain. We made a similar remark in Section 12.4.2.

Now to get the product-form solution, we require that the transition probabilities of the embedded Markov chain $\mathcal{Z}'$ have a certain form. Let $q(\mathbf{n}, \mathcal{E})$ denote the probability that a set $\mathcal{E}$ of transitions fires following an enabling point that has marking $\mathbf{n}$. (Remember that by "firing" we mean the absorption of tokens, and $\mathbf{n}$ is the marking before this absorption. Also, in the continuous time case, the set $\mathcal{E}$ will contain only one transition.) The desired form for q is as follows[5]

$$q(\mathbf{n}, \mathcal{E}) = \frac{\phi(\mathbf{n} - \mathcal{I}(\mathcal{E}))\chi(\mathcal{E})}{\Phi(\mathbf{n})} \tag{7.2}$$

where the $\Phi(\mathbf{n})$ function ensures that all transition probabilities in marking $\mathbf{n}$ sum to 1. Let $\mathcal{T}(\mathbf{n})$ denote the set of all transitions that can fire in the marking $\mathbf{n}$. Then,

$$\Phi(\mathbf{n}) = \sum_{\eta \in \mathcal{T}(\mathbf{n})} \phi(\mathbf{n} - \mathcal{I}(\eta))\chi(\eta) \tag{7.3}$$

The functions ϕ and χ are nonnegative but otherwise arbitrary. There is nothing mysterious about these functions. Given the Petri net model, we first compute the transition probabilities $q(\mathbf{n}, \mathcal{E})$, and from there identify the ϕ and χ functions. Since $\mathbf{n} - \mathcal{I}(\mathcal{E})$ is the marking after the firing, the ϕ term concerns the marking after state transition and χ with the state transition itself. The Φ term is merely for normalization and can be ignored until ϕ and χ have been computed. As an example in Fig. 12-13, transitions t_1 and t_2 are enabled in the marking shown.

[5] With a vector representation of bags, the subtraction in $\mathbf{n} - \mathcal{I}(\mathcal{E})$ is a perfectly meaningful operation.

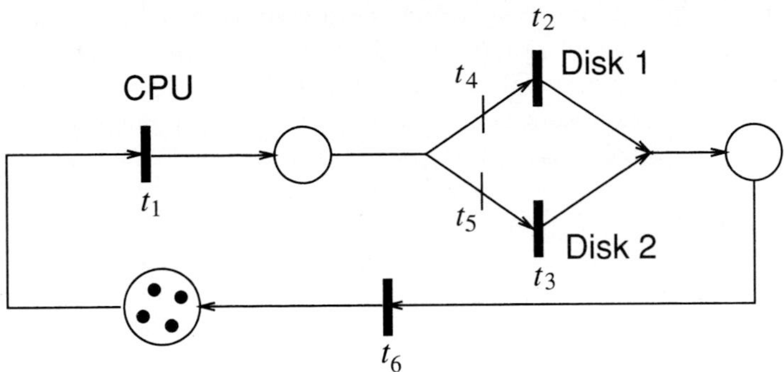

FIGURE 12-14: A timed Petri net representation of a queuing network.

Let the mean enabling rates of these be μ_1 and μ_2. The current state is $\mathbf{n} = (1, 1, 1, 0, 0, 0, 0, 0)$ and

$$q(\mathbf{n}, t_1) = \frac{\mu_1}{\mu_1 + \mu_2} \qquad q(\mathbf{n}, t_2) = \frac{\mu_2}{\mu_1 + \mu_2} \tag{7.4}$$

If t_1 fires (i.e., absorbs tokens) first, the resulting state is $\mathbf{n}^1 = (0, 0, 1, 0, 0, 0, 0, 0)$, and if t_2 fires first, it is $\mathbf{n}^2 = (1, 0, 0, 0, 0, 0, 0, 0)$. We can let $\chi(t_1) = \mu_1$, $\chi(t_2) = \mu_2$, and $\phi(\mathbf{n}^1) = \phi(\mathbf{n}^2) = 1$, which yields $\Phi(\mathbf{n}) = \mu_1 + \mu_2$. This is a valid choice, since we have chosen χ functions to be independent of the marking. (Of course, we should choose the same $\chi(t_1)$ function for every state in which transition t_1 is enabled. A similar comment applies to $\chi(t_2)$.) Intuitively, it also makes sense to choose the two ϕ functions to be identical, because no transition is enabled in either $\mathbf{n}^1$ or $\mathbf{n}^2$. However, this is not the only possible choice.

Let $p(\mathcal{D}, \mathcal{E})$ denote the probability that the input bag absorbed by the transitions in the set $\mathcal{D}$ when they fire is transformed into the input bag of the transitions in the set $\mathcal{E}$. Notice that according to the condition given above, $p(\mathcal{D}, \mathcal{E})$ could only be 0 or 1. However, we can generalize product-form Petri nets to allow for *probabilistic routing*. This generalization is essential to cover product-form queuing networks as a special case. The idea is to allow an input bag $\mathcal{D}$ to be probabilistically transformed into one of several output bags. The modeling of this situation will require immediate transitions and switching probabilities. Fig. 12-14 shows a Petri net model of a central-server type of queuing network, where the transition t_1 represents the CPU, and t_2 and t_3 represent disks. Assuming AF semantics, the immediate transitions t_4 and t_5 are essential since, otherwise, the conflict between t_2 and t_3 will be resolved solely by the race condition rather than by user-defined routing probabilities. We can allow for such a situation in our solution technique by simply letting $p(t_1, t_2) = q$ and $p(t_1, t_3) = 1 - q$ (and ignoring the immediate transitions). So, henceforth, we shall allow $p(\mathcal{D}, \mathcal{E})$ to be any valid probability.

We can determine $p(\mathcal{D}, \mathcal{E})$ directly from the topological properties of the given Petri net. We can view the relevant bags as states of a discrete parameter Markov chain RC, called the *routing chain*, with $p(\mathcal{D}, \mathcal{E})$ as the transition probabilities. It can be shown that under the product-form conditions, this Markov chain will consist of a set of disjoint ergodic subchains. Therefore, the steady-state distribution for RC, denoted $\pi(\mathcal{D})$, $\mathcal{D} \subseteq \mathcal{T}$, can be obtained by solving equation (5.2.8). Actually, the normalization is not required for our purposes, so the only relevant equations to solve are

$$\pi(\mathcal{D}) = \sum_{\forall adj(\mathcal{E},\mathcal{D})} \pi(\mathcal{E})p(\mathcal{E},\mathcal{D}) \tag{7.5}$$

where the notation $adj(A, B)$ means that B is adjacent to A, i.e., $p(A, B) > 0$. Since RC may consist of several disjoint subchains, this system really applies to each connected set of states.

As an example, in Fig. 12-13, $p(t_1, t_3) = 1$ because after t_1 has finished firing, it transforms its input bag to the input bag t_3. (Recall that $p(\mathcal{D}, \mathcal{E})$ can only be 1 or 0 here, since we do not have any probabilistic routing.) Assuming that we are dealing with a continuous time Petri net in Fig. 12-13, we get three disjoint chains, each having individual transitions as states. The states of chain 1 are $\{t_1, t_3, t_7\}$, those of chain 2 are $\{t_4, t_5\}$, and those of chain 3 are $\{t_2, t_6\}$. Each chain cycles through its states sequentially (e.g., t_1 to t_3 to t_7 back to t_1 for chain 1), as should be obvious from Fig. 12-13. Since the normalization of probabilities is not important here, we can thus let $\pi(s) = 1$ for each state s of each of the three chains.

Let $f(\mathcal{D}) = \pi(\mathcal{D})/\chi(\mathcal{D})$ where χ is the function introduced above. Thus, in Fig. 12-13, we have $f(t_1) = 1/\mu_1$, $f(t_2) = 1/\mu_2$, etc. The next step is to define a function $g(\mathbf{n})$ that has the following property: For every *adjacent pair* $(\mathcal{D}, \mathcal{E})$ with respect to any marking $\mathbf{n}$

$$\frac{g(\mathbf{n} + \mathcal{I}(\mathcal{E}))}{g(\mathbf{n} + \mathcal{I}(\mathcal{D}))} = \frac{f(\mathcal{E})}{f(\mathcal{D})} \tag{7.6}$$

We can compute the g function systematically during the reachability graph generation as follows: Start with $g(\mathbf{n}_0) = 1$ for the initial marking $\mathbf{n}_0$. Then, during a generation step, if the marking $\mathbf{n}$ changes to $\mathbf{n}' = \mathbf{n} - \mathcal{I}(\mathcal{D}) + \mathcal{I}(\mathcal{E})$, we let

$$g(\mathbf{n}') = g(\mathbf{n})f(\mathcal{E})/f(\mathcal{D}) \tag{7.7}$$

This procedure can also detect situations where the product-form conditions are violated, since in that case the following could happen: When a marking is revisited during the reachability graph generation, we are forced to choose a different g function than the one already chosen. Obviously, a valid $g(\mathbf{n})$ must be a product of terms of type x^m where x is a constant and m is a simple function of the number of tokens in some places. The precise form of the powers depends on the synchronization constraints that the Petri net enforces. For example, $g(\mathbf{n})$ in Fig. 12-13 is given by

$$g(\mathbf{n}) = \left(\frac{\mu_2}{\mu_6}\right)^{n_6} \left(\frac{\mu_4}{\mu_5}\right)^{n_8} \left(\frac{\mu_1}{\mu_7}\right)^{n_7} \left(\frac{\mu_1}{\mu_3}\right)^{\min(n_4, n_5+n_8)} \tag{7.8}$$

Having determined $g(\mathbf{n})$, we can finally write the product-form solution as

$$P(\mathbf{n}+\mathcal{I}(\mathcal{E}),\mathbf{n}) = \phi(\mathbf{n})g(\mathbf{n}+\mathcal{I}(\mathcal{E}))\chi(\mathcal{E})/G \tag{7.9}$$

where G is the normalization constant to ensure that all probabilities sum to 1. From this, we can also get expressions for marginal probabilities P_e and P_f. By substituting $\mathbf{n}-\mathcal{I}(\mathcal{E})$ for $\mathbf{n}$ in equation (7.9), summing over all possible $\mathcal{E}$'s, and using equation (7.3), we have

$$P_e(\mathbf{n}) = \Phi(\mathbf{n})g(\mathbf{n})/G \tag{7.10}$$

Also by summing equation (7.9) over all $\mathcal{E}$'s such that $\mathbf{n}+\mathcal{I}(\mathcal{E})$ is feasible (i.e., in the reachability set $\mathcal{R}$), we get

$$P_f(\mathbf{n}) = \frac{\phi(\mathbf{n})}{G} \sum_{\forall\mathcal{E}\in\mathcal{T},\ \mathbf{n}+\mathcal{I}(\mathcal{E})\in\mathcal{R}} g(\mathbf{n}+\mathcal{I}(\mathcal{E}))\chi(\mathcal{E}) \tag{7.11}$$

These solutions look very different from the ones for a product-form queuing network, but the latter can be derived easily as a special case. The current solution is in form of a product of three functions, namely ϕ, g, and χ. The first two of these depend on the marking (or state), whereas the last one only depends on the structural aspects. Now suppose that we view a queuing network as a Petri net by considering each station as a transition (as in Fig. 12-14). The PF condition does not hold here because of probabilistic routing, but we have already seen how to handle that. Now to get the ϕ term for this case, we have to examine the embedded chain at transition points. The transition probabilities of this chain, and hence ϕ will come out in terms of the service rates of individual stations. If the stations are load-dependent, the transition probabilities will be marking-dependent, thereby also yielding a product of capacity functions. The chain RC would now describe the routing behavior of the customers and will have only one recurrent subchain (assuming that the network is well-formed). Thus, the solution to equation (7.5) will simply yield the visit ratios. Therefore, the g function can be chosen as a product $v_1^{n_1} \times \cdots \times v_M^{n_M}$. It follows that the resulting solution will look like the familiar solution in equation (6.3.8). The solution will not be identical to (6.3.8) since we are still dealing with an embedded Markov chain at transition points, instead of the actual continuous time chain, but the conversion is trivial. The details are explored in Exercise 12.12. In a general Petri net, because of conflicts, generation/destruction of tokens, etc., the transitions do not have a uniform behavior; therefore, the solution is much less explicit.

12.8 Exercises

1. Show a Petri net representation of the classical reader-writer problem with n readers and one writer. You will need arcs with multiplicity n for this. Basically, the idea is that the firing of a write transition grabs all n tokens, whereas a reader grabs only one token. Extend this solution for the case where there are multiple writers.
2. Are classical Petri nets adequate to represent the problem where the number of readers is unbounded? Show a solution to this problem using as few inhibitor arcs as possible. Refine this solution and the one in Exercise 12.1 to implement the policy that as soon as a writer becomes ready to write, no more readers are allowed to start reading. Is this refinement dependent on whether the number of readers is finite or unbounded?
3. Show that the coverability problem of classical Petri nets is NP space-hard by reducing the reachability problem to it. That is, given a marking m in a Petri net $\mathcal{P}_1$, construct another Petri net $\mathcal{P}_2$ such that m is reachable in $\mathcal{P}_1$, if and only if $\mathcal{P}_2$ has a reachable marking $m' \succ m$. Here the "$\succ$" relation must be interpreted in a special way since $\mathcal{P}_2$ may not have the same set of places as $\mathcal{P}_1$. In particular, we could construct $\mathcal{P}_2$ by adding some places and transitions to $\mathcal{P}_1$. Then the coverability of m by m' should also apply with respect to the portion of state vector that involves the places of $\mathcal{P}_1$. Use a similar approach to prove that k-boundedness and liveness problems are also NP space-hard.
4. Give an example of a Petri net that is not live, but the coverability tree does not have sufficient information to draw this conclusion. Do the same with respect to the reachability property. (Hint: Consider a situation where no firing is possible in a state that in the coverability tree will be represented by a vector having two or more ω's.)
5. Consider the Petri net in Fig. 12-6. Suppose that the firing of transitions t_1 and t_2 generates a and b respectively, those of t_3 and t_4 an empty string. What language does this Petri net generate if the goal state is any state with more than two tokens in place p_1? How is this language related to the language generated when the goal state is defined by place p_1 containing exactly two tokens?
6. When dealing with marked graphs, it is customary to eliminate places and instead put tokens on the arcs. The transitions now take the role of nodes of a graph. Show that in a marked graph the token count on any directed loop (or circuit) is invariant under any transition firing. Using this, show that a marked graph is live if and only if it has no token-free directed circuit.
7. Show that a classical Petri net is recurrent if and only if there exists a realizable column vector x of strictly positive integers such that $A^T x \geq 0$.
8. Consider two multiserver FCFS, exponential service stations connected in tandem, each with two servers. The first station has a capacity of 3 whereas the second has a capacity of 2. (Here capacity refers to the number of

customers allowed at the station.) If a customer cannot move to the second station because of capacity limitation, it stays at station 1. Customers come from outside to station 1 according to a Poisson process. If a customer cannot get into station 1, it blocks for an exponential amount of time in station 1's queue and tries again. (Blocked customers do not need any attention from the server but do hold up positions in the "waiting room".) Construct a GSPN model of this system and identify the Q' matrix for its embedded Markov chain. What difficulties do you encounter in solving this model? Suggest possible ways of overcoming them.

9. Modify the models in figures 12-11 and 12-12 for the NF semantics, i.e., for the case where tokens are removed when a timed transition starts firing. Since this change allows you to specify switching probabilities directly for the timed transitions, can you remove any of the immediate transitions from the model in this case? Does this change result in a smaller state space?

10. Suppose that all transitions denoted by t_4 in Fig. 12-12 have the same firing rate $\mu = 0.5$, and $\mu_1 = 0.1$. Suppose that the processor accesses memory 1 with probability q, and each of memories 2 and 3 with probability $(1-q)/2$ for some $0 < q < 1$. What random switches are important for this problem? Write down the Q' matrix for this model by suitably choosing all random switches. (Try to maximize the number of zeros in the Q' matrix for choosing irrelevant random switches.) Follow the efficient computation procedure of Section 12.3.1 and compute the modified matrix $\mathcal{A}$. Characterize the performance of this system as a function of the parameter q.

11. Suppose that in Exercise 12.10, we are dealing with discrete time, and μ, μ_1 now represent the unconditional firing probabilities. Determine the Q' and $\mathcal{A}$ matrices for this system as well. Study this system as well for different values of q.

12. Specialize the results in Section 12.7 to a continuous-time SPN that uses a pure AF semantics and the corresponding chain RC contains but one recurrent subchain. Using this, show how you can model an ordinary single-chain closed queuing network as a timed Petri net, and derive the solution in equation (6.3.8).

Bibliographic Notes

Classical Petri nets were originally defined by C.A. Petri in 1962 and have been the subject of intensive research since. The book by Peterson (1984) discusses properties of classical Petri nets and their several variations. It shows that the reachability problem of classical Petri nets must be at least P space-hard. The definitive result was proved later in Mayr (1981). Peterson's book contains a detailed discussion on Petri net languages and their closure properties, a topic that we mentioned only briefly. Free-choice Petri nets were introduced by Hack in

1972. Murata (1989) provides an excellent up-to-date survey of the applications and structural analysis of Petri nets. Molloy (1987) presents a polynomial time algorithm for checking if an arbitrary net is structurally bounded. The analysis is based on the fact that a structurally bounded net must have an S-invariant and $AY \leq 0$ for some Y. The problem then reduces to checking whether a linear program has a feasible solution (which is known to be polynomially solvable).

Deterministic timed Petri nets were first examined by Ramchandani in 1974. Ramamoorthy and Ho (1980) presents the throughput analysis of timed marked graphs and shows that in a recurrent marked graph, all transitions have the same cycle time. Since each loop in a marked graph conserves the number of tokens, the cycle time of a transition can be obtained by dividing the total delay across a loop by the number of tokens on the loop. Another interesting result is that *an arbitrary safe and persistent Petri net can be transformed into a marked graph, and thus can be analyzed using the same techniques*. This paper also shows that the problem of verifying whether an arbitrary timed Petri net can achieve a given throughput is NP-complete. The proof goes by reducing the set partitioning problem to this problem. Associating deterministic time with places is suggested in Sifakis (1980).

Stochastic Petri nets (SPN's) with exponentially distributed firing times are explored in Molloy (1982). The GSPN model was proposed in Marsan, Balbo and Conte (1984). The extensions to the GSPN model that exploit structural properties and introduce priorities are presented in Marsan, et al. (1987) and Balbo, et al. (1987). Blakemore (1989) examines both graphical and matrix-oriented methods for efficient elimination of vanishing states. Chen, Bruell and Balbo (1989) discusses various ways of modeling firing times that have an exponential stage representation. Dugan, et al. (1984) discusses a few situations where arbitrarily distributed firing times can be allowed.

Discrete time SPN's with geometrically distributed firing times are explored in Molloy (1985) and those with deterministic time in Razouk and Phelps (1985). The latter also introduced the idea of associating resources with transitions. The GTPN model is described in Holliday and Vernon (1987). Our multiprocessor modeling example is taken from Marsan, Balbo, and Conte (1986). This book discusses other approaches (probabilistic, queuing theoretic) for modeling memory and bus contention in multiprocessor systems. Marsan, et al. (1989) discusses a different execution semantics in stochastic Petri nets with arbitrarily distribute firing times.

Ciardo (1987) compares the modeling power of various classes of stochastic Petri nets. Henderson and Taylor (1990) shows that queuing networks with batch movement of customers and correlated routing have product-form solution under certain restrictions. Henderson, Lucic and Taylor (1989) applies these ideas to stochastic Petri nets to give the solutions that we presented in Section 12.7. Henderson and Taylor (1991) shows that if a SPN does not satisfy the product-form condition, it is still possible to get partial but exact results, as we mentioned in Section 12.7. Florin and Natkin (1991) shows matrix-analytic solutions for *closed synchronized Petri nets*, i.e., recurrent and bounded Petri nets with constant firing rates.

Colored Petri nets were first proposed in Jensen (1981). A recent article on the subject is Jensen (1987). Billington (1989) proposes some further extensions to such nets in terms of place capacities and threshold testing. Colored stochastic Petri nets are studied in Zenie (1985). Colored version of GSPN's are reported in Chiola and Franceschinis (1989). State aggregation in colored Petri nets without generating reachability graph is studied in Dutheillet and Haddad (1989). High-level Petri nets are explored in Genrich and Lautenbach (1981), and reachability analysis for them is explored in Huber, et al. (1984). Lin and Marinescu (1988) discusses stochastic high-level Petri nets involving token attributes and predicates, and discuss how to construct the corresponding Markov chain. Sanders and Meyer (1987, 1989) discuss *stochastic activity nets*, which are well-suited for performability studies. Balbo, Bruell, and Ghanta (1988) discusses the use of flow-equivalent aggregation of subnets for approximately solving complex GSPN models.

CHAPTER

13

Selected Applications

In this chapter we shall study the application of the techniques discussed in previous chapters to the modeling of various aspects of modern computer systems. In Section 13.1, we examine the modeling of cyclic polling systems, such as the token-ring local area networks. We also discuss conservation laws for polling systems and show how they can be used to obtain approximations for mean waiting times.

Section 13.2 concerns the problem of design, as opposed to simply the analysis. The goal here is to choose system parameters so as to optimize some measure of performance. Here we study two important optimization problems: optimal placement of a set of files among the nodes of a distributed system, and optimal traffic routing among a set of nodes.

Section 13.3 concerns the solution of queuing network models when the jobs are not atomic entities but instead are composed of a number of tasks with certain precedence relationships between them. We present exact analysis of certain simple instances of this problem, and an approximate solution for the general problem.

Section 13.4 concerns the modeling of reliability aspects of fault-tolerant computer systems. We introduce various measures of interest and show how they can be computed. Since steady-state analysis is largely inapplicable in such applications, an important goal here is to briefly discuss transient analysis of Markov chains.

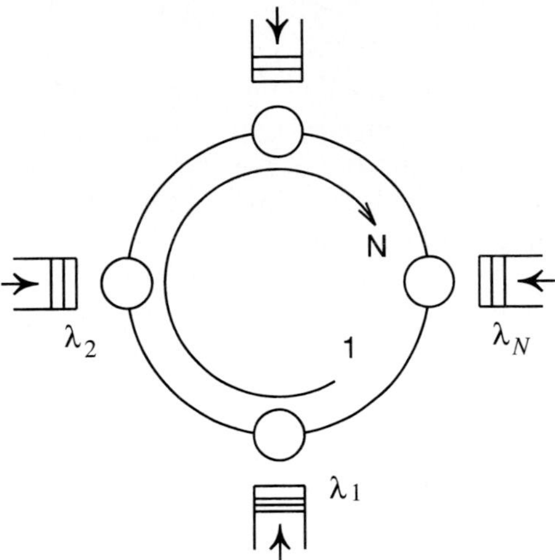

FIGURE 13-1: A polling system.

13.1 Analysis of Polling Systems

In a polling system, a number of stations are served by a single-server who polls the stations in a selected order, as shown in Fig. 13-1. Customers requiring service arrive independently and queue up at one of these stations. When the server polls a station, one or more of the customers that are present there may be served, depending on the service discipline. When the server departs from a station, there may be some time delay before the next station can be polled. This time delay is usually termed the *switch-over time*. Although polling systems arise in many applications, the token-ring local area network (LAN) is one of the most common examples of such a system.

In a token ring network, a number of nodes (or stations) are connected together via links in the form of a ring. When a station wishes to transmit data to another station on the ring, it frames this data into one or more *packets* and transmits each packet over the ring. At any time, at most one station is allowed to transmit on the ring, and the control of the transmission is arbitrated via a *token*. A token is a unique bit pattern that is constantly circulated around the ring. A station that has data to transmit monitors this ring, and when it detects a "free" token, it seizes the token (by altering the bit pattern) and transmits one or more packets before releasing the token. In modeling the token ring network as a queuing system, the token is modeled as a single-server, and the packets constitute the customers that require service. The service time for each customer is the time taken to transmit the packet on the ring. The overhead involved in passing the token from one station to the next, including the associated token propagation time, is modeled by the switch-over time.

13.1.1 Polling Disciplines

At each station of a polling system, the customers are usually served according to the FCFS discipline; therefore, the service discipline in a polling system only specifies two aspects (a) polling order, and (b) number of packets transmitted on each poll. In many cases, the polling order is cyclic, and we shall assume this to be the case in our discussions. Some of the popular packet-removal disciplines are exhaustive, gated, nonexhaustive, and limited. Under the *exhaustive service* discipline, all the customers that are present at the station at the polling instant are served. In addition, the customers that arrive at the station while the server is present there are also served; the server leaves the station only when the station is empty. In the *gated service* discipline, only those customers that are present at the station at the polling instant are served in the current cycle; customers who arrive while the server is present at the station are served in a subsequent visit by the server. In the *nonexhaustive service* discipline, exactly one customer is served when the station is polled and is found to be nonempty. In the *limited service* discipline, up to k (for some given k) customers are served when a station is polled. Nonexhaustive service is most popular in practice because it provides a small *cycle time* and avoids the starvation of lightly loaded stations by heavily loaded ones.

A number of schemes exist that also allow *prioritized service* at certain stations. One way of doing this is to have the server poll high priority stations more than once during a polling cycle. Another technique would be to serve more customers per poll at a high priority station. One extreme case of this is where the high priority stations are served exhaustively, whereas the others are served nonexhaustively.

There are many other polling schemes that have been specified and modeled. For example, in *time-limited service* scheme, there is an upper limit on the amount of time that the server can spend at a station when it is polled. In this section we shall restrict our attention to systems in which the stations are all served either using the exhaustive or nonexhaustive service. The analysis for the gated service case is similar to the one for the exhaustive service case, and is not presented. It is implicitly assumed that the server polls each station exactly once during a polling cycle.

13.1.2 The M/G/1 Vacation Model

Consider the behavior of the system from the point of view of a random observer who is positioned at some station i in the system. This observer sees the server poll station i at certain points in time. At these polling instants, if there is at least one customer waiting for service at station i, then the server serves one or more of these customers depending on the service at this station. Serving a customer takes a random amount of time, which can follow a general distribution. Following this, the server disappears from this station for a random amount of time during which it is busy polling and switching between other stations. In effect, the server takes a *vacation* from station i. Thus, *if the distribution of the vacation time can be obtained, each station can be studied in isolation as an M/G/1 queuing system with server vacations.* In general, however, obtaining vacation-time distribution is a very difficult problem.

Let M denote the number of stations in the system and let the polling sequence be $1, 2, \ldots, M$ and then back to station 1. Customers for service arrive at station i according to a Poisson process with rate λ_i. It is assumed that the buffer at each station is infinite, and that no customer is turned away. The time taken to service a customer at station i is a random variable, S_i, which has a mean s_i and second moment $s_i^{(2)}$. As usual we let $\rho_i = \lambda_i s_i$ denote the utilization of the server at station i. We also let ρ denote the total server utilization; i.e., $\rho = \sum_{i=1}^{M} \rho_i$. The time taken by the server to switch between station i and station $i+1$ is a random variable ω_i, which has a mean θ_i. The first two moments of the sum of the switch-over times are denoted by Θ and $\Theta^{(2)}$, respectively.

13.1.3 Mean Cycle and Waiting Times

We first obtain the expression for the *cycle time*, CT, which is defined as the expected time for the server to complete one poll of all the stations. It can be obtained rather easily for both exhaustive and nonexhaustive service. Note that for the system to be stable, the average number of customers arriving to station i during a cycle must equal the average number of customers served at station i during a cycle. Obviously, the former, and hence the latter, is $\lambda_i CT$. Since each customer requires s_i units of service, the average time spent at station i in a cycle is $\rho_i CT$ where $\rho_i = \lambda_i s_i$. Therefore, we can write $CT = \sum_{i=1}^{M}(\theta_i + \rho_i CT)$. This gives the following expression for CT

$$CT = \Theta/(1-\rho) \tag{1.1}$$

Obviously, a necessary condition for stability is $\rho < 1$. This condition is sufficient for an exhaustive service system but not so for a nonexhaustive one. The problem is that in the latter case, at most one customer is served per polling cycle, which means that some of the queues may grow unbounded even though $\rho < 1$. Therefore, we have an additional requirement that the expected number of arrivals during a cycle time is less than 1. That is,

$$\max_i \lambda_i CT < 1 \tag{1.2}$$

We now show how to obtain the mean waiting time W_i at station i in a vacation system *under exhaustive service assuming that the first two moments of the vacation time are known*. The analysis for the nonexhaustive service system is very similar and is left as an exercise. Let the random variable V_i denote the duration of the vacation from station i, and let v_i and $v_i^{(2)}$ denote the first two moments of V_i, respectively. If these two moments are known, it is relatively straightforward to obtain the mean waiting time experienced by a customer arriving at station i. In this case, it will be convenient to consider this system as a single station vacation system, and we drop the subscript that indicates the particular station.

Consider the distribution of the number of customers present in the system, as seen by an arriving customer. It can be shown (see Section 4.2.5) that this distribution is the same as that seen by a random observer. We shall use p_n to denote the probability that the arriving customer sees n customers present at the station. Let x denote the fraction of time that the server is away on vacation from the station, and $\tilde{x}$ the same fraction given that there is at least one customer present at the station. Because the server is always on vacation when there are zero customers at the station, it is clear that $x = p_0 + (1 - p_0)\tilde{x}$. Since ρ is the server utilization, we also have $x = 1 - \rho$. Therefore,

$$\tilde{x} = \frac{1 - \rho - p_0}{1 - p_0} \tag{1.3}$$

Let R denote the mean response time, and $R(n)$ the mean response time for a tagged customer $\mathcal{A}$ who finds n customers present in the system. Then

$$R = W + s = \sum_{n=0}^{\infty} p_n R(n) \tag{1.4}$$

Consider the case where $\mathcal{A}$ finds the system empty. In this case, the server has to be on vacation and the arriving customer interrupts a vacation that has a residual life (see Section 9.2.1) of $v^{(2)}/2v$. The expected time in the system for this customer is

$$R(0) = \frac{v^{(2)}}{2v} + s \tag{1.5}$$

Suppose, on the other hand, that $\mathcal{A}$ finds $n > 0$ customers present at the station on arrival. Then, there are two possibilities:

1. $\mathcal{A}$ finds the server on vacation. The fraction of time this occurs is, on the average, $\tilde{x}$. In this case, the customer interrupts a special vacation, which has an expected residual life of $v^{(2)}/2v$. Since the customer at the head of the line is served following this vacation, the expected time until the departure of the customer at the head of the line is $v^{(2)}/2v + s$.
2. $\mathcal{A}$ finds the server serving a customer. The fraction of time this occurs is, on the average, $(1 - \tilde{x})$. The expected time until the departure of the customer at the head of the line is simply the expected residual life of that customer, and is given by $s^{(2)}/2s$.

These two terms give the delay caused to $\mathcal{A}$ due to the customer at the head of the line. If $\mathcal{A}$ finds n customers at the station, $n - 1$ of those will cause an additional delay of $(n - 1)s$ units (for $n > 0$). Finally, $R(n)$ will also include the service time s of $\mathcal{A}$ itself. It thus follows that for $n > 0$, we have

$$R(n) = \tilde{x}\left[\frac{v^{(2)}}{2v} + s\right] + (1 - \tilde{x})\left[\frac{s^{(2)}}{2s}\right] + n\, s \tag{1.6}$$

Substituting this in equation (1.4), we get

$$\begin{aligned} R &= \left[\frac{v^{(2)}}{2v} + s\right][p_0 + \tilde{x}(1-p_0)] + \left[\frac{s^{(2)}}{2s}\right](1-\tilde{x})(1-p_0) + s\sum_{n=1}^{\infty} np_n \\ &= \left[\frac{v^{(2)}}{2v} + s\right](1-\rho) + \left[\frac{s^{(2)}}{2s}\right]\rho + s\sum_{n=1}^{\infty} np_n \qquad (1.7) \end{aligned}$$

Note that from Little's law we can set $\sum_n np_n = \lambda(W+s)$. Therefore, from equation (1.7),

$$W = \frac{\lambda s^{(2)}}{2(1-\rho)} + \frac{v^{(2)}}{2v} \qquad (1.8)$$

Observe that the expression for the mean waiting time in this M/G/1 vacation system decomposes into two terms, the first of which is just the mean waiting time in the standard M/G/1 queuing system studied in Section 9.3.1.

Example 13.1 A single processor attends to requests that arrive according to a Poisson process with rate 0.16 per unit time. The time to process each request is a random variable with mean 5 units, and a coefficient of variation $\sqrt{0.4}$. When the processor completes all waiting requests, it is switched to perform a self-diagnosis. Following this, it is switched back to process any requests that may have arrived during this period. If there are no requests waiting at this time, then the processor is again switched into the self-diagnostic mode. The time taken to switch the processor between the two modes of operation is deterministic and takes 0.1 units of time. The time to perform the self-diagnosis is a random variable with mean 1 unit and a coefficient of variation $\sqrt{2}$. The intent here is to obtain the mean waiting time of an arbitrary request for service that is made on this processor.

Solution We are given $\lambda = 0.16$, and $s = 5$; hence, $\rho = 0.80$, which meets the stability requirement for the exhaustive service system. Since $CV_S^2 = 0.4, s^{(2)}$ is easily obtained as $5^2(1+0.4) = 35$. The time that the processor is not attending to these requests forms the vacation period.

The switching time to and from the vacation can be lumped with the real vacation time in order to give an effective vacation time V. The first moment of V, denoted v, is simply $0.1 + 1 + 0.1 = 1.2$. Since this is the expected total switching time in a cycle, the cycle time is given by $v/(1-\rho) = 1.2/0.2 = 6$. Because the switching periods are deterministic, the variance of V is 2. Hence the second moment of V, denoted $v^{(2)}$, is obtained as $(1.2)^2+2 = 3.44$. The mean waiting time W is then obtained from equation (1.7) as W=15.72. □

13.1.4 Markovian Analysis and Conservation Laws

The approach typically followed here is to identify a discrete time Markov chain embedded in the system at appropriate points in time. Consider an exhaustive service system with M stations and let n_i denote the number of customers at station i. Also let $\mathbf{n} = (n_1, \ldots, n_M)$ denote the state of the system. We shall use the discrete random variable A_i to represent the system state at the instant in time that the server polls station i, and the discrete random variable D_i to represent the system state at the instant the server departs station i, $1 \leq i \leq M$. Let $PA_i(\mathbf{n}) = Pr(A_i = \mathbf{n})$, and $PD_i(\mathbf{n}) = Pr(D_i = \mathbf{n})$. With $\mathbf{z} = (z_1, \ldots, z_M)$, let

$$\Phi_{A_i}(\mathbf{z}) \triangleq \sum_{n_1=0}^{\infty} \sum_{n_2=0}^{\infty} \cdots \sum_{n_M=0}^{\infty} PA_i(\mathbf{n}) z_1^{n_1} \cdots z_M^{n_M} \tag{1.9}$$

denote the z-transform of A_i. Analogously, let $\Phi_{D_i}(\mathbf{z})$ denote the z-transform of D_i. We shall express $\Phi_{A_{i+1}}(\mathbf{z})$ in terms of $\Phi_{D_i}(\mathbf{z})$, and $\Phi_{D_i}(\mathbf{z})$ in terms of $\Phi_{A_i}(\mathbf{z})$. This will give a recursive expression for $\Phi_{A_{i+1}}(\mathbf{z})$ in terms of $\Phi_{A_i}(\mathbf{z})$, which can be solved. For clarity, we only derive the relationship between $\Phi_{A_{i+1}}(\mathbf{z})$ and $\Phi_{A_i}(\mathbf{z})$ for a system with two stations and leave the derivation for the general case as an exercise. Once we obtain this recursive relationship, we can obtain the mean waiting times as we show subsequently.

Let us denote by $\mathcal{P}_i(k;t)$ the probability that k customers arrive at station i in a time t. Since these arrivals form a Poisson process, $\mathcal{P}_i(k;t)$ is given by

$$\mathcal{P}_i(k;t) = \frac{(\lambda_i t)^k}{k!} \exp(-\lambda_i t) \quad \text{for } k \geq 0; \quad 1 \leq i \leq M \tag{1.10}$$

Recall that ω_i is the random variable that denotes the switch-over time between station i and $i+1$. Let $f_{\omega_i}(t)$ denote its density function and $\Psi_{\omega_i}(.)$ the Laplace transform of its density. Consider the state A_2 at the instant that the server polls (arrives at) station 2. We express $PA_2(n_1, n_2)$ in terms of $PD_1(.,.)$, based on the number of arrivals that occur during the random amount of time ω_1, as follows:

$$PA_2(n_1, n_2) = \sum_{k_2=0}^{n_2} PD_1(0, k_2) \int_{t=0}^{\infty} \mathcal{P}_1(n_1;t)\mathcal{P}_2(n_2 - k_2;t) f_{\omega_1}(t)\, dt \tag{1.11}$$

In the above equation we use the fact that when the server departs a station, the number of customers left behind at this station is always 0. Taking z-transforms on both sides of equation (1.11) and simplifying, we get

$$\Phi_{A_2}(z_1, z_2) = \sum_{k_2=0}^{\infty} z_2^{k_2} PD_1(0, k_2) \mathcal{I}(k_2, z_1, z_2) \tag{1.12}$$

where

$$\begin{aligned} \mathcal{I}(k_2, z_1, z_2) &= \int_{t=0}^{\infty} \sum_{n_2=k_2}^{\infty} \mathcal{P}_2(n_2 - k_2;t) z_2^{n_2-k_2} \sum_{n_1=0}^{\infty} \mathcal{P}_1(n_1;t) z_1^{n_1} f_{\omega_1}(t)\, dt \\ &= \int_{t=0}^{\infty} e^{\sum_{i=1}^{2} \lambda_i (z_i - 1)t} f_{\omega_1}(t)\, dt \\ &= \Psi_{\omega_1}[\lambda_1(1 - z_1) + \lambda_2(1 - z_2)] \end{aligned} \tag{1.13}$$

Therefore, by substituting in (1.12), we get

$$\Phi_{A_2}(z_1, z_2) = \Phi_{D_1}(0, z_2)\Psi_{\omega_1}[\lambda_1(1 - z_1) + \lambda_2(1 - z_2)] \quad (1.14)$$

To obtain a relation between $\Phi_{D_1}(0, z_2)$ and $\Phi_{A_1}(.,.)$, we need to use the concept of a busy period. Suppose that the server arrives after a vacation to find $j > 0$ customers waiting in the queue. This initiates a sequence of j independent busy periods to clear all the customers. Let $f_{\beta^*(j)}(t)$ denote the distribution of this j–busy period. Then,

$$PD_1(0, n_2) = PA_1(0, n_2) + \sum_{j=1}^{\infty}\sum_{k_2=0}^{n_2} PA_1(j, k_2)\int_0^{\infty} \mathcal{P}_2(n_2 - k_2; t) f_{\beta^*(j)}(t)\, dt \quad (1.15)$$

and taking z-transforms, this gives

$$\Phi_{D_1}(0, z_2) = \Phi_{A_1}(\Psi_{\beta_1}(\lambda_2(1 - z_2)), z_2) \quad (1.16)$$

where $\Psi_{\beta_i}(.)$ denotes the Laplace transform of a busy period at station i. Thus, from equations (1.14) and (1.16), we get

$$\Phi_{A_2}(z_1, z_2) = \Phi_{A_1}(\Psi_{\beta_1}(\lambda_2(1 - z_2)), z_2)\Psi_{\omega_1}(\sum_{i=1}^{2}\lambda_i(1 - z_i)) \quad (1.17)$$

The expression for the general system with M stations under the exhaustive service is obtained in a similar manner. It is

$$\Phi_{A_{i+1}}(\mathbf{z}) = \Phi_{A_i}(z_1, \ldots, z_{i-1}, \Psi^*_{\beta_i}, z_{i+1}, \ldots, z_M)\Psi^*_{\omega_i} \quad (1.18)$$

where

$$\Psi^*_{\beta_i} = \Psi_{\beta_i}\left(\sum_{m \neq i}\lambda_m(1 - z_m)\right) \quad (1.19)$$

$$\Psi^*_{\omega_i} = \Psi_{\omega_i}\left(\sum_{m=1}^{M}\lambda_m(1 - z_m)\right) \quad (1.20)$$

Let us see how to obtain the mean waiting times using equation (1.18). Let $\mathbf{e}$ denote a vector of all 1's and define

$$f_{ij} = \left.\frac{\partial\Phi_{A_i}(\mathbf{z})}{\partial z_j}\right|_{\mathbf{z}=\mathbf{e}} \quad \text{and} \quad f^{(2)}_{ijk} = \left.\frac{\partial^2\Phi_{A_i}(\mathbf{z})}{\partial z_j \partial z_k}\right|_{\mathbf{z}=\mathbf{e}} \quad (1.21)$$

The term f_{ij} denotes the expected number of customers present at station j when the server polls station i. In particular, f_{ii} denotes the expected number of customers present at station i when the server polls station i. Similarly, the term $f^{(2)}_{iii}$ denotes the second moment of the number of customers present at station i when the server polls station i. It can be shown that the mean waiting time W_i and $f^{(2)}_{iii}$ are related as follows:

$$W_i = f^{(2)}_{iii}\left(\frac{(1 - \rho)}{2\lambda_i^2\Theta(1 - \rho_i)}\right) + \frac{\lambda_i s_i^{(2)}}{2(1 - \rho_i)} \quad (1.22)$$

For each $i = 1, \ldots, M$, we differentiate equation (1.18) once with respect to $z_j, j = 1, \ldots, M$, and set $\mathbf{z} = \mathbf{e}$ to obtain a system of M^2 equations in the unknowns f_{ij}. These equations have a special structure which allows the unknowns f_{ij} to be determined explicitly as:

$$f_{ij} = \lambda_j \left[\sum_{k=j}^{i-1} \theta_k + \sum_{k=j+1}^{i-1} \rho_k CT \right] \quad \text{for } i \neq j \tag{1.23}$$

$$f_{ii} = \lambda_i CT(1 - \rho_i) \tag{1.24}$$

These equations are explained intuitively as follows. Since the server departs from station j leaving zero customers behind, the expected number of customers present at station j when station i is polled is equal to the expected number of arrivals at j during the time it takes the server to get to station i following the departure from station j. At every station k the server encounters enroute to station i, an expected time of $\rho_k CT$ is spent to service the customers at that station. This is followed by a switchover time of expected length θ_k to move to the next station. This explains the expression for f_{ij}. The expected number of customers present at station i, at the instant it is polled, is simply the expected number of customers who arrive at station i during a vacation from that station. Since the vacation from station i has duration $CT(1 - \rho_i)$, this explains the expression for f_{ii}.

Next, we differentiate equation (1.18) twice with respect to j and k, and set $\mathbf{z} = \mathbf{e}$ to obtain a system of $M^2(M + 1)/2$ linear equations in the unknowns $f_{ijk}^{(2)}$, and the f_{ij}'s which have just been determined. These equations can now be solved to obtain the $f_{iii}^{(2)}$'s and thereby the mean waiting times. (Note that $f_{ijk}^{(2)} = f_{ikj}^{(2)}$ and hence there are less than M^3 equations.) The approach outlined above is a classical one, based on generating functions, and requires the solution of $O(M^3)$ equations. Other approaches have been proposed which require less computational effort to obtain the mean waiting times. Some of these approaches are mentioned in the bibliographic notes.

An expression similar to equation (1.18) can be derived for a general system with M nodes under the nonexhaustive service. Let

$$\Psi_{S_i}^* = \Psi_{S_i} \left[\sum_{m=i}^{M} \lambda_m (1 - z_m) \right] \tag{1.25}$$

Then

$$\Phi_{A_{i+1}}(\mathbf{z}) = \frac{\Phi_{A_i}(\mathbf{z}) - \Phi_{A_i}(\mathbf{z} - z_i e_i)}{z_i} \Psi_{S_i}^* \Psi_{\omega_i}^* + \Phi_{A_i}(\mathbf{z} - z_i e_i) \Psi_{\omega_i}^* \tag{1.26}$$

Unfortunately, we cannot carry through the above analysis for the nonexhaustive service case. In fact, obtaining mean waiting times under nonexhaustive service is an unsolved problem in general. The interested reader is referred to the bibliographic notes for additional material on this topic.

Next we study *conservation laws* for polling systems. As usual, these laws provide an equation for a weighted sum of mean waiting times in terms of the input parameters. However, because of the pseudo-conservative nature of a polling system, the laws are difficult to derive, and we shall state them here without proof. These laws can be obtained even for the case where some of the stations use exhaustive service, some use nonexhaustive service, and some others use the gated service discipline. The laws are useful in at least two ways: they provide the exact mean waiting times in the case of symmetric systems, and facilitate the development of approximations in others. For the exhaustive service system, the conservation law is given by

$$\sum_{i=1}^{M} \rho_i W_i = \frac{\rho}{2(1-\rho)} \sum_{i=1}^{M} \lambda_i s_i^{(2)} + \rho \frac{\Theta^{(2)}}{2\Theta} + \frac{\Theta}{2(1-\rho)} \left[\rho^2 - \sum_{i=1}^{M} \rho_i^2 \right] \tag{1.27}$$

For the nonexhaustive service system, the conservation law is given by

$$\sum_{i=1}^{M} \rho_i (1-\lambda_i CT) W_i = \frac{\rho}{2(1-\rho)} \sum_{i=1}^{M} \lambda_i s_i^{(2)} + \frac{\rho \Theta^{(2)}}{2\Theta} + \frac{\Theta}{2(1-\rho)} \left[\rho^2 + \sum_{i=1}^{M} \rho_i^2 \right] \tag{1.28}$$

Note that with these conservation laws, it is easy to obtain the mean waiting times for completely symmetric systems; namely, systems where each station has identical characteristics. Thus, by setting $\rho_k = \rho_i$ for all k, the mean waiting time at a station in the symmetric exhaustive service system, is given by

$$\rho_i W_i = \frac{\rho_i}{2(1-\rho)} \sum_{i=1}^{M} \lambda_i s_i^{(2)} + \rho_i \frac{\Theta^{(2)}}{2\Theta} + \frac{\Theta}{2(1-\rho)} (M\rho_i^2 - \rho_i^2) \tag{1.29}$$

from which, we get

$$W_i = \frac{\sum_{i=1}^{M} \lambda_i s_i^{(2)}}{2(1-\rho)} + \frac{\Theta^{(2)}}{2\Theta} + \frac{\Theta}{2(1-\rho)} (M-1)\rho_i \tag{1.30}$$

Note from equation (1.30) that the first term on the right-hand side is just the mean waiting time that would be experienced by a customer in an ordinary M/G/1 queuing system with arrival rate $\lambda = \sum_{i=1}^{M} \lambda_i$ (see Section 9.3.1).

For a symmetric nonexhaustive service system, the mean waiting times are obtained from equation (1.28), in an analogous manner, from

$$W_i(1-\lambda_i CT) = \frac{\sum_{i=1}^{M} \lambda_i s_i^{(2)}}{2(1-\rho)} + \frac{\Theta^{(2)}}{2\Theta} + \frac{\Theta}{2(1-\rho)} (M+1)\rho_i \tag{1.31}$$

13.1.5 Approximations for Mean Waiting Times

As noted above, obtaining exact mean waiting times for polling systems can be difficult in general. This has motivated the need for obtaining these values approximately, and a nun ber of approximations have been proposed. We present one of these techniques for the exhaustive service system, and another technique for the nonexhaustive service system. These techniques have been extensively validated with simulation, and usually produce fairly accurate estimates of the mean waiting times.

First consider exhaustive service systems. Here we will assume that the switch-over times are deterministic. It was observed earlier in this section that if the first and second moments of the vacation from a station are known, then we can obtain the mean waiting times from equation (1.8). For the general exhaustive service system, this is given by

$$W_i = \frac{\lambda_i s_i^{(2)}}{2(1-\rho_i)} + \frac{v_i^{(2)}}{2v_i} \tag{1.32}$$

In order to obtain the first two moments of the vacation time, we first analyze the system with two stations and obtain these moments exactly. The analysis is then heuristically extrapolated to the case where there are more than two stations. Let T_i denote the time spent by the server at station i per polling cycle, and let t_i denote its expected value. Applying the arguments used in Section 13.1.3 for obtaining the cycle time, we have $t_i = \rho_i CT$. Thus, v_i is easily obtained from equation (1.1), as

$$v_i = CT - t_i = CT(1-\rho_i) = \Theta\frac{1-\rho_i}{1-\rho} \tag{1.33}$$

To obtain $v_i^{(2)}$, let the random variable K_i denote the number of messages waiting at station i when the server polls this station. Note that T_i is the sum of K_i independent 1-busy periods. Let β_i denote the duration of a 1-busy period at station i. Let $k_i = E[K_i]$, $b_i = E[\beta_i]$, and $b_i^{(2)} = E[\beta_i^2]$. The first two moments of β_i are obtained from equation (9.3.26) using s_i and ρ_i in place of $E[S]$ and ρ. Let $\text{Var}(A)$ denote the variance of a random variable A. In terms of K_i and β_i, the variance of T_i is then given by the following expression, which is obtained by conditioning on the value of K_i

$$\text{Var}(T_i) = k_i \text{Var}(\beta_i) + \text{Var}(K_i) b_i^2 \tag{1.34}$$

Since K_i is just the number of arrivals at station i during a vacation from station i, k_i is easily obtained as $k_i = \lambda_i v_i$. Therefore, using a relationship similar to the one in equation (9.3.5), we obtain

$$\text{Var}(K_i) = \lambda_i^2 \text{Var}(V_i) + \lambda_i v_i \tag{1.35}$$

Obviously, if we can determine $\text{Var}(V_i)$, we can obtain $v_i^{(2)}$ and thereby W_i. For an arbitrary M, the above equations are not sufficient to determine $\text{Var}(V_i)$. However, when $M = 2$, we can obtain $\text{Var}(V_i)$ as follows. Note that in this case the vacation from station 1 differs from the time the server spends at station 2 only by the deterministic time Θ. Hence,

$$\text{Var}(T_1) = \text{Var}(V_2) \quad \text{and} \quad \text{Var}(T_2) = \text{Var}(V_1) \tag{1.36}$$

From equations (1.33) through (1.36), after some modest algebra, we obtain the variance of V_i, $i = 1, 2$, as

$$\mathrm{Var}(V_i) = \frac{\Theta}{(1-\rho)^2} \frac{\lambda_k s_k^{(2)}(1-\rho_i)^2 + \lambda_i s_i^{(2)} \rho_k^2}{1-\rho_i-\rho_k+2\rho_i\rho_k}, \qquad i = 1, 2, ; \; k = 3 - i \quad (1.37)$$

For the general model with $M > 2$, the heuristic assumption is that the variance of the vacation time is approximated by an expression similar to equation (1.37), namely,

$$\mathrm{Var}(V_i) = \frac{\Theta}{(1-\rho)^2} \sum_{k=1,k\neq i}^{M} \frac{\lambda_k s_k^{(2)}(1-\rho_i)^2 + \lambda_i s_i^{(2)} \rho_k^2}{1-\rho_i-\rho_k+2\rho_i\rho_k} \quad (1.38)$$

From equations (1.38), (1.32) and (1.33), noting that $v_i^{(2)} = \mathrm{Var}(V_i) + v_i^2$, the desired approximate expression for the mean waiting times is obtained as

$$W_i = \frac{\lambda_i s_i^{(2)}}{2(1-\rho_i)} + \frac{(1-\rho_i)CT}{2} + \frac{(1-\rho)\mathrm{Var}(V_i)}{2\Theta(1-\rho_i)} \quad (1.39)$$

The above expression is exact for the symmetric system. Interestingly enough, even though the expression for the mean waiting times is obtained through an approximate analysis, it satisfies the conservation law.

Example 13.2 Consider a two-station polling system operating under exhaustive service discipline. The switch-over times are deterministic and equal to 0.1 in either direction. Requests arrive to stations 1 and 2 according to a Poisson process with rates 0.10 and 0.11 respectively. The time taken to service the requests are random variables, with means 4 and 5, and coefficients of variations 1 and $\sqrt{2}$ respectively. Obtain the mean waiting times for the requests at both stations.

Solution The input parameters are $\lambda_1 = 0.10$, $\lambda_2 = 0.11$, $s_1 = 4$, $s_2 = 5$, $CV_{S_1} = 1$, and $CV_{S_2} = \sqrt{2}$. The second moments of the service times are obtained as $s_1^{(2)} = 32$, $s_2^{(2)} = 75$. In this case, $\Theta = 0.2$, and $\rho = \rho_1 + \rho_2 = 0.4 + 0.55 = 0.95$. Hence the system is stable, and the cycle time is given by $\Theta/(1-\rho) = 0.2/(1-0.95) = 4$.

Since $\Theta/(1-\rho)^2 = 80$ and $1 - \rho_1 - \rho_2 + 2\rho_1\rho_2 = 0.49$, the variances of the two vacations are obtained from equation (1.37) as

$$\begin{aligned} \mathrm{Var}(V_1) &= (80/0.49)(\lambda_2 s_2^{(2)}(1-\rho_1)^2 + \lambda_1 s_1^{(2)} \rho_2^2) = 642.94 \\ \mathrm{Var}(V_2) &= (80/0.49)(\lambda_1 s_1^{(2)}(1-\rho_2)^2 + \lambda_2 s_2^{(2)} \rho_1^2) = 321.31 \end{aligned}$$

From equation (1.33), $v_1 = CT(1-\rho_1) = 2.4$ and $v_2 = CT(1-\rho_2) = 1.8$. Therefore,

$$v_1^{(2)} = v_1^2 + \mathrm{Var}(V_1) = 648.70 \quad \text{and} \quad v_2^{(2)} = v_2^2 + \mathrm{Var}(V_2) = 324.55$$

Hence, from equation (1.32) we have $W_1 = 137.81$ and $W_2 = 99.318$. As a cross-check, these values of W_i may be validated using the conservation law for exhaustive systems given by equation (1.27). □

Next, we consider nonexhaustive service systems. A fairly simple approximation scheme is obtained here, using the conservation law given by equation (1.28). Consider an arbitrary customer who arrives to station i. This customer interrupts a cycle that is already in progress and will end when the server returns to poll station i. Following this, the server needs to complete as many cycles as there are customers ahead of the arriving customer before service begins on the arriving customer. Each of these cycles will include a service at station i. Let n_i denote the expected number of customers at station i seen by an arriving customer, and CT_i the expected length of a conditional cycle that always includes a service at station i. Then, W_i consists of two components: (1) the expected residual life $\tilde{r}_i$ of the cycle which the arriving customer interrupts, and (2) the expected length of time for the server to complete n_i cycles, each of length CT_i. Because of the PASTA property, $n_i = Q_i = \lambda_i W_i$, which means that $W_i = \tilde{r}_i + \lambda_i W_i CT_i$. Thus,

$$W_i = \frac{\tilde{r}_i}{1 - \lambda_i CT_i} \tag{1.40}$$

In equation (1.40), there are two unknowns, $\tilde{r}_i$, and CT_i. An (approximate) expression for CT_i is obtained using a similar reasoning as was used to obtain the cycle time. Since CT_i always consists of a service at station i,

$$CT_i = \Theta + s_i + \sum_{m=1, m \neq i}^{M} \alpha_{im} s_m \tag{1.41}$$

where α_{im} is the probability that the conditional cycle with expected length CT_i includes a service at station m. We approximate α_{im} as $\lambda_m CT_i$. Since $\lambda_m s_m = \rho_m$, we get the following expression for CT_i.

$$CT_i = \frac{\Theta + s_i}{1 - \rho + \rho_i} \tag{1.42}$$

Note that under heavy traffic, it is possible that $\lambda_m CT_i$ may exceed 1, and thus cannot be interpreted as a probability. In such cases, evaluating CT_i may require some iteration, as will be illustrated by an example below.

The approximation for $\tilde{r}_i$ is obtained by assuming that it is the same for every station, i.e., $\tilde{r}_i = \tilde{r}$. Therefore,

$$W_i = \tilde{r}/(1 - \lambda_i CT_i) \tag{1.43}$$

Substituting W_i in the conservation law (1.28), we get

$$\sum_{i=1}^{M} \frac{\rho_i (1 - \lambda_i CT)\tilde{r}}{(1 - \lambda_i CT_i)} = g(\rho) \tag{1.44}$$

where $g(\rho)$ is the right-hand side of equation (1.28). Noting that

$$\sum_{i=1}^{M} \rho_i \frac{(1-\lambda_i CT)}{(1-\lambda_i CT_i)} = \sum_{i=1}^{M} \rho_i \frac{1-\rho+\rho_i}{1-\rho} = \frac{(1-\rho)\rho + \sum_{i=1}^{M} \rho_i^2}{1-\rho} \tag{1.45}$$

we get the following expression for $\tilde{r}$

$$\tilde{r} = \frac{(1-\rho)g(\rho)}{(1-\rho)\rho + \sum_{i=1}^{M} \rho_i^2} \tag{1.46}$$

The mean waiting times are now obtained from equations (1.43), (1.46), and (1.42).

Example 13.3 Consider a three station polling model operating under the nonexhaustive service. The input parameters for this system are as follows: $\lambda_1 = 0.6$, $\lambda_2 = \lambda_3 = 0.2$; all service-time distributions are exponential with $s_1 = s_2 = s_3 = 0.8$. All switch-over times are exponential with a mean of 0.05. Find the approximate mean waiting times for this model.

Solution For this system, $\rho = 0.8$ and $\Theta = 0.15$. Hence, the cycle time is $\Theta/(1-\rho) = 0.75$. For this system the additional check on stability is to determine whether $\max_i \lambda_i CT < 1$. Here, the maximum value of λ_i occurs at $i = 1$, and is equal to 0.6. Clearly, the conditions for stability are satisfied. We now use equation (1.46) to obtain the value of $\tilde{r}$. For this, we must first calculate $s_i^{(2)}$ and $\Theta^{(2)}$. All $s_i^{(2)}$'s are the same, and since the service times are exponentially distributed, $s_i^{(2)} = 2s_i^2 = 1.28$. Noting that the switch-over times are mutually independent, it can be shown that $\Theta^{(2)} = \sum_{i=1}^{M} \mathrm{Var}(\omega_i) + \Theta^2$ (the reader should verify this). This gives $\Theta^{(2)} = 0.03$. Hence, from equation (1.46), $\tilde{r} = 1.3521739$.

Now, let us obtain the mean waiting time at station 2. For this, we need to obtain CT_2, which is the conditional cycle time given that there is a service at station 2 during this cycle time. From equation (1.42), we have

$$CT_2 = (\Theta + s_2)/(1-\rho+\rho_2) = 0.95/0.36 = 2.6389$$

However, if we now substitute this value of CT_2 in equation (1.42), we get $\alpha_{21} = \lambda_1 CT_2 = 1.5833$, which is greater than 1. Hence, we need to re-evaluate CT_2 constraining the contribution towards this cycle time from station 1 to be a mean service time. In other words, CT_2 is re-evaluated as $CT_2 = \Theta + s_2 + s_1 + \alpha_{23}s_3$. Now, substituting $\alpha_{23} = \lambda_3 CT_2$, we get $CT_2 = \Theta + s_2 + s_1 + \rho_3 CT_2$. Collecting terms involving CT_2, we finally get

$$CT_2 = (\Theta + s_1 + s_2)/(1-\rho_3)$$

and this evaluates to $CT_2 = 2.08333$. Note that this value of CT_2 ensures that $\alpha_{23} < 1$. With $CT_2 = 2.08333$, W_2 is obtained from equation (1.43) as 2.318. For comparison, the value of W_2 obtained through simulation is 1.92. □

13.2 Problems in Performance Optimization

In this section we examine the problem of design, as opposed to analysis, where the objective is to find optimum values of input parameters that yield the desired values of the output parameters of interest. This optimization may require evaluating the model for several sets of input parameters, and is thus much harder than the analysis problem. We shall study two important optimization problems here: the optimal file-allocation problem in distributed systems, and the optimal routing of traffic in computer networks.

13.2.1 File-Allocation Problem

The *file-allocation problem* (FAP) entails allocating a set of F distinct files among a set of M computer installations (stations), such that a given performance index is optimized. This problem has been shown to be a complex one, and work on it has proceeded in two directions. One direction is toward obtaining an allocation that minimizes some cost function, typically consisting of storage costs and/or communication costs, subject to some constraints on the performance. The other direction is toward obtaining an allocation that optimizes some performance parameter of the network (e.g., weighted throughput or mean response time). In this section we model the FAP as a queuing network optimization problem, with the objective of minimizing the weighted mean response time.

Consider a network of computers where the file requests originating at each computer have potentially different characteristics. The customers in the model are the processes making requests for files located on various computers. We can think of each customer type accessing the desired files in some sequence. The results of a request typically generate some information that is transmitted back to the customer originating the request. Some information may also be transmitted between files in a request sequence. These characteristics naturally lead to a multiple-chain closed queuing network model, where each customer type corresponds to a separate chain. Let K denote the number of chains, and $\mathbf{N} = (N_1, \ldots, N_K)$ the population vector. We shall assume that the communication delays are negligible compared to the time taken to retrieve a file located at a station. The mean time to complete a typical request for a customer chain is its cycle time. We shall minimize a weighted summation of these cycle times over all the chains.

Processing each file in a typical request sequence imposes a certain amount of work on the system. In particular, processing file f for a chain r customer takes τ_{rf} operations. We denote the work capacity (i.e., operations per second) of station i as θ_i. Let x_{if} denote a variable that is set to 1 if file f is allocated to station i and to 0 otherwise. Thus, an allocation of the F files is given by the vector $X = \{x_{if}\}$. This allocation generates a mean service time demand $d_{ir}(X)$

by customer chain r at station i, which is given by

$$d_{ir}(X) = \sum_{f=1}^{F} x_{if}\tau_{rf}/\theta_i \tag{2.1}$$

Let $D_r(X)$ represent the total mean service time demand by the rth customer chain on the system. Then

$$D_r(X) = \sum_{i=1}^{M} d_{ir}(X) \tag{2.2}$$

Denote by $CT_r(\mathbf{N}, X)$ the cycle time of chain r customers when the network population is $\mathbf{N}$, and the allocation vector is X. Then the optimization problem, henceforth denoted as $P1$, can be written as follows:

$$\begin{array}{lll} P1: & \min \sum_{r=1}^{K} \beta_r \; CT_r(\mathbf{N}, X) & \\ \text{s.t.:} & \sum_{i=1}^{M} x_{if} = 1, \quad f = 1..F & \text{(single copy only)} \\ & x_{if} \in \{0,1\} \text{ for } f = 1..F, \; i = 1..M & \text{(integer assignments only)} \end{array}$$

where β_r's are the specified weights, that can be adjusted to reflect the relative importance of various chains. Problem $P1$ is an integer-programming problem with a highly nonlinear objective function. As such, even under the product-form assumption, it is very difficult to solve. One approach is to approximate the objective function. Let $R_{ir}(\mathbf{N}, X)$ denote the mean waiting time for a chain r customer at station i under allocation X and let $v_{ir}(X)$ denote the visit ratio for chain r customers at station i with this allocation. Then the mean residence time at station i for a chain r customer in a cycle of length $CT_r(\mathbf{N}, X)$ is given by $R^*_{ir}(\mathbf{N}, X) = v_{ir}(X)R_{ir}(\mathbf{N}, X)$. Clearly,

$$CT_r(\mathbf{N}, X) = \sum_{i=1}^{M} R^*_{ir}(\mathbf{N}, X) \tag{2.3}$$

From the MVA algorithm, $R^*_{ir}(\mathbf{N}, X)$ can be written as

$$\begin{aligned} R^*_{ir}(\mathbf{N}, X) &= d_{ir}(X)\,[1 + Q_i(\mathbf{N} - e_r, X)] \\ &= d_{ir}(X)\left[1 + \sum_{j=1}^{K} Q_{ij}(\mathbf{N} - e_r, X)\right] \end{aligned} \tag{2.4}$$

The first-order approximation made here is that the mean queue lengths are proportional to the mean service time demands at the stations; i.e., we assume that

$$Q_{ij}(\mathbf{N} - e_r, X) \approx [N_j - \delta(j, r)]\frac{d_{ij}(X)}{D_j(X)} \tag{2.5}$$

where $\delta(j,r) = 1$ for $j = r$, and 0 otherwise. With this approximation to the mean queue length, the mean residence time is given by

$$R^*_{ir}(\mathbf{N}, X) = d_{ir}(X)\left[1 + \sum_{j=1}^{K} \frac{d_{ij}(X)N_j}{D_j(X)} - \frac{d_{ir}(X)}{D_r(X)}\right] \tag{2.6}$$

For simplicity, we shall assume that all stations in the network are homogeneous, i.e., they all process work at the same rate θ. Hence, from equation (2.2)

$$D_r(X) = \sum_{i=1}^{M}\sum_{f=1}^{F} x_{if}\tau_{rf}/\theta \tag{2.7}$$

Therefore, from equation (2.3), we have

$$D_r(X) = \frac{1}{\theta}\sum_{f=1}^{F} \tau_{rf} \tag{2.8}$$

Note that $D_r(X)$ is independent of the allocation and can be written as D_r. From equations (2.3) and (2.6), we have

$$\beta_r CT_r(\mathbf{N}, X) = \beta_r \sum_{i=1}^{M} d_{ir}(X)\left[1 + \sum_{j=1}^{K} N_j d_{ij}(X)/D_j - d_{ir}(X)/D_r\right] \tag{2.9}$$

Using equation (2.1) to express $d_{ij}(X)$, after some elementary algebra we obtain the following equation for the objective function

$$\sum_{r=1}^{K} \beta_r CT_r(\mathbf{N}, X) = \sum_{r=1}^{K} \beta_r D_r + \sum_{i=1}^{M}\sum_{f=1}^{F}\sum_{g=1}^{F} c_{fg}x_{if}x_{ig} \tag{2.10}$$

where

$$c_{fg} = \sum_{r=1}^{K} \frac{\beta_r \tau_{rf}}{\theta^2}\left(\sum_{j=1}^{K} \frac{N_j \tau_{jg}}{D_j} - \frac{\tau_{rg}}{D_r}\right) \tag{2.11}$$

The first term in the objective function is now a constant and can be removed. When $f = g$, the product $x_{if}x_{ig}$ is either 1 or 0, and a fixed cost of $\sum_{f=1}^{F} c_{ff}$ is always incurred no matter where the file f is stored. Hence, the terms where $f = g$ can also be removed from the objective function. Therefore, problem $P1$ can be reformulated as follows:

$$P1': \quad \min \sum_{i=1}^{M} \sum_{f=1, f\neq g}^{F} \sum_{g=1}^{F} c_{fg}x_{if}x_{ig}$$

$$\text{st:} \quad \sum_{i=1}^{M} x_{if} = 1 \quad \text{for } f = 1..F, \quad x_{if} \in \{0,1\},\ i \in 1..M$$

Problem $P1'$ can be interpreted as follows. Consider a completely connected weighted graph where the vertices in the graph correspond to the files 1 through F. In this graph, the weight on the edge connecting two files f and g is given by $w(f, g) = c_{fg} + c_{gf}$, and this represents a measure of the queuing delays that would be induced if these two files were to be placed at the same node. The problem, then, is to partition these F vertices among M groups such that the sum of the weights on the edges $w(f, g)$ in each group is minimized.

Example 13.4 Suppose that there are five files, labeled 1 through 5. These five files are to be allocated among two stations. Suppose that the weights $w(f, g)$, $f, g = 1..5$, have been obtained as follows:

$$\begin{array}{lllll} w(1,2) = 10 & w(1,3) = 5 & w(1,4) = 7 & w(1,5) = 11 & w(2,3) = 12 \\ w(2,4) = 7 & w(2,5) = 12 & w(3,4) = 4 & w(3,5) = 14 & w(4,5) = 8 \end{array}$$

Evaluate the objective function value for problem $P1'$ for the following allocations: (a) $x_{11} = x_{22} = x_{32} = x_{41} = x_{51} = 1$, and (b) $x_{12} = x_{21} = x_{32} = x_{42} = x_{51} = 1$.

Solution In the first allocation, files 1, 4, and 5 are allocated to station 1, and files 2 and 3 are allocated to station 2. Here the sum of the weights of the edges in group 1 (station 1) is $w(1, 4) + w(1, 5) + w(4, 5) = 26$, and the corresponding sum for group 2 (station 2) is $w(2, 3) = 12$. The sum of weights over all groups is $26 + 12 = 38$.

In the second allocation, files 1, 3, and 4 are allocated to station 2, whereas files 2 and 5 are allocated to station 1. The sum of the weights of the edges in group 1 is $w(2, 5) = 12$, and the corresponding sum for station 2 is $w(1, 3) + w(1, 4) + w(3, 4) = 16$. The sum of the weights over all groups is $12 + 16 = 28$. Clearly, this allocation will be preferred.

The objective function in problem $P1'$ is far easier to evaluate than the complex function in problem $P1$. No doubt, the evaluation gives an approximate value. However, as the solution approaches the optimum value, the approximation has generally been observed to be sufficiently accurate based on extensive numerical validation. Problem $P1'$ is still a hard problem, and the corresponding decision problem can be shown to be NP-complete. The search for the optimum is now effected using a heuristic interchange technique. This approach returns allocations that are usually within 2% to 3% of the optimum value in most cases. □

13.2.2 Optimal Routing in Computer Networks

For the FAP, we considered an approximation scheme to assist in the search for the optimum. We now consider an exact solution technique for the problem of optimal routing in computer networks. This is a problem that has been extensively studied in the last two decades and has led to the development of several routing techniques. Many of these techniques model the network as an open queuing network and several efficient algorithms exist under this assumption. However, these models are not always accurate for computer networks. Most data networks in existence usually provide end-to-end virtual circuit with some form of flow control on each virtual circuit. In such cases the number of packets on each virtual circuit is limited to a fixed value called the window size. This suggests that a closed queuing network is more appropriate for modeling these networks.

Consider a network where a source computer (or node) is transmitting messages to a destination node. These messages travel to the destination passing through zero or more intermediate nodes via a set of communication channels. (See Fig. 13-2.) There are M communication channels, and each channel is modeled as a load-independent station in this network. We assume that the time a message spends at a node is negligible. However, there can be a queue of messages forming at the source node; therefore, the source is also modeled as a load-independent station, designated as station 0.

We assume that the source node always has one or more messages in its queue waiting to be delivered at the destination. We also assume that as soon as a message is delivered at the destination, an acknowledgment is instantaneously given to the source node. Suppose that the window size is N. Based on the above assumptions, as soon as an acknowledgment is received by the source node, another message is released by it into the network. As a result, there are always N unacknowledged messages in the network at any point in time. The resulting single-chain closed queuing network model of this network has $M+1$ load-independent stations, numbered $0 \mathinner{..} M$, where node 0 is the source node. Given the service rates μ_i, $i = 0 \mathinner{..} M$ and N, the routing problem is to find the visit ratios $\mathbf{v} = \{v_i\}$, $i = 1 \mathinner{..} M$, such that the overall cycle time $CT(N, \mathbf{v})$ is minimized. Without any loss of generality we assume that $v_0 = 1$.

In general, let there be M' intermediate nodes. Each message departing the source travels through zero or more intermediate nodes via one or more channels. Let $IN(m)$ = the set of channels leading into node m, and $OUT(m)$ = the set of channels leading out of node m, $m = 1 \mathinner{..} M'$. Then the optimal routing problem is formally defined as

$$\begin{aligned} & \min \; CT(N, \mathbf{v}) \\ \text{s.t.:} \quad & v_i \geq 0 \quad \text{for } i = 1 \mathinner{..} M \\ & \sum_{i \in IN(m)} v_i = \sum_{i \in OUT(m)} v_i \quad \text{for } m = 1 \mathinner{..} M' \end{aligned} \tag{2.12}$$

We shall assume that our queuing network model satisfies the product-form assumptions. Let $G(N, \mathbf{v})$ denote the normalization constant for this network for a given $\mathbf{v}$, and let $\lambda(N, \mathbf{v})$ denote the corresponding throughput (as measured at either the source or the destination). We assume that all messages generated at the source reach the destination. Thus, from the throughput theorem, we have

$$CT(N, \mathbf{v}) = \frac{N}{\lambda(N, \mathbf{v})} = \frac{NG(N, \mathbf{v})}{G(N-1, \mathbf{v})} \tag{2.13}$$

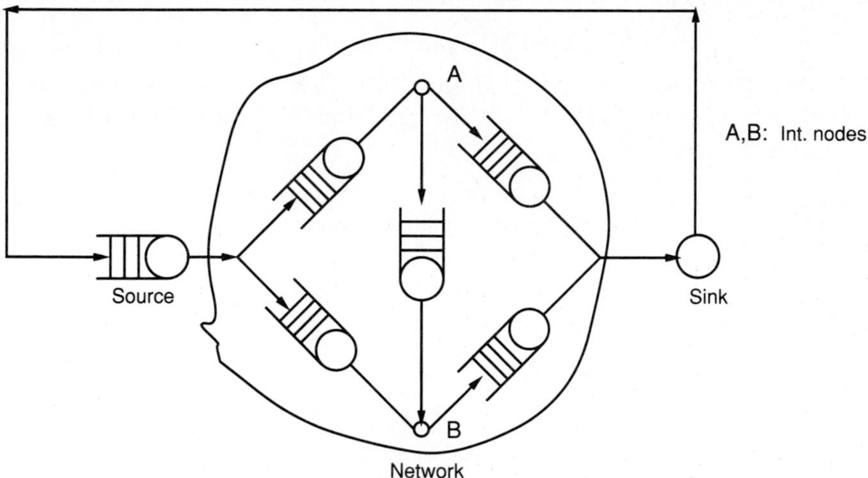

FIGURE 13-2: A queuing model of a computer network.

From equation (10.5.4), we have

$$\frac{\partial}{\partial v_i} G(N, \mathbf{v}) = \frac{G(N, \mathbf{v})}{v_i} Q_i(N, \mathbf{v}) \tag{2.14}$$

To solve the optimal routing problem, we first need to evaluate the partial derivative $\frac{\partial}{\partial v_i} CT(N, \mathbf{v})$. From equations (2.13) and (2.14), we get

$$\frac{\partial CT(N, \mathbf{v})}{\partial v_i} = \frac{NG(N-1, \mathbf{v})G(N, \mathbf{v})[Q_i(N, \mathbf{v}) - Q_i(N-1, \mathbf{v})]}{v_i G^2(N-1, \mathbf{v})}$$

which simplifies to the following

$$\frac{\partial}{\partial v_i} CT(N, \mathbf{v}) = \frac{CT(N, \mathbf{v})}{v_i} [Q_i(N, \mathbf{v}) - Q_i(N-1, \mathbf{v})] \tag{2.15}$$

Define a weight for station i as $w_i = \frac{1}{CT(N,\mathbf{v})} \frac{\partial}{\partial v_i} CT(N, \mathbf{v})$. Suppose that there are J possible paths from the source to the destination. Denote by ϕ_j the jth such path. Clearly, each path uses one or more stations to transfer the message from the source to the destination. The total message flow can be split among these paths. Let q_j be the proportion of the total flow from source to destination that is routed through path ϕ_j. We have $\sum_{j=1}^{J} q_j = 1$. The q_j's are termed as the path probabilities that are to be selected so that the overall cycle time is minimized. Observe that station 0 is on every path. From the definition of the visit ratios, we have

$$v_i = \sum_{i \in \phi_j} q_j \quad \text{for} \quad i = 1 .. M \tag{2.17}$$

The weight of the path ϕ_j is given by $w(\phi_j) = \sum_{i \in \phi_j} w_i$.

1. Set $n = 0$. Choose $\mathbf{v}^{(0)}$, the initial value for the vector of visit ratios.
2. For the given visit ratio vector, obtain the cycle time and related performance measures using the MVA algorithm. Compute the station weights w_i, $i = 1 .. M$.
3. Using the set of weights obtained in step 2, solve a *shortest path problem*. Let $\mathbf{v}^*$ denote the visit ratio vector obtained by sending a unit flow along the shortest path. Note that in this vector, all stations on the shortest path have a visit ratio equal to 1 and all other stations have a visit ratio equal to zero.
4. Compute the incremental delay $b^{(n)}$ and b^* for the vectors $\mathbf{v}^{(n)}$ and $\mathbf{v}^*$, respectively, where
$$b^{(n)} = \sum_i w_i v_i^{(n)} \quad \text{and} \quad b^* = \sum_i w_i v_i^* \tag{2.16}$$
5. (Stopping rule). If $|b^{(n)} - b^*| < \varepsilon$, where $\varepsilon > 0$ is a properly chosen tolerance, then stop; otherwise, go to step 6.
6. Find the value $\alpha, 0 \leq \alpha \leq 1$, such that the flow $\mathbf{v}' = (1-\alpha)\mathbf{v}^{(n)} + \alpha\mathbf{v}^*$ minimizes $CT(N, \mathbf{v})$. Set $\mathbf{v}^{(n+1)} = \mathbf{v}'$.
7. Set $n = n + 1$, and go to step 2.

FIGURE 13-3: The flow deviation (FD) algorithm.

The routing of the messages is specified by the particular choice of the path probabilities. For a given choice of these path probabilities, we can think of the product $w(\phi_j)CT(N, \mathbf{v})$ as being the marginal delay for path ϕ_j. In other words, an increase Δq in the routing probability of path ϕ_j causes an increase of $w(\phi_j)CT(N, \mathbf{v})\Delta q$ in the overall cycle time. Intuitively, at the optimal flow pattern, all paths in use (i.e., all paths for which $q_j > 0$) must have the same marginal delay. Otherwise, if there are two paths ϕ_1 and ϕ_2 in use, such that $w(\phi_1) > w(\phi_2)$, then one can always reduce the cycle time by shifting Δq traffic from path ϕ_1 to path ϕ_2. The corresponding reduction in delay is given by $\Delta CT(N, \mathbf{v}) = \Delta q CT(N, \mathbf{v})[w(\phi_1) - w(\phi_2)]$. Thus, the obvious choice for reducing the cycle time is to shift traffic from one or more paths onto the shortest path.

The algorithm for obtaining the optimal routing, termed the *flow deviation* (FD) algorithm, is shown in Fig. 13-3. The FD algorithm is initialized with a given feasible set of values for the visit ratio vector $\mathbf{v}$. One such vector may be obtained by sending all the flow through path 1, by setting $q_1 = 1$. We let n denote the iteration number.

It can be shown that the function $CT(N, \mathbf{v})$ is convex in $\mathbf{v}$. Hence, any local minimum is a global minimum. Convergence to the global minimum is guaranteed because in each iteration, there is an improvement in the objective function. If no improvement is found, the algorithm stops.

13.3 Analysis of Jobs with Internal Concurrency

Much of our discussion on queuing analysis until now assumed that each customer (or job) receives service sequentially. In dealing with concurrent and parallel programs we come across situations where each job consists of a number of *tasks* with some precedence relations between them. The internal structure of such jobs can be represented by a *task graph* (TG). Depending on the availability of processors, several tasks of the same job could receive service simultaneously. The synchronization requirements between tasks complicate the analysis considerably. In this section, we shall study the performance analysis of such situations.

13.3.1 Generalized Task Graphs

Task graphs are a popular way of representing the internal structure of concurrent programs. The *classical task graphs* are acyclic graphs that contain only the well-known *fork* and *join* (also called *AND-join*) nodes. *Extended task graphs* also include *branch* and *merge* nodes, which allow modeling of loops and conditional branches. Extended task graphs are inadequate for representing situations where several tasks may be initiated concurrently, but not all of them have to finish. For this, we introduce a *max node* in extended task graphs, which requires only one computation to finish among a set of *competing computations*. We call the resulting model a *generalized task graph* (GTG).

A task graph can be viewed as a high-level timed Petri net where the tasks behave like timed transitions and each arc implicitly passes through a single-input, single-output place. With this in mind, we can freely use the Petri net terminology.[1] For example, it is convenient to view the task graph execution in terms of "tokens" moving along its arcs (or places) and firing the tasks (or transitions). We could use any type of timing semantics, but for convenience we assume it to be AF/SS. The execution of a task graph starts in a *marking* M_0 wherein there is one token on the *initial arc* a_s, and none on others. The execution terminates whenever a marking, in which there is a token on the *terminal arc* a_d, is reached. With each task node we associate an input label (IL) and an output label (OL), which indicate its *firing rule*. These labels could be $*$, $+$ or @. The first two of these concern extended task graphs, and we shall explain them first.

Let i be some node of the task graph. Then $OL[i] = *$ indicates the fork operation at this node; i.e., when the execution of task t_i is finished, one token will be released along each of the outgoing arcs of node i. The label $IL[i] = *$ represents a join operation; i.e., one token is accepted from each of the incoming arcs of node i, and task t_i becomes active. (The task remains inactive until this happens.) The labels $OL[i] = +$ and $IL[i] = +$ represent, respectively,

[1] The reader is urged to review sections 12.1.1, 12.1.2, and 12.2.1, since we shall be using the concepts discussed there extensively.

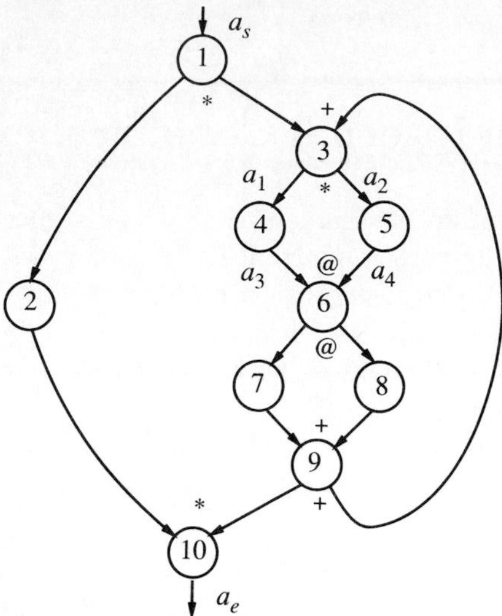

FIGURE 13-4: A generalized task graph.

the branch (i.e., nondeterministic selection) and merge operations. These also have obvious interpretations in terms of the token movement. Fig. 13-4 shows the use of these labels. Here the completion of task t_1 initiates the execution of tasks t_2 and t_3, and therefore, $OL[1] = *$. Task t_{10} can be initiated only after tasks t_2 and t_9 have completed, and therefore, $IL[10] = *$. Task t_3 can be initiated either because of the completion of task t_1 or of task t_9, and therefore $IL[3] = +$. Finally, the completion of task t_9 can initiate either task t_{10} or task t_3 (but not both), which means $OL[9] = +$. Notice that each time this task graph is initiated, the computation between nodes 3 and 9 will be repeated a certain number of times. This looping capability would not be possible without the branch and merge nodes.

We call a node i with $IL[i] = @$ as a *max node*. This label represents the *OR-join* type of situation; i.e., as soon as any of its predecessor computation finishes, task t_i can be initiated. For example, in Fig. 13-4, task t_6 can start execution as soon as task t_4 or task t_5 are finished. Although this behavior is identical to the one for a merge node, the two types of nodes are used in different contexts. An OR-join is used in situations where several tasks may be started in parallel (with a fork), but only one of them has to finish. This means that some action must be taken with respect to the *loser tasks*. In contrast, a merge node is intended for merging together various branches of a probabilistic branch node, and thus does not involve any "competing tasks".

A max node is useful for representing parallel implementation of state space search problems (theorem proving, query processing in replicated databases, VLSI layout, etc.) where several paths may be explored in parallel, but we only care for one of the probes to succeed. Modeling of fault-tolerant systems requires the more general k-out-of-n type selection capability, but that can also be im-

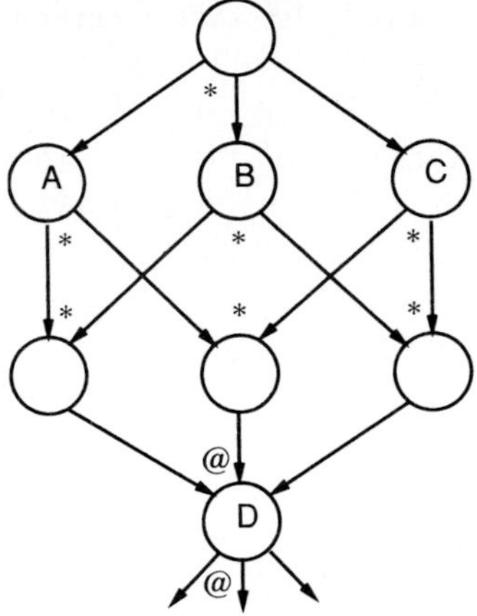

FIGURE 13-5: A 2-out-of-3 operation implemented via a max node.

plemented using the max node. Fig. 13-5 shows how the behavior of a triple modular redundant (TMR) system can be represented using the max node. Here node D should fire if at least two of the three subsystems, represented as tasks A, B, and C, succeed.

An output label of @ is also allowed, but is interpreted in a special way. First, such a label can appear on the output-end of only a max node. We call the combination a $\frac{@}{@}$ node. Although not necessary, we shall assume that a $\frac{@}{@}$ node has an equal number of input and output arcs, with a one-to-one mapping between them. This mapping is used in selecting the next task to be executed following the firing of the $\frac{@}{@}$ node. This is illustrated in Fig. 13-4. Here t_5 represents a computation that must finish by some deadline. The timer task for enforcing the deadline is represented by task t_4. Task t_6 can be assumed to be "null"; i.e., take zero time. If the timer expires before t_5 finishes, task t_7 (i.e., the exception handler) is initiated. If instead, t_5 finishes before the deadline, the control goes to task t_8. (To avoid clutter, we have kept the mapping implicit in this example; i.e., we have assumed a left-to-right association between the input and the output arcs.)

As indicated above, a max-node specification is incomplete without the rules for handling the *loser tasks*. For example, suppose that in Fig. 13-4, task t_4 finishes before task t_5. Then the completion of task t_5 is irrelevant for further progress of the task graph, and to avoid problems in the case of loops, we must abort it (i.e., remove the corresponding token from the task graph). In general, any ongoing computations that could potentially disrupt the functioning of the max node, must be aborted. Therefore, with each max node t_i, we associated a set of arcs, known as its *enabling set*, denoted ${}^{@}t_i$. It can be defined as follows:

1. If x is an input arc of node i, then $x \in {}^{@}t_i$.
2. If x is an input arc of a predecessor node of i and there exists a marking in which x and the input arcs of node i are both marked, then $x \in {}^{@}t_i$.

Notice that because of the assumption of AF semantics, the tokens are not absorbed by active tasks until the computation is finished. Therefore, to abort computations, it is enough to simply remove tokens on the input arcs. This is the reason for defining the enabling set in terms of the arcs. According to this definition, in Fig. 13-4, ${}^{@}t_6 = \{a_1, a_2, a_3, a_4\}$. Notice that even though node 3 is a predecessor of node 6, ${}^{@}t_i$ cannot get marked simultaneously with a_3 or a_4. Therefore, the input arcs of node 3 do not belong to ${}^{@}t_6$. The enabling set of a max node can be constructed using reachability analysis on some relevant portion of the task graph; however, under certain weak restrictions, the reachability analysis can be avoided. We shall omit discussion on these restrictions here.

A generalized task graph (GTG) may not represent a meaningful parallel computation, because (1) it may suffer from deadlock, (2) certain tasks may never be processed, and (3) a task may be reinstantiated while it is already being processed. We call a task graph *well-formed* or *legal* if it is free of these problems. Checking for the legality of a task graph is a fundamental problem, and can be addressed by exploiting the equivalence between task graphs and restricted classes of Petri nets. In this respect, *classical task graphs are equivalent to decision-free Petri nets and extended task graphs to free-choice Petri nets*. The Petri net representation for a GTG requires the ability to count, which makes them more powerful than the extended task graphs. In the following, we briefly characterize well-formed GTG's.

There are two fundamental properties for characterizing well-formed task graphs: liveness and safeness. To define these, let M_0 denote the initial marking in which only the initial arc is marked, and let $\mathcal{M}$ denote the corresponding reachability set. We say that a task t is *live* if there exists a marking in $\mathcal{M}$ that can fire t; otherwise t is *dead*. This definition is different from the one in Section 12.1.2, since we no longer insist that t be firable starting from any marking in $\mathcal{M}$. We say that *the task graph is live*, if from every marking in $\mathcal{M}$, there exists a sequence of firings of tasks that enables the terminal task. Note that the liveness of a task graph (TG) is not equivalent to the liveness of its terminal task. The reason for defining task-liveness as different from the TG-liveness is that in any given execution of the TG, we always want the terminal task to fire, but other tasks may or may not fire. The definition of safeness is identical to the one for Petri nets; i.e., a task graph is *safe* if there is at most one token on any arc in every marking in $\mathcal{M}$. We call a task graph *well-formed* if and only if (a) it is live, (b) it is safe, and (c) each of its tasks is live.

Fig. 13-6 shows four examples of illegal task graphs. The TG in Fig. 13-6(a) is neither live nor safe because if arc (3,4) is selected at node 3, the terminal task t_6 cannot fire, but task t_4 is initiated twice. All tasks in the TG of Fig. 13-6(b) are live (with our definition), but there is a sequence of firings such that the terminal task cannot fire, hence the TG is dead. Such a sequence starts out with $(t_1, \ldots, t_6, t_2)$, after which t_4 can fire, but t_5 cannot, which in turn means that t_7 cannot fire. The TG of Fig. 13-6(c) is live but unsafe because task t_5 gets initiated twice. Fig. 13-6(d) shows a live and safe TG in which task t_8 is dead. (Firability of task t_8 is not crucial here because of the max node.)

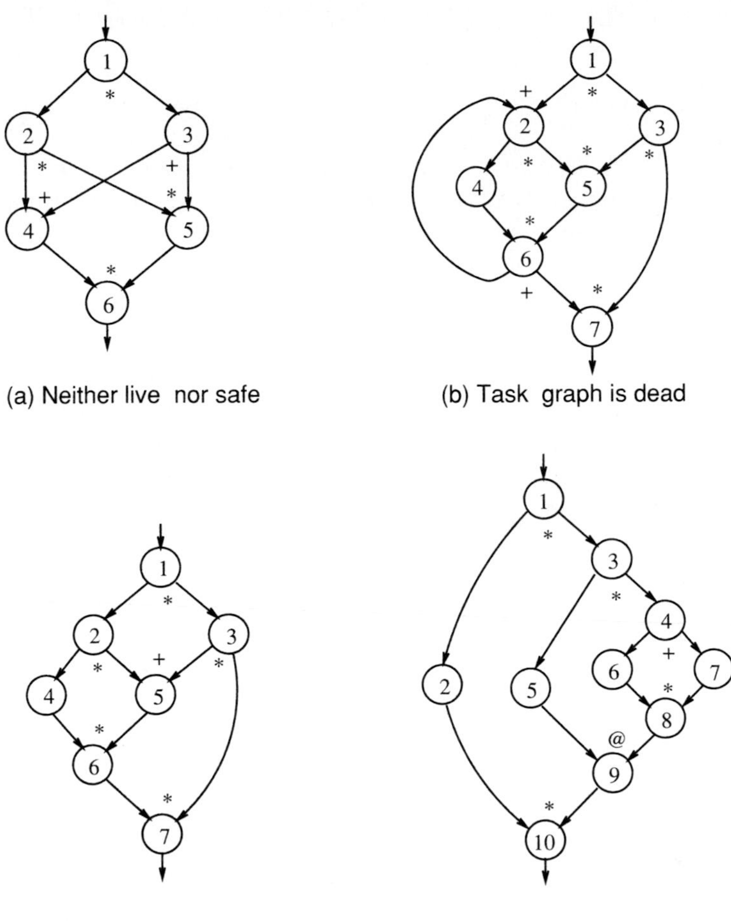

(a) Neither live nor safe

(b) Task graph is dead

(c) Live but not safe

(d) Live but t_8 is dead

FIGURE 13-6: Illustration of some illegal task graphs.

Now we state the main results on well-formedness. If we connect the initial and terminal arcs of a TG, we call the resulting TG a *persistent task graph* or PTG. It is easy to show that the original TG is well-formed if and only if its PTG is live and safe. Thus, a straightforward approach for checking legality is to generate the reachability set for the PTG and examine each marking for liveness and safeness properties. This will have exponential complexity in the number of tasks. Unfortunately, we cannot do any better in the worst case since the legality problem for free-choice Petri nets (and hence for GTG's) is NP-complete. However, by exploiting the structural properties we can often do much better in the average case. This is done in terms of traps and siphons, which are constructed much as stated in Section 12.1.3. (A label @ is treated much like + in this construction.) The final result, under some mild restrictions, turns out to be similar to the one for free-choice Petri nets. That is,

Lemma 13.1 (Liveness theorem). A GTG is live if and only if every siphon contains a trap.

□

Let us denote the type of a node i using the notation $\frac{IL[i]}{OL[i]}$. In this notation, if the label could be arbitrary, we shall denote it as "$\cdot$". It is easy to see from Lemma 13.1 that a GTG whose tasks are all either of types $\frac{*}{*}$ and $\frac{@}{*}$, or of types $\frac{+}{+}$ and $\frac{@}{+}$, is live. As for the safeness problem, we need to consider all subtask graphs defined over the siphons. That is, we have the following result:

Lemma 13.2 (Safeness theorem). A live PTG is safe if and only if for each of its minimal siphon S, the persistent subtask graph σ_S defined over it is safe. Furthermore, σ_S is safe if and only if for every pair of nodes t_1 and t_2 such that (a) t_1 is of $\frac{\cdot}{*}$ type, (b) t_2 is of $\frac{+}{\cdot}$ type, and (c) t_2 is a successor of t_1, t_1 and t_2 belong to different biconnected components.

□

A few special results now follow easily. First, a GTG whose tasks are all either of types $\frac{*}{*}$ and $\frac{@}{*}$, or of types $\frac{+}{+}$ and $\frac{@}{+}$, is well-formed. Second, for the special case where there are no $\frac{@}{\cdot}$ nodes, we can conclude Hack's theorem in Lemma 12.2 as a special case.

13.3.2 Multiserver with 1-Level Task Graphs

In this section we consider the problem of analyzing the performance of an isolated M/M/c system where the jobs consist of k tasks, all of which can be executed in parallel. The job arrivals are Poisson with rate λ, and the service time of the ith task of a job is exponentially distributed with mean rate of $\mu(i)$. The analysis has obvious applications in studying the performance of a tightly-coupled multiprocessor system running parallel programs. We consider the following two cases:

1. Max node semantics where only one of the k tasks needs to be processed. This situation arises in parallel-search algorithms, as mentioned above.
2. Fork-join semantics where all k tasks must be processed. This situation arises when the given problem can be partitioned into several subproblems, all of which can be run in parallel.

1. Jobs with Max node Semantics

Let c denote the number of servers (or processors) in the system, and let $c = qk+r$ for $0 \le r < k$. Here the "quotient" q represents the number of jobs that can be fully loaded simultaneously. We assume that $q \ge 1$, because, otherwise, it is useless to have k subtasks. If we adopt the policy of allocating as many tasks of a job simultaneously as possible, we will have at most one job with partial allocation of r processors. There are $m = \binom{k}{r}$ ways of choosing r tasks for a partial allocation from a total of k tasks. We can number these possibilities sequentially from $1..m$. We assume that whenever a partial allocation is to be done, we choose among these possibilities equiprobably. Also, whenever a fully loaded task completes and there is also a partially loaded task, we load all remaining tasks of the latter and then consider the situation as if a new partial allocation is to be made. Then the state of the Markov chain can be described by the pair (n, j) where n is the number of jobs in the system and $j \in 1..m$. For $n \leq q$, there is no partial loading, and the behavior is exactly as for a M/M/q system. That is, the initial q probabilities can be obtained in terms of $P(0,0)$ using the standard M/M/q formula. For the rest, let us define the partial generating function as

$$G_j(z) = \sum_{n=q+1}^{\infty} z^n P(n,j) \qquad \text{for } j = 1..m \tag{3.1}$$

Using the global balance equations for $n \geq q$, it is easy to obtain an expression for $G_j(z)$. We shall omit the details and only report the final result in the following:

$$G_j(z) = \frac{\lambda P(q,0) z^{q+1}}{[\lambda - \lambda z + \eta(j)] \sum_{i=1}^{m} \frac{\eta(i)-\lambda z}{\lambda - \lambda z + \eta(i)}} \tag{3.2}$$

Let $V(i)$ denote the set of indices of the allocated tasks of a partially allocated job. Then the $\eta(i)$ parameter is defined as follows:

$$\eta(i) = \sum_{j=1}^{k} \mu(j) + \sum_{j \in V(i)} \mu(j) \tag{3.3}$$

The rest of the analysis is now routine. For example, $P(0,0)$ can be found by the requirement that $\sum_{n=0}^{q} P(n,0) + \sum_{j=1}^{m} G_j(1) = 1$. The number of jobs in the system is simply $1/k$th the number of tasks. Applying Little's law, we easily get the job response time.

2. Jobs with Fork-join Semantics

Here we assume that all tasks of a job have the same mean service time ($= 1/\mu$). However, it is possible to let the number of splits be a random variable, henceforth denoted as K. Let $\alpha_1, \alpha_2, \ldots$ denote the mass function of K, and $\Phi_K(z)$ its generating function. Thus, each job spawns some number of statistically identical tasks, all of which must be processed. Then, the system can be modeled as a classical $M^{(X)}/M/c$ queue, i.e., a M/M/c queue fed by bulk arrivals. The analysis of this system is much like that of the $M^{(X)}/M/1$ system in Section 5.6.1. Using the global balance equations, it is easy to find the z-transform of the number of tasks in the system, and it turns out to be

$$\Phi(z) = \frac{A(z)\mu(z-1)}{\lambda z[1 - \Phi_K(z)] + c\mu(z-1)} \qquad \text{where } A(z) = \sum_{i=0}^{c-1} (c-i)\pi_i z^i \tag{3.4}$$

where π_i is the probability of an initial state i. Here $\pi_1, \ldots, \pi_{c-1}$ can be computed in terms of π_0 using the global balance equations. Let $\rho = \lambda/\mu$. Then, $\pi_1 = \rho\pi_0$, and for $0 < n < c$,

$$(n+1)\pi_{n+1} = (n+\rho)\pi_n + \rho\sum_{i=0}^{n-1}\alpha_{n-i}\pi_i \tag{3.5}$$

Thus, we can obtain the moments of the number of tasks in the system as usual. A more interesting problem is to find the average *job response time* R_{job}. We can write this as $R_{\text{job}} = W' + E[S]$ where W' is the average waiting time of the first task of a job to go into service, and $E[S]$ is the average time needed from then on to service all tasks of the job. To get W', we start with an expression for the waiting line length L. Obviously $L = Q - \rho$, where ρ is the average number of busy servers. That is,

$$L = Q - c + \sum_{i=0}^{c-1}(c-i)\pi_i \tag{3.6}$$

where the summation term gives the average number of idle servers. In this expression, Q can be obtained as $\Phi'(1)$, as usual. Note that W' is different from W, the average waiting time of a random task. W' has two components:

1. Delay caused by customers that the first task finds waiting upon arrival. Since the jobs arrive according to a Poisson process, the PASTA property (see Section 9.2.1) holds for the first task to go in service. Therefore, the waiting line length seen by the first task is L, which implies that the delay caused by it is simply $L/(c\mu)$.
2. If all servers are busy (which happens with probability $1 - \sum_{i=0}^{c-1}\pi_i$), the task must wait for the residual life of a task in service. Since the service-time distribution is exponential, the residual life is simply $1/(c\mu)$.

Summing the two terms, we get the following expression for W'

$$W' = \frac{L + 1 - \sum_{i=0}^{c-1}\pi_i}{c\mu} \tag{3.7}$$

Let us now see how $E[S]$ can be computed. For this, we shall first compute the *conditional expectation* $E[S|k]$, i.e., the expected service time of a tagged job $\mathcal{A}$ that consists of k tasks. Let $s_{i,n}$ denote the mean service time of a job that had exactly i tasks scheduled initially and still has n tasks to be completed (waiting or in service). It is easy to verify that $s_{i,n}$'s must satisfy the following difference equations

$$\begin{aligned}
s_{1,1} &= 1/\mu \\
s_{n,n} &= s_{n-1,n-1} + 1/(n\mu) \qquad \text{for } 1 \le n \le c \\
s_{c,n} &= 1/(c\mu) + s_{c,n-1}, \qquad \text{for } n > c \\
s_{i,n} &= 1/(c\mu) + i\, s_{i,n-1}/c + (c-i)s_{i+1,n}/c, \qquad \text{for } 1 \le i < \min(c,n)
\end{aligned} \tag{3.8}$$

For example, let us consider the fourth equation. Since $i < \min(c, n)$, all c processors must be busy following the allocation of i tasks of $\mathcal{A}$. Therefore, the completion rate in "state" (i, n) is $c\mu$. Because of the exponential service-time distribution, any one of the c tasks in service is equally likely to be completed next; therefore, the probability that the completed task will belong to the job $\mathcal{A}$ is simply $q = i/c$. Thus, with probability q, we go to "state" $(i, n-1)$, and with probability $1-q$ we go to "state" $(i+1, n)$. (Since not all tasks of $\mathcal{A}$ have yet been scheduled, a new task of $\mathcal{A}$ will be put into service immediately in both cases.)

If all servers are busy when $\mathcal{A}$ is at the head of the queue, then only one of its tasks can be allocated initially. If $i < c$ servers are busy, we can initially schedule $\min(k, c-i)$ servers for $\mathcal{A}$. Therefore, $E[S|k]$ can be obtained as

$$E[S|k] = (1 - \sum_{i=0}^{c-1} \pi_i) s_{1,k} + \sum_{i=0}^{c-1} \pi_i s_{\min\{k,c-i\},k} \tag{3.9}$$

Finally, we can obtain $E[S]$ as

$$E[S] = \sum_{k=1}^{\infty} E[S|k] Pr(K = k) \tag{3.10}$$

13.3.3 Multiserver with 2-Level Task Graphs

In this section we consider the same problem as in the last section except that the job is now represented by a 2-level tree. That is, each job consists of a header task or *phase-1 task*, and k subtasks or *phase-2 tasks*. The header task can be one of three types $+$, $*$, or @, and identifies the nature of jobs. The label $+$ means a probabilistic select among the phase-2 tasks following the execution of the phase-1 task. The label $*$ means a standard fork-join semantics; i.e., all phase-2 tasks must be executed for the job to be finished. The label @ represents a standard max node semantics; i.e., several phase-2 tasks may be started, but only one needs to finish, and all others are aborted at that time. We assume that all phase-2 tasks are statistically identical. The service rates of phase-1 and phase-2 tasks are μ_1 and μ_2 respectively.

If the jobs are of $+$ type, there is no internal concurrency, and the problem is uninteresting. (The problem reduces to a M/G/c system for which we can easily obtain bounds as discussed in Section 9.2.4). So, we consider only the other two cases.

Before starting, we need to specify the policy for selecting between the two types of tasks. From a practical point of view, it seems most reasonable to give higher priority to phase-2 tasks; i.e., whenever a processor is freed, give it to a phase-2 task, if there are any. This strategy minimizes the number of partially processed jobs in the system and thereby the response time. Fortunately, this is also the easiest to analyze, since it ensures a finite upper bound on the number of phase-2 tasks in the system. In contrast, a nonprioritized scheme would result in a potentially unbounded number of tasks of both types, thereby requiring two-dimensional z-transforms for analysis.

1. Jobs with Fork-join Semantics

Let n_i denote the number of phase-i tasks in the system and s_i the number of phase-i tasks in service. Obviously, $s_2 = \min(c - s_1, n_2)$, $0 \le s_1 \le c$, and because of the priority mechanism $0 \le n_2 \le k(c - s_1)$. We can represent the state of the system by the triple (n_1, n_2, s_1). Let us define the partial generating functions as follows:

$$\Phi(z, n_2, s_1) = \sum_{i=s_1}^{\infty} z^i P(i, n_2, s_1) \qquad s_1 = 0\,..\,c,\; n_2 = (c - s_1)\,..\,(c - s_1)k \quad (3.11)$$

We could then get $O(kc^2)$ simultaneous linear equations for $\Phi(z, n_2, s_1)$ using the global balance condition. These equations can be put in the matrix form $AX = B$. Here the vector X can be expressed as $(X_c, X_{c-1}, \ldots, X_0)$ where X_i is itself a vector of $\Phi(z, n_2, i)$'s with $n_2 = (c-i), \ldots, (c-i)k$. Vector B can similarly be viewed as the vector $(B_c, B_{c-1}, \ldots, B_0)$ where B_i is itself a vector compatible with X_i. The square matrix A can also be a viewed as a $(c+1) \times (c+1)$ matrix of matrices. It is interesting to note that A is block tridiagonal. Each element A_{ii} is itself a square matrix of size $(c-i)(k-1)+1$, whereas the elements $A_{i,j-1}$ and $A_{i,j+1}$ are rectangular matrices compatible with A_{ii}. The main difficulty in dealing with this system is that the z-transform involves c initial probabilities, of which $c-1$ must be obtained from the poles of the generating function. This requires obtaining the denominator symbolically using the $AX = B$ system. The overall complexity of computing the generating function is rather high $[O(k^5c^9)]$, because of the need of a lot of symbolic computation. Fortunately, this system can also be put in M/M/1 canonical form with complex boundary behavior and thus has an explicit matrix-geometric solution.

Note that the direct solution only gives the queue-length moments of individual tasks of each type. Our main concern in solving the problem is finding the overall job response time. We examine this problem briefly now. Let T denote the job response time. Then,

$$E[T] = E[T_1] + E[W] + E[S] \quad (3.12)$$

where $E[T_1]$ is the average response time for phase-1 tasks, and $E[W]$ is the average time that phase-2 tasks of a job wait in queue before the first task in its group enters the server. (Since phase-2 tasks come into being only when phase-1 finishes, it is correct to add $E[W]$ to $E[T_1]$.) $E[S]$ is the average service time required to complete all phase-2 tasks of the job once the first phase-2 task starts execution. Of these, $E[T_1]$ can be obtained as usual, but the other two are more involved. $E[W]$ is obtained by considering the distribution seen by the phase-2 tasks of a job when they are generated and $E[S]$ by a technique similar to the one when no header is present. Again, for brevity, we omit the details. The general results from the analysis are finishes, it is correct to add $E[W]$ to $E[T_1]$.) $E[S]$ is the average service time required to complete all phase-2 tasks of the job once the first phase-2 task starts execution. Of these, $E[T_1]$ can be obtained using the moment generation property of z-transforms, but the other two are more involved. $E[W]$ is obtained by considering the distribution seen by the phase-2 tasks of a job when they are generated and $E[S]$ by a technique similar to the one when no header is present. Again, for brevity, we omit the details. The general results from the analysis are as expected. The job response time increases with number of splits, and decreases with the number of processors. Since this system is conservative, the expression for utilization (and hence the stability condition) is trivial to find. In particular, $U = \lambda/(c\mu_1) + k\lambda/(c\mu_2)$.

2. Jobs with Max node Semantics

Here again, the state of the system can be represented by the triple (n_1, n_2, s_1) with the same interpretations and range of values for n_i and s_i as for the fork-join case. Furthermore, since all phase-2 tasks are removed as soon as one of them finishes, n_2 is further restricted to be a multiple of k. Thus, we can identify a state by the triplet (n_1, i, j) where $i = n_2/k$ and $j = s_2 - i$. (Here j represents the number of duplicate phase-2 tasks being processed.) Next we write balance equations for $P(n, i, j)$ and then find the partial generating functions $\Phi(z, i, j)$ as usual. This will result in a large number of simultaneous equations that must be solved symbolically. However, a careful look at the equations reveals a number of symmetries that can be exploited to do the solution in $O(c^5)$ time instead of $O(c^6)$ time. Here again we encounter the difficulty that the equations contain c unknown probabilities; therefore, we must have $c - 1$ poles of the generating function in the unit disk. The details are extremely involved and are omitted. Note that the abortion of loser phase-2 tasks of a job makes this system nonconservative; therefore, even the stability condition is nontrivial to get. However, once the generating functions are known, the computation of job response time is easy. Let T denote the job response time. Then we can write

$$E[T] = E[T_1] + E[T_2] \tag{3.13}$$

where T_i is the response time of phase-i. This simple relationship results from the fact that (a) phase-2 tasks of a job come into being only after the phase-1 task is done, and (b) only one of the phase-2 tasks need to finish for the job to be completed. $E[T_i]$'s can be computed easily from the moment generating property and Little's law. In applying Little's law to phase-2, note that the throughput is λ, rather than $k\lambda$, since only one task is allowed to finish and all others are destroyed immediately.

We can note some interesting results for this system. Fig. 13-7 shows a plot of job response time as a function of k for different values of the loading factor ρ (assuming $\mu_1 = \mu_2 = \mu$). The response time decreases as the number of phase-2 tasks increases, thereby making the parallel execution of phase-2 tasks worthwhile. However, there is no significant gain in increasing the number of phase-2 tasks beyond some rather small limit (four in this case). The response

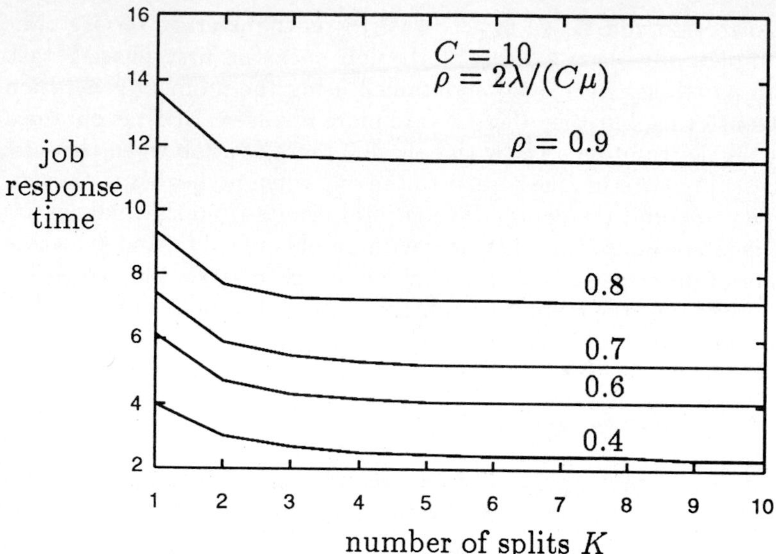

FIGURE 13-7: Job response time at different values of k and ρ.

if prioritized scheduling is abandoned or the service-time distribution is non-exponential, the problem immediately becomes intractable. This points to the need for approximate analysis. In the next subsection we present one possible approach for dealing with arbitrary task graphs.

13.3.4 Analysis of Queuing Networks

In this section we consider the analysis of a closed queuing network driven by jobs with internal concurrency. The stations of the network may represent different devices (CPU, channels, etc.) or entire nodes in a distributed system. Fig. 13-8 shows the overall structure of the queuing system. The "arrival station" is a delay-server whose purpose is to generate jobs. In a real system, this station would be a terminal or a work-station submitting the jobs. We assume that all N jobs are represented by a common underlying extended task graph, whose tasks have exponentially distributed service times.[2] We shall number the jobs as $1..N$. We also allow for a *passive resource constraint* (e.g., the memory or buffer limitation) inside the central subsystem (CS) portion of the network. The passive resource is represented by *tokens*, and each task needs to acquire one token in order to execute inside the CS.

When job $j \in 1..N$ leaves the *arrival station*, all its K tasks are created. Of these, the *initial task* is put at the end of the *blocked queue*, and all others into the jth *enter queue*. Tasks are loaded into the CS from the blocked queue according to a FCFS policy and executed. When a running task belonging to

[2]The branch and merge nodes allow a common underlying task graph representation even when the jobs in the real system have differing structures.

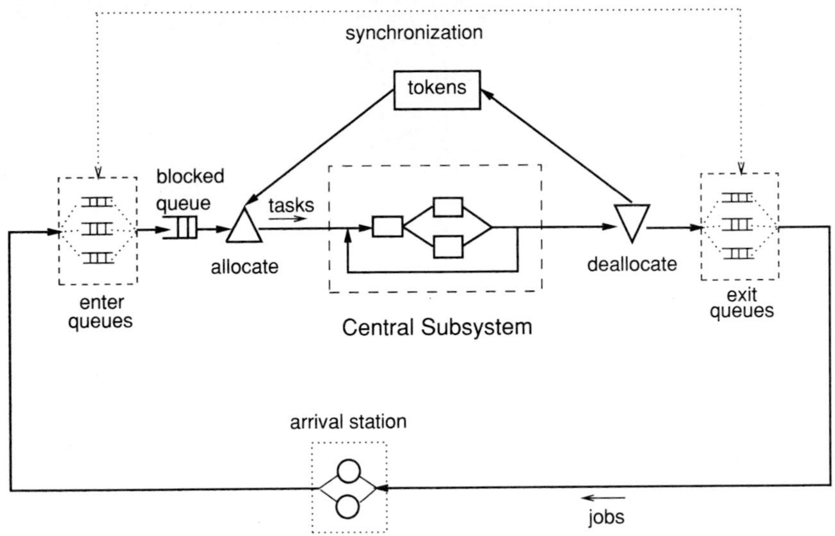

FIGURE 13-8: A model of a computer system running jobs with internal concurrency.

the jth job leaves the CS, it is put into the jth *exit queue*. A task from an enter queue is removed and put into the blocked queue immediately after its precedence conditions are satisfied (i.e., an appropriate set of its predecessor tasks are present in the jth exit queue). After the terminal task belonging to the jth job arrives at its exit queue, all the tasks in the jth exit queue are removed from the system, and a new job is created, which goes to the arrival station.

At any time, a task may be in one of three states: inactive, blocked, or loaded. The last two refer to the situations where a task is waiting to get a token (after its precedence conditions have been satisfied) or executing inside the CS. In both cases, we call the task as *active*. In other cases, we call the task as *inactive*. The delays that a task t encounters are its blocking delay B_t, its CS response time $R_t^{(cs)}$, and its average inactive period ID_t. The total task response time, denoted R_t, is simply $R_t^{(cs)} + B_t$. (All parameters here are average values.) The *loading probability* of task t, denoted ρ_t, is defined as the probability that task t is loaded given that it is active.

The input parameters of the system are the task graph topology, delay at the external arrival station (ED), job population (N), number of available tokens (M), CS structure, and the service demand of each task at each station (D_{tk}). The performance parameters of interest are task response time (R_t), job response time (R) and throughput (λ), and *token utilization* (U). Here U is defined as the average fraction of tokens in use.

The solution technique is approximate and involves iterating between two different models. The first model is the *high-level task graph* (HLTG) model, whose purpose is to estimate *synchronization delays*. These delays are those

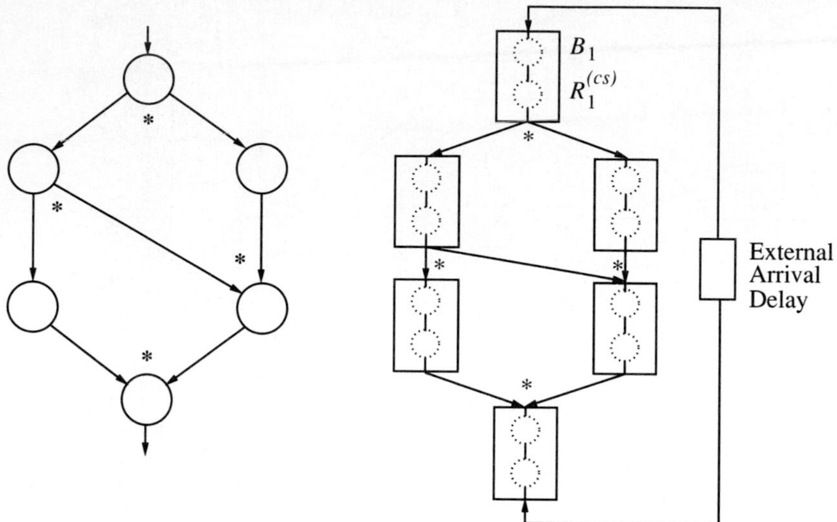

FIGURE 13-9: A task graph and its HLTG model.

caused because of the precedence constraints. The second model is the *high-level queuing network* (HLQN) model, whose purpose is to compute the queuing and blocking delays. The HLTG model is calibrated by using the results of the HLQN model and vice versa. The HLTG model is identical to the original task graph except that (a) it has an extra node representing the external arrival delay, which is connected to the initial and the final arcs, and (b) the average processing time of task t is its response times R_t. Fig. 13-9 shows a sample task graph and the corresponding HLTG model. There are N HLTG models, one for each job.

The main assumption in solving a HLTG model is that the processing times of its nodes are exponentially distributed, and we shall comment on its accuracy later. Under this assumption, we can represent the behavior of a HLTG by a Markov chain with states given by $\mathbf{S} = (s_1, \ldots, s_K)$, where s_i is 1 if the ith task is active and 0 otherwise. The state transition rates are governed by the completion rates $1/R_t$'s. Note that the state (0,...,0) represents the situation where all tasks of a job are inactive; i.e., the job is at the arrival station. The solution to this Markov chain provides us the distribution of the number of active tasks. For brevity, we shall indicate the use of this distribution for further calculations without giving any actual equations.

We first estimate the loading probability ρ_t as $R_t^{(cs)}/R_t$. Assuming that each task acts independently, we could then compute $\beta_t^{(s)}(j|\mathbf{S})$, which is the probability that j tasks of types other than t are loaded (and none of type t are loaded) given that the system is in state $\mathbf{S}$. (The superscript s on β indicates that we are talking about a single job right now.) Furthermore, by assuming that each job itself acts independently, we can compute $\beta_t(j|n)$, which is the probability that j tasks of type other than t are loaded, given that a total of n tasks of type

t are active. (Here we are talking about all N jobs; therefore, n ranges from 0 to N). We could then compute $\alpha_t(j|n)$, which denotes the probability that j tasks of type t are loaded when n tasks of the same type are active. Let $\mathbf{L}_t(j,n)$ denote the vector of the average number of tasks of each type that are loaded in the CS when n tasks of type t are active, j of which are loaded. The components of $\mathbf{L}_t(j,n)$ can also be computed from the HLTG by simple probabilistic arguments.

The HLTG model also gives us the throughput λ_t of each task t. Let λ_0 denote the throughput of the *initial task*. This is the same as the effective departure rate from the arrival station; therefore, by the utilization law $\lambda_0 = P(0,\ldots,0)/ED$. The throughputs of other tasks are then computed by multiplying this by their respective *flow rates*. These flow rates can be computed easily from linear equations relating token flow rates of various nodes in the task graph. It is important to realize that these throughputs are on a per job basis, rather than for all N jobs. With this in mind and applying Little's law to the entire network, we can compute ID_t as $1/\lambda_t - E[R_t]$.

Next, we consider the HLQN model. There is one such model for each of the K task types. The HLQN model for task t is a closed, single chain network with population of N that consists of two stations: a delay station representing the inactive period ID_t, and a flow-equivalent aggregate station representing the CS. We have already seen how to estimate ID_t. The only thing remaining is to estimate $\mu_t(n)$, the mean service rate of the aggregate station when there are n type t tasks there. We estimate $\mu_t(n)$ by using Norton's theorem, much as we did in Section 8.2.1 to model memory constraints. Let $\mathbf{x} = (x_1,\ldots,x_K)$ denote the population vector of the CS, and $\phi_t(\mathbf{x})$ the corresponding mean departure rate of type t tasks. We can compute this last parameter by solving the CS in isolation with population $\mathbf{x}$. Then by using the same ideas as in modeling memory constraints in a multiple-chain environment, we can write

$$\mu_t(n) \approx \sum_{j=1}^{n} \alpha_t(j|n)\, \phi_t[\mathbf{L}_t(j,n)] \tag{3.14}$$

Thus, we can calibrate and solve the HLQN model much as in Section 8.2.1. This gives us R_t and $R_t^{(cs)}$, which can be used for the next iteration on the HLTG.

Let us look at some experimental results concerning the expense and accuracy of the approximation. Over 244 test cases, the average absolute relative errors for the system throughput, token (or resource) utilization, and task response times were found to be 5.9%, 7.9%, and 9.5% respectively. The average tolerance error in response time, defined as the absolute error divided by the cycle time, was 1.5%. Generally, the algorithm performs very well when the token utilization is less then 90% and the task graph is such that the assumption of exponentially distributed response times is reasonable. However, in other cases, it may lead to severe errors.

13.4 Modeling Fault-Tolerant Systems

In this section, we consider the measures of interest for fault-tolerant computer systems and their estimation. We shall discuss both the classical reliability and more general performability concepts in this regard. In either case, much of the analysis is based on the Markovian modeling concepts discussed in Chapter 5. However, unlike pure performance modeling, a steady-state analysis is either meaningless or inadequate. For example, no steady state can exist in a non-repairable system. Even in a repairable system, the failures typically are too infrequent and repairs are too prompt to have any significant impact on the long-term behavior. Yet, the behavior of the system after failure and during repair is of utmost importance. Thus, the main emphasis of this section will be on transient analysis.

13.4.1 Reliability Modeling

The *reliability* of a system, denoted $R(t)$, is defined as the probability that the system remains operational by time t given that it was started in perfect condition at time 0. Let T denote the time of first failure and $F(t)$ its distribution function. Then $R(t) = P(T > t) = 1 - F(t)$. The fractional rate of change in $F(t)$ is known as the *hazard rate* or *failure rate*, denoted $\lambda(t)$. Expressed in terms of $R(t)$, it is given by

$$\lambda(t) = -\frac{1}{R(t)}\frac{dR(t)}{dt} \tag{4.1}$$

If T is exponentially distributed, $\lambda(t)$ is independent of t and is simply the rate parameter of the distribution. Depending on the situation, an increasing failure rate (e.g., when modeling the effect of "aging") or a decreasing failure rate (e.g., when modeling the maturing of a fabrication process) may be more realistic. A common distribution in reliability modeling is the *Weibull distribution*, for which

$$\lambda(t) = \frac{1}{F(t)}\frac{dF(t)}{dt} = \alpha\beta(\beta t)^{\alpha-1} \tag{4.2}$$

The rate for this distribution increases with t if $\alpha > 1$ and decreases if $\alpha < 1$.

There are a few other measures closely related to reliability. The *mission time*, sometimes also known as *life-time*, is defined as the time t when $R(t)$ drops below a given threshold. When comparing two systems, one can use the ratio of their life times, often called *mission time improvement*, as an indicator of how much better one system is over the other. The mean of the distribution $F(t)$ is called "mean time to failure" (MTTF). Similarly, we can define mean time to repair (MTTR), and mean time between failures (MTBF) which is MTTF + MTTR. The availability (or, more accurately, the *steady-state availability*), defined as the probability of the system being operational, is then given by MTTR / MTBF. However, if a preventive maintenance is involved, the real availability could be different from this.

As an example of the application of the above concepts, consider the problem of aircraft maintenance. Suppose that the aircraft has a constant failure rate λ of one per two years of *continuous flying time*, but it goes through maintenance every d hours. Each maintenance takes, on the average, h hours, and restores the aircraft to the perfect operating condition. Then the availability of the aircraft is $d/(d+h)$, even though the MTTF would be a very long time period. Now, suppose that it is considered risky to fly the aircraft if the probability of failure increases to 0.0001. Then, it is easy to calculate the mission time, which will give the maximum time for which the aircraft can be flown between successive maintenance events.

Let $\mathcal{S}$ denote the system of interest. In general, $\mathcal{S}$ will consist of a number of components, some of which are possibly redundant. The redundancy may be helpful in fault detection (as in self-checking circuits), in fault masking (as in N-modular systems), in continuous operation (as in hot or cold standby systems), or in graceful degradation (as in transparent multiprocessing systems). In any case, the redundancy will allow $\mathcal{S}$ to tolerate a certain number of component failures before $\mathcal{S}$ becomes unable to provide an adequate level of service (in terms of fault-detection ability, masking ability, adequate performance level, etc.) Henceforth, by a *nonoperational* or *down* system, we shall only mean that it cannot provide an adequate level of service. That is, a total loss of functionality is not required for the system to become "nonoperational". Suppose that each component of the system fails independently and the operational status of the entire system depends only on which components are functional and which are not. Then there are three ways of representing the failure behavior: (a) reliability block diagrams, (b) success diagrams, and (c) fault trees. In the following, we discuss each one of these briefly.

A *reliability block diagram* (RBD) represents the logical structure of the system with respect to the reliability of its component. A series connection between a set of components means that each component must be operational for that subsystem to be operational, and a parallel connection means that only one of the components need be operational. Thus, if $R_i(t)$ is the reliability of the ith component, the overall reliability R of a subsystem consisting of k components is given by

$$R = \begin{cases} \prod_{i=1}^{k} R_i(t) & \text{for series connection} \\ 1 - \prod_{i=1}^{k}(1 - R_i(t)) & \text{for parallel connection} \end{cases} \tag{4.3}$$

In general, the reliability block diagram may be an arbitrary series-parallel network, but it is still trivial to compute the overall reliability recursively. The *success diagram* is similar, except that it does not need to be series-parallel. An example is shown in Fig. 13-10(a). Here the system is considered operational if a path from source to destination exists. To analyze such a model, we first condition it on the operability of certain key components so that the resulting situation is series-parallel and then use the same method as for a reliability block diagram. For example, in Fig. 13-10(a), conditioning on the failed state of component B amounts to removing B, thereby creating a series-parallel network shown in Fig. 13-10(b). The case in which B works amounts to shorting out B,

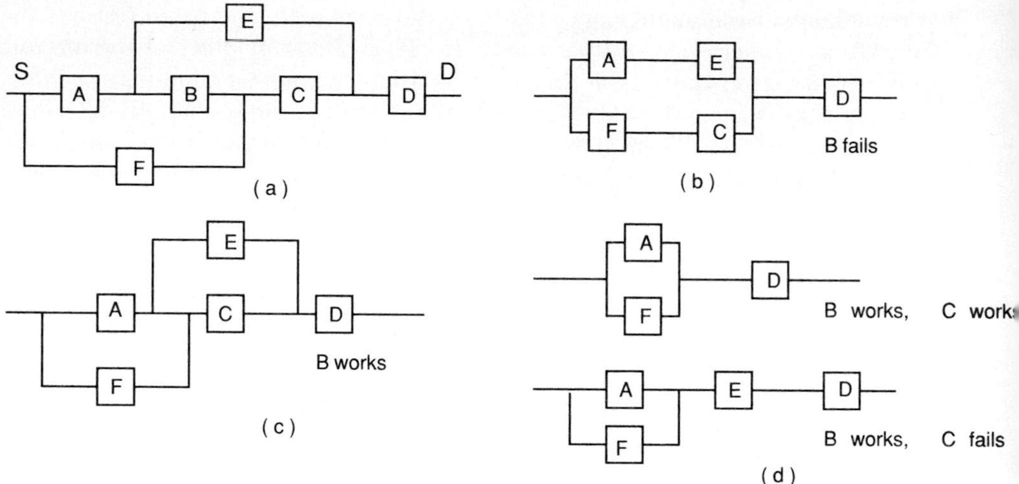

FIGURE 13-10: Use of success diagram in evaluating reliability.

and is shown in Fig. 13-10(c). Since this is still not a series parallel network, it requires further conditioning, shown in Fig. 13-10(d). Let R_1, R_2, and R_3 denote, respectively, the reliabilities of the three subsystems shown in the right-half of Fig. 13-10. Then

$$R_{\text{sys}} = (1 - R_B)R_1 + R_B[R_C R_2 + (1 - R_C)R_3] \tag{4.4}$$

Fault trees represent all sequences of failures leading to system failure in a tree-like fashion. They can be thought of as another way of representing the reliability block diagram. The root of the tree represents the event that the entire system has failed, and its ith child represents the event that the ith subsystem has failed. Each subsystem can be further decomposed into smaller subsystems, thereby giving an arbitrary tree structure. The label on a node indicates how the failure of the children affects this node. The node types are usually *k-out-of-n*, meaning that if k or more children out of a total of n fail, the node itself will fail. Of course, series and parallel connections are special cases of such a node. Finding the overall reliability is again straightforward. In some cases, however, the failure of a lower-level component may affect two or more higher-level components (e.g., a common power-supply module). In such cases, we get general acyclic graphs instead of trees. The computation now would require conditioning, as for the success diagrams. Exercises 13.12 through 13.14 explore this topic further.

13.4.2 Performability Measures

The notion of reliability alone is inadequate to characterize a complex computing system. First, reliability only deals with the time until a failure, whereas we may be interested in the amount of work that the given system $\mathcal{S}$ can accomplish before the failure occurs. The notion of "work" may be defined as the number of jobs processed, instructions executed, packets transmitted, etc., depending on the situation. This parameter is of independent interest since as the individual components fail, the *work capacity* of $\mathcal{S}$ may decrease until at some point it falls below the acceptable level (which we call system failure). Second, the notion of reliability specifies system behavior only until the first failure, and thus does not cover repairable systems in general. (The repair may only amount to recovery in the case of a *soft failure* such as a machine crash.) The additional measures of interest for a (possibly repairable) system $\mathcal{S}$ at time t, given that it starts operating at time 0, include

1. Instantaneous availability: $Pr(\mathcal{S}$ is operational at time $t)$.
2. Interval availability: fraction of time during $(0, t)$ when $\mathcal{S}$ was up.
3. Cumulative performance: total work accomplished during the time $(0, t)$.
4. Computation capacity: average work rate during the time $(0, t)$.

Cumulative performance was originally defined as *performability*. Since the second and fourth measures are closely related to it, we shall collectively refer to the last three as performability measures. It is important to note that *all performability measures are random variables*. Therefore, we may want to characterize performability measures either in terms of their distribution or only the expected values. As usual, expected values are easy to compute, but yield much less information. Although the performability measures are defined for finite time intervals, it is sometimes desirable to obtain their limiting values (as $t \to \infty$), if they exist. In this regard, it is important to know if the repair is *perfect* or *imperfect*. The repair is called imperfect if there is a finite probability that the system cannot be repaired. The absence of repair is one special case of imperfect repair. Imperfect repair may occur in other situations because of fault-coverage problems. Note that the limiting cumulative performance does not exist under perfect repair. Also, *if the system is ergodic, the limiting interval availability is the same as instantaneous availability*.

The combinatorial methods introduced in the last section are intended primarily for computing instantaneous measures. For example, given the reliability or the instantaneous availability of various subsystems at time t, we can easily compute that measure for the entire system at time t. Obviously, such an approach cannot be used to compute time interval-dependent parameters. The combinatorial methods also cannot handle several other features of the real systems. One such feature is the interdependence between the behaviors of various components. For example, a component may become more prone to failure or take longer to repair if some others are in a failed state. In some cases, the failure/repair rates may themselves be time-dependent. Also, it is typically unrealistic to assume that the failures or repairs are "clean"; i.e., they affect a component in a well-defined way. The failure of a component may go undetected until it causes enough corruption to bring the entire system down. A simple way to view this situation is to postulate that there are two types of faults: the detectable and undetectable ones, each showing a different type of behavior. Undetectable faults, when they eventually cause visible effects, may be too far gone to repair. Even for detectable faults, the repair procedure may not be followed correctly, or there may be failures during the repair. The notion of *coverage* is often used to account for such unusual situations. Coverage can be defined as the probability that the system can be repaired or reconfigured correctly following a failure. It is important to account for coverage in computing reliability measures; otherwise, the results may be overly optimistic. For example, suppose that a system consists of two subsystems, one operational and one standby, each with a reliability of 0.9999. Then under ideal conditions, the failure probability of the duplexed system will be 10^{-8}. However, if the coverage for a proper switch-over operation is only 0.99, the failure probability, P_f, increases by two orders of magnitude, since

$$P_f = 10^{-4} \times [0.01 + 0.99 \times 10^{-4}] > 10^{-6}$$

In accounting for the more complex behavior, it is natural to think of the system as being in a particular "state" with respect to the operational status of its components, and the failures/repairs causing transitions between these states. If the failure/repair-time distributions are memoryless, we can use a Markov chain to model such situations, and we shall assume this to be the case. (As usual, more general distributions can also be handled using either the method of stages, or in some cases, an embedded Markov chain.) The state description of such a model could include arbitrary information, but typically it indicates the number of components in each operational state (working, failed, recovering, etc.). In a Markovian model, it is easy to postulate multiple types of failures and repairs, state-dependent (and even time-dependent) failure/repair rates, coverage parameters, and the work capacity in each state. The last attribute can be modeled as the *reward rate* of a state, thereby leading to a *Markov reward model*. One example of reward rate in a state i is the throughput, which by definition, is the rate at which the jobs can be processed in state i.

Our analysis of Markov reward models is based on an important assumption that is easy to overlook. Suppose that we start a job while the system is in state i. It is possible that before the job finishes, the system transits to another state. If the job processing time is not memoryless, such a change of state would couple the performance and reliability models. This complication can be avoided if we can do the logical decomposition as suggested in Section 8.4.1. That is, we assume that *the failures/repairs occur infrequently as compared with job arrivals/services*; therefore, we can ignore the end-effects.

Let $r(t)$ denote the reward rate at time t. This is simply the reward rate of whatever state the system happens to be at time t. Then we can define the following performability measures:

Accumulated reward: $Y(t) = \int_0^t r(\tau)\, d\tau$

Accumulated reward rate: $W(t) = Y(t)/t$

Let us see the usefulness of $Y(t)$ and $W(t)$ by taking some specific types of reward processes. Consider a system with $n+1$ states, numbered $0\,..\,n$. Let r_i, the reward rate in state i, be the throughput in state i. Also let $\pi_i(t)$ denote the state of the system at time t. Then

$Pr(Y(t) > y)$: Probability of completing y jobs by time t.

$Pr(W(t) > w)$: Probability that the average completion rate is $> w$ during time $(0, t)$.

$\sum_{i=0}^{n} r_i \pi_i(t)$: Expected throughput *at* time t.

Next suppose that if the system is considered operational in state i, then $r_i = 1$, otherwise $r_i = 0$. Then,

$Pr(Y(t) > y)$: Probability that the system was up longer than y time units during time $(0, t)$.

$Pr(W(t) > w)$: Probability that the fraction of time the system was up during time t is larger than w.

$\mathrm{E}(W(t))$: Expected interval availability during time $(0, t)$.

$\sum_{i=0}^{n} r_i \pi_i(t)$: Instantaneous availability at time t.

Let us consider one more application. Suppose that we are interested in finding if the *mean* response time provided by the system, denoted R, is below some threshold x. Here the variability in R comes because the system may transit between states having different processing capacities; for any given state, we only consider the mean response time. Let R_i denote the mean response time in state i, and λ_i the throughput in this state. (It is assumed that R_i and λ_i are finite in every state $i \in 0\,..\,n$.) Let t denote the observation period, and τ_i the total time spent in state i during this time. Then $\sum_{i=0}^{n} \lambda_i \tau_i R_i$ gives the cumulative average response time of $\sum_{i=0}^{n} \lambda_i \tau_i$ jobs processed during time t. Therefore,

$$Pr(R \le x) = Pr\left[\frac{\sum_{i=0}^{n} \lambda_i \tau_i R_i}{\sum_{i=0}^{n} \lambda_i \tau_i} \le x\right] = Pr\left[\sum_{i=0}^{n} (R_i - x)\lambda_i \tau_i \le 0\right] \tag{4.5}$$

which implies that if we choose the reward rate $r_i = (R_i - x)\lambda_i$, the probability that the accumulated reward $Y(t)$ is negative gives the desired answer.

13.4.3 Evaluation of Performability Measures

In this section we discuss the evaluation of both the expected values and distributions of the performability measures $Y(t)$ and $W(t)$. Consider a continuous parameter Markov chain, denoted $\mathcal{Z}$, having n states. Let $\phi_i(\tau)$ denote the binary random variable that takes the value 1 if the system is in state i at time τ and zero otherwise. By definition then,

$$Y(t) = \int_0^t r(\tau)\,d\tau = \int_0^t \sum_{i=0}^{n} r_i\phi_i(\tau)\,d\tau \tag{4.6}$$

Obviously, $E[\phi_i(\tau)]$ gives the probability that the system will be found in state i at time τ. Therefore,

$$E[Y(t)] = \sum_{i=0}^{n} r_i \int_0^t \pi_i(\tau)\,d\tau \tag{4.7}$$

That is, the expected value of $Y(t)$ can be computed if the state probabilities are known. Let $\Pi(t)$ denote the row vector of $\pi_i(t)$'s, and let Q be the transition rate matrix of $\mathcal{Z}$. Then $\Pi(t)$ satisfies the Chapman-Kolmogorov differential equation $\Pi'(t) = \Pi(t)Q$. [See equation (5.2.15)]. This equation can be solved by standard methods, some of which we shall study in the next section. However, if we do not need $\pi_i(\tau)$'s for other purposes, we can avoid the integration in equation (4.7). Let $L_i(t) = \int_0^t \pi_i(\tau)\,d\tau$, and let $\mathbf{L}(t)$ denote the row vector of $L_i(t)$'s. By integrating both sides of equation (5.2.15), we get $\Pi(t) - \Pi(0) = \mathbf{L}(t)Q$, which means that

$$\frac{d\mathbf{L}(t)}{dt} = \mathbf{L}(t)Q + \Pi(0) \tag{4.8}$$

This equation is similar to (5.2.15), except for the *forcing function* $\Pi(0)$. However, since this forcing function is a constant, the solution is easy to get using standard methods for solving nonhomogeneous first-order differential equations (e.g., by assuming that the solution is of the form $G(t)e^{Qt}$ and then determining the vector $G(t)$). The solution is given by

$$\mathbf{L}(t) = \Pi(0)Q^{-1}(e^{Qt} + I) + \Pi(0)e^{Qt} \tag{4.9}$$

Therefore, from equation (4.7) we have

$$E[Y(t)] = \sum_{i=0}^{n} r_i L_i(t) = \mathbf{r}\mathbf{L}^T(t) \tag{4.10}$$

Once $E[Y(t)]$ is known, $E[W(t)]$ can be computed as $E[Y(t)]/t$. Thus, expected performability measures are easy to get.

Next, let us consider limiting distributions as $t \to \infty$. There are two cases of interest. First suppose that the repair is perfect and the system is ergodic. Then $\lim_{t\to\infty} Y(t)$ is not defined, but $W(\infty)$ is. For an ergodic system, the sample average must be the same as the time average (see Section 5.3.4). That is, if π_i denotes the steady-state probability, we have

$$\lim_{t\to\infty} \frac{1}{t}\int_0^t \phi_i(\tau)\,d\tau = \lim_{t\to\infty} \pi_i(t) = \pi_i \tag{4.11}$$

Therefore, we get the following intuitively obvious equation for $W(\infty)$:

$$W(\infty) = \sum_{i=0}^{n} r_i \pi_i \tag{4.12}$$

Notice that unlike $W(t)$, $W(\infty)$ is not a random variable but merely a constant. From equation (4.11), this fact can also be seen as a consequence of the *law of large numbers*. Now, suppose that $r_i = 1$ for states where the system is considered operational and 0 otherwise. Then, equation (4.12), which is the correct expression for interval availability according to our definition, can also be interpreted as giving the instantaneous availability. This steady-state availability is also given by MTTF/MTBF as claimed in Section 13.4.1.

With imperfect repair, there must be a set of absorbing states such that the Markov chain, denoted $\mathcal{Z}$, eventually settles in one of them. We assume that the reward rate in the absorbing states is zero. Thus, it is meaningful to speak of $Y(\infty)$, but $W(\infty)$ will drop to zero. Let $\mathcal{A}$ denote the set of absorbing states, and $\mathcal{B}$ the remaining set of states. Let T denote the total time until absorption, and let τ_i denote the time spent in state $i \in \mathcal{B}$ during the interval $(0, T)$. Then,

$$Y(\infty) = \sum_{\forall i \in \mathcal{B}} r_i \tau_i \tag{4.13}$$

Let μ_{ij} denote the transition rate from state i to state $j \neq i$ and let $\mu_i = \sum_{\forall j \neq i} \mu_{ij}$. From the Markovian property, we know that on any visit to state i, the time spent in state i is exponentially distributed with mean $1/\mu_i$. Now consider a slightly different Markov chain $\mathcal{Z}'$ whose state space is the same, but the transition rates have been changed to μ_{ij}/r_i. Thus, the average residence time of state i in $\mathcal{Z}'$ will be r_i/μ_i. Therefore, if $\mathcal{Z}$ spends τ_i time units in state i during the period $(0, T)$, $\mathcal{Z}'$ will spend $r_i \tau_i$ time units. That is, if $\mathcal{Z}$ is absorbed in time T, $\mathcal{Z}'$ will be absorbed in time $Y(\infty)$. In other words, T', the time to absorption for $\mathcal{Z}'$ is simply $Y(\infty)$. Therefore,

$$Pr(Y(\infty) \leq t) = Pr(T' \leq t) = \sum_{\forall i \in \mathcal{A}} \pi'_i(t) \tag{4.14}$$

where $\pi'_i(t)$'s are the transient state probabilities for $\mathcal{Z}'$. Thus, *the limiting distribution of $Y(t)$ for $\mathcal{Z}$ can be obtained from the transient state probabilities of $\mathcal{Z}'$.*

Let us now turn to performability distributions for finite t. Since $W(t)$ is related to $Y(t)$ by a constant, it suffices to compute the distribution of $Y(t)$. Here we separately consider the situations with and without repair. Without repair, no state will be visited more than once; i.e., the Markov chain will be *acyclic*. In this case, it is possible to set up a recursion to express the work done in an n-stage system in terms of the work done in an $n-1$ state system. Without loss of generality, we assume that there is but one absorbing state in the system. We denote this as state 0 and assume its reward rate to be zero. Let us denote the cumulative work for an n-stage system by $Y(n, t)$. Notice that *because of* *the lack of repair, we must choose the starting state for computing $Y(n,t)$ as n itself*. In fact, this is the reason why we can compute parameters for a n-state system in terms of those for a $(n-1)$-state system. Let $\delta(x)$ denote the *indicator function* for predicate x; i.e., $\delta(x) = 1$ if x is true, and zero otherwise. Also let $q_{ij} = \mu_{ij}/\mu_i$ denote the transition probability from state i to state j. Then,

$$\begin{aligned} Pr[Y(n,t) > y] &= \sum_{i=0}^{n-1} \int_0^t \mu_n e^{-\mu_n \tau} q_{ni} Pr[Y(i,t-\tau) > y - r_n\tau]\, d\tau \\ &\quad + \delta(r_n t > y) e^{-\mu_n t} \end{aligned} \tag{4.15}$$

This equation results by considering the following two cases: (a) the system transits to some state $i < n$ at time $\tau < t$, where it earns at least $y - r_n\tau$ reward, or (b) the system stays in state n for the entire duration t and accumulates more than y reward. The probability of transiting to some other state in an interval $d\tau$ at time $\tau < t$ is $\mu_n e^{-\mu_n\tau}$, and that of staying in state n until time t is $e^{-\mu_n t}$. It is possible that $r_n\tau > y$ at the time of transition even though the entire time period t has not elapsed; therefore, we adopt the convention that $Pr[Y(i,t) > x] = 1$ for any i and t if $x < 0$.[3] Equation (4.15) gives us an implicit expression for the distribution $F_{Y(n,t)}$, and hence of the density function of $f_{Y(n,t)}$. To proceed further, we take its *double Laplace transform*, i.e., Laplace transform with respect to both y and t, henceforth denoted as $\Psi_n(s,u)$. That is,

$$\Psi_n(s,u) = \int_{y=0}^{\infty} \int_{t=0}^{\infty} f_{Y(n,t)}(y) e^{-ut} e^{-sy}\, dt\, dy \tag{4.16}$$

where y transforms into s and t transforms into u. Applying the properties of Laplace transforms, it is easy to get the following expression for $\Psi_n(s,u)$. (See Exercise 13.16).

$$\Psi_n(s,u) = \frac{1}{\mu_n + sr_n + u} + \frac{\mu_n}{\mu_n + sr_n + u} \sum_{i=0}^{n-1} q_{ni} \Psi_i(s,u) \tag{4.17}$$

This is a triangular system of equations in Ψ_i's, $i = 0..n$, and can be solved symbolically by repeated back substitutions. The result is

$$\Psi_n(s,u) = \frac{1}{\mu_n + sr_n + u} + \sum_{i=0}^{n} \sum_{j=0, j\neq i}^{n} \frac{h_n(j,i)/[(\mu_j - \mu_i) + s(r_j - r_i)]}{\mu_i + sr_i + u} \tag{4.18}$$

where the coefficients $h_n(i,j)$'s are given by

$$h_n(i,j) = \sum_{m=\max(i,j), m\neq j}^{n-1} \frac{q_{nm}\mu_n h_m(i,j)}{(\mu_n - \mu_m) - [(r_n - r_j)(\mu_i - \mu_j)/(r_i - r_j)]} \tag{4.19}$$

Equation (4.18) can be inverted easily in both variables (one at a time) to get a closed-form expression for the distribution of $Y(n,t)$, as explored in Exercise

[3]Because of this, the lower limit of $i = 0$ in the summation is significant even though we have assumed that no reward is earned in state 0.

13.17. The complementary distribution turns out to be

$$Pr[Y(n,t) > y] = \sum_{i=0}^{n} \sum_{j=0, j\neq i}^{n} \frac{h_n(j,i)}{\mu_j - \mu_i} e^{-\mu_i t} \exp\left[-\frac{\mu_j - \mu_i}{r_j - r_i}(y - r_i t)\delta(y > r_i t)\right] + e^{-\mu_n t}\delta(y \leq r_n t) \qquad (4.20)$$

Note that the distribution is mixed exponential with $h_n(j,i)$'s as coefficients. The computational complexity is $O(n^3)$ because although the expression has $O(n^2)$ terms, the recursive computation of h_n's takes $O(n^3)$ time. Also note that the solution requires that all states have distinct failure rates and the reward rate is not proportional to failure rates. These requirements are a consequence of the way equations (4.19) and (4.20) are expressed. It is certainly possible to take appropriate limits and get expressions when these assumptions do not hold. Also, equation (4.20) is needed only if we are specifically interested in the distribution of $Y(n,t)$. If the moments suffice, we can get them directly from equation (4.18). In particular, let

$$G_k(u) = (-1)^k \frac{\partial^k \Psi_n(s,u)}{\partial s^k}\bigg|_{s=0} \qquad (4.21)$$

This gives the ordinary Laplace transform of kth order moment of reward with respect to time. The inversion of this transform will give us the kth order moment of the reward earned as a function of time. Similarly, if we let

$$H_k(s) = (-1)^k \frac{\partial^k \Psi_n(s,u)}{\partial u^k}\bigg|_{u=0} \qquad (4.22)$$

we get the ordinary Laplace transform of the kth order moment of the time with respect to the reward. The inversion of this transform will give us the kth order moment of the time needed to a earn a given reward.

When repairs are involved, whether perfect or imperfect, the Markov chain becomes cyclic and finding distributions becomes more involved. However, it can be shown that *as* $t \to \infty$, *the distribution of* $Y(t)$ *becomes Gaussian*. This result, along with methods to compute the mean and variance of $\lim_{t\to\infty} Y(t)$, can be used as one distributional approximation for large t. It is also possible to derive recursions starting from an equation similar to equation (4.15). Let $Y(n,t)$ denote the accumulated reward by time t if the system is started in state n. With repairs, the system may come back to state n, therefore, the right-hand side of equation (4.15) will now involve all states of the system, henceforth denoted as N, independent of where the system started. Another difference is that the state 0 (the absorbing state) no longer exists. Thus, equation (4.15) becomes

$$Pr[Y(n,t) > y] = \sum_{i=1}^{N} \int_0^t \mu_n e^{-\mu_n \tau} q_{ni} Pr[Y(i, t-\tau) > y - r_n \tau]\, d\tau + \delta(r_n t > y) e^{-\mu_n t} \qquad (4.23)$$

Taking double Laplace transforms, we get an equation identical to (4.17) except that the summation limit goes from 1 to N for any n. That is, we no longer have a triangular system of equations in Ψ_i's, and an explicit symbolic solution becomes very complex. Instead, we put these equations in a matrix form. For this, let Q denote the matrix of q_{ij}'s, $\mathbf{e} = [1, \ldots, 1]$, $\mathbf{r} = [r_1, \ldots, r_N]$, $\mathbf{\Psi} = [\Psi_1, \ldots, \Psi_N]$, $\boldsymbol{\mu} = [\mu_1, \ldots, \mu_N]$, and

$$A(\mathbf{x}) = \left[\frac{1}{x_1 + \mu_1}, \ldots, \frac{1}{x_N + \mu_N}\right] \tag{4.24}$$

Note that all vectors are column vectors here. Then the matrix form of the double Laplace transform becomes

$$\mathbf{\Psi}(s,u) = A(u\mathbf{e} + s\mathbf{r}) + \Delta(\boldsymbol{\mu}) \cdot \Delta[A(u\mathbf{e} + s\mathbf{r})]Q\mathbf{\Psi}(s,u) \tag{4.25}$$

where $\Delta(\mathbf{x})$ means that a column vector $\mathbf{x}$ is made into a square matrix by putting its elements along the diagonal. We thus get the following solution

$$\mathbf{\Psi}(s,u) = [I - \Delta(\boldsymbol{\mu}) \cdot \Delta(A(u\mathbf{e} + s\mathbf{r}))Q]^{-1} A(u\mathbf{e} + s\mathbf{r}) \tag{4.26}$$

Let $R = \Delta(\mathbf{r})$, and let $Q^* = \Delta(\mu)(Q - I)$ be the transition rate matrix of the original continuous time Markov chain. (Note that Q is the transition probability matrix.) As shown in Exercise 13.19, equation (4.26) can be simplified to give

$$\mathbf{\Psi}(s,u) = (uI + sR - Q^*)^{-1}\mathbf{e} \tag{4.27}$$

This equation can be inverted in parameter u to give the ordinary Laplace transform of the reward earned as a function of time t

$$\Psi(s,t) = \exp(Q^*t - sRt) \cdot \mathbf{e} \tag{4.28}$$

We could now invert this numerically to get the distribution of $Y(n,t)$ for $n = 1 \mathinner{..} N$. If only moments are needed, we can instead differentiate equation (4.28) with respect to s. Let $M^k(t)$ denote the column vector of the kth order moments of $Y(n,t)$. We could then obtain the following recursive expression for $M^k(t)$ from equation (4.27).

$$M^{k+1}(t) = (k+1)\int_0^t e^{Q^*(t-\tau)} \cdot R \cdot M^k(\tau)\,d\tau \tag{4.29}$$

The computation of both the distribution and moments requires the evaluation of the exponential of a matrix, i.e., e^{Q^*t}. In the next section, we shall discuss some methods for this. An approach that avoids the computation of *matrix-exponential* is to solve the simultaneous equations for $\Psi_n(s,u)$ symbolically in s and u. It can be shown that the resulting expression can be written as a sum of terms of the type $[u - \lambda_j(s)]^{-k}$ where $\lambda_j(s)$'s are eigenvalues of the matrix $(Q^* - sR)$. This form is suitable for symbolic inversion. The resulting one-dimensional Laplace transform could then be inverted numerically to get the distribution. The entire process takes $O(N^3)$ steps.

In some cases, the characterization of the reward rate r_i in state i may need an elaborate performance model. For example, in a multiprocessor system, r_i may be defined as the throughput and would require solving a performance model. Since we have assumed that failures/repairs occur infrequently, we can solve the performance model independently for each state.

13.4.4 Transient Analysis of Markov Chains

In Section 5.2 we derived equations for the transient solution of both discrete and continuous parameter Markov chains. For the discrete parameter case, the transient solution is obtained by using the recursion $\Pi(n+1) = \Pi(n)Q$. (Throughout this section we assume that the Markov chain has only a finite number of states, denoted N; therefore, such recursions can be used.) For the continuous parameter case, however, we need to solve the differential equation (5.2.15). There are three ways to go about this: (a) use the explicit solution $\Pi(t) = \Pi(0)\exp(Qt)$, (b) use numerical integration of $\Pi'(t) = \Pi(t)Q$, and (c) find the solution by considering an embedded discrete parameter chain. We now briefly look at each one of these methods.

The main difficulty in using the explicit solution is in evaluating the matrix exponential $\exp(Qt)$. By definition, for any matrix A, we have

$$\exp(A) = I + A + \frac{A^2}{2!} + \frac{A^3}{3!} + \cdots \tag{4.30}$$

By the *Cayley-Hamilton theorem*, a matrix A also satisfies its own characteristic equation $\det(A - \lambda I) = 0$. Thus, we can express $\exp(A)$ as a matrix polynomial of degree $d \leq N - 1$, where d is the number of distinct nonzero eigenvalues of A. Once the representation of $\exp(A)$ is known, the computation takes only $O(d)$ matrix operations. This method can also be applied for $A = Qt$ where t is retained as a symbolic parameter. In fact, it is possible to get a generic formula for $\exp(Qt)$ with t retained symbolically. In the following we shall show how this is done for the special case where all eigenvalues of Q are distinct. The key property that we use in this case is that Q can be diagonalized. In the general case, it is still possible to obtain an expression for $\exp(Qt)$ using the *Jordan form* of Q, but we shall not discuss it here. Let $\mathbf{\Lambda} = \Delta(\lambda_1, \ldots, \lambda_N)$ denote the diagonal matrix of eigenvalues of Q, and $\mathbf{X} = (\mathbf{x}_1, \mathbf{x}_2, \ldots, \mathbf{x}_N)^T$ the square matrix whose *ith row* $\mathbf{x}_i$ is the *left eigenvector* of Q corresponding to the eigenvalue λ_i; i.e., $\mathbf{x}_i Q = \lambda_i \mathbf{x}_i$ for $i \in 1..N$. Then from elementary linear algebra, we know that Q can be *diagonalized* as $\mathbf{X}^{-1}\,\mathbf{\Lambda}\,\mathbf{X}$. This leads to the following representation of $\exp(Qt)$:

$$\exp(Qt) = \sum_{i=1}^{N} Z_i e^{\lambda_i t} \tag{4.31}$$

where the matrices Z_i's are given by $\mathbf{y}_i\,\mathbf{x}_i$ where $\mathbf{y}_i$ is the right (or column) eigenvector corresponding to the eigenvalue λ_i. That is, $\mathbf{y}_i$ is the solution to the equation $Q\mathbf{y}_i = \lambda_i \mathbf{y}_i$. It can be shown that Z_i can be expressed in the following alternate form

$$Z_i = \prod_{j=1, j\neq i}^{N} (Q - \lambda_j I) \Big/ \prod_{j=1, j\neq i}^{N} (\lambda_i - \lambda_j) \tag{4.32}$$

Notice that to use these formulae, we need to first compute all eigenvalues. This can be done in $O(N^3)$ time using standard methods, such as the *QR-algorithm*.

This could be expensive when N is large. The main advantage of this method is that we get the final result as a function of t, which can be evaluated directly for any value of t. In contrast, the next two methods only give numerical answers, and require more and more computation as t increases.

The solution by *numerical integration* follows the standard approach of solving differential equations numerically, so we describe the method only briefly. The differential equation for state i is

$$\frac{d\pi_i(t)}{dt} = \sum_{j=1}^{N} \pi_j(t) q_{ji} \tag{4.33}$$

(Remember that q_{ij}'s here are transition rates, rather than transition probabilities and $q_{ii} = -\sum_{j\neq i} q_{ij}$). If we consider the Taylor series expansion of $\pi_i(t+h)$ around t, we get

$$\pi_i(t+h) = \pi_i(t) + h\pi_i'(t) + \frac{h^2}{2}\pi_i''(t) + \cdots \tag{4.34}$$

By successive differentiation of equation (4.33) and substitution, we can express $\pi_i^{(k)}(t)$ (the kth order derivative) for any k in terms of $\pi_j(t)$'s alone. Thus, by truncating the Taylor series at a desired point, we can compute $\pi_i(t+h)$ from $\pi_j(t)$'s. This provides us with a way of numerically stepping through time starting with the initial distribution $\Pi(0)$. Since the computation of higher-order derivatives by this technique is expensive, we can use finite approximations like $f'(x) \approx [f(x+h) - f(x)]/h$ for any function f, to estimate high order derivatives. The main disadvantage of numerical integration is that each step h introduces some error and therefore, the results for a large t may be unreliable. A related disadvantage is that as the transition rates (i.e., off-diagonal elements of Q) increase, the step-size h will have to be reduced to obtain the same level of accuracy.

The last method is known as *uniformization* or *randomization*. It computes the state probabilities of the original continuous parameter chain $\mathcal{Z}$ via the probabilities for an embedded Markov chain $\mathcal{Z}^*$. Let q denote the magnitude of the largest element of Q and $Q^* = Q/q + I$. From equation (5.2.18), we can identify Q^* as the transition probability matrix of a discrete parameter chain $\mathcal{Z}^*$, whose steady-state distribution is the same as that of $\mathcal{Z}$. We can also establish a relationship between their transient distributions. Let $\Pi^*(n)$ denote the distribution after the nth transition of $\mathcal{Z}^*$. Obviously, $\Pi^*(0) = \Pi(0)$, and

$$\Pi^*(n) = \Pi^*(n-1)Q^* \tag{4.35}$$

which implies that $\Pi^*(n) = \Pi(0)(Q^*)^n$. The transient solution of $\mathcal{Z}$ can be expressed as

$$\Pi(t) = \Pi(0)e^{Qt} = \Pi(0)e^{qt(Q^*-I)} = \Pi(0)e^{-qt}e^{qtQ^*} \tag{4.36}$$

Now by the Taylor series expansion of e^{qtQ^*}, and using the expression for $\Pi^*(n)$, we get

$$\Pi(t) = \sum_{n=0}^{\infty} \Pi^*(n) \frac{(qt)^n e^{-qt}}{n!} \tag{4.37}$$

We note that equation (4.37) holds for any value of t (and not just at the transition points). It also has a simple probabilistic interpretation. The second term in equation (4.37) is merely the Poisson distribution with rate q. Since $\mathcal{Z}^*$ is a discrete parameter chain, we can place its transition points in real time arbitrarily without affecting anything. So we let the transition points be located such that the number of transitions in a given interval has Poisson distribution with rate q. Then $\Pi^*(n)$ gives the system state, given that n transitions occur during time t. Thus, equation (4.37) follows from the definition of conditional probability.

Now, to solve $\mathcal{Z}$, we only have to solve $\mathcal{Z}^*$ using the recursion (4.35). Since this recursion does not modify Q^*, it can also effectively exploit the sparseness of Q^*. The only difficulty is that equation (4.37) involves an infinite summation. One way to deal with this is to truncate the summation at some value, say k. Since $\Pi^*(n) \leq \mathbf{e}$, a safe way to choose k is to let

$$1 - \sum_{n=0}^{k} \frac{(qt)^n e^{-qt}}{n!} < \varepsilon \tag{4.38}$$

where ε is the chosen error bound. We can, of course, do the computations in equations (4.37) and (4.38) along with the recursion in (4.35) so that appropriate k is computed on the fly.

A different method is to use the limiting distribution $\Pi^*(\infty)$, if it exists. For this, as we go through the recursion (4.35), we watch for the convergence of the solution and choose k such that $\max_i |\Pi^*(k+1) - \Pi^*(k)| < \varepsilon$ for some small ε. Since (4.35) essentially amounts to applying the *power method*, the rate of convergence depends on the subdominant eigenvalue of Q^*. If the convergence is fast, we can safely regard $\Pi^*(k+1)$ as the limiting distribution $\Pi^*(\infty)$. In other cases, we may be able to determine $\Pi^*(\infty)$ by independent means. For example, if the chain $\mathcal{Z}$ is ergodic, we can compute $\Pi^*(\infty)$ easily from the steady-state equations. Also, if the system eventually settles in one of the absorbing states, the limiting distribution can usually be obtained by inspection. In any case, by letting $\Pi(n) = \Pi(\infty)$ for $n > k$, equation (4.37) gives us the following approximation:

$$\Pi(t) \approx \sum_{n=0}^{k} [\Pi^*(n) - \Pi^*(\infty)] \frac{(qt)^n e^{-qt}}{n!} + \Pi^*(\infty) \tag{4.39}$$

One important issue that we have neglected to address in the above is that of *stiffness*. Informally, a Markov chain is called stiff if it includes certain events that are fast and others that are slow. For example, in a reliability model, the repair time is usually much smaller compared with the interfailure time. Let q denote the largest nondiagonal element of the transition rate matrix Q, and T the time period over which we want to obtain the transient solution. Stiffness means that $qT \gg 1$. Suppose that we use numerical integration to obtain the solution. For good accuracy, we must choose the step-size h such that $qh \ll 1$; i.e., the probability of a transition in time h is small. However, this means that a large number of steps will be needed. Furthermore, the presence of both very small and very large entries in Q will cause serious roundoff errors. We now briefly discuss a decomposition-based approach to deal with such situations.

The situation here is similar to the one considered in Section 8.4, except that now we are dealing with transient solutions instead of the steady-state solutions. We decompose the states of the original Markov chain $\mathcal{Z}$ into two nonempty subsets, say Ω_F and Ω_S, as follows. A state in Ω_F is such that at least one transition out of it is fast (i.e., has a large rate), whereas a state in Ω_S has only slow transitions out of it.[4] The solution steps are as follows:

1. Remove all slow transitions from $\mathcal{Z}$. As a result, each slow state will either become a sink or will be completely isolated. Let $C_1, \ldots, C_{k-1}$ denote the nontrivial, strongly connected components thus obtained. (By nontrivial, we mean the components that have at least two states.) Let C_k contain all other fast states. Let $\mathcal{Z}_i$ denote the subchain corresponding to C_i, $i = 1\,..\,k-1$. These subchains are obtained by removing from C_i any transitions to/from states not in C_i.

2. Each of the subchains $\mathcal{Z}_i$ will be ergodic and reach steady state quickly (compared with the behavior of slow states). Solve $\mathcal{Z}_i$'s to get the steady-state probabilities, denoted π_{ij} for state j inside the aggregate i.

3. Aggregate each $\mathcal{Z}_i$ into a single macrostate exactly as we did in Section 8.4.2, e.g., by using equation (8.4.8). This will reduce $\mathcal{Z}$ to an aggregated chain, say $\mathcal{Z}^*$, containing $|\Omega_S| + k - 1 + |C_k|$ states. Solve $\mathcal{Z}^*$ to get the transient state probabilities $x_i(t)$, where i is an aggregated state. (For this, we set $x_i(0)$, $i = 1\,..\,k-1$, to be sum of initial probabilities of all states in C_i.)

4. If j is a state in C_i, $i = 1\,..\,k-1$, estimate its transient probability $\pi_j(t)$ as simply $\pi_{ij}x_i(t)$. (This is the same as we did in Section 8.4.2.)

Note that the chain $\mathcal{Z}^*$ still suffers from stiffness, so we solve it in a special way. Let A denote the transition rate matrix of $\mathcal{Z}^*$. Let us put the slow states and $k-1$ aggregated states in group 1, and the remaining $|C_k|$ fast states in group 2. This grouping induces a similar grouping of the matrix A. Then the Chapman-Kolmogorov equation $\mathbf{x}'(t) = \mathbf{x}(t)\,A$ for computing the transient probabilities $\mathbf{x}(t)$ of chain $\mathcal{Z}^*$ can be written as

$$\mathbf{x}_1'(t) = \mathbf{x}_1(t)A_{11} + \mathbf{x}_2(t)A_{21} \quad \text{and} \quad \mathbf{x}_2'(t) = \mathbf{x}_1(t)A_{12} + \mathbf{x}_2(t)A_{22} \qquad (4.40)$$

However, since the states in group 2 are fast, we can assume that they quickly reach steady state, i.e., $\mathbf{x}_2'(t) = 0$. This gives us the following nonstiff differential

[4] A fast state may well have incoming transitions with small rates. Similarly, a slow state may have incoming transitions with large rates.

equation for group 1:

$$\mathbf{x}_1'(t) = \mathbf{x}_1(t)[A_{11} - A_{12}A_{22}^{-1}A_{21}] \tag{4.41}$$

which can be solved by standard methods already discussed above. We could then determine $\mathbf{x}_2(t)$ using the equation $\mathbf{x}_2(t) = -\mathbf{x}_1(t)A_{12}A_{22}^{-1}$.

13.5 Exercises

1. In Section 13.1.3, we obtained the mean waiting time for a customer in a vacation system using the exhaustive service. Do a similar analysis for a nonexhaustive service system.

2. Follow through the steps required to obtain equation (1.16 that gives the z-transform of D_1 in terms of the z -transform of A_1. Start with the expression given for PD_1 in terms of PA_1.

3. Extend the analysis presented in Section 13.1.4, to consider a system with more than 2 stations, and obtain equation (1.18).

4. In Section 13.1.5, follow through the algebra required to obtain the expression for $\text{Var}(V_m)$ in equation (1.37), using equations (1.33) through (1.36).

5. Consider a nonexhaustive service system with 16 stations where $\rho = 0.80$ and $\rho_2 = \ldots = \rho_{16} = \rho_1/150$. The switch-over times are deterministic, with $\Theta = 21$ units. The service times are exponentially distributed with a mean of 2048 units. Obtain the mean waiting times at the stations.

6. In Example 13.3, obtain the mean waiting time at station 1. For comparison, the corresponding value for W_1 obtained through simulation is 9.09.

7. Consider the following modification to the approximation presented in Section 13.1.5 for the nonexhaustive service system. Suppose that station i has high utilization (≥ 0.7) and has an arrival rate at least twice that of the other stations. Since service is almost certain at such a station, we remove this station from the system, and absorb its effect into the switch-over times. In the modified system, everything remains the same except that the switch-over time $\omega_{i-1}' = \omega_{i-1} + \tau_i + \omega_i$, with $E(\tau_i) = \lambda_i CTs_i$, and $E(\tau_i^2) = \lambda_i CTs_i^{(2)}$. Here τ_i takes into account possible service in i in the original model. Clearly when $\lambda_i CT$ is close to 1, then the other stations should behave very similar in both models.

   Obtain the mean waiting time at station 2 in Example 13.3 using this modification. This should give $W_2 = 1.48$. You should note that this modification need not always improve on earlier estimates (as in this case).

8. Now redo Example 13.3 when all parameters are the same except that the switch-over times are exponentially distributed with mean 0.10, instead of 0.05. The simulation results for this case are $W_1 = 53.87$, $W_2 = W_3 = 2.37$. Use the modification suggested in Exercise 13.7 for stations 2 and 3, and compare the resulting values with the simulation results.

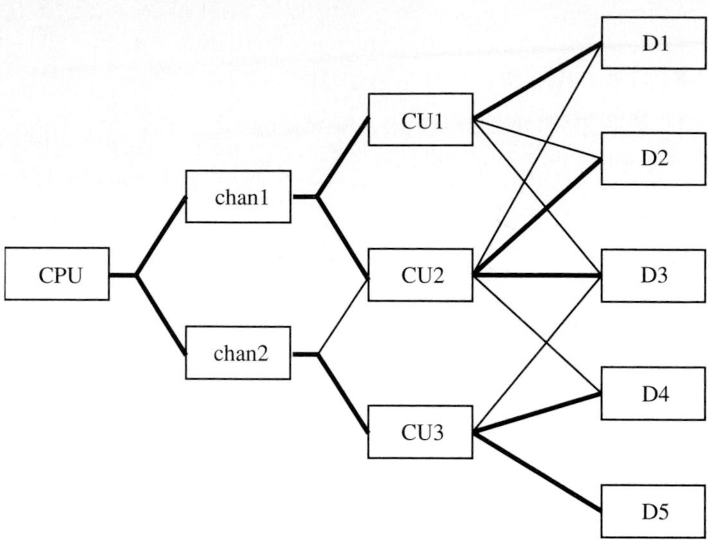

FIGURE 13-11: An I/O system model with multiple paths.

9. Show that a GTG is well-formed if and only if its persistent task graph is live and safe. Using this result, devise a method for checking the well-formedness of GTG's based on the reachability graph. (Note that the reachability graph could be infinite, but we do not have to generate unsafe states.)

10. Consider the system of Section 13.3.2 when the jobs are of type @ and $r = 0$. Show that the $\Phi(z)$ for this system is the same as for a M/M/q system. Explain this result intuitively.

11. Derive the generating function $\Phi(z)$ in equation (3.4) for a $M^{(X)}/M/c$ queue. Assuming that the bulk size is fixed at k, also obtain an expression for the job response time.

12. Consider the IO subsystem shown in Fig. 13-11. (Treat both heavy and normal lines equally.) All components of the same type have identical performance and reliability characteristics. Let $R_d = 0.995$, $R_u = 0.999$, and $R_h = 0.9999$ be the steady-state availabilities of individual disk-drives, control-units, and channels, respectively. Find the *dependability* of each disk-drive, defined as the probability that the drive remains accessible.

13. In Exercise 13.12, suppose that only the paths shown in heavy lines are the primary paths, and an explicit switch-over is needed to utilize other path segments. Let $C = 0.999$ denote the probability that a switch-over will be made successfully. Recompute the dependabilities under this assumption.

14. Repeat the calculations in Exercise 13.12 assuming that drives $(2, 3)$ and $(4, 5)$ are *mirrored*, i.e., all writes are done in parallel to both drives and a read can occur from either drive.

15. Solve equation (4.8) to obtain the solution in (4.9). Now consider a two-

state Markov chain with arbitrary transition rates. (The corresponding Q matrix will have only two distinct rates, since all elements in a row must sum to 0.) Using the Cayley-Hamilton theorem, compute e^{Qt}.

16. Starting with equation (4.15), first obtain Laplace transform with respect to t using the shift and convolution properties and the Laplace transform for the unit-step function. Next take Laplace transform with respect to y and obtain equation (4.17).
17. Do a partial-fraction expansion of equation (4.18). Then using the identity that $\mathcal{L}(\nu e^{-\nu t}) = \nu/(\nu + s)$, obtain equation (4.20).
18. Suppose that in Exercise 13.17, $r_i \propto \mu_i$ for all i. Starting with equation (4.18), obtain the appropriate solution.
19. Since $A(u\mathbf{e} + s\mathbf{r})$ can be written as $\Delta(A(u\mathbf{e} + s\mathbf{r})) \cdot \mathbf{e}$, simplify equation (4.26) using the identities $(\Delta(\mathbf{x}))^{-1} = \Delta(1/x_1, \ldots, 1/x_N)$, $\Delta(\mathbf{x})\Delta(\mathbf{y}) = \Delta(\mathbf{y})\Delta(\mathbf{x})$, and $A^{-1}B^{-1} = (BA)^{-1}$. Now let $R = \Delta(\mathbf{r})$ and $Q^* = \Delta(\mu)(Q - I)$, and derive equation (4.27).
20. Show that equation (4.27) is the Laplace transform of equation (4.28).

Bibliographic Notes

The seminal work on the modeling and analysis of polling systems is usually attributed to Cooper and Murray (1969), which analyzes the exhaustive service system with zero switch-over times. The analysis of the general system in Section 13.1.4 is based on this work. A number of other papers have appeared since then on the modeling and analysis of polling systems. For exhaustive systems with nonzero switch-over times, Ferguson and Aminetzah (1985) obtains the mean waiting times by solving a set of M^2 equations, where M is the number of stations. Sarkar and Zangwill (1989) significantly improves on these results, and obtains the mean waiting times by solving a system of M equations in M unknowns. For the nonexhaustive system, obtaining the mean waiting times is still an open problem (except for a few limited results). For a comprehensive survey of the analysis of polling systems, the reader may refer to Takagi (1986, 1990). Doshi (1990) provides another survey of techniques for analyzing single-server systems with server vacations. The conservation laws for polling systems were first presented in Watson (1984). Boxma and Groenendijk (1987) presents an elegant derivation of the conservation laws for a mix of service disciplines. Conservation laws have been obtained for a wide variety of polling systems including systems in which the server consults a polling table to decide which station to next switch to (Boxma, Groenendijk and Weststrate 1988), and systems in which the server switches in a nondeterministic manner between stations (Srinivasan 1991).

Our approximation for the exhaustive service system is taken from Bux and Truong (1983), whereas the one for the nonexhaustive system is taken from Boxma and Meister (1986). Approximation schemes for nonexhaustive service systems are also presented in Kuehn (1979) and Srinivasan (1988), among many others. Kant (1987) presents an approximate analysis for a network of polling systems connected together in a hierarchical manner by appropriately modeling the individual polling systems as nodes in a closed queuing network.

The file-allocation problem has been analyzed under various assumptions and with different objective functions. A survey of some of the earlier work on this problem appears in Dowdy and Foster (1982). The presentation in this chapter is based on the work in Srinivasan and Kant (1987). The optimal routing problem in closed queuing networks presented in this chapter is based on work in Kobayashi and Gerla (1983). Further work on the subject appears in Robertazzi and Lazar (1985). Bannister and Trivedi (1983), among others, considers the problem of file allocation in a fault-tolerant environment. Pattipati and Wolf (1990) presents an approach to the file-allocation problem based on calculus of variations by viewing the mean value theorem as a nonlinear difference equation.

The problem of well-formedness of acyclic extended task graphs was first examined by Baer in 1968. Hack (1975) presents necessary and sufficient conditions for the liveness and safeness of free-choice Petri nets based on the ideas of traps and siphons. Generalized task graphs are introduced in Kant (1990) and further refined in Ghodsi and Kant (1991). Several researchers have considered the analysis of isolated queues with simple structure for the jobs. Fork-join task graphs without the header task are considered in Heidelberger and Trivedi (1982, 1983); Nelson and Tantawi (1988); and Nelson, Towsley, and Tantawi (1988). Nelson (1990) analyzes a somewhat more general situation, where a processed job may be fed back into the system with some probability. Kim and Agrawala (1989) obtains the transient solution and steady-state solutions under nonexponential service-time distributions assuming $K = M$ and using the concept of virtual waiting time. The exact analysis of fork-join task graphs with the header task may be found in Kant, Suen, and Liaw (1991), and the analysis of those with max node can be found in Ghodsi and Kant (1990). In these works, it is assumed that any task can be allocated to any processor. A more difficult problem is the one where the subtasks are assigned to individual processors immediately upon fork. This problem has been solved exactly in Flatto and Hahn (1984) and Flatto (1985) for $K = 2$. Nelson and Tantawi (1988) proposes an approximation for $K > 2$.

Baccelli, Makowski, and Schwartz (1989) provides lower and upper bounds on response time for a fork-join queue based on the concept of stochastic ordering. Baccelli, Massey, and Towsley (1989) provides similar bounds for feed-forward networks of fork-join queues. Thomasian and Bay (1986) and Kapelnikov (1987) consider analysis of closed queuing networks running jobs with internal concurrency. These methods are primarily intended for networks of unit population. Mak (1987) presents a mean value analysis based algorithm for a similar system with the further restriction that the task graphs are series-parallel type. The algorithm presented in Section 13.3.4 that allows arbitrary task graphs, arbitrary population and resource constraints, is taken from Ghodsi and Kant (1989).

The material on reliability modeling is classical and may be found in most books dealing with the subject of fault-tolerant computing. For example,

Siewiorek and Swarz (1982) discusses both combinatorial and Markov modeling techniques and shows the analysis of various classical techniques of enhancing reliability (N-modular redundancy, standby spare, etc.). Johnson (1989) and Trivedi (1982) are among other relevant books on the topic.

The concept of performability was introduced in Meyer(1980, 1982), and has been studied extensively since then. Smith, Trivedi, and Ramesh (1988) and Iyer (1987) provide recent surveys on the subject. Beaudry (1978) and Huslende (1981) provide some early but important results in the area. The $O(N^3)$ algorithm for computing performability distribution for nonrepairable systems comes from Donatiello and Iyer (1987). Iyer, Donatiello, and Heidelberger (1986) discusses the computation of performability moments for repairable systems, and shows that the distribution approaches the normal distribution asymptotically. Smith, Trivedi, and Ramesh (1988) also discusses an $O(N^3)$ algorithm for computing performability distribution for repairable systems based on the inversion of double Laplace transforms. Reibman, Smith, and Trivedi (1989), and Reibman and Trivedi (1989) provide an overview of the major techniques for solving Markov and Markov-reward models. One such technique, which we did not discuss, is based on solving a set of partial differential equations for the performability measure with respect to time and reward variables. The randomization technique for obtaining transient solutions is developed in Gross and Miller (1984). Silva and Gail (1989) discusses the randomization approach for solving performability models. Bobbio and Trivedi (1986) presents the aggregation technique for handling stiff Markov chains. Moler and Van Loan (1978) discusses nineteen different ways to compute the exponential of a matrix.

Part III

Appendices

APPENDIX A

Notation

M Number of stations in the network (numbered $1 \mathinner{..} M$).

K Number of chains in the network (numbered $1 \mathinner{..} K$).

Ω The entire network; i.e., the set of stations $1 \mathinner{..} M$.

Ω_{LD} A subset of Ω containing indices of all load-dependent stations.

$\mathbf{N}$ Population vector. $\mathbf{N} = (N_1, \ldots, N_K)$, where N_r is the population of chain r.

N Magnitude of $\mathbf{N} = \sum_{r=1}^{K} N_r$. Also denotes the population in single-chain networks.

$\mathbf{n}_i$ Occupancy vector at station i. $\mathbf{n}_i = (n_{i1}, \ldots, n_{iK})$, where n_{ir} is the number of chain r customers at station i. Magnitude of $\mathbf{n}_i$ is denoted as n_i.

$\vec{\mathbf{n}}$ State of the entire network; i.e., $\vec{\mathbf{n}} = (\mathbf{n}_1, \ldots, \mathbf{n}_M)$ where $\mathbf{n}_i$ is the occupancy vector at station i.

$\mathbf{0}$ Vector with all elements zero. Dimensionality depends on the context.

e_r A unit vector in the rth dimension. For single-chain networks, the relevant space is the M-dimensional state space of the network. For multiple-chain networks, the relevant space is the K-dimensional state space of a station.

e_{ir} A unit vector in the cross-product space of stations and chains. That is, this vector represents the presence of a chain r customer at station i in the network.

$\mu_{ir}(\mathbf{n})$ Inherent service rate for chain r customers at station i at occupancy vector of $\mathbf{n}$. Also, we define $1/\mu_{ir}(\mathbf{n})$ as $s_{ir}(\mathbf{n})$.

$\mu^*_{ir}(\mathbf{n})$ Effective service rate for chain r customers at station i at occupancy vector of $\mathbf{n}$. Also, we define $1/\mu^*_{ir}(\mathbf{n})$ as $s^*_{ir}(\mathbf{n})$.

μ°_{ir} Basic service rate for chain r customers at station i; i.e., $\mu_{ir}(e_r)$.

s°_{ir} Basic service time of chain r customers at station i. $s^\circ_{ir} = 1/\mu^\circ_{ir}$.

CV_{ir} Coefficient of variation of service time for chain r customers at station i.

$C_i(n)$ (Chain-independent) capacity function for station i at total load of n; i.e., $C_i(n) = \mu_{ir}(n)/\mu^\circ_{ir}$. By definition, $C_i(0) = 0$, and $C_i(1) = 1$.

$C_{ir}(\mathbf{n})$ (Chain-dependent) capacity function for station i at load $\mathbf{n}$; i.e., $C_{ir}(\mathbf{n}) = \mu_{ir}(\mathbf{n})/\mu^\circ_{ir}$.

q_{ijr} Routing probability for chain r customers from station i to station j. An argument, if used, indicates the state-dependence.

v_{ir} Visit ratio (or relative throughput) of chain r customers at station i.

u_{ir} Relative utilization of chain r customers at station i; defined as $v_{ir}\mu^\circ_{ir}$.

$nc(r)$ Number of classes in chain r. Unless stated otherwise, $nc(r) = 1$.

$\Lambda_r(N_r)$ Total external arrival rate for open chain r when the network contains N_r chain r customers.

$\Lambda_{ir}(N_r)$ External arrival rate of chain r customers to station i when the network contains N_r chain r customers. If s denotes the source node, then $\Lambda_{ir}(N_r) = q_{sir}\Lambda_r(N_r)$.

$P_i(\mathbf{n}|\mathbf{N})$ Random observer's distribution; i.e., the probability that the occupancy vector at station i is $\mathbf{n}$ when the network population is $\mathbf{N}$.

$P_i(n|\mathbf{N})$ Aggregated distribution; i.e., the probability of finding n customers (considering all chains) at station i, given that the population vector is $\mathbf{N}$.

$PA_{ir}(\mathbf{n}|\mathbf{N})$ Arriver's distribution; i.e., the probability that a chain r customer arriving at station i finds $\mathbf{n}$ customers there when the network population is $\mathbf{N}$.

$PD_{ir}(\mathbf{n}|\mathbf{N})$ Departer's distribution; i.e., the probability that a chain r customer departing from station i leaves behind $\mathbf{n}$ customers, when the network population is $\mathbf{N}$.

$\lambda_{ir}(\mathbf{N})$ Throughput of chain r at station i, given that the population vector is $\mathbf{N}$.

$U_{ir}(\mathbf{N})$ Utilization of chain r at station i, given that the population vector is $\mathbf{N}$. This is always defined as $\lambda_{ir}(\mathbf{N})s^{\circ}_{ir}$.

$Q_{ir}(\mathbf{N})$ Average queue length of chain r at station i (including customers in service), as seen by a random observer.

$L_{ir}(\mathbf{N})$ Average waiting line length of chain r at station i (excluding customers in service), as seen by a random observer.

$R_{ir}(\mathbf{N})$ Average response time of chain r customers at station i.

$W_{ir}(\mathbf{N})$ Average waiting time of chain r customers at station i.

$CT_{ir}(\mathbf{N})$ Average cycle time of chain r customers with respect to station i.

$\lambda_i(\mathbf{N})$ Overall throughput of station i at population $\mathbf{N} = \sum_{r=1}^{K} \lambda_{ir}(\mathbf{N})$.

$U_i(\mathbf{N})$ Overall utilization of station $i = \sum_{r=1}^{K} U_{ir}(\mathbf{N})$.

$Q_i(\mathbf{N})$ Overall average queue length at station $i = \sum_{r=1}^{K} Q_{ir}(\mathbf{N})$.

$L_i(\mathbf{N})$ Overall average waiting line length at station $i = \sum_{r=1}^{K} L_{ir}(\mathbf{N})$.

$R_i(\mathbf{N})$ Overall average response time at station $i = Q_i(\mathbf{N})/\lambda_i(\mathbf{N})$.

$W_i(\mathbf{N})$ Overall average waiting time at station $i = L_i(\mathbf{N})/\lambda_i(\mathbf{N})$.

$CT_i(\mathbf{N})$ Overall cycle time with respect to station i.

$V_i(n_i)$ Product of capacities for station i (when the capacity is chain-independent). Defined as $\prod_{j=1}^{n_i} C_i(j)$.

$V_i(\mathbf{n}_i)$ Product of capacities for station i (when the capacity is chain-dependent). Defined in equation (6.6.5).

$X_i(\mathbf{n}_i)$ Unnormalized probability of finding $\mathbf{n}_i$ customers at station $i = \frac{n_i!}{V_i(n_i)} \prod_{r=1}^{K} \frac{u_{ir}^{n_{ir}}}{n_{ir}!}$

$G(\mathbf{N}, \Omega)$ Normalization constant for network Ω at population $\mathbf{N}$.

$f_X(..)$ Density (mass) function for a continuous (discrete) random variable X.

$F_X(..)$ Distribution function for a continuous or discrete random variable X.

$E(g(X))$ Expected value of function $g(X)$.

$\mathrm{Var}(X)$ Variance of the random variable X.

$\mathrm{Cov}(X, Y)$ Covariance of the random variables X and Y.

$\mathcal{C}_X(\theta)$ Characteristic function of X (discrete or continuous) $= E[e^{i\theta X}]$.

$\Phi_X(z)$ z-transform of the mass function of a nonnegative discrete random variable X. Defined as $\sum_{n=0}^{\infty} f_X(n)z^n$.

$\Psi_X(s)$ Laplace transform of the density function of a nonnegative continuous random variable X.

$\mathcal{Z}$ Denotes a Markov chain. $\mathcal{Z}^*$ is also used when two Markov chains are involved.

Q Transition rate (probability) matrix for a continuous (discrete) parameter Markov chain. The symbols Q^* and Q' are also used for the same purpose.

$\Pi(t)$ A row vector $[\pi_0(t), \pi_1(t), \ldots]$ giving the state probabilities of a Markov chain at time t. For steady-state distribution, the argument t is omitted.

Pr General notation for the probability of an event.

$\mathbf{e}$ A vector of all 1's. Dimensionality depends on the context.

Notes

1. The notations for single-chain networks follow by just removing the chain subscript from the symbol, and are not listed explicitly.
2. For open networks, the population indicator is removed; e.g., Q_{ir}, R_{ir}, etc.
3. When a chain consists of multiple classes, the last subscript gives the class number; e.g., v_{irc} is the visit ratio of class c customers of chain r at station i.
4. The primary symbols for stations, classes, and chains are as follows: i, j for stations; r, k for chains; and c, d for classes. *Keeping this convention in mind should make the equations much more readable.*
5. When both scalars and vectors are involved, boldface (and sometimes uppercase) letters are used for matrices and vectors, and lowercase letters for scalars. For example, $\boldsymbol{\alpha}$ refers to a vector, α_i to an element of $\boldsymbol{\alpha}$, and α to its magnitude (1-norm).
6. Uppercase letters are generally used for random variables, except when conflicts might arise with standard symbols listed above. In the latter case, script letters are used to denote the random variables. For example, $\mathcal{R}$ denotes the random variable for response time, because R is reserved for the mean response time.
7. In isolated places, some of the symbols listed above are used in a different context, but this should not cause confusion. For example, in Chapter 3, Q refers to total variation and e_j, e_{ij} to main and interaction effects.
8. Only the frequently used symbols are listed above. Chapter 4 uses many other symbols, but they are not needed elsewhere.

APPENDIX

B

Introduction to Probability Theory

In this appendix we provide a brief overview of the probability theory. The material is intended to be a refresher and is not targeted toward readers unfamiliar with the subject. The topics that are particularly important in the context of performance modeling (e.g., stage type distributions and characteristic functions) have received particular attention. The discussion assumes familiarity with elementary calculus.

B.1 Basic Concepts

In this section we discuss the fundamental concepts of events and their probabilities, properties of the probability measure, distribution and density functions, expectation and moments of a random variable, functions of a random variable, and some inequalities that are often useful in dealing with the probabilities.

B.1.1 Events and the Probability Measure

Probability is defined as the triple $\{\Omega, \omega, Pr\}$ where Ω is the *sample space*, defined as a set of all possible *outcomes* of an experiment or *sample points*; $\omega \subset \Omega$ is an *event* that includes all outcomes of interest; and $Pr(\omega)$ is the probability measure associated with the event ω. This measure must satisfy the following properties: $0 \le Pr(\omega) \le 1$, $Pr(\Omega) = 1$, and $Pr(\phi) = 0$, where ϕ is the *null event*, i.e., the event that does not include any sample points. For example, if we count the number of arrivals during a given time period, each possible value is a sample point, and the specification like "at least two arrivals" characterizes an event (or a subset of the sample space) with which we can associate a probability measure.

Since events are merely sets, we can use various properties of sets to properly assign probabilities to nonelementary events. The familiar *Venn diagram* representation of sets is particularly useful in this regard. For example, let A and B be two events, and consider the events $U = A \cup B$ and $I = A \cap B$. Then U includes the sample points of both A and B, and thus $Pr(U)$ represents the probability that either A or B occurs. Similarly, I includes only the sample points common to both A and B and thus $Pr(I)$ represents the probability that both A and B occur together. Henceforth, we shall write $Pr(A \cap B)$ as $Pr(A, B)$ also. It is easy to see from a Venn diagram representation that

$$Pr(A \cup B) = Pr(A) + Pr(B) - Pr(A \cap B) \tag{1.1}$$

Obviously, if A and B are *mutually exclusive events*, i.e., have no sample points in common, then $A \cap B = \phi$. In this case, $Pr(A \cup B) = Pr(A) + Pr(B)$. Since $\text{Pr}(\Omega) = 1$, it also follows that A and B are *complementary events* (i.e., nonoverlapping and covering the entire sample space) if and only if $Pr(B) = 1 - Pr(A)$.

Let $Pr(A|B)$ denote the conditional probability of occurrence of A, given that B has already occurred. Then,

$$Pr(A, B) = Pr(A|B)Pr(B) \tag{1.2}$$

We call A and B *independent* if $Pr(A, B) = Pr(A)Pr(B)$. Obviously, if A and B are independent, $Pr(A|B) = Pr(A)$ and $Pr(B|A) = Pr(B)$. That is, the occurrence of one event does not tell us anything about the other. Also, if A and B are independent and mutually exclusive, $Pr(A \cap B) = Pr(A)Pr(B) = 0$, which means that one of the two events must be null. If A, B, and C are three events, it is easy to verify that

$$Pr(A, B|C) = Pr(A|B, C)Pr(B|C) \tag{1.3}$$

Let $B_1, \ldots, B_n$ denote a set of mutually exclusive events (or subsets) that span the entire sample space, and A some other event. Using the definition of conditional probability, it is then easy to verify that

$$P(B_i|A) = \frac{P(A|B_i)P(B_i)}{\sum_{j=1}^{n} P(A|B_j)P(B_j)} \tag{1.4}$$

B.1.2 Random Variables and Distributions

A random variable can be thought of as a function that maps outcomes (or sample points) to numbers. A *continuous random variable* is a mapping of outcomes to the real line, whereas a *discrete random variable* can be considered as a mapping of outcomes to integers. At times, it is convenient to speak of a random variable that takes only a countable set of values, except that those values are real numbers. Such a random variable also fits our definition of a discrete random variable, since we could easily associate a unique integer with each of its values. That is, we could view the actual values as a one-to-one function of an integer-valued random variable.

A discrete random variable N can be characterized by its *distribution function*, denoted $F_N(n)$, and defined as $F_N(n) = Pr(N \leq n)$. We can also speak of its density or *probability mass function*, denoted $f_N(n)$, defined as $f_N(n) = Pr(N = n)$. The following properties apply to these functions

$$F_N(n) = \sum_{i=-\infty}^{n} f_N(i), \qquad F_N(-\infty) = 0, \qquad F_N(+\infty) = 1 \tag{1.5}$$

Here we have chosen the lower limit of $-\infty$ for generality; in most of the performance modeling applications, the random variables are nonnegative, thereby requiring the lower limit of 0. Note that $F_N(n)$ is monotonic nondecreasing in the range 0 to 1, whereas $f_N(n)$ is nonnegative. Now consider two discrete random variables N and K. Then $f_{N,K}(n,k) = Pr(N = n, K = k)$ is called the *joint density* function, and $F_{N,K}(n,k) = Pr(N \leq n, K \leq k)$ is called the *joint distribution* function. Clearly,

$$F_{N,K}(n,k) = \sum_{i \leq n} \sum_{j \leq k} f_{N,K}(i,j) \tag{1.6}$$

Note that $F_{N,K}(-\infty, k) = F_{N,K}(n, -\infty) = 0$ for any n and k. $F_{N,K}(n,k)$ is monotonic nondecreasing with respect to n and k, and $F_{N,K}(\infty,\infty) = 1$. We can obtain individual or *marginal distribution* of these random variables as $F_N(n) = F_{N,K}(n,\infty)$ and $F_K(k) = F_{N,K}(\infty,k)$. The *marginal density* of N can be obtained as

$$f_N(n) = \sum_{k=-\infty}^{\infty} f_{N,K}(n,k) = F_{N,K}(n,\infty) - F_{N,K}(n-1,\infty) \tag{1.7}$$

We define the *conditional density* of N with respect to K as

$$f_{N|K}(n|k) = Pr(N = n|K = k) = f_{N,K}(n,k)/f_K(k) \tag{1.8}$$

where the last equation follows from the definition of the conditional probability. Similarly, we can define *conditional distribution* as

$$F_{N|K}(n|k) = Pr(N \leq n|K = k) = \frac{1}{f_K(k)} \sum_{i=-\infty}^{n} f_{N|K}(i,k) \tag{1.9}$$

If N and K are *independent*, we have $f_{N|K}(n|k) = f_N(n)$, which further implies that

$$f_{N,K}(n,k) = f_N(n) f_K(k) \tag{1.10}$$

Using this, or the fact that $Pr(N \leq n|K \leq k) = Pr(N \leq n)$, we also have

$$F_{N,K}(n,k) = F_N(n)F_K(k) \tag{1.11}$$

Let us now turn to continuous random variables. For such a variable X, $\Pr(X = x) = 0$ for any x. The *distribution function* is defined as $F_X(x) = \Pr(X \leq x)$ and the *density function*, if it exists, as

$$f_X(x) = \lim_{\Delta \to 0} \frac{Pr(x < X \leq x + \Delta)}{\Delta} = \frac{dF_X(x)}{dx} \tag{1.12}$$

$F_X(x)$ is monotonic nondecreasing in the range of 0 to 1 and $f_X(x)$ is non-negative. Consider two continuous random variables X and Y. Then the *joint distribution* of X and Y, denoted $F_{X,Y}(x,y)$, is simply $\Pr(X \leq x, Y \leq y)$. Assuming that the limit in the following equation exists, the *joint density* function is given by

$$\begin{aligned} f_{X,Y}(x,y) &= \lim_{\Delta x \to 0, \Delta y \to 0} \frac{\Pr(x < X \leq x + \Delta x, \quad y < Y \leq y + \Delta y)}{\Delta x \Delta y} \\ &= \frac{\partial^2 F_{X,Y}(x,y)}{\partial x \partial y} \end{aligned} \tag{1.13}$$

From which, the *marginal density* of X can be obtained as

$$f_X(x) = \int_{-\infty}^{\infty} f_{X,Y}(x,y)\, dy \tag{1.14}$$

Using the definition of conditional probability and equation (1.12), we have

$$Pr(X \leq x|y < Y \leq y + \Delta y) \approx \frac{\int_{-\infty}^{x} f_{X,Y}(\tau, y)\, d\tau\, \Delta y}{f_Y(y)\Delta y}$$

Therefore, by taking the limit as $\Delta y \to 0$, we get the *conditional distribution* of X as

$$F_{X|Y}(x|y) \triangleq \Pr(X \leq x|Y = y) = \frac{1}{f_Y(y)} \int_{-\infty}^{x} f_{X,Y}(\tau, y)\, d\tau \tag{1.15}$$

and the conditional density as

$$f_{X|Y}(x|y) = \frac{\partial F_{X|Y}(x,y)}{\partial x} = \frac{f_{XY}(x,y)}{f_Y(y)} \tag{1.16}$$

Note that these equations are identical (except that the summation changes into an integral) to equations (1.9) and (1.8). If X and Y are independent, $Pr(X \leq x|Y \leq y) = Pr(X \leq x)$. Therefore, by the definition of the conditional probability, we get

$$F_{X,Y}(x,y) = F_X(x)F_Y(y) \quad \text{and} \quad f_{X,Y}(x,y) = f_X(x)f_Y(y) \tag{1.17}$$

which are again identical to their discrete counterparts.

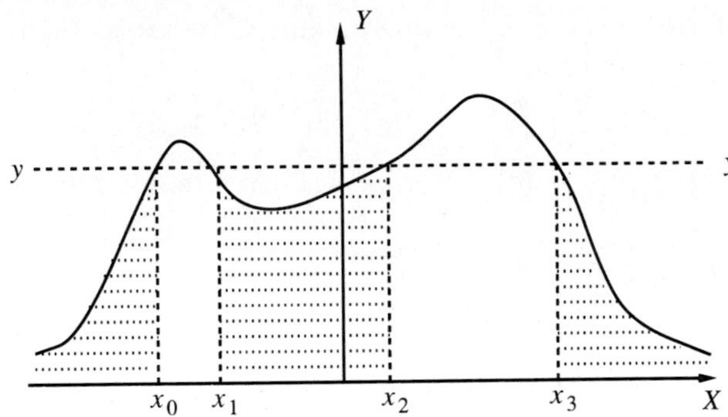

FIGURE B-1: A function of a random variable.

B.1.3 Functions of a Random Variable

The function of a random variable can be defined in the same way as a function of an ordinary variable. Let X denote a random variable and $Y = g(X)$ some function. Then, if X takes a value x, the random variable Y will take a value $g(x)$. Let us see how to obtain the distribution of Y from that of X. Fig. B-1 shows an arbitrary function $Y = g(X)$ defined over the entire real line $(-\infty, +\infty)$. By definition, $F_Y(y) = Pr(Y \leq y) = Pr(g(X) \leq y)$. The horizontal line defines the regions where $g(X)$ is no greater than y. We can identify a sequence of $2n$ intersection points for these regions, denoted as $x_0, x_1, \ldots, x_{2n-2}, x_{2n-1}$.[1] Then from Fig. B-1, we have

$$Pr(g(X) \leq y) = Pr(X \leq x_0) + Pr(X > x_{2n-1}) + \sum_{i=1}^{n-1} Pr(x_{2i-1} \leq X < x_{2i})$$

Therefore,

$$F_Y(y) = F_X(x_0) + \sum_{i=1}^{n-1}[F_X(x_{2i}) - F_X(x_{2i-1})] + [1 - F_X(x_{2n-1})] \tag{1.18}$$

This provides us with a general method for finding the distribution of an arbitrary function of a random variable. If the function $g(X)$ has a unique inverse, we can use the following simpler approach

$$F_Y(y) = Pr[g(X) \leq y] = Pr[X \leq g^{-1}(y)] = F_X[g^{-1}(y)] \tag{1.19}$$

Example B.1 Compute the distribution of $g(X)$ for the following two cases:

1. X is uniformly distributed over the interval $[-1, +1]$ and $g(X) = X^2$.
2. X has the density $f_X(x) = \mu e^{-\mu x}$ and $g(X) = e^X$.

[1] As shown, $g(x)$ should be increasing at x_0; if not, we assume that $x_0 = -\infty$. Similarly, $g(x)$ should be decreasing at x_{2n-1}; if not, we assume that $x_{2n-1} = +\infty$.

Solution For part (1), the function $Y = X^2$ is *not* uniquely invertible. Using the approach for the general case, we have

$$F_Y(y) = Pr(Y \le y) = Pr(-\sqrt{y} < X \le \sqrt{y}) = F_X(\sqrt{y}) - F_X(-\sqrt{y})$$

The uniform density is given by $f_X(x) = 1/2$ for $|x| \le 1$. Therefore, by integration, we get

$$F_X(x) = \begin{cases} (x+1)/2 & -1 \le x \le 1 \\ 0 & x < -1 \\ 1 & x > 1 \end{cases} \tag{1.20}$$

Substituting and simplifying, we get

$$F_Y(y) = \begin{cases} \sqrt{y} & 0 \le y \le 1 \\ 0 & y < 0 \\ 1 & y > 1 \end{cases}$$

By differentiation, we get $f_Y(y) = 0.5y^{-0.5}$ in the range $0 \le y \le 1$ and zero elsewhere. In part (2), the function is uniquely invertible; therefore,

$$F_Y(y) = F_X[g^{-1}(y)] = F_X(\ln y) = 1 - e^{-\mu \ln y} \quad \text{for} \quad \ln y \ge 0$$

which gives $F_Y(y) = 1 - y^{-\mu}$ for $y \ge 1$. □

B.1.4 Expectation and Moments

Consider some function $g(X)$ of a random variable X. If X is discrete, then the *expected value* of $g(X)$, denoted $E[g(X)]$, is defined as

$$E[g(X)] = \sum_{n=-\infty}^{\infty} g(n) Pr(X = n) \tag{1.21}$$

and if X is continuous,

$$E[g(X)] = \int_{-\infty}^{\infty} g(x) f_X(x)\, dx \tag{1.22}$$

$E[X^k]$ is called the kth *moment* of X. $E[X]$ is also called the *mean*. For convenience, we will also denote $E[X]$ as s. The quantity $E[(X-s)^k]$ is known as the kth *central moment* of X. For $k = 2$, this moment is known as the *variance* and denoted as $\mathrm{Var}(X)$ or σ_X^2. We shall call its square root σ_X the *standard deviation.*[2] Note that

$$\mathrm{Var}(X) = E[(X-s)^2] = E[X^2] - s^2 \tag{1.23}$$

The quantity $CV_X = \sigma_X / s$ is called the *coefficient of variation*. It is a dimensionless number and gives an idea of the variability of the distribution. A coefficient of variation equal to 1 is considered "normal" and corresponds to the exponential distribution. Two other useful dimensionless numbers for describing properties of a distribution are:

[2] In statistics literature, standard deviation often refers to the square root of sample variance. Following the terminology for the mean, we shall call that quantity *sample standard deviation.*

(a) $E[(X-s)^3]/E[X^2]^{3/2}$, which measures the *skewness* or asymmetry of the distribution, and

(b) $E[(X-s)^4]/E[X^2]^2$, which measures the rate of decay of the distribution around the mean.

Often, one also needs the notions of *joint expectation* and *joint moment*. Let $X_1, \ldots, X_n$ be a set of continuous random variables. Then their joint expectation is the expected value of the product $X_1 \times \cdots \times X_n$, and is given by

$$E[X_1 \cdots X_n] = \int_{-\infty}^{\infty} \cdots \int_{-\infty}^{\infty} x_1 \cdots x_n f_{X_1 \ldots X_n}(x_1, \ldots, x_n) dx_1 \cdots dx_n \qquad (1.24)$$

where the argument of the integral contains a product of x_1 through x_n. We can modify this definition appropriately if any of the X_i's are discrete. The notion can be generalized by allowing arbitrary powers of X_i's. Thus, $E[X_1^2 X_2^3]$ is a joint moment of X_1 and X_2 of order $(2,3)$. Yet another concept of interest is that of *factorial moment*. Let us define the product

$$< X, m >= X(X-1) \cdots (X-m+1)$$

Then $E[< X, m >]$ is known as the mth order factorial moment of X. Using an equation similar to (1.24), we could also define the *joint factorial moment* as the expected value of the products of $< X_i, m_i >$'s, usually denoted as $E[< X_1, m_1 > \cdots < X_n, m_n >]$.

Now we look at some properties of the expectation operator. From the definition in equations (1.21) and (1.22), it follows that this operator is linear, i.e.,

$$E\left[\sum_{i=1}^{k} g_i(X_i)\right] = \sum_{i=1}^{k} E[g_i(X_i)] \qquad (1.25)$$

irrespective of whether X_i's are mutually independent. In particular, the first moment of a sum of random variables is always the sum of first moments of these random variables. If X_i's are independent, we also have the following property

$$E\left[\prod_{i=1}^{k} g_i(X_i)\right] = \prod_{i=1}^{k} E[g_i(X_i)] \qquad (1.26)$$

This property follows from the fact that if X_i's are independent, their joint density is a product of individual densities. In particular,

$$\text{Var}\left(\prod_{i=1}^{k} X_i\right) = \prod_{i=1}^{k} \text{Var}(X_i) \qquad (1.27)$$

It is also easy to show that (under the assumption of independence) a similar property holds with respect to the sum of variances, i.e.,

$$\text{Var}\left(\sum_{i=1}^{k} X_i\right) = \sum_{i=1}^{k} \text{Var}(X_i) \qquad (1.28)$$

The expected value of a *nonnegative* random variable can be expressed in terms of its *complementary distribution function* $F_X^{(c)}(x)$. If X is continuous, a simple integration by parts yields

$$E[X] = \int_0^\infty x f_X(x)\,dx = \int_0^\infty F_X^{(c)}(x)\,dx = \int_0^\infty Pr(X \geq x)\,dx \tag{1.29}$$

whereas if X is discrete, a rearrangement of summands yields

$$E[X] = \sum_{k=1}^{\infty} kPr(X = k) = \sum_{k=1}^{\infty} Pr(X \geq k) \tag{1.30}$$

The *conditional expectation* of $g(X)$, denoted $E[g(X)|y]$, is defined as the expected value of $g(X)$ given that Y has the specified value y. That is, if X is continuous,

$$E[g(X)|y] = \int_{-\infty}^{\infty} g(x) f_{X|Y}(x|y)\,dx \tag{1.31}$$

A similar definition can be written down when X is discrete. As an example of the usefulness of this concept, let X denote the waiting time of a customer at a station and Y as the service time. Then $E[X|y]$ is the mean waiting time of all those customers whose service time requirement is y. This is the *conditional waiting time* measure discussed in Section 8.3.5.

Note that $E[g(X)|y]$ can be regarded as an ordinary function of y. With a slight change in the point of view, we can write conditional expectation as $E[g(X)|Y]$ and regard it as a function of the random variable Y. This view allows us to speak of the expected value of $E[g(X)|Y]$ itself. From equation (1.31), it is then easy to see that

$$E[g(X)] = E\{E[g(X)|Y]\} \tag{1.32}$$

This is a practically useful relationship, since it is often easier to first find the conditional expectation and then the *total expectation*. For example, let $Z = X_1 + \cdots + X_N$ where X_i's are *iid* (independent, identically distributed) with the common mean denoted as $E[X]$. Also, suppose that N itself is a random variable, independent of X_i's. Then equation (1.32) implies that

$$E[Z] = E[E(Z|N)] = E[N\,E(X)] = E(N) \times E(X) \tag{1.33}$$

A further use of equation (1.32) is explored in Exercise B.3.

B.1.5 Some Inequalities

We start with the concepts of correlation and covariance. Let X_1 and X_2 be two random variables with $E[X_1] = s_1$ and $E[X_2] = s_2$. Their *covariance* is defined as

$$\text{Cov}(X_1, X_2) = E\left[(X_1 - s_1)(X_2 - s_2)\right] = E[X_1X_2] - E[X_1]E[X_2] \tag{1.34}$$

Obviously, if X_1 and X_2 are independent, $\text{Cov}(X_1X_2) = 0$. Unfortunately, the opposite is not true; i.e., $\text{Cov}(X_1X_2)$ *can be 0 even if* X_1 *and* X_2 *are mutually dependent*. For example, if $X_2 = X_1^2$, and X_1 is uniformly distributed over the interval $(-1, 1)$, we have

$$E[X_1X_2] = E[X_1^3] = 0 \quad \text{and} \quad E[X_1]E[X_2] = 0 \cdot E[X_1^2] = 0$$

That is, $\text{Cov}(X_1, X_2) = 0$, but X_1 and X_2 are totally interdependent! Because of this, covariance is not a reliable indicator of the degree of dependence in general. However, it does accurately reflect the *linear dependence* or *correlation* between two variables. To see this, consider the random variables $Y_i = (X_i - s_i)/\sigma_i$ where σ_i is the standard deviation of X_i. Obviously, $E[Y_i^2] = 1$. Since $E[(Y_1 \pm Y_2)^2]$ can never be negative, we have

$$E[Y_1^2] + E[Y_2^2] \pm 2E[Y_1Y_2] \geq 0 \quad \Rightarrow \quad |E[Y_1Y_2]| \leq 1$$

Now substituting back for X_i's, we get

$$\text{Cov}(X_1, X_2) \leq \sigma_1\sigma_2 \quad \text{and} \quad \text{Cov}(X_1, X_2) \geq -\sigma_1\sigma_2 \tag{1.35}$$

which can also be put in the following compact form

$$|\text{Cov}(X_1, X_2)| \leq \sigma_1\sigma_2 \tag{1.36}$$

In view of this relation, it is useful to define a dimensionless measure known as the *correlation coefficient*, denoted $\rho_{X_1X_2}$.

$$\rho_{X_1X_2} = \frac{\text{Cov}(X_1, X_2)}{\sigma_1\sigma_2} \tag{1.37}$$

Obviously then, $-1 \leq \rho_{X_1X_2} \leq +1$, and it is shown in Exercise B.2 that $|\rho_{X_1X_2}|=1$, if and only if X_1 and X_2 are linearly-dependent. If $\rho_{X_1X_2} = 0$, we say that X_1 and X_2 are *uncorrelated*.

There are a few other useful inequalities involving expectations. The first such inequality is called the *Cauchy–Schwarz inequality*, which states

$$(E[X_1X_2])^2 \leq E[X_1^2]E[X_2^2] \tag{1.38}$$

To prove this, we start with equation (1.34), and apply the first part of equation (1.35).

$$\begin{aligned}(E[X_1X_2])^2 &= [\text{Cov}(X_1, X_2) + s_1s_2]^2 \leq \sigma_1^2\sigma_2^2 + 2s_1s_2(\sigma_1\sigma_2) + s_1^2s_2^2 \\ &\leq \sigma_1^2\sigma_2^2 + s_1^2s_2^2 + s_1^2\sigma_2^2 + s_2^2\sigma_1^2 = (\sigma_1^2 + s_1^2)(\sigma_2^2 + s_2^2)\end{aligned}$$

where we have used the inequality $2xy \leq x^2 + y^2$ for any x and y.

The next result, known as the *Markov inequality*, allows us to say something about the distribution when only the mean is known:

$$Pr(X \geq x) \leq E[X]/x \tag{1.39}$$

Of course, this inequality makes sense only for $x > E[X]$. The proof of this inequality follows trivially from the definition of $E[X]$, since

$$E[X] \geq \int_x^\infty t f_X(t)\, dt \geq \int_x^\infty x f_X(t)\, dt = x Pr(X \geq x)$$

Needless to say, the upper bound given by the Markov inequality could be very loose. If the variance is also known, a better bound is given by the *Chebychev inequality*. For any $\alpha > 1$, we have

$$Pr\Big[|X - E[X]| \geq \alpha\sigma_X\Big] \leq 1/\alpha^2 \tag{1.40}$$

To prove this inequality, we replace X with $(X - E[X])^2$ and x by $\alpha^2\text{Var}(X)$ in the Markov inequality, and use the fact that for any Z and z, $Pr(Z^2 \geq z^2) = Pr(|Z| \geq z)$. Chebychev's inequality can also be "turned around" to get a lower bound, i.e.,

$$Pr\Big[|X - E[X]| \leq \alpha\sigma_X\Big] \geq 1 - 1/\alpha^2 \tag{1.41}$$

One application of the Chebychev inequality is in obtaining the *weak law of large numbers*. Suppose that we have a set of n *iid* random variables $X_1, \ldots, X_n$ with mean s and a finite variance σ^2. Let $\overline{X}$ denote their arithmetic average. Clearly, $\text{Var}(\overline{X}) = \sigma^2/n$, and hence by the Chebychev inequality, $Pr(|\overline{X} - s| \geq x) \leq \sigma^2/(nx^2)$. Therefore, in the limit as $n \to \infty$, for any value x,

$$\lim_{n\to\infty} Pr(|\overline{X} - s| \geq x) = 0 \tag{1.42}$$

That is, as $n \to \infty$, the sample mean approaches the expected value.

B.2 Summary of Selected Distributions

In this section, we briefly present some discrete and continuous distributions and their properties. Only those distributions that are most useful in performance modeling are included.

B.2.1 Discrete Distributions

Bernoulli: Here the discrete random variable, denoted N throughout this section, can only take two values. Without loss of generality, let $Pr(N = 1) = p$ and $Pr(N = 0) = 1 - p$. Then,

$$E[N] = p, \qquad \sigma_N^2 = p(1-p) \tag{2.1}$$

Example application: Utilization measurement, e.g., let $U = 1$ if the device is busy and 0 otherwise. Then U has Bernoulli distribution, and the purpose of measurement is to estimate p.

Binomial: Consider an experiment whose outcome is a success or failure. Let p be the probability of success. Let N denote the number of successes in n independent replications of the experiment. Then N has the binomial distribution given by

$$B(n,k,p) \triangleq Pr(N=k|n) = \binom{n}{k} p^k(1-p)^{n-k} \tag{2.2}$$

For this distribution, $E[N] = np$, and $\sigma_N^2 = np(1-p)$. If $N_1, \ldots, N_n$ are n *iid* random variables with Bernoulli distribution, then it is easy to verify that $N = N_1 + \cdots + N_n$ has the binomial distribution given in equation (2.2).

Example application: Result of making several utilization measurements.

Poisson: Consider the occurrence of some event such that in a small time interval Δt, the probability of occurrence of one event is $\lambda\Delta t$, and the probability of more than one event is negligible; i.e., of order $(\Delta t)^2$. Let $N(t)$ denote the number of events occurring in interval t. Then $N(t)$ has the Poisson distribution given by

$$Pr[N(t)=n] = \frac{e^{-\lambda t}(\lambda t)^n}{n!} \tag{2.3}$$

To prove this result, let $f(n,t) = Pr[N(t)=n]$. There are only two possibilities during time δt: one arrival or no arrival. Therefore, we can write the following equation for $f(n,t)$.

$$f(n, t+\Delta t) = f(n-1,t)\lambda\Delta t + f(n,t)(1-\lambda\Delta t)$$

which yields the following differential-difference equation

$$f'(n,t) = [f(n-1,t) - f(n,t)]\lambda \tag{2.4}$$

It is now easy to verify that equation (2.3) is a solution to equation (2.4). (See Exercise B.5.)

For the Poisson distribution, $E[N] = \sigma_N^2 = \lambda t$. Poisson distribution has a number of other interesting properties, which are discussed in Section 5.1.3.

Example application: Number of jobs arriving at a computing facility during a given time period.

Geometric: Consider an experiment whose outcome is a success or failure. Let p be the probability of success. Let N denote the number of independent replications needed to obtain success for the first time. Then N has the geometric distribution given by

$$Pr(N=n) = (1-p)^{n-1}p, \quad n = 1,2,3,\ldots \tag{2.5}$$

For this distribution, $E[N] = 1/p$ and $\sigma_N^2 = (1-p)/p^2$. In some applications, we want N to represent the number of failures before a success. In such cases,

$$Pr(N=n) = (1-p)^n p, \quad n = 0,1,2,\ldots \tag{2.6}$$

For this case, $E[N] = (1-p)/p$, but the variance remains the same.

Example application: Number of CPU "bursts" a job needs before it is completed, or number of times a message must be retransmitted to ensure error-free reception. Geometric distribution is the discrete counterpart of the exponential distribution. It has the memoryless property, which makes it attractive in analytic modeling.

Negative Binomial: Consider the same situation as for the geometric distribution, but now let N denote the number of failures before the kth success. Then N has negative binomial distribution given by

$$Pr(N = n) = \binom{n+k-1}{n}(1-p)^n p^k \tag{2.7}$$

For this distribution $E[N] = k(1-p)/p$ and $\sigma_N^2 = k(1-p)/p^2$. Note that if in the geometric distribution, we only count the number of failures, the negative binomial random variable will be a sum of k independent geometric random variables.

B.2.2 Continuous Distributions

Exponential: Let X denote a nonnegative continuous random variable. The exponential distribution is then characterized by the following density and distribution functions

$$f_X(x) = \mu e^{-\mu x} \quad \text{and} \quad F_X(x) = 1 - e^{-\mu x} \tag{2.8}$$

For this distribution, $E[X] = 1/\mu$ and $\text{Var}(X) = 1/\mu^2$. The coefficient of variation, CV_X, is then simply 1.

Example application: Running time of a job with $1/\mu$ as the mean. Because of its memoryless property, exponential distribution is of prime importance in performance modeling. As shown in Exercise B.8, this distribution can be considered to be a limiting case of the geometric distribution.

Erlang: Let $X_1, \ldots, X_n$ be *iid* random variables having exponential distribution with mean $1/\mu$. Then $X = X_1 + \cdots + X_n$ has n-stage Erlang distribution. We shall later see that the density of X can be obtained as the convolution of the densities of X_i's. Therefore,

$$f_X(x) = \frac{\mu(\mu x)^{n-1}}{(n-1)!}e^{-\mu x}, \qquad F_X(x) = 1 - e^{-\mu x}\sum_{j=0}^{n-1}\frac{(\mu x)^j}{j!} \tag{2.9}$$

Also,

$$E[X] = nE[X_i] = n/\mu \quad \text{and} \quad \text{Var}(X) = n\sigma_{X_i}^2 = n/\mu^2 \tag{2.10}$$

Therefore, $CV_X = 1/\sqrt{n}$.

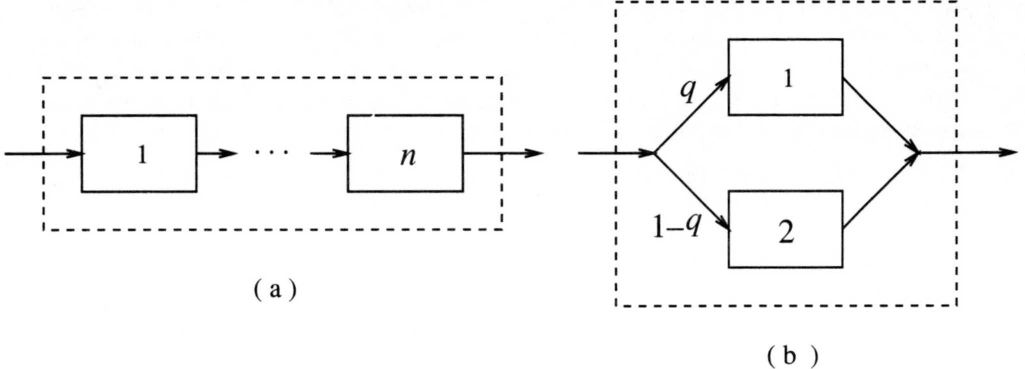

FIGURE B-2: Erlang and hyperexponential distributions.

A service station with n-stage Erlang distribution can be viewed as consisting of n exponential sub-stations or *stages* connected in series, as shown in Fig. B-2(a). Only one customer is allowed inside the dotted box, and it receives service sequentially from each stage. This view is useful in the Markovian analysis of queuing systems where the service time and/or the interarrival time has Erlang distribution. For this distribution, $CV_X \leq 1$ and decreases rather slowly with the number of stages. Distributions related to the exponential distribution that give $CV_X < 1$ are known as *hypo-exponential*.

Example application: Useful for modeling processing times at devices where the variability is low; e.g., the service time at a paging disk.

Hyperexponential: Let X_1 and X_2 denote two exponentially distributed random variables with means $1/\mu_1$ and $1/\mu_2$ respectively. Suppose that the random variable X assumes the values of X_1 with probability q, and the values of X_2 with probability $1-q$. Then the density of X is given by

$$f_X(x) = q\mu_1 e^{-\mu_1 x} + (1-q)\mu_2 e^{-\mu_2 x} \tag{2.11}$$

This is known as a two-stage hyperexponential distribution. Its mean and variance are given by

$$E[X] = \frac{q}{\mu_1} + \frac{1-q}{\mu_2} \tag{2.12}$$

$$\text{Var}(X) = \frac{q(2-q)}{\mu_1^2} + \frac{1-q^2}{\mu_2^2} - \frac{2q(1-q)}{\mu_1\mu_2} \tag{2.13}$$

Let X denote the service time of a customer at a station. Then we can view the station as consisting of two exponential substations (or stages) connected in parallel, as shown in Fig. B-2(b). The two stages have mean service times of $1/\mu_1$ and $1/\mu_2$ respectively, and an arriving customer goes to the first stage with probability q. Again, this view is important in the Markovian analysis of systems using hyperexponential distribution. It is easy to show that $CV_X > 1$; moreover, it is possible to obtain an arbitrarily large value for CV_X by choosing q and μ_1/μ_2 appropriately. Thus, even though we can consider an n-stage hyperexponential distribution for $n > 2$, that generalization is rarely needed. This is in contrast to the Erlang case, where n determines CV_X.

Example application: Processing time at devices with high variability; e.g., the service time at the CPU.

Gamma: This is a generalization of the Erlang distribution, where the parameter n is replaced by a real number α. It has the following density function

$$f_X(x) = \frac{\mu(\mu x)^{\alpha-1}}{\Gamma(\alpha)} e^{-\mu x} \tag{2.14}$$

where $\Gamma(\alpha)$ is the gamma function. For this distribution, $E[X] = \alpha/\mu$, $\text{Var}(X) = \alpha/\mu^2$ and $CV_X = 1/\sqrt{\alpha}$. The main point of the generalization is that any $CV_X \leq 1$ can be achieved. Unfortunately, this distribution does not have an exponential stage representation; therefore, its use in performance modeling is limited.

Branching Erlang: This is also a generalization of the Erlang distribution that does have the stage type interpretation, as shown in Fig. B-3. It differs from the Erlang distribution in that a customer can leave the system after finishing service in any stage (rather than just the nth stage). Also, the service time in each stage could be different. Let X denote a random variable with branching Erlang distribution, X_i the duration of the ith stage, and $E[X_i] = 1/\mu_i$. Then X takes on the values of X_1 with probability q_1, the values of $X_1 + X_2$ with probability $(1 - q_1)q_2$, etc. Define

$$Y_i = \sum_{j=1}^{i} X_j \quad \text{and} \quad \delta_i = q_i \prod_{j=1}^{i-1}(1 - q_j) \tag{2.15}$$

where the products over empty ranges are assumed to be 1. Then the density of X is given by

$$f_X(x) = \sum_{i=1}^{n} \delta_i f_{Y_i}(x) \tag{2.16}$$

which gives the following expressions for the first two moments

$$\begin{aligned} E[X] &= \sum_{i=1}^{n} \delta_i \sum_{j=1}^{i} \frac{1}{\mu_j} \\ E[X^2] &= \sum_{i=1}^{n} \delta_i \left[\sum_{j=1}^{i} \frac{1}{\mu_j^2} + \left(\sum_{j=1}^{i} \frac{1}{\mu_j} \right)^2 \right] \end{aligned} \tag{2.17}$$

This distribution is also known as *Coxian*, after Cox, who first proposed it. Apart from the stage type representation, the main significance of this distribution is

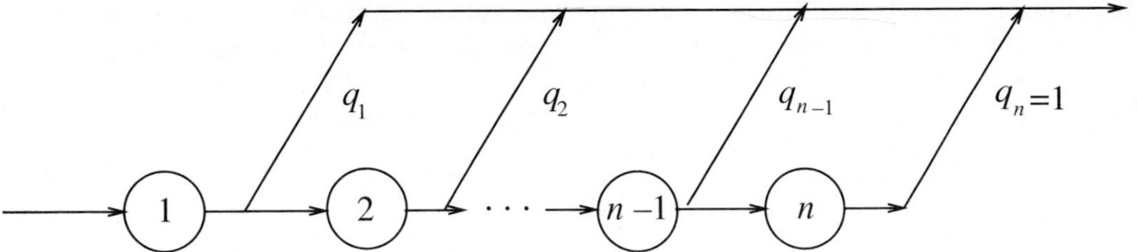

FIGURE B-3: Pictorial representation of the branching Erlang distribution.

that any coefficient of variation (CV) larger than $1/\sqrt{n}$ can be achieved. In fact, if we are only trying to match a given mean and coefficient of variation, we can make simplistic choices for all but two parameters. In particular, for $CV < 1$, it is enough to let $E[X_1] = \cdots = E[X_n]$ and $q_2 = \cdots = q_{n-1} = 0$. For $CV > 1$, we can choose $n = 2$, which gives only three unknown parameters. One of these is typically chosen by requiring that each stage contribute equally to the mean. It is easy to specialize equation (2.17) for these cases.

Branching Erlang distribution is *closed* under addition; i.e., if X_1 and X_2 are independent and have a branching Erlang distribution, then so does X_1+X_2.

Example application: Exponential stage approximation for arbitrarily distributed service times. Such an approximation is crucial for using Markov chain based analysis.

Generalized Stage-type Distribution: We saw that we can get $CV_X < 1$ by connecting exponential stages in series, and $CV_X > 1$ by connecting stages in parallel. This immediately leads to the possibility of having arbitrary series-parallel networks of exponential stages. In the Laplace transform domain, each series subnetwork will yield a term like $\prod_i \frac{\mu_i}{s+\mu_i}$, where μ_i is the service rate of the ith stage in the subnetwork. Similarly, a parallel connection will yield a weighted summation over terms like these. Thus, any series-parallel network will have a rational Laplace transform. Conversely, *any service time density with a rational Laplace transform can be represented as a series-parallel network of exponential stages*. Since a series-parallel network can be described recursively, it is easy to come up with recursive expressions for its moments. We shall leave the details as an exercise. The branching Erlang distribution can be viewed as a special type of series-parallel network. It can be shown that any density function with a rational Laplace transform can be represented by a branching Erlang network, provided that we are willing to let its parameters be complex-valued.

The idea can be generalized further by removing the restriction of series-parallel structure. We can even allow a customer to visit a stage more than once (i.e., have cycles in the network). The main motivation for these generalizations is to obtain a very general behavior using a small number of stages and retaining real-valued parameters. The resulting distributions are known as *phase-type distributions* and are studied in Section 9.5. These distributions show a number of closure properties, as described there.

Normal Distribution: Let X denote a continuous random variable defined over the entire real line. The normal or *Gaussian distribution* is specified by the following density function

$$f_X(x) = \frac{1}{\sqrt{2\pi}\sigma} \exp\left[\frac{-(x-s)^2}{2\sigma^2}\right] \tag{2.18}$$

where s is the mean and σ is the standard deviation. We shall denote this distribution as $\mathcal{N}(s, \sigma)$. No closed form is possible for the distribution function. Since s and σ can be chosen arbitrarily, any CV_X can be obtained. The normal distribution derives its importance from the following interesting result:

Central Limit theorem: Let $X_1, X_2, \ldots, X_n$ be a set of random variables with means $s_1, s_2, \ldots, s_n$ and standard deviations $\sigma_1, \sigma_2, \ldots, \sigma_n$, such that (1) s_i, σ_i, and s_i/σ_i are finite, and (2) all X_i's are mutually independent. Then as $n \to \infty$, we have

$$\frac{\sum_{i=1}^n X_i - \sum_{i=1}^n s_i}{\sqrt{\sum_{i=1}^n \sigma_i^2}} \to \mathcal{N}(0,1) \tag{2.19}$$

That is, for large n, the arithmetic average of $X_1, \ldots, X_n$ is approximately normally distributed. Notice that nothing is assumed regarding the distribution of X_i's. If X_i's themselves have normal distribution, then their average also has normal distribution, irrespective of the value of n. That is, *the normal distribution is closed under summation*. In practice, the independence requirement in the central limit theorem may not be met; therefore, one often uses a *meta-form of central limit theorem*, which states that the distribution approaches normal even if X_i's are weakly inter-dependent.

Because the normal variate can take negative values, this distribution is not useful for representing parameters like service times, resource requirements, etc. However, the central limit theorem makes it useful in characterizing error and the cumulative result of several different types of effects.

There are a number of useful distributions related to the normal distribution. Section 3.2 discusses two of them, namely the t-distribution and the χ^2-distribution. Yet another one is the *F-distribution*, which is useful for comparing the variance of the performance parameters of two systems. If X_1 and X_2 are independent and have a χ^2-distribution, then the ratio X_1/X_2 has the F-distribution.

Example application: Suppose that a set of floating-point data is processed by a series of steps, each one of which has different roundoff error characteristics. Then we could assume that the roundoff errors in the final result have approximately normal distribution. Another example is the data analysis from measurement or simulation, where each X_i corresponds to a separate observation from the system.

B.3 Characteristic Functions

In this section, we study various types of characteristic functions or "transforms" of the density function of a random variable and show their usefulness. For discrete random variables, one mostly uses the *z-transform*, or *probability generating function*, and we study that first. Next, we discuss the *Laplace transform*, which is useful for continuous random variables. Both of these transforms are intended primarily for nonnegative random variables and are particularly important in performance modeling for this reason. In dealing with random variables that can take both positive and negative values, one often uses the general characteristic function, which we discuss in Section B.3.3.

B.3.1 The Z-Transform

The z-transform of a discrete, *nonnegative* random variable N, denoted $\Phi_N(z)$, can be defined as follows:

$$\Phi_N(z) = E[z^N] = \sum_{n=0}^{\infty} z^n f_N(n) \tag{3.1}$$

As an example, suppose that N has Poisson distribution with a mean of λt. Then,

$$\Phi_N(z) = \sum_{n=0}^{\infty} \frac{(\lambda t)^n e^{-\lambda t}}{n!} z^n = e^{-\lambda t} \sum_{n=0}^{\infty} \frac{(\lambda t z)^n}{n!} = e^{-\lambda t(1-z)} \tag{3.2}$$

The z-transform has a number of interesting properties that make it useful in solving Markovian models. In stating these properties, we shall use the notation $\mathcal{Z}()$ to mean the z-transform of the enclosed expression.

1. *Moment generation:* By repeated differentiation, it is easy to verify that

$$\mathcal{Z}\left[\frac{n!}{(n-k)!} f_N(n)\right] = z^k \frac{d^k \Phi_N(z)}{dz^k} \tag{3.3}$$

   In particular, we have $\mathcal{Z}[nf_N(n)] = z\Phi'_N(z)$. From equations (3.1) and (3.3) we can conclude that $\Phi_N^{(k)}(z)$ evaluated at $z = 1$ gives the kth factorial moment of N, i.e.,

$$\Phi_N^{(k)}(1) = E[N(N-1)\cdots(N-k-1)] \tag{3.4}$$

   In particular, $E[N] = \Phi'_N(1)$ and $\text{Var}(N) = \Phi''_N(1) + \Phi'_N(1)[1 - \Phi'_N(1)]$.

2. *Convolution theorem:* Let K and L be two independent nonnegative discrete random variables and $N = K + L$. Then the mass function of N is the convolution of the mass functions of K and L. This can be proved as follows:

$$Pr(N = n) = \sum_{k=0}^{n} Pr(K = k, L = n - k) = \sum_{k=0}^{n} f_K(k) f_L(n-k) \tag{3.5}$$

Also, the z-transform of N (i.e., that of the mass function of N) is the product of the z-transforms of K and L.

$$\Phi_N(z) = E[Z^N] = E[Z^{K+L}] = E[Z^K]E[Z^L] = \Phi_K(z)\Phi_L(z) \tag{3.6}$$

Therefore, the convolution in the probability domain translates to product in the z-transform domain.

3. *Shift and scaling:* The following properties follow directly from the definition of z-transforms. For simplicity, we have dropped the subscript indicating the random variable from the functions f and Φ.

$$\mathcal{Z}[f(n) - f(n-1)] = (1-z)\Phi(z) \tag{3.7}$$

$$\mathcal{Z}[f(n+k)] = \frac{\Phi(z)}{z^k} - \sum_{j=0}^{k-1} \frac{f(j)}{z^{k-j}} \tag{3.8}$$

$$\mathcal{Z}[f(n-k)] = z^k\Phi(z) \tag{3.9}$$

$$\mathcal{Z}[a^n f(n)] = \Phi(az) \tag{3.10}$$

$$\mathcal{Z}[f(n/k)] = \Phi(z^k), \qquad n = 0, k, 2k, 3k, \ldots \tag{3.11}$$

Exercise B.9 explores a few more properties of z-transforms.

Because of these properties, z-transforms can be used for solving systems of difference equations that arise naturally when dealing with Markov chains. The technique is to first obtain the z-transform of the desired function and then invert it to retrieve the function. There are two ways to do the inversion: (a) use Taylor series expansion of $\Phi(z)$, and (b) obtain a partial-fraction representation of $\Phi(z)$ using standard techniques and then invert term by term. The *Taylor series expansion* around $z = 0$ yields

$$\Phi(z) = \sum_{n=0}^{\infty} \frac{\Phi^{(n)}(0)z^n}{n!} \triangleq \sum_{n=0}^{\infty} f(n)z^n \tag{3.12}$$

Comparing the two summations term-by-term, we get the following interesting relationship between the function $f(n)$ and its z-transform $\Phi(z)$, often known as the *intermediate value theorem.*

$$f(n) = \frac{1}{n!}\frac{d^n\Phi(z)}{dz^n}\bigg|_{z=0} \tag{3.13}$$

We shall illustrate the *partial-fraction expansion* method by a simple example, but at the same time make some general comments as well.

Example B.2 Invert the following z-transform using partial-fraction expansion and obtain $f(n)$.

$$\Phi(z) = \frac{z^2(z+4) - 6(z+1)}{z^2 + 4z - 6} \tag{3.14}$$

Solution The first step is to check whether the numerator has higher powers of z than the denominator. If so, we have to do a long division to rectify this situation. With our $\Phi(z)$ function, a long division reduces it to

$$\Phi(z) = z + \Phi^*(z) \qquad \text{where} \quad \Phi^*(z) = -6/(z^2 + 4z - 6)$$

Here the z term will invert to $u_0(n-1)$ (see Section E.4). Therefore, we shall only work with $\Phi^*(z)$ function from now on. The next step is to find the roots of the denominator. These are $z = -2 \pm \sqrt{10}$. Then we can write

$$\Phi^*(z) = \frac{A}{(z + 2 - \sqrt{10})} + \frac{B}{(z + 2 + \sqrt{10})}$$

where A and B are some constants. Notice that the above is a valid form since both roots are simple. If we had a root r of multiplicity 2, we would have to use two terms for it, one of type $A_1/(z-r)$ and the other $A_2/(z-r)^2$. Similar comments apply to the roots of higher multiplicity. Now to evaluate these constants, we simply find the *residue* of $\Phi^*(z)$ at the corresponding root. The term A_j for a root r of multiplicity k is given by $\lim_{z\to r} \frac{1}{(k-j)!} \frac{d^{k-j}}{dz^{k-j}} \left[(z-r)^k \Phi^*(z)\right]$. Therefore,

$$\begin{aligned} A &= \lim_{z \to -2+\sqrt{10}} (z + 2 - \sqrt{10})\Phi(z) = -3/\sqrt{10} \\ B &= \lim_{z \to -2-\sqrt{10}} (z + 2 + \sqrt{10})\Phi(z) = 3/\sqrt{10} \end{aligned}$$

By applying the inversion formula $(z+a)^{-1} \to (-1)^n a^{-(n+1)}$, we get the corresponding time function, denoted $f^*(n)$.

$$f^*(n) = \frac{3}{\sqrt{10}} \left[(\sqrt{10} - 2)^{-n-1} - (-2 - \sqrt{10})^{-n-1}\right] \tag{3.15}$$

□

Example B.3 Consider the following system of difference equations for a function $P(n)$, $n = 0..\infty$

$$P(n+1) = (1+\rho)P(n) - \rho P(n-2), \qquad n = 2, 3, 4, \ldots \tag{3.16}$$

along with the conditions $P(2) = (1+\rho)P(1)$ and $P(1) = \rho P(0)$. Solve this system and obtain an expression for $P(n)$.

Solution A convenient way of solving this system is to first obtain the z-transform. For this, we multiply both sides of equation (3.16) by z^n, sum from $n = 2$ to ∞, and express the terms using $\Phi(z)$. After simplification, which involves the use of $P(1)$ and $P(0)$, this yields

$$\Phi(z) = P(0)/(1 - \rho z - \rho z^2) \tag{3.17}$$

To invert $\Phi(z)$, we use the partial-fraction approach. For this, we first find the roots of the denominator. The roots are $(-1 \pm r)/2$ where $r = \sqrt{1+4/\rho}$. Therefore, by using the partial-fraction expansion technique of the previous example, we have

$$\Phi(z) = \frac{-P(0)}{r\rho}\left[\frac{1}{z+0.5+0.5r} - \frac{1}{z+0.5-0.5r}\right]$$

The inversion and simplification yields the following solution for $P(n)$

$$P(n) = \frac{\rho^n P(0)}{r2^{n+1}}\left[(1+r)^{n+1} - (1-r)^{n+1}\right] \tag{3.18}$$

□

B.3.2 Laplace Transform

The Laplace transform of a nonnegative continuous random variable X, denoted $\Psi_X(s)$, is defined as

$$\Psi_X(s) = E[e^{-sX}] = \int_0^\infty e^{-sx} f_X(x)\,dx \tag{3.19}$$

The properties of Laplace transforms closely parallel those of z-transforms, so we mention them only briefly. In the following, we use $\mathcal{L}()$ to denote the Laplace transform of the enclosed expression. Laplace transforms are usually needed when dealing with time dependence; therefore, we shall use t instead of x in stating the properties. Also, we shall omit the subscript indicating the random variable from $f(t)$ and $\Psi(s)$, since the properties apply to any integrable function $f(t)$. By definition, it follows that

$$\frac{d^n\Psi(s)}{ds^n} = \int_0^\infty e^{-st}(-t)^n f(t)\,dt = \mathcal{L}\left[(-t)^n f(t)\right] \tag{3.20}$$

That is, multiplication by t in the time domain results in the derivative with respect to s in the transform domain. This immediately gives the following moment generation property

$$E[X^n] = (-1)^n \left.\frac{d^n\Psi(s)}{ds^n}\right|_{s=0} \tag{3.21}$$

The opposite property also holds. That is, the multiplication by s in the transform domain results in the derivative in the time domain.

$$\mathcal{L}[f^{(n)}(t)] = s^n\mathcal{L}[f(t)] - \sum_{i=1}^{n} s^{n-i} f^{(n-i)}(0) \tag{3.22}$$

This property is easily shown by repeated integration by parts. For example,

$$\begin{aligned}\mathcal{L}[f'(t)] &= \int_0^\infty e^{-st} f'(t)\,dt = f(t)e^{-st}\Big|_0^\infty + s\int_0^\infty f(t)e^{-st}\,dt \\ &= -f(0) + s\mathcal{L}[f(t)]\end{aligned} \tag{3.23}$$

For the *convolution property*, let $X = X_1 + \cdots + X_n$ where X_i's are all mutually independent. Then,

$$\Psi_X(s) = E[e^{-sX}] = E[e^{-sX_1}]E[e^{-sX_2}]\cdots E[e^{-sX_n}] \tag{3.24}$$

Therefore, $\Psi_X(s) = \Psi_{X_1}(s)\Psi_{X_2}(s)\cdots\Psi_{X_n}(s)$.

Since the density of X is a convolution of the densities of X_i's, we again have the result that the convolution in the time domain translates into the product in the transform domain. Other properties of Laplace transforms are explored in Exercise B.10.

Just as z-transforms are useful for solving difference equations, Laplace transforms are useful for solving differential equations. Because of equation (3.22), the application of Laplace transform to a linear differential equation will convert it into an algebraic equation, which can be solved and the result inverted. The following example illustrates various methods of inversion.

Example B.4 Let $Y_1, \ldots, Y_n$ denote independent, identically distributed random variables having exponential distribution with mean $1/\mu$. Let $X = Y_1 + \cdots + Y_n$. Find the Laplace transform of the density of X and from there the density function, mean, and variance of X.

Solution From the discussion on the Erlang distribution, we already know that X has n-stage Erlang distribution with mean n/μ. However, the purpose of the exercise is to formally show this using Laplace transforms. The density function for Y_i, $i = 1 \mathinner{..} n$ is $f_{Y_i}(y) = \mu e^{-\mu y}$. Using the definition of Laplace transform and the convolution property, we get

$$\Psi_X(s) = [\Psi_Y(s)]^n = \mu^n/(s+\mu)^n \tag{3.25}$$

where Y stands for any Y_i, since they have identical distributions. Now to get $f_X(x)$, we must invert equation (3.25). There are two ways to do the inversion, and it is instructive to look at both of them.

1. Application of the properties of the Laplace transform. Since

   $$\mathcal{L}\left[\mu \exp(-\mu x)\right] = \mu/(s+\mu) \tag{3.26}$$

   The property in equation (3.20) yields

   $$\frac{d^{n-1}}{ds^{n-1}}\left[\frac{\mu}{s+\mu}\right] = \frac{(\mu)(-1)^{n-1}(n-1)!}{(s+\mu)^n} = \mathcal{L}\left[(-x)^{n-1}\mu e^{-\mu x}\right]$$

   which means that the inverse transform of $\mu^n/(s+\mu)^n$ is $(\mu x)^{n-1}\mu e^{-\mu x}/(n-1)!$, which is the same as $f_X(x)$ in equation (2.9). In general, before applying the properties, it is useful to do a partial-fraction expansion of the expression. (Our present expression is already in the desired form, so no expansion was needed.)

2. Direct evaluation of the inversion integral. Let c be some point on the positive real line such that $\Psi_X(s)$ does not have any poles with real part larger than c. Consider a closed region C consisting of the entire space to the left of the line $[c-i\infty, c+i\infty]$ where $i=\sqrt{-1}$. It can be shown that

$$f_X(x) = \frac{1}{2\pi i}\int_{c-i\infty}^{c+i\infty} e^{sx}\Psi_X(s)\,ds \tag{3.27}$$

The evaluation of this integral is usually done using the *Cauchy's residue theorem*, which states that the integral of a function $g(s)$ over a closed contour C is the summation over the residues of $g(s)$ at each one of its poles inside C.[3] The *residue* of $g(s)$ at a pole s_0 of order k is given by

$$res(s_0) = \lim_{s\to s_0}\frac{2\pi i}{(k-1)!}\frac{d^{k-1}[(s-s_0)^k g(s)]}{ds^{k-1}} \tag{3.28}$$

To apply this theorem, let $g(s) = e^{sx}\mu^n/(s+\mu)^n$. This function has only one pole, of order n, at $s=-\mu$ and is analytic everywhere else. Therefore, by the Cauchy's residue theorem, we get

$$f_X(x) = \frac{\mu^n}{(n-1)!}\lim_{s\to-\mu}\frac{d^{n-1}e^{sx}}{ds^{n-1}} = \frac{\mu^n x^{n-1}}{(n-1)!}\lim_{s\to-\mu} e^{sx} = \frac{\mu(\mu x)^{n-1}e^{-\mu x}}{(n-1)!}$$

The mean and variance of X can be computed by inspection here, since the overall mean (variance) must be the sum of means (variances) of individual stages. Another way is to use the moment generation property in equation (3.21), which gives $E[X] = -\Psi'_X(0) = n/\mu$ and $E[X^2] = \Psi''_X(0) = n(n+1)/\mu^2$. Therefore, $\text{Var}(X) = n/\mu^2$. □

B.3.3 General Characteristic Function

The general *characteristic function* or *moment generating function* of a probability distribution, denoted as $\mathcal{C}_X(\theta)$, is defined as

$$\mathcal{C}_X(\theta) = E[e^{i\theta X}] = \begin{cases} \displaystyle\sum_{n=-\infty}^{\infty} e^{i\theta n}P(X=n) & \text{if } X \text{ is discrete} \\ \displaystyle\int_{-\infty}^{\infty} e^{i\theta x} f_X(x)dx & \text{if } X \text{ is continuous} \end{cases} \tag{3.29}$$

where $i=\sqrt{-1}$. Note that unlike the Laplace and z-transforms, the general characteristic function does not require that the random variable X only take nonnegative values. Also, both z-transform and Laplace transform are special cases of this function. For the z-transform, we replace $e^{i\theta}$ with z, and for Laplace transform with e^{-s}. We shall illustrate the use of $\mathcal{C}_X(\theta)$ via an example.

[3] $g(s)$ must be analytic everywhere over C except for a finite number of points inside C.

Example B.5 Let X denote a discrete random variable with binomial distribution $B(n, k, p)$. Let s_X and σ_X denote the mean and standard deviation of X. Find the characteristic function of $Y = (X - s_X)/\sigma_X$. By taking the limit of this as $n \to \infty$, show that the distribution approaches the standard normal distribution.

Solution Since X takes a discrete set of values, so does Y; however, the values of Y are not integers. This requires a bit of care in dealing with the characteristic functions. By definition,

$$\mathcal{C}_X(\theta) = \sum_{k=0}^{n} e^{i\theta k} Pr(X = k) = \sum_{k=0}^{n} e^{i\theta k} Pr[Y = (k - s_X)/\sigma_X]$$

Let $\theta' = \sigma_X \theta$. Then we can write the above equation as

$$\mathcal{C}_X(\theta) = e^{i\theta' s_X/\sigma_X} \sum_{k=0}^{n} e^{i\theta'(k-s_X)/\sigma_X} Pr[Y = (k - s_X)/\sigma_X] = e^{i\theta' s_X/\sigma_X} \mathcal{C}_Y(\theta')$$

For a Bernoulli random variable Z, obviously $C_Z(\theta) = (1 - p) + pe^{i\theta}$. Since the binomial random variable X is a sum of n *iid* Bernoulli random variables, we get $C_X(\theta) = [1 + p(e^{i\theta} - 1)]^n$. Therefore,

$$\mathcal{C}_Y(\theta) = e^{-i\theta s_X/\sigma_X} \left[1 + p(e^{i\theta/\sigma_X} - 1)\right]^n \tag{3.30}$$

Now to prove that the distribution of Y approaches normal as $n \to \infty$, we let $\mathcal{C}_Y^*(\theta) = \ln[\mathcal{C}_Y(\theta)]$. Obviously,

$$\mathcal{C}_Y^*(\theta) = -i\theta s_X/\sigma_X + n \ln\left[1 + p(e^{i\theta/\sigma_X} - 1)\right] \tag{3.31}$$

By definition, $s_X = np$ and $\sigma_X = \sqrt{np(1-p)}$. Therefore, as n increases, for a given θ, $e^{i\theta/\sigma_X}$ must decrease. Using the Maclaurin series expansion, we have

$$e^{i\theta/\sigma_X} = 1 + \frac{i\theta}{\sigma_X} + \frac{(i\theta)^2}{2\sigma_X^2} + \frac{(i\theta)^3}{6\sigma_X^3} + \cdots \qquad \approx 1 + \frac{i\theta}{\sigma_X} - \frac{\theta^2}{2\sigma_X^2} + o\left(\frac{1}{n}\right)$$

where $o(x)$ denotes terms that decrease faster than x. Therefore, from equation (3.31),

$$\begin{aligned}
\ln\left[1 + p(e^{i\theta/\sigma_X} - 1)\right] &= \ln\left[1 + \frac{i\theta p}{\sqrt{np(1-p)}} - \frac{\theta^2 p}{2np(1-p)} + o\left(\frac{1}{n}\right)\right] \\
&= \frac{i\theta p}{\sqrt{np(1-p)}} - \frac{\theta^2}{2n} + o\left(\frac{1}{n}\right)
\end{aligned} \tag{3.32}$$

where we have used Maclaurin series expansion for $\ln(1 + x)$, i.e.,

$$\ln(1 + x) = x - \frac{x^2}{2} + \frac{x^3}{3} - \cdots$$

Substituting equation (3.32) in equation (3.31), we get $C_Y^*(\theta) = -\theta^2/2 + n\, o(1/n)$. Now taking the limit as $n \to \infty$, we get $\lim_{n\to\infty} C_Y^*(\theta) = -\theta^2/2$. Therefore,

$$\lim_{n\to\infty} \mathcal{C}_Y(\theta) = e^{-\theta^2/2} \tag{3.33}$$

It is easy to verify that the characteristic function of the standard normal distribution is $e^{-\theta^2/2}$. Thus, the distribution of Y and hence that of X, approaches the normal distribution. This is, of course, to be expected from the Central Limit theorem. □

B.4 Exercises

1. Let $X_1, \ldots, X_n$ be a set of independent continuous random variables. Find the density and distribution of $\max(X_1, \ldots, X_n)$ and $\min(X_1, \ldots, X_n)$. Determine these functions for the special case where each X_i is exponentially distributed with rate μ_i.

2. Show that in equation (1.36) the equality holds if X_1 and X_2 are linearly-dependent. Also show the opposite by proving that

$$E\left[[(X_1 - s_1) - \tfrac{\sigma_1}{\sigma_2}(X_2 - s_2)]^2\right] = 0 \tag{4.1}$$

   (This is sufficient because if the expected value of a non-negative random variable is zero, the random variable itself must be identically zero.)

3. Using $g(X) = X$ and $g(X) = X^2$ respectively in equation (1.32), and the definition of variance, show that

$$\text{Var}(X) = E[\text{Var}(X|Y)] + \text{Var}[E(X|Y)] \tag{4.2}$$

4. Suppose that X is uniformly distributed in the range $0\,..\,2\pi$ and let $Y = \sin(X)$. Find the density and distribution function of Y.

5. Solve the differential-difference equation (2.4) and verify that it yields the Poisson distribution. Use the following two methods:

   (a) Solve the equation for $n = 0$, substitute the result and get a differential equation for $n = 1$. Solve this equation and then get a differential equation for $n = 2$, etc., until the pattern emerges.

   (b) Take the Laplace transform and then the z-transform of the equation. Invert the two transforms in sequence to get the solution.

6. Derive a simple branching Erlang representation for distributions for which the first three moments are known.

7. Find recursive expressions for the moments of distributions represented by arbitrary series-parallel networks of exponential stages.

8. Consider a discrete model of service time duration. That is, the basic time unit has duration δ, and at the end of each such time unit, the service may complete with probability q. Let T denote the service time. Obviously, $Pr(T = n\delta)$ is then described by the geometric distribution. Now consider the limit as $\delta \to 0$ while δ/q stays constant. Show that the limiting distribution is exponential.

9. Show that the z-transform has the following additional properties:

   Initial value theorem: $\Phi(0) = f(0)$.
   Final value theorem: $\lim_{z\to 1}(1-z)\Phi(z) = f(\infty)$.

10. Show that the Laplace transform has the following additional properties:

    (a) Division in the time domain gives integral in the transform domain

$$\mathcal{L}\left[\frac{f(t)}{t^n}\right] = \int_{s_1=s}^{\infty} ds_1 \int_{s_2=s_1}^{\infty} ds_2 \cdots \int_{s_n=s_{n-1}}^{\infty} \Psi(s_n)\, ds_n \tag{4.3}$$

    (b) Division in the transform domain gives integral in the time domain

$$\mathcal{L}\left[\int_0^t f(u)\, du\right] = \frac{\Psi(s)}{s} \tag{4.4}$$

    (c) Shift in the transform domain results in multiplication by an exponential factor in the time domain

$$\mathcal{L}\left[e^{at} f(t)\right] = \Psi(s-a) \tag{4.5}$$

    (d) Shift in the time domain results in multiplication by an exponential factor in the transform domain

$$\mathcal{L}[f(t-a)] = e^{-as}\Psi(s) \tag{4.6}$$

    (e) Initial and final value theorems

$$\lim_{s\to\infty} s\Psi(s) = \lim_{t\to 0} f(t) \quad \text{and} \quad \lim_{s\to 0} s\Psi(s) = \lim_{t\to\infty} f(t) \tag{4.7}$$

11. Find the z-transforms of all discrete distributions discussed in Section B.2.1. Similarly, find the Laplace transforms for all continuous distributions in Section B.2.2.

Bibliographic Notes

Many texts are available on both introductory and advanced probability theory. For example, Feller (1966) (in two volumes) provides an in-depth coverage of the subject. Some of the books slanted toward performance modeling are Trivedi (1982), Kleinrock (1975), Law and Kelton (1982), and Kobayashi (1978). In particular, Chapter 2 of Kobayashi (1978) provides concise yet excellent coverage of the basic probability theory as it applies to performance modeling. Law and Kelton (1982) is unique in its detailed listing of important properties of a large number of distributions.

APPENDIX C

A Suggested Modeling Project

This appendix describes a typical interactive computer system and shows how to construct both simulation and analytic models for it. The material is intended to be used as a semester-long project for a performance modeling course. The project has two main goals: (1) to provide some experience in modeling real systems, and (2) to test the student's ability to apply concepts learned from the text. Like the text itself, the project also emphasizes analytic modeling, though simulation forms an essential part of the model validation and can be used for other purposes as well. It is assumed that the simulation and analysis will be done using high level software packages so that the effort in writing and debugging simulation/analysis programs remains minimal.

C.1 Project Overview

The main purpose of this project is to construct a realistic model of an interactive computer system, validate it, and use it in a performance-tuning and/or system-upgrade study. Although the emphasis of the project is on analytic modeling, certain aspects of the system behavior cannot be modeled accurately without help from simulation. Therefore, we shall really be constructing a hybrid model.

We shall call our system SYS-A.

We shall first describe SYS-A much as it might be discussed in a hardware or an operating system manual. Many of these details may be irrelevant for modeling, but have been included to illustrate the process of abstraction that is needed in modeling any real system. This applies to both simulation and analysis, although different levels of abstraction are usually needed for the two cases. Details pertaining to such abstractions are discussed later. The analytic model is intended to use solution techniques for closed product-form queuing networks and their heuristic extensions. It is possible to use extended analytic modeling techniques for certain aspects (memory constraints, I/O subsystem, etc.), but these are not discussed. Even within the confines where we are operating, there is no unique way of doing analytic modeling, and simplifying assumptions are needed in many instances.

The project can be accomplished in several steps, as listed below. The ordering of these steps assumes that the material is covered in the class as suggested in the Preface. In particular, it is assumed that the simulation will be discussed early on, and the core material on product-form network based analytic modeling will have been covered by the time step (4) of the project is started.

1. Construction of a pure simulation model. The simulation model and its calibration is explained at length, although several trivial calculations will be required. The model can be developed in steps. For example, memory allocation/deallocation and spooling may be ignored to start with. It would be helpful to avoid hard-coding the calibration parameters in the program, so that changes can be made easily.
2. Running the simulation model and determining confidence intervals for system throughput, response times of individual stations, average memory fragmentation, utilization of spool area buffers, etc. By obtaining appropriate data from simulation, one can also come up with exercises in experiment design, regression analysis, selection among alternates, etc.
3. Constructing and calibrating a simple analytic model of the system that ignores memory constraints and uses only the features directly available in the analytic solution package. It is assumed that the solution package can handle at least the product-form networks directly. It is possible to do this part before the details of solution techniques have been covered in the class.
4. Heuristic modeling of memory constraints and complex scheduling disciplines. This requires techniques from sections 8.2 and 8.3 (along with necessary background material from Chapter 7). It is assumed that the analysis package allows interfacing with the user code.
5. Estimation of memory fragmentation from the simulation and the use of this information to further refine the analytic model. Validation of the resulting hybrid model against simulation.
6. Tuning and upgrade phase; deciding how the performance could be improved, making the change, and verifying the results. Possible changes

are file migration, change in CPU time slice, scheduling changes, memory compaction, change in main memory size, change in disk speed, etc. More details on this are contained in Section C.3.3. Upgrades should be applied only if absolutely necessary.

7. Modeling of more complex features such as multiprocessing, channel contention, and synchronization delays. The details of this are discussed in Section C.4.

C.2 Operational Details of SYS-A

In this section we briefly describe the pertinent hardware and operating system details of SYS-A.

C.2.1 Hardware Configuration

The hardware configuration of SYS-A is as follows: one CPU, three I/O channels (CH_1, CH_2, and CH_3), one line printer (LP), and N terminals. CH_1 controls a fast disk D_1 which holds the operating system and system utilities. CH_2 controls a regular disk D_2, which is used for all user files. CH_3 controls the line printer. Detailed hardware specifications are given below:

CPU: Maximum memory capacity = 32 Mbytes.
Total currently installed memory = 8 Mbytes.
First $(2000 + 80N)$ KB of memory are occupied by the O/S.
Remaining memory is available for user programs.

D_1: Number of cylinders (L_1) = 320, numbered 0 to 319.
Number of surfaces (with one head per surface) = 10.
Seek time across n cylinders, denoted $ST(n)$, is given by

$$\mathrm{ST}(n) = \text{if } n \leq 20 \text{ then } 2n \text{ else } 20 + 1.0n \text{ (in milliseconds)}$$

Block (sector) size = 1 KB; Number of sectors/track = 50.
Rotation speed = 3,000 revolutions/minute.
Retraction time from cylinder $L_1 - 1$ to 0 = $\frac{1}{4}$th of the scan time.
(Scan time is the time to seek last cylinder from cylinder 0).

D_2: Number of cylinders (L_2) = 200, numbered 0 to 199.
Number of surfaces (with one head per surface) = 10.
Seek time = 2 ms/cylinder (constant).
Block (sector) size = 1 KB; Number of sectors/track = 50.
Rotation speed = 1,500 revolutions/minute.
Retraction time from cylinder $L_2 - 1$ to 0 = $\frac{1}{4}$th of the scan time.

LP: Average print speed = 0.50 ms/character.
Line width = 128 chars max (not needed in modeling)

The command language interpreter is written as a pure procedure; therefore, there is only one copy of it shared among all terminal processes. The terminal processes do, however, need separate space for data area and I/O buffers. This explains the dependence of the space occupied by the O/S on N, the number of terminals. The channels in SYS-A remain permanently connected to the devices controlled by them; therefore, a channel and its device can be treated as a single entity. Thus, in the model, CH_1 and D_1 refer to the same service station. The same is true with respect to CH_2 and D_2, or CH_3 and LP.

As usual, all heads on a disk are mounted on a single arm and move in synchronism. The head selection time can be assumed to be zero, which allows all tracks on a cylinder to be read sequentially without any intervening delays. The seek and I/O operations on a disk are started by its channel. After starting a seek operation, the channel waits for the disk controller to signal when the disk head is positioned on the desired cylinder. The channel then provides the disk controller with the starting sector and the number of contiguous sectors to be read/written. The disk controller can read any number of contiguous sectors on a cylinder without any intervening delays.

C.2.2 System Operation

We assume that all N terminals are in use for the entire period of observation. Each terminal user issues a command and then waits for the response. We assume that one command execution requires running exactly one user program. (It may, of course, involve the execution of several portions of the O/S). Running a program involves the following steps: (a) obtain required main memory, (b) swap in the program from D_1 or D_2, (c) run the program until it completes or is aborted, and (d) release the main memory. While the program is running, it may go through several cycles of computation and I/O. Part of the I/O might be directed to the line printer. Since the line printer cannot be shared among concurrent processes, it is *spooled*, i.e., while the program is running, all its output is written to the disk. When the program completes, the output can be dumped on the printer. The printing is handled by a system process called PRINT. Other than this, the O/S essentially has the monolithic structure. In the following, we describe the various management policies used by SYS-A.

1. Processor Management

There are only $N + 1$ processes of direct interest, one printer process, and N terminal processes. The PRINT process is I/O-bound and requires no direct use of the CPU. The processes waiting to use the CPU are held in a ready list (RL). The processes on RL are scheduled according to the round-robin policy with a time-slice of TS milliseconds. The context switching overhead is constant (denoted S_{sw}) and is estimated by direct measurement. Since the operating system structure is monolithic, each process may spend part of its time executing some O/S routines. This time is counted toward the processes' own execution time.

The O/S is permanently resident in the memory and thus the O/S routines do not involve any loading.

2. I/O Management

For channel CH_i ($i = 1..3$), we have a list IOL_i that holds the processes using or waiting to use channel CH_i. The PRINT process circulates only between IOL_1 and IOL_3. If there is nothing for the PRINT process to print, it still stays in IOL_1 but in a "not eligible for scheduling" state. It will become eligible for scheduling on the next completion of a program that generates some printout. All processes on IOL_1 are scheduled according to the SCAN policy. Processes on IOL_2 are served according to the C-SCAN policy. Both lists are ordered by increasing cylinder numbers so that the dispatching does not require any search and can be implemented easily.

All three channels can operate in parallel with the CPU; however, the bus access conflicts between the channels and the CPU result in the slowdown of all devices. The (multiplicative) degradation factor, denoted γ, depends on many factors and is obtained experimentally. The other CPU overhead contributed by the channels is that of I/O initiation and the service of I/O completion interrupts. The servicing of I/O completion interrupts takes priority over the regular processing and preempts it. The average I/O trap/interrupt service time (including all list manipulations, scheduling, and context switches) is measured and denoted as S_I. If another interrupt is generated while the CPU is servicing one, the new interrupt is queued until the first one has been fully processed. All queued interrupts are handled in FCFS manner. The interrupted process is resumed after all pending interrupts have been serviced. To make sure that each process gets a complete time slice, the timer (used for round-robin scheduling) is stopped before servicing an interrupt. The timer is restarted when the interrupted process is resumed.

3. File Management

The file system of SYS-A uses a multi-level mapped allocation scheme that allows large files to be stored. The file system tries to keep the blocks of small and medium sized files together as far as possible (in rotational ordering, contiguous on the same track, contiguous on the same cylinder, on adjacent sectors of the same track/cylinder, etc.). However, to avoid large concentrations of used blocks in certain portions of the disk (which could make incremental growth of files very inefficient), the file system deliberately spreads out files that require more than one cylinder to store. The technique is as follows: Whenever the file exceeds a multiple of one cylinder (= 250 blocks), the file system generates a random number $\mathcal{D}$ with expected value of $d = 5$. The next set of 250 blocks are staggered by $\mathcal{D}$ cylinders. Thus, if the 250th block is on cylinder n, the storage of the 251st block will start at mod$(n + d', L)$th cylinder, where d' is the generated random number and L is the total number of cylinders on the disk. Of course, a group of 250 blocks may itself span several cylinders because of the lack of contiguous space, but in storing such blocks the file system does not do any deliberate staggering.

To take advantage of any existing contiguity, the user or system processes that want to read/write multiple blocks make only one request to the file manager. The file manager decomposes this request into requests for individual blocks and puts the requests into the disk scheduler queue. This allows the disk scheduler to perform I/O with minimum seek and rotational delays. A disk reorganization process runs in the background every night when the load is low to ensure that the disk does not get too fragmented. However, this process does not compact everything (because that would be useless, given the incremental nature of growth and shrinkage of files). Instead, this process only swaps blocks belonging to different files on the same and adjacent cylinders so as to reduce seek and rotational delays (while leaving the holes intact or even increasing them!). Thus, there is always some amount of fragmentation for medium to large files. Since the user makes only one I/O request for all the blocks, we can think of the transfer as a single operation except that it has embedded seeks that reduce the effective transfer rate. The reduction factor depends on the size of the I/O request. Some measurements were taken on SYS-A to quantify this aspect and are reported later.

To facilitate sequential access, every block in every file has a pointer field that takes 4 bytes; therefore, each block contains only 1020 bytes of data. This field either points to the next block or is null. Every file has always one more block allocated to it than necessary. This ensures that when a newly allocated block is written for the first time, the file system already knows the next block that it points to and thus can supply this information without extra disk I/O.

The line printer is spooled to disk D_1. The spool area is not a hard partition on the disk, but merely a directory on the disk (i.e., it is not located in any specific part of the disk). Spool files are organized like ordinary files and can be as large as an ordinary file. The only thing special about a spool file is that the file manager keeps track of whether the process that created the spool file is finished. This is essential since a spool file becomes eligible for printout only when the creating process is finished. The eligible spool file is printed out by the PRINT process, block by block. To print a block, the PRINT process obtains the next block from D_1 via CH_1 into a main memory buffer, then puts it out to the line printer via CH_3.

4. Memory Management

The memory allocation in SYS-A is based on the dynamic partioned allocation scheme without full compaction. The list of free blocks is maintained in the order of increasing addresses, and the allocation is done using the first-fit algorithm. Since the straightforward first-fit algorithm tends to create many small blocks at the head of the list, we modify the scheme slightly by treating the list as a circular list and starting the search where it left off the last time. On deallocation, the freed block is merged with the adjacent free blocks, if any. If there are any

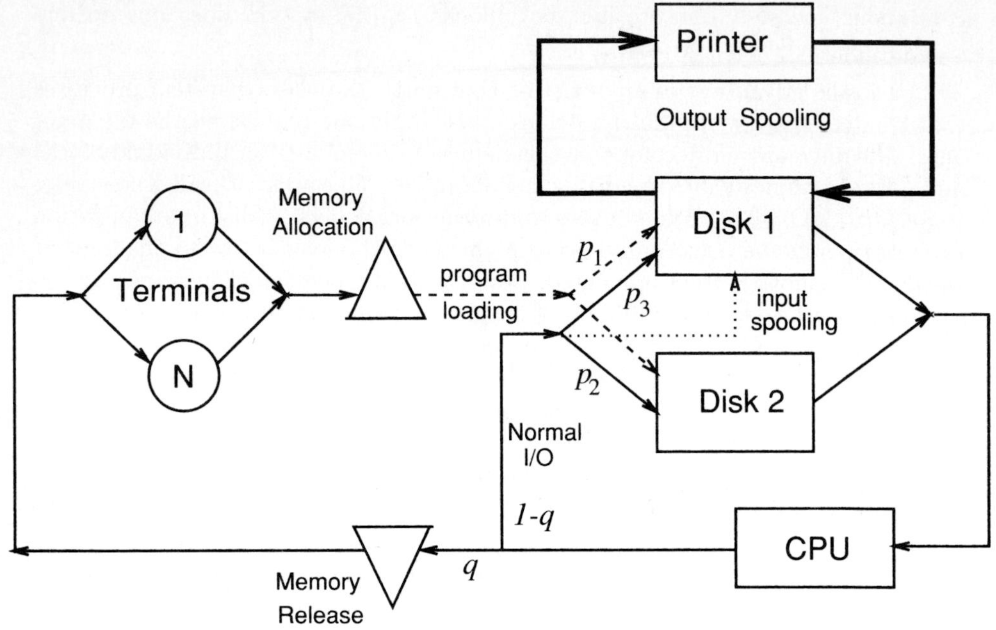

FIGURE C-1: A queuing network model for SYS-A.

waiting memory requests at this point, allocation is attempted. The queue of memory requests is ordered by request size, with the smallest-size request at the head of the queue. Every time the allocation routine runs, it attempts to allocate as many requests as possible, starting at the head of the queue. Allocation is also attempted if a new request arrives and goes at the head of the queue (i.e. has a size smaller than those of the existing requests). Notice that our allocation policy will starve large requests if the memory is heavily used. The average running time of the memory management component of the O/S (on each invocation) is measured and is denoted as S_M.

C.3 Model Construction

When modeling a complex system such as the one just described, one must pay careful attention to the details to be included. A direct representation of every detail of the real system would only result in a model that cannot be calibrated, validated, or solved/simulated efficiently. A queuing network oriented model is shown in Fig. C-1, and is described next.

C.3.1 Model Description

The terminal station represents the N active terminals on the system. Each of the N users thinks for a while, issues a command, and then waits for the response.

Therefore, each of the N terminal processes can be identified as a customer in the model. The time needed for the display of the results generated by the previous command is included in our definition of think time; therefore, the think time is the same as the service time of the customers at the terminal. On exit from the terminal station, a customer goes through the program loading and processing phase and eventually returns to its terminal for another round. The return corresponds to the beginning of display of the computer's response on the terminal screen. Obviously, the time spent by the customer outside the terminal is the *system response time*. The terminal behaves like a delay station and no waiting line can form there. For modeling purposes, the commands issued at the terminal are irrelevant; instead, we need only to characterize the distribution of the think time.

A customer departing from the terminal station arrives at the memory allocation station. The memory allocation policy and scheduling discipline were specified in Section C.2.2. The service time at this station ($= S_M$) is small, but the customer will be blocked if the required memory is not available. The only other parameter needed is the distribution of memory request size. This is specified later in Table C.2. Note that the allocated memory is retained until the customer exits the *central subsystem*.

After the memory has been obtained, the program must be loaded from the disk into the allocated memory space. This job is done by CH_1 or CH_2 station, depending on whether the program is on D_1 or D_2. Therefore, after exiting the memory allocation station, a customer enters either D_1 or D_2. (As stated earlier, we could also say that the customer enters either CH_1 or CH_2). Disk D_1 contains all system-supplied programs such as compilers and editors, whereas D_2 contains all user-written programs. The choice is specified by the routing probability p_1, which gives the fraction of time that a customer goes to a particular disk. Note that this use of D_1 and D_2 is only for loading the program into memory. The use of D_1 or D_2 by a running program for performing I/O is distinct from this and will be discussed later.

The distribution of the cylinder requested and the scheduling discipline for both disks is given later in Table C.2. The service time at D_1 and D_2 consists of three components: seek delay, rotational delay, and transfer delay. Estimation of these is discussed in Section C.3.3. The head may also move during the transfer, because not all the requested blocks will be on the same cylinder. Although this movement is a random variable, only its expected value, denoted $\delta(n)$, is available from measurements. (Here n is I/O request size in blocks.) This function is given in Table C.1. For example, the table shows that if a file of size 128 blocks is transferred, the head will move over 0.83 cylinders on the average during the transfer itself.

The numbers in this table correspond to files that take no more than a cylinder to store. Files larger than one cylinder are staggered, on the average, by an amount d (see Section C.2.2); therefore, the net movement in loading a large file of size n blocks is given by

$$\delta(n) = d\lfloor n/250 \rfloor + \delta(n \bmod 250) \tag{3.1}$$

n	$\delta(n)$
16	0.06
32	0.18
64	0.39
128	0.83
250	1.90

TABLE C.1: Head displacement as a function of transfer size.

The cylinders can be thought of as wrapping around; i.e., cylinder 0 immediately follows the last cylinder. Thus, during an I/O operation, the forward incremental movement of the head may involve retracting the head from the last cylinder to cylinder 0. We can estimate the probability of this happening as $1/L$ where L is the total number of cylinders on the disk. Thus, the time spent in moving over cylinders during a transfer of n blocks from disk i, denoted $\theta_i(n)$, is given by

$$\theta_i(n) = \delta(n)[r_i/L_i + t_i(1 - 1/L_i)] \tag{3.2}$$

where r_i is the head retraction time and t_i is the time to step over one cylinder of disk i.[1] The values of r_i and t_i were specified in Section C.2.1. When switching from one cylinder to the next, some rotational delay may be encountered before the first block is accessed. In fact, some rotational delay may occur because not all blocks on a cylinder are contiguous. Because the blocks are maintained more or less in rotational order by the disk reorganization program, it is safe to assume that a single rotation is adequate to access all blocks on a given track. That is, the effective file transfer rate, given that the head stays on the same cylinder can be assumed to be 1/2 of the peak transfer rate computed from the hardware characteristics given in Section C.2.1.

After loading, the program is ready to execute. Thus, after exiting from D_1 or D_2, the customer enters the CPU. Note that the queue of customers at the CPU is the *ready list* RL. The queuing discipline at CPU is round-robin and the service-time distribution is given in Table C.2. If the CPU service ends because the customer makes an I/O request, the customer will go to D_1 or D_2 to do I/O. On the other hand, if the service ends because of completion or abortion, the customer enters the memory release station. The destination is specified probabilistically by the routing probability q. Note that a given job will go through a certain number of computation-I/O cycles before it is completed. The number of cycles required is geometrically distributed with a mean of $k = 1/q$.

After releasing the memory, the customer returns to the terminal station. (The system will attempt to allocate memory to waiting requests, if any, at this point.)

A customer going to the disks may require the following types of I/O operations: (a) loading a program into memory, (b) normal disk I/O during program

[1]During transfer, the stepping would occur one cylinder at a time, so t_i represents the basic stepping time even if the disk has nonlinear seek characteristics (e.g., disk D_1).

execution, or (c) writing the output bound for LP into a spool file from the main memory buffer. To distinguish between various types of I/O activities, we use the concept of classes. A customer normally belongs to class 1 (shown in solid lines). Thus, normal I/O at D_1 and D_2 is considered a class 1 activity. Program loading is considered a class 2 activity. That is, on exit from the memory allocation station, a class 1 customer unconditionally changes to class 2 (shown in dashed lines). On exit from the disk stations, a customer reverts back to class 1. Spooling is considered as class 3 activity. A customer coming from the CPU toward the disks changes over to class 3 with probability $1 - p_2 - p_3$ (shown in dotted lines). After service at D_1, the customer reverts back to class 1. The sole purpose of introducing classes is, of course, to have different calibration parameters for them. The scheduling discipline at both disks is class-independent. The transfer size for classes 1 and 2 is given in Table C.2. Class 3, of course, transfers only one block at a time.

The behavior of the PRINT process can be represented by using the concept of chains. Fig. C-1 contains two chains. The PRINT process moves in chain 2 (shown in heavy lines). All other processes move in chain 1. As explained earlier, the PRINT process stays at D_1 in ineligible state if there is no block for it to print. When it becomes eligible and is scheduled, the PRINT process reads the next block to be printed from D_1 into a main memory buffer called PRINTBUFF. It then moves over to CH_3 and prints out the contents of PRINTBUFF on the line printer. Obviously, there is never any waiting line at CH_3 since the PRINT process is the only customer to visit it. After exiting CH_3, the PRINT process goes back to D_1 in eligible or ineligible state depending on whether there are any more blocks that can be printed.

The service time of the PRINT process at D_1 can be obtained from the disk block size. Its service time at CH_3 is obviously the time required to print one block on the line printer. To accurately tell when the PRINT process will or will not be in an eligible state at D_1, we must keep track of the outputs generated by all N user processes. For each user process n, $n = 1..N$, let us define two counters IBCNT[n] and EBCNT[n], both initialized to 0. These give, respectively, the number of output blocks generated by process n that are ineligible and eligible for printout. Whenever process n exits D_1 after receiving service as a class 3 customer, IBCNT[n] is incremented by 1. When process n completes (i.e., proceeds to the memory release station), the current value of IBCNT[n] is added to EBCNT[n], and IBCNT[n] is reset to 0. Whenever the PRINT process exits D_1 (and thereby picks up one block for printout), the appropriate EBCNT is decremented by 1. If the PRINT process arrives at D_1 and finds all EBCNT values 0, it must change to an ineligible state. It will be made eligible again whenever some process generates some output and completes. By looking at the snapshots of these counter arrays during modeling, we can tell (a) if the line printer is too slow or too fast for the workload given to it, and (b) if the spooled files are occupying too much of disk space.

C.3.2 Modeling of Minor Overheads

In this section, we explain the modeling of the effect of miscellaneous sources of overhead. The first such effect is caused by memory allocation and release since the corresponding stations *do not* operate in parallel with the CPU. Note that memory allocation and deallocation is done once for each program execution (rather than once for each CPU burst). Therefore, the CPU service time must be increased by the amount $2S_M/v_{cpu}$ where v_{cpu} is the visit ratio of the CPU relative to the terminals.

The second effect arises owing to bus conflicts. Since the slowdown in CPU owing to bus conflicts is γ, we need to reduce the CPU service rate by this amount. The seek time and rotational latency at disk stations are not affected by bus conflicts because their channels do not grab system bus during this time. But the transfer rate must be reduced by the factor γ also. This degradation should be applied to the peak transfer rate (i.e., before factoring in the effect of rotational latency during multiblock transfers).

The third effect is due to handling of various kinds of traps, I/O interrupts, and timer interrupts. Although it is possible to explicitly model trap/interrupt handling, there is little point in doing so since the effect is rather small. Let λ_I denote the average number of I/O traps and interrupts generated per second, and S_I the average time needed to service a trap/interrupt. Then each second, $S_I\lambda_I$ seconds are spent in servicing traps and interrupts. In other words, the effective processing rate of the CPU is reduced by the factor $(1 - S_I\lambda_I)$. The process-switching overhead reduces the effective rate further. Since the overhead of providing TS milliseconds of service is S_{sw} ms, the time needed to provide 1 second worth of service is $(TS + S_{sw})/TS$ seconds. Let T_{cpu} denote the basic service time of a program at CPU, and T'_{cpu} the corresponding time with overhead taken into account. It follows that

$$T'_{cpu} = \frac{2S_M/v_{cpu} + T_{cpu}(1 + S_{sw}/TS)}{\gamma(1 - S_I\lambda_I)} \tag{3.3}$$

where we have assumed that memory allocation/deallocation is not subject to round-robin scheduling and thus its duration is not expanded by the $(1+S_{sw}/TS)$ factor. This is the result of monolithic O/S structure. If memory management were to be handled by an ordinary process, it too would be subject to the overhead of round-robin scheduling.

C.3.3 Model Calibration and Validation

We now give all remaining calibration parameters. In the following, the notation unif(a, b) means uniform distribution in the closed interval $[a, b]$. The notation Expo(a) means exponential distribution with mean of a. Similarly the notations Hyper(a, b) and Erlang(a, b) denote hyperexponential and Erlang distributions with mean a and *coefficient of variation* b.

All necessary parameters can now be computed. Remember that for D_1 and D_2, the service time is determined from the seek time, rotational delay, and

Terminals: $N = 12$; Think time: Expo(4000) ms.

Program size: Empirical distribution defined as (range, probability).
Range is in blocks. Distribution is uniform over the range.
(16–128, 0.10), (129–256, 0.17), (257–512, 0.23),
(513–1024, 0.30), (1025–2048, 0.15), (2049–4096, 0.05).

CPU station: TS = 5.0 ms; Service time: Hyper(25, 2) ms.
Speed degradation due to bus contention: $\gamma = 0.90$.
Context switch time: $S_{sw} = 50$ μsec.
Trap/interrupt handling time: $S_I = 200$ μsec.

I/O request size: unif(1, 13) blocks.
Scheduling disciplines: SCAN for D_1, C-SCAN for D_2.
Cylinders accessed by requests to D_1 = unif(0, $L_1 - 1$).
Cylinders accessed by requests to D_2 = unif(0, $L_2 - 1$).

Memory allocation/deallocation time: $S_M = 2$ ms.
Trap and interrupt rate: $\lambda_I = 20{*}N$ per second.

Routing probabilities: $p_1 = 0.7$, $p_2 = 0.56$, $p_3 = 0.3$, $q = 0.1$.

TABLE C.2: Calibration parameters for the SYS-A model.

transfer time. In simulation, we explicitly keep track of the desired and current cylinder numbers; therefore, we can compute the seek time exactly and delay the requesting customer by this amount. In contrast, the analytic model must estimate seek delay indirectly, as explained next. Other than this, the calibration is identical for both simulation and analytic modeling. Let d_{ij} denote the overall service time of some request at disk i for class j. We can obtain d_{ij} as $\alpha_i + \beta_{ij}$ where α_i represents the seek time portion and β_{ij} the rest.

Let us start with details for the simulation. Here we know the "target" cylinder number on which a given transfer starts. The target for a request is selected by generating a random number with the distribution given in Table C.2. Scheduling of a disk operation is governed by the current and target head positions and the scheduling policy. When a request is scheduled, the following actions must be performed: (a) compute the seek time α_i and delay the requesting customer by this amount, (b) set current head position to the target position, (c) compute the β_{ij} portion of service time, and (d) start the operation. The computation of β_{ij} is common to both simulation and analysis and will be described shortly. One point to keep in mind, however, is that the head may move during the transfer. This movement can be obtained using the δ function and used to further adjust the head position. (Since the δ function gives fractional numbers, we round the result to the nearest integer.) Notice that the complexity of the I/O operation precludes the simplistic situation where the simulation package generates a random number for the service time of transactions according to a given distribution. Instead, each transaction that comes in must compute for itself the total service time at the disk. Most simulation packages provide facilities to do so. Typically, the approach is to let a transaction compute and store the service time in a variable, which is local to the transaction. The simulation then only needs to know the identity of the local variable where the actual service time will be found.

Accurate computation of α_i part for analytic modeling is difficult. One possibility is to develop detailed heuristic MVA equations for estimating seek delays under the real scheduling discipline. Here we shall use only a simple model. Since the distribution of the cylinders accessed by the I/O requests is uniform, it is reasonable to assume (for the purposes of modeling) that all requests are equally spaced. We shall consider the head also as one of the "cylinders", that is, if n requests are present, we think of a situation where there are $n+1$ equally spaced points on the disk, one of which represents the head, and the remaining n the requests. This gives α_i as a function of n, henceforth denoted as $\alpha_i(n)$. For C-SCAN discipline, we have

$$\alpha_i(n) = \frac{r_i + n \times ST[L_i/(n+1)]}{n+1} \quad \text{for} \quad n = 1, 2, 3, \ldots \tag{3.4}$$

where r_i is the retraction time. The numerator in this expression is the time needed to make one round of the disk. During this time, all n requests would have been served, and the head would return to the original position for a second round. This expression also applies to SCAN discipline if we set $r = 0$. Notice that the state dependence of α_i makes the overall service time d_{ij} also state-dependent. That is,

$$d_{ij}(n) = \alpha_i(n) + \beta_{ij} \tag{3.5}$$

It is clear that $d_{ij}(n)$ cannot be expressed as a product of $d_{ij}(1)$ (the class-dependent basic service rate) and a class-independent capacity function $C_i(n)$. It is easy to verify using equation (6.6.3) that $C_{ij}(n) = d_{ij}(1)/d_{ij}(n)$ *does not* even satisfy product-form restrictions. Thus, further approximation is needed. One possibility is to choose the basic service time b_{ij} as simply $d_{ij}(1)$, and compute an "averaged" capacity function that weights different classes according to their visit ratios. That is,

$$C_i(n) = \frac{\sum_{\forall j} d_{ij}(1)v_{ij}}{\sum_{\forall j} d_{ij}(n)v_{ij}} \tag{3.6}$$

This approximation is only a heuristic without any mathematical justification, and may not work well if the load-dependence is very pronounced.

Let us now see how to determine β_{ij}. This part is, of course, common to both simulation and analytic modeling. The peak transfer rate, denoted η_i for disk i, can be computed from the data given in Section C.2.1. In the discussion that follows, we assume that η_i is expressed in terms number of *blocks* transferred per second. Because of the bus contention, the usable rate is only $\gamma\eta_i$. This rate applies only to single-block transfers (i.e., to class 3 at D_1). Each transfer may involve some rotational delay, which can be assumed to be 1/2 of the revolution time. Therefore, for class 3, we have

$$\beta_{i3} = 1/(\gamma\eta_i) + \text{rev\_time}/2 \tag{3.7}$$

The situation is somewhat more complex for multi-block transfers that occur for classes 1 and 2. In particular, seek and latency delays may occur while the transfer is taking place. To account for these, we compute an *effective transfer rate* first. As discussed in Section C.3.1, the effective rate can be estimated as $\gamma\eta_i/2$ given that no seek occurs. The effect of the rotational latency at the beginning of the transfer *is included here* and need not be considered separately. Thus, if the request size is n_j blocks, we have

$$\beta_{ij} = n_j \times 2/(\gamma\eta_i) + \theta_i(n_j) \qquad \text{for} \quad j = 1, 2 \tag{3.8}$$

where the θ_i function is given in equation (3.2). These expressions for β_{ij}'s can be used to specify transfer time in as much detail as necessary. For simulation, it is desirable to use the distribution. The distribution of β_{i3} is governed by that of rotational delay, since the first term in the RHS of equation (3.7) is a constant. That is, the distribution is of β_{i3} is uniform. The distribution of β_{i1} and β_{i2} is governed by those of n_1 and n_2 and can again be computed easily. (You may ignore the fact that $\delta(n)$ is also a random variable.) For analytic modeling, we can use the first or first two moments.

The service time at CH_3 is the time needed to print out *exactly one* disk block. Since the output of each program is started from a new block, the last block of the output may not be completely full. It is enough to assume that the last block is half-full and estimate the fraction of half-full blocks. Let k denote the average number of blocks of output generated by a program. Obviously, $k = (1-p_2-p_3)(\frac{1}{q}-1)$. Then we can assume that $k-1$ blocks are completely full and one is half full. Thus, on the average, each block contains only $(1-1/2k)*1020$ bytes of data. Using the LP speed, the service time at CH_3 can be obtained. (Note that both in simulation and analysis, the service time at CH_3 is computed as a constant, i.e., it has zero variance.) For analytic modeling of the blockage of the PRINT process in the ineligible state, we exploit the fact that the throughput of chain 2 must be the same as the throughput of class 3 of chain 1. This would, no doubt, require an iterative solution that determines the blockage time for the PRINT process by enforcing throughput equalization. This is not needed for simulation, since the spooling details to the extent of maintaining the IBCNT and EBCNT arrays can be included directly. Note that the simulation need not maintain any linked lists of spool blocks.

We now discuss a few other issues. The average CPU service time should be increased as indicated in equation (3.3). Since the given time slice is small compared with average CPU service time, the scheduling discipline at CPU can be assumed to be PS for analytic modeling. Under PS discipline, the service-time distribution becomes irrelevant and can be assumed to be exponential. (For simulation, we still use the round-robin discipline and hyperexponential distribution, as specified in Table C.2). The service-time distribution at the terminals can be assumed to be exponential. We have already seen that the service time at CH_3 is a constant. (Since CH_3 and terminals are delay stations, the service-time distribution at these stations is actually irrelevant for analytic modeling.) We have already seen how to get distributional characteristics at D_1 and D_2. In simulation, we can use the exact scheduling disciplines at these stations (namely

SCAN and C-SCAN). For analysis, we can assume FCFS discipline since the effect of SCAN/C-SCAN scheduling is already taken into account in determining the α_i portion of the service time.

Memory allocation/deallocation can be done exactly in the simulation model. (Minor optimizations, such as starting the search from a different point each time, can be ignored in simulation as well, as their effect is likely to be minimal.) For analytic modeling, we need to use the technique in Section 8.2.1, taking into account the portion of memory unusable because of fragmentation. Since we are considering the system in steady state, a certain amount of fragmentation will be constantly present. Let σ denote the standard deviation of the program size. For part (4) of the project in Section C.1, the amount of unused memory can be estimated as σN. For part (5), the fragmentation should be estimated by simulation.

The simulation should follow the recommendations in Chapter 3 in determining the length of the transient duration, length of individual runs, number of replications, construction of confidence intervals, etc. Obtain enough data points so that the half-width of the 95% confidence interval for the system response time is no more than 5% of the sample mean. Compare the results against those obtained from the analysis. If there are serious discrepancies, attempt to explain them and refine the analytic model. Once you are satisfied that the model is reasonable, do the following:

1. Determine the optimum number of terminals as given by equation (4.3.8) (which obviously ignores the effect of memory constraints). Solve the model for N varying from 1 to 20. Plot the mean system response time as a function of N. From this plot estimate a value of N^* and compare it with the value given by equation (4.3.8). Explain any discrepancies.
2. Set N to N^* and examine the results to see how the system performance could be improved. Consider the following possibilities (a) migrating files from one disk to another, (b) changing the line printer speed, (c) doubling the memory size, and (d) adding one more disk, similar to disk 2, and shifting enough load from disks 1 and 2 to make all disks equally loaded. Evaluate only those possibilities that appear promising.
3. Evaluate, by simulation, the effect of doing full compaction of memory whenever there is enough noncontiguous space to allocate a new request. Assume that a memory-to-memory word (= 4 bytes) move requires 400 nanoseconds.
4. Study the impact of changes to CPU time-slice duration on the performance. Choose time-slices of 2 ms and 10 ms.

C.4 Modeling Enhancements

We consider two types of enhancements to SYS-A (a) multiprocessing at command level, and (b) sharing of a single channel between the two disks. These are described below along with hints for modeling.

Suppose that the command interpreter in SYS-A works like the Unix™ shell. That is, when a user issues a command, a new process is created for handling the command. If the command is suffixed with an ampersand (&), the command interpreter puts the process in the background and immediately becomes ready to take the next command; otherwise, the user must wait for the command completion. There are two aspects to consider in the modeling of this aspect: (a) increased concurrency resulting from the larger number of processes, and (b) contention among various processes for terminal I/O and for attention from the user. To model (a), we need to determine the average number of simultaneous commands issued by one user, say α. Assume that α =1.4. To model (b), we consider the terminal station as a multiserver with N servers. Then the situation is equivalent to the one where the system has αN customers, but only N terminals.

Suppose that both disks of SYS-A are controlled by a single channel. To simplify things, assume that the disks do not have the rotational position sensing (RPS) mechanism. Then the disk I/O will go as follows: a request (customer) arrives at a disk station and waits until it is selected by the disk scheduler (according to SCAN or C-SCAN discipline). The seek operation is then started on the requested disk. This operation does need the channel, but only momentarily. When the seek is completed, the channel must be connected to the requested disk before the transfer can begin. Thus, the request may have to be blocked if the channel is busy transferring data from the other disk. After getting the channel, the customer (or request) must wait for the rotational delay before the data transfer can begin. Thus, the service time at a disk station consists of four factors. An approximate modeling of this is discussed in Section 8.2.5 and can be used here as well. The only thing to keep in mind is that because of the SCAN/C-SCAN policies, the seek times become load-dependent. (The hypothetical channel station is still load-independent.) The model can be solved iteratively.

APPENDIX

D

Performance Tuning Using Solver

In this appendix, we use a concrete example to illustrate how to identify bottlenecks in an interactive computer system and tune it to get better performance. We also briefly mention a number of other issues that the reader can pursue for a more thorough study of the system. The tuning study necessarily requires the use of an analytic modeling package that can handle closed queuing networks. Here we use such a package, known as *Solver*, which was developed by the author.[1] A brief discussion of its features, particularly those used in the program of this section, is provided in the following.

D.1 Overview of Solver

Solver is designed for obtaining steady-state solutions of queuing networks that can be tackled by the mean value analysis algorithm and its heuristic extensions. Some of the salient features of Solver are listed below:

1. A Solver program can define several models and manipulate them arbitrarily. In particular, the following operations apply to models: splitting

[1] Solver package, language reference manual, and Unix-style manual entry are available from the author.

a model into two, deleting stations and chains, renumbering stations and chains, saving models into and loading them from files, creating in-memory copies of models, modifying calibration parameters of a model (possibly based upon results obtained by solving other models), and solving models analytically.

2. Solver provides a Pascal-like language for manipulating models, programming solution techniques, input/output, etc. It defines a set of *standard variables* to deal with various input and output parameters of the models. Several built-in functions exist to deal with a given parameter (e.g., the service time) for a group of stations and/or chains.

3. Solver provides several output options to cast the results from model solution in desired format. (Some of these options are used in the program presented later.)

4. Models in Solver allow all scheduling disciplines discussed in Section 8.3. Stations with PF scheduling disciplines can have arbitrary (but chain-independent) capacity functions, whereas others can have the restricted functions that can be represented by the SS-net and SD-net approximations discussed in Section 8.3.6.

5. Solver is primarily oriented towards closed networks with one class per chain and provides both unidirectional and bidirectional MVA algorithms. However, facilities are provided for handling other aspects, especially the solution techniques discussed in Section 8.2.

Solver programs are interpreted directly, which is convenient but slow. All variables are initially given an "undefined" value, so that the use of uninitialized variables can be detected. Here are a few specific details that would be useful in reading the tuning-program given later.

Solver provides C-style operators such as "+ =" or "− =" meaning that the left-hand side should be incremented or decremented by the right hand side. The "$" in the write statement is for extra newlines, and "#" to begin a comment. The names of standard variables should be mostly self-explanatory. For example, `vratio` stands for visit ratio and can be thought of as a two-dimensional array indexed with station number and chain number. (This is only a user's view; the implementation may use a different data structure.) If the last index is omitted, it is assumed to indicate chain 1. Thus, `vratio[3]` means the visit ratio of chain 1 at station 3. This convention allows easy handling of single-chain models. A few other standard variables are as follows: `stime[s,c]` (service time of station s chain c), `cvsqr[s,c]` (squared coefficient of variation), `popul[c]` (population of chain c), `thruput[s,c]` (throughput), `resptime[s,c]` (response time), `qlength[s,c]` (queue length), `mprob[s,n]` (marginal probability of station s at total load of n), `fn_ind[s]` (capacity function number of station s), `fn_bnd[f]` (saturation point of capacity function f), `fn_val[f,n]` (value of the capacity function f at load n), `nq` (number of queues in the model), `nchn` (number of chains in the model), etc. These variables are not declared, but otherwise can be used like any other variable. (For safety, however, certain standard variables are

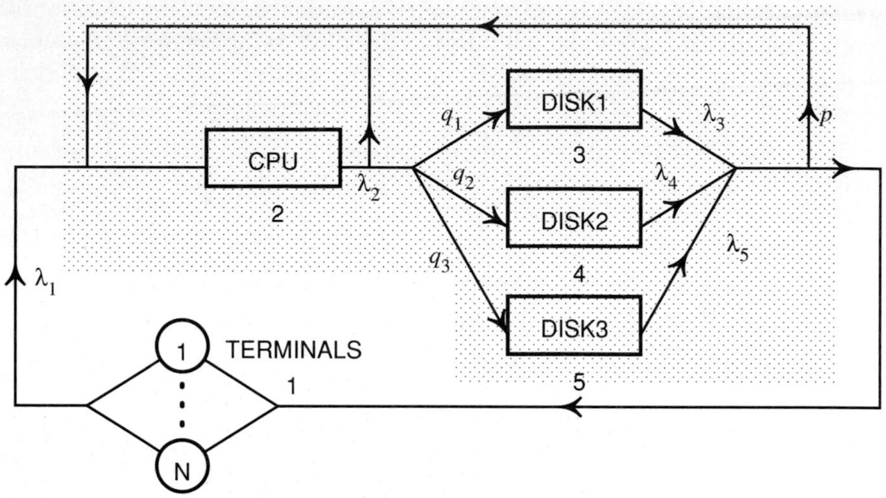

FIGURE D-1: A model of an interactive system.

restricted to be read-only.) All variables in Solver are known globally (i.e., have global names), but local storage instances can be created for them by declaring them of type `value` inside a procedure. For example, in procedure `compute` given later, fresh local storage is allocated to `vratio` and `stime`, with the result that any changes to them inside the procedure are not retained upon return.

D.2 Tuning a Paging System

In this section we analyze an interactive computer system consisting of some number of terminals, one CPU, one paging disk, and two file-disks. Henceforth, we shall number the terminal station as 1, CPU as 2, paging disk as 3, and file-disks as 4 and 5. Thus, the model consists of five stations, the first of which is delay type and the other four are load-independent. The queuing network model of the system is shown in Fig. D-1. The shaded portion of the network represents the *central subsystem*, which is responsible for processing user commands. The population of the network is N, which is the same as the number of active terminals.

We wish to examine this system assuming constant memory to find out how many terminals it can support, what the bottleneck devices are, and how the system could be tuned to give better performance. Because of the constant memory size, as the *degree of multiprogramming* (DMP) increases, so does the paging rate. The DMP in this system corresponds to the number of users inside the central subsystem, and thus fluctuates between 0 and N. The *life-time curve*, or the mean time between page faults that require disk I/O as a function of DMP, is known and is shown in Fig. D-2.

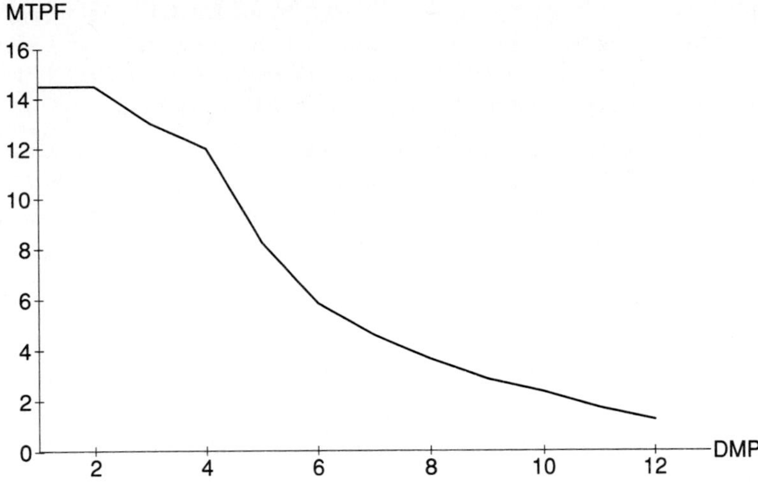

FIGURE D-2: The life-time curve for the paging system.

D.2.1 The Solver Program

The Solver program for this problem is shown in Section D.3. It starts out by declaring some variables including the array `sys_tput` that will be used to hold the throughput of the central subsystem in isolation. Next, we declare two loading functions. Function 1 specifies the life-time curve (with a value of 14.5 for DMP=1 and DMP=2, 13.0 for DMP=3, etc.). Function 2 is a dummy for now, and will be used for defining the capacity of the aggregate station in Norton's equivalent.

Next, we define the base models that we wish to use. Here we have only one such model, called `FULL`, that specifies the entire network. Its structure should be self-explanatory for the most part. The scheduling disciplines are as shown. The `unif-ps` discipline refers to the ordinary processor sharing discipline. The specification "a 1" for each station after the scheduling discipline line means that none of the stations carries a general or specialized (i.e., an SS-net or SD-net type) capacity function. All service times are assumed to be exponentially distributed; therefore, the coefficient of variation is 1.0 for all the stations. The population N is specified as 12. The visit ratios represent the number of times each device is visited during the execution of a command. That is, the visit ratio of the terminal is 1. The visit ratios of the two file-disks (150 and 250) are also as specified; however, those for the CPU and the paging disk are essentially dummy numbers. The problem is that the number of visits to the paging disk is determined by the life-time curve, and thus depends on the DMP. We shall see its computation shortly. From Fig. D-1, the visit ratio of the CPU is 1 plus the sum of the visit ratios of all disks; therefore, it too must be computed explicitly.

All service times are given in milliseconds. The average *think-time* is 40 seconds and the average time to read/write a page cluster is 12.43 ms for disks 1

& 2, and 29.64 ms for disk 3. However, the number given for the CPU (= 3 sec) is not really its service time. Service time is defined as the time on a per visit basis, but three seconds is the total CPU time *over all visits to the CPU*. This is again because we do not know the visit ratio of the CPU a priori.

Let us start examining the main program in the given Solver code. Because of the DMP dependence of the calibration parameters, we solve the model `FULL` in two steps using Norton's theorem. We first split the `FULL` model into two submodels: one called `CENTRAL` consisting of everything except the terminals, and the other called `OUTER`, which consists of the terminal and the flow equivalent aggregate of the `CENTRAL` model. This kind of splitting is done automatically by the `splitmodel` statement. The first model in this statement (i.e., `CENTRAL`) replaces the current model in the work area following a split, and the second model is saved. *The stations are automatically numbered by a split*; therefore, in the `CENTRAL` model, station 1 is the CPU, station 2 is the paging disk, and stations 3 & 4 are the file-disks.

Since the population of the `CENTRAL` model represents the DMP, we first calibrate and solve this model with DMP ranging from 1 to 12. This is done in the procedure `compute`. (Ignore the various option settings in this procedure; they are only for tabulating the results.) For each DMP, we first compute `vratio[2]`, the visit ratio of the paging disk. At a given DMP level, `vratio[2]` is obviously the `duration` divided by the mean time between page faults at that DMP. The latter is obtained from the array `fn_val[1]`. We could then compute the visit ratio and the service time of the CPU. Following the calibration, we solve the model (using the `solve` statement) and use the results to compute the system throughput, denoted `sys_tput`. The system throughput is simply the rate at which the jobs would have gone from the central subsystem to the terminals. (The multiplication by 1000 is needed because `sys_tput` is expressed in the units of jobs/sec, whereas `thruput[1]` is in the units of jobs/ms.)

By Norton's theorem, `sys_tput` should be the load-dependent service rate of the aggregate station in the `OUTER` model. Thus, after the `CENTRAL` model has been solved, we can load the `OUTER` model into the work area, calibrate its station 2, and solve this model. (See the main program.) Function 2 in the program is used to specify the capacity function derived from `sys_tput`. This calibrated model is saved for later use, though we don't really have any such use in this program.

D.2.2 Interpretation of Results

The output generated by the Solver program is also listed in Section D.3. Tables 1 and 2 give results for the *original* `CENTRAL` model, i.e., the model without tuning. Several things can be seen from these. As Table 2 shows, the central subsystem throughput increases at first, then becomes stagnant, and finally drops. To see the reasons for this, we look at Table 1, which lists utilizations of CPU, paging disk, and the file-disks. We see that the second file-disk (i.e., station 4) becomes a bottleneck at the DMP of only 4. But an increase in DMP increases the page fault rate also, and the paging disk (i.e., station 2) also begins to suffer. Since more and more processes get stuck to do page I/O, the load on the other devices decreases. Consequently, we see a drop in the utilization of other stations *including the second file-disk*. The system throughput also drops as a result. Note that the maximum throughput is achieved at DMP of 5, and this throughput is rather small. If the DMP is increased to 10 or beyond, the paging disk becomes almost completely saturated. Throughout the whole range, the first file-disk (station 3) remains lightly loaded and does not play any important role in the system performance.

One may be tempted to conclude from these results that the system needs a faster file-disk; however, we should not propose such expensive solutions without a careful study of the system. We should first see if some tuning of the system would improve the performance. This is a particularly important point to remember because a poorly thought out hardware-upgrade solution may even make the performance worse. It is easy to see that by making the second file-disk faster, we would effectively throw more load at the paging disk, thereby saturating it even faster. Thus, although a higher maximum throughput will result, it will occur at a lower DMP. That is, if we were expecting to support more terminals (which requires obtaining good performance at higher DMP's) we would have actually hurt ourselves by making the upgrade! This is shown in Table 5 where the second column shows `sys_tput` as a function of DMP when the second file-disk is made twice as fast.[2]

There is also another pitfall to note. Suppose that we only solved the model (or performed actual measurements) when most of the terminals are active. Then as Table 1 indicates, we would conclude that the system "obviously" needs a faster paging disk. We might even think that the conclusion is safe because it was drawn based upon the data for a heavily loaded system. In effect, we would completely miss the fact that the second file-disk is the first one to become the bottleneck as the load increases. In fact, putting a faster paging disk will saturate the second file-disk even faster among the two file-disks. Thus, although we will be able to support a higher DMP (and hence a larger number of terminals), the increase in the optimum throughput will be insignificant. This should be clear from the third column of Table 5 which shows `sys_tput` when the paging disk is made twice as fast.

Let us now consider the tuning strategy. Since the first file-disk remains lightly loaded throughout, but the second one is the first to become a bottleneck, it is clear that the first action should be to move some load from the second file-disk to the first. This can be done by swapping the more frequently used files (or file systems) of the second file-disk with the less frequently used files of the first. In terms of our model, this would affect the visit ratios of the two disks. It is intuitively obvious that a balanced load would work the best. Therefore, we reduce the visit ratio of station 4 by 132 and increase that of station 3 by the same amount. This is done in the second call to `compute` procedure in the program above.

[2]The code for generating Table 5 is not included in the Solver program as shown.

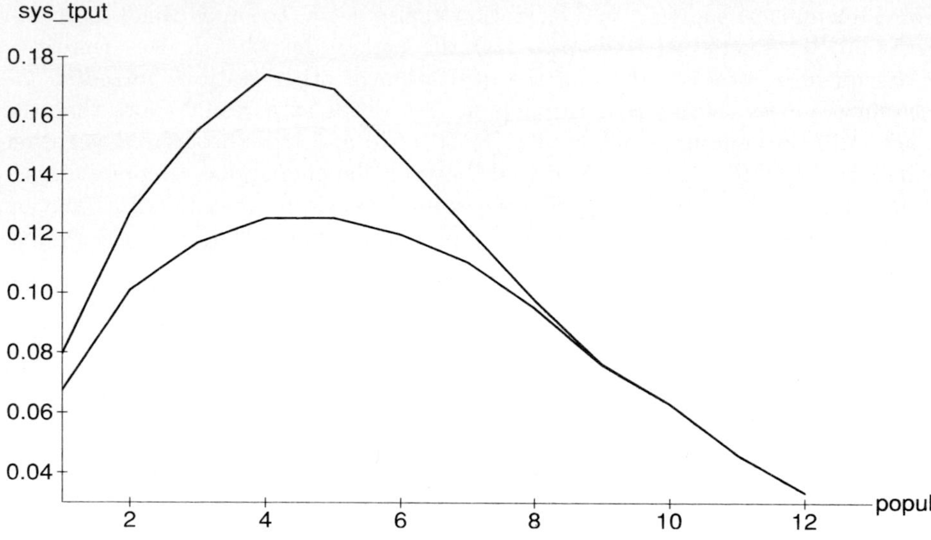

FIGURE D-3: System throughput (a) without and (b) with tuning.

Let us examine the results from the *modified* CENTRAL model, given in Tables 3 and 4. As a result of load balancing, the utilizations of the two file-disks remain almost equal throughout. Also, the maximum utilization is now 61%, which means that the file-disks do not become bottlenecks. (So disk 3 was not the problem, after all!) Fig. D-3 shows the system throughput graphically for both the untuned and the tuned systems. The shape of both curves is similar, as expected, but the tuning increases the maximum throughput from 0.125 to about 0.174, a 40% increase. The paging disk still becomes a bottleneck eventually, but at a *lower* DMP. Also, the maximum throughput is now achieved at a *lower* DMP. This may seem anomalous, but it is an expected behavior. The reason is that a well-tuned system will attain its optimum performance at a smaller load than a mistuned system. It is clear that the only limiting device in the tuned system is the paging disk. So, if we want to achieve an even higher throughput, a faster paging disk will help now. The last column in Table 5 shows sys_tput for a tuned system with the paging disk made twice as fast. Both the maximum throughput and the number of terminals that can be supported increase significantly. The behavior also becomes smoother than in Table 4 because of the availability of more service capacity in the system.

Let us now see how the overall system will behave with tuning. For this, we solve the aggregated 2-station OUTER model, where station 1 is the terminal and station 2 represents the CENTRAL model. The results are shown in the last data set and are interesting. It is seen that the throughput increases with the number of active terminals (or N) until $N = 9$ and then begins to fall off. At $N = 10$ the change is not significant, but any further increase in N makes a drastic change. A careful look will reveal why. As we go from $N = 10$ to $N = 11$, the queue length at station 2 of the aggregated model (which is the same as DMP) crosses over its optimum value of 4, the paging disk begins to choke, and the throughput drops. Once again, the sudden change is the result of tuning! *A tuned system quickly uses up all its capacity, and so any overloading will deteriorate the performance significantly*. The untuned system will not show such a sharp change. The results show clearly that this system cannot support more than 10 terminals. (One can also verify that the tuned model with twice-as-fast a paging disk can support 13 terminals.) The bottleneck analysis illustrated in Section 4.3.2 will also give similar results, though we will not be able to examine the behavior in such detail without actually solving the model.

D.2.3 Issues for Further Study

It would be instructive to study this system further to see how the performance can be improved. Notice that after tuning we find that the paging disk becomes a bottleneck beyond DMP of 5. Thus, any further improvement should somehow reduce the paging overhead. The first thing to examine in this regard is the parameters related to paging (replacement policy, cluster size for page I/O, page caching mechanism, etc.); however, since these require a very detailed system description, we shall not consider them here. At the hardware level, we can do two things to reduce paging: (a) increase the main memory size, and (b) replace the paging disk with a faster disk. From cost considerations, option (a) should be looked at first. More main memory would allow a larger portion of a program's working set to be resident and thereby increase the mean time between page faults. Suppose that we increase the memory by the (multiplicative) factor α. We can expect the page fault rate to go down by this factor also. Study the system for $\alpha = 2$. That is, find out which device now becomes the bottleneck, at what DMP, and how many terminals can be supported by the system. Do the same for $\alpha = 4$. (We cannot make α arbitrarily high because of the limitations on how much memory the system can support.)

In the analysis above, we assumed that the service-time distributions are all exponential. It is probably more reasonable to assume that the coefficient of variation at the disks is 0.5. Repeat the analysis with this change. Would you expect any significant changes in the overall behavior?

Now include a second chain in the model that represents batch jobs. This chain goes through only stations 2 through 5 and has N' jobs circulating through it. Each batch job requires 1500 ms of total service at the CPU. A batch job exiting the CPU goes to one of the three disks, and from the disks back to the CPU. The service times at the disks are the same as for chain 1, but $v_{32} = 80$, $v_{42} = 50$. Of course, the visit ratios of the paging disk and the CPU depend on the overall DMP (including both chains) and must be computed for each DMP value. Repeat the entire analysis for this more complicated case. Also examine the effect of increasing chain 2 population on the number of terminals that can be supported. Obviously, chain 2 will load the stations of the central subsystems further; however, since the loading pattern of chain 2 is different from that of chain 1, the bottlenecks may shift. Thus, for example, you will find that station

4 does not become a bottleneck quite as quickly. Examine carefully how the utilizations of various devices change with chain populations and explain the behavior intuitively.

D.3 Program Listing and Output

```
#Model of a paging system with a CPU, a paging disk, and two file-disks.
#Declaration part
   integer ind, amount
   real    duration, vtemp, sys_tput(15)
   char    mess(14)
#
#Loading Function Declarations
#  function 1: saturation_point(=12) list-of-values
#  function 2: saturation_point(=1)  value
#A '*' is needed in function 1 to avoid error messages.
#
functions
  list*(1) 12 14.5 14.5 13.0 12.0 8.25 5.85 4.60 3.65 2.85 2.35 1.72 1.25
  list(2) 1 1
end
#
#model definition.
models
  FULL:                                               #name of the model
    5  1                                              #no of stns and chains
    delay  unif_ps   fcfs     fcfs     fcfs      #sch. discip of each stn
      a 1    a 1      a 1      a 1      a 1      #std capacity functions
     40000  3000.0   12.43    12.43    29.64     #Service times of chain1
      1.0    1.0      1.0      1.0      1.0      #coeff of var for chain1
      1.0    401      1.0      150      250      #visit ratios for chain1
    12                                                #population vector
end;
#
  procedure compute(amount, mess)
  value vratio, stime        #locally re-allocated variables
  begin
    writeln(outfile,$,' ':30, mess)
#   Calculate visit ratios of stations 3&4 (in the central model) assuming
#   that "amount" load is transferred from station 4 to station 3.
    vratio[3] += amount; vratio[4] -= amount
    vtemp := 1 + vratio[3] + vratio[4];
#
#   Misc option settings to get utilization tables
    option[1] := 110;        #Exact solution, auto-plot mode
    option[4] := 301411421   #First three table columns
    option[5] := 431441      #Fourth and fifth table columns
    option[6] := 1013        #left margin 10, generate labels, tbl mode
    option[7] := 091094094   #Format for table columns
```

```
    option[9] := 100          #Plot label only on top
    option[10] := ord(' ')  #separate table columns by blanks
#
#   Compute visit ratios and CPU service time. Solve the model.
    for ind := 1 to fn_bnd[1] do
      vratio[2] := duration/fn_val[1,ind];
      vratio[1] := vtemp + vratio[2];
      stime[1] := duration/vratio[1];
      popul[1] := ind
      solve                   #Solve for each population level.
      sys_tput[ind] := 1000*thruput[1]/vratio[1];
    endfor
#
#   Compute and print system throughput
    writeln(outfile,$,$,' ':25,'popul[1]':10,'sys_tput':10)
    for ind := 1 to fn_bnd[1] do
       writeln(outfile,' ':25, ind:3,' ':4, sys_tput[ind]:10:5)
    endfor
  end
#
#main program
begin
#  The last-declared model is loaded into the workspace automatically;
#  therefore, the "current" model is FULL.
#  Split FULL into 2 parts: CENTRAL={2,3,4,5}, OUTER={1,a} where a is
#  the aggregate station. The first model becomes "current".
   splitmodel(CENTRAL, OUTER, 1)
   duration := stime[1]
   compute(0, 'ORIGINAL MODEL')          #Solve the original model.
   writeln(outfile,$)
   compute(132, 'MODIFIED MODEL')        #Solve the tuned model.
#
#  Load outer model and calibrate it using sys_tput for the tuned model.
   loadmodel(OUTER, 1)
   stime[1] /= 1000; stime[2] := 1/sys_tput[1];
#  Define the basic service time (using Norton's theorem).
   fn_ind[2] := 2; fn_bnd[2] := fn_bnd[1]
#  Set up capacity function number and saturation point.
   for ind := 1 to fn_bnd[1] do
      fn_val[2,ind] := sys_tput[ind]/sys_tput[1]
   endfor
   savemodel               #save current model (not really necessary)
#
#  Set option[1] to print results for each population level.
   option[1] := 121; option[9] := 4
   writeln(outfile, $,' ':30,'COMPOSITE MODEL',$)
   solve                      #Solve composite model
end
```

Please note that the output below has been altered slightly for ease in reference and presentation. In particular, the labeling of tables on the side is not program generated.

ORIGINAL MODEL

TABLE 1:

popul[1]	util[1,1]	util[2,1]	util[3,1]	util[4,1]
1.0	0.2021	0.1732	0.1256	0.4991
2.0	0.3026	0.2594	0.1880	0.7473
3.0	0.3502	0.3349	0.2177	0.8651
4.0	0.3751	0.3886	0.2331	0.9265
5.0	0.3755	0.5657	0.2334	0.9275
6.0	0.3588	0.7623	0.2230	0.8861
7.0	0.3308	0.8938	0.2056	0.8170
8.0	0.2850	0.9706	0.1771	0.7040
9.0	0.2284	0.9961	0.1419	0.5641
10.0	0.1890	0.9996	0.1175	0.4668
11.0	0.1384	1.0000	0.0860	0.3418
12.0	0.1006	1.0000	0.0625	0.2484

TABLE 2:

popul[1]	sys_tput
1	0.06736
2	0.10085
3	0.11675
4	0.12504
5	0.12516
6	0.11958
7	0.11026
8	0.09501
9	0.07613
10	0.06299
11	0.04612
12	0.03352

MODIFIED MODEL

TABLE 3:

popul[1]	util[1,1]	util[2,1]	util[3,1]	util[4,1]
1.0	0.2386	0.2045	0.2788	0.2781
2.0	0.3806	0.3262	0.4447	0.4437
3.0	0.4647	0.4443	0.5429	0.5417
4.0	0.5215	0.5402	0.6094	0.6080
5.0	0.5067	0.7634	0.5920	0.5907
6.0	0.4371	0.9287	0.5107	0.5096
7.0	0.3645	0.9848	0.4258	0.4249
8.0	0.2931	0.9982	0.3425	0.3417
9.0	0.2293	0.9999	0.2679	0.2673
10.0	0.1891	1.0000	0.2209	0.2204
11.0	0.1384	1.0000	0.1617	0.1613
12.0	0.1006	1.0000	0.1175	0.1172

TABLE 4:

popul[1]	sys_tput
1	0.07953
2	0.12685
3	0.15489
4	0.17385
5	0.16890
6	0.14570
7	0.12148
8	0.09770
9	0.07642
10	0.06302
11	0.04612
12	0.03352

TABLE 5:

popul[1]	Untuned Fast-2FD	Untuned Fast-PD	Tuned Fast-PD
1	0.08976	0.07374	0.08858
2	0.14198	0.10723	0.13885
3	0.17133	0.12219	0.16930
4	0.19019	0.12916	0.19006
5	0.17931	0.13162	0.19979
6	0.14928	0.13238	0.20134
7	0.12226	0.13241	0.19656
8	0.09779	0.13114	0.18011
9	0.07642	0.12610	0.15042
10	0.06302	0.11699	0.12575
11	0.04612	0.09164	0.09224
12	0.03352	0.06703	0.06704

COMPOSITE MODEL

QUEUE	S.TIME	CVSQR	VRATIO	QLENGTH	RESP-TIME	THROUGHPUT	UTIL-FAC
			Chain 1	Population = 1			
1 0	40.0000	1.000	1.000	0.7608	4.000e+01	1.902e-02	0.7608
2 1	12.5745	1.000	1.000	0.2392	1.257e+01	1.902e-02	0.2392
			Chain 1	Population = 2			
1 0	40.0000	1.000	1.000	1.4999	4.000e+01	3.750e-02	1.4999
2 1	12.5745	1.000	1.000	0.5001	1.334e+01	3.750e-02	0.4715
			Chain 1	Population = 3			
1 0	40.0000	1.000	1.000	2.2140	4.000e+01	5.535e-02	2.2140
2 1	12.5745	1.000	1.000	0.7860	1.420e+01	5.535e-02	0.6960
			Chain 1	Population = 4			
1 0	40.0000	1.000	1.000	2.9002	4.000e+01	7.250e-02	2.9002
2 1	12.5745	1.000	1.000	1.0998	1.517e+01	7.250e-02	0.9117

```
QUEUE   S.TIME   CVSQR  VRATIO  QLENGTH  RESP-TIME   THROUGHPUT UTIL-FAC

                        Chain 1  Population = 5
 1 0  40.0000  1.000   1.000   3.5533  4.000e+01   8.883e-02  3.5533
 2 1  12.5745  1.000   1.000   1.4467  1.629e+01   8.883e-02  1.1170

                        Chain 1  Population = 6
 1 0  40.0000  1.000   1.000   4.1635  4.000e+01   1.041e-01  4.1635
 2 1  12.5745  1.000   1.000   1.8365  1.764e+01   1.041e-01  1.3089

                        Chain 1  Population = 7
 1 0  40.0000  1.000   1.000   4.7112  4.000e+01   1.178e-01  4.7112
 2 1  12.5745  1.000   1.000   2.2888  1.943e+01   1.178e-01  1.4810

                        Chain 1  Population = 8
 1 0  40.0000  1.000   1.000   5.1577  4.000e+01   1.289e-01  5.1577
 2 1  12.5745  1.000   1.000   2.8423  2.204e+01   1.289e-01  1.6214

QUEUE   S.TIME   CVSQR  VRATIO  QLENGTH  RESP-TIME   THROUGHPUT UTIL-FAC

                        Chain 1  Population = 9
 1 0  40.0000  1.000   1.000   5.4249  4.000e+01   1.356e-01  5.4249
 2 1  12.5745  1.000   1.000   3.5751  2.636e+01   1.356e-01  1.7054

                        Chain 1  Population =10
 1 0  40.0000  1.000   1.000   5.3635  4.000e+01   1.341e-01  5.3635
 2 1  12.5745  1.000   1.000   4.6365  3.458e+01   1.341e-01  1.6861

                        Chain 1  Population =11
 1 0  40.0000  1.000   1.000   4.7469  4.000e+01   1.187e-01  4.7469
 2 1  12.5745  1.000   1.000   6.2531  5.269e+01   1.187e-01  1.4922

                        Chain 1  Population =12
 1 0  40.0000  1.000   1.000   3.4717  4.000e+01   8.679e-02  3.4717
 2 1  12.5745  1.000   1.000   8.5283  9.826e+01   8.679e-02  1.0914
```

APPENDIX

E

Selected Tables

The tables in sections E.1 and E.2 are taken with permission from *Simulation Modeling and Analysis*, by Law and Kelton, McGraw-Hill, 1982.

E.1 Critical Points of t Distribution

Let X be a random variable with standard t distribution with n degrees of freedom. Then if the listed value is x, it means that $Pr(X \le x) = 1 - \alpha$. Since t distribution is symmetric, this also means that $Pr(X \ge -x) = 1 - \alpha$.

n	$\alpha = 0.1$	$\alpha = 0.05$	$\alpha = 0.025$	$\alpha = 0.01$	$\alpha = 0.005$	$\alpha = 0.001$
1	3.078	6.314	12.706	31.821	63.657	318.310
2	1.886	2.920	4.303	6.965	9.925	22.327
3	1.638	2.353	3.182	4.541	5.841	10.215
4	1.533	2.132	2.776	3.747	4.604	7.173
5	1.476	2.015	2.571	3.365	4.032	5.893
6	1.440	1.943	2.447	3.143	3.707	5.208
7	1.415	1.895	2.365	2.998	3.499	4.785
8	1.397	1.860	2.306	2.896	3.355	4.501
9	1.383	1.833	2.262	2.821	3.250	4.297
10	1.372	1.812	2.228	2.764	3.169	4.144

n	$\alpha = 0.1$	$\alpha = 0.05$	$\alpha = 0.025$	$\alpha = 0.01$	$\alpha = 0.005$	$\alpha = 0.001$
11	1.363	1.796	2.201	2.718	3.106	4.025
12	1.356	1.782	2.179	2.681	3.055	3.930
13	1.350	1.771	2.160	2.650	3.012	3.852
14	1.345	1.761	2.145	2.624	2.977	3.787
15	1.341	1.753	2.131	2.602	2.947	3.733
16	1.337	1.746	2.120	2.583	2.921	3.686
17	1.333	1.740	2.110	2.567	2.898	3.646
18	1.330	1.734	2.101	2.552	2.878	3.610
19	1.328	1.729	2.093	2.539	2.861	3.579
20	1.325	1.725	2.086	2.528	2.845	3.552
21	1.323	1.721	2.080	2.518	2.831	3.527
22	1.321	1.717	2.074	2.508	2.819	3.505
23	1.319	1.714	2.069	2.500	2.807	3.485
24	1.318	1.711	2.064	2.492	2.797	3.467
25	1.316	1.708	2.060	2.485	2.787	3.450
26	1.315	1.706	2.056	2.479	2.779	3.435
28	1.313	1.701	2.048	2.467	2.763	3.408
30	1.310	1.697	2.042	2.457	2.750	3.385
40	1.303	1.684	2.021	2.423	2.704	3.307
60	1.296	1.671	2.000	2.390	2.660	3.232
120	1.289	1.658	1.980	2.358	2.617	3.160
∞	1.282	1.645	1.960	2.326	2.576	3.090

TABLE E.1: Values of $t_{n,\alpha}$.

E.2 Selection among Alternate Designs

In these tables, P_0 is the probability of correct selection, n is the sample size, and k is the number of systems. In the tables for h_2 and h_3, m is the size of the subset that we wish to select. The omitted values are those where the required restriction on P_0 does not hold.

P_0	n	$k=2$	$k=3$	$k=4$	$k=5$	$k=6$	$k=7$	$k=8$	$k=9$	$k=10$
0.90	20	1.896	2.342	2.583	2.747	2.870	2.969	3.051	3.121	3.182
0.90	40	1.852	2.283	2.514	2.669	2.785	2.878	2.954	3.019	3.076
0.95	20	2.453	2.872	3.101	3.258	3.377	3.472	3.551	3.619	3.679
0.95	40	2.386	2.786	3.003	3.150	3.260	3.349	3.422	3.484	3.539

TABLE E.2: Parameter h_1 for given values of p_0, n, and k.

m	$k=3$	$k=4$	$k=5$	$k=6$	$k=7$	$k=8$	$k=9$	$k=10$
				$P_0 = 0.90,\ n = 20$				
2	1.137	1.601	1.860	2.039	2.174	2.282	2.373	2.450
3		0.782	1.243	1.507	1.690	1.830	1.943	2.038
4			0.556	1.012	1.276	1.461	1.603	1.718
5				0.392	0.843	1.105	1.291	1.434
6					0.265	0.711	0.971	1.156
7						0.162	0.603	0.861
8							0.075	0.512
				$P_0 = 0.90,\ n = 40$				
2	1.114	1.570	1.825	1.999	2.131	2.237	2.324	2.399
3		0.763	1.219	1.479	1.660	1.798	1.909	2.002
4			0.541	0.991	1.251	1.434	1.575	1.688
5				0.381	0.824	1.083	1.266	1.408
6					0.257	0.693	0.950	1.133
7						0.156	0.587	0.841
8							0.072	0.497

m	$k=3$	$k=4$	$k=5$	$k=6$	$k=7$	$k=8$	$k=9$	$k=10$
				$P_0 = 0.95,\ n = 20$				
2	1.631	2.071	2.321	2.494	2.625	2.731	2.819	2.894
3		1.256	1.697	1.952	2.131	2.267	2.378	2.470
4			1.021	1.458	1.714	1.894	2.033	2.146
5				0.852	1.284	1.539	1.720	1.860
6					0.721	1.149	1.402	1.583
7						0.615	1.038	1.290
8							0.526	0.945
9								0.449
				$P_0 = 0.95,\ n = 40$				
2	1.591	2.023	2.267	2.435	2.563	2.665	2.750	2.823
3		1.222	1.656	1.907	2.082	2.217	2.325	2.415
4			0 990	1.420	1.672	1.850	1.987	2.098
5				0.824	1.248	1.499	1.678	1.816
6					0.695	1.114	1.363	1.541
7						0.591	1.004	1.252
8							0.505	0.913
9								0.430

TABLE E.3: Parameter h_2 for given values of p_0, n, m, and k.

m	$k=3$	$k=4$	$k=5$	$k=6$	$k=7$	$k=8$	$k=9$	$k=10$
				$P_0=0.90,\ n=20$				
2	2.342	2.779	3.016	3.177	3.299	3.396	3.477	3.546
3		2.583	3.016	3.251	3.411	3.532	3.629	3.709
4			2.747	3.177	3.411	3.571	3.691	3.787
5				2.870	3.299	3.532	3.691	3.811
6					2.969	3.396	3.629	3.787
7						3.051	3.477	3.709
8							3.121	3.546
9								3.182
				$P_0=0.90,\ n=40$				
2	2.283	2.703	2.928	3.081	3.195	3.285	3.360	3.424
3		2.514	2.928	3.151	3.302	3.415	3.505	3.579
4			2.669	3.081	3.302	3.451	3.564	3.653
5				2.785	3.195	3.415	3.564	3.675
6					2.878	3.285	3.505	3.653
7						2.954	3.360	3.579
8							3.019	3.424
9								3.076

m	$k=3$	$k=4$	$k=5$	$k=6$	$k=7$	$k=8$	$k=9$	$k=10$
				$P_0=0.95,\ n=20$				
2	2.872	3.282	3.507	3.662	3.779	3.873	3.952	4.019
3		3.101	3.507	3.731	3.885	4.001	4.094	4.172
4			3.258	3.662	3.885	4.037	4.153	4.246
5				3.377	3.779	4.001	4.153	4.269
6					3.472	3.873	4.094	4.246
7						3.551	3.952	4.172
8							3.619	4.019
9								3.679
				$P_0=0.95,\ n=40$				
2	2.786	3.175	3.386	3.530	3.639	3.725	3.797	3.858
3		3.003	3.386	3.595	3.738	3.845	3.931	4.002
4			3.150	3.530	3.738	3.879	3.986	4.071
5				3.260	3.639	3.845	3.986	4.092
6					3.349	3.725	3.931	4.071
7						3.422	3.797	4.002
8							3.484	3.858
9								3.539

TABLE E.4: Parameter h_3 for given values of p_0, n, m, and k.

E.3 Selected Laplace Transform Pairs

We denote the Laplace transform of a continuous function $f(x)$, $x \geq 0$ as $\Psi(s)$ or $\Psi_f(s)$ and define it as $\int_0^\infty e^{-sx} f(x)dx$. In the following, "TD" stands for "transform domain".

$$
\begin{aligned}
\alpha f(t) + \beta g(t) \quad &\text{(linearity)} &\Longleftrightarrow\quad & \alpha\Psi_f(s) + \beta\Psi_g(s) \\
f(t/a) \quad &\text{(scaling)} &\Longleftrightarrow\quad & a\Psi(as) \\
f(t-a) \quad &\text{(time shift)} &\Longleftrightarrow\quad & e^{-as}\Psi(s) \\
e^{at} f(t) \quad &\text{(TD shift)} &\Longleftrightarrow\quad & \Psi(s-a) \\
f'(t) \quad &\text{(time derivative)} &\Longleftrightarrow\quad & s\Psi(s) - f(0) \\
f^{(n)}(t) \quad &\text{(time derivative)} &\Longleftrightarrow\quad & s^n\Psi(s) - \sum_{i=1}^{n} s^{n-i} f^{n-i}(0) \\
t^n f(t) \quad &\text{(TD derivative)} &\Longleftrightarrow\quad & (-1)^n \frac{d^n\Psi(s)}{ds^n} \\
\frac{f(t)}{t} \quad &\text{(TD integration)} &\Longleftrightarrow\quad & \int_s^\infty \Psi(u)\, du \\
\int_0^t f(u)\, du \quad &\text{(time integration)} &\Longleftrightarrow\quad & \frac{\Psi(s)}{s} \\
f(t) \bullet g(t) \quad &\text{(time convolution)} &\Longleftrightarrow\quad & \Psi_f(s)\Psi_g(s) \\
\int_0^\infty f(t)\, dt \quad &\text{(integral property)} &\Longleftrightarrow\quad & \Psi(0) \\
\lim_{t\to 0} f(t) \quad &\text{(initial value thrm)} &\Longleftrightarrow\quad & \lim_{s\to\infty} s\Psi(s) \\
\lim_{t\to\infty} f(t) \quad &\text{(final value thrm)} &\Longleftrightarrow\quad & \lim_{s\to 0} s\Psi(s)
\end{aligned}
$$

$$
\begin{aligned}
u_0(t-a) \quad \text{(unit impulse)} &\Longleftrightarrow e^{-as} \quad \Rightarrow \quad u_0(t) \Longleftrightarrow 1 \\
U_0(t-a) \quad \text{(unit step)} &\Longleftrightarrow e^{-as}/s \quad \Rightarrow \quad 1 \Longleftrightarrow 1/s \\
t^{n-1}/(n-1)! &\Longleftrightarrow 1/s^n \\
\frac{t^{n-1}e^{-at}}{(n-1)!} &\Longleftrightarrow \frac{1}{(s+a)^n} \quad \Rightarrow \quad e^{-at} \Longleftrightarrow \frac{1}{s+a} \\
t^{\alpha-1}e^{-at}/\Gamma(\alpha) &\Longleftrightarrow 1/(s+a)^\alpha \\
\sin(at)/a &\Longleftrightarrow 1/(s^2+a^2) \\
\cos(at) &\Longleftrightarrow s/(s^2+a^2) \\
\sin(at)/t &\Longleftrightarrow \tan^{-1}(a/s) \\
\frac{e^{-bt} - e^{-at}}{t} &\Longleftrightarrow \ln\left(\frac{s+a}{s+b}\right)
\end{aligned}
$$

E.4 Selected z-Transform Pairs

We denote the z-transform of a function $f(n)$, $n = 0, 1, 2, \ldots$ as $\Phi(z)$, defined as $\Phi(z) = \sum_{n=0}^{\infty} z^n f(n)$. In the following, "TD" stands for "transform domain".

$$
\begin{array}{rrcl}
\alpha f(n) + \beta g(n) & \text{(linearity)} & \Longleftrightarrow & \alpha\Phi_f(z) + \beta\Phi_g(z) \\
f(n) - f(n-1) & \text{(difference)} & \Longleftrightarrow & (1-z)\Phi(z) \\
\sum_{k=0}^{n} f(k) & \text{(cumulation)} & \Longleftrightarrow & \dfrac{\Phi(z)}{1-z} \\
f(n+k) & \text{(right shift)} & \Longleftrightarrow & \dfrac{\Phi(z)}{z^k} - \sum_{j=0}^{k-1} z^{j-k} f(j) \\
f(n-k) & \text{(left shift)} & \Longleftrightarrow & z^k \Phi(z) \\
a^n f(n) & \text{(TD scaling)} & \Longleftrightarrow & \Phi(az) \\
f(n/k) & \text{(time scaling)} & \Longleftrightarrow & \Phi(z^k), \qquad n = 0, k, 2k, 3k, \ldots \\
n f(n) & \text{(TD derivative)} & \Longleftrightarrow & z\Phi'(z) \\
\dfrac{n!}{(n-k)!} f(n) & \text{(TD derivative)} & \Longleftrightarrow & z^k \dfrac{d^k \Phi(z)}{dz^k} \\
f(n) \bullet g(n) & \text{(time convolution)} & \Longleftrightarrow & \Phi_f(z)\Phi_g(z) \\
\Phi(0) & \text{(initial value thrm)} & \Longleftrightarrow & f(0) \\
\lim_{z\to 1}(1-z)\Phi(z) & \text{(final value thrm)} & \Longleftrightarrow & f(\infty) \\
P(n) & \text{(intermediate value thrm)} & \Longleftrightarrow & \dfrac{1}{n!} \dfrac{d^n \Phi(z)}{dz^n}\bigg|_{z=0}
\end{array}
$$

$$
\begin{array}{rrcll}
u_0(n-k) & \text{(unit pulse)} & \Longleftrightarrow & z^k & \\
U_0(n-k) & \text{(unit step)} & \Longleftrightarrow & z^k/(1-z) & \\
 & \dfrac{1}{a^{n+1}} & \Longleftrightarrow & \dfrac{1}{a-z} & \Rightarrow \; a^n \Leftrightarrow \dfrac{1}{1-az} \\
 & \dfrac{n}{a^n} & \Longleftrightarrow & \dfrac{az}{(z-a)^2} & \Rightarrow \; n \Leftrightarrow \dfrac{z}{(z-1)^2} \\
 & \dfrac{n+1}{a^{n+2}} & \Longleftrightarrow & \dfrac{1}{(z-a)^2} & \Rightarrow \; n+1 \Leftrightarrow \dfrac{1}{(z-1)^2} \\
 & \dfrac{n^2}{a^{n+1}} & \Longleftrightarrow & \dfrac{z(z+a)}{(a-z)^3} & \Rightarrow \; n^2 \Leftrightarrow \dfrac{z(1+z)}{(1-z)^3} \\
 & \dbinom{n+m}{n} a^n & \Longleftrightarrow & 1/(1-az)^{m+1} & \\
 & 1/n! & \Longleftrightarrow & e^z &
\end{array}
$$

References

Frequently occurring journal and conference names have been abbreviated in the following. JACM stands for *Journal of ACM*, CACM for *Communications of the ACM*, TC for *Transactions on Computers*, TSE for *Transactions on Software Engineering*, TOCS for *Transactions on Computer Systems*, BSTJ for *Bell System Technical Journal*, Perf-Eval for *Performance Evaluation Journal*, PNPM for *Conference on Petri nets and Performance Models*, and Sigmetrics for *ACM Conference on Measurement and Modeling.* The location information for the following is also omitted: North Holland, which is based in Amsterdam, The Netherlands; PNPM 87 conference, that took place in Madison, WI; PNPM 89 conference, that took place in Kyoto, Japan. Old articles whose contents are readily available in books or in newer articles have generally been omitted.

Agrawal, S. C. and J. P. Buzen, "The Aggregate Server Method for Analyzing Serialization Delays in Computer Systems," *ACM-TOCS*, vol. 1, no. 2, pp. 116–143, 1983.

Agrawal, S. C., *Metamodeling: A Study of Approximations in Queueing Models*, MIT Press, Cambridge, MA, 1985.

Agre, J. R. and S. K. Tripathi, "Approximate Solution to Multichain Queueing Networks with State Dependent Service Rates," *Perf-Eval*, vol. 5, pp. 45–55, 1985.

Akyildiz, I. F., "Mean Value Analysis for Blocking Queueing Networks," *IEEE-TSE*, vol. 14, pp. 418–428, April 1988.

Akyildiz, I. F. and A. Sieber, "Approximate Analysis of Load Dependent General Queueing Networks," *IEEE-TSE*, vol. 14, pp. 1537–1545, Nov. 1988.

Akyildiz, I. F., "Product Form Approximations for Queueing Networks with Multiple Servers and Blocking," *IEEE-TC*, vol. 38, pp. 99–114, Jan. 1989.

Akyildiz, I. F. and H. Von Brand, "Central Server Models with Multiple Job Classes, State Dependent Routing and Rejection Blocking," *IEEE-TSE*, vol. 15, pp. 1305–1312, Oct. 1989.

Baccelli, F., W. A. Massey, and D. Towsley, "Acyclic Fork-Join Queueing Networks," *JACM*, vol. 36, pp. 615–642, July 1989.

Balbo, G., G. Chiola, G. Franceschinis, and G. M. Roet, "On the Efficient Construction of the Tangible Reachability Graph of Generalized Stochastic Petri Nets," *PNPM*, pp. 136–145, Aug. 1987.

Balbo, G., S. C. Bruell, and S. Ghanta, "Combining Queueing Networks and Generalized Stochastic Petri-Nets for the Solution of Complex Models of System Behavior," *IEEE-TC*, vol. 37, pp. 1251–1268, Oct. 1988.

Bannister, J. A. and K. S. Trivedi, "Task Allocation in Fault-Tolerant Distributed Systems," *Acta Informatica*, vol. 20, pp. 261–281, 1983.

Bard, Y., "A Model of Shared DASD and Multipathing," *CACM*, vol. 23, pp. 564–572, Oct. 1980.

Bard, Y., "Modeling I/O Systems with Dynamic Path Selection and General Transmission Networks," *ACM Sigmetrics*, vol. 10, pp. 118–129, 1982.

Baskett, F., K. M. Chandy, R. R. Muntz, and F. G. Palacios, "Open, Closed, and Mixed Networks of Queues with Different Classes of Customers," *JACM*, vol. 22, pp. 248–260, April 1975.

Beaudry, M. D., "Performance-Related Reliability Measures for Computing Systems," *IEEE-TC*, vol. 27, pp. 540–547, June 1978.

Billington, J., "Extensions to Colored Petri Nets," *PNPM*, pp. 61–69, Dec. 1989.

Blakemore, A., "The Cost of Eliminating Vanishing Markings from Generalized Stochastic Petri Nets," *PNPM*, pp. 85–92, Dec. 1989.

Blondia, C., "The N/G/1 Finite Capacity Queue," *Stochastic Models*, vol. 5, no. 2, 1989.

Bobbio, A. and K. S. Trivedi, "An Aggregation Technique for the Transient Analysis of Stiff Markov Chains," *IEEE-TC*, vol. 35, pp. 803–814, Sept. 1986.

Bondi, A. B., "The Response Time of Priority Classes Under Preemptive Resume in M/G/m Queues," *ACM Sigmetrics*, vol. 12, pp. 195–201, Aug. 1984.

Bondi, A. B. and Y. M. Chuang, "A New MVA-Based Approximation for Closed Queuing Networks with a Preemptive Priority Server," *Perf-Eval*, vol. 8, pp. 195–221, 1988.

Boudec, J-Y. Le, "A BCMP Extension to Multiserver Stations with Concurrent Classes of Customers," *ACM Sigmetrics*, vol. 14, pp. 78–91, May 1986.

Box, G. E. P., W. G. Hunter, and J. S. Hunter, *Statistics for Experimenters: An Introduction to Design, Data Analysis and Model Building*, John Wiley, New York, 1978.

Boxma, O. J., F. P. Kelly, and A. G. Konheim, "The Product Form for Sojourn Time Distributions in Cyclic Exponential Queues," *JACM*, vol. 31, pp. 128–133, 1984.

Boxma, O. J. and B. Meister, "Waiting Time Approximations for Cyclic-Service Systems with Switchover Times," *ACM Sigmetrics*, vol. 14, no. 1, pp. 254–262, 1986.

Boxma, O. J. and W. P. Groenendijk, "Pseudoconservation Laws in Cyclic-Service Systems," *J. of Applied Probability*, vol. 24, pp. 949–952, 1987.

Boxma, O. J. and W. P. Groenendijk, and J. A. Weststrate, "A Pseudoconservation Law for Service Systems with a Polling Table," *Center for Mathematics and Computer Science, Netherlands*, Report OS-R8813, August 1988.

Brandwajn, A., "Fast Approximate Solution of Multiprogramming Models," *ACM Sigmetrics*, vol. 10, pp. 141–149, 1982.

Brandwajn, A., "Models of DASD Subsystems with Multiple Access Paths: A throughput driven approach," *IEEE-TC*, vol. 32, pp. 451–463, 1983.

Brandwajn, A., "Efficient Approximation for Models of Multiprogramming with Shared Domains," *ACM Sigmetrics*, vol. 12, pp. 186–191, 1984.

Bruell, S. C., G. Balbo, and P. V. Afshari, "Mean Value Analysis of Mixed, Multiple Class BCMP Networks with Load Dependent Service Stations," *Perf-Eval*, vol. 4, pp. 241–260, 1984.

Bryant, R. M., A. E. Krzesinski, M. S. Lakshmi, and K. M. Chandy, "The MVA Priority Approximation," *ACM-TOCS*, vol. 2, pp. 335–359, 1984.

Bucher, I. Y. and M. DePrycker, "On the Development of a Measurement System for High Level Language Program Statistics," *IEEE-TC*, vol. 31, pp. 883–891, Sept. 1982.

Burkhart, H. and R. Milen, "Performance Measurement Tools in a Multiprocessor Environment," *IEEE-TC*, vol. 38, pp. 725–737, May 1989.

Bux, W. and H. L. Truong, "Mean-Delay Approximation for Cyclic Service Queueing Systems," *Perf-Eval*, vol. 3, no. 3, pp. 187–196, 1983.

Buzen, J. P., "Computational Algorithms for Closed Queueing Networks with Exponential Servers," *CACM*, vol. 16, pp. 527–531, Sept. 1973.

Buzen, J. P. and P. J. Denning, "Measuring and Calculating Queue Length Distributions," *IEEE Computer*, vol. 13, pp. 33–46, April 1980. (A special issue on Analytic Queueing Models).

Buzen, J. P. and A. W. Shum, "A Unified Operational Treatment of RPS Reconnect Delays," *ACM Sigmetrics*, vol. 15, pp. 78–92, 1987.

Calzarossa, M. and D. Ferrari, "A Sensitivity Study of the Clustering Approach to Workload Modeling," *Perf-Eval*, vol. 6, pp. 25–33, March 1986.

Chandy, K. M., U. Herzog, and L. Woo, "Approximate Analysis of General Queueing Networks," *IBM-JRD*, vol. 19, pp. 43–49, 1975.

Chandy, K. M., J. H. Howard, and D. F. Towsley, "Product Form and Local Balance in Queuing Networks," *JACM*, vol. 24, pp. 250–263, April 1977.

Chandy, K. M. and D. Neuse, "Linearizer: A Heuristic Algorithm for Queueing Network Models of Computer Systems," *CACM*, vol. 25, pp. 126–134, 1982.

Chandy, K. M. and A. J. Martin, "A Characterization of Product-Form Queuing Networks," *JACM*, vol. 30, pp. 286–299, April 1983.

Chaudhry, M. L. and J. G. C. Templeton, *A First Course in Bulk Queues*, John Wiley, 1983.

Chen, P., S. C. Bruell, and G. Balbo, "Alternate Methods for Incorporating Non-exponential Distributions into Stochastic Timed Petri-nets," *PNPM*, pp. 187–197, Dec 1989.

Chiola, G., M. A. Marsan, and G. Balbo, "Product-Form Solution Techniques for the Performance Analysis of Multiple-Bus Multiprocessor Systems with Nonuniform Memory References," *IEEE-TC*, vol. 37, pp. 532–540, May 1988.

Chiola, G. and G. Franceschinis, "Colored GSPN Models and Automatic Symmetry Detection," *PNPM*, pp. 50–60, Dec. 1989.

Ciardo, G., "Toward a Definition of Modeling Power for Stochastic Petri Net Models," *PNPM*, pp. 54–65, Aug. 1987.

Coffman, E. G. and P. J. Denning, *Operating Systems Theory*, Prentice-Hall, Englewood Cliffs, 1973.

Conway, A. E. and N. D. Georganas, "RECAL - A New Efficient Algorithm for the Exact Analysis of Multiple-Chain Closed Queueing Networks," *JACM*, vol. 33, pp. 768–791, Oct. 1986.

Conway, A. E. and N. D. Georganas, "Decomposition and Aggregation by Class in Closed Queueing Networks," *IEEE-TSE*, vol. 12, pp. 1025–1040, Oct. 1986.

Conway, A. E., E. D. Silva, and S. S. Lavenberg, "Mean Value Analysis by Chain of Product Form Queueing Networks," *IEEE-TC*, vol. 38, pp. 432–442, March 1989.

Cooper, R. B. and G. Murray, "Queues Served in Cyclic Order," *BSTJ*, vol. 48, pp. 675–689, March 1969.

Courtois, P. J., *Decomposability: Queueing and Computer System Applications*, Academic Press, New York, 1977.

Courtois, P. J. and P. Semal, "Bounds for the Positive Eigenvectors of Nonnegativ Matrices and their Approximations by Decomposition," *JACM*, vol. 31, pp. 804–825, 1984.

Curnow, H. J. and B. A. Wichman, "A Synthetic Benchmark," *Computer Journal*, vol. 19, pp. 43–49, Feb. 1976.

Dallery, Y. and R. Suri, "Approximate Disaggregation and Performance Bounds for Queueing Networks with Multiple-Server Stations," *ACM Sigmetrics*, vol. 14, pp. 111–128, May 1986.

Das, M. N. and N. C. Giri, *Design and Analysis of Experiments*, Halsted Press, New York, 1986.

Denning, P. J. and J. P. Buzen, "The Operational Analysis of Queueing Network Models," *ACM Computing Surveys*, vol. 10, no. 3, pp. 225–261, Sept. 1978.

Disney, R. L. and P. C. Kiessler, *Traffic Processes in Queuing Networks*, Johns-Hopkins, Baltimore, MD, 1987.

Donatiello, L. and B. R. Iyer, "Analysis of a Composite Performance Reliability Measure for Fault-Tolerant Systems," *JACM*, vol. 34, no. 1, pp. 179–199, Jan. 1987.

Dongarra, J., J. Martin, and J. Worlton, "Computer Benchmarking: Paths and Pitfalls," *IEEE Spectrum*, pp. 38–43, July 1987.

Doshi, B., "Single Server Queues with Vacations," *Performance Analysis of Communication Systems*, Elsevier Science Publisher B.V. (North Holland), 1990.

Dowdy, L. W. and D. V. Foster, "Comparative Models of the File Assignment Problem," *ACM Computing Surveys*, vol. 14, no. 2, pp. 287–313, 1982.

Dudewicz, E. J. and S. R. Dalal, "Allocation of Measurements in Ranking and Selection with Unequal Variances," *Sankhya*, vol. B37, pp. 28–78, 1975.

Dudewicz, E. J. and Z. A. Karian, eds., *Tutorial on Modern Design and Analysis of Discrete-Event Computer Simulations*, IEEE Computer Society, Los Angeles, CA, 1985.

Dugan, J. B., K. S. Trivedi, R. M. Geist, and V. F. Nicola, "Extended Stochastic Petri Nets: Applications and Analysis," *Performance '84*, pp. 507–519, North Holland, Dec. 1984.

Duncan, R., "A Survey of Parallel Computer Architectures," *IEEE Computer*, vol. 23, pp. 5–17, Feb. 1990.

Dutheillet, C. and S. Haddad, "Aggregation of States in Colored Stochastic Petri Nets: Application to a Multiprocessor Architecture," *PNPM*, pp. 40–49, Dec. 1989.

Eager, D. L. and K. C. Sevcik, "Performance Bound Hierarchies for Queueing Networks," *ACM-TOCS*, vol. 1, no. 2, pp. 99–115, 1983.

Eager, D. L. and K. C. Sevcik, "An Analysis of an Approximation Algorithm for Queuing Networks," *Perf-Eval*, vol. 4, pp. 275–284, 1984.

Eager, D. L. and K. C. Sevcik, "Bound Hierarchies for Multiple Class Queueing Networks," *JACM*, vol. 33, pp. 179–206, Jan. 1986.

Eager, D. L., J. Zahorjan, and E. D. Lazowska, "Speedup vs Efficiency in Parallel Systems," *IEEE-TC*, vol. 38, pp. 408–423, March 1989.

Feller, W., *An Introduction to Probability Theory and its Applications*, John Wiley, New York, 1966. (in two volumes)

Ferguson, M. J. and Y. J. Aminetzah, "Exact Results for Nonsymmetric Token Ring Systems," *IEEE Transactions on Communications*, vol. COM-33, pp. 223–231, March 1985.

Ferrari, D., *Computer Systems Performance Evaluation*, Prentice-Hall, Englewood Cliffs, 1978.

Ferrari, D., G. Serazzi, and A. Zeigner, *Measurement and Tuning of Computer Systems*, Prentice-Hall, Englewood Cliffs, 1983.

Ferrari, D., "On the Foundation of Artificial Workload Design," *ACM Sigmetrics*, vol. 12, pp. 8–13, 1984.

Flatto, L. and S. Hahn, "Two Parallel Queues Created by Arrivals with Two Demands I," *SIAM J. of Applied Math*, vol. 44, pp. 1041–1053, Oct. 1984.

Flatto, L., "Two Parallel Queues Created by Arrivals with Two Demands II," *SIAM J. of Applied Math*, vol. 45, pp. 861–878, Oct. 1985.

Florin, G. and S. Natkin, "Generalization of Queuing Network Product Form Solutions to Stochastic Petri nets," *IEEE-TSE*, vol. 17, pp. 99–107, Feb. 1991.

Fujimoto, R. M., "Parallel Discrete Event Simulation," *CACM*, vol. 33, pp. 31–54, Oct. 1990.

Gelenbe, E. and I. Mitrani, *Analysis and Synthesis of Computer Systems*, Academic Press, New York, 1980.

Gelenbe, E. and G. Pujolle, *Introduction to Queueing Networks*, John Wiley, New York, 1987.

Genrich, H. J. and K. Lautenbach, "System Modeling with High Level Petri Nets," *Theoretical Computer Science*, vol. 13, pp. 109–136, 1981.

George, J. A. and J. W.-H. Liu, *Computer solution of sparse positive definite systems*, Prentice-Hall, Englewood Cliffs, 1981.

Ghodsi, M. and K. Kant, "Performance Modeling of Concurrent Systems Under Resource Constraints," *Proc. of Parallel Computing '89*, pp. 589–594, Elsevier Science Publishers, North Holland, Sept. 1989.

Ghodsi, M. and K. Kant, "Performance Analysis of Parallel Search Algorithms," *Perf-Eval*, vol. 13, pp. 67–81, Sept. 1991. (Also appeared in Performance'90.)

Ghodsi, M. and K. Kant, "Well-Formed Generalized Task Graphs," *Proc. of 3rd Intl. Conf. on Parallel and Distributed Systems*, pp. 344–351, Dec. 1991.

Gordon, W. J. and G. F. Newell, "Closed Queueing Systems with Exponential Servers," *Operations Research*, vol. 15, pp. 254–265, April 1967.

Greenberg, A. G. and J. McKenna, "Solution of Closed Product Form Queuing Networks Via the RECAL and Tree-RECAL Methods on a Shared Memory Multiprocessor," *ACM Sigmetrics*, pp. 127–135, May 1989.

Gross, D. and D. R. Miller, "The Randomization Technique as a Modeling Tool and Solution Procedure for Transient Markov Processes," *Operations Research*, vol. 32, pp. 343–361, 1984.

Gross, D. and C. M. Harris, *Fundamentals of Queueing Theory, 2nd edition*, John Wiley, New York, 1985.

Hack, M., "Decidability Questions for Petri-Nets," Ph.D. thesis, Report #161, Project MAC, MIT, 1975.

Heffes, H. and D. M. Lucantoni, "A Markov-Modulated Characterization of Packetized Voice and Data Traffic and Related Statistical Multiplexer Performance," *IEEE J. on Selected Areas in Communications*, vol. 4, pp. 856–868, Sept. 1986.

Heidelberger, P. and K. S. Trivedi, "Queueing Network Models for Parallel Processing with Asynchronous Tasks," *IEEE-TC*, vol. 31, pp. 1099–1108, Nov. 1982.

Heidelberger, P. and K. S. Trivedi, "Queueing Network Models for Programs with Internal Concurrency," *IEEE-TC*, vol. 32, pp. 73–82, Jan. 1983.

Heidelberger, P. and S. S. Lavenberg, "Computer Performance Evaluation Methodology," *IEEE-TC*, vol. 33, pp. 1195–1220, Dec. 1984.

Henderson, W., D. Lucic, and P. G. Taylor, "A Net Level Performance Analysis of Stochastic Petri Nets," *J. of Australian Math Society*, vol. 31, pp. 176–187, 1989. (Special issue on Telecommunications)

Henderson, W. and P. G. Taylor, "Open Networks of Queues with Batch Arrivals and Batch Services," *Queuing Systems*, vol. 6, pp. 71–88, 1990. (The previous paper in this issue discusses closed networks with batch services.)

Henderson, W. and P. G. Taylor, "Embedded Processes in Stochastic Petri nets," *IEEE-TSE*, vol. 17, pp. 108–116, Feb. 1991.

Hennessy, J. L. and D. A. Patterson, *Computer Architecture: A Quantitative Approach*, Morgan Kauffmann, San Mateo, CA, 1990.

Henrici, P., *Applied and Computational Complex Analysis*, Wiley Interscience, 1988. In two volumes. Original date 1975. Published by Wiley in 1988 under its Classics Series.

Holliday, M. A. and M. K. Vernon, "A Generalized Timed Petri Net Model for Performance Analysis," *IEEE-TSE*, vol. 13, pp. 1297–1310, Dec. 1987.

Holliday, M. A. and M. K. Vernon, "Exact Performance Estimates for Multiprocessor Memory and Bus Interference," *IEEE-TC*, vol. 36, pp. 76–85, Jan. 1987.

Hordijk, A. and N. Vandijk, "Networks of Queues with Blocking," *Performance '81*, pp. 51–65, North-Holland, 1981.

Hoyme, K. P., S. C. Bruell, P. V. Afshari, and R. Y. Kain, "A Tree-Structured Mean Value Analysis Algorithm," *ACM-TOCS*, vol. 4, pp. 178–185, May 1986.

Hsieh, C.-T. and S. S. Lam, "Two Classes of Performance Bounds for Closed Queueing Networks," *Perf-Eval*, vol. 7, pp. 3–30, 1987.

Huber, P., A. M. Jensen, L. O. Jepsen, and K. Jensen, "Towards Reachability Trees for High-Level Petri-Nets," in *Advances in Petri nets '84*, ed. G. Rozenberg, pp. 215–233, Springer-Verlag, Berlin, 1984.

Huslende, R., "A Combined Evaluation of Performance and Reliability for Degradable Systems," *ACM Sigmetrics*, vol. 10, pp. 157–164, 1981.

Hwang, K. and F. Briggs, *Computer Architecture and Parallel Processing*, McGraw-Hill, 1984.

Irani, K. B. and I. H. Onyuksel, "A Closed Form Solution for the Performance Analysis of Multiple Bus Multiprocessors," *IEEE-TC*, vol. 33, pp. 1004–1012, Nov. 1984.

Iyer, B. R., L. Donatiello, and P. Heidelberger, "Analysis of Performability for Stochastic Models of Fault-Tolerant Systems," *IEEE-TC*, vol. 35, pp. 902–907, Oct. 1986.

Iyer, B. R., "Recent Results in Performability Analysis," in *Current Advances in Distributed Computing and Communications*, ed. Y. Yemini, pp. 50–64, Computer Science Press, Rockville, MD, 1987.

Jackson, J. R., "Jobshop-Like Queueing Systems," *Management Science*, vol. 10, pp. 131–142, 1963.

Jacobson, P. A. and E. D. Lazowska, "A Reduction Technique for Evaluating Queueing Networks with Serialization Delays," *Performance '83*, pp. 45–59, North-Holland, 1983.

Jain, R., *The Art of Computer Systems Performance Analysis*, John Wiley, New York, 1990.

Jensen, K., "Colored Petri nets and the Invariant Method," *Theoretical Computer Science*, vol. 14, pp. 317–336, 1981.

Jensen, K., "Colored Petri Nets," in *Lecture Notes in Computer Science: Petri nets*, vol. 254, pp. 248–299, Springer-Verlag, Berlin, Feb. 1987.

Johnson, B. W., *Design and Analysis of Fault-Tolerant Digital Systems*, Addison-Wesley, Reading MA, 1989.

Joyce, J., G. Lomow, K. Slind, and B. Unger, "Monitoring Distributed Systems," *ACM-TOCS*, vol. 5, pp. 121–150, May 1987.

Kant, K., "Performance Analysis of Hierarchical Ring Networks," *Proc. of 12th Conference on Local Computer Networks*, pp. 95–108, Oct. 1987.

Kant, K., "Application Level Modeling of Parallel Machines," *ACM Sigmetrics*, vol. 16, pp. 83–93, May 1988.

Kant, K., "Analysis and Synthesis of Generalized Task Graphs," *Proc. of 2nd Intl. Conf on Parallel and Distributed Systems*, pp. 570–577, Nov. 1990.

Kant, K., J. Suen, and F. C. Liaw, "Analysis of a Fork-Join System with Headers," Technical Report, Dept. of Computer Science, Penn State Univ., Nov 1991.

Kant, K., "MVA Modeling of SJN Scheduling," *Perf-Eval*, vol. 15, pp. 41–61, March 1992.

Kapelnikov, A., "A Modeling Methodology for the Analysis of Concurrent Systems and Computations," Ph.D. thesis, Computer Science Dept, UCLA, July 1987

Keilson, J. and L. D. Servi, "A Distributional Form of Little's Law," *Operations Research Letters*, vol. 7, no. 5, pp. 223–228, October 1988.

Kelly, F. P., "Networks of Queues," *Advances in Applied Probability*, vol. 8, pp. 416–432, June 1976.

Kelly, F. P., *Reversibility and Stochastic Networks*, John Wiley, New York, 1979.

Kelly, F. P. and P. K. Pollett, "Sojourn Times in Closed Queueing Networks," *Advances in Applied Probability*, vol. 15, pp. 638–656, 1983.

Kerola, T., "The Composite Bound Method for Computing Throughput Bounds in Multiple Class Environments," *Perf-Eval*, vol. 6, pp. 1–9, 1986.

Kerola, T. and H. Schwetman, "Monit: A Performance Monitoring Tool for Parallel and Pseudo-Parallel Programs," *ACM Sigmetrics*, vol. 15, pp. 163–174, May 1987.

Kim, C. and A. K. Agrawala, "Analyis of the Fork-Join Queue," *IEEE-TC*, vol. 38, pp. 250–255, Feb. 1989.

King, P., *Computer and Communications Systems Performance Modeling*, Prentice-Hall, Englewood Cliffs, 1990.

Kleijnen, J. P. C., *Statistical Techniques in Simulation, Part 1*, Marcel Dekker, 1974.

Kleinrock, L., *Queueing Systems, Vol 1: Theory*, John Wiley, New York, 1975.

Kleinrock, L., *Queueing Systems, Vol 2: Computer Applications*, John Wiley, New York, 1976.

Kobayashi, H., *Modeling and Analysis: An Introduction to System Performance Evaluation Methodology*, Addison-Wesley, Reading, MA, 1978.

Kobayashi, H. and M. Gerla, "Optimal Routing in Closed Queueing Networks," *ACM-TOCS*, vol. 1, no. 4, pp. 294–310, 1983.

Kritzinger, P., S. van Wyk, and A. Krzesinski, "A Generalization of Norton's Theorem for Multiclass Queueing Networks," *Perf-Eval*, vol. 2, pp. 98–107, 1982.

Kriz, J., "Throughput Bounds for Closed Queueing Networks," *Perf-Eval*, vol. 4, pp. 1–10, 1984.

Krzesinski, A. and J. Greyling, "Improved Lineariser Methods for Queueing Networks with Queue Dependent Centres," *ACM Sigmetrics*, vol. 12, pp. 41–51, Aug. 1984.

Krzesinski, A. E. and P. Teunissen, "Multiclass Queuing Networks with Population Size Constraints," *ACM Sigmetrics*, vol. 13, pp. 128–139, Aug. 1985.

Krzesinski, A. E., "Multiclass Queueing Networks with State-Dependent Routing," *Perf-Eval*, vol. 7, pp. 125–143, 1987.

Kuehn, P. J., "Multiqueue Systems with Non-Exhaustive Service," *BSTJ*, vol. 58, no. 3, pp. 671–698, 1979.

Lam, S. S., "Queuing Networks with Population Size Constraints," *IBM-JRD*, pp. 370–378, July 1977.

Lam, S. S., "Dynamic Scaling and Growth Behavior of Queueing Network Normalization Constants," *JACM*, vol. 29, pp. 492–513, 1982.

Lam, S. S. and Y. L. Lien, "A Tree Convolution Algorithm for the Solution of Queueing Networks," *CACM*, vol. 26, pp. 203–215, 1983.

Lavenberg, S. S. and M. Reiser, "Stationary State Probabilities at Arrival instants for Closed Queueing Networks with Multiple Types of Customers," *J. of Applied Probability*, vol. 17, pp. 1048–1061, 1980.

Lavenberg, S. S., *Computer Performance Modeling Handbook*, Academic Press, New York, 1983.

Law, A. M. and W. D. Kelton, *Simulation Modeling and Analysis*, McGraw-Hill, New York, 1982.

Lazowska, E. D. and J. Zahorjan, "Multiple Class Memory Constrained Queueing Networks," *ACM Sigmetrics*, vol. 10, pp. 130–140, 1982.

Lazowska, E. D., J. Zahorjan, G. S. Graham, and K. C. Sevcik, *Quantitative System Performance–Computer System Analysis Using Queueing Network Models*, Prentice-Hall, Englewood Cliffs, 1984.

Lin, C. L. and C. M. Marinescu, "Stochastic High-Level Petri Nets," *IEEE-TC*, vol. 37, pp. 815–825, July 1988.

Lipovski, G. J. and M. Malek (Eds.), *Parallel Computing: Theory and Comparisons*, John Wiley, New York, 1987.

Lubeck, O., J. Moore, and R. Mendez, "A Benchmark Comparison of Three Supercomputers: Fujitsu Vp-200, Hitachi S810/20, and Cray X-Mp/2," *IEEE Computer*, vol. 18, pp. 10–23, Dec. 1985.

Lucantoni, D. M., "New Results on Single Server Queue with a Batch Markovian Arrival Process," Tech. Rep. AT&T Bell Labs, Holmdel, NJ, 1990.

Lucantoni, D. M., K. S. Meier-Hellstern, and M. F. Neuts, "A Single Server Queue with Server Vacations and a Class of Nonrenewal Arrival Processes," Tech. Rep. AT&T Bell Labs, Holmdel, NJ, 1990.

MacDougall, M. H., "A Class of Generalized Stochastic Petri Nets for the Performance Evaluation of Multiprocessor Systems," *ACM-TOCS*, vol. 2, pp. 93–122, 1984.

Mak, V. W. K., "Performance Prediction of Concurrent Systems," Ph.D. thesis, Computer Systems Lab, Stanford Univ., CA, Dec. 1987.

Marsan, M. A. and R. A. Marie, "An Approximate Analytical Method for General Queueing Networks," *IEEE-TSE*, vol. 5, pp. 530–538, 1979.

Marsan, M. A., G. Conte, and G. Balbo, "A Class of Generalized Stochastic Petri Nets for the Performance Evaluation of Multiprocessor Systems," *ACM-TOCS*, vol. 2, pp. 93–122, 1984.

Marsan, M. A., G. Balbo, and G. Conte, *Performance Evaluation of Multiprocessor Systems*, MIT Press, Cambridge, MA, 1986.

Marsan, M. A., G. Balbo, G. Chiola, and G. Conte, "Generalized Stochastic Petri Nets Revisited: Random Switches and Priorities," *PNPM*, pp. 44–53, Aug. 1987.

Marsan, M. A. and G. Balbo, et al., "The Effect of Execution Policies on the Semantics of Analysis of Stochastic Petri Nets," *IEEE-TSE*, vol. 15, pp. 825–831, July 1989.

Mayr, E., "An Algorithm for the General Petri Net Reachability Problem," *SIAM J. of Computing*, vol. 13, pp. 441–460, Aug. 1984.

McKenna, J., D. Mitra, and K. G. Ramakrishnan, "A Class of Closed Markovian Queueing Networks: Integral Representations, Asymptotic Expansions, and Generalizations," *BSTJ*, vol. 60, pp. 599–641, 1981.

McKenna, J. and D. Mitra, "Integral Representations and Asymptotic Expansions for Closed Markovian Queueing Networks: Normal Usage," *BSTJ*, vol. 61, pp. 661–683, 1982.

McKenna, J. and D. Mitra, "Asymptotic Expansions and Integral Representations of Moments of Queue Lengths in Closed Markovian Networks," *JACM*, vol. 31, pp. 346–360, 1984.

McKenna, J., "Asymptotic Expansions of the Sojourn Time Distribution Functions of Jobs in Closed, Product-Form Queuing Networks," *JACM*, vol. 34, pp. 985–1003, Oct. 1987.

Meyer, J. F., "On Evaluating the Performability of Degradable Computing Systems," *IEEE-TC*, vol. 22, pp. 720–731, Aug. 1980.

Meyer, J. F., "Closed-Form Solutions of Performability," *IEEE-TC*, vol. 31, pp. 648–657, July 1982.

Miller, B. P., C. Macrander, and S. Sechrest, "A Distributed Programs Monitor for Berkeley Unix," *Proc. of the 5th Intl Conference on Distributed Computing Systems*, pp. 43–54, IEEE Computer Society, Denver, Colorado, May 1985.

Mitra, D. and J. McKenna, "Asymptotic Expansions for Closed Markovian Networks with State Dependent Service Rates," *JACM*, vol. 33, no. 3, pp. 568–592, 1986.

Moler, C. B. and V. Van Loan, "Nineteen Dubious Ways of Computing the Matrix Exponential," *SIAM Reviews*, vol. 20, pp. 801–836, 1978.

Molloy, M. K., "Performance Analysis Using Stochastic Petri Nets," *IEEE-TC*, vol. 31, pp. 913–917, Sept. 1982.

Molloy, M. K., "Discrete Time Stochastic Petri Nets," *IEEE-TSE*, vol. 11, pp. 417–423, April 1985.

Molloy, M. K., "Structurally Bounded Stochastic Petri Nets," *PNPM*, pp. 156–163, Aug. 1987.

Morrison, J. A. and D. Mitra, "Heavy-Usage Asymptotic Expansions for the Waiting Time in Closed Processor-Sharing Systems with Multiple Classes," *Advances in Applied Probability*, vol. 17, pp. 163–185, 1985.

Murata, T., "Petri nets: Properties, Analysis and Applications," *Proc. of IEEE*, vol. 77, pp. 541–580, April 1989.

Nelson, R., D. Towsley, and A. N. Tantawi, *Performance Analysis of Parallel Processing Systems*, 14, pp. 532–540, April 1988.

Nelson, R. and A. N. Tantawi, "Approximate Analysis of Fork-Join Synchronization in Parallel Queues," *IEEE-TC*, vol. 37, pp. 739–743, June 1988.

Nelson, R., "A Performance Evaluation of a General Parallel Processing Model," *ACM Sigmetrics*, pp. 13–26, May 1990.

Neuse, D. and K. M. Chandy, "HAM: The Heuristic Aggregation Method," *ACM Sigmetrics*, vol. 11, no. 4, pp. 195–212, 1982.

Neuts, M. F., "A Versatile Markovian Point Process," *J. of Applied Probability*, vol. 16, pp. 764–769, 1979.

Neuts, M. F., *Matrix Geometric Solutions in Stochastic Models: An Algorithmic Approach*, Johns-Hopkins, Baltimore, MD, 1981.

Neuts, M. F., "Matrix-Analytic Methods in Queuing Theory," *European J. of Operations Research*, vol. 15, pp. 2–12, 1984.

Neuts, M. F., *Structure of Stochastic Matrices of M/G/1 Type and Their Applications*, Marcel-Dekker, New York, 1990.

Noetzel, A. S., "A Generalized Queueing Discipline for Product Form Network Solutions," *JACM*, vol. 26, no. 4, pp. 779–793, Oct. 1979.

Oney, W. C., "Queuing Analysis of the Scan Policy for Moving Head Disks," *JACM*, vol. 22, pp. 397–412, July 1975.

Onvural, R. O., "Survey of Closed Queuing Networks with Blocking," *ACM Computing Surveys*, vol. 22, pp. 83–122, June 1990.

Pattipati, K. R., M. M. Kostreva, and J. L. Teele, "Approximate Mean Value Analysis Algorithms for Queuing Networks: Existence, Uniqueness and Convergence Results," *JACM*, vol. 37, July 1990.

Pattipati, K. R. and J. Wolf, "A Calculus of Variations Approach to File Allocation Problems in Computer Systems," *ACM Sigmetrics*, pp. 126–133, May 1990.

Pawlikowski, K., "Steady-state Simulation of Queuing Processes: A Survey of Problems and Solutions," *ACM Computing Surveys*, pp. 123–170, June 1990.

Payne, J. A., *Introduction to Simulation*, McGraw-Hill, New York, 1982.

Peterson, J. L., *Petri Net Theory and the Modeling of Systems*, Prentice-Hall, Englewood Cliffs, 1981.

Pittel, B., "Closed Exponential Networks with Saturation," *Mathematics of Operations Research*, vol. 4, pp. 367–378, Nov. 1979.

Price, W. J., "Benchmark Tutorial," *IEEE Micro Magazine*, vol. 9, pp. 28–43, Oct. 1989.

Raatikainen, K. E. E., "Approximating Response Time Distributions," *ACM Sigmetrics*, vol. 17, pp. 190–199, May 1989.

Ramamoorthy, C. V. and G. S. Ho, "Performance Evaluation of Asynchronous Concurrent Systems using Petri Nets," *IEEE-TSE*, vol. 6, pp. 440–449, May 1980.

Razouk, R. and C. V. Phelps, "Performance Analysis using Timed Petri Nets," *Proc. of IFIP WG 6.1, Fourth Intl. workshop*, pp. 561–576, North Holland, 1985.

Rege, K. M. and B. Sengupta, "Response Time Distributions in a Multiprogrammed Computer with Terminal Traffic," *Perf-Eval*, vol. 8, pp. 41–50, 1988.

Reibman, A., R. M. Smith, and K. S. Trivedi, "Markov and Markov Reward Model Transient Analysis: An Overview of Numerical Techniques," *European J. of Operations Research*, vol. 40, pp. 257–267, 1989.

Reibman, A. and K. S. Trivedi, "Transient Analysis of Cumulative Measures of Markov Model Behavior," *Communication, Statistics and Stochastic Models*, Marcel Dekker, New York, pp. 683–710, 1989.

Reiser, M. "A Quarter Century of Performance Evaluation - Where Do We Stand?," *Perf-Eval*, vol. 12, no. 1, pp. 1–4, January 1991.

Reiser, M. and S. S. Lavenberg, "Mean Value Analysis of Closed Multichain Queueing Networks," *JACM*, vol. 27, no. 2, pp. 313–320, 1980.

Robertazzi, T. G. and A. A. Lazar, "On the Modeling and Optimal Flow Control of the Jacksonian Network," *Perf-Eval*, vol. 5, pp. 29–43, 1985.

Rose, C. A., "A Measurement Procedure for Queuing Network Models of Computer Systems," *ACM Computing Surveys*, vol. 10, no. 3, pp. 263–280, Sept. 1978. (A special issue on queuing network models).

Ross, S. M., *Applied Probability Models with Optimization Applications*, Holden-Day, San Francisco, 1970.

Ross, S. M., *Stochastic Processes*, John Wiley, New York, 1983.

Sanders, W. H. and J. F. Meyer, "Performability Evaluation of Distributed Systems using Stochastic Activity Networks," *PNPM*, pp. 111–125, Aug. 1987.

Sanders, W. H. and J. F. Meyer, "Reduced Base Model Construction Methods for Stochastic Activity Networks," *PNPM*, pp. 74–84, Dec. 1989.

Sarkar, D. and W. I. Zangwill, "Expected Waiting Time for Nonsymmetric Cyclic Queueing Systems - Exact Results and Applications," *Management Science*, vol. 35, pp. 1463–1474, Dec. 1989.

Sauer, C. H. and K. M. Chandy, *Computer Systems Performance Modeling*, Prentice-Hall, Englewood Cliffs, 1981.

Sauer, C. H., "Computational Algorithms for State-Dependent Queueing Networks," *ACM-TOCS*, vol. 1, pp. 67–92, Feb. 1983.

Segall, Z. and L. Rudolph, "PIE: A Programming and Instrumentation Environment for Parallel Processing," *IEEE Software*, vol. 2, pp. 22–37, Nov. 1985.

Sevcik, K. C. and I. Mitrani, "The Distribution of Queueing Network States at Input and Output Instants," *JACM*, vol. 28, pp. 358–371, 1981.

Shanthikumar, J. G. and R. G. Sargent, "A Unifying View of Hybrid Simulation/Analytic Models and Modeling," *Operations Research*, vol. 31, pp. 1030–1052, 1983.

Shanthikumar, J. G. and D. D. Yao, "Throughput Bounds for Closed Queueing Networks with Queue-Dependent Service Rates," *Perf-Eval*, vol. 9, pp. 69–78, 1988.

Siewiorek, D. P. and R. S. Swarz, *The Theory and Practice of Reliable System Design*, Digital Press, Bedford, MA, 1982.

Sifakis, J., "Performance Evaluation of Systems using Nets," in *Net Theory and Applications*, ed. W. Brauer, pp. 307–319, Springer-Verlag, Berlin, 1980.

Silva, E. D., S. S. Lavenberg, and R. R. Muntz, "A Perspective on Iterative Methods for the Approximate Analysis of Closed Queueing Networks," in *Mathematical Computer Performance and Reliability*, ed. A. Hordijk, pp. 225–244, North-Holland, 1984.

Silva, E. D. and R. R. Muntz, "Approximate Solutions for a Class of Non-Product Form Queuing Networks," *Perf-Eval*, vol. 7, pp. 221–242, 1987.

Silva, E. D. and R. Muntz, "Simple Relationships among Moments of Queue Lengths in Product Form Queueing Networks," *IEEE-TC*, vol. 37, pp. 1125–1130, Sept. 1988.

Silva, E. D. and S. S. Lavenberg, "Calculating Joint Queue Length Distributions in Product Form Queueing Networks," *JACM*, vol. 36, pp. 194–207, Jan. 1989.

Silva, E. D. and H. R. Gail, "Calculating Availability and Performability Measures of Repairable Computer Systems using Randomization," *JACM*, vol. 36, pp. 171–193, Jan. 1989.

Silva, E. D. and R. R. Muntz, "A Note on the Computational Cost of the Linearizer Algorithm for Queuing Networks," *IEEE-TC*, vol. 39, pp. 840–842, June 1990.

Simmons, M., R. Koskela, and I. Bucher, eds., *Instrumentation of Future Parallel Computing Systems*, pp. 239–250, Addison-Wesley, 1990.

Smith, R. M., K. S. Trivedi, and A. V. Ramesh, "Performability Analysis: Measures, an Algorithm and a Case Study," *IEEE-TC*, vol. 37, pp. 406–417, April 1988.

Spirn, J. R., "Queuing Models with Random Selection for Service," *IEEE-TSE*, vol. 5, pp. 287–289, May 1979.

Srinivasan, M. M. and K. Kant, "On the Analysis of Approximation Algorithms for Closed Queuing Networks," Dept. of IOE, Univ. of Michigan, Ann Arbor, MI, Sept. 1986.

Srinivasan, M. M. and K. Kant, "The File Allocation Problem - A Queueing Network Optimization Approach," *Computers and Operations Research*, vol. 14, no. 5, pp. 349–361, 1987.

Srinivasan, M. M., "Successively Improving Bounds on Performance Measures for Single Class Product Form Queueing Networks," *IEEE-TC*, vol. 36, pp. 1107–1112, Sept. 1987.

Srinivasan, M. M., "On Extending the Scope of Bounding Techniques for Closed Queueing Networks," *Large Scale Systems Journal*, vol. 12, no. 2, pp. 125-141, 1988.

Srinivasan, M. M., "Nondeterministic Polling Systems," *Management Science*, vol. 37, no. 6, pp. 667–681, June 1991.

Srinivasan, M. M., "An Approximation for Mean Waiting Times in Cyclic Server Systems with Non-Exhaustive Service," *Perf-Eval*, vol. 9, no. 1, pp. 17–33, 1988.

Stephens, L. E. and L. W. Dowdy, "Convolutional Bound Hierarchies," *ACM Sigmetrics*, pp. 120–133, 1984.

Stewart, G. W., "Computable Error Bounds for Aggregated Markov Chains," *JACM*, vol. 30, pp. 271–285, 1983.

Stewart, W. J., "A Comparison of Numerical Techniques in Markov Modeling," *CACM*, vol. 21, pp. 144–152, Feb. 1978.

Strelen, J., "A Generalization of Mean Value Analysis to Higher Moments: Moment Analysis," *ACM Sigmetrics*, vol. 14, May 1986.

Suri, R., "Robustness of Queueing Network Formulas," *JACM*, vol. 30, pp. 564–594, 1983.

Suri, R., "Generalized Quick Bounds for Performance of Queueing Networks," *Computer Performance*, vol. 5, pp. 116–120, 1984.

Suri, R., "A Concept of Monotonicity and its Characterization for Closed Queueing Networks," *Operations Research*, vol. 33, pp. 606–624, May-June 1985.

Svobodova, L., *Computer Performance Measurement and Evaluation Methods: Analysis and Application*, North-Holland, 1976.

Takagi, H., *Analysis of Polling Systems*, The MIT Press, Cambridge, MA, 1986.

Takagi, H., "Queueing Analysis of Polling Models: An Update," in *Stochastic Analysis of Computer and Communication Systems*, pp. 267–318, Elsevier Science Publishers B. V., North-Holland, 1990.

Thomasian, A. and P. F. Bay, "Analytic Queuing Network Models for Parallel Processing of Task Systems," *IEEE-TC*, pp. 1045–1054, Dec. 1986.

Towsley, D. F., "Queueing Network Models with State-Dependent Routing," *JACM*, vol. 27, pp. 323–337, April 1980.

Trivedi, K. S., *Probability and Statistics with Reliability, Queueing, and Computer Science Applications*, Prentice-Hall, Englewood Cliffs, 1982.

Tucci, S. and C. H. Sauer, "The Tree MVA Algorithm," *Perf-Eval*, vol. 5, pp. 187–196, 1985.

Wagner, D. B. and E. D. Lazowska, "Parallel Simulation of Queuing Networks: Limitations and Potentials," *ACM Sigmetrics*, pp. 146–155, May 1989.

Watson, K., "Performance Evaluation of Cyclic Service Strategies – A Survey," *Performance '84*, pp. 521–533, North Holland, 1984.

Weicker, R. P., "Dhrystone: A Synthetic Systems Programming Benchmark," *CACM*, vol. 27, pp. 1013–1030, Oct. 1984.

Wilhelm, N. C., "A General Model for the Performance of Disk Systems," *JACM*, vol. 24, pp. 14–31, Jan. 1977.

Wolff, R. A., *Stochastic Modeling and Theory of Queues*, Prentice-Hall, Englewood Cliffs, 1989.

Yang, C. Q. and B. P. Miller, "Performance Measurements for Parallel and Distributed Programs: A Structured and Automatic Approach," *IEEE-TSE*, vol. 15, pp. 1615–1629, Dec. 1989.

Zahorjan, J., J. N. P. Hume, and K. C. Sevcik, "A Queueing Model of a Rotational Position Sensing Disk System," *Canadian J. of Operations Research*, vol. 16, pp. 199–216, Oct. 1978.

Zahorjan, J., K. C. Sevcik, D. L. Eager, and B. Galler, "Balanced Job Bound Analysis of Queueing Networks," *CACM*, vol. 25, pp. 132–141, 1982.

Zenie, A., "Colored Stochastic Petri Nets," *Proc. of IEEE Intl. Workshop on Timed Petri Nets*, pp. 262–271, Torino, Italy, July 1985.

Zuberek, W. M., "Timed Petri Nets and Preliminary ," *Proc. of the 7th Annual Symposium on Computer Architecture*, pp. 88–96, 1980.

Index